THE MONETARY STATE

MONETARY STATECRAFT & THE ARCHITECTURE OF FINANCIAL POWER.

JAG DESAINT

To God — the breath within every breath, the silence beneath every word, the light that holds the stars and the spaces between them. You are the river and the ocean, the question and the answer, the beginning that never began and the end that never comes. This work is yours, as all things are. I am simply grateful to have been the hand that wrote it.

- Jag DeSaint

TABLE OF CONTENT

PART EIGHT

FAILURE MODES AND FINAL DOCTRINE

HOW THE SYSTEM BREAKS NEXT, AND HOW TO REDESIGN IT

PART NINE

APPENDIX

RESEARCH, REFERENCE REGISTER, SOURCE CONCORDANCE, GLOSSARY +

PREFACE

MONETARY STATECRAFT & THE ARCHITECTURE OF FINANCIAL POWER.

The first time the machine reveals itself, it does not feel like economics. It feels like a delay that arrives with no explanation and then lingers long enough to become a story. A transfer that should have been ordinary sits in a pending state long enough to turn certainty into suspicion. A shipment that should have cleared sits on a dock because a single data field is "incomplete," and nobody with authority is willing to call the incompleteness finished. A treasury desk that should have rolled funding at 9:00 is still waiting at 11:00, watching the day's cutoffs turn from routine into threat. Nothing has "collapsed," yet everything has changed, because the argument has returned. Money exists to end arguments. When it cannot, the entire order becomes negotiable again, and negotiation under stress is another name for power.

That is where this book begins. Not with a definition, not with a slogan, not with a parable about barter, but with the moment closure fails and the state's real burden becomes visible: deciding which obligations are allowed to end, and on what terms, and who must wait while the system decides what it is willing to recognize as real.

You do not need another morality play about greed and fear. You already live inside the machine. You have watched "technical" choices become political events. You have watched eligibility lists change faster than speeches. You have watched a marginal haircut adjustment do more to tighten the economy than a month of public guidance. You have watched corridor admissibility tighten and felt domestic autonomy compress without a single formal decree. You have watched a platform change a rule, rename a risk category, adjust a threshold, and quietly rewrite who counts as routine.

If you have ever left a crisis meeting with the sensation that the public story and the real story did not occupy the same universe, you already understand the premise.

The premise is severe and operational. Money is not primarily a coin, a note, or a policy variable. Money is a governed architecture of claims, ledgers, priorities, and settlement pathways. In calm, the architecture hides inside routine. In stress, it becomes visible as behavior: everyone tries to upgrade into the claim that ends the argument with the least residual risk. That is what a run is, whether it is a bank run, a collateral run, a corridor run, or a flight into the apex settlement claim. The hierarchy is always there. Crisis is merely the moment the system stops pretending otherwise.

The implication is the reason this book exists. The real power of a monetary order is not the power to print symbols. It is the power to define upgrade rights: who can convert, at what speed, through which institutions, with what documentation, with what collateral, under what legal priority, with what reversibility, and with what loss allocation when capacity is scarce. Whoever controls those gates controls the monetary position in practice, even if someone else controls the headlines.

This is not theory for its own sake. This is the map of where sovereignty lives now. Sovereignty lives in finality. Sovereignty lives in the authoritative ledger. Sovereignty lives in collateral eligibility and haircut discipline. Sovereignty lives in who may clear, who may net, who may settle, and who may be treated as routine rather than as exception. Sovereignty lives in corridor admissibility, in the translator chokepoints that convert one regime's legibility into another's, and in the ability to keep essentials moving when the system is forced into triage.

The world is entering a period where these levers are no longer background. They are the battlefield.

Parallel rails are being built. Standards are diverging. Compliance is thickening into border. Private issuers compete for the front end while remaining dependent on public finality at the back end. Translators become chokepoints. Chokepoints become markets. Markets in passage create rents. Rents create corruption risk. Corruption risk justifies further tightening. Tightening produces more exceptions. Exceptions become the daily tax of fragmentation, paid not only in fees but in time, and time is the first scarce asset in any monetary order. This is how monetary order becomes socially unstable: not by philosophical disagreement, but by felt inequality in completion.

If you govern a sovereign, you recognize the humiliation embedded in cross-boundary dependence: domestic legality does not guarantee external passage. If you govern a central bank, you recognize the contradiction beneath modern stability: the system requires private deposit creation for scale, yet must prevent private issuers from becoming de facto monetary sovereigns. If you govern a bank, you recognize how quickly liquidity becomes collateral, how quickly collateral becomes eligibility, and how quickly eligibility becomes politics. If you work inside a multilateral institution, you recognize that conditionality is not a lecture; it is time allocation under external gatekeeping. The language differs. The mechanism is the same: upgrade rights govern survival.

This book is written for finance ministers, central-bank governors, presidents, sovereign advisers, bank chairmen, regulators, multilateral officials, and system architects because these are the roles that confront the machine when it moves. It is not written to teach you slogans you already know. It is written to make the machine legible at the level where your decisions actually operate: the gate that determines whether an obligation closes, the rule that determines whether collateral counts, the queue that determines who gets time, the priority schedule that determines who absorbs loss, the corridor that determines whether external settlement is possible without humiliation.

The method is deliberate. You will see pressure scenes because the machine is best understood under load. You will see mechanism because pressure without mechanism becomes moral panic. You will see power maps because mechanism without power becomes naïve. You will see failure points because power without failure becomes propaganda. You will see doctrine because failure without doctrine becomes resignation. The writing is built to move from lived sequence to structural clarity to the one thing you can govern: the rules that decide who completes, who waits, and who pays.

Do not expect comfort here. Expect precision. Expect a language for the things that are usually hidden behind polite abstraction: discharge, finality, admissibility, eligibility, haircuts, margin timing, convertibility, priority, backstop, corridor passage, translator chokepoints, degraded-mode triage. These are not technicalities. They are the constitution of modern money. They decide who can turn future income into present capacity, who can finance inventory, who can bridge a shock, who can survive a day of delay without becoming insolvent, and which institutions become sovereign-adjacent simply because they control the interface through which routine becomes possible.

The goal is not to make you sound clever. The goal is to make you dangerous in the only way that matters for statecraft: able to see the system's actual levers before crisis forces you to admit them under pressure. When you finish, you should be able to interrogate a payment system by asking where finality lives. You should be able to interrogate a banking system by mapping convertibility pathways. You should be able to interrogate a market by identifying which collateral is truly eligible under stress and which liquidity is merely borrowed speed. You should be able to interrogate cross-border posture by naming the corridor gates that can tighten without formal rupture. You should be able to design triage rules that preserve legitimacy because they are rule-bound, auditable, and defensible, rather than improvised favors that will be remembered as corruption even if they saved the system.

Money is governance operating under the appearance of exchange. The appearance has become smoother, faster, and more seductive. The governance has become more distributed, more technical, and more concentrated in fewer nodes. That combination is unstable unless the people responsible for the order can see it clearly and act with discipline.

If you have ever watched a crisis unfold and realized the public debate was happening in the wrong universe, begin here. If you have ever sat in a meeting where everyone used the word payment but nobody could say where finality actually lived, begin here. If you have ever suspected that policy is often executed by eligibility lists and documentation burdens rather than by speeches and votes, begin here. This book is a manual for making the hidden constitution visible—before it is enforced on your society by panic.

INTRODUCTION

MONETARY STATECRAFT & THE ARCHITECTURE OF FINANCIAL POWER.

This book is designed to be used, not admired. Read it the way you would read a field directive prepared for people who cannot afford surprise: with a pen, a mandate, and the expectation that you will apply it to a living system that already has seams, already has dependencies, and already has gatekeepers you did not appoint. If you read it as commentary, you will take away phrases. If you read it as doctrine, you will take away control. By the end, you should be able to map your system's settlement endpoint, convertibility pathways, collateral discipline, corridor dependence, and concentration nodes into a practical redesign agenda rather than a set of opinions.

Begin with a discipline. Each time you encounter a sentence that sounds like economics, ask which gate it implies. The gate is the real content. Confidence is usually a statement about convertibility. Liquidity is usually a statement about collateral eligibility and time. Stability is usually a statement about finality, priority, and backstop credibility. Market functioning is usually a statement about dealers, margins, and settlement pathways. When a speech says resilience, ask what degraded mode actually means and who decides what throttles. When a memo says integrity, ask what holds become routine and how exceptions are handled. If you can name the gate, you can govern. If you cannot name the gate, you are operating inside rules you did not make.

Read each chapter in three passes. The first pass is for sequence. Identify the completion path the chapter is describing: initiation, authorization, posting, clearing, settlement, discharge. Identify where the path can stall. Identify which actor controls the stall. The second pass is for hierarchy. Identify which claims are treated as upgradeable and which are treated as conditional. Identify what makes a claim high-grade in practice: eligibility, haircut discipline, custody mobility, corridor admissibility, and the speed at which it becomes usable under stress. The third pass is for crisis behavior. Ask what happens when fear arrives: which queues form, which haircuts widen, which margins accelerate, which corridors tighten, which translators become chokepoints, which backstops become unavoidable, and which priorities become politically explosive.

Do not skim the pressure scenes. They are not decoration. They are how the machine becomes visible. In calm, systems hide hierarchy inside routine and interface. Under load, hierarchy becomes behavior. Treat every scene as a test case. Where does closure actually occur. Who can prevent it. What proof is demanded. What discretion is exercised. What is the first reasonable tightening that turns into the second, and then becomes the new normal.

Use the book as an audit, not as a narrative. After any chapter that lands, pause and write the equivalent mechanism in your own jurisdiction or institution. Name your settlement endpoint. Name your authoritative ledger. Name the legal basis that defends finality. Name the reversal channels and their limits. Name your convertibility pathways as upgrade rights and list the gates that can tighten. Name your collateral eligibility map and the triggers that widen haircuts or accelerate margin. Name your custody dependencies and where legal time can freeze financial time. Name your queue and triage rules in degraded mode, including who can override and what audit record is produced. Name your concentration nodes and your tested substitutes. Name your corridor dependencies for essentials and the documentation burdens that govern passage. If you cannot name them, you have found your first vulnerability, and it is not theoretical.

Read with two clocks running. The first is ordinary life: payroll, rent, inventory, fuel, shipping, and the daily belief that money will complete with the quiet reliability people mistake for nature. The second is crisis time: cutoffs, margin calls, intraday liquidity, and the hours in which a system can slide from routine to panic through delays that look small until they compound. This book is about how the second clock governs the first, and how legitimacy collapses when ordinary life is forced to live on crisis time without being told.

Use the chapters strategically when you need immediate value. If you are rebuilding payment rails or responding to outages, begin with discharge, finality, sequence, and degraded-mode triage, then move to concentration and operational resilience. If you are watching secured funding tighten, begin with collateral chains, haircuts, margin timing, and the mechanics of forced liquidation. If you are facing sovereign constraint or corridor tightening, begin with reserve order, cross-boundary passage, admissibility, and the distinction between access, passage, and finality. If you are designing development finance, begin with multilateral time allocation and development-credit architecture, then map how domestic bankability interacts with external settlement requirements. If you are confronting private rails, stable-value claims, or programmable policy, read the interface chapters as sovereignty relocation into identity, custody, and platform governance, not as novelty.

Keep one discipline throughout: separate speed from finality. Many modern failures come from systems that are fast but not final, or final but not explainable, or final in one perimeter and contestable in another. Each time you catch yourself using payment as if it were a single state, stop and ask which state you actually mean. Authorization is not posting. Posting is not settlement. Settlement is not discharge if reversal remains broad. Ambiguity is where legitimacy dies, because ambiguity invites the belief that someone else has a faster lane and a softer rulebook.

Keep a second discipline, quieter but more decisive: separate law from interface. Interfaces flatter certainty. Law enforces it, or does not. When an interface tells a citizen complete while the system retains discretion to reverse, the citizen is being asked to trust appearance. The citizen will comply in calm. The citizen will revolt in stress. The state must never build legitimacy on appearance. Appearance collapses the moment delays and reversals arrive.

Use the end matter as your meeting kit. The glossary standardizes language. The checklists force gate-mapping. The red flags section gives early warning questions. The concordance and audit matrix let you move from doctrine to the rule texts and standards that define what is enforceable. If you treat these pages as operational tools rather than as appendices, you will extract the book's real value.

Expect discomfort. This book treats certain abstractions as cover stories and certain technical settings as constitutional power. That is deliberate. A system governed by cover stories cannot survive an era of fragmentation, strategic exclusion, and private interface competition without improvisation. Improvisation is how legitimacy collapses because it allocates time and loss through discretion, and discretion will be remembered as favoritism even when it saved the system.

Disagree like an operator. If a chapter feels wrong, name the gate you believe it misweights, then stress-test your alternative gate against crisis behavior. Ask whether your gate still holds when collateral must move quickly, when margin accelerates, when corridors tighten, when custody freezes, and when degraded mode forces triage. Doctrine improves through stress testing, not through rhetoric.

Apply this in calm. Crises do not create rules. Crises reveal the rules already embedded in the machine. If you wait for crisis to discover your gates, your gates will be discovered for you, publicly, and at the worst moment. The time to govern the machine is when it is quiet enough to be redesigned, and when legitimacy is still a reservoir rather than a ration.

PART ONE

ORIGIN OF AUTHORITY

HOW MONEY BECOMES ENFORCEABLE POWER

The late hour in a capital has a particular sound: the sealed hush of offices that do not truly close, the soft cadence of staff moving paper without speaking, the persistent glow of terminals that keep time for markets in other hemispheres. A finance minister can stare at inflation prints, debt-service curves, reserve balances, and funding ladders until morning and still miss the more dangerous truth: the monetary position of a state is not defined by slogans, nor by symbols, nor by the elegance of its framework. It is defined by whether its claims clear, whether its priorities hold in court and under stress, whether enforcement reaches the points where value is recorded and released, and whether institutions can still command time when confidence collapses into speed.

Money begins as promise. Promise becomes power only when it becomes enforceable. That conversion is the hinge of monetary history and the hinge modern officials are trained to treat as background noise. Training begins too high on the stack, where rates, targets, and public statements appear as levers. The lever arm lives lower: in the rules that decide what counts as payment, whose record becomes official, whose claim is senior in insolvency, whose default is punished, whose delay is tolerated, and whose survival is protected behind the language of stability. Monetary sovereignty is not a possession. It is a capability: the capability to impose a hierarchy of claims and make that hierarchy hold when the system is stressed, disputed, or attacked.

"Money is a ranking of claims made credible by enforcement."

That sentence feels abstract until enforcement becomes uncertain. Without an enforceable ledger, the economy does not become freer. It becomes smaller. Trade retreats into proximity. Credit collapses into personal networks, threats, and informal protection. Complexity stops compounding because the future cannot be reliably assigned. A society that cannot record obligations in a trusted way cannot scale supply chains, cannot fund mobilization without improvising seizure, and cannot convert productivity into long-term coordination. The ledger is not a technical convenience. It is the social machine that allows strangers to cooperate at scale.

The earliest monetary systems were therefore not coin systems. They were accounting systems: inventories of obligations maintained by institutions with the power to certify, arbitrate, and punish. Names differed across civilizations; function did not. They measured, marked, reconciled, and enforced. This is the first monetary technology: a recognized record that defines discharge by law, binding third parties and terminating disputes beyond the consent of the two counterparties. When discharge is recognized by authority, it ends in a way that can be audited, taxed, collateralized, and enforced. That is the quiet violence and the quiet mercy of monetary order: it closes arguments by declaring finality.

Coinage enters as a second-stage compression of authority into a portable standard. The coin is not valuable because it is metallic. It is valuable because it carries an issuer's legal order: a unit recognized for settlement, a unit protected against certain disputes, a unit accepted in payment to the sovereign itself, and a unit backed by punishments for refusal, counterfeiting, and noncompliance. Coinage scales governance. It makes obligation legible to administrators, collectible by tax authorities, auditable by treasuries, and deployable by armies. When rule expands, it does not merely export soldiers and goods. It exports an enforceable unit of account and the institutions that defend its acceptability. Currency becomes rule because it turns plural local obligation into a system that can be ranked, taxed, and mobilized.

A second illusion must be broken: the belief that monetary history is a parade of improved instruments. It is not an engineering story where the best tool wins on design merit. It is a jurisdiction story. A currency dominates when its issuer can defend acceptability, secure settlement channels, and enforce claims across enough territory that others must coordinate around it. Monetary order is the expansion of a governance perimeter built from law, tax, courts, payment rails, coercive capacity, and—when the system matures—institutions designed to absorb panic without rewriting the entire political settlement each time confidence breaks.

Convertibility is where these issues become surgical. Convertibility is a pledge to upgrade a claim into a superior claim on demand. Under metallic regimes, the superior claim is the metal. Under later architectures, the superior claim is final settlement within the legal hierarchy of the system: the form of payment treated as discharged beyond dispute, not merely credited, not merely acknowledged, but completed under statute. Convertibility is often described as restraint. It is also a method of governing expectations. It forces reserve discipline, it forces attention to outflows, and it forces leaders to confront the fact that confidence is not a mood but a constraint. When convertibility is credible, circulation widens because the upgrade promise stabilizes hierarchy. When convertibility is doubted, the promise becomes an accelerant: everyone tries to upgrade at once, and hierarchy reveals itself through queues, suspensions, selective protection, and official language that insists nothing has changed while quietly changing who gets paid first.

The recurring pattern under stress is recognizable because it is procedural. The public line remains continuity while the operational line becomes triage. Payment is slowed without saying it is slowed. Redemption is deferred without saying it is deferred. Priorities are rewritten in practice before they are rewritten in statute. The first act is administrative: a window shortened, a list narrowed, a process "reviewed." The second act is legal: emergency authority, temporary restrictions, reclassification of eligible claims, a narrowed definition of discharge. The third act is political: a justification that reframes hierarchy as necessity. In that sequence, money stops being habit and becomes visible as governance: a contested ranking of claims managed through institutions that decide, under pressure, whose time will be honored and whose time will be taken.

One can watch the machinery work in a single night in a system that has promised upgrade on demand and discovers that the crowd has begun to run. A treasury meets with its monetary authority before dawn. A redemption desk is closed "for orderly processing." A narrow set of institutions is offered access to superior settlement at a penalty rate, while the public is directed to accept deferred instruments that remain legal tender but no longer behave as equivalent. A list of acceptable collateral is tightened. A court circular is issued to prioritize certain payment obligations over others in insolvency, so that a chosen set of claims will still clear even if the broader system does not. The press line is reassurance. The operational reality is that hierarchy has been redrawn to protect core settlement and preserve internal order. In that moment, the monetary constitution reveals itself as a set of priorities enforced by time, not merely by law.

War is the moment monetary geometry is exposed and then bent. War is not an external shock that merely pressures a system. War is a design environment that rewards administrative speed and punishes regimes that cannot fund themselves fast enough to survive. In war, the question "What is money?" becomes operational: money is the claim that can be accepted quickly enough to keep procurement continuous and internal order intact. Under that pressure, convertibility can become a strategic liability. The issuer can keep the anchor and lose the war, or cut the anchor and buy time. States frequently choose time, then spend years pretending the decision was temporary.

Fiat is not freedom. Fiat relocates constraint. Under convertibility, constraint sits in the reserve. Under fiat, constraint sits in legitimacy: legitimacy of taxing power, legitimacy of enforcement, legitimacy of institutions that can keep the claim hierarchy stable without collapsing into arbitrary confiscation, disorderly inflation, or selective protection so blatant that it tears the coalition that underwrites the currency. A fiat order is disciplined, but its discipline is institutional and political rather than metallic. It is less visible, more contested, and more prone to strategic error by leaders who mistake discretion for capacity.

Domestic finality and cross-border finality are not the same problem: the first is enforced by a single legal order, while the second is enforced by overlapping jurisdictions that can recognize, delay, ring-fence, or refuse each other's discharge when fear returns.

> "Every monetary order is a peace treaty between claims; crisis is the moment the treaty is read aloud."

This is why the transition from emergency finance to durable architecture is the decisive moment in monetary statecraft. When an anchor is cut, the debts remain, the distributional winners and losers remain, and hierarchy has already been rewritten by necessity. The question that follows is never merely how to restore stability. It is how to rebuild enforceability at scale: how to make settlement final across borders, how to manage convertibility expectations without inviting runs, how to build backstops without inviting permanent moral hazard, and how to embed advantage inside structures that present as neutral coordination. The modern monetary world did not emerge because humanity discovered a cleaner theory. It emerged because the world required an enforceable architecture that could scale beyond borders without collapsing into permanent payment disputes and recurrent panics. Stability was built, and dependence was encoded, often in the same stroke.

To understand the origin of authority is to stop asking whether money is "real" and start asking the questions that govern power in practice: which authority makes a claim enforceable, which ledger makes it official, which courts assign priority, which rails grant finality, which institutions provide emergency liquidity, and which political coalitions keep the architecture credible when costs must be allocated. The state does not control money by declaring it. It controls money by controlling the machinery that turns claims into settlement.

CHAPTER 1

THE FIRST CLAIM

EXCHANGE WITHOUT AUTHORITY

The argument did not begin with theory. It began with a refusal to accept delivery as complete. A buyer's agent stood beside stacked bundles and counted again, slower the second time, as if pace could convert doubt into certainty. A carrier's clerk watched with the flat patience of a man who had heard the same dispute in a dozen ports. The seller's representative insisted the shortfall was imaginary, or already priced, or the fault of weather that had scattered cargo before the convoy reached the quay. The goods sat in front of them, present, measurable, and still the transaction remained unsettled. No one trusted the other's count. No one accepted the other's testimony. Each demanded a conclusion that would bind the others and bind whoever would finance the next shipment.

Exchange without authority fails here because it lacks a recognized end-state. It can produce agreement when cooperation is cheap and conflict is costly. It cannot reliably produce closure when incentives diverge, when distance thins reputation into rumor, when time introduces temptation, and when third parties require certainty before they extend credit. A market can host bargaining. It cannot, on its own, create an act that forces unwilling parties to treat an obligation as discharged. The first claim in any system is therefore not a coin and not a price. It is a claim that the obligation has ended, and a claim that this ending will be honored beyond the immediate participants.

Immediate swap survives because it ends itself. Serious economies do not. The moment exchange stretches across time, quality, and distance, trade becomes a chain of promises: provision now, delivery later; delivery now, inspection later; partial performance argued as completion; loss alleged after transit; payment deferred until resale; inventory pledged before it is sold. At that point the governing problem stops being equivalence and becomes enforceability: when does a promise become binding, and when does its discharge become a fact outsiders must accept. A society without enforceable closure retreats into narrow circles where memory substitutes for record and retaliation substitutes for court. Scale does not fail as a shortage of clever instruments; it fails as a shortage of binding endings.

"United States coins and currency (including Federal reserve notes and circulating notes of Federal reserve banks and national banks) are legal tender for all debts, public charges, taxes, and dues."

Read as engineering, not ceremony, the line is a design decision about closure. It declares that a defined instrument ends disputes by rule in the domains named. It binds third parties to treat tender as discharge. It installs a public answer to the question exchange cannot escape: when a debtor offers the recognized instrument, does the obligation end, or does the argument continue under a different mask. The invention of money, at scale, is the invention of that public answer and the apparatus required to make it real.

The popular barter story misplaces the bottleneck. It treats barter as baseline, then money as clever solution to coincidence of wants. That story flatters the idea that money is a tool selected for convenience, and it trains officials to look for objects rather than mechanisms. The deeper sequence runs through record and obligation. Systems that scale begin with measures, schedules, and enforceable promises, because large societies are built on credit: promises carried forward, netted, transferred, and pledged. The instrument that circulates on the surface arrives later as the traveling skin of a deeper mechanism: discharge, enforceability, and ranking under scarcity.

Begin, then, where monetary authority begins: with the unit of account. A unit of account does not need to be carried in the pocket. It needs to be shared in the mind and enforced in the record. It allows a society to compare unlike obligations and offset them against one another. Without a unit, each dispute is unique and each settlement is negotiated from scratch. With a unit, obligations can be aggregated, balanced, discounted, postponed, transferred, and netted. The unit makes obligation speakable at scale. It turns a pile of unique bargains into a coherent domain of comparable claims.

The unit of account also creates the first bridge between the world as it is and the world as it can be financed. Once obligations can be expressed in a stable measure, they can be priced over time. That pricing over time is interest, whether named or hidden. Interest is the rate at which a society converts uncertainty into compensation. Yet interest cannot do its job if the underlying obligation is not enforceable. Without enforceability, the premium becomes arbitrary, and the premium becomes power: whoever can enforce privately charges less to friends and more to outsiders, and the economy organizes itself around protection rather than productivity. A unit of account without enforceability creates sophistication in language and disorder in practice.

Language alone is insufficient. A unit is speech. A ledger is adjudication. The unit allows obligations to be stated; the ledger decides which statements become official record and which remain mere assertion. A ledger is not neutral bookkeeping. It is a ranking machine. It determines who is authorized to write and who must merely speak. It determines which evidence is admissible and which is ignored. It determines what correction procedures exist and which errors become permanent. It determines whether a claim is transferable, whether it can be pledged as collateral, whether it can be offset against other obligations, and what penalties follow when it is dishonored. The ledger's rules decide which promises can be monetized and which remain personal, local, and fragile.

Once record is recognized, claims begin to travel, and the social physics of trade changes. A claim written into recognized record can be transferred, pledged, inherited, taxed, and netted. It can be purchased without the buyer needing to know the debtor personally, because enforceability is no longer carried solely by private threat. A claim outside recognized record travels only as far as the claimant's ability to pressure acceptance. That is the first separation between a society of exchange and a society of money: money is the condition under which claims circulate without requiring the claimant's private force to accompany them.

That separation is not only commercial. It is constitutional. Once claims circulate, the question becomes who has the right to create recognized claims and under what constraints. The right to record is the right to grant economic mobility. The right to deny record is the right to impose economic immobility. In small worlds, that power hides behind custom. In larger worlds, it hardens into offices, courts, charters, and licensed institutions. The architecture of money begins to look like paperwork. The paperwork is the point. Paperwork is how a society chooses whose promises count.

This is the first monetary politics: not the politics of prices, but the politics of admissibility and recognition. Who may be recorded. Which obligations may be recognized. Which assets may be pledged. Which disputes may be heard. Which errors may be corrected. Which claims are treated as senior when collateral is seized. These look like technicalities until one notices what technicalities decide. They decide who can turn future income into present capacity, who can finance inventory, who can bridge a season, who can survive a shock, and who must liquidate at the worst moment. The distributional map of a society is embedded in the ledger's entry rules long before it is argued in public.

In practice, the politics begins with mundane decisions that later become unchallengeable conventions. Which witnesses are acceptable. Which seals or marks satisfy proof. Which forms of pledge are valid. Which documents must be produced for transfer. Which obligations can be assigned to a third party. Which claims can be offset, and which must be paid gross. Which fees attach to registration. Which offices can interpret ambiguity. Each decision creates a cost. Each cost creates an exclusion. Each exclusion creates a class of actors who must either pay to enter, submit to a patron, or stay small. The ledger is not only a record of obligations; it is a machine that manufactures economic shape.

The strategic pass begins where the institutional pass ends. Ledger authority is not mere administration; it is capacity and leverage. Whoever controls recognized record controls the conversion channel from private promise to public credit. That control includes the power to grant access, to impose documentation burdens, to demand collateral, to slow processing, to widen or narrow eligibility, and to deny recognition entirely. In calm periods, those powers look like procedure. In stress, they become time-allocation. Who settles today. Who is queued until tomorrow. Who is told to accept a substitute instrument. Who is forced to sell assets to obtain the recognized claim. Time-allocation becomes solvency-allocation the moment funding depends on timely settlement, and solvency-allocation becomes political allocation the moment failure spills into employment, supply, and public order.

This is why a reader trained in policy must stop picturing money as a thing and start picturing money as an administrative perimeter. Inside the perimeter, claims enjoy recognition. Outside the perimeter, claims rely on private enforcement. The perimeter is drawn by rules: documentation, identity, jurisdiction, admissibility, collateral eligibility, and the right to access the recognized mechanism of discharge. When the perimeter is wide, the economy can scale. When the perimeter narrows, credit shrinks and trade becomes expensive. When the perimeter becomes unstable, panic begins, because panic is what happens when actors realize access to discharge may not be available on the terms they assumed.

Return to the port dispute, not as a scene of frustration but as a map of system requirements. The buyer wants certainty about quantity and quality. The seller wants certainty about payment. The carrier wants certainty about liability boundaries. The financier wants certainty about enforceability and priority if the deal collapses. Each wants a conclusion that survives appeal to a third party. Without that, the financier prices uncertainty as a premium, or refuses entirely. Trade continues, but it continues smaller, slower, and more expensive. Scale becomes expensive because closure becomes negotiable.

In a world that has not yet built enforceable closure, the port dispute does not end with payment. It ends with a bargain under threat. The buyer withholds settlement until the seller offers concessions. The seller threatens to blacklist the buyer from future shipments. The carrier threatens to refuse future carriage without advance payment. Each party seeks to convert uncertainty into advantage. The bargain may resolve that one shipment, but it increases the cost of the next. The next financier sees the precedent and demands higher compensation or more collateral. The next seller insists on harsher terms. Over time, the market becomes a series of guarded transactions rather than a platform for growth. The price system still exists, but it is a thin skin stretched over a deeper problem: discharge is not rule, it is negotiation.

The next invention is discharge, because discharge is the legal event that ends an obligation with finality recognized by third parties. Discharge does two things simultaneously. It gives the creditor certainty that successful tender ends the dispute. It gives the debtor certainty that tender ends the creditor's right to pursue. Without recognized discharge, the debtor never knows when the obligation is truly closed. Without recognized discharge, the creditor never knows whether refusal will be treated as default or as invitation to renegotiate under pressure. Uncertainty forces exchange back toward familiarity because familiarity substitutes, poorly, for enforceable closure.

"If tender of payment of an obligation to pay an instrument is made to a person entitled to enforce the instrument and the tender is refused, there is discharge, to the extent of the amount of the tender, of the obligation of an indorser or accommodation party..." ([law.cornell.edu](https://www.law.cornell.edu/ucc/3/3-603?utm_source=chatgpt.com))

Notice what this does. It is not sentimental about willingness. It is structural about containment. It treats certain forms of tender as sufficient to prevent liabilities from cascading even if acceptance is refused. A monetary order does not merely persuade parties to settle; it creates rules that stop disagreements from propagating into chains of secondary liability. This is the invisible purpose of discharge doctrine: to substitute a public rule for private escalation.

Discharge is the quiet violence and the quiet mercy of monetary order. It is violence because it closes disputes by rule, binding even the unwilling. It is mercy because it prevents perpetual pursuit. It converts the open-ended threat of retaliation into a bounded outcome the order recognizes. A society that can define discharge can expand credit because parties can trust that obligations, once performed, will be treated as ended. A society that cannot define discharge caps credit through fear, and fear makes the economy smaller than it could be.

Yet discharge by itself does not end fragility. It relocates fragility into the definition of what counts as acceptable tender and into the institutions that decide whether tender is valid. A debtor can offer payment that is formally permitted, but the creditor can still dispute adequacy, timing, or authenticity. The order answers these disputes by tightening proof. Tightened proof imposes cost. Cost imposes exclusion. Exclusion changes who can transact at scale. A society that improves enforceability by raising documentary burdens can unintentionally concentrate commerce in the hands of those who can afford compliance. Money, then, is always a compromise between openness and certainty, and the compromise is never neutral.

Once discharge exists, finality becomes the next necessity. Finality is the point after which reversal is not permitted. Without a defined point of finality, no one can rely on payment as completed, and every chain remains subject to clawback anxiety. Participants hoard optionality because reversibility makes the past unsafe. That hoarding raises the cost of trade, increases the appetite for immediate settlement assets, and encourages defensive behavior that looks like prudence and functions like paralysis. Finality lowers the cost of coordination by allowing participants to treat the past as settled and direct attention to the next transaction.

"Settlement fund transfers are irrevocable and unconditional no later than when the derivatives clearing organization's accounts are debited or credited." ([ecfr.gov](https://www.ecfr.gov/current/title-17/chapter-I/part-39/subpart-B/section-39.14?utm_source=chatgpt.com))

Modern language, ancient requirement. A payment that can be reversed after it is treated as settled does not end arguments; it relocates them. Finality is the difference between settlement and mere messaging, between discharge and mere crediting, between a ledger that governs and a ledger that records intentions. In the absence of finality, every participant prices reversal as risk, and risk becomes spread, haircuts, collateral hoarding, and eventually refusal.

Finality produces hierarchy because not all settlement is treated as equally final under stress. Some forms of settlement are treated as final beyond dispute, while others are treated as conditional, revocable, or subject to delay. In calm conditions, the hierarchy is mostly invisible because the order behaves as if equivalence holds. In stress, equivalence breaks. People reach for the highest-grade claim because it ends arguments with the least residual risk. Lower-grade claims are accepted only with conditions, discounts, or suspicion. A hierarchy that had been submerged in routine becomes visible as behavior.

Once hierarchy becomes visible, the political character of money becomes impossible to deny. The highest-grade claim is not better because it is morally superior. It is better because it carries more enforceability and fewer contingencies. It is closer to finality. The crucial point is that the ladder of claims is built, not discovered. It is built out of legal definitions, institutional access, documentation requirements, and the ability to convert one claim into another through recognized pathways. When those pathways are wide and trusted, the economy behaves expansive. When they are narrow or doubted, the economy behaves defensive.

This ladder also determines who can survive a temporary disruption and who is forced into permanent loss. The actor who can reach final settlement can wait. The actor who cannot must sell. The actor who must sell sells into disadvantage, because desperation has a price. In every monetary order, there is a price for being far from finality. That price appears as discount, spread, haircut, and forced liquidation, but its source is institutional: distance from the recognized event that ends disputes.

A society that expands credit must also decide how to allocate loss when promises collide with scarcity. This is where legal priority enters as the hidden constitution of money. Priority decides who gets paid first when value is insufficient. Priority decides which claims are protected and which are sacrificed. Priority decides whether public charges outrank private charges, whether secured claims outrank unsecured claims, whether certain obligations outrank others by policy rather than contract, and whether emergency can rewrite the order. Priority is not an appendix. It is one of the central ways a political order expresses itself in monetary form.

The first time a community experiences multiple creditors competing for the same limited assets, it discovers that enforceability alone is not enough. Enforceability produces collection; it does not produce order. Without priority rules, insolvency becomes a race to the debtor's door. Races become violence or privatized protection. Privatized protection becomes fragmentation. Priority prevents continuous brawling over the remains of default by forcing a ranking on scarcity, and by forcing the ranking to be recognized by third parties whose acceptance determines whether the order can move on.

Here the reader should hold a hard fact in mind: every monetary regime is a regime of loss assignment. In good years, the assignment is quiet because losses are small and spread. In bad years, the assignment becomes explicit because losses are concentrated and time becomes scarce. When officials speak about stability, they often mean preservation of an ordering of claims that allows settlement to continue even while some claims are subordinated. Stability is not the absence of loss. It is the administration of loss without dissolving the settlement perimeter.

A second vignette makes the priority machine visible without requiring grand crisis. A workshop that produces essential components suffers a fire. Orders are delayed. Cash flow collapses. The owner has three immediate creditors: a secured lender with a pledge on inventory and machinery, a supplier owed for raw materials, and workers owed wages. There are also public charges. All parties agree on the facts. The conflict is not about truth; it is about rank. Without a recognized priority schedule, each creditor attempts self-help. The lender sends agents to seize equipment. The supplier attempts to attach inventory at the door. Workers threaten to block removal. The public authority threatens penalty. The outcome becomes a contest of force and speed.

With a priority schedule, the contest becomes procedure. The secured claim is recognized first against pledged collateral. Wages may be granted special status by policy. Public charges have defined rank. Unsecured trade claims fall behind. The decision is not moral purity; it is system continuity. If wages are not protected, production stops everywhere because labor refuses to extend trust. If secured claims are not recognized, collateral cannot support credit and funding retreats. If public charges are not enforced, the authority loses revenue and enforcement capacity. Priority is thus a constitutional compromise about which forms of continuity are most important to preserve. The regime reveals its values in the order in which it pays.

The transition that matters for statecraft is therefore not from barter to coin. It is from exchange as personal contest to exchange as governed settlement. The instrument that circulates on the surface, whether commodity, coin, note, or ledger entry, is the interface. Beneath it sits the machine: discharge definitions, record authority, finality points, default penalties, and priority schedules. The invention of money is the invention of that machine.

To see the machine rather than the interface, consider a market-town that has outgrown kinship enforcement. Traders arrive from surrounding regions. Inventory is financed on promise. The local forum begins registering obligations because informal memory no longer keeps pace. A buyer disputes a shipment and refuses to settle. The seller petitions the registry. The clerk requires sworn statements and weighs them against the carrier's manifest. The forum orders the buyer to tender the recognized instrument by a fixed hour. The buyer tenders, then attempts to attach conditions. The clerk rejects the conditions, records the tender, and the forum treats the obligation as discharged under rule.

The dispute should end there, yet it expands because a second creditor appears, claiming the buyer's warehouse is already pledged. A third arrives with public charges. A fourth appears with unsecured trade claims. The forum must assign priority because the assets cannot satisfy all claims. It orders the pledged collateral to satisfy the secured claim first. It orders public charges next. It orders unsecured claims last, with the remainder, if any. The decision does not create abundance. It creates order. The town does not discover money as an object. It installs money as procedure: end disputes, rank claims, preserve continuity by preventing violence from becoming the default collection mechanism.

The reader should notice the shift. The town has not solved a technical puzzle. It has built a governance apparatus that makes commerce scalable. It has created a recognized place where statements become entries, where entries become enforceable obligations, where tender becomes discharge, where discharge becomes finality, and where scarcity is handled through priority rather than through violence. This is the point at which the authority, in whatever form it takes, becomes the keeper of the monetary perimeter.

In that scene, one sees the first sovereign act: not taxation, not minting, not speech, but recognized closure of dispute. Once closure exists, other sovereign capacities follow. The authority can demand settlement of obligations to itself in the recognized instrument, creating demand. The authority can spend using the instrument, distributing claims that circulate. The authority can enforce using the instrument, making discharge real. Demand creation alone does not build a monetary order. Demand creation without enforceability produces coercion without credibility. Enforceability without legitimacy produces order without acceptance. A durable regime sits between: enough enforcement to end disputes, enough legitimacy to keep acceptance broad.

Tax acceptance is necessary but insufficient. It creates the floor of demand. It does not create the ceiling of trust. Trust, in the institutional sense, is the expectation that discharge will be honored and that priority will be applied predictably. When priority becomes arbitrary, trust becomes fragile. When discharge becomes conditional, trust becomes expensive. When finality is doubted, trust becomes hoarding. Money is not sustained by belief. It is sustained by the predictable operation of closure and ranking.

At this point the reader can see why banking, later, will become unavoidable. Once claims are transferable, they invite intermediation. Someone specializes in evaluating claims, recording them, and converting them into more liquid forms. Intermediation begins as convenience, then becomes infrastructure. The moment it becomes infrastructure, it becomes a public concern. The authority cannot allow the infrastructure to rewrite discharge and priority privately without destabilizing the settlement perimeter. The state may tolerate private intermediation, but it cannot tolerate private sovereignty over finality.

The coin arrives as a later compression of authority into a portable standard. Its significance is not material. Its significance is that it carries discharge recognition into the hand. A coin is a traveling assertion that a unit will be accepted within the issuer's domain for defined obligations, and that refusal carries consequence. A note is a traveling assertion of similar form, tied either to a claim on superior settlement or to acceptance for obligations to the issuer. A ledger entry is a traveling assertion through networks of recognition: it travels when counterparties and institutions accept the ledger as authoritative and treat its settlement as final. The surface differs. The interior function stays constant: money is a governed ranking of claims that ends disputes.

That constancy should discipline modern intuitions. A payment card, a mobile transfer, a stable balance in a banking interface, a wholesale repo claim, a tokenized unit in a custody system: each appears as money to the holder to the extent it can reliably discharge obligations without being questioned. Each fails as money to the extent it cannot. The difference is not branding. It is proximity to finality and certainty of recognition. The machine is still discharge and priority, executed through faster rails and broader networks of record.

There are multiple routes into monetary architecture, and the routes matter because they shape institutional temperament later. One route centralizes record early through storehouse administration. Obligations are recorded as inventory flows. Settlement is enforced through administrative power that can seize, penalize, or exclude. Another route emerges through merchant networks and commercial forums. Obligations are recognized through contract practices that harden into enforceable rules. Settlement is enforced through courts whose legitimacy grows with predictable dispute resolution. The first route emphasizes allocation, procurement, and taxation. The second emphasizes contract, transferability, and netting across counterparties. Both routes converge on the same necessity: scalable trade requires a recognized forum that can define discharge, enforce default, and rank claims under scarcity.

The next step in scale is netting, and netting is where money becomes system rather than series. If every obligation had to be settled gross, in full, one by one, the economy would require an immense stock of settlement assets. Netting reduces that need by offsetting claims and obligations across a network. Netting is not merely efficiency. It is governance. It requires rules about who may participate, what counts as eligible claim, how disputes are resolved, when positions are calculated, and what happens when one participant fails. Netting is also the first mechanism that makes private obligations look like public infrastructure, because it creates a shared dependence on a common calculation.

A simple example reveals the stakes. Three merchants trade in a triangle. Each owes one and is owed by another. Without netting, each must obtain settlement assets to pay gross, even though their obligations cancel in aggregate. With netting, the system calculates the residual and settles only the remainder. The difference is not arithmetic; it is the institutional ability to declare the net as binding. If one merchant disputes the calculation or refuses settlement, the triangle collapses back into bilateral conflict. The netting forum therefore must have authority to enforce the calculation and punish refusal, otherwise netting remains optional and cannot support scale.

Netting introduces a new kind of fragility: default contagion. When obligations are offset, each participant's ability to receive depends on others' ability to pay. The forum must therefore define default containment. It must define collateral rules, margin rules, contribution rules, and loss-sharing rules. This is the early outline of clearing. Clearing is the institutionalization of netting under enforceable procedure. The reason to preview it here is structural: the first claim in money is enforceable closure, but closure at scale is achieved through networks, and networks require institutions that can impose binding calculations. The ledger, in Chapter 2, becomes not only record but operating system: it becomes the platform on which netting, clearing, and finality are produced.

A third vignette shows how cross-boundary exchange turns discharge into leverage even before modern geopolitics. A trader sells goods across a jurisdictional boundary and is paid in an instrument treated as full discharge at home. The seller's home forum recognizes it as settlement. Yet the buyer's forum contests it as insufficient and holds the obligation open until another form of tender is delivered. The seller, thinking he has been paid, extends new credit and ships again. The buyer, operating under a different discharge regime, treats the first obligation as unresolved and uses that to press terms on the second. The conflict is not about honesty. It is about whose closure rule governs.

In the absence of bridge institutions, such conflicts multiply. Merchants retreat into narrow corridors where they know which forum will rule and which instrument will be accepted. The bridge institutions that later emerge are not neutral conveniences. They are systems of recognition: standardized documents, accepted dispute forums, and intermediaries who can translate claims into forms that will be treated as discharge on both sides. The intermediary charges for that translation. The intermediary also gains influence because the intermediary can delay, deny, or condition translation. In primitive form, this is already the logic of correspondent relationships and cross-border payment permissioning. The first claim inside the port dispute becomes the first claim across borders: the claim that an obligation has ended, and the claim that this ending will be honored by those who matter.

The convergence of the domestic and the cross-boundary is the real pressure point for the modern state. Domestic finality is enforced by a single legal order. Cross-boundary finality is enforced by overlapping jurisdictions that may recognize, delay, ring-fence, or refuse each other's discharge. This difference explains why global trade tends to consolidate around a smaller set of widely accepted discharge instruments and widely trusted forums. It also explains why the issuer or gatekeeper of those instruments gains structural advantage: not because others admire it, but because others need the closure it provides.

The first fragility follows from the first invention. If money is the mechanism that ends arguments, crisis is the moment when too many arguments arrive simultaneously and the order cannot end them all without selecting winners. Selection appears first as delay. Delay is the oldest form of rationing. An authority can preserve the appearance of continuity by slowing settlement, narrowing eligibility, and quietly changing which claims receive timely discharge. A regime that can still command time can survive panic. A regime that loses control of time sees hierarchy exposed through runs, freezes, and forced liquidation.

The second fragility is exclusion. Any mechanism that creates binding discharge also creates gatekeeping. Someone decides who can hold the discharge instrument, who can access recognized record, who can participate in clearing, whose collateral is acceptable, whose identity is admissible, and whose claims are subordinated. Exclusion is not a side effect. It is how order is maintained under constraint. Access to discharge is a form of membership. Loss of access is a form of force. That is why monetary order is never only an economic order. It is an inclusion order, enforced through the gates of settlement.

The boundary of the order turns these truths into leverage. Trade across jurisdictions is trade across competing discharge regimes. A claim that settles an obligation inside one legal order may not settle it in another. A ledger entry treated as final here may be contested there. A priority schedule that governs insolvency here may be ignored there. Exchange across distance therefore depends on bridges of equivalence: standardized documents, accepted forums, shared evidentiary rules, common definitions of finality, and intermediaries who translate claims across boundaries. Those bridges are not neutral. They can be priced, delayed, constrained, or denied. The authority that controls the bridge controls the speed and cost of cross-boundary settlement, and speed and cost determine who can participate at scale.

Gatekeeping across boundaries creates dependency. Deny discharge, and trade becomes smaller. Delay discharge, and financing becomes expensive. Condition discharge, and domestic policy becomes constrained because domestic actors must preserve access to external finality and external dispute forums. The logic is old, only the machinery changes. The first claim inside the port dispute is the first claim inside any wider order: the claim that an obligation has ended, and the claim that the ending will be honored by those who matter.

A serious counterargument insists that money can arise without authority through market selection of a convenient commodity or token, then sustain itself through custom and mutual interest. Limited forms can arise that way in small networks with repeated dealing and shared norms. The argument fails at scale and fails under stress. Custom cannot reliably bind third parties who were not present. Custom cannot assign legal priority when multiple creditors compete for the same scarce assets. Custom cannot provide emergency liquidity without immediate conflict over who bears the loss. When fear makes everyone prefer the highest-grade claim immediately, custom yields to gates, and gates require authority.

The practical conclusion for statecraft is immediate. When officials speak as if money is issued at the top and obeyed below, they underestimate the real levers. The levers sit in the recognition of discharge, the enforcement of default, the assignment of priority, the definition of finality, and the control of settlement pathways that convert private claims into public facts. A state that does not control those points does not fully control its monetary position. It may set policy instruments. It may publish targets. Yet its capacity will be conditioned by whoever controls the recognized ledger of finality, the rules of access, the gateways of cross-boundary settlement, and the legal architecture that determines whose claims survive when stress arrives.

The first claim, then, is not a claim about value. It is a claim about authority. It is the claim that an obligation has ended because the order says it has ended, and that the order has the power to make that ending real. Once a society accepts that claim, it has crossed the threshold into monetary order. It has also accepted the permanent truth that money is governance operating under the appearance of exchange.

CLOSING DOCTRINE

Money begins when discharge is defined and enforced as a public fact that binds third parties, because only then can an obligation end in a way that survives dispute, distance, and changing incentives. The unit of account supplies the shared language that makes unlike obligations comparable, but the ledger supplies the institution that makes obligations admissible as proof, transferable as claims, and punishable when dishonored, which is why societies do not scale on barter logic or on custom alone once strangers and time enter the chain. Ledger authority is sovereign capacity in practice because it controls who may access official record, what documentation burdens must be met to obtain recognition, and how time is allocated when stress turns settlement into a queue, and queues decide who remains liquid and who is forced into loss.

Settlement finality is the nonnegotiable hinge because without an irrevocable point after which reversal is not permitted, every payment remains contestable, every chain remains vulnerable to clawback fear, and credit shrinks into caution as actors hoard the highest-grade claim and refuse to extend terms. Legal priority is the hidden constitution of money because insolvency is where the regime proves which claims it will protect and which it will sacrifice, translating political order into a ranking of recoveries that determines who can finance themselves cheaply and who must pay a premium to survive uncertainty. Delay is the oldest crisis instrument because time is the first rationed asset when finality becomes scarce, and rationing by time becomes rationing by solvency as soon as obligations are funded through rolling credit and settlement access. Monetary power is therefore exercised at the gates of record, tender, finality, and priority, not in the symbol printed on an instrument, because the decisive question is never what the object is called but whether it can terminate dispute, clear through the recognized ledger, and hold its rank when fear forces the hierarchy to show itself.

CHAPTER 2

LEDGER RULE

THE BIRTH OF ENFORCED TRUST

The correction request arrived folded twice, pressed flat, and carried like contraband. The trader's agent kept his voice low while the room filled behind him—men waiting to register cargo, to swear out delivery claims, to have a seal verified, to pay a fee that always seemed to rise the week after a bad storm. Two witnesses stood close enough to hear every word and far enough apart to look independent.

The clerk did not ask whether the trader deserved mercy. He did not ask whether the counterparty was cruel. He asked for the only questions that mattered in that room: who had authority to amend, what proof would be accepted, and whether notice had been served. Behind him, a thick book lay open at the day's entries, the ink along the margin still glossy where it had not yet fully set.

The question was not arithmetic. It was whether the record could be changed without teaching everyone in line that the record was negotiable.

A ledger begins as a quiet object and ends as a constitution. At first it is only a place to put obligations so memory does not have to carry them. Later it becomes the institution that decides which obligations can be enforced, transferred, pledged, netted, discharged, and ranked when scarcity arrives. The difference is not ink or medium. The difference is rule—rule that survives pressure, and pressure that arrives more often than polite histories admit.

The first claim of any monetary order is closure: that an obligation has ended, and that the ending will be honored beyond the two people who made the deal. Ledger rule is the next claim, and it is harder: that the record is authoritative enough to bind strangers, reliable enough to support transfer, and disciplined enough to survive correction without collapsing into opportunistic rewriting. If closure ends the argument, ledger rule determines whose version of the argument can even be heard.

Trust in money is often described as mood. Mood matters, but it follows mechanics. A creditor extends terms because the creditor expects enforceability. A buyer pays because the buyer expects discharge. A third party finances because the third party expects that if the deal goes wrong, a forum will assign priority in a way that makes recovery legible. A stranger accepts a claim because the stranger expects the record will be recognized and the dispute forum will enforce it. None of this requires affection. It requires an operating system people do not have to renegotiate every morning.

Ledger rule supplies that operating system by settling four questions that exchange cannot settle on its own. Who may write. What counts as evidence. When an entry becomes official. How correction occurs without becoming a second market in favors. Every monetary order is a set of answers to those four questions. They can be wise or crooked, open or exclusionary, modern or ancient. Yet they must exist, and they must be applied with enough consistency that people can plan across time.

A line like that looks like housekeeping. It is a border checkpoint. It decides which promises will be treated as enforceable obligations and which will remain socially negotiable stories. It decides what can be proven without hauling the original parties into the same room. It decides what can be assigned to third parties, pledged, netted, and enforced without turning every transaction into a trial. In practice, what counts as record determines which parts of an economy are financeable and which remain trapped in the informal—respected by neighbors, ignored by outsiders.

A ledger does not create truth. It creates a governable substitute for truth. Memory, testimony, and reputation can be accurate, but they do not scale because they do not bind third parties cheaply. The ledger creates a public object that can be relied upon, contested in a forum, and defended by enforcement. Once obligation can be detached from relationship and attached to procedure, trade stops needing kinship as its engine. That is the moment specialization stops being risky and starts being rational.

Yet the ledger also creates its own problem. The moment entries exist, people will contest them. They will allege error, forgery, coercion, omission, mismeasurement, or "misunderstanding." The ledger becomes powerful only when it is paired with a forum that can decide which contests matter and which do not. Ledger and tribunal grow together for the same reason locks and keys do: one invites attack, the other sets boundaries.

The tribunal does not need marble columns to be real. It can be a registrar's desk with delegated authority, a merchant forum with chartered rules, a guild committee, an administrative office, a clearing association with membership votes and fines. The label is secondary. The function is primary: it is where record becomes enforceable fact. Once that place exists, the economics of time changes. Planning becomes less gamble and more calculation. Financing becomes possible because priority can be defined and enforced. Investment becomes possible because claims can be transferred with predictable defenses.

The opening scene is an illustrative composite. It is not a claim about one documented petition in one named port. It is the pattern any scalable record regime must produce: a narrow, boring, brutally specific channel for correction that preserves legitimacy by being predictable, evidentiary, and bounded. If a regime never corrects, it becomes cruel and brittle. If it corrects too easily, it becomes corruptible and fragile. Ledger rule is the compromise between those failures. That compromise is never merely technical.

The first lever is admission to the record. Admission sounds clerical. It is distributive power. If one class of actor's obligations are recognized and another class's are not, credit becomes available to one and unavailable to the other. If one class can satisfy documentation burdens cheaply and another cannot, the cost of capital becomes a function of institutional status. The rulebook decides which promises can become claims that travel.

The second lever is identity. Record cannot be enforced if authorship is fog. In early regimes identity is seals, marks, witnesses, oaths, recognized scribes, and sanctions for falsification. In mature regimes it is signatures, licenses, registration numbers, audit trails, and control systems that make denial expensive. Identity integrity is what turns penalty from threat into reality. A ledger without identity becomes a theater of forgery. A ledger with identity becomes a platform for credit.

The third lever is evidence. This is where ledger rule becomes a doctrine of reality. The order must decide what it will treat as proof when parties disagree. It must decide whether testimony is sufficient, whether contemporaneous records are privileged, whether routine recordkeeping has special credibility, whether certain forms are required for transfer, and what happens when proof is missing.

"A record ... made at or near the time ... kept in the course of a regularly conducted activity..." (Business records logic reflected in modern evidence rules; source: uscourts.gov)

The phrase "regularly conducted activity" is not moral praise. It is a design shortcut. Routine records are harder to fabricate without leaving traces. They are more likely to be contemporaneous with the event. They tend to be consistent across time because they are produced even when no dispute is expected. The system elevates these records because it needs a scalable way to treat some information as more reliable than competing testimony. That is enforced trust: trust manufactured by procedures that make lying costly and detectable.

The fourth lever is correction, and correction is where legitimacy is won or lost. A regime must allow errors to be fixed, but it must also make fixes difficult enough that opportunism does not become a business model. Correction needs notice rules, evidence thresholds, adjudication steps, and a point of finality beyond which correction becomes rare and painful. Otherwise the past can be rewritten cheaply, and if the past can be rewritten cheaply, the future cannot be financed. Credit retreats into immediate settlement because no record can be trusted to endure.

The fifth lever is audit. Audit is the bloodstream of credibility. It is how outsiders accept claims without personally trusting every clerk who touched the ledger. Audit imposes external discipline on internal recordkeeping. It gives third parties confidence that the book is not fictional. That confidence becomes liquidity: claims circulate because the market accepts the procedures that produced them.

The sixth lever is penalty. Without penalty, record is suggestion. With penalty, record becomes binding. Penalty can be financial, legal, exclusionary, reputational, or physical, depending on the regime. The mix changes across history. The requirement does not. Dishonoring recorded obligations must carry consequence. Falsifying entries must carry consequence. Obstructing dispute resolution must carry consequence. Otherwise the ledger becomes paper theater and the economy drifts back toward private enforcement.

It helps to see the ledger as a machine with a lifecycle, because lifecycle reveals where power sits. A claim begins as an entry, but it does not become money-like until it survives four gates. Entry: stated in the unit of account and recorded by an authorized writer. Admissibility: treated as credible proof in dispute. Enforceability: backed by consequence for nonperformance. Transferability: capable of being sold or pledged so the transferee can rely on the record without inheriting unlimited litigation. When those gates exist, the claim can travel. When they fail, the claim becomes relational again, dependent on who you know and what force you can apply.

This lifecycle is also where power changes shape. In a memory world, the stronger party can rewrite history by insisting the past occurred differently. In a record world, the stronger party must contest the record, which is costlier and riskier. But procedural fluency becomes its own advantage. The advantage shifts from strength to literacy, from literacy to access, and from access to control. Ledger rule does not abolish power. It changes its camouflage.

Transferability is the hinge that turns record into market. A recorded obligation becomes dangerous and useful once it can be assigned. Transferability allows creditors to convert promises into liquidity by selling them. It allows buyers to accept claims because they can later convert them. It also makes fraud scalable. The regime must therefore design rules of transfer that balance liquidity against authenticity. Who may endorse. What counts as endorsement. What warranties attach. Which defenses travel. When a transferee takes free of certain disputes. These rules decide whether a claim behaves like money or behaves like a lawsuit.

Money is not trust without conflict. Money is trust with conflict contained. If every transferee inherits every dispute, the claim becomes illiquid. If transferees take free of too many defenses, fraud becomes profitable. So the regime creates a managed zone of trust: certain claims circulate with limited contamination, and disputes are channeled into predictable remedies rather than allowed to poison every subsequent holder. That is negotiability as governance.

A second illustrative composite shows the tension without romance. A small merchant sells a claim to a larger dealer for immediate funds. The merchant knows the debtor is slow. The dealer assumes the record will be enforced. The debtor later claims the underlying goods were defective and refuses to pay. If the dealer must relitigate the entire underlying dispute, the claim was not liquid; it was merely reassigned litigation. If the debtor is barred from raising legitimate defenses, the regime becomes predatory. Ledger rule solves this by separating claim-types and defense-types, defining which disputes can travel and which cannot, and defining evidentiary burdens that make fraud expensive without making liquidity impossible.

Once claims can be transferred, intermediation becomes inevitable. Someone will specialize in evaluating claims, recording them, converting them into more liquid forms, and charging a spread. Intermediation starts as convenience and becomes infrastructure. Once it becomes infrastructure, it becomes public concern. The authority cannot allow infrastructure to rewrite discharge and priority privately without destabilizing the settlement perimeter. This is why banking is not an accidental industry. It is ledger rule institutionalized under permission.

The ledger therefore creates two layers of sovereignty. There is visible sovereignty of statutes and tribunals. There is operational sovereignty of access. Access to the ledger determines participation in the economy's most valuable processes: credit creation, collateral transformation, clearing, netting, and settlement. Whoever can grant or deny access can impose conditions that look like administrative requirements and function like policy. This is quiet control: power exercised without speeches.

Ledger rule becomes fully monetary only when it scales beyond a single book and a single forum. Multiple ledgers appear: merchant ledgers, storehouse ledgers, guild registers, court registers, bank ledgers. Actors attempt to settle obligations recorded in one place using entries from another. This creates a recognition fight: which ledger will be treated as authoritative for discharge. If one ledger's entries cannot discharge obligations in another domain, the economy fragments into islands of settlement.

The first solution is standardization. It is dull, and it is the foundation of scale. Standardized measures, standardized contract terms, standardized forms of proof, standardized identity marks, standardized signature practices, standardized timestamps, standardized dispute procedures. Standardization reduces verification costs. Reduced verification cost increases liquidity. Liquidity increases scale. Standard-setting also shifts power to the institutions that certify compliance. Standards are never neutral. They draw boundaries around participation.

The second solution is hierarchy. Some ledgers are treated as superior because they are associated with stronger enforcement, higher legitimacy, and broader acceptance. Those superior ledgers become settlement endpoints. Other ledgers become subordinate—convertible into the superior ledger under conditions. This is where the hierarchy of money begins in institutional reality: not as a theory of instruments, but as a practical question of which record is treated as final.

The third solution is netting. If every obligation had to be settled gross, in full, one by one, the economy would require an immense stock of settlement assets. Netting reduces that need by offsetting obligations across a network. Netting is not merely efficiency. It is governance. It requires rules about who may participate, what claims are eligible, when the net is calculated, how disputes are handled, and what happens when a participant fails. A binding net is a public fact produced by a forum, not a friendly agreement among equals.

A triangle makes it visible. Three merchants trade in a loop. Each owes one and is owed by another. Without netting, each must obtain settlement assets to pay gross even though their obligations cancel in aggregate. With netting, the forum calculates residuals and settles only the remainder. If one merchant refuses an unfavorable net, the loop collapses back into bilateral conflict. So the netting forum must have authority to enforce the calculation and punish refusal. Otherwise netting is optional, and optionality becomes fragility at exactly the wrong moment.

This is where clearing becomes unavoidable. Clearing is netting institutionalized under enforceable procedure. It turns a web of bilateral promises into a governed platform with defined membership, collateral rules, margin rules, and default procedures. Clearing is ledger rule in motion. It is also the first major concentration of systemic risk, because it centralizes dependence.

Membership is where the ledger shows its teeth. A clearing forum must decide who may join. That decision is not merely commercial. It is a political perimeter. A member can net and settle on privileged terms. A nonmember must settle gross through intermediaries, pay more, wait longer, or remain outside the most liquid markets. Membership becomes a form of citizenship inside the monetary machine.

The clearing vignette is also an illustrative composite. A fast-growing trading house petitions to join. It has volume, but it lacks institutional sponsorship and a collateral profile that comforts the incumbents. The forum responds with requirements: higher initial margin, tighter collateral eligibility, slower settlement windows, more frequent audits, and a probation period long enough to feel like a message. The trading house can comply only by tying up capital—slowing growth—or by paying an established member to clear on its behalf—transferring profit and control upward. The forum calls it prudence. It is also a distributional decision about who may access the cheapest form of settlement. Ledger rule at scale is a hierarchy of access.

The continuity from Chapter 1 matters. Closure created the first claim. Record makes that claim enforceable beyond the parties. Together they generate the next inevitability: governed networks for netting and settlement. Those networks cannot function without rules that bind. Binding rules create winners because they allocate time, cost, and access. Enforced trust is never free and never neutral. It is purchased through governance choices that assign friction to some and privilege to others.

The question becomes what makes a ledger regime legitimate enough to endure. Legitimacy is not popularity. It is acceptance of outcomes as binding even by those who dislike them. For ledger rule, legitimacy rests on three pillars. Predictability: rules are stable enough that actors can plan. Correction: errors can be fixed through credible channels. Bounded discretion: officials cannot rewrite record arbitrarily without consequence.

Audit and correction become constitutional here. Strong audit with weak correction produces oppressive brittleness. Strong correction with weak audit produces corrosive uncertainty. Balance is a monetary asset. It lowers spreads, reduces hoarding, and expands willingness to accept claims from strangers, because it teaches the market that the record is reliable and not cruel.

Modern readers often assume digitization solves these problems. It does not. It changes tempo. A digital ledger can preserve injustice more efficiently. A cryptographic signature can authenticate exclusion as well as inclusion. A data standard can produce interoperability for some and isolation for others. The medium changes speed; it does not change power. Governance remains: who writes, who audits, who enforces, and how disputes are closed.

The private-record counterargument must be treated honestly. Private record can scale farther than casual observers expect when membership sanctions are strong, exclusion is credible, and reputational systems are tied to enforcement. Merchant networks can generate real liquidity inside their perimeter. Yet the boundary remains structural. Private record cannot compel recognition outside the perimeter without public endorsement or private coercion. The moment claims must settle against obligations outside the club, the private ledger must translate into a recognized public forum or remain a closed loop. Large monetary orders cannot remain closed loops. Obligations cross boundaries. Insolvencies spill. Political legitimacy is tested by outcomes that affect nonmembers.

The final step that completes ledger rule is settlement finality. A ledger that cannot produce final settlement is a ledger of intentions, not a ledger of discharge. Finality is where record becomes reality: where an entry is no longer a claim about the world but a change in the world the order will defend.

"Final settlement is defined as the irrevocable and unconditional transfer of an asset or financial instrument, or the discharge of an obligation... in accordance with the terms of the underlying contract." (CPMI, BIS; source: bis.org)

The definition matters because it ties ledger rule to the endpoint of monetary authority. If final settlement is not defined, or if it is defined but not defended, chains remain vulnerable to reversal, dispute, and hoarding. Enforced trust requires a point at which the order says, without apology: the argument is over. Ledger rule is how that point can be reached predictably.

The chapter began at a counter where an entry might be amended. It ends at the definition of final settlement because that is where amendment must stop. A ledger regime must choose where to stop rewriting the past, otherwise it cannot finance the future. The birth of enforced trust is the birth of a record that can be corrected within narrow channels, defended against opportunism, used for transfer, used for netting, and carried into finality that third parties must honor.

CLOSING DOCTRINE

Ledger rule is sovereignty expressed as procedure rather than proclamation, and procedure is where power hides when it intends to endure. The authority that governs the ledger governs the economy's reality by deciding who may write into the official record, what counts as admissible proof when parties disagree, when an entry becomes official enough to bind third parties, and how errors can be corrected without turning correction into a market in favors. A unit of account provides the language that makes obligations comparable, but the ledger provides the forum that makes obligations enforceable, transferable, and punishable when dishonored, which is why the unit alone never produces scale unless record and enforcement travel with it. Enforced trust is not a mood and not a cultural virtue; it is manufactured through regular process, auditability that makes fabrication detectable, and credible penalty that makes defection costly, so that strangers can cooperate without requiring personal affection or private protection.

Correction is the legitimacy hinge because a regime that never corrects becomes brittle and unjust, while a regime that corrects too freely becomes corrosive and uncertain, teaching creditors that the past can be rewritten cheaply and therefore the future cannot be financed at reasonable cost. The ledger's discipline is completed only when transferability is made safe enough to support liquidity without making fraud profitable, which requires managed containment of dispute so that claims can circulate without dragging unlimited litigation into every transaction. Netting and clearing are ledger rule at scale because they take the ledger from passive record to active machinery: a forum calculates binding residuals, defines who may participate, sets collateral and margin rules that determine who can remain solvent under stress, and applies default handling that prevents one failure from turning every promise into a contest of speed and violence. A ledger becomes fully monetary only when it can reach final settlement, meaning an irrevocable and unconditional discharge that third parties must honor under the terms of the underlying contract, because without that endpoint the record remains a statement about intention rather than an event that ends argument and allows the system to move forward.

CHAPTER 3

CURRENCY AND CONQUEST

EMPIRE AS MONETARY TECHNOLOGY

The first time a conquered town paid in the conqueror's unit, the transaction looked ordinary enough to disappear into the day's accounting. A levy was assessed, a receipt was marked, grain was carried into a storehouse, and a clerk ticked an entry that did not care who had pleaded in the square the week before. That ordinary appearance was not incidental; it was the point. Conquest that stays visible as violence must be repeated, and repetition is expensive, loud, and brittle. Conquest that becomes currency can be administered, audited, and routinized, which is to say it can be made cheap enough to last. The durable empires were never only machines of force; they were machines of standardization that turned force into an operating system: a unit in which obligations were counted, a record in which they were recognized, a forum in which they were enforced, and a schedule in which the unit had to be produced by subjects regardless of what they thought of the stamp.

Currency is often taught as a medium of exchange, as if its primary virtue were convenience. In statecraft it is a medium of governance, and its primary virtue is not convenience but compulsion disguised as normality. A unit becomes power when it becomes the default language of obligation and the default instrument of discharge, and when the institutions that recognize discharge are strong enough that strangers accept the unit without insisting on private guarantees. The deeper mechanism is not the object in the hand; it is the perimeter behind the object. When the perimeter is coherent, the unit feels natural. When the perimeter is weak, the unit feels like tribute and produces evasion corridors, barter substitutes, and private settlement regimes that fracture the sovereign's command. Currency is the traveling skin of enforceability: it carries a promise that obligations can end cleanly, and it carries a threat that refusal will be punished through courts, gates, and seizure rather than through personal retaliation.

Empire's monetary breakthrough begins with an act that sounds fiscal and is in fact constitutional: tax payable in the unit. A unit that must be delivered to the authority on schedule creates demand that cannot be politely declined. It forces households, merchants, and local elites to obtain the unit repeatedly, and repetition builds habit faster than persuasion ever will. Habit becomes circulation, circulation becomes pricing, and pricing becomes the illusion that the unit is simply what value is. A modern formulation makes the design brutally explicit: "Coins and currency ... are legal tender for all debts, public charges, taxes, and dues." (31 U.S.C. §5103.) Read as engineering, the sentence does not celebrate money; it defines discharge as a public fact in specified domains. A unit that can extinguish tax obligations becomes more than a token among merchants because it is wired into the obligations that bind people to authority, and because failure to obtain it can be punished without negotiation. That is how a unit becomes unavoidable without requiring affection.

Demand alone, however, does not become dominance unless the empire builds the machinery that makes payment predictable. A sovereign can require a unit and still fail if the unit cannot travel reliably, if counterfeit is rampant, if records are inconsistent, if forums disagree, or if enforcement is porous enough that evasion becomes normal. Tax creates demand; machinery creates confidence that tender ends arguments. The combination is what allows the unit to function as governance rather than as raw extraction. When machinery is weak, the empire must keep showing weapons because procedure cannot carry the load. When machinery is strong, coercion retreats behind routine and routine begins to look like commerce. Subjects learn to comply not because they are convinced but because the cost of noncompliance becomes constant, predictable, and unpleasant, while compliance becomes the shortest path to lawful standing, enforceable title, and access to wider markets.

The machinery expands through channels that look administrative and function as domination. The first is measure. Empires standardize weights, measures, and accounting units because governance needs comparability. Without comparability, taxation becomes arbitrary, procurement becomes corruptible, and audit becomes theater. Standardization reduces dispute and reduces the discretion of local intermediaries who profit from ambiguity, but it also erodes local autonomy because local measure is local sovereignty in miniature, an ability to define equivalence on one's own terms. When the center imposes measure, it is asserting that the center will decide what counts and that local count will be treated as inferior, which is why standardization produces resistance that looks cultural and is in fact economic. The second channel is the forum. A unit becomes dominant when official dispute resolution calculates damages, enforces contracts, and assigns priority in the imperial unit. Once that happens, local obligation is pulled into the imperial record even when the parties never consciously "adopted" it, because the only outcomes that matter are the outcomes the forum will enforce. The third channel is the gate. Licenses, permits, charters, registries, toll points, and market permissions force obligations into the imperial record, turning legal access into a currency decision: adopt the unit and the forms, or remain in a shrinking corridor where credit is expensive because enforceability is uncertain. The subject may describe adaptation as voluntary. The empire knows the choice is conditioned by its control of gates.

A composite scene shows the conversion of force into routine without needing famous episodes. A provincial merchant brings a complaint to a registrar because the counterparty has begun trading with outsiders who refuse elder decisions. The registrar insists on standardized forms, demands proof in a format local practice never required, charges a fee that is small once and painful when repeated, and schedules a hearing date that implicitly rations time. The merchant can comply and gain access to broader routes and stronger enforcement, or refuse and remain inside a local corridor where counterparties demand immediate settlement and where every dispute must be resolved by reputation, threat, or private patronage. The choice is framed as modernization, but the deeper truth is migration from one recognition regime to another, and currency is the interface through which that migration becomes survivable. The merchant learns quickly that the empire's unit is not merely what he pays; it is what grants him standing, what makes his claims transferable, and what allows his obligations to end without having to bargain in the street.

The unit's dominance also reorganizes loyalty by reorganizing time. In many local orders, obligations are seasonal and negotiable; repayment can be socially mediated; arrears can be handled through status. An imperial schedule is different. It is calendared, external, and enforced. The subject must obtain the unit on time, which changes production choices, storage choices, and trade choices. By making payment a timed obligation, the empire becomes the manager of the subject's calendar, and calendar control is deeper than visible coercion because it disciplines daily life. A subject who must obtain the unit repeatedly will choose crops, routes, and counterparties that supply it, and those choices pull the subject into imperial markets even when the subject's loyalties remain local. This is how the unit becomes a tool of incorporation: it aligns survival with participation.

Distribution infrastructure matters as much as demand. Soldiers must be paid, officials must be salaried, roads and ports must be maintained, procurement must settle cleanly, and each of these tasks depends on whether the unit is accepted broadly enough that administration does not require constant seizure. Durable empires invest in credibility not as benevolence but as cost reduction. Credibility here is not merely stability of purchasing power; it is predictability of acceptance and predictability of discharge. A unit can fluctuate in value and still govern if it remains the required discharge instrument for taxes and enforceable obligations, while a unit can be stable and still fail if acceptance is contested, recordkeeping is unreliable, or forums do not enforce discharge consistently. The coin in the hand is the smallest visible part of the machine; the machine is what allows strangers to accept payment without asking who will back them if payment is refused later. The empire backs them, not out of kindness, but because acceptance is the empire's administrative fuel.

Monetary compromise is often intelligence rather than weakness. Empires tolerate local units in peripheral domains while requiring taxes in the imperial unit, allowing local instruments for small trade while forcing large obligations into imperial settlement. This creates hierarchy inside the empire: local claims circulate at the edges, while the imperial claim settles at the center. Over time the hierarchy pulls activity toward the center because the center is where discharge is strongest and credit is cheapest, and "cheapest" here means closest to the point where argument truly ends. Integration feels like convenience. It is also consolidation of power because integration means more transactions terminate under imperial rules and fewer terminate under local discretion. Those closest to the center—licensed intermediaries, chartered merchants, registrars, magistrates—gain privileged access to the strongest discharge and the lowest friction, while those farther away pay a premium in worse terms, higher collateral demands, and more frequent exposure to dispute. That premium is not a moral judgment; it is the price of being far from finality.

The unit becomes harder to dislodge once it is embedded in property. When land title is recorded and enforced in the imperial record, the unit becomes wired into the property system because property becomes financeable only through recognized title. Enforceable title becomes collateral, collateral becomes credit capacity, and credit capacity becomes survival advantage when seasons turn. At that point monetary governance and property governance fuse. The empire that controls the translation of property into enforceable collateral controls the credit capacity of its subjects, and that capacity can be expanded for allies and constrained for rivals without theatrical decrees, through registry rules, court delays, licensing conditions, and documentation burdens that feel procedural and function as political control. Resistance to standardization is therefore not only cultural; it is a defense of local rents and local autonomy, because local measures, local forums, and local registries are sources of power that the empire is actively replacing.

The modern continuity is direct even when uniforms have changed. Monetary dominance can operate through network control rather than territorial control, but the mechanism is the same: a unit backed by enforceable discharge, supported by legal and institutional machinery, demanded through obligations to the center, and exported through trade and finance. A network formulation makes the governance character of cross-border payment explicit: "No member shall ... impose restrictions on the making of payments and transfers for current international transactions." (Articles of Agreement, Article VIII, Section 2(a).) The sentence is written as a prohibition, but its existence proves the point: payments and transfers are treated as a governed domain, subject to permission and supervision. Whoever can influence those channels—through approval, denial, delay, documentation burden, or compliance gating—can shape trade and finance far beyond their borders. The gate has moved from a physical checkpoint to a procedural one, but the lever is the same: access to recognized discharge.

A counterargument must be conceded because it is partly true and widely believed. Currency dominance can look like market preference for stability and liquidity, and preferences do matter. Traders prefer units that hold purchasing power; creditors prefer predictable enforcement; markets coordinate around instruments that reduce dispute. The concession stands. Yet the boundary condition is decisive: the instrument becomes most useful because it is embedded in an enforcement perimeter and because its issuer or its governing network can defend the infrastructure that makes discharge credible at scale. Preference follows power because power shapes which preferences can be safely expressed and which claims can be trusted to survive dispute. Liquidity is not a natural attribute; it is an institutional gift granted by recognition and defended by enforcement.

The endpoint that makes hierarchy real is final settlement, because final settlement is where record becomes reality and where reality becomes governable. A definition used in payment-system doctrine states it plainly: "Final settlement [is] the irrevocable and unconditional transfer ... or the discharge of an obligation ... in accordance with the terms of the underlying contract." (CPMI glossary definition of final settlement.) This is why so many systems converge around a smaller set of trusted settlement nodes. The unit closest to widely accepted final settlement does not merely enjoy prestige; it enjoys the ability to lower its own cost of governance and raise the cost of participation for others by controlling the pathways through which obligations are definitively extinguished.

CLOSING DOCTRINE

Conquest that becomes currency becomes administration, and administration is cheaper than repeated violence because it converts force into routine procedure that subjects can predict and therefore accommodate, even when they resent the center. A currency dominates when timed obligations to authority, enforceable forums, registries, and gates force obligations into a common unit and make discharge predictable enough that strangers accept claims without requiring private protection or private retaliation. Standardization of measure and record is monetary technology because it reduces dispute and lowers verification costs while eroding local autonomy by replacing local equivalence with central equivalence, and because it shifts advantage to those who can satisfy documentation and access burdens cheaply. Hierarchy inside an empire begins as tolerated plurality and ends as enforced settlement at the center, because the center offers stronger discharge and therefore cheaper credit, drawing activity inward and embedding dependence in the structure of everyday commerce. Monetary dominance is not pure preference; liquidity follows the perimeter of credible discharge, and credible discharge is defended by institutions that can delay, deny, condition, or punish, even when the justification is written in administrative language rather than political confession.

CHAPTER 4
CONVERTIBILITY DISCIPLINE
THE ANCHOR THAT GOVERNS STATES

The line outside the redemption window is never only a line. It is a referendum conducted without ballots, measured in footsteps and hours, and decided before any official statement can be drafted. Men arrive with folded notes and stamped receipts, women with small bags and tight mouths, merchants with ledgers under their arms, and clerks sent by employers who do not want to be seen in public. Nobody stands there to make a speech. Each person is making a calculation that is colder than panic: if an ordinary claim can be upgraded into a superior claim on demand, then delay is information, and refusal is confession. In a convertibility regime, the first crack is not a headline; it is a pause at a counter, a whispered instruction to return tomorrow, and a glance toward the back room where the reserve asset is kept.

Convertibility is the most elegant trap a sovereign can set for itself because it translates legitimacy into a promise that can be demanded at the worst possible moment. It is described as prudence, as restraint, as a commitment that keeps the state honest. That description is not wrong, but it is incomplete. Convertibility is a constitutional arrangement about hierarchy, a public guarantee that certain claims can be redeemed into superior settlement under defined conditions. The guarantee makes ordinary instruments circulate with less friction because holders believe upgrade is available. The same guarantee makes crisis sharper because doubt concentrates demand for upgrade and turns rumor into a run on the mechanism itself. The anchor governs the state not by inspiring virtue but by making weakness measurable in reserves and measurable in time, because the promise is testable and the test is performed by anyone who can reach the window.

The modern mind treats convertibility as a historical stage, a primitive constraint that technocrats outgrew. That dismissal misses why convertibility remains the purest demonstration of monetary architecture. It forces every participant to confront the hierarchy of claims in explicit form. It clarifies the difference between a claim that is merely accepted and a claim that is final, and it does so through procedure rather than persuasion. When a regime promises conversion into superior settlement, it is promising to defend a boundary: the boundary between ordinary money and the higher-grade asset that ends disputes beyond appeal. When that boundary becomes permeable only for the privileged or only after delay, the regime reveals its true constitution without needing to say a word, and the public learns that monetary equality was always an administrative story.

Convertibility is not a story about whether people like the currency. It is a story about what people are entitled to demand in exchange for it, and about whether the issuer can honor the demand when honoring it becomes inconvenient. If the upgrade is credible, the system enjoys a gift: ordinary claims circulate broadly because holders treat them as nearly equivalent to the superior claim, and the reserve asset is not hoarded because hoarding feels unnecessary. If the upgrade is doubted, the gift becomes a curse: everyone seeks the superior claim at once, and the issuer discovers that confidence is not a mood but an operational constraint. The reserve stock drains whether the issuer enjoys the rhetoric or not, and the drain forces decisions that no committee can finesse with language.

A commercial formulation, written for ordinary instruments, captures the deeper architecture of convertibility because it defines the nature of a promise that can be demanded rather than requested. "An instrument is a 'negotiable instrument' if it is an unconditional promise or order to pay a fixed amount of money ... payable to bearer or to order ... payable on demand or at a definite time." (Uniform Commercial Code §3-104.) Payable on demand is not a poetic phrase. It is a design choice that shifts leverage from issuer to holder. A regime that makes upgrade available on demand, whether directly to households or indirectly through banks, is offering liquidity as a right rather than a favor. Rights stabilize circulation in calm periods and destabilize regimes in stress because rights cannot be rationed quietly without becoming political, and the state's first instinct under stress is always to ration.

The anchor governs states because it forces political choice to show up as reserve arithmetic. In a convertibility regime, the state cannot expand claims indefinitely without confronting outflows of the reserve asset. Deficits that require imports, procurement that draws on external supply, capital flight driven by political fear, banking stress that triggers internal hoarding, all appear as demand for the superior claim. Reserves are not an abstract symbol of "confidence." They are the resource that makes the promise credible. When reserves drain, the state is forced into choices that are normally postponed: tighten credit, raise taxes, cut spending, borrow at punishing terms, impose gates, or suspend convertibility and admit that hierarchy has changed. The anchor does not prevent political conflict; it forces conflict into visible tradeoffs.

Convertibility regimes are built on definitions that look technical and are in fact distributive. The system must specify what counts as the redeemable claim and what counts as the reserve asset. It must specify where redemption occurs, who is eligible, what documentation is required, what hours apply, what fees apply, and what exceptions exist in emergency. Each specification is a gate, and gates create hierarchy. If only banks can redeem, banks occupy a higher rung than households, and the household's "right" becomes mediated by the bank's willingness to convert on the household's behalf. If redemption requires documentation that only large firms can produce quickly, large firms receive time and small firms receive delay. If redemption is limited to certain windows, access is rationed by geography and schedule. Convertibility is marketed as an equal promise. In operation it is a hierarchy of permissions wrapped in public language.

The first visible symptom of stress in such a regime is almost always administrative. Redemption forms become more detailed. Verification becomes slower. Hours become shorter. Larger requests are asked to return tomorrow. The language used is always ordinary: orderly processing, routine checks, verification for security. The effect is never ordinary. Under convertibility, delay is rationing, and rationing is a signal that the superior claim is scarce. A regime can survive if it can ration without triggering a rush. It fails when rationing becomes visible enough that people infer the book is thin. In a convertibility system, time is the first battleground because time is the first thing the issuer can control without formally breaking the promise, and the public learns quickly to treat time as the regime's honest statement.

The second symptom is legal. Emergency authority is invoked. Eligibility is narrowed. Fees are raised. Redemption is limited to certain counterparties. Redemption is converted into a staged process with waiting periods. The language remains calm while the hierarchy becomes explicit. In effect, the regime is rewriting the upgrade promise by procedural means, moving from on demand toward on permission. The decision is rarely described as a change in hierarchy. It is described as a measure to protect stability, which is the regime's way of saying that the promise is too expensive to honor universally.

The third symptom is social. Those closest to the redemption mechanism obtain the superior claim; those farthest away receive substitutes. A large merchant clears through privileged channels. A small shopkeeper is told to accept delay. A wage earner holds a claim that is still "money" in name but is no longer money in function because it cannot be upgraded when needed. The regime's ranking becomes visible in the distribution of time. Convertibility therefore exposes a truth the political class prefers to keep obscure: monetary systems allocate privilege by controlling access to final settlement. The anchor makes that allocation impossible to hide because it forces the question of who gets the upgrade and who does not.

When convertibility is truly honored, it generates a paradoxical stability. People do not constantly redeem because redemption is available. The promise reduces the need to exercise the promise. The reserve stock can therefore be smaller than the total stock of circulating claims, which is why convertibility regimes can operate for long periods without daily crisis. The system runs on the expectation of upgrade rather than on continuous upgrade. Yet this is precisely what makes the regime vulnerable to shifts in belief. Because reserves are fractional relative to claims, a large swing in redemption demand is existential. Convertibility is stable until it is not, and the transition can be fast because the architecture creates a funnel for demand.

Banking turns that funnel into a machine. Banks issue liabilities that function as money because holders expect those liabilities to be convertible, directly or indirectly, into the settlement asset that ends disputes beyond appeal. Under an anchor regime, that expectation tightens. Deposit holders care less about slogans and more about the speed with which deposits can become the superior claim. Intermediaries, sensing this, hoard reserves, shorten maturities, and demand higher-quality collateral. Merchants begin to refuse lower-grade instruments except at a discount. The discount is not a moral judgment; it is a risk premium for uncertain upgrade. The anchor, by making the hierarchy explicit, forces the private sector to behave as a risk manager rather than as a storyteller.

This is where the state discovers a cruel asymmetry: the promise is uniform, but the ability to exercise the promise is not. Households can stand in lines. Large institutions can move through corridors. If redemption is mediated through banks, banks can ration households while redeeming for themselves, and the state will call it stability because it preserves the banking interface that keeps payments running. If redemption is direct, households can drain reserves quickly, and the state will call it disorder because it forces the state to choose between honoring the promise and defending the reserve stock. Either way, the anchor governs by forcing the same question with different faces: whose claims are upgraded first when the superior claim is scarce.

The anchor also governs through external channels. Convertibility is never purely domestic because the reserve asset is often acquired through trade balances, external borrowing, or political arrangements that can be tightened when the state looks weak. The state that promises redemption is acknowledging a dependency: it must maintain channels that allow it to acquire and hold the superior claim. When those channels are influenced by foreign creditors, foreign trade partners, or external intermediaries, convertibility becomes a lever others can pull. A sovereign can insist it is independent while its reserve position tells the truth. When reserves are abundant, sovereignty feels natural. When reserves are scarce, sovereignty becomes negotiation with external conditions, and domestic monetary stress becomes foreign policy in the form of outflows.

The deepest misunderstanding in convertibility crises is the idea that "speculators" cause collapse. People test promises when incentives make testing profitable and when information suggests the promise is thin. Under convertibility, the promise is testable by design, and the test is simple: present the claim, demand the superior claim, observe the response. If the response is prompt and unquestioned, confidence strengthens. If the response is delayed, conditional, or partial, confidence weakens. The act of testing drains reserves, so the test becomes self-fulfilling even when the testers are not malicious. Convertibility regimes are therefore games of time and perception, but the pieces are legal and physical. The reserve stock drains whether or not the state enjoys the moral vocabulary it uses to describe the drain.

The moral vocabulary exists because convertibility regimes often require contraction to survive. If reserves are finite and claims are large, then defending convertibility requires adjustment somewhere: contraction of credit, contraction of demand, contraction of imports, contraction of wages, contraction of political promises. Leaders speak of honesty, solidity, and discipline because those words create social support for painful policies. Yet the pain is not produced by morality; it is produced by arithmetic. The anchor is a tool for forcing contraction. The language is a tool for selling it.

The pattern of crisis management under convertibility is predictable because the corridor of choices is narrow. First comes administrative rationing, because rationing buys time without formally breaking the promise. Then comes legal narrowing, because narrowing reduces the population that can demand upgrade. Then comes emergency borrowing, because borrowing replenishes reserves and signals both determination and vulnerability. Then comes defensive tightening, because tightening reduces outflows and makes the economy smaller to fit the reserve constraint. Then either stabilization occurs or suspension arrives. The pattern matters not as history trivia but as a diagnosis of how a commitment governs: it forces sequences that would otherwise be politically negotiable into a set of actions that are nearly compelled by the design of the promise.

The first added pressure scene begins where real governance begins: a closed room with tired people and a balance sheet that refuses to be persuaded. The cabinet meets at dusk, the long table littered with drafts of emergency decrees, the smell of ink and stale coffee mixing with the more metallic smell of fear. The treasury has one set of numbers. The monetary authority has another. The banking supervisor has a third. The trade ministry arrives with a fourth, insisting that if import settlement fails for critical goods, the next crisis will be shortages, not merely exchange rates. Nobody speaks in slogans. They speak in maturities, schedules, and obligations that will hit the window tomorrow morning.

The decision is not framed as "defend the anchor" or "abandon the anchor," because those phrases are political poison. It is framed as a sequence of operational choices. Should the state raise the policy rate overnight to slow outflows, knowing this will hit domestic borrowers and trigger layoffs that will reduce tax revenues? Should it limit redemption to banks only, knowing that households will interpret that as confiscation of rights and merchants will reprice goods immediately? Should it announce an emergency holiday for "reconciliation," knowing that the holiday is a confession to anyone who understands what holidays mean? Should it commit reserves to backstop banks' settlement, knowing that defending domestic payments may drain the reserve stock faster than any household line could?

The governor of the monetary authority speaks last, not out of drama but out of habit. He does not claim heroism. He claims arithmetic. If the state uses reserves to rescue banks and preserve domestic payments, the anchor may fail externally because reserves are drained. If the state refuses reserves to banks, domestic payments freeze, which will destroy commerce, tax collection, and public order, and then the anchor will fail anyway because the state will be forced into seizure and improvisation. The room recognizes a truth nobody wants to write in a communiqué: convertibility is not a single promise but a ranking of promises. The state must decide which obligations will be treated as superior in practice when the superior claim is scarce.

They choose a triage plan because convertibility regimes always end up triaging when stress is real. Redemption is restricted by counterparty class rather than by formal admission of suspension. Banks receive access under penalty rates and tighter collateral eligibility. Large import settlement receives priority because shortages would produce political failure faster than inflation statistics. Households are told that redemption remains available, but only within daily limits and with additional verification, which is rationing in polite clothing. The press statement will say the regime remains intact. The operational plan will say the regime has become administered. In the morning, merchants will price goods as if the plan is the truth, because merchants respond to the operational plan, not to the press line.

The consequence arrives immediately and quietly. A bank that knows it can obtain the superior claim at the window, even at penalty, gains leverage over depositors who cannot. Depositors become aware of this leverage, and their behavior changes. Some withdraw to hold physical claims. Some move deposits to institutions rumored to have better access. Some demand higher wages or faster payment because they sense that time is becoming expensive. The banking supervisor watches the flows and sees the shape of a new hierarchy forming inside the old one: not merely who can redeem, but who can redeem without waiting, and waiting is the difference between liquidity and insolvency when obligations mature daily.

That room also shows why convertibility is geopolitical even before anyone mentions foreign creditors. Once the state begins triage, outsiders infer weakness. The price of emergency borrowing rises. Trade partners demand settlement in the superior claim rather than in the domestic claim. External lenders shorten maturities. The state is forced to spend reserves not only to honor redemption, but to keep external channels open long enough to import essentials. Convertibility turns foreign perception into domestic constraint because perception controls outflows, and outflows control the reserve stock that makes the promise credible. The anchor is a domestic commitment and an external exposure at the same time, and that dual character is why it governs so ruthlessly.

The second added pressure scene shows the external channel in motion, because sovereign weakness is often discovered not in speeches but in term sheets. An emissary is sent to an external lender, not with a flourish but with a folder of numbers and a request that is framed as routine liquidity support. The meeting is cordial. The response is conditional. There will be assistance, but only against specified collateral, only with covenants that limit domestic discretion, only with reporting requirements that effectively install external observation inside domestic administration, and only with a timetable that forces contraction faster than the political cycle can absorb. The lender does not need to say "your sovereignty is reduced." The covenants say it. Convertibility regimes, when stressed, often trade autonomy for reserves, because reserves are the key to defending the promise.

The state returns with the offer and pretends it is a victory, because the alternative is to admit that the window may not be honored tomorrow. The finance minister reads the conditions and sees that the offer is not simply money. It is governance. It dictates which expenditures will be cut, which taxes must rise, which public enterprises must be reorganized, which banking practices must be altered, and which capital movements must be monitored. The conditions are presented as stabilization. They function as re-ranking. The state will keep the anchor for now, but it will keep it by accepting a narrower corridor of domestic choice. The state is buying time with autonomy, and convertibility regimes always end up buying time with something.

Back home, implementation becomes the real crisis. Tightening credit reduces import demand but also reduces employment. Reduced employment reduces revenues. Reduced revenues increase deficit pressure. Deficit pressure increases the temptation to issue claims that will later be demanded at the window. The state is forced into a feedback loop in which defending the anchor requires contraction that weakens the fiscal base that supports the anchor. The only way out is either exceptional growth, exceptional political cohesion, or a redefinition of the promise. The first two are rare under crisis pressure. The third is suspension dressed as reform.

This is why convertibility discipline is not merely a monetary discipline but a discipline imposed on the entire administrative machine. It forces the state to align fiscal capacity, banking stability, trade flows, and political tolerance around a reserve constraint. It forces the state to treat time as a resource that can be allocated, not merely as a background condition. It forces the state to treat access as a privilege that must be managed, not as a right that can be honored universally at all moments. Convertibility regimes can endure for long periods when the external position is strong and the political coalition is coherent. They fail when external channels tighten, domestic coalitions fracture, or banking becomes too large a promise to be honored inside the reserve constraint.

The role of legal discharge rules becomes more visible as the regime strains. A modern formulation, though written for ordinary instruments, reveals the deeper intent of monetary law in stressed regimes: "If tender of payment ... is made ... and the tender is refused, there is discharge, to the extent of the amount of the tender, of the obligation ..." (Uniform Commercial Code §3-603.) The significance in convertibility crises is not the specific parties contemplated by the rule but the purpose: the order needs closure rules that prevent disputes from cascading. When redemption is delayed or refused, the state tries to preserve closure by redefining what counts as tender, substituting instruments that preserve legal discharge while weakening practical equivalence, and narrowing who may demand the superior claim. It is an attempt to keep the legal machine running when the economic machine is straining, because legal closure is the last line of defense against private escalation.

Suspension is the moment the constitution is read aloud. Official language will describe suspension as temporary, orderly, necessary, designed to protect the public, designed to prevent hoarding, designed to stop speculation. Whatever the justification, the fact remains: the upgrade promise has been rewritten. The hierarchy of claims has changed. The old superior claim is now scarce enough that the state is choosing who can obtain it and who cannot. Once that choice is made, the regime is no longer a pure convertibility regime. It has become an administered hierarchy, and administered hierarchy is a different form of sovereignty with different political costs. The regime can survive suspension, but it cannot pretend suspension is not a constitutional change because citizens and creditors experience the change as an alteration of rights and an alteration of the meaning of money in their hands.

The most revealing aspect of suspension is what the state protects. It rarely protects everyone equally. It protects core settlement. It protects external obligations that, if defaulted, would cut off trade. It protects institutions whose failure would freeze domestic payments. It protects the minimum machinery needed to keep the economy functioning, and it allows other claims to bear delay, discount, or loss. That selection is never purely technical. It is policy in its most literal form: deciding which claims will remain close to finality and which claims will be pushed away. Convertibility forces the state to reveal priorities earlier than it would prefer. Under discretionary regimes, priorities can hide behind language. Under convertibility, priorities appear as who gets redemption and who does not, and the public learns to read the hierarchy through access.

The coalition question is inseparable from the arithmetic. In calm periods, convertibility is popular because it signals strength and restrains debasement. In stress, convertibility becomes unpopular because it demands visible sacrifice in order to preserve reserves. It demands tight credit when unemployment is rising. It demands higher taxes when revenues are falling. It demands cuts when politics wants expansion. The state learns that anchors are not maintained by doctrine alone; they are maintained by coalitions willing to pay. When the coalition fractures, the anchor becomes vulnerable because the state will choose domestic survival over external credibility. That choice is rational, but it is costly. It transforms the meaning of claims and forces a re-pricing of risk that can last for years because participants now treat the upgrade promise as conditional rather than automatic.

Convertibility also clarifies the relationship between domestic law and cross-boundary settlement. A state can declare its notes acceptable for domestic obligations, but convertibility is a promise about external equivalence, about whether domestic claims can be exchanged into the form demanded abroad. When external equivalence is credible, domestic claims circulate more easily because merchants and creditors do not fear being trapped. When external equivalence is doubted, domestic claims become provincial, and provincial money is more expensive because it carries convertibility risk that must be priced into every long-term contract. Convertibility turns international position into domestic cost, binding the domestic economy to external channels in a way that becomes visible only when the channels tighten.

The anchor that governs states is therefore not metaphor. It is a set of gates, schedules, reserve constraints, and triage decisions that reorganize behavior across the entire economy. It trains merchants to price in hierarchy, trains banks to hoard and ration, trains governments to prioritize reserves, trains citizens to interpret delay as weakness, and trains foreign creditors to treat domestic politics as an input into redemption probability. It can produce stability by constraining discretion, but it produces fragility by making the constraint testable. The same architecture that creates confidence in calm periods becomes the architecture of runs in stress periods. The state that adopts convertibility does not merely choose a monetary regime; it chooses a method by which its own future choices will be governed.

CLOSING DOCTRINE

Convertibility is discipline because it converts monetary legitimacy into an upgrade promise that can be demanded rather than requested, and that single design decision forces the state to live inside reserve arithmetic and time rationing instead of inside rhetoric. The upgrade path stabilizes ordinary circulation when it is credible because holders treat lower-grade claims as nearly equivalent to superior settlement, but the same path becomes a funnel when doubt appears, concentrating demand for the superior claim and turning administrative delay into evidence that reshapes prices and behavior faster than any announcement can repair. Eligibility rules, documentation burdens, redemption windows, and verification procedures are not neutral implementation details; they are distributive gates that decide who receives time and who receives loss, and the moment those gates tighten the regime becomes administered hierarchy even if the press line denies it. Suspension is not merely an emergency measure; it is a visible rewriting of the monetary constitution, a re-ranking of claims that cannot be concealed because citizens and creditors experience it as a change in rights, and the lasting cost of that change is the re-pricing of the state's credibility across domestic payments, bank stability, external settlement, and the political coalition required to carry contraction when reserves run thin.

CHAPTER 5
WAR FINANCE
THE MOMENT CONSTRAINT BREAKS

War does not introduce new money. War reveals what money has always been by forcing the state to spend first, at scale, under deadline, while the public still believes rules are rules. In peacetime, constraint can be narrated as prudence, and choices can be disguised as preference. In war, the state discovers which constraints are real, which are political theater, and which can be rewritten the moment survival is priced above precedent. The first sign is never a grand speech. It is a procurement officer holding a contract that must be honored now, an import invoice that cannot be delayed, and a domestic tax base that cannot be expanded fast enough to keep pace with the burn rate. Money becomes a calendar problem. The state either finds time inside its finances, or it manufactures time by changing the meaning of obligations.

A war economy is a violence economy, but the violence is not only on the battlefield. It is also in the claim structure. The state must mobilize labor, materials, transport, and industrial capacity, and it must do so through contracts that require payment. If the state cannot pay, it cannot command. If it pays in a way that destroys confidence, it may command briefly and then lose the domestic economy behind it. War finance is the craft of holding the settlement perimeter together while pulling resources forward from the future, and pulling them forward fast enough that survival is not outbid by delay. The mechanism is not mystery. It is re-ranking: which claims are treated as sacred, which are stretched, which are converted into forced loans, and which are quietly diluted through price dynamics that are never described as confiscation.

The war constraint breaks at the point where normal revenue and normal borrowing no longer match the required rate of expenditure. Taxes can rise, but taxes have a political and administrative speed limit. Borrowing can expand, but borrowing has a credibility and absorption limit, because the market's capacity to hold sovereign paper is not infinite when uncertainty is rising and private needs are rising at the same time. Convertibility regimes, if they exist, impose an additional constraint: reserves drain as imports rise, and redemption demand rises as fear rises, making the upgrade promise expensive at the same moment procurement needs the superior claim most. The state meets a corner and discovers a rule of survival that is older than its slogans: when time is scarce, constraints are rewritten.

The legal mind has always admitted, in narrow form, that ordinary restraints can be suspended when survival is invoked, and the admission matters because it reveals the state's self-understanding. "The privilege of the writ of habeas corpus shall not be suspended, unless when in cases of rebellion or invasion the public safety may require it." (U.S. Constitution, Article I, Section 9, Clause 2.) The power of the line is not its legal domain. It is the recognition that ordinary rights, ordinary procedures, and ordinary constraints can be altered when existential danger is claimed. War finance is the economic version of that logic, and it rarely announces itself as suspension. It begins as temporary measures, wartime expedients, special facilities, emergency authorizations, and patriotic appeals. The content is always the same: the state is asserting a higher claim on resources than the market would voluntarily grant at peacetime prices, and it is building the administrative means to make that claim real.

The first war-finance instrument is taxation, because taxation is the cleanest claim the state can assert. It is clean because it does not pretend to be voluntary and it does not pretend to be a market transaction. Yet taxation cannot carry the whole burden because it cannot be raised fast enough or far enough without tearing the coalition required to fight. War states learn quickly that taxation is both revenue and signal. It demonstrates seriousness, it reduces reliance on monetary expansion, and it distributes sacrifice in visible form. Yet it also hits consumption and investment at the wrong moment, when production must expand and morale must be managed. Tax becomes a pacing tool as much as a funding tool, calibrated to extract without triggering collapse of compliance or collapse of output.

The second instrument is borrowing, and borrowing begins as persuasion and ends as structure. Early on, the state issues obligations and relies on voluntary demand, pricing the bonds to attract buyers and framing purchase as both investment and duty. The rhetoric matters because the state is selling not just yield but confidence in continuity. As the burden grows, persuasion becomes insufficient, and borrowing becomes entwined with the financial system's plumbing. Banks are encouraged, then expected, then required to hold sovereign paper because bank balance sheets are one of the largest reservoirs of captive demand in any economy. Insurance pools are guided toward sovereign holdings because their liabilities are long and their investment mandates can be shaped. Pension institutions are leaned on because they are designed to absorb duration. This is not a conspiracy and it is not sentiment. It is statecraft under constraint: war finance uses intermediation architecture to transform voluntary lending into structured absorption.

The third instrument is administered price, because war states attempt to hold the domestic price level within a politically survivable corridor. Inflation is a tax that is neither legislated nor evenly distributed. It punishes fixed incomes, rewards debtors, destroys savings, and can fracture the social order behind the war effort. Yet inflation is also the natural consequence of pulling demand forward while production is being reallocated toward conflict needs. The state therefore fights a two-front war: it fights external enemies and it fights internal price dynamics. When it cannot prevent inflation mechanically, it attempts to control its visibility and distribution through rationing, price controls, wage guidance, and priority allocations of scarce goods. These are not merely social policies. In wartime they are monetary governance by another name because they determine how scarcity is shared and how nominal expansion becomes real price movement rather than political breakdown.

The moment the constraint truly breaks is the moment the state stops pretending that voluntary choice will deliver the needed resources. This is where the logic of bills, notes, and compelled credits emerges, even if the instruments are routed through banking channels rather than printed as obvious paper. A constitutional boundary line, written to deny sub-sovereigns a particular form of monetary improvisation, reveals what is at stake in the broader architecture: "No State shall ... emit Bills of Credit." (U.S. Constitution, Article I, Section 10, Clause 1.) The significance is not only the target. It is the recognition that issuing credit as money is a sovereignty function that must be governed because it can be abused. War does not abolish that logic. War pressures it. When central authority needs resources faster than taxes and voluntary bonds can deliver, it stretches the credit boundary, often through privileged banking channels and emergency instruments that look like loans and behave like money because they settle procurement immediately while being rolled over indefinitely.

A first pressure scene makes the mechanism unavoidable. The procurement office receives bids for critical materials that cannot be substituted, and the suppliers demand settlement terms tighter than any peacetime contract would tolerate. They have their reasons.

Their own upstream providers are demanding cash. Transport is constrained. Insurance is expensive. Workers demand wage increases to compensate for scarcity and fatigue. The procurement officer offers sovereign paper, but the supplier asks a simple question that strips away propaganda: can this paper be converted into settlement without delay, and can it be used to pay taxes and wages on schedule without discount. The procurement officer realizes he is not negotiating price; he is negotiating discharge quality. If the supplier doubts discharge, the supplier adds a premium, demands collateral, or refuses. The war effort is now being priced by the hierarchy of claims.

The treasury responds by opening facilities and changing rules, and each change is a quiet re-ranking. Certain institutions are granted direct access to funding against specified collateral. Certain payments are prioritized in clearing. Certain instruments are declared acceptable for certain obligations, with the implicit message that refusal will not be tolerated. The result is not merely liquidity. It is coercive harmonization of acceptance. The state is building a tunnel through the market's skepticism by turning skepticism into a legal and administrative problem rather than a pricing problem, and by making settlement predictable for suppliers who would otherwise ration production. This is war finance's essential move: it converts a funding gap into a governance project.

The second pressure scene occurs when borrowing meets its absorption limit. A bond issue is planned with confidence because the state's need is immense and the financial system has been cooperative. The auction arrives and demand is thinner than expected, not because the market is immoral but because private actors need liquidity for their own survival, because uncertainty has raised the value of cash-like claims, and because rumors of future controls have made everyone cautious. The weak auction forces a decision that cannot be dressed up. Either the state offers higher yields and admits risk has risen, compounding future cost, or the state creates a buyer of last resort through the banking system, converting the war bond from a voluntary instrument into a structurally absorbed instrument. When the buyer of last resort appears, it is rarely described as monetization. It is described as stabilization. The economic reality is that the boundary between fiscal and monetary function has been intentionally blurred to secure time.

This is where the absorption mechanism becomes concrete rather than rhetorical. Banks are told that sovereign paper will carry privileged regulatory treatment, that it will be eligible as high-grade collateral at public facilities, and that it will count favorably in liquidity calculations compared with private claims whose value is now uncertain. Reserve and liquidity rules are adjusted so that holding sovereign paper becomes the cheapest way to remain compliant. Supervisors communicate, sometimes directly and sometimes through silence, that a bank holding insufficient sovereign paper will be scrutinized as uncooperative or unsafe. The architecture does the coercion without needing to say the word. Banks respond rationally. They buy. They fund purchases through deposit growth and short-term borrowing. They rely on the expectation that the monetary authority will keep the system liquid enough that the paper can be carried. War borrowing, at scale, becomes a joint enterprise: issuance by the treasury, absorption by the banking system, and backstopping by the monetary authority, all coordinated through eligibility rules that translate policy into balance-sheet necessity.

War collapses the comforting division between fiscal and monetary authority because survival demands a single coordinated claim on resources. The treasury issues. The monetary authority supports. The banking system distributes. The regulator adjusts eligibility and capital treatment to make holdings possible. The payments operator protects settlement continuity so procurement does not stall. Each institution performs a task that looks technical and is political because it shapes who bears the burden of funding and who receives the first access to scarce goods. In peacetime, these functions can be separated and debated as policy. In war, separation is a luxury, and debate is often replaced by necessity.

The quiet center of war finance is financial repression, whether named or not. Repression is not a moral slur; it is a description of tools used to channel savings into the state at manageable cost. It includes caps on yields, guidance on portfolio holdings, reserve requirements that create demand for sovereign claims, restrictions on alternative assets, and capital controls that prevent flight. These tools are rarely announced as repression because the word is politically poisonous. They are described as stability measures, patriotic measures, emergency measures. Yet their function is simple: keep the sovereign's cost of funds below what a fully free market would demand under existential uncertainty. Without that, the war effort is priced out by the market's fear. With that, the burden is shifted onto savers, onto holders of fixed claims, and onto those without access to inflation hedges. War finance is a distribution engine. It cannot avoid distribution; it can only choose which distribution is tolerable.

The street-level distribution scene shows why repression cannot stand alone. A ration office opens before dawn, and the line forms with the grim discipline of people who have learned that lateness is hunger. A clerk stamps cards with a practiced motion that has become the rhythm of survival, while an inspector walks the queue looking for the familiar signs of fraud: altered ink, mismatched names, counterfeit seals. Across the street, a small shopkeeper argues with a supplier who will no longer deliver without payment in the most acceptable claim available, and the shopkeeper's anger has a target because prices have become a daily insult. At a factory gate, workers demand wage adjustments not out of greed but out of arithmetic, because controlled prices on some goods have pushed scarcity into uncontrolled prices on others, and wages that once purchased a week of living now purchase a fraction. The manager cannot grant the demand without raising prices, and cannot raise prices without violating controls, and cannot violate controls without inviting penalty. The war state, attempting to hold the economy together, has turned the wage bargain into a monetary dispute and the ration stamp into a settlement instrument.

In that environment, inflation is not a statistic. It is a moral accusation aimed at whoever is perceived to be protected from scarcity. Workers believe merchants are cheating. Merchants believe suppliers are hoarding. Suppliers believe the state is paying favored contractors first. The rumor structure is always wrong in detail and correct in essence: someone is closer to finality than someone else. The state responds by tightening enforcement, expanding rationing categories, and prosecuting obvious profiteering, but enforcement cannot eliminate the underlying mechanism because the underlying mechanism is the state's own need to pull resources forward. The state can choose how the pain is distributed, but it cannot choose a painless war finance. The consequence for monetary governance is immediate. Wage controls, price controls, rationing, and enforcement become substitutes for interest rates and reserve ratios, because they determine which claims are honored in real terms and which claims are diluted through scarcity and queues.

Convertibility, if it exists, becomes the point where internal and external constraints collide. Defending convertibility drains reserves, but abandoning it risks collapsing confidence and accelerating inflation. War states often choose a middle path first: restrict convertibility, narrow eligibility, delay redemption, and attempt to preserve the appearance of the promise while administratively rationing its exercise. Delay becomes signal. Signal becomes run. The state then either suspends or accepts an external dependency large enough to replenish reserves, which becomes its own form of constraint. War finance therefore teaches a brutal lesson: anchors govern, but anchors can also be sacrificed when the cost of honoring them exceeds the cost of changing them, and the sacrifice is rarely framed as failure because failure is politically unusable during mobilization.

The inner logic of wartime sacrifice is priority. The state elevates its own claims and its own survival needs above ordinary contract expectations. Procurement contracts are enforced with urgency. Taxes are collected with force. Certain creditors are protected to preserve payment continuity. Other creditors are told to wait, restructure, or accept loss. This is not an accident. It is the state revealing its hierarchy. Legal priority is always the hidden constitution of money, but war makes the constitution explicit because scarcity is no longer hypothetical. When the state chooses which obligations will be honored first, it is choosing which sectors continue to exist, and it is choosing which households will experience the war as deprivation and which will experience it as income.

War also forces an institutional innovation that hides in paperwork: the state builds administrative capacity to measure, record, and police economic life at higher resolution. Rationing requires identification. Controls require registries. Procurement requires supply-chain mapping. Tax enforcement requires better records. Bond absorption requires supervision of intermediaries. What begins as emergency apparatus often outlives the emergency because institutions do not like giving up capacity once built. War finance therefore changes not only the monetary regime but the administrative state. The state learns how to see the economy more clearly, and seeing more clearly is a form of power that persists after the cannons quiet.

The state also learns that inflation is not merely an outcome; it is a tool it may accept when other tools are exhausted. Inflation can erase parts of the real debt burden, reducing future tax requirements. It can transfer resources from holders of cash-like claims to the issuer, functioning as a diffuse tax that is hard to vote against because it is not legislated. Yet inflation corrodes legitimacy, and legitimacy is itself a war asset because legitimacy keeps factories running and keeps soldiers' families fed without rebellion. The state therefore tries to keep inflation within a corridor that is politically survivable, and when it cannot, it seeks scapegoats, controls, and moral language that can redirect anger away from fiscal reality. War finance is as much management of perception as it is management of balance sheets, but perception management only works when paired with enforceable control over the gates of settlement and supply.

The final war-finance truth is that constraint breaks, then is rebuilt in a new form. The old constraint might have been convertibility. The new constraint might be debt capacity. The old constraint might have been balanced budgets. The new constraint might be controlled inflation plus capped yields. The old constraint might have been legal limits on issuance. The new constraint might be institutional limits enforced by coordinated banks, regulators, and payments. War does not create a free-for-all. War creates a reconstituted discipline with a new hierarchy at its core. A regime that survives war finance is a regime that can rewrite constraints without dissolving discharge, because if discharge dissolves, the war effort becomes impossible and domestic order collapses behind the front.

CLOSING DOCTRINE

War finance is the moment constraint breaks because survival requires spending at a speed and scale that outpaces normal revenue and voluntary borrowing, forcing the state to convert a funding gap into an enforceable governance project that re-ranks claims, channels savings, and protects settlement continuity under scarcity. Taxes provide the cleanest extraction but cannot carry the full burden without breaking the coalition required to fight, while borrowing begins as persuasion and becomes structured absorption as banks and long-horizon institutions are guided and compelled into sovereign holdings through eligibility rules, supervisory pressure, and privileged liquidity treatment that make refusal expensive and compliance rational. Financial repression, rationing, and controlled allocation are not deviations from normal order but the instruments by which the state manufactures time, limits inflation's political damage, and keeps procurement supplied by making acceptance and priority enforceable even when markets would otherwise demand punitive yields or refuse to deliver critical inputs. The state emerges with a revised constitution of money: thicker administrative capacity, a blurred boundary between fiscal and monetary function, and a redefined hierarchy that persists because the machinery built to win survival rarely dismantles itself voluntarily, and because the distributional choices embedded in wartime finance tend to harden into the postwar architecture of claims.

CHAPTER 6

THE RESERVE BLUEPRINT

DESIGNING THE POSTWAR ORDER

The war ended, but the balance sheets did not. They sat on desks like unexploded ordnance: emergency debts piled into maturities that did not fit peacetime revenues, ration systems that had trained populations to accept administrative priority, banking systems swollen with sovereign paper, and external obligations that would not accept patriotic language as payment. In the first months after the guns quieted, governments spoke in the public vocabulary of victory and reconstruction, but their private vocabulary was narrower and more urgent. They spoke of settlement, of shortages, of shipping and fuel, of wage pressure, of import invoices that required an outside discharge instrument, and of a single question that returned because it governed every other one. What would be treated as final payment across borders, and who would control access to it when stress arrived.

A postwar order is often described as a peace project. In monetary terms it is an engineering project built out of fear: fear that competitive devaluations would return, fear that capital flight would turn domestic politics into a hostage situation, fear that external settlement crises would force austerity so brutal it would dissolve legitimacy, fear that banking systems would fracture under the weight of obligations created under emergency conditions. The blueprint that emerged was not a classroom model and it was not a philosopher's diagram. It was a design for survival in peacetime, meaning a design for predictable discharge across borders that did not require repeated improvisation. It treated money as architecture: rules, records, priority, and final settlement, extended beyond a single jurisdiction and made credible enough that trade could expand without every invoice turning into a diplomatic incident.

The reserve question sat at the center because reserves are the bridge between domestic law and external settlement. A state can declare its domestic instrument good for taxes and dues and enforce that declaration through courts and penalties. It cannot declare external counterparties satisfied by that same instrument unless those counterparties are willing to accept it, and willingness is not moral; it is institutional. External acceptance depends on convertibility into a claim the outside world treats as final, or on a network of agreements and backstops that make the domestic claim behave as if it were final even when it is not. Postwar designers understood that without a reserve architecture, states would drift back into the same loop: external deficits, reserve drain, currency panic, capital controls imposed in haste, trade collapse, and political radicalization. The blueprint was an attempt to turn that loop into a managed corridor of adjustment.

The first design choice was to stop pretending that cross-border monetary order could be built on pure market spontaneity. Domestic monetary systems can be governed by a sovereign perimeter. Cross-border settlement requires coordination among sovereign perimeters, and coordination does not appear by accident when survival incentives are in play. The blueprint therefore began with institutions that could standardize expectations: about exchange rates, about access to temporary liquidity, about the legitimacy of certain controls in certain circumstances, and about what "adjustment" would mean when a country's external position became unsustainable. The intention was not to eliminate stress. The intention was to prevent stress from becoming a chain reaction that turned monetary disputes into geopolitical rupture.

The founding language of the postwar institution is polite, and it is operationally sharp. Its purposes included promoting exchange stability, maintaining orderly exchange arrangements, avoiding competitive exchange depreciation, and making resources available "under adequate safeguards." (International Monetary Fund, Articles of Agreement, Article I.) That last phrase is the spine, because safeguards are how a reserve order gives time without dissolving discipline. A system that gives time without safeguards becomes an unlimited credit line that invites delay and manipulation. A system that imposes safeguards without time becomes a punishment regime that drives states into unilateral improvisation. The blueprint's claim was that procedure could do what fear could not: make adjustment survivable enough to be politically enacted while keeping the settlement perimeter credible enough that trade would continue.

The second design choice was a managed convertibility regime at the international level, because convertibility without management collapses into runs, while management without convertibility collapses into closed blocs. The compromise was a world in which exchange rates were anchored through declared par values and adjusted through a process meant to be disciplined rather than improvisational. The designers were not naive. They knew parities would be tested by productivity differences, by capital flows, by domestic politics, and by the scars left by war. Their goal was not to freeze reality. Their goal was to create a system in which parity changes could occur without competitive panic and without destroying the credibility of cross-border contracts. The exchange rate was treated as a settlement parameter, not as a weapon to export pain.

The constitutional flavor of this approach is clear in the obligations that members accepted. "Each member undertakes to collaborate with the Fund and other members to assure orderly exchange arrangements and to promote a stable system of exchange rates." (International Monetary Fund, Articles of Agreement, Article IV, Section 1.) The sentence matters because it captures the ambition of the blueprint: a promise to restrain the temptation to treat the exchange rate as a domestic valve rather than as a shared condition of cross-border settlement. It could never be perfectly enforced, and the architects understood that. Yet even imperfect enforcement changes behavior when it creates an expectation that certain moves will trigger institutional response rather than merely market reaction, and when it makes the political cost of unilateral competitive depreciation higher than the fiscal relief it offers.

The third design choice was to treat capital mobility as a variable rather than as a moral absolute. The blueprint did not demand immediate openness because immediate openness would have made the reserve problem worse by allowing panic to drain reserves faster than any institution could replenish them. The system implicitly accepted sequencing: rebuild domestic capacity, stabilize fiscal and banking systems, then widen openness as credibility strengthened. This was not idealism. It was triage made systematic. Capital controls were no longer merely desperate improvisation; they were potential instruments inside a governed corridor, tolerated so long as they did not destroy the system's core function, which was to keep current transactions and trade settlement from collapsing into blockade by paperwork.

The reserve blueprint also had to address the blunt fact that the world needed a settlement asset trusted beyond any single devastated fiscal base. The designers relied on a layered structure: domestic currencies for domestic life, a small number of internationally acceptable claims for cross-border settlement, and an institutional mechanism to supply temporary liquidity to countries under stress so that trade could continue while adjustment occurred. The reserve asset had to be scarce enough to discipline, but not so scarce that it strangled growth. That balance is the defining problem of reserve design because scarcity is both stabilizer and destabilizer. Scarcity stabilizes by forcing adjustment; scarcity destabilizes by making panic profitable and by turning external deficits into political crises. The blueprint tried to move scarcity from raw market panic into managed procedure by providing a lender of time.

Conditional liquidity was the instrument that made the corridor plausible, and it required oversight because conditionality without monitoring is theater. The institution was therefore given a surveillance role that is often treated as bureaucratic and is in fact constitutional. The institution was empowered to oversee the international monetary system and to exercise "firm surveillance" over members' exchange rate policies. (International Monetary Fund, Articles of Agreement, Article IV, Section 3.) "Firm" is the revealing word. It signals that the system was designed to be governed, not merely observed, and that states were accepting an external view into their domestic policy choices because without that view, coordination collapses into suspicion and suspicion collapses into hoarding and controls. Surveillance is not an insult to sovereignty in this blueprint; it is the price of operating a shared settlement perimeter without constant crisis.

The blueprint's brilliance, and its danger, lay in what it implied about sovereignty. Domestic monetary sovereignty is often described as the right to issue and regulate one's own currency. The postwar order treated sovereignty as conditional on participating in shared constraints framed as necessary for stability. That meant the reserve order would always contain conflict. Countries would demand autonomy during domestic stress, while the reserve order would demand adjustment to protect cross-border settlement. This conflict is not a design flaw. It is the tension the blueprint was built to process, because a world of sovereign states cannot eliminate conflict; it can only choose whether conflict is processed through procedure or through panic. The blueprint attempted to replace the old pattern of humiliation and collapse with a pattern of negotiated adjustment and time-lending, without pretending that adjustment could be painless.

The distributional problem sits beneath every reserve system and determines whether the corridor holds. A reserve order must decide, in practice, who bears the cost of adjustment: deficit countries, surplus countries, or the institution that provides liquidity. If deficit countries bear all costs rapidly, the system becomes politically explosive because austerity arrives as humiliation and unemployment arrives as proof that external rules are governing domestic life. If surplus countries bear costs, surplus countries resist because they treat their position as virtue and their surpluses as deserved reward. If the institution bears costs through unlimited liquidity, discipline dissolves and the reserve claim becomes unstable. The blueprint attempted to distribute the burden through conditional assistance, staged adjustment, and a moral vocabulary of cooperation that made discipline easier to sell domestically, but moral vocabulary cannot erase distribution. It can only postpone the moment when distribution becomes visible as protest.

The reserve order is also a credit order, and this is where multilateral development lending becomes central rather than decorative. Stabilization lending buys time. Development lending builds capacity. A postwar economy cannot remain stable externally if it lacks the productive base to earn reserves through exports, or the infrastructure to replace imported essentials, or the institutional capacity to mobilize domestic savings without constant flight. Liquidity assistance can keep trade flowing for months. It cannot, by itself, build a port, an energy grid, a transport network, or a domestic industrial base that reduces external vulnerability. Development credit is therefore the slower engine inside the reserve blueprint, designed to shift a country's structure so that future balance-of-payments stress is less frequent and less fatal.

This is why development institutions are not merely charity banks; they are structural stabilizers that work through credit architecture. When a development lender finances energy infrastructure, the effect is not only electricity. It is reserve resilience, because energy independence reduces the need to spend scarce external claims on fuel imports during stress. When a development lender finances transport or logistics, the effect is not only commerce. It is reserve earning capacity, because exports become possible at scale and at lower cost. When a development lender finances agricultural productivity, the effect is not only output. It is a reduction in the domestic political pressure that triggers import surges and external deficits. The blueprint's logic is that stability is not produced only by defensive austerity; stability is produced by altering the structure that makes austerity inevitable. Development credit, in this sense, is macroeconomic statecraft executed through project finance and institution building.

Development lending also creates its own gates, and gates create power. Conditions are attached to procurement, to governance, to reporting, to legal reforms, to currency management, and to the priority given to repayment. These conditions are defended as safeguards to protect lender resources and as reforms to protect project success. They function, in practice, as levers over domestic policy. This is not a scandal; it is the inevitable character of credit when the creditor is an institution with a mandate and the borrower is a state with a constrained external position. The development gate is slower than the liquidity gate, but it is often deeper because it shapes the borrower's legal and administrative structure, and structure determines future bargaining power.

The first pressure scene in the postwar blueprint is not a summit. It is a finance ministry on a weekday morning, with a staff meeting that has the exhausted tone of people managing shortages as if shortages were weather. The import desk reports that fuel shipments require settlement in the external claim, not in domestic promises. The tax desk reports that raising rates further will trigger evasion and unrest. The labor desk reports wage pressure because ration systems have frayed and black markets are thickening. The monetary desk reports reserve depletion and rising demand for conversion because merchants fear they will be trapped in domestic claims when external settlement is required. The minister does not ask a philosophical question. The minister asks which obligations must be honored today to avoid collapse tomorrow. The answer is predictable and humiliating: imports that keep lights on, payments that keep banks liquid, and external settlements that keep trade routes open. In that question the blueprint becomes real, because "reserve" stops being a statistic and becomes the boundary between ordinary administration and political crisis.

The institutional corridor changes what the minister can do without detonating confidence. Instead of choosing between immediate austerity and uncontrolled devaluation, the minister can pursue a third path: obtain temporary external liquidity under conditions that are politically painful but not immediately fatal, and use the borrowed time to implement adjustment without dissolving the domestic coalition. The corridor does not remove pain. It sequences pain. It prevents a liquidity problem from becoming a solvency and legitimacy collapse overnight. It also turns the institution into a lender of time, and time is the most valuable commodity in a balance-of-payments crisis because time determines whether policy can be enacted gradually or must be enacted violently. The institution that lends time becomes a quiet sovereign over the tempo of domestic politics in distressed states, because tempo determines whether a government survives long enough to implement the measures it promises.

The second pressure scene occurs at the border between economics and politics, where the reserve order's logic becomes unpopular. A government signs an agreement that requires cutting subsidies or tightening credit, and the street interprets the agreement not as stabilization but as surrender. Opposition leaders call it foreign control.

Workers call it theft. Merchants call it chaos. The cabinet calls it necessity. The reserve blueprint reveals its most dangerous feature here: it forces domestic politics to internalize external constraints, and internalizing external constraints always produces legitimacy contest. The regime survives only if the domestic coalition can be convinced that pain is shared fairly, that the alternative is worse, and that adjustment is temporary rather than permanent subordination. This is why reserve systems rely on moral vocabulary. The vocabulary is not sentimental. It is political technology for persuading domestic coalitions to accept externally imposed constraints without treating them as conquest.

The added surplus-country scene is where the blueprint's asymmetry is exposed, because the system can discipline deficit countries more easily than it can discipline surplus countries. In a surplus capital, officials sit in comfortable rooms with thick folders of export numbers and reserve accumulation charts that feel like moral proof. They do not speak of adjustment. They speak of prudence, competitiveness, and domestic stability. Their banking sector is healthy, their currency is trusted, and their political coalition is allergic to any move that would reduce surplus by expanding domestic demand. The institution sends a delegation with the language of symmetry: the system cannot function if only deficit countries adjust; surplus hoarding starves global liquidity and forces contraction elsewhere. The officials listen politely, then return to domestic priorities. They may offer small gestures: modest lending, symbolic contributions, cooperative statements. They avoid structural change because their electorate experiences structural change as self-inflicted harm.

The delegation's leverage is limited, and that limitation is structural rather than personal. A deficit country needs access to time. A surplus country already has time because it has reserves. The institution can condition lending; it cannot easily condition surplus behavior. It can criticize; criticism is weak against abundance. It can recommend; recommendations do not move electorates. This is where the reserve blueprint reveals a core truth: a system built to manage stability must still live with asymmetry of bargaining power because states with reserves can ignore procedure longer than states without reserves. The blueprint can soften the consequences by lending time to deficit countries and by framing surplus behavior as shared responsibility, but it cannot compel symmetrical adjustment without a political authority that does not exist at the international level. In that sense, the reserve blueprint is a machine designed to manage a world it cannot govern fully.

The distributional logic therefore returns with sharper edges. Deficit countries experience conditions as humiliation. Surplus countries experience pressure as unfair intrusion. The institution experiences its own mandate as permanent negotiation with power. Yet the blueprint still matters because the alternative is worse: uncoordinated panic that turns every external imbalance into a currency crisis and every currency crisis into trade fragmentation. The postwar order's practical achievement was not perfection. It was creating a repeatable corridor of response: monitoring, conditional liquidity, negotiated adjustment, and development credit that slowly alters structure so the same crisis does not recur endlessly.

The pairing of liquidity and development is the part most often misunderstood by those who treat the system as purely monetary. Liquidity without development is a treadmill: time is borrowed, adjustment is imposed, growth is strangled, reserves remain scarce, and the next crisis arrives on schedule. Development without liquidity is a dream: projects may be funded, but external settlement crises can still collapse the economy before projects mature. The blueprint tried to combine them so that time could be used for transformation rather than merely for survival. In doing so it created an international credit architecture that functions like a state's internal credit architecture: a central stabilizer that manages short-term runs and a development engine that builds the productive base that makes runs less likely.

The reserve blueprint also created a template of reporting, surveillance, and standard-setting that outlives any single era. Standardized reporting makes crises legible. Surveillance makes manipulation harder to hide. Standard-setting reduces verification costs and allows trade to expand without each contract requiring bespoke political assurances. Yet standard-setting also creates a bureaucracy of judgment, because standardized procedures require interpretation and interpretation is power. This is why the system is always contested. Those who control the standards shape participation. Those who control surveillance shape legitimacy. Those who control conditionality shape domestic sequencing. The architecture is presented as neutral stability. It is stability with politics inside it.

The postwar reserve blueprint can therefore be read as the moment monetary statecraft becomes explicit international architecture. War taught states that constraint can be rewritten when survival demands it. The postwar order attempted to build a system in which rewriting did not occur through unilateral improvisation but through governed adjustment. It did not eliminate the state's ability to act. It attempted to channel action into procedure so trade and settlement could keep functioning long enough for politics to remain politics rather than become emergency. The cost of that channel is sovereignty traded for time. The benefit of that channel is fewer collapses that turn monetary stress into geopolitical rupture.

CLOSING DOCTRINE

The postwar reserve blueprint is an engineering response to fear, built to keep cross-border settlement from turning every external deficit into domestic political collapse and every domestic panic into trade fragmentation. It functions by creating a governed hierarchy of external discharge in which exchange stability is pursued through managed arrangements, liquidity is supplied as borrowed time under safeguards, and capital mobility is treated as a variable to be sequenced rather than a moral absolute, because uncontrolled mobility turns reserve scarcity into a run and a run into a legitimacy crisis. The system inevitably reshapes sovereignty because it replaces the blunt constraint of pure convertibility with institutional constraint: access, conditionality, surveillance, and negotiated adjustment that can preserve continuity while imposing political cost, and that political cost becomes the decisive battlefield inside deficit states. The pairing of stabilization liquidity with development credit is not an accessory; it is the structural attempt to turn borrowed time into productive capacity so that reserve stress becomes less frequent and less fatal, even as the conditions attached to credit create their own gates of influence over domestic law, procurement, and policy sequencing. The system's central fragility is asymmetry: deficit countries can be disciplined because they need time, surplus countries resist adjustment because they already possess time in the form of reserves, and the institution can monitor and persuade but cannot compel symmetry without a political authority that does not exist; the blueprint therefore endures only to the extent that its procedures are perceived as fair enough, and its distributions tolerable enough, that states prefer the corridor of managed adjustment to the chaos of unilateral panic.

PART TWO
THE FIAT REGIME
HOW CENTRAL BANKS MANUFACTURE CREDIBILITY AND CONTROL TIME

The first night the anchor fails, nobody calls it failure. The communiqué is drafted in calm language and read in the measured voice that states use when they are trying to sound like inevitability. The doors of conversion are described as temporarily adjusted, the window is described as suspended for orderly administration, the public is described as protected from disorder, and the press is invited to treat the event as technical. Outside the building, the market reads the truth faster than the public can. The price of the currency moves first, then the price of credit, then the price of imports, then the price of labor, and each movement is a verdict on whether the state still governs time or has begun to be governed by it. The fiat regime begins not as philosophy and not as innovation for its own sake, but as triage: the state chooses to stop promising an upgrade into a scarce external claim and instead promises that its own liabilities will remain acceptable enough, stable enough, and enforceable enough that domestic life can continue without every stress episode turning into a run on reserves.

Fiat is often described as currency without backing, a negative definition that invites caricature. In statecraft, fiat is substitution, not absence. The anchor once forced discipline through reserve drain and redemption, imposing a hard constraint that could override domestic politics. The new regime imposes discipline through credibility engineering: the managed expectation that the state will defend internal purchasing power within a politically survivable corridor, keep the payments machine running in stress, and prevent the credit structure from collapsing into a contest of who can reach settlement first. This is not freedom from constraint. It is a change in the instrument through which constraint is applied, from a scarce reserve asset that governs the state's calendar to an institutional apparatus that governs expectations, liquidity, and the price of time itself. The shift is not cosmetic. Under an anchor regime, legitimacy rests on the credibility of redemption. Under fiat, legitimacy rests on the credibility of purchasing power and on the credibility of crisis containment, and those credibilities are tested not at a window but in wages, rents, food prices, borrowing costs, and the daily ease with which obligations can be discharged without discounts and delays.

The legal skeleton remains, and it becomes more important because it replaces convertibility as the ultimate guarantee of closure inside the jurisdiction. "Coins and currency ... are legal tender for all debts, public charges, taxes, and dues." (31 U.S.C. §5103.) The significance is not national romance; it is mechanical finality. The state asserts that its instrument can end disputes in the domains named, binding third parties to treat tender as discharge. Under convertibility, legal force is reinforced by the upgrade promise into a superior asset. Under fiat, legal force must do more work because the upgrade promise is absent. The state is, in effect, declaring that finality is achieved not by redeeming into an external reserve claim but by the state's own power to define discharge, enforce it through courts, and sustain acceptance through the institutions that keep banking and payments functioning.

That foundation does not solve the problem the anchor once solved: external equivalence. A state can enforce domestic discharge, but it cannot compel foreign counterparties to treat its instrument as final unless those counterparties believe they can convert it, hedge it, or use it to settle other obligations that matter to them. This is where fiat becomes a regime of time control. The monetary authority must manage interest rates and liquidity conditions so holding the currency does not feel like holding a melting claim, and so holding bank liabilities denominated in that currency does not feel like holding a conditional promise that will be frozen at the first sign of stress. The key variable is not only the price level but the structure of expectations about the future price level, because in a fiat order the public's willingness to hold claims depends on whether tomorrow is believed to be roughly governable. When tomorrow ceases to feel governable, the public does not merely complain; it flees into substitutes, hoards goods, shortens contracts, demands higher wages, and converts every transaction into a vote against the state's credibility.

The hierarchy of claims does not disappear under fiat; it is domesticated and partially concealed. The state's liabilities sit at the top domestically because they define what discharges obligations to the state and because the courts and enforcement apparatus make that definition consequential. Bank liabilities function as money because they are expected to be convertible into state settlement through clearing and backstops, and because the state stands behind the payment system when panic tries to turn payment into paralysis. Below bank liabilities sit private instruments whose acceptability depends on collateral, market confidence, and the continued operation of funding markets that can dry up in hours. The fiat regime is therefore an attempt to keep the top rung stable enough that the rest of the ladder does not become a panic machine every time conditions turn. It is the domestication of the hierarchy rather than its abolition, and it is the replacement of the redemption window with a set of institutional windows—discount access, collateral eligibility, settlement finality rules, supervisory forbearance—that determine who receives liquidity when it matters.

In practice, the fiat regime arrives through choices made under pressure, not through doctrine written in calm. External settlement crises kept forcing internal contraction, and internal contraction kept producing political revolt. Governments learned that defending an external anchor could destroy domestic legitimacy, and that domestic legitimacy is not a soft factor but the precondition for collecting taxes, enforcing contracts, and maintaining the coalition that makes governance possible. The fiat regime is the regime in which the state chooses to defend domestic governability first and accept that external settlement will be managed through negotiated arrangements, market pricing, and institutional backstops rather than through a universal promise of redemption. The regime's central challenge is that the anchor's simplicity is gone. Instead of one promise—redeem—you now have many promises: contain inflation enough to preserve legitimacy, contain crises enough to preserve payments, contain bank failure enough to preserve credit, and do all of it while markets and households continuously test credibility through the price of time.

A statutory mandate, written in the sober language of long-run objectives, reveals the new discipline the state imposes on itself, not as morality but as operational assignment. "The Board of Governors ... shall maintain long run growth of the monetary and credit aggregates ... so as to promote effectively the goals of maximum employment, stable prices, and moderate long-term interest rates." (Federal Reserve Act, 12 U.S.C. §225a.) The phrasing matters because it acknowledges the fiat regime's core tension: price stability and employment stability are both political necessities, and they often collide. The fiat state therefore lives inside a constant trade: preserve purchasing power without destroying employment, defend credibility without breaking the credit machine, tighten policy without freezing payments, loosen policy without igniting a spiral that collapses legitimacy. Central banking becomes the craft of managing those tolerances, and the tolerances are social as well as financial because the public experiences policy not as a chart but as whether rent is payable, whether wages keep pace, whether loans remain serviceable, and whether the banking system still feels like money rather than like a promise that could be paused.

The fiat regime's real novelty is not that money is no longer convertible; it is that credibility must be manufactured continuously through institutions that operate in public view and under political attack. When inflation rises, the public experiences it as taxation without vote. When disinflation is imposed, the public experiences it as unemployment and bankruptcy imposed to restore credibility. The legitimacy of the regime depends on whether the state can keep both pains within tolerable limits while preserving the appearance—and the reality—of procedural fairness in who is protected and who is sacrificed during crisis containment. The questions that will govern everything that follows are therefore not academic. Who receives liquidity first when panic hits. Which collateral is treated as acceptable when funding markets freeze. Which institutions are rescued to preserve payments. Which households bear inflation as silent tax. Which workers bear unemployment as the price of restored credibility. Fiat is governance under continuous test, and the test is administered daily through settlement, credit, and prices rather than through a redemption window.

CHAPTER 7
INFLATION AND LEGITIMACY
WHEN PRICES BECOME POLITICS

The wage meeting was scheduled for ninety minutes and lasted five hours because nobody in the room could afford to pretend the calendar still mattered more than the price level. The employer's team arrived with forecasts, credit terms, and the tired confidence of people who had already run the numbers through every tolerable scenario. The workers' representatives arrived with grocery receipts, rent notices, and the blunt arithmetic of a life where "inflation" was not a statistic but a weekly ambush. The opening offer was rejected within minutes, not as theater but as disbelief. A raise that lagged the bills did not read as compromise; it read as a transfer. The employer pointed to margins and borrowing costs and explained that price increases could not be passed through indefinitely. The workers pointed to shelves and said the pass-through had already happened. By the third hour the vocabulary shifted from economics to legitimacy, because legitimacy is what remains when every side can prove its pain and nobody can prove the other side's duty to absorb it.

In a fiat regime, inflation is the moment money stops feeling like infrastructure and starts feeling like politics. Under an anchor regime, legitimacy is tested at the upgrade window: can a claim be converted into superior settlement without delay and without discretion. Under fiat, legitimacy is tested in the domains no government can quarantine from judgment: food, fuel, rent, wages, and the cost of borrowing. The state can enforce legal tender and preserve settlement finality, but it cannot legislate felt purchasing power. It must defend it, or defend the public belief that it will be defended within a corridor that keeps domestic life governable. When that belief breaks, people do not need doctrine to recognize the breach. They shorten contracts, demand indexing, hoard durable goods, move into substitutes, and treat the currency as a claim to be spent quickly rather than held. Those behaviors are not cultural quirks; they are rational adaptations to a claim that is melting through time.

Inflation becomes political because it is distribution disguised as arithmetic, and distribution is never neutral. It does not fall evenly across a population. It targets the wrong people first: wage earners who cannot renegotiate weekly, households on fixed incomes, small firms with long receivables, tenants whose leases reset after a year, and savers whose balance sheets are built around nominal promises. It rewards debtors and punishes creditors, but the deeper divide is not debtor versus creditor; it is who can reprice versus who cannot. Firms with market power can push prices through quickly. Workers without bargaining power cannot. Large institutions can place assets into instruments that reprice. Households often cannot. Inflation therefore redistributes not only wealth but dignity, because dignity in a modern monetary order is the belief that the unit is not quietly selecting winners while the state speaks as if stability were still intact.

The state's first defense is always language, because language buys time before measures do. Officials describe inflation as transitory, as supply-driven, as localized, as a sequence of shocks that will pass. Sometimes this is accurate. Price spikes can occur without becoming regime inflation. The problem is that fiat lives on expectations, and expectations are not managed by accuracy alone. Expectations are managed by credibility, and credibility is a history of whether the authorities have been willing to impose pain on powerful interests when necessary. The public does not only ask whether inflation will fall. The public asks whether it will be forced down, and whether the burden of forcing it down will be shared or selectively assigned. In that question, inflation becomes politics even before it becomes extreme, because the argument is no longer about causes but about who will be made to pay for correction.

A mandate line captures the official claim that a fiat order requires: an institution tasked with stabilizing prices without pretending politics can be erased. "The Board of Governors... shall maintain long run growth of the monetary and credit aggregates... so as to promote effectively the goals of maximum employment, stable prices, and moderate long-term interest rates." (12 U.S.C. §225a.) The sentence is an assignment of impossible balance. It binds legitimacy to objectives that can collide in the short run: price stability and employment continuity. If the monetary authority protects employment at the expense of prices, households experience inflation as taxation without vote. If it protects prices at the expense of employment, households experience disinflation as job loss imposed to preserve a credibility that can feel creditor-owned. Either way, the institution is governing distribution while insisting it is only governing aggregates.

The mechanism by which inflation becomes politics begins with the unit of account itself. The unit is a compression device: it allows obligations to be stated, compared, and enforced. Inflation degrades that compression by making the unit's meaning unstable through time. Parties add clauses and contingencies because the future unit is no longer trusted. Long-term contracts include adjustment terms. Short-term contracts become default. Firms demand shorter payment terms. Workers demand more frequent wage resets. Landlords rewrite leases. Lenders widen spreads and shorten maturities. When this shift becomes widespread, inflation is not only a rise in prices; it is a reconfiguration of time. The state is losing its ability to persuade the public to hold nominal promises across months and years, and once that holding behavior weakens, the credit machine becomes brittle because modern credit is built on the willingness to accept time risk inside money.

The classic instrument used to arrest this process is the policy rate, which is the administered price of time. Raising the rate is not primarily a signal; it is rationing credit by design. It constrains borrowers, raises the hurdle rate for investment, and changes the valuation of assets used as collateral. In a fiat regime, it is also a threat to political order, because higher rates translate into layoffs, business failures, and fiscal stress as debt service costs rise. This is why inflation is rarely defeated by rates alone unless the political coalition is willing to tolerate the resulting unemployment and bankruptcies. A monetary authority can tighten aggressively and still fail if fiscal policy refuses to adjust and wage-price institutions embed inflation through indexing and repricing norms. Inflation is monetary plus institutional, and institutions are where politics lives.

The institutional channel is where credibility is manufactured or lost. Credibility is not the announcement of a target. Credibility is the belief that the authority will do what it says even when doing so is unpopular and costly. Targets are promises about future purchasing power, which means targets are implicit promises about how much pain will be imposed to restore stability if it is threatened. When targets are trusted, wage bargaining stays anchored, firms do not preemptively raise prices to protect margins, and lenders do not build large inflation premia into rates. When targets are doubted, the private sector does the rational thing: it front-loads protection. That front-loading becomes inflationary because protective repricing is itself price movement, and the economy begins to behave as if the future were ungoverned. Credibility therefore has a self-reinforcing structure: it stabilizes behavior when trusted and accelerates behavior when doubted.

The most dangerous phase is the middle zone where inflation is high enough to change behavior but low enough for officials to believe it can be talked down. In that zone, the public adapts while the state remains rhetorically committed to stability without executing the full suite of actions stability requires. Contracts shorten, bargaining hardens, and the unit begins to lose its time-bridging role. By the time policy shifts decisively, inflation is no longer merely a price phenomenon. It is embedded in contract structure, in wage norms, and in business models that assume continuous repricing. Restoring stability then becomes not a technical adjustment but a political campaign against an entire way of doing business, and campaigns produce casualties that must be justified or legitimacy collapses in the attempt to save credibility.

A treaty line, written to govern a shared unit where local narratives cannot defend value, states the doctrine without softness: "The primary objective... shall be to maintain price stability." (TFEU Article 127(1).) The bluntness matters because it reveals how a fiat order protects itself when it cannot rely on redemption. A shared unit cannot survive if its meaning through time becomes contested, because contestation becomes fragmentation, and fragmentation destroys the payment perimeter that makes a shared unit useful. The line is not devotion to a number; it is devotion to governability, because price instability turns the unit into a political object fought over in wage rounds, rent resets, and budget seasons, and a unit fought over that way stops functioning as a neutral language of obligation.

The power map inside inflation politics is therefore not only "monetary authority versus treasury." It is an architecture of repricing speed and access to settlement. Large firms can change prices quickly. Organized labor can change wages quickly when bargaining power exists. Households with little bargaining power experience lag. Banks transmit tightening through lending and deposit pricing. Payment operators transmit stress through the speed of settlement and the terms of liquidity. The state, meanwhile, is both referee and participant because it controls fiscal outlays, tax schedules, and the legal discharge boundary. Inflation becomes political when these actors move at different speeds and blame each other for the drift, and when the public concludes that the rules of adjustment are being written to protect some balance sheets and sacrifice others.

The added pressure scene begins where the fiat regime's legitimacy is actually manufactured: a late-night rate decision with fiscal officials waiting in adjacent rooms, not to interfere openly, but because everyone knows that a rate move is also a distribution move. The monetary committee studies inflation prints, wage settlements, and market-implied expectations, but the numbers do not argue by themselves. One faction insists that credibility is slipping and that delay will embed inflation into contracts, making later tightening harsher and more socially destructive. Another faction insists that the banking layer is already straining under higher funding costs and collateral repricing, and that an aggressive move risks freezing credit and triggering a cascade that will force reversal, which would destroy credibility in a different way. In the corridor outside, fiscal staff run the debt-service projections and see the immediate consequence: tightening raises the state's own cost of borrowing, which pressures budgets, which pressures taxes, which pressures wage demands, which feeds the inflation politics the rate move is supposed to contain. The decision is not only whether to raise. It is whether the state's pain will be paid through unemployment now or through inflation later, and whether either path can be framed as fair enough that consent survives.

The vote is taken, and the statement is drafted to sound like inevitability rather than choice, because fiat requires the public to believe the future is governable. The next morning the labor market reads the decision as signal and threat. Employers harden wage offers because they expect demand to soften. Workers harden wage demands because they expect bills to keep rising until disinflation is proven in their own receipts. Banks reprice credit, which pressures marginal firms first, because marginal firms are always the first to pay for tightening. The state then faces the second-order legitimacy problem: the central authority can raise the cost of time, but it cannot decide whose time becomes worthless. That decision is made in layoffs, in bankruptcies, in rent arrears, and in which firms are deemed too important to fail when the credit machine creaks.

Inflation politics becomes unavoidable in fiscal indexing choices because indexing reveals who the state is willing to protect. If benefits are indexed quickly while wages lag, wage earners feel raided. If taxes are not indexed, households experience bracket creep as a second inflation tax. If public-sector wages are indexed while private wages are not, private workers see favoritism. If neither is indexed, social unrest grows because the state appears indifferent to the unit's failure. Each indexing decision is a legitimacy decision disguised as administration. Fiat regimes often try to hide these decisions behind formulas, but formulas are still choices about which losses are socialized and which are individualized. The more inflation persists, the more these choices accumulate into a public model of state behavior, and once that model becomes "they solve budgets by shrinking my life," the currency becomes a political object rather than a common instrument.

The temptation to treat inflation as an acceptable tax is therefore always present, and sometimes it is defended as pragmatic. Inflation reduces the real burden of public debt. It can ease fiscal stress without explicit austerity. It can soften real wage rigidity by allowing real wages to fall without nominal cuts. It can facilitate relative price adjustment. These claims can be true. The problem is that inflation performs them by eroding the currency's claim to neutrality. Once the public believes inflation is being used as an instrument, the public starts protecting itself, and protection behavior changes the economy's time structure. Debt contracts demand higher premia. Lenders demand collateral with inflation resilience. Households move out of nominal savings. Wage bargaining hardens. The tax becomes less efficient because the public learns to evade it through balance-sheet rearrangement. Inflation, used repeatedly, becomes fiscal poison because it destroys the cheapness of borrowing that modern states rely on.

The central bank is drawn into this dilemma through its role as guardian of settlement and liquidity. In a fiat regime, the bank is not only a rate-setter. It is the backstop that prevents panic from turning payment into paralysis. Inflation intensifies the demand for speed because when the unit is losing meaning through time, actors demand settlement faster, shorten credit terms, and prefer claims closer to final settlement. A payment doctrine line clarifies why finality matters to inflation politics even when people never say the word. "Final settlement... is the irrevocable and unconditional transfer... or the discharge of an obligation." (CPMI Glossary, definition of final settlement.) When inflation raises the premium on speed, the hierarchy of claims becomes more visible: the highest-grade claim is the one that settles without dispute and without delay. Lower tiers face discounts, haircuts, and refusal. The monetary authority tightening into inflation is therefore tightening into hierarchy stress, because it is simultaneously reducing liquidity and increasing the value of liquidity. If it breaks the plumbing, credibility collapses. If it protects plumbing too generously, inflation expectations may drift. Fiat legitimacy depends on balancing these constraints in a way the public can tolerate and the market can believe.

A serious fiat regime therefore tries to build credibility as architecture rather than as personality. It builds a target framework not as a slogan but as a constraint system that binds the institution across leadership changes. It builds communication not as public relations but as an attempt to condition expectations to reduce the unemployment cost of disinflation. It builds operational independence not as moral purity but as a barrier against fiscal dominance, because fiscal dominance is the condition under which monetary policy becomes servant of debt service and inflation becomes a budget tool rather than a stability constraint. It tries to align fiscal practice, monetary practice, and bargaining norms so inflation does not become embedded. This alignment is hardest precisely when inflation is high, because every group wants protection first and protection demands conflict.

The chapter began with a wage meeting because wages are where inflation becomes a political verdict. When workers demand indexing, they are declaring the unit untrusted across time. When employers resist indexing, they are resisting a regime change in the contract structure of the economy. When the state urges restraint, it is asking one group to subsidize credibility for all, and the success of that request depends on whether sacrifice is perceived as shared and whether the state is seen imposing discipline on other powerful actors as well. In a fiat regime, disinflation is not only a policy; it is a coalition project, and the coalition fails when inflation is experienced as selective extraction rather than shared adjustment.

The counterargument insists societies can live with moderate inflation and that obsession with stability is creditor ideology. There is truth here, and a fiat regime that treats any deviation from a target as existential will impose unnecessary unemployment and protect asset owners at the expense of labor. Moderate inflation can coexist with growth when bargaining institutions are stable and fiscal policy is coherent. The danger is not moderate inflation itself. The danger is the credibility threshold where behavior shifts into defensive repricing, contract shortening, and indexing, because once that shift occurs, inflation is no longer a level effect; it becomes an acceleration process embedded in norms and contracts. Statecraft is not worship of a number. It is maintaining the architecture that keeps expectations from slipping across the threshold where inflation becomes self-protective equilibrium and legitimacy becomes the casualty.

The strategic implication is direct. Inflation is not only an economic variable; it is a legitimacy variable that determines how much sovereign capacity a state can mobilize without revolt. A state facing external stress, security stress, or supply stress cannot rely on fiat flexibility if inflation has already eroded trust in the unit. In that condition, every fiscal expansion is interpreted as inflationary, every easing as surrender, every tightening as cruelty, and the state loses degrees of freedom precisely when it needs them. Price stability, understood properly, is preservation of maneuver. It keeps the unit stable enough that the state can borrow, tax, spend, and backstop without triggering immediate flight into substitutes or immediate political collapse.

CLOSING DOCTRINE

Inflation becomes politics because it transforms the unit of account from trusted infrastructure into contested distribution, and once the unit is contested the state cannot ask society to carry time risk inside nominal claims without paying for that risk through indexing, defensive repricing, and shortened contracts that weaken credit and erode governability. In a fiat regime, price stability is not a technocratic preference; it is a legitimacy anchor that preserves sovereign maneuver by keeping expectations from crossing the threshold where inflation becomes embedded acceleration and where the hierarchy of money collapses into a scramble for settlement speed and real assets. Credibility is not speech; it is the demonstrated willingness to impose discipline even when discipline produces unemployment and fiscal pain, coupled with the operational capacity to protect payment finality so tightening does not break the plumbing and force reversal that would destroy trust. The governing problem is therefore institutional coherence and procedural fairness: fiscal practice, monetary practice, and wage-price bargaining must be aligned enough that stabilization does not become a war between social groups, and the distribution of pain during both inflation and disinflation must be visibly nonselective, because inflation perceived as insider protection becomes legitimacy collapse even before it becomes macroeconomic collapse.

CHAPTER 8

CUTTING THE ANCHOR

THE FLOATING WORLD IS BORN

The decision was presented as a temporary measure, because temporary language is how states soften permanent turns. The room was small, the papers were thick, and the anxiety was not about ideology; it was about arithmetic and credibility under deadline. Foreign monetary authorities had been converting accumulated claims into reserve assets at a pace that made the promise look less like a standard and more like a run conducted by governments. Domestic politics wanted growth and jobs, not a recession induced to defend a redemption window most voters never touched. The treasury wanted room to fund. The monetary authority wanted room to stabilize. The international system wanted continuity without admitting that continuity was already cracking. When the announcement came, it sounded controlled, managerial, and calm. Beneath the surface it was an admission that the old constitution of external equivalence had become too expensive to honor.

"I have directed the suspension, on a temporary basis, of convertibility of our currency into reserve assets." (Head-of-state address announcing suspension of convertibility, August 1971.) The hinge is not the person. The hinge is the verb. Suspend is a constitutional act in monetary form. It is the state admitting that redemption, the hard discipline of external equivalence, will no longer govern domestic policy. Temporarily is the protective mask, a way to tell creditors and allies that the old hierarchy still exists while the machinery begins to behave as if it does not. In that single line, the postwar reserve blueprint was revised under pressure, not by treaty and not by conference, but by executive necessity.

Before the suspension, the system lived on a double promise that was always fragile. The domestic promise was that the state's liabilities would discharge obligations within its jurisdiction because law and enforcement made them final enough for ordinary life. The external promise was that a defined pathway existed from accumulated claims into a superior settlement asset, and that this pathway would remain open in principle, not merely by courtesy. That external promise elevated the currency into an apex instrument for the postwar order because it made private and public claims behave as if they could always reach the top of the hierarchy. Yet the promise also created the classic vulnerability of convertibility: when confidence tightens, everyone reaches for the upgrade path, and the upgrade path cannot serve everyone simultaneously without draining the reserve stock that makes the promise credible.

The late fixed-rate years were not a morality play about virtue and vice. They were a conflict between constraints that could not be held together indefinitely. A state wanted domestic autonomy to manage employment and growth. It wanted stable exchange rates to preserve trade and avoid competitive devaluation. It faced increasing cross-border mobility of claims that allowed foreign holders to test the system quickly when doubts emerged. The more the system succeeded in rebuilding trade and finance, the more it created the conditions that made the peg hard to defend. Claims accumulated abroad as global liquidity demand grew, and those accumulated claims were a standing invitation to redemption under the old rules. A world that used one country's liabilities as reserve instruments was always asking that country to supply liquidity to the world while remaining disciplined enough that the world would trust the supply. That tension was structural. It could be managed for a time. It could not be denied forever.

The break therefore cannot be understood as a mere change in exchange-rate technique. It was a change in where sovereignty lived. Under an anchor regime, sovereignty is conditioned by the obligation to defend external equivalence, meaning a state must sometimes impose domestic pain to preserve the external promise. Under the floating world, the state refuses that conditioning. It chooses to defend domestic governability first, and to let the external value of its liabilities be priced in markets that can move faster than treaties. This choice does not remove discipline. It relocates it. Discipline becomes the price level and the cost of time, not the reserve stock and the redemption window. The state trades a single hard constraint for a continuous test: inflation legitimacy, interest-rate credibility, and the stability of a banking system that now sits on a currency whose external value can move sharply and whose import channel can transmit that movement straight into domestic politics.

A governing line from the international monetary order reads like aspiration until it is read as system engineering: "Each member undertakes to collaborate ... to assure orderly exchange arrangements and to promote a stable system of exchange rates." (International Monetary Fund, Articles of Agreement, Article IV, Section 1.) Stability after the anchor is cut is no longer the mechanical consequence of a redemption rule. It becomes a policy project. It must be manufactured through cooperation, through credibility, through reserve management, and through occasional intervention that is never admitted as intervention until after the fact. The promise of stability survives, but the method changes from redemption to governance, and governance is always slower and messier than a rule because governance must operate through expectations and through institutions that can lose legitimacy when they impose pain.

The floating world did not eliminate hierarchy; it made hierarchy more dependent on institutions and more sensitive to perception. The top claim within each jurisdiction remained the public settlement instrument, but the cross-border ranking of those instruments became a market judgment shaped by financial depth, geopolitical confidence, and the credibility of crisis containment. A currency that could be sold in size without collapsing its price gained advantage. A state that could backstop its banking system without igniting sustained inflation gained advantage. A market with deep settlement infrastructure and predictable law gained advantage. These are not abstract virtues. They are operational capacities. In the floating era, the strongest currency is not the one with the prettiest doctrine. It is the one whose issuer can convince the world that its liabilities will retain meaning through time, that its payment architecture will not freeze when stress arrives, and that its crisis responses will not rewrite the hierarchy arbitrarily.

The immediate consequence of cutting the anchor was exposure. Exchange rates became channels through which domestic politics, external confidence, and capital flows could punish each other without delay. A government that overstimulated could see its currency fall, raising import prices and accelerating inflation. A government that tightened harshly could see unemployment rise, triggering political revolt and policy reversal that markets would price instantly. A monetary authority that hesitated could see expectations drift. A monetary authority that overreacted could break its banking layer. The floating world is therefore the world in which policy is no longer protected by a fixed parity story. Every decision prints a price.

The added pressure scene occurs in the first full year after the float, when the new regime stops being a headline and becomes a routine conflict over whose pain is acceptable. The finance minister arrives with a fiscal plan that assumes growth will rescue revenue, and the plan depends on credit remaining cheap enough that firms keep hiring and households keep spending. The monetary authority arrives with inflation prints that look less like noise and more like drift, and drift is the enemy in a fiat regime because drift teaches households to expect more drift. The minister argues that tightening will produce recession, and recession will produce political collapse, and political collapse will produce policy reversal that will unanchor expectations anyway. The monetary authority argues that easing will entrench inflation, and entrenched inflation will destroy legitimacy, and destroyed legitimacy will force harsher tightening later under worse conditions. The argument is not about ideology. It is about sequencing: whether to pay through unemployment now or through inflation later, whether the coalition can survive either payment, and whether external markets will punish delay faster than domestic politics can absorb discipline.

In the old regime, the reserve stock and redemption window would have forced the decision by draining. In the new regime, the decision is forced by expectation. The currency's external value moves as the debate leaks into market interpretation, and the move feeds back into domestic prices through imports, which feeds back into wage bargaining, which feeds back into inflation prints. The state discovers that the float is not a release from constraint but a conversion of constraint into feedback loops. It must govern loops, not defend a window. Governing loops requires institutions that can act decisively without appearing capricious, because caprice is what breaks expectations. The minister and the monetary authority therefore negotiate not only policy but narrative: what pain can be framed as necessary, what pain can be blamed on external shocks, and what pain will be interpreted as betrayal. The fiat regime begins here, in this friction between two necessities that cannot be fully reconciled: preserving purchasing power and preserving employment continuity, while the exchange rate broadcasts every hesitation.

Cutting the anchor also changed how states could wage economic conflict. Under a fixed regime, devaluation is a dramatic act, a breach that can be condemned. Under a floating regime, currency movement can be framed as market outcome even when policy is deliberately shaping it. This ambiguity widened the space for strategic behavior: interest-rate policy as exchange-rate policy, liquidity policy as capital-flow policy, regulatory tightening as monetary defense. It also widened the space for misunderstanding and accusation, because every currency move can be interpreted as either market discipline or statecraft. The floating world is therefore not merely more flexible. It is more politically combustible, because it turns exchange value into a permanent arena of interpretation and contestation.

The final settlement layer did not become less important after the anchor was cut; it became more important because the hierarchy now depended on whether claims could remain money-like under stress without an external redemption promise. "Final settlement... is the irrevocable and unconditional transfer... or the discharge of an obligation." (CPMI Glossary, definition of final settlement.) In a floating world, fear does not funnel into a reserve window. It funnels into settlement speed, into safe claims, into the top tier of the hierarchy inside and across borders. When exchange rates move and confidence tightens, participants demand instruments closest to final settlement and institutions closest to the backstop. The floating regime therefore increases the premium on payment architecture and on credible last-resort capacity, because those are the mechanisms that keep fiat from becoming a melting claim in crisis.

The official defense of cutting the anchor is straightforward: the old promise had become incompatible with domestic stability and global liquidity demand, and maintaining it would have required pain that could not be politically carried. This defense is not cynical. It is often correct as strategic logic. The counterargument is equally serious: cutting the anchor removed a hard constraint that disciplined fiscal behavior and protected savers, and it opened the door to inflationary finance, political capture, and repeated cycles of boom and bust. Both claims contain truth because the anchor was both discipline and fragility. The peg could impose virtue through constraint, but it could also impose crisis through reserve drain. Fiat can impose maneuver through flexibility, but it can also impose abuse through discretion. The statecraft question is not which world is morally superior. The question is which set of constraints can be governed without collapsing legitimacy.

The shift into the floating world is therefore the threshold where money becomes explicitly a policy regime rather than a conversion rule. From this point, the central bank's toolkit becomes the instrument of sovereign credibility. Targets, guidance, and signals will be built to anchor expectations where reserve promises once anchored them. Balance sheets will be used to backstop markets where convertibility once supplied confidence. Legal and regulatory frameworks will be tightened to sustain the hierarchy where the old system relied on an external promise. The float is the breach; the fiat regime is the construction erected to keep that breach from widening into disorder.

CLOSING DOCTRINE

Cutting the anchor is not the end of discipline; it is the relocation of discipline from reserve arithmetic and redemption into credibility, inflation legitimacy, and the governance of time through interest rates, liquidity backstops, and settlement architecture. A fixed promise fails when accumulated claims can test it faster than the reserve stock can sustain and when the issuer cannot politically carry the domestic pain required to defend external equivalence; a floating regime survives only if the issuer can manufacture stability through institutions that keep purchasing power governable and final settlement continuous in stress. The floating world expands sovereign maneuver in the short run, but it turns exchange value into a permanent referendum on institutional credibility, and it makes the hierarchy of money more dependent on the state's capacity to backstop liquidity without igniting sustained inflation and to impose disinflation without collapsing the coalition that makes governance possible.

CHAPTER 9

CREDIBILITY ENGINEERING

TARGETS, GUIDANCE, AND THE PUBLIC SIGNAL

The meeting ended, but the statement did not. It sat on the table as a draft that everybody pretended was merely wording, even though the room understood it would function as policy before the first rate move ever arrived. The market was not waiting for the decision; it was waiting for the sentence that would tell it how to interpret the next six months of sentences. A single adjective could steepen a yield curve. A single omission could trigger a repricing that would tighten conditions more violently than any committee wanted to admit it could control. Staff argued over the placement of a clause that looked like grammar and behaved like sovereign capacity, because in a fiat regime the public signal is not commentary layered atop policy. It is one of the mechanisms by which policy becomes real.

Convertibility discipline governed by threat. A scarce reserve asset could be demanded, and the demand forced adjustment whether politicians enjoyed it or not. Once that discipline is cut away, the state must manufacture an alternative anchor that can hold the unit of account inside a tolerable corridor without requiring an external redemption promise. That anchor is credibility, and credibility in the fiat regime is not reputation in the abstract. It is structured belief about future behavior: that the monetary authority will defend price stability enough to preserve legitimacy, will defend liquidity enough to preserve settlement, and will accept the political pain required to do both when the objectives collide. The machinery for producing that belief is mandate, instrument, and communication, but communication is the part the public touches directly, and what the public touches is what becomes politics when trust frays.

A statutory mandate makes the role explicit in the least romantic language possible, assigning the authority responsibility to promote stable prices alongside employment and sustainable long-term borrowing conditions. "Shall... maintain... so as to promote effectively the goals of maximum employment, stable prices, and moderate long-term interest rates." (Central banking statute, mandate clause.) The sentence is not ornament; it is institutional cover. It gives the authority a legal spine for choices that will otherwise be interpreted as elective cruelty or elective indulgence. It also exposes the tension that makes credibility engineering unavoidable. Stable prices and maximum employment can be aligned for long stretches, then collide abruptly, and when they collide the public signal becomes the battlefield over which objective will be prioritized and for how long.

Credibility engineering begins with an admission that feels humiliating to technocrats and liberating to statecraft. In a fiat regime, policy operates through expectations as much as through arithmetic. Rates matter because they set the cost of time today, but guidance matters because it shapes the expected cost of time tomorrow, and tomorrow is where most of the balance sheet lives. Mortgages, corporate debt, infrastructure finance, inventory credit, municipal funding, and asset valuations are long-dated claims whose present value is a function of anticipated policy paths. If the authority can shape that anticipated path, it can tighten or ease conditions without moving the policy rate as aggressively, because markets do part of the work by repricing ahead of action. If it cannot shape the anticipated path, it must do more work through blunt moves, and blunt moves generate political backlash faster because they are easier to feel and harder to explain.

The target is the simplest public device for compressing the future into a number. It takes the sprawling complexity of wages, rents, commodity shocks, exchange swings, and credit cycles and claims the authority will steer the system toward a defined stability corridor. The target is not the mechanism. It is the claim that a mechanism exists and will be used. That claim matters because in fiat, the public's willingness to hold nominal promises depends on whether the future price level is believed to be governable enough. Once the public believes the authority has no anchor, wage bargaining demands indexing, firms preemptively reprice, and lenders demand inflation premia that become inflationary in their own right. The target is therefore not primarily about optimality. It is about preventing a behavioral regime change in which everyone treats the unit as unreliable through time.

A second institutional tradition states the discipline with fewer concessions because a shared unit cannot survive if its meaning through time is treated as negotiable. "The primary objective... shall be to maintain price stability." (Monetary union treaty, price-stability clause.) The bluntness is instructive. When an authority is embedded in a shared unit and cannot rely on a single national fiscal narrative to defend legitimacy, it needs a simple public commitment that can be repeated until it becomes reflex. That simplicity is not naivety. It is recognition that credibility is a public asset that can be lost quickly and rebuilt slowly, and that complex commitments invite political capture because complexity lets every faction hear what it wants to hear.

Guidance is where targets become actionable, and it is also where the power map becomes visible. The authority can pledge stability while quietly communicating tolerance for inflation to protect employment.

It can pledge employment support while quietly communicating willingness to accept recession to restore the unit's meaning. The public signal is the method for shaping which interpretation dominates without writing the interpretation into law. Guidance can be explicit, through projected paths and conditional commitments, or implicit, through tone, sequencing, and what the authority chooses to emphasize. In either form, guidance is narrative converted into market action: words move yields and spreads, yields and spreads move credit conditions, and credit conditions move the real economy before a committee meets again.

This is why the sentence on the table matters more than the committee's private certainty. Private certainty is cheap. Public credibility is expensive. The authority must sound committed without sounding trapped, because sounding trapped invites markets to test the trap. It must sound flexible without sounding permissive, because sounding permissive invites wage bargaining to treat the target as optional. It must sound legible without surrendering its ability to surprise, because surprise is sometimes required to break a drift in expectations. The signal therefore operates in a corridor between clarity and ambiguity, and the corridor is not aesthetic. It is the space in which the authority preserves maneuver while preventing maneuver from being interpreted as caprice.

The first practical mechanism of credibility engineering is conditionality. Guidance is rarely a pure promise. It is a promise tied to conditions: inflation persistence, labor tightness, funding stress, or external shocks. Conditionality is the authority's attempt to pre-commit without becoming hostage. Yet conditionality also creates vulnerability. If the public believes conditions can be redefined whenever pain arrives, conditionality becomes a loophole and the signal becomes cheap talk. Credibility is built when conditions are specified clearly enough that the public can see the line, and when the authority later acts as if the line is real even when acting is unpopular. Credibility is lost when conditions are used as a way to avoid doing what the framework implies.

The second mechanism is repetition. Fiat legitimacy is learned behavior. The authority repeats its commitment until the public's default assumption becomes that the commitment will be defended. This is not propaganda in the crude sense. It is conditioning the time horizon of an economy. When people believe stability will be defended, they accept long-term nominal contracts at lower premia, and those lower premia make the economy less fragile because fewer actors are forced into defensive repricing. Repetition therefore reduces the cost of later stabilization by reducing the degree to which inflation becomes embedded in contracts.

The third mechanism is legibility, which is often mislabeled as virtue. Publishing rationales, projections, and decision logic makes the authority interpretable, and interpretability shapes markets. Interpretability can reduce panic by shrinking the space for rumor. It also narrows discretion because published commitments can be thrown back as accusation. The authority accepts this trade because credibility is the objective: a narrower corridor of discretion in exchange for a lower probability of expectation drift. Yet interpretability also creates an arena for conflict because every actor will attempt to interpret signals in a way that serves its balance sheet, and those interpretations can become self-reinforcing if enough participants trade on them.

The fourth mechanism is the strategic use of surprise, deployed sparingly because surprise is expensive. Surprise can damage trust in calm periods, but it can be necessary when expectations drift into an equilibrium the authority must break. Predictable guidance can become a cage. The authority may need to act more aggressively than signaled to convince the public the line is real. This is the paradox of guidance. Guidance stabilizes by shaping expectations, but guidance also risks boxing the authority into the very expectations it shaped. Credibility engineering therefore requires occasional demonstrations that stability outranks comfort, because comfort is what the public demands in the short run and what destroys the unit in the long run when inflation becomes tolerated drift.

The power structure beneath guidance is not subtle. Those who can move quickly benefit. Those who cannot move quickly pay. When the authority signals tightening, asset prices fall before wages adjust. Borrowing costs rise before rents fall. Firms with flexible pricing protect margins more easily than households protect budgets. When the authority signals easing, asset prices can rise quickly, benefiting holders of long-duration claims, while wage growth may lag. Guidance therefore redistributes even when the authority insists it is only transmitting information. The distribution follows the time structure: who holds long-duration assets, who holds variable-rate liabilities, who is a net borrower, who is a net saver, and who can reprice contracts quickly. Credibility engineering is inseparable from legitimacy politics because a signal that repeatedly benefits the same balance sheets becomes politically contested even if it stabilizes inflation.

The chapter's pressure scene belongs inside drafting, because the draft is where legitimacy is negotiated. Staff proposes a sentence committing to hold policy restrictive "for some time" until inflation returns to target. One member insists the phrase is permissive and will unanchor wage bargaining. Another insists it is rigid and will box the authority into overtightening if a funding market seizes. A third insists on an explicit clause about monitoring financial conditions, because financial stability is the hidden constraint in every inflation fight: tighten too far and the credit machine breaks; loosen too far and the unit drifts. They settle on a compromise that reads balanced, then the market reads it as a tilt, and the tilt becomes the day's policy. The authority discovers again that its signal is not evaluated by intent but by its effect on ranked claims.

The next morning, the currency moves, the curve adjusts, and spreads widen or tighten as the market updates its model of the authority's willingness to impose pain. The public sees none of this directly, but it experiences consequences in loan offers, in employer behavior, and in the speed at which landlords and retailers reprice. The signal has entered the economy and begun allocating time. This is why credibility engineering is not a communications chapter in the trivial sense. It is about how the state uses language to prevent the economy from shortening itself into a series of immediate transactions driven by distrust.

The critique of this project must be treated honestly because it is serious. The critique insists targets and guidance often protect creditors, that stability language justifies unemployment imposed on labor, and that claimed neutrality hides distributive choices that should be subject to democratic contest. The critique is not frivolous. Disinflation can be achieved through recession, and recession is a weapon that hits the vulnerable first. The defense is also serious. Without a credible stability anchor, inflation becomes a continuous tax that erodes the unit's meaning, destroys long-term contracting, and ultimately reduces employment and growth by making the economy short-term and defensive. The statecraft question is not whether distribution exists. The question is whether distribution is governed openly enough to preserve legitimacy while preserving stability enough to preserve maneuver.

The hidden danger of credibility engineering is self-referential performance. Authorities begin managing the public signal for its own sake, treating market reaction as the objective rather than as information about whether policy is aligned with stability and legitimacy. In that failure mode, the signal becomes a fragile idol. Necessary action is avoided because officials fear surprising markets, and necessary flexibility is avoided because officials fear accusations of inconsistency. Credibility then collapses not because the institution is too weak, but because it becomes captive to the performance of credibility. The remedy is doctrinal discipline: keep the signal tied to a coherent framework, keep conditions defined, keep actions consistent with the stated hierarchy of objectives, and accept that some market displeasure is the price of maintaining the unit's meaning through time.

Credibility engineering reaches into plumbing through its effect on settlement preference. When inflation is feared, actors demand settlement speed and short maturities. When stability is trusted, actors accept longer maturities and hold nominal claims with less defensive posture. A payment doctrine definition clarifies the endpoint the system is trying to protect when it protects trust. "Final settlement... is the irrevocable and unconditional transfer... or the discharge of an obligation." (Payment-system glossary, definition of final settlement.) The public signal's job is to keep the hierarchy from becoming a stampede toward the top claim at the first sign of drift. When the signal fails, the stampede begins: collateral haircuts widen, funding shortens, and liquidity becomes scarce precisely when everyone demands it. Guidance is thus not only about inflation. It is about preventing expectation drift from turning into structural fragility in the ranked-claims architecture of modern money.

The chapter closes where it began, with the sentence on the table. The authority's power in fiat is not that it can command prices directly. Its power is that it can command expectations indirectly, and that by commanding expectations it can reduce the amount of brute force it must apply later. A credible signal is sovereign capacity because it allows the state to borrow and spend without igniting immediate flight, allows private contracts to extend across time without constant repricing, and allows crises to be met with backstops without instantly unanchoring the unit. A weak signal is not merely a public relations problem. It is a fracture in the architecture that holds the fiat regime together.

CLOSING DOCTRINE

In the fiat regime, the public signal is a policy instrument because expectations are the transmission channel through which the state governs the price of time and stabilizes the unit of account without an external redemption rule. Targets compress the future into a commitment that restrains defensive repricing, guidance shapes the anticipated path of constraint so markets do part of the tightening or easing before action, and credibility is earned only when the authority enforces its own conditions even when enforcement is unpopular and costly. Communication is sovereignty operating through legibility: it allocates time across ranked claims by moving yields, spreads, and repricing speeds, and it becomes political the moment the distribution of those effects is perceived as selective. A regime that treats the signal as performance rather than as binding framework becomes captive to its own rhetoric, and when rhetoric detaches from action the unit loses meaning through time, the economy shortens into defensive contracting, and fragility returns through the same mechanism the signal was meant to prevent.

CHAPTER 10
BALANCE SHEET SOVEREIGNTY
BACKSTOPS, QE, AND PERMANENT INTERVENTION

The call does not come in the language of ideology. It comes in the language of collateral schedules and settlement deadlines. A desk reports that the market for the safest long-duration claims has become one-way, not because the claims changed overnight, but because the dealers who normally warehouse risk have reached their own funding limits and no longer want to stand between panic and price. Another desk reports that a benchmark spread has begun to gap, which means margin calls are coming, which means forced sales are coming, which means the next round of price discovery will not be valuation but liquidation. Someone says liquidity, but what the room means is time, because time is the only commodity that can prevent a market stress from becoming a funding cascade. The problem is simple and obscene: the state must decide whether to let private balance sheets discover reality in public, or to interpose its own balance sheet as the place where reality can be absorbed without breaking the payment machine.

The fiat regime's great promise is that the state will not be governed by an external redemption window. Its hidden cost is that the state must now govern the internal hierarchy continuously, and that governance increasingly runs through its balance sheet. Earlier monetary authority could pretend that it merely set the short price of time and allowed markets to do the rest. That fiction dies the first time a market freeze threatens settlement finality, because finality is not optional in a modern economy. When credit chains are long, collateral chains are layered, and payment obligations mature by the hour, the state's power is not only its ability to define tender or publish targets. Its power is its ability to turn its own liabilities into the claim nobody inside the jurisdiction can refuse, and to use that claim to buy, lend against, or guarantee what the private system is dumping in panic. That is balance sheet sovereignty: the capacity to convert public authority into market functioning by placing the state's own balance sheet between fear and forced liquidation.

A monetary balance sheet is often described as an accounting surface, as if the numbers were descriptive rather than decisive. In the fiat regime it is closer to a weapons platform. The asset side is not a portfolio in the ordinary sense; it is a map of which claims the state is willing to treat as fundable when markets are refusing to fund them. The liability side is not merely money creation; it is the ranked claims architecture through which settlements occur, through which banks meet reserve needs, and through which the private sector decides which promises are safe enough to hold through the night. When the state expands its balance sheet, it is not merely injecting reserves. It is altering the hierarchy by widening the set of assets that can be upgraded into settlement-grade claims. When it contracts, it narrows that upgrade path and forces private holders to carry more time risk on their own.

The mechanism is straightforward and therefore dangerous. Large-scale purchases replace a private holder with the state. A security that was funding itself through private markets now funds itself through the state because the state has bought it and paid with its own liabilities. Those liabilities are special not because they are paper or digits, but because they settle. They are the claim that ends argument inside the jurisdiction because the state can make them final through the settlement system and through law. The immediate effect is mechanical: yields move, spreads compress, and the price of time falls. The deeper effect is political: a chosen set of asset holders receives relief through higher prices and easier refinancing, while everyone else receives the secondary effects through jobs, wages, taxes, and the cost of living. Balance sheet sovereignty is distribution executed through procedure.

A hinge definition from the payment canon is the quiet driver of every large-scale intervention, even when nobody says it aloud: "Final settlement... is the irrevocable and unconditional transfer... or the discharge of an obligation." (Payment-system glossary, definition of final settlement.) The point is not elegance. The point is that a fiat order cannot survive a generalized doubt about whether obligations end on time, because once obligations stop ending cleanly, every contract becomes a negotiation under fear, and fear shortens everything. When the safest benchmark claims stop trading, the system loses its yardstick for collateral value. When collateral value becomes disputed, funding becomes scarce. When funding becomes scarce, institutions hoard the top claim and payment speed slows. Once payment speed slows, finality itself becomes suspect, and the fiat state is forced to respond not to stabilize prices in the abstract, but to keep the settlement perimeter from turning into a queue that becomes a run.

This is why the public description of these operations is always smaller than their real function. The public hears purchases and thinks stimulus. The machinery hears purchases and thinks keep the hierarchy from collapsing into binary refusal. The state's balance sheet is not deployed to make people feel wealthy. It is deployed to prevent the credit system from converting a market shock into a payment freeze, because a payment freeze is not a market event but a sovereignty event. It is the moment the state's unit stops behaving like a unit and starts behaving like a contested claim.

The chapter's first pressure scene belongs inside the design phase of intervention, because that is where distribution hides beneath technical criteria. The committee does not debate abstractions. It debates eligibility. Which maturities count. Which counterparties may sell directly. Whether purchases should concentrate in the benchmark claims that anchor discounting across the whole system, or spread into the riskier edges where the panic is actually forming. Whether the state should accept impaired collateral with a meaningful haircut, or only pristine collateral that is already fundable somewhere. Each choice has a clean technical justification and a messy political shadow. Buy only benchmark claims and you stabilize the reference curve, but you may abandon the stressed credit that employs people and finances inventories. Buy the stressed credit and you may preserve jobs, but you place public legitimacy at risk by visibly rescuing private balance sheets. Accept only pristine collateral and you protect the public balance sheet, but you may fail to stop the run because the run is happening in assets the market has stopped trusting. Accept broader collateral and you stop the run, but you invite accusations that administrative eligibility has converted private mistakes into public safety.

The causal chain is rarely visible to the public, so it must be stated without decorative language. A dealer funds long-duration paper in a short-term market. Volatility rises, haircuts widen, and the dealer must either post more collateral or sell. The sale depresses the price of the paper. That lower price forces mark-to-market losses on other holders, who then face their own margin calls and become sellers as well. If the state buys the paper or lends against it at a less destructive haircut, the chain slows. The price stabilizes enough that the next seller can wait. Waiting is the difference between a liquidity stress and a balance-sheet collapse. This is what QE and its cousins do in their cleanest operational form. They do not abolish losses. They rearrange the time at which losses must be realized, and in rearranging time they decide which institutions survive long enough to matter tomorrow.

A collateral vignette makes the point concrete without leaning on any famous crisis. A pool of mortgage-linked claims that had traded as routine collateral suddenly finds no bid because one segment of the market has reported losses and nobody knows how far correlation runs. Funding desks widen haircuts by habit and fear. A holder that was solvent under hold-to-maturity arithmetic becomes distressed under margin arithmetic because the collateral must now support more funding with less recognized value. If the state declares the pool eligible at a substantial haircut, the pool becomes fundable again, not because the market has regained faith, but because the state has built a bridge from disputed collateral into settlement liquidity. If the state refuses eligibility, forced sales continue, margin calls multiply, and institutions that were merely illiquid become insolvent by sequence. The line between eligibility and ineligibility is not a neutral line. It is a survival line.

That survival line is why market neutrality is usually a half-truth. A program may be neutral within its chosen perimeter, buying proportionally or according to a rule. The act of choosing the perimeter is already non-neutral. It determines which claims deserve stabilization and which claims must continue discovering pain in public. Perimeter choice is the hidden politics of every balance-sheet intervention. It decides whether the state is defending the benchmark core, defending employment-heavy credit, defending public borrowing conditions, or defending a mixture that can later be described as technical but was always distributive in practice. The stronger the intervention, the less plausible the fiction that it is merely administrative.

The second pressure scene arrives through a different channel: the collateral chain that nobody sees until it snaps. A small dealer funds inventory with overnight borrowing. The borrowing is secured by a stack of benchmark claims. The dealer has pledged those claims once already to another counterparty, and the chain continues because in calm times the system treats these claims as effectively money. A rumor hits the market that benchmark liquidity is thinning, not because credit has worsened, but because everyone wants the same exit at once. Haircuts rise by a few points, which is a polite way of saying that the dealer must find cash immediately. The dealer sells what it can, which is the very benchmark claim others are also selling. The price slips. The slip triggers a margin call at another node that uses the same claim as collateral. Another sale follows. The chain amplifies. The state watches this and understands the dirty truth: it is not rescuing bad credit; it is rescuing the assumption that certain collateral is cash-like enough to hold the system together. If that assumption fails, the whole credit machine becomes a set of isolated balance sheets refusing one another, and refusal is how payment freezes begin.

The state responds by placing its balance sheet where private balance sheets are trying to retreat. It buys, not because buying is morally satisfying, but because buying is the only way to create a buyer when the market's rational move is to stop being one. It lends, not because lending is generosity, but because term funding is the only way to prevent forced sales from setting the price for an entire class of collateral. It signals, not as theater, but because signals condition whether the next haircut is wider or narrower, and haircuts are the gears of panic. The intervention looks like a market operation. It functions like a constitutional operation because it decides whether the unit remains a unit or becomes a battlefield.

Balance sheet sovereignty also changes private management long before the next panic arrives. A bank treasurer who lives through one rescue does not return to the old world unchanged. Internal liquidity policy is rewritten. Some buffers are increased to satisfy supervisors and internal committees, but others are reduced because the treasurer has learned that the public sector will not allow deep disorder in the core. The treasurer shortens private alarm horizons, assuming that if market depth vanishes in benchmark claims the sovereign balance sheet will step in before the firm is forced into suicide pricing. Risk committees still talk about prudence, but prudence now includes planning around intervention. The firm's model of tail risk has been politicalized. What once counted as catastrophe now counts as a public-sector liquidity event. This is how extraordinary operations become part of ordinary private behavior without anybody announcing the constitutional revision openly.

The same shift occurs in the dealer community, only faster and with less shame. Dealers start carrying thinner warehouse capacity in normal times because they know that if benchmark markets stop functioning the state will likely restore two-way flow before total paralysis is allowed to spread. Treasury departments inside large firms change how they think about safe assets. A claim is not safe merely because its credit looks pristine. It is safe because it is likely to sit inside the sovereign defense perimeter when stress arrives. That distinction quietly rewrites portfolio construction across the system. Some assets now command lower spreads not because their fundamental cash flows are better, but because they are believed to be politically backstoppable. The state has not merely calmed markets. It has rewritten the map of what markets think they are.

The third pressure scene, and the one that births permanent intervention as a structural risk, arrives after the panic is contained. The balance sheet is now large enough that it cannot be ignored even by those who never cared about operations. Markets want reassurance that support will remain until stability is undeniable. Politicians want reassurance that support will not become permanent subsidy. Banks and dealers want assurance that liquidity will not be withdrawn while fragile structures still depend on it. Households want assurance that inflation will not become the silent payment for financial rescue. The state discovers that exit is not the mirror image of entry. Entry is fear, and fear creates coalition. Exit is distribution, and distribution fractures coalition. When the state shrinks its balance sheet, it raises the price of time, lowers asset prices, tightens conditions, and returns duration risk to private hands. That tightening can be economically necessary and politically ruinous because the beneficiaries of easy conditions are concentrated and vocal, while the beneficiaries of restored discipline are diffuse and often do not connect their relief to balance sheet decisions.

This is where permanent intervention ceases to be a slogan and becomes a structural trap. If every serious stress now elicits the same answer—expand the balance sheet, stabilize key markets, compress spreads, then promise eventual normalization—the system learns that normalization is conditional and rescue is reliable. Private portfolios are then built around the expectation that deep drawdowns in systemically central claims will trigger sovereign absorption. The state may still impose haircuts, conditions, and stigma, but the broad lesson survives: the sovereign balance sheet is part of the market's architecture. At that point, exit becomes less a technical challenge than a constitutional one. How does a state restore market discipline when the market's current valuations already assume the state will not tolerate genuine liquidation in the core.

The temptation is to treat this as a communications problem, to reassure markets that normalization will be gradual and that stability is the priority. That is necessary and insufficient. The real constraint is behavioral. Once private actors have built strategies around a public backstop, the withdrawal of the backstop is experienced not as normalization but as betrayal of the model. Those actors will sell earlier, lobby harder, and punish faster because they have learned that the state moves when the system screams. The state then faces a choice: normalize and tolerate disorder, or delay normalization and tolerate creeping dependence. The public sees the choice as a morality play. The machinery sees it as a timing problem inside a hierarchy: withdraw too quickly and you force liquidation; withdraw too slowly and you embed the expectation that liquidation will never be allowed in the core.

A fourth scene makes the exit trap harder. The authority announces that purchase reinvestments will slow and that balance sheet runoff will begin in an orderly, preannounced way. Inside official rooms this is treated as discipline. In markets it is treated as a test. Dealers pull in risk. Leveraged holders shorten duration. Treasury desks across the private system begin hoarding cash because nobody wants to be caught funding the same claims the state is no longer absorbing. Yields rise more quickly than the announcement's authors expected. The move spills from benchmark claims into mortgages, then into corporate funding, then into municipal borrowing. None of this is a panic in the theatrical sense. It is more dangerous than panic because it looks orderly while quietly raising the price of time across the economy. A housing project is delayed because financing terms no longer work. A business line is shelved because rollover risk has become too expensive. A local authority cuts planned spending because refinancing now threatens its budget. The state then confronts the ugliest possibility in all normalization efforts: the system may need support not because it is panicking, but because it has quietly reorganized itself to require public balance-sheet presence as a normal condition.

This is where balance sheet sovereignty changes the meaning of independence. Independence is often framed as insulation from politics. In practice, balance sheet operations are politics by other means because they reshape asset prices, credit availability, and fiscal funding conditions. When the state's balance sheet holds large quantities of public debt, the boundary between monetary operations and fiscal consequence becomes harder to defend, even when intent is not fiscal. Higher rates now matter not only for employment and inflation, but for public debt service, budget fights, and the political viability of discipline. Fiscal dominance does not need to be declared. It can emerge as gravitational pull, because a large balance sheet turns interest rates into a budget weapon and balance sheet shrinkage into a visible tightening that elected officials will resist.

The fifth pressure scene shows that pull in a way that does not require slogans. Treasury staff arrives with financing projections and quietly requests stability in borrowing conditions because refinancing will otherwise require either unpopular taxes or unpopular cuts. The monetary authority arrives with inflation drift and quietly requests restraint in fiscal expansion because the unit's credibility is fraying. Both requests are reasonable. They are also incompatible in the short run. If borrowing costs rise sharply, budgets break. If borrowing costs are suppressed indefinitely, inflation legitimacy breaks. The state discovers that its balance sheet has become the arena where these conflicts are negotiated, because purchases and backstops can keep borrowing conditions smooth while tightening can restore purchasing power. The balance sheet is now not only a market tool but a political bargaining surface.

A sixth scene unfolds outside official rooms, where legitimacy is either preserved or lost. A household does not care about maturity transformation as a phrase, but it cares that asset prices are climbing while rents climb too, and it notices that every intervention aimed at stabilizing markets seems to arrive faster than any intervention aimed at stabilizing ordinary life. A small business owner does not parse duration risk, but notices that benchmark markets get rescue language while local credit lines get repriced with no ceremony. A pension committee notices that lower yields raise the value of liabilities and push the fund into riskier assets just to maintain return assumptions, which means the same intervention that stabilized the system today may be seeding tomorrow's fragility in another corner. The public description says stabilization. The lived description says hierarchy. This is why permanent intervention is not only a financial issue. It is a civic issue, because repeated use of the sovereign balance sheet can teach the population that continuity is protected for the core and rationed for the edges. Once that lesson hardens, every future intervention begins from a legitimacy deficit.

The strongest counterargument should be stated without defensiveness because it is right about the risk. Repeated intervention creates moral hazard, distorts price discovery, subsidizes leverage, and embeds a political economy in which asset owners are repeatedly protected while those without financial assets are told to accept inflation or austerity as the price of stability. That description is not paranoia. It is a map of the legitimacy danger. If the state repeatedly upgrades private risk into public safety, private risk-taking will increase and the next intervention will have to be larger. If the state suppresses risk premia for too long, capital will be misallocated and fragility will grow under the surface. If the state holds the price of time too low for too long, inflation legitimacy can fracture and the political coalition that tolerated earlier interventions can turn hostile.

The defense is also real. A modern economy organized around collateralized funding, benchmark claims, and timed settlement obligations cannot survive repeated liquidity freezes without accepting collapse on a scale that would tear through employment, taxation, savings, and political order. The state is therefore not choosing between purity and compromise. It is choosing between imperfect intervention and destructive liquidation. That is why balance sheet sovereignty is not an aberration inside the fiat regime. It is one of the regime's core capacities. Once redemption discipline is gone, the state must defend the hierarchy internally, and its balance sheet is one of the few instruments powerful enough to do that at speed.

The governing problem is not whether to intervene, but how to draw and defend the perimeter. A durable perimeter preserves finality, imposes haircuts where possible, forces private recapitalization where necessary, and keeps the public signal clear enough that support is understood as defense of the payment core rather than as a standing guarantee of asset prices. It must also make room for actual failure. Equity must be allowed to burn. Management must be removed where negligence or recklessness made the intervention necessary. Creditors close enough to the edge must sometimes bear loss, or the state will lose the moral authority to defend the center. Balance sheet sovereignty without loss discipline is not stabilization. It is hierarchy capture.

A short hinge line from the book's canon states the danger with the right bluntness: external liquidity can preserve stability while quietly reducing autonomy. The domestic analogue is just as severe. Public purchases and backstops can preserve internal stability while quietly reducing future policy freedom, because the state becomes more exposed to asset prices, more entangled with fiscal funding conditions, and more vulnerable to accusations that any tightening is betrayal. This is the permanence trap in its pure form. The state uses its balance sheet to protect maneuver, then discovers maneuver has been traded away to maintain the very system it protected.

The discipline required after intervention is therefore harder than the intervention itself. It requires regulators to force stronger private liquidity buffers even while markets are celebrating restored calm. It requires supervisors to resist lobbying for the old thin margins and soft assumptions that looked efficient before the panic. It requires the monetary authority to tolerate some repricing and some discomfort as the cost of reintroducing private responsibility into markets that have been taught to expect sovereign absorption. It requires fiscal authorities not to mistake smoother borrowing conditions for a permanent invitation to fund every conflict with duration. Most of all, it requires the state to remember that its balance sheet is not the system's natural home. It is the emergency room. The more comfortable markets become living there, the sicker the constitution of the system becomes.

The chapter closes on the simplest proposition the system teaches under stress. A state that can expand its balance sheet can buy time.

A state that cannot expand its balance sheet is governed by the market's demand for immediate liquidation. Buying time is not free. It is a transfer of risk from private hands to public legitimacy. Whether that transfer is tolerable depends on whether the state can keep finality intact, keep inflation governable, and keep the public persuaded that the hierarchy is being managed for continuity rather than for privilege. In the fiat regime, the balance sheet is not the afterthought of policy. It is one of the primary locations where monetary authority becomes real.

CLOSING DOCTRINE

Balance sheet sovereignty is the capacity to defend settlement finality by converting public liabilities into time, using purchases and backstops to prevent fire-sale liquidation from becoming systemic refusal. Large-scale intervention does not eliminate hierarchy; it governs hierarchy by widening the upgrade path from private assets into settlement-grade claims, and that widening is always distribution through eligibility, haircut, maturity, and access. The political danger is habituation: once markets learn that deep stress in core claims will trigger sovereign absorption, private pricing begins to lean on public capacity and withdrawal becomes a crisis of its own, forcing the state to choose between disorder now and dependence later. A durable fiat regime therefore requires perimeter discipline: intervene to preserve finality, force private loss where possible, and withdraw support slowly enough to avoid collapse but firmly enough to prevent rescue from becoming the system's constitution, because a balance sheet that cannot shrink without panic is no longer a stabilizer but a governor of the state itself.

CHAPTER 11

THE LEGAL CORE

TENDER, TAX, PRIORITY, AND ENFORCEMENT

The dispute did not begin with philosophy. It began with a refusal at a counter. A payer slid across a stack of instruments with the easy confidence of someone who believed money was whatever could be circulated and accepted often enough. The clerk did not raise her voice. She pointed to the rule displayed beside the payment window and repeated a sentence that sounded petty until the room understood it was sovereign. Only the state's settlement instrument would discharge this obligation, in this office, on this date. The payer argued that the instrument in hand was liquid, widely used, and accepted by merchants without complaint. The clerk did not argue about convenience. She argued about closure. The question was not whether the instrument could purchase goods. The question was whether it could end a public obligation as a public fact, binding on third parties, immune to later dispute, and enforceable by the same authority that demanded payment.

The fiat regime is often described through its visible tools: the cost of time, the public signal, the emergency backstop, the sovereign balance sheet. Those are the moving parts. Beneath them sits a harder structure without which none of the visible machinery can hold for long. The legal core is that structure. Tender defines what ends an obligation within the jurisdiction. Tax defines what the population must periodically obtain in order to remain inside the law without penalty. Priority defines which claims survive scarcity with dignity and which are sacrificed first. Enforcement turns each of those definitions from suggestion into social fact. Without this core, credibility engineering becomes theater, balance sheet intervention becomes gift, and the unit of account loses the coercive skeleton that makes strangers trust it across time.

Tender is the first hinge because it solves the closure problem in the most explicit way law can solve anything. A tender rule does not say the state's instrument is useful. It says the instrument can end the relevant obligation if offered according to rule. "Legal tender for all debts, public charges, taxes, and dues." (Tender clause in the monetary statute.) The brutal elegance of that line is that it compresses the entire closure architecture into a sentence. The state is not merely issuing a liability. It is defining the liability as the instrument that discharges obligations in the domains named. Under an anchor regime, that closure is reinforced by the promise that the liability can be upgraded into a superior reserve claim. Under fiat, the closure rule must do more work because the upgrade promise is gone. The law becomes the first machine that makes the state's claim money-like even before markets or habit ratify it.

Yet tender on its own is not enough to sustain a fiat order. A population may accept the state's instrument for convenience and still flee it when stress rises, unless a stronger and more repetitive demand exists. That stronger demand is tax. Tax is the second hinge because it creates unavoidable periodic demand backed by penalty. A state does not need every private contract to specify its instrument if it can specify that public obligations to the state must be discharged in that instrument, and then punish failure. This is the point at which monetary design stops pretending to be voluntary. A person or firm may prefer to transact in substitutes. At certain dates, under certain rules, they must obtain the state's instrument or confront sanctions. Tax therefore does what no amount of rhetoric can do on its own: it creates recurrent demand that is not merely cultural or convenient, but legally compelled.

That compulsion is often misunderstood as a theoretical claim about value. It is more practical and more severe than that. Tax does not prove an instrument is stable, just, or efficient. It proves the state can create a floor of demand for it by making compliance depend on possession. That floor matters because the banking system builds on it. Deposits are trusted more easily when the unit into which they clear is also the unit in which taxes must be paid. Wages are negotiated more naturally in that unit because it is the unit households must periodically secure. Contracts are written in that unit because courts and public obligations recognize it. The tax boundary is therefore not an appendix to the monetary order. It is one of the main reasons the order becomes hard to escape without exiting the legal and administrative world that surrounds ordinary economic life.

The state does not rely on outright prohibition to protect this position. It often relies on inconvenience, and inconvenience is one of the most underrated instruments of sovereign force. A substitute instrument may remain lawful for private use while becoming burdensome the moment it approaches tax, payroll, reporting, or settlement interfaces governed by the state. Documentation demands rise. Delays appear. Source-of-funds questions multiply. Reporting thresholds tighten. Dispute resolution becomes slower and more expensive. None of this needs to be theatrical. It only needs to raise the compliance cost enough that the state's own instrument becomes the path of least resistance for anyone who expects to remain in regular contact with formal institutions. In a fiat regime, dominance is often protected less by spectacular prohibition than by bureaucratic asymmetry.

This is where the legal core starts shaping behavior before any judge, collector, or supervisor appears. A landlord who expects taxes, utilities, and mortgage obligations to clear most easily in the state's unit prices rent in that unit even if tenants ask for alternatives. A payroll department that knows withholding, reporting, and penalties all run through official channels refuses anything that complicates remittance. A supplier facing thin margins and slow receivables demands invoices in the unit that courts and tax offices will recognize without argument. A local lender discounts collateral more heavily if title, perfection, or enforcement is uncertain. These are not grand constitutional moments. They are repetitive acts of preference shaped by the legal core. The monetary order survives not only because law exists in books, but because law becomes habit in billing rooms, payroll systems, lease clauses, and credit committees.

Priority is the third hinge because scarcity is where the monetary constitution stops pretending to be abstract. In ordinary conditions, many claims circulate as if they are near-equivalent. A supplier extends trade credit because payment seems likely. A bank extends a secured loan because collateral seems sufficient. An employee works because wages seem collectible. An investor buys a claim because expected order appears intact. Scarcity tests every one of those assumptions. When the debtor cannot satisfy all claimants, law must rank. Without ranking, insolvency becomes a race to seize, and a race to seize becomes private enforcement, and private enforcement destroys the predictability on which scalable credit depends. Priority does not create value. It creates order under insufficiency.

A standard priority principle can be stated in a line so dry that it disguises its violence: secured claims are satisfied from designated collateral before residual claimants share what remains. (Priority rule in the insolvency framework.) What sounds technical is in fact one of the most important sentences in the monetary order. It determines which creditors can lend cheaply because law will protect them in failure. It determines which borrowers can finance on tolerable terms because they possess assets that can anchor senior claims. It determines whether suppliers price trade credit loosely or defensively, whether wages are treated as protected obligations or as casualties of collapse, and whether public charges outrank private bargains when the system needs to preserve its own fiscal claims. Priority is the hidden constitution of credit because future lending costs are shaped by today's ordering of yesterday's wreckage.

The chapter's first pressure scene makes this visible where it always becomes visible: in a courtroom after failure. A mid-sized firm has collapsed. The file is thick with claims that each look righteous from the vantage point of the holder. A secured lender points to perfected rights over a collateral pool and insists that the bargain was clear. Suppliers point to unpaid deliveries and insist that without them the firm would never have operated long enough for the lender to earn its priority. Workers point to unpaid wages and insist that labor should not be treated as a disposable residual. A public authority points to unpaid charges and insists that public obligations cannot be made junior to private opportunism. The tribunal does not negotiate social theory. It applies ranking. In doing so, it does more than close a case. It teaches the market what future promises are worth. Those who are protected in failure will finance more cheaply in the next cycle. Those who are sacrificed in failure will price that sacrifice into every future bargain. The decision is not merely legal. It is monetary.

Priority also determines whether collateral can function as a bridge from private risk into public liquidity. A claim becomes fundable not only because its cash flows look sound, but because the legal architecture surrounding it is reliable enough that a lender believes it can seize, perfect, liquidate, and outrank competing claims if things go wrong. This means collateral value is partly legal value. A warehouse of goods, a property claim, or a receivable stream is not just an economic asset. It is a legal pathway through which a creditor expects to preserve position under stress. If that pathway is ambiguous, collateral becomes less valuable, lending becomes more expensive, and whole sectors of the economy become dependent on relationship finance instead of scalable credit. The legal core therefore governs liquidity long before a crisis, because it shapes what can be pledged in the first place and at what haircut.

The fourth hinge is enforcement, because a tender rule without enforcement is suggestion, a tax rule without enforcement is aspiration, and a priority rule without enforcement is an invitation to fraud and delay. Enforcement gives closure its bite. It turns due dates into deadlines rather than preferences. It makes tax demand more than a moral request. It turns perfected rights from elegant paperwork into seizable reality. It also defines the perimeter of the formal economy, because the reach, speed, and predictability of enforcement determine whether actors are willing to rely on law rather than on relationship, intimidation, or private collateral networks. A monetary system that cannot enforce becomes local, slow, and fragile, because trust must then travel on memory and reputation rather than on documents and procedure.

Enforcement does not only mean punishment. It also means standardization. Forms are recognized or rejected. Records are privileged or discounted. Signatures, timestamps, notices, filing systems, and registry order matter because enforceability depends on whether a third party can reconstruct the obligation without needing every original participant physically present. A claim that lives only in private memory cannot travel far. A claim embedded in recognized record can travel, be sold, be pledged, and be financed. This is why the legal core governs the fiat regime in two directions at once. It governs downward into daily transactions by defining what counts as payment and compliance. It governs upward into the credit hierarchy by defining which claims are admissible, transferrable, seizable, and rankable when stress arrives.

The second pressure scene is less dramatic than a courtroom and often more important. A small business tries to remit a public obligation using an instrument popular in its commercial niche but outside the state's preferred channels. The attempt does not trigger a raid or a ban. It triggers paperwork. The remittance is flagged for review. A notice requests source documentation, transaction logs, counterparties, conversion evidence, and an explanation for deviation from ordinary channels. The owner experiences the request as harassment. The state experiences it as perimeter defense. The effect is the same either way. The alternative instrument becomes slower, more expensive, and more legally vulnerable the moment it approaches the tax boundary. The state does not need to outlaw substitutes to make them secondary. It only needs to make them administratively awkward where the formal economy meets public authority. In a fiat regime, awkwardness is often enough to preserve primacy.

The legal core also determines how the banking layer remains money-like. Deposits are trusted not only because banks are supervised or because backstops exist, but because the legal framework makes deposit claims recognizable, settlement claims final, collateral rights enforceable, and failure procedures legible enough that panic does not begin from total uncertainty. A payment system can only remain fast if participants believe that incoming funds will be final and that outgoing obligations will not later be unwound arbitrarily. A credit system can only remain broad if creditors believe they can enforce rights without waiting so long that the right decays into fiction. Law is what turns settlement infrastructure into usable confidence. Without law, the ledger is a rumor.

A third pressure scene shows this in miniature through a collateral-perfection dispute. A lender extended credit against a receivables pool and believed it held senior rights because the filing was made and the notices were sent. A rival claimant arrives after the borrower fails and argues that the filing was defective, a notice was mistimed, and a carve-out in the governing agreement leaves part of the pool outside the lender's perfected reach. The fight does not remain inside paper. Liquidation is delayed while the tribunal untangles the chain. The collateral cannot be sold cleanly because buyers do not want to purchase a lawsuit masquerading as an asset. Recovery values fall while the dispute runs. Workers wait longer. Suppliers recover less. The failed borrower's remaining inventory deteriorates because the financing needed to preserve going-concern value evaporates. A technical ambiguity in perfection becomes a real-economy loss because law did not provide a clean enough bridge from promise to recovery. This is why the legal core is not decorative. When it is ambiguous, liquidity dies before insolvency is even finished speaking.

A fourth pressure scene belongs not in court but in a warehouse district. A distributor, already facing thin margins, begins shortening payment terms for smaller buyers after watching two enforcement proceedings drag on for months. Nothing in the law has changed on paper, but everyone in the district has learned the same lesson: even a formally valid claim can decay while the system decides how valid it really is. The distributor now demands partial prepayment. Buyers respond by cutting inventories. Truck routes run half-full. A local lender sees slower turnover and marks the borrowers as riskier. Credit tightens. None of this shows up first as a grand monetary event. It shows up as less trust carried through ordinary commerce. This is how legal weakness transmits into monetary weakness: not only through dramatic failure, but through horizon-shortening in thousands of minor decisions that make the economy smaller, meaner, and more defensive.

Tender, tax, priority, and enforcement therefore form a chain. Tender defines closure. Tax creates nonoptional demand. Priority assigns order under collapse. Enforcement makes all three actionable. Break any link and the fiat regime can continue for a while through habit and improvisation, but it loses one of the main reasons strangers accept its unit without demanding immediate conversion into harder claims. Break several links and the regime becomes performative, relying on speeches and emergency measures to compensate for the decay of its legal skeleton. That kind of regime can survive for a time. It cannot scale with dignity.

The strongest counterargument insists that this legal core is simply organized coercion in polite clothing, that tender rules discipline creditors for the state's convenience, that tax demand forces artificial acceptance, that priority tends to favor those already rich enough to secure senior claims, and that enforcement is often selective. This critique is serious and sometimes accurate. A fiat regime can become predatory if it uses its legal core to protect insiders, suppress alternatives, and distribute losses downward. Yet the alternative to a rule-bound legal core is not freedom in any meaningful commercial sense. It is fragmentation. Without a recognized closure instrument, every dispute remains open longer. Without a tax instrument, the state either seizes arbitrarily or starves. Without priority, insolvency becomes a scramble. Without enforcement, the economy shrinks into private trust networks, private sanctions, and high transaction costs. The statecraft problem is not whether coercion exists. The problem is whether coercion is predictable enough, bounded enough, and visibly fair enough to preserve consent while still performing the work that money requires.

This is why the legal core is also a legitimacy engine. People comply not only because they fear punishment, but because they believe the basic architecture is legible enough that planning is worth the effort. A firm borrows because it believes the collateral regime is real. A household accepts wages in the unit because taxes and ordinary payments will recognize it tomorrow. A supplier extends terms because it believes ranking and enforcement will not dissolve into arbitrary discretion if the buyer fails. If that belief weakens, every actor shortens horizon. Shorter horizons mean more cash hoarding, faster repricing, less trade credit, more defensive contracting, and weaker investment. The legal core therefore shapes macroeconomic behavior through micro-level confidence in procedure. It is the place where boring rules become growth or stagnation.

The design challenge is unforgiving. Tender must be broad enough to deliver closure but not so broad that every unstable substitute can claim equal status at the public window. Tax enforcement must be strong enough to sustain demand but not so punitive that the monetary order is experienced as extraction theater. Priority must be stable enough for credit to be priced, but flexible enough that emergency can protect continuity when mechanical rank would create political collapse. Enforcement must be credible enough to deter evasion but bounded enough that it does not become arbitrary force. These balances are not solved once. They are maintained continuously, and failure at maintenance is one of the main ways a fiat regime loses quiet confidence before it loses visible control.

The modern implication is severe and easy to miss. Monetary sovereignty is not only about the central authority's ability to create reserves or set the cost of time. It is also about whether the legal core remains strong enough that the state's unit keeps its privileged path through the formal economy without requiring constant emergency support. A regime with weak closure rules, slow enforcement, ambiguous priority, and porous tax demand can still print and purchase. It cannot rely on law to carry confidence. It will need more visible intervention, more administrative discretion, and more rhetorical effort to do work that a stronger legal core would do quietly. In that sense, legal weakness is monetary weakness even before prices or exchange values reveal it.

That is also where this chapter locks back into the ones that came before it. When the legal core weakens, credibility engineering must work harder because the public signal is no longer riding on a trusted enforcement skeleton. Balance-sheet intervention must work harder because more claims arrive at the public perimeter in damaged form after private enforcement and private liquidity already failed. Last-resort lending becomes more politically toxic because the public sees rescue after preventable disorder rather than rescue in defense of a functioning rule-set. A weak legal core therefore does not merely create local friction. It pushes the whole fiat regime toward louder, larger, and more discretionary interventions. Once that happens repeatedly, the state begins to govern by exception what it should have governed by rule.

The chapter closes with the hardest truth in the quietest form. A monetary order is never only a matter of belief. It is belief backed by closure, demand, ranking, and force. When those four are predictable, people call the system normal. When those four become patchy, people begin improvising around it long before they openly rebel against it. The legal core is what keeps improvisation from becoming monetary pluralism at the edges and monetary weakness at the center.

CLOSING DOCTRINE

The fiat regime is sustained by legal architecture before it is sustained by rhetoric: tender defines discharge, tax defines unavoidable demand, priority defines the hierarchy of loss under scarcity, and enforcement makes each definition real enough that strangers are willing to plan across time. Legal tender is the closure instrument that ends disputes inside the jurisdiction, tax acceptance is the demand engine that keeps the unit nonoptional, legal priority is the hidden constitution that determines which promises can be financed cheaply because law will protect them in failure, and enforcement is the perimeter that prevents the system from collapsing into private bargaining and private violence. Policy discretion operates on top of this core, but it cannot replace it; when the legal core is predictable and credible, claims travel and credit scales, and when it is ambiguous or experienced as selective, the economy shortens into defensive contracting, substitutes press at the edges, and the state must use more visible force to achieve what clear law would have achieved quietly.

PART THREE
THE PAYMENT STATE
WHO CLEARS, WHO SETTLES, WHO GETS PAID FIRST

The illusion of money is strongest at the moment it moves cleanly. A salary arrives before breakfast. A supplier is paid before the truck reaches the dock. A securities trade closes without either side seeing the machinery that decided whose claim counted, whose message was recognized, which ledger updated first, and what would have happened if one participant failed three minutes before the final instruction. Smooth payment is the most successful disguise in the monetary order because it makes architecture feel like convenience. What looks effortless to the user is usually the product of queues, netting rules, liquidity buffers, default procedures, collateral demands, messaging standards, access hierarchies, legal finality, and operational routines so tightly maintained that most people mistake them for nature. They are not nature. They are rank made operational.

The payment state begins where ordinary confidence ends. It begins in the moment one message is held back, one institution is asked for more collateral, one participant is forced to prefund while another is allowed to settle against incoming flows, one bank's clients are told that transfers will post later while another bank's clients continue moving through the day as if no stress existed. In those moments the public sees delay. The system sees classification. It sees the hierarchy it had spent years hiding inside routine. Payment architecture is not neutral sequencing. It is a machinery for deciding whose obligations become final on time and whose obligations must wait at the edge of certainty while the center protects itself.

Earlier chapters established the legal skeleton of fiat and the central authority's role in manufacturing credibility, absorbing panic, and defending the settlement perimeter when markets begin to refuse one another. That story now moves into the chamber where credibility either becomes routine or fails in public. Money does not rule because it is named. It rules because it clears. A unit of account can be legally recognized, tax-backed, and rhetorically defended, yet still become a weak monetary instrument if its payments architecture is slow, exclusionary, reversible, fragile under stress, or dependent on external intermediaries that can ration access. The payment state is the part of the monetary order where sovereignty stops speaking in doctrine and starts acting in sequence. Who can enter the queue. Who may net before paying gross. Which institutions can transform private claims into final settlement without delay. Which actors must wait for end-of-day balances while others settle in apex claims continuously. These are not technical curiosities. They are one of the main ways a society decides who receives speed, who receives safety, and who receives subordination.

A modern monetary system is therefore not merely a stock of instruments. It is a choreography of ranked claims moving through permissioned channels. Deposits behave like money because they can usually be converted into higher-grade settlement through the banking system without visible friction. Wholesale claims behave like money when clearinghouses, reserve access, and secured funding pathways make them fundable on acceptable terms. Cross-border claims behave like money only if messaging, sanctions compliance, settlement windows, correspondent confidence, and legal recognition all hold together long enough for discharge to occur. Every one of those conditions is contingent. Every one is governed. The payment state is the name for that governance when it becomes infrastructure rather than proclamation.

This is also the point where the hierarchy of money becomes impossible to romanticize. People often imagine the monetary order as a set of symbols backed by trust. Symbols matter. Trust matters. But when pressure arrives, what matters first is routing. Which message is accepted. Which institution is recognized as good for funds. Which claims can be netted rather than settled gross. Which positions receive intraday liquidity. Which failures trigger containment and which failures are allowed to contaminate the queue. In calm periods, the answer is hidden because the system functions so smoothly that differences in status appear cosmetic. In stress, the queue reveals the constitution. Some participants move through the center and receive time from the architecture itself. Others are pushed outward, asked for more collateral, delayed by compliance, forced into prefunding, or cut off altogether. The payment state is where ranked claims become a lived experience of precedence.

A pressure scene makes the point more honestly than a definition. A regional bank begins the day expecting ordinary flows. By midmorning, one of its larger counterparties is being questioned by the market, not yet failed, not yet rescued, simply doubted. Doubt widens haircuts on one side of the system and caution slows outgoing payments on the other. The regional bank's customers still see balances on their screens, still think in terms of my money, still assume the transfer they initiated at nine will settle by noon. Inside the machinery, the bank is now being asked for more collateral to secure the same intraday movement that cost less yesterday. A larger institution with cleaner access to the center continues moving through the queue with little visible friction. By midday, one bank's clients discover that payroll will arrive late while another bank's clients do not even know a hierarchy was activated. This is the payment state stripped of euphemism. The claims did not change character in moral terms. Their route through the hierarchy changed, and that change was enough to decide whose ordinary life would continue uninterrupted and whose would be forced to wait.

The regional bank is not the only one reading the event. Corporate treasury desks begin to redraw their internal maps before any official notice is published. A manufacturer shifts a portion of its operating cash away from the bank whose payments slowed and toward the institution whose position in the queue appears stronger. A payroll processor quietly revises cutoff times and requires earlier prefunding from clients it now considers operationally weaker. A supplier narrows credit terms for customers banking at institutions that seem one layer farther from the settlement core. Nothing dramatic has happened in public. No headline announces a constitutional turn. Yet the payment state has already spoken in a language every operating business understands: speed has become a credit signal, and delay has become a ranking mechanism. The queue does not merely move money. It teaches the economy whom to trust.

The strategic significance of this Part is therefore larger than plumbing. Payment architecture determines whether monetary sovereignty is real or ceremonial. A state that issues a respected unit but depends on foreign messaging channels, foreign correspondents, foreign cloud concentration, or foreign legal finality to move that unit across borders does not fully command its own monetary position. A state whose retail rails are fast but whose wholesale liquidity is brittle has not solved payments; it has improved the surface. A state whose banks create abundant deposits but whose clearing and settlement architecture concentrates hidden fragility at a few nodes has built a monetary order that looks broad in expansion and narrow in panic.

The questions in this Part are severe because they are constitutional questions asked through operational sequence. Who clears. Who settles. Who gets paid first. Who is allowed to remain liquid. Who becomes dependent.

The retail surface matters precisely because it is so smooth. A citizen judges the monetary order by whether wages arrive, cards clear, transfers post, and bills disappear from the list of pending obligations. Retail speed creates political legitimacy because it makes the state's settlement instrument feel close, ordinary, and reliable. Yet retail smoothness can coexist with wholesale fragility so severe that a few stressed institutions can force the central machinery into emergency posture. This split is one of the central facts of the modern system. The public experiences speed. The system survives on liquidity ladders, queue discipline, and collateral transformation it would rather never have to explain. A payment state that masters retail but neglects wholesale resilience builds trust on top of a fault line. A payment state that masters wholesale discipline but neglects retail speed creates a monetary order that is safe for institutions and irritating for citizens. The durable system must govern both layers at once.

The contrast between retail ease and wholesale fragility is not cosmetic. It is one of the main ways a payment system preserves legitimacy while concentrating risk in places ordinary users never see until they are forced to. A card tap at a grocery counter feels instantaneous, but the apparent simplicity often rests on a stack of intraday exposures, private guarantees, netted obligations, and deferred settlement sequences that can become political in a single afternoon if one core node begins to wobble. The household thinks the payment is complete because the interface says approved. The system knows the deeper truth: approval is often the front end of a chain whose finality depends on multiple institutions remaining liquid, synchronized, and recognized through the close of day. The retail surface is therefore a political shield. It hides the extent to which "easy money movement" for the public depends on wholesale institutions being granted time by the architecture.

A second scene belongs on that surface, because it is where hierarchy becomes visible to ordinary life. A payroll run is submitted on schedule by a medium-sized employer. At the user level nothing appears unusual. Employees expect funds at dawn. During the night, however, one intermediary in the chain is reclassified as riskier and another is asked for additional liquidity support before processing can continue at full speed. The result is not a collapse. It is something more revealing. A portion of the employees are paid on time because their accounts sit inside institutions closer to the favored center. The rest receive credits hours later, after manual routing and additional checks. To the worker waiting for rent to clear, a payment delay is a life problem. To the system, it is a queue-management choice. That difference is what makes payment architecture constitutional rather than merely operational. It allocates not only speed, but practical dignity.

The cross-border dimension makes the hierarchy even harsher. Domestic payment order can be defended through law, reserve access, and the sovereign backstop. Cross-border order depends on recognition by others. A claim can be perfectly valid at home and still move badly abroad if messaging is interrupted, if compliance flags multiply, if correspondent appetite narrows, or if foreign institutions decide that speed now belongs only to cleaner, larger, more politically protected participants. In that space, payment architecture becomes geopolitical architecture. A state may discover that its unit is sovereign internally and conditional externally, and conditionality at the border is one of the sharpest limits on any monetary system that imagines itself autonomous. The payment state is therefore also the place where domestic hierarchy meets international hierarchy and learns which one is stronger under stress.

A second pressure scene shows how quietly that border can harden. An exporter believes the sale is complete because the contract is signed and the goods are loaded. The domestic bank accepts the payment instruction. The message moves outward, then stalls. A compliance review is triggered in an institution the exporter has never heard of, in a jurisdiction the exporter did not choose, under standards the exporter cannot contest in real time. Inventory sits. Working capital tightens. A supplier at home waits for payment that depends on a chain now frozen far beyond the exporter's legal reach. No law at home has changed. No court has ruled. No central authority has spoken publicly. Yet sovereignty has already been rationed because the payment could not cross the architecture fast enough to remain ordinary. This is the modern border in one of its purest forms: not a wall against goods, but a gate against finality.

The cross-border payment order is especially brutal because dependence can masquerade as interoperability. A state may believe it participates in a global system when in fact it merely rents access to one. Messages are formatted elsewhere, screened elsewhere, queued elsewhere, and finally recognized through institutions that can at any moment slow movement without formally prohibiting it. In good times this dependence looks like efficiency. In stress it reveals itself as conditional sovereignty. A domestic payment obligation may be enforceable in local law and fully funded in local balance-sheet terms, yet still remain incomplete because an external gatekeeper has not granted the final movement. That gap between legal validity and operational completion is one of the defining vulnerabilities of the payment state in an interconnected world.

This is why clearing and settlement cannot be treated as service functions. Clearing is not merely calculation. It is a system for deciding what can be offset, who must fund gross, and which obligations are allowed to survive by being netted against one another before scarce settlement assets are demanded. Settlement is not merely delivery. It is the point at which argument ends or fails to end. A participant allowed to net before paying gross uses the architecture itself as a source of time. A participant forced to prefund must arrive with time already purchased. That distinction can determine whether an institution is competitive in calm and whether it survives in crisis. The difference between a payment participant and a payment dependent is often nothing more glamorous than the rules governing when funds must arrive and in what form.

The opening doctrine of this Part is simple enough to be dangerous: money becomes governing power only when payment architecture can convert legal recognition into final settlement at scale, under stress, and across distance without losing control of priority. That is why the chapters ahead move from deposit creation to clearing, from clearing to cross-border gatekeepers, from gatekeepers to retail rails, from retail rails to shadow liquidity, and from shadow liquidity to token rails. Each chapter descends into a deeper chamber of the same structure. Deposits are not merely liabilities. They are privately manufactured money under public rule. Clearinghouses are not service platforms. They are default triage wrapped in netting logic. Cross-border messaging is not communication. It is a permission system for international monetary life. Retail rails are not convenience. They are the interface that hides the state by making state-backed closure feel instantaneous. Shadow liquidity is not an anomaly. It is the part of the system that behaves like money until the hierarchy tightens and reveals that it never fully was. Token rails are not novelty. They are an attempt to redesign sequence, programmability, and concentration risk inside the claims architecture itself.

A payment system that works well is almost invisible. A payment system that breaks forces the public to discover, all at once, that modern money is not a thing but an order of movement. That is why this Part cannot be a detour into infrastructure. It must be read as the section in which the book shows how monetary rule is exercised minute by minute, file by file, message by message, queue by queue. The legal core explained why the state's instrument can demand obedience. The payment state explains how that obedience is routed, sequenced, delayed, privileged, hidden, and sometimes weaponized. If the previous Part showed how central authorities manufacture credibility and control time, this Part shows where time is actually allocated.

The deepest truth is unpleasant and operational. Payment architecture does not merely process the economy. It sorts it. It sorts institutions by access, claims by grade, transactions by urgency, and failures by whether they are containable or contagious. It assigns friction selectively, sometimes intentionally, sometimes because every system with finite liquidity must rank even when it claims neutrality. That ranking is why payment architecture is one of the main places where sovereignty becomes visible to institutions long before it becomes visible to the public. A bank treasurer knows whether the state trusts a claim by whether the claim can fund in the center. A dealer knows whether a market is politically central by whether the settlement core will defend it under stress. A firm knows whether its bank is inside the favored perimeter by whether payments keep moving when others begin to stall. The public learns the same lesson only when inconvenience reaches wages, rents, payroll, and inventory. By then the hierarchy has already spoken.

This is also why the payment state is inseparable from legitimacy. A system that clears beautifully for the center and clumsily for the edge will eventually be understood as a hierarchy rather than a service. A system that settles instantly for asset markets and slowly for households will eventually be experienced as a ranking of social importance. A cross-border architecture that allows some claims to move globally while forcing others through repeated checks, delays, and dependencies is not merely administering risk. It is expressing power. The more the state wants payment architecture to remain invisible, the more carefully it must govern these asymmetries, because once ordinary users begin to feel them consistently the payment order stops looking like infrastructure and starts looking like a constitution they never voted on but live under every day.

The reader should therefore approach the chapters ahead with a harder frame. This is not the place where the book pauses for mechanics. It is the place where the book shows that mechanics are rule. Deposits, clearing, cross-border channels, retail rails, shadow liquidity, and tokenized claims are not side systems orbiting around money. They are the channels through which money is ranked, accelerated, delayed, protected, and denied. If a state wishes to know whether it truly governs its monetary order, it should ask not only what it issues or what it targets, but what it can clear, what it can settle, how quickly it can defend finality, and who must ask permission before their claim can move.

The hardest implication is the simplest one. Payment architecture is where sovereignty is rationed minute by minute. It is where law becomes clock time, where priority becomes queue position, where public backing becomes intraday liquidity, and where abstract monetary hierarchy becomes the difference between payroll arriving before rent is due and payroll arriving after the landlord has already charged the fee. If previous Parts established that money is governed architecture, this Part establishes where the architecture actually governs. The command of money is not complete when the state issues, taxes, targets, or backstops. It is complete only when the state can move claims through the order of finality without surrendering control over sequence, access, and priority at the very moments when speed becomes power.

CLOSING DOCTRINE

The payment state is the part of the monetary order in which sovereignty becomes sequence: legal recognition becomes queued movement, hierarchy becomes timing, and priority becomes lived experience through speed, collateral demand, netting privilege, and finality access. Money is not fully governing power until it can clear and settle at scale under stress and across distance without surrendering control of who gets time and who must wait. A payment architecture that is smooth only on the surface but brittle in wholesale or dependent at the border is not a complete monetary order; it is a partial one whose sovereignty can be interrupted where movement matters most. The chapters that follow therefore do not descend into secondary infrastructure. They descend into the operational constitution of money itself.

CHAPTER 12
THE DEPOSIT ENGINE
PRIVATE MONEY UNDER PUBLIC RULE

The customer believed she was moving her own money. She woke before sunrise, opened the banking application, and saw the ordinary reassurance people now treat as natural: a number, available, stable, unquestioned. Her rent would leave at noon. Her wages had arrived overnight. A grocery order had already cleared. Somewhere else, a small firm's payroll file was being released against receipts that had not yet fully settled. In another district, a contractor ordered materials before breakfast because incoming customer payments were expected by afternoon. None of these people thought they were touching a fragile structure. They thought they were using money. The system knew better. What they were using was a layered promise manufactured privately, stabilized publicly, and tolerated only because a larger architecture stood behind it with rules for convertibility, liquidity, enforcement, and finality. A bank deposit looks simple because the state has spent more than a century making complexity disappear behind a number on a screen.

This chapter begins with the claim most societies now live inside without seeing: most money in daily life is not issued directly by the sovereign center. It is manufactured by commercial banks. The state names the unit, taxes in it, protects its legal core, supplies the apex settlement asset, and backstops the perimeter when panic rises. Yet the balances households and firms actually use for wages, rents, invoices, subscriptions, payroll, supply purchases, and savings are overwhelmingly bank liabilities. The deposit engine is therefore the place where the modern monetary order reveals one of its least intuitive truths. Public money governs the system. Private money fills it. The state does not monopolize the creation of everyday money. It governs the terms under which private institutions may create promises that behave as money because they are expected to clear into higher-grade claims on demand.

That arrangement only survives because different layers of society are allowed, encouraged, and sometimes forced to see the same thing differently. The household sees a salary balance and experiences continuity. The shop owner sees incoming card receipts and experiences working liquidity. The payroll clerk sees enough funds to press send and assumes wages will become available in all the right places by morning. A bank treasurer looking at the same day sees concentration risk, settlement timing, expected outflows, collateral capacity, and the possibility that one large corporate client may shift balances before noon. A supervisor sees something harder still: a private institution whose liabilities are being treated by the public as money while the institution itself remains a leveraged balance sheet vulnerable to misjudgment, duration strain, and flight. Sameness at the surface is therefore not a fact. It is a maintained appearance. That appearance is one of the state's greatest political achievements and one of its most delicate burdens.

A deposit must therefore be understood as architecture rather than metaphor. It is not stored value. It is a bank's liability to its customer, a promise to deliver settlement through the payment system in the named unit of account. The customer experiences it as possession. The bank experiences it as funding. The central authority experiences it as a private claim whose money-like quality depends on reserve access, supervisory rule, liquidity support, legal enforceability, and the wider public's belief that convertibility into final settlement will hold when tested. That difference in vantage point matters because it shows where power sits. The public thinks deposits are money because the interface teaches them to. The system treats deposits as conditionally money-like because the public architecture keeps them close enough to finality that everyday life can proceed without everyone demanding conversion all the time.

A hard sentence from the governing tradition captures the truth more clearly than the polite language of retail banking ever does: the process by which banks make loans creates deposits. The importance of that sentence is not scholastic. It overturns the folk belief that banks first gather savings and then lend them onward. In the actual sequence of modern banking, a creditworthy borrower is approved, the bank writes an asset to itself in the form of a loan, and writes a matching liability to the borrower in the form of a deposit. The bank has not transferred preexisting money from one pocket to another. It has manufactured a new private claim denominated in the state's unit. That claim will survive as money only if the bank can settle the payments that flow from it, fund the liquidity it requires, and preserve confidence that the deposit remains convertible into higher-grade settlement when the customer or another bank demands it.

The elegance of that sequence hides its violence. A bank can create a deposit in an instant. It cannot create the conditions under which everyone else will go on treating that deposit as if it were equivalent to every other deposit regardless of circumstance. The borrower sees spendable funds. The banker sees an earning asset and a liability that may soon move. The treasurer sees an exposure to payment flow. The supervisor sees a private institution manufacturing public life under rule. The sequence becomes constitutional not at the moment the loan is signed, but at the moment the newly created deposit is spent. If the borrower pays a supplier who banks elsewhere, reserves must move. If the supplier immediately pays wages, more deposits must clear outward. If enough such outflows occur while depositors are already shifting balances toward stronger institutions, what looked like profitable credit creation becomes a referendum on convertibility. "Loans make deposits" is therefore only the opening line. The real sentence is longer and harsher: loans make deposits, deposits make payment obligations, payment obligations test reserves, and reserve strain determines whether private money remains socially acceptable as money.

The origin of this structure lies in a practical problem older than central banking. Trade expanded faster than coin could comfortably move. Merchants needed instruments that could travel through ledger entries, not only through metal. Households and firms needed somewhere to hold claims that were safer and more convenient than carrying settlement assets physically. Banks emerged as institutions willing to accept funds, honor payment instructions, and extend credit against future cash flow or collateral. Their liabilities became money-like because enough people accepted them in daily exchange and enough merchants believed they could be redeemed or transferred onward without argument. The innovation was not simply institutional. It was political. Once bank liabilities became socially important, the state had to decide whether to leave them as private promises exposed fully to private ruin or pull them into a governed hierarchy in which convertibility, reserve access, and emergency support could preserve broader order.

The answer was never pure laissez-faire for long, because bank money scales into systemic dependence quickly. If households are paid in deposits, if firms manage working capital in deposits, if suppliers invoice in deposits, and if taxes are remitted through deposit accounts, then a bank failure is no longer the fall of a private house. It becomes a threat to the payment state itself. The state therefore enters the scene in stages: defining the legal perimeter, licensing entry, setting capital and liquidity conditions, offering access to reserves directly or indirectly, standardizing clearing, protecting smaller depositors to prevent social panic, and ultimately lending against collateral when the system begins to refuse its own private money. The deposit engine is private in manufacture and public in survivability. That is the arrangement. It is not an accident.

"Loans make deposits." The line is often used as if it settles the matter by cleverness alone. It does not. It opens the real question. If banks can manufacture deposit money through lending, what prevents money from becoming merely the private appetite of balance sheets. The answer is hierarchy. A bank can write deposits into existence, but it cannot by itself write the apex settlement asset into existence. If deposit holders spend, if funds leave the institution, if counterparties doubt the bank, if withdrawals rise, or if interbank payments turn one-sided, the bank must meet those outflows through reserves or other settlement grade claims. That need disciplines private money creation more harshly than the retail user usually sees. The bank can create a deposit with a keystroke. It cannot guarantee the long-run money-like quality of that deposit without access to a larger architecture that stands above it.

The chapter's first pressure scene belongs here because it reveals the arrangement better than a definition. A mid-sized bank has expanded aggressively into business lending during a period of calm. Its loans looked prudent, its margins acceptable, its deposit base stable. Then one month changes the tone of the market. A few large customers begin transferring funds toward institutions perceived to sit closer to the sovereign center. Nothing theatrical occurs at first. Branches remain open. The application still shows balances. But by midday the treasury desk is monitoring reserve needs with a new kind of attention. Outgoing payments are heavier than incoming flows. The bank can continue honoring transfers, but only by drawing down liquid assets and borrowing against collateral. The customers think they are moving money between equivalent institutions. The system knows the truth. They are testing whether one private issuer's liabilities still enjoy the same degree of public confidence as another's. In a deposit regime, a transfer is never just a transfer. It is a referendum on convertibility and perceived sovereign proximity.

The household does not experience that referendum in treasury language. It experiences it as lateness, fee risk, embarrassment, and the sudden discovery that the phrase my money conceals a chain of permissions. A parent expects wages to arrive before a utility debit. A utility company does not care that an interbank outflow strained one institution's reserve position before the file completed. A landlord's system charges its fee automatically. The family sees the same number appear later in the day and is told the payment was delayed, not denied. To the household, that distinction feels insulting. To the architecture, it is profound. Delay means the deposit remained inside the hierarchy but fell to a lower rank in sequence for a few hours. The family has just experienced what the treasurer already knew: sameness is maintained only while the system can afford to maintain it.

The firm experiences the same contradiction at a larger scale. A supplier's treasurer sees that customer receipts at one bank are becoming less reliable in timing than customer receipts at another. Contracts are not immediately rewritten, but internal assumptions are. Cutoff times are moved earlier. Credit terms shorten. More cash is held against expected friction. A firm that had been operating with lean treasury buffers begins behaving as if some deposits are slightly less immediate than others. No public authority announces a new class system for money. Yet one has begun to appear inside treasury practice. This is how the deposit illusion becomes intimate. The household learns it through payroll timing and fees. The firm learns it through settlement discipline and working-capital caution. The supervisor learns it through liquidity reports that show private rank re-emerging beneath the public fiction of equality.

The deposit engine therefore runs on an illusion that must be preserved but must never be believed too literally by those governing it. The illusion is sameness. A wage deposit at one licensed institution appears equal to a wage deposit at another because daily commerce would become unmanageable if everyone continuously priced bank-specific risk into ordinary transactions. Sameness is politically useful and economically necessary. But it is not metaphysically true. Deposits differ in resilience according to the balance sheet that issued them, the quality of the bank's assets, the stability of its funding, its access to collateralized liquidity, its importance to the payment system, and the public expectation that the authorities will or will not allow it to fail messily. In normal times, the state suppresses visible differences because equality at the interface is part of what makes deposit money workable. In stress, differences reappear all at once, and then the hierarchy speaks in spread, delay, outflow, and queue position.

This is why the word deposit is so misleadingly passive. It sounds like safekeeping. It sounds like storage. In practice it is a balance-sheet claim produced inside a structure of leverage. The bank has not placed the depositor's funds untouched in a vault awaiting return. It has woven liabilities and assets together through maturity mismatch, liquidity management, collateral use, and payment commitments. The depositor is funding part of that structure whether the depositor thinks in those terms or not. The bank depends on the fact that not all depositors will demand apex settlement at once, just as the depositor depends on the expectation that if enough people do demand it at once the state will not let the entire hierarchy disintegrate into private panic. Deposits are therefore both ordinary and constitutional. That duality is what makes them dangerous to misunderstand.

A second hinge line sharpens the architecture without reducing it to slogan: every deposit is a private promise made credible by public rule. That sentence matters because it places the burden where it belongs. The private bank manufactures the liability. The public system decides whether that liability will clear, how it will be supervised, whether it will be insured, what liquidity standards will restrain its growth, how it may access reserves, and under what conditions it may be supported or closed. Remove the public rule and deposits become private credit instruments whose acceptability varies widely by issuer and circumstance. Strengthen the public rule and deposits become so uniformly money-like that the public forgets private manufacture ever mattered. The modern deposit regime exists between those poles. It must allow enough private balance-sheet expansion to finance the economy while maintaining enough public control that private money creation does not become private monetary sovereignty.

The political contradiction sits there in full view. The state needs private deposit creation because scale requires distributed credit judgment, local balance-sheet reach, and the capacity to turn innumerable private opportunities into spendable claims without routing every decision through a public bureau. But the state must constantly prevent those same private issuers from becoming de facto monetary sovereigns. A bank that can create the balances households and firms use daily holds a kind of delegated public power whether the legal system says so or not. If left ungoverned, that power would let private institutions decide not only which borrowers get funded, but which sectors, regions, and households receive more spendable claims and on what terms, all while relying on the state to preserve confidence when trouble arrives. The state therefore faces a permanent constitutional labor: it must recruit private balance sheets into public money creation while denying them the right to become autonomous rulers of the unit.

The mechanism of deposit creation is not mysterious once stripped of ritual language. A borrower is approved for a loan. The bank records an asset on its own books: the borrower's obligation to repay. At the same moment, it records a liability: a deposit balance credited to the borrower. That deposit can now be spent. Once spent, it may remain within the same institution or leave for another. If it remains, the bank enjoys relatively cheap funding and can support the new liability with its own asset base and liquidity planning. If it leaves, the bank must settle through reserves or reserve-like claims. The quality of the underlying loan matters over time because loan failure weakens the bank's capital and eventually its credibility. The timing of payment flows matters immediately because reserve outflows can tighten the institution faster than asset quality alone would suggest. The deposit engine therefore binds long-term credit judgment to short-term payment survival. That is one of its deepest fragilities and one of its greatest powers.

This duality is why bank money creation expands in waves. In optimism, asset quality is assumed, deposit outflows are manageable, collateral is easily funded, and the banking system writes more promises into the economy because the system expects those promises to remain close enough to finality. In fear, the same system becomes selective. Deposits migrate. Funding shortens. Collateral haircuts widen. Banks stop seeing every approved loan as a future income stream and start seeing every new deposit as a possible future outflow. The engine that expands money in calm becomes the channel through which money-like confidence contracts in stress. Modern monetary management is inseparable from that cycle because central authorities are not merely setting rates against an abstract stock of money. They are trying to influence the appetite and restraint of a private deposit machine that manufactures most of what the public uses as money.

The transition from loan creation to payment stress is where the chapter's true burden sits. A loan committee approves a credit line for a local manufacturer. At the instant of approval, the system has created new purchasing power. The manufacturer sees inventory, wages, expansion. The bank sees yield and customer growth. But the moment the manufacturer spends, the deposit begins testing the bank's relationship to the payment core. Wages leave in batches. Suppliers bank elsewhere. Tax withholdings move out through formal channels. What began as a profitable asset now generates a pattern of reserve demands. If the bank's funding base is stable, the machine hums. If depositors are already migrating, if wholesale funding is tightening, or if market doubt has raised the cost of collateralized liquidity, then the very act of money creation becomes a stress event. This is where "loans make deposits" stops being clever and becomes constitutional. A private institution has created a claim that society will treat as money only if the issuer can survive the payment consequences of its own credit judgment.

The chapter's second pressure scene belongs inside that loan committee, because that is where public money quietly becomes private decision. A local manufacturer seeks a larger revolving facility to finance inventory and payroll expansion. The firm's orders look healthy. Its collateral is acceptable. Under one set of expectations the bank approves and a new deposit appears, flowing outward through wages and supplier payments within days. Under another set of expectations the committee worries about wholesale funding conditions, possible deposit migration, and the cost of replacing lost balances if confidence turns. The same borrower can therefore receive money or be denied it not because the state changed the unit of account, but because a private institution inside a public rule-set recalculated how much private money it was willing to create. This is one of the least democratic yet most powerful features of the deposit regime. Everyday money supply is profoundly shaped by credit committees, treasury desks, asset-liability committees, and supervisory expectations long before it is shaped by the public's imagination of government money.

That should not be mistaken for a claim that banks are sovereign in their own right. They are powerful, but they are nested power. Their power is delegated, conditioned, surveilled, and periodically punished. Capital requirements restrain how much loss a bank can absorb before its liabilities become socially dangerous. Liquidity rules restrain how much short-term instability can hide beneath apparently stable funding. Reserve arrangements determine the terms on which deposit outflows can be settled. Supervisory examinations do not simply assess prudence. They govern how much private money creation the state is willing to tolerate from a given institution under prevailing conditions. Deposit protection, where offered, is not only depositor protection. It is a political technology for preserving sameness at the interface by reducing the incentive for smaller depositors to run at the first sign of trouble. Every one of these devices tells the same story: private money is permitted only inside a disciplined public perimeter.

The banking system also teaches a more uncomfortable truth. Not all deposits are equal in how they fund the institution, and not all depositors behave the same way under stress. Retail deposits tied to salary, bill payment, and ordinary household routine often move more slowly than large corporate balances or the money of institutions that can shift at speed. That means banks are constantly classifying their own liabilities according to expected stickiness, cost, and stress behavior. From the user's standpoint a deposit is a deposit. From the bank's standpoint one deposit is durable funding and another is flight risk wearing a current-account label. This internal classification matters because it shapes lending appetite, pricing, liquidity buffers, and ultimately the pace of money creation itself. The deposit engine is social at the surface and actuarial underneath.

A third pressure scene shows how that hidden classification becomes visible in policy and pain. A rumor spreads that one segment of the banking sector holds more fragile assets than previously assumed. Households do not parse the rumor in detail, but treasury professionals do. Large balances begin migrating from regional institutions into banks thought to sit closer to the state's settlement core. Nothing has failed outright. Yet within hours the money-like quality of deposits has begun to stratify. One institution can still create deposits confidently because incoming balances strengthen its position. Another becomes cautious because every new loan it makes could leave as a transfer before the day is done. The public hears discussion of confidence. The architecture reveals something harder: deposit money is always partly a ranking of issuers, and stress merely forces that ranking into the open.

A fourth scene belongs at the household edge, because the system's abstraction becomes political there. A family with wages deposited at a smaller institution assumes ordinary continuity until a landlord's debit posts before an incoming payroll credit that has been delayed by routing friction. The money appears on the same day, but the sequence has changed, and the fee is charged before the family can prove the system, not their behavior, created the shortfall. To the architecture this is a byproduct of queue pressure and liquidity preference. To the household it is the state allowing one promise to clear slower than another while still calling both money. This is how deposit hierarchy becomes political resentment. The public does not need to understand reserve drains to understand that not all balances behave equally when pressure arrives.

This is why the state cannot regard bank deposits as just another private product. They are the interface through which households experience the monetary order and through which firms finance daily life. If the state wants taxes paid, wages stable, invoices credible, consumption continuous, and the payment system politically acceptable, it must preserve broad confidence that deposits remain convertible into final settlement without bank-by-bank discrimination at the retail level. But if it preserves that confidence too generously, it encourages banks and depositors alike to treat all private money as equally backstopped regardless of risk. The governing challenge is therefore permanent. Preserve enough sameness to prevent disorder. Preserve enough difference to preserve discipline. That balance is one of the deepest constitutional tensions in the modern monetary state.

"A bank is a dealer in its own liabilities." The line deserves to be read slowly because it strips away sentiment. A bank does not simply intermediate existing money. It issues promises, prices them, funds itself through them, and manages the conditions under which the public continues to treat those promises as money-like. The line also reveals why supervision can never be a secondary concern. If banks are dealers in liabilities that society uses as money, then weakness in supervision is not merely a prudential lapse. It is an opening through which private misjudgment can become public monetary instability. A bad loan is not only a future credit loss. In sufficient size, it is a threat to the quality of liabilities people thought were plain money.

The deposit engine also reaches beyond banking into the macroeconomy more directly than public debate usually admits. Credit expansion creates deposits and therefore purchasing power. Contraction destroys deposits or slows their creation and therefore slows nominal activity. When a bank writes a mortgage, a business line, or a construction facility, it is not merely transferring resources. It is enlarging spendable claims inside the economy. When banks pull back, the reverse occurs. This is why debates over inflation, housing, productive investment, and financial fragility cannot be resolved by staring only at central-bank balance sheets or public deficits. The broad behavior of the deposit engine matters as much or more because that is where most everyday money appears, circulates, and disappears. The central authority influences the engine. It does not directly replace it in normal times.

This does not mean the state is subordinate to banks. It means the state governs through a hybrid monetary constitution. Public authority supplies the apex unit, settlement architecture, legal core, and emergency backstop. Private banks manufacture the circulating liabilities most people treat as money. The arrangement is efficient in one sense because it decentralizes credit judgment and lets money creation respond to local opportunities and sectoral demand. It is dangerous in another because profit-seeking institutions create public money-like claims under conditions that can always drift toward fragility, herding, maturity mismatch, and political leverage over the state when panic arrives. Hybrid systems are productive because they mix capacities. They are unstable because they mix motives.

The strongest counterargument insists that this arrangement is exactly the problem. If banks can create money through lending, then credit booms, asset bubbles, inequality in access, and crisis transmission are not accidental defects but structural features. The critique is serious. Credit committees allocate purchasing power unevenly. Property-backed lending often outruns productive lending because collateral is easier to price than future enterprise. Regions, sectors, and classes with better balance sheets receive more money creation on better terms. Banks may prefer refinancing existing assets over financing new production because the former looks safer inside prevailing supervisory and market conditions. These are not random distortions. They are consequences of allowing private institutions to create socially central liabilities inside a profit-bearing model.

The defense is also serious. A purely public money system would face different rigidities: bureaucratic credit allocation, slower local knowledge, politicized lending channels, and an immense concentration of operational burden in the state. The modern banking system evolved because decentralized judgment, even when flawed, could finance commerce, housing, inventories, payroll, and local enterprise more flexibly than direct state issuance alone. The question is therefore not whether private deposit creation is pure. It is whether it can be governed tightly enough that its productive capacities outweigh its destabilizing tendencies. That is the real constitutional argument. Not markets versus state, but governed private money versus the alternatives.

The present-day implication is severe. Any authority that believes it governs money while ignoring the balance-sheet logic of commercial banking is governing only the crest of the wave. Deposit creation determines the pace at which the unit enters housing, payroll, trade credit, inventory cycles, and asset markets. Deposit migration determines which institutions are stable enough to continue creating money under stress. Deposit protection and liquidity backstops determine whether sameness at the interface survives when private differences become visible. A central authority can publish targets and speeches all week; if the deposit engine is seizing, retrenching, or concentrating dangerously, the real monetary constitution is already changing beneath the words.

This is why the chapter belongs at the opening of the payment state. Before queues can be managed, before netting can save time, before cross-border gatekeepers can ration access, there must be claims worth moving. Deposits are those claims in daily life. They are the first chamber where private promise enters public architecture and becomes usable money under rule. If the reader sees only banking in this chapter, the chapter has failed. The real subject is the state's decision to let private balance sheets manufacture public life under supervision, and the permanent consequences of that decision for sovereignty, fragility, hierarchy, and control.

The contradiction should now be stated in its final form because this chapter lives or dies on whether it can carry the weight of it. The state needs private deposit creation because without it the monetary order loses scale, local responsiveness, and much of the practical elasticity through which everyday economic life is financed. But the state must also prevent private issuers from becoming de facto monetary sovereigns, because the moment a private balance sheet can create the balances society relies on without meaningful public constraint, the state is left underwriting a money system it no longer truly governs. The modern deposit regime is therefore not a stable peace between public and private. It is a managed tension in which the state borrows private flexibility while constantly policing the frontier where flexibility becomes autonomy. That frontier is the constitutional heart of modern money.

CLOSING DOCTRINE

The deposit engine is the modern monetary compromise in its purest form: private institutions manufacture the liabilities most people use as money, while public rule determines whether those liabilities remain close enough to final settlement to function as ordinary life. Deposits are not stored sovereign money but privately issued promises stabilized by legal recognition, reserve architecture, supervision, and backstop capacity. Their money-like quality depends on convertibility, not sentiment. Their expansion depends on bank credit judgment, not simple prior savings. Their survival under stress depends on whether the state preserves sameness at the interface without erasing discipline beneath it. A system that forgets deposits are private promises will subsidize fragility. A system that forgets deposits are socially central will tolerate failures it cannot politically carry. A system that forgets private issuers must never become autonomous rulers of the unit will eventually discover that it has delegated monetary sovereignty farther than it intended and retained more liability than it can safely bear. The modern monetary state lives inside that tension and is judged by how well it governs it.

CHAPTER 13
CLEARINGHOUSES AND FINALITY
QUEUES, NETTING, AND DEFAULT CONTAINMENT

The payment looked finished long before it was safe. A trade had been agreed, matched, confirmed, and sent forward through the day's machinery with the smoothness that makes modern finance feel inevitable to those who never have to watch the pipes. Screens showed progression. Messages were accepted. Internal systems marked the exposure as moving toward completion. Yet inside the chain that mattered most, the obligation had not ended. It had only entered a governed interval in which sequence, collateral, netting rights, and the failure of one participant could still force everyone else to discover what they had mistaken for money was really a ranked claim waiting for permission to become final. In ordinary speech, people say a payment is made when the instruction is sent. In the architecture that governs modern finance, a payment is made only when the system agrees the argument is over and has enough authority to make that ending stick.

This chapter begins where convenience becomes law in motion. The deposit chapter established that private institutions manufacture most of the balances the public treats as money. That truth alone does not explain how a system holding millions of offsetting obligations survives each day without demanding gross settlement of every promise in apex claims at the moment of creation. The answer is clearing. Clearinghouses and related settlement institutions do not merely process traffic. They decide how much traffic must actually be funded, in what order, against what collateral, under which default rules, and at whose expense when one participant fails before the queue is complete. If the deposit engine is the chamber in which private promises are created under public rule, clearing is the chamber in which those promises are sorted, compressed, and tested against the possibility of failure.

A modern payment and market system would be impossible if every claim had to settle gross, immediately, and separately in the highest form of money. The demand for apex settlement assets would be overwhelming, daily liquidity needs would become punitive, and the price of moving ordinary obligations would rise high enough to slow commerce, securities markets, and the broader credit system. Netting emerged because scale required compression. But compression is not innocent. The moment obligations are offset against one another rather than funded in full one by one, somebody must decide which claims are eligible to net, when the calculation becomes binding, what collateral protects the residual exposure, and how the failure of one member will be contained so that the whole system does not discover too late that it had economized on liquidity by concentrating fragility. Clearinghouses are therefore not conveniences layered on top of money. They are authorities inside money's operating system.

The first illusion is completion. Market participants move through the day surrounded by status indicators that create the feeling of closure: submitted, matched, accepted, confirmed. These words are useful for operations and dangerous for legitimacy because they blur sequence into certainty. A message can be accepted while the obligation remains contingent. A trade can be confirmed while the netting cycle has not yet hardened into binding position. An instruction can be released while the settlement asset has not yet been delivered in a form the system treats as beyond reversal. The system survives by separating these states and controlling how the public interprets them. If the public confuses message completion with finality, the first serious failure will feel like betrayal because people will believe the system rewrote the past rather than merely finished the sequence.

That distinction deserves sharper edges because modern payment language is designed to comfort. A bank message can be complete as communication while remaining incomplete as settlement. A payment can be operationally released while still legally vulnerable to interruption, offset, queue reprioritization, collateral failure, compliance hold, insolvency stay, or the collapse of a participant that had been counted on to supply the other side of completion. Messaging completion means the instruction has entered the architecture in a recognized form. Legal finality means the architecture has passed the point at which ordinary reversal is no longer available and third parties must treat the obligation as ended. Between those two states sits the true territory of the payment state: a governed middle in which risk is compressed, sequence is rationed, and time itself is allocated by rule.

A hard proposition therefore belongs near the front of the chapter. Finality is not the sending of an instruction. It is the recognized point at which the system withdraws permission to dispute the payment as unpaid. That withdrawal is an act of authority. It is also an act of triage. It protects continuity by limiting reversibility, and it imposes harshness by making some errors, injustices, and regrets non-reversible once the threshold has passed. Without that harshness, scale collapses because every participant must treat every completed payment as provisional and therefore hold more liquidity, shorten more relationships, and behave as if the past is unsafe. With it, scale becomes possible because the past can be treated as closed enough to build future risk on top. Clearing is the machine that brings the system to that threshold daily without requiring the highest-grade settlement asset to be present in full for every gross obligation.

The chapter's first pressure scene belongs inside a queue because queues reveal constitutional truth better than theory. A participant enters the afternoon owing funds on one side of the clearing system while expecting to receive slightly more on the other. Under ordinary conditions this is routine. Outgoing obligations are covered by incoming flows and the participant finishes the day with little drama. Then doubt attaches to one of its counterparties. Risk controls tighten. Intraday credit becomes less generous. One instruction is held until collateral is increased. Another participant, more central and better collateralized, continues moving through the queue with little visible friction. The first participant is now living inside a distinction the public rarely sees: some institutions are allowed to use the system itself as a source of time, while others must arrive with time already purchased in the form of extra liquid assets and pre-positioned collateral. Nothing has failed outright. Yet hierarchy is already at work. The queue is not neutral. It is the place where the system decides whose obligations deserve to move first and whose must wait while certainty is re-priced.

Clearing exists because bilateral settlement wastes liquidity and multiplies contagion. When markets were smaller, obligations could be settled pair by pair and dependence was easier to monitor. As volume grew and claims formed webs rather than lines, bilateral settlement became a tax on liquidity and a generator of cascades. Each participant had to prepare for multiple simultaneous demands. Each payment consumed balance-sheet capacity. Each delay threatened another delay. Clearing solved this by moving from a world of many separate confrontations to a world of governed aggregation. Claims are gathered, validated, offset, compressed into net residuals, collateralized, and then settled through a sequence designed to survive failure. The savings are real. The concentration is also real. Clearing lowers the liquidity requirement of the system by replacing gross funding with institutional trust in a controlled machine. That is efficiency. It is also dependency.

The mechanics are plain once stripped of jargon. Participants send obligations into a recognized process. The process validates eligibility, membership, timing, and integrity. Claims are matched. Offsetting positions are netted. Residuals are calculated. Those residuals are margined, queued, and eventually settled in a higher-grade asset according to rules that must be operationally precise and legally binding. The strategic meaning is harder. Clearing decides how much liquidity is demanded, who is permitted to economize on gross settlement, which participants must contribute resources to enter the protected circle, and how much the center trusts each member not to detonate the day's arithmetic if it comes under stress. Clearing is not beneath power. It is one of the places power resides.

Membership is therefore not a technical detail. It is a rank. A direct member can net more efficiently, fund more cheaply, and exploit the time value created by the system itself. An indirect participant pays more, waits longer, and depends on the intermediary's fear regime. In calm times this difference looks like a pricing nuance. In stress it becomes survival. Access to clearing is a form of citizenship inside the payment state. Restricted access is a form of subordination even when the same legal currency is used by both sides.

A second pressure scene makes that subordination visible without calling it politics. A fast-growing financial intermediary has volume but not standing. It clears through a larger sponsor. On quiet days it pays a fee and lives with it. On stressed days the sponsor tightens collateral demands, shortens deadlines, and delays pass-through settlement until its own position is protected. The smaller institution's clients experience the result as late settlement and higher financing costs. Management discovers that it was not purchasing a service. It was renting a place in the queue. The economy claims equality of money at the surface. The payment state expresses inequality of access beneath it.

Clearinghouses also change the shape of risk. Bilateral dependence spreads anxiety horizontally. Central clearing concentrates it vertically. By stepping between counterparties or by serving as the recognized central processor of obligations, the clearing institution reduces bilateral uncertainty and can improve discipline and transparency. It also becomes a single point that must be trusted by everyone at once. The question becomes whether the clearing institution can absorb the failure of a member without losing the market's belief in the netted world it administers. That belief is what prevents the system from reverting to gross defensive behavior that demands far more apex liquidity than exists comfortably.

Default containment is therefore the core constitutional function of clearing. Margin calls, default funds, member contributions, loss waterfalls, and emergency rulebooks exist to make one participant's failure survivable for the rest. These devices are usually described as prudence. They are also pre-written ranking. A margin call is the system telling a participant to prove it deserves to remain inside the circle. A default fund is a pre-negotiated ordering of whose resources absorb loss after the failed member is exhausted. A loss waterfall is the social order of pain encoded as operational protocol. The public rarely sees the waterfall until the day it matters, and then it wonders why the sacrifice looks predetermined. It is predetermined because it had to be, or the system would be negotiating loss distribution in real time while liquidity drained away.

A third pressure scene belongs at the moment a member actually fails. A large participant misses a variation call near the end of the day. The clearing institution must choose quickly: declare default, seize collateral, auction positions, draw on mutual resources, suspend flows, and, if necessary, request emergency liquidity from the sovereign architecture. Each minute matters because uncertainty spreads faster than explanation. Surviving members do not only care about their own exposures. They care whether the clearing institution can defend the system's belief that the queue remains governed and that net positions will be honored as calculated. If belief holds, the failure becomes containable. If belief breaks, participants begin hoarding liquidity and doubting future netting cycles, which means the advantage of compression unwinds into a scramble for gross funding. In that moment, the clearing institution becomes an emergency government of market time.

The consequences reach beyond finance faster than polite narratives admit. A major firm rolling short-term funding finds that the spread it pays for working capital is now wider because the market is charging for uncertainty about whether netting and settlement will remain smooth through the week. A supplier shortens payment terms because it no longer wants to be the unpaid creditor inside a chain that could freeze if an upstream intermediary is delayed. A regional exporter discovers that trade finance terms have tightened because foreign counterparties are uncertain about settlement speed across the border. None of these actors are members of the clearing institution. They are downstream of it. That is the point. Clearing is often defended as a market efficiency tool, yet its failure modes transmit into ordinary commerce by changing the price of time and the willingness to extend credit. The payment state does not stay inside financial districts. It leaks into inventory cycles, wage cycles, and household cash flow the moment settlement confidence wobbles.

An intimate scene makes the indirect reach even harder to ignore. A midsized distributor expects payment from a major customer on Thursday because the customer's payment message was sent on Wednesday and marked as processed by its bank. The distributor, trusting the surface language, schedules its own supplier payments and a payroll release for Thursday afternoon. Then a clearing delay ripples backward through a chain the distributor never sees. The customer's instruction was complete as message, but the underlying obligation had not yet crossed into legal finality. Net positions were recalculated, an intermediary's collateral was questioned, and the payment sat inside a governed interval longer than anyone at the distributor had imagined possible. By late afternoon the distributor is drawing on an expensive emergency line to avoid missing payroll. Nothing has been stolen. No one has openly defaulted. Yet the difference between operational completion and legal finality has just appeared as financing cost, managerial humiliation, and thinner margins. To the distributor, the system did not "work a little slower." It silently changed the price of time.

A household experiences the same distinction with even less vocabulary and more pain. A parent receives a message that salary has been sent. The employer's portal shows complete. The bank application shows pending. A rent debit is presented before the credit crosses the final threshold into usable balance. A fee posts. A grocery purchase is declined. Hours later the salary becomes available and everyone in the chain insists the payment was processed correctly. That answer is technically tidy and socially corrosive. What the household learns is not the vocabulary of settlement states. It learns that "sent" is not the same as "final," and that the system reserves the right to make ordinary life live inside that difference. This is where clearing and finality become political. Not in the abstract design of the queue, but in the moment an ordinary person discovers that messaging completion is a comfort word while legal finality is the real event.

Legal finality matters because without it the system pays twice. If settled instructions can be unwound casually through later legal dispute or insolvency ambiguity, participants must treat yesterday's completion as provisional and therefore hold more liquidity and shorten relationships. Finality narrows the domain in which after-the-fact reversal is permitted. That narrowing lowers the premium demanded for participation and is one of the hidden sources of scale. Yet finality also means some injustices become non-reversible once the threshold is crossed. That harshness is not an incidental defect. It is one of the operating principles of a high-scale economy. The system chooses continuity over reopenability because reopenability at scale becomes paralysis. The governance challenge is therefore to ensure that access to the finality perimeter is not allocated carelessly, because the more privileged the institution, the more dangerous its errors become once finalized.

The distinction between messaging and finality must therefore be guarded at the language level as well as the legal level. A system that advertises immediacy while relying on multi-stage conditionality is always one crisis away from legitimacy damage. It can survive that damage if the public rarely feels the gap. It cannot survive it indefinitely if firms and households begin experiencing the gap as routine cost. This is why payment design is never only engineering. It is a politics of description. The system chooses which stages to expose, which stages to hide, and which words to use when something is not yet final but must be treated as ordinary enough that people keep building life around it. The more that descriptive layer diverges from the legal and operational layer, the more inevitable the eventual resentment becomes.

Netting alters liquidity geography as well. In a gross world, institutions must hold more immediately available funding against daily obligations. In a netted world, they can economize on balances because offsetting claims reduce what must actually move in final settlement. That saves costs and enlarges scale. It also means the system becomes dependent on timely net calculations and the institutions that perform them. A delay in netting is not merely inconvenience. It is a sudden increase in effective liquidity demand. Participants expecting to settle only residual positions may find themselves scrambling for cash or eligible collateral because the compression they were relying on has not yet been delivered. This is one of the quiet ways clearing governs markets. By deciding when netting becomes authoritative, the system decides when liquidity can safely remain idle and when it must appear.

The strategic implication is severe. Any authority that thinks it governs money but does not command or effectively shape the clearing and settlement core is governing only the visible layer. Clearing and settlement institutions decide how stress is processed before any official speech occurs. They decide which institutions remain liquid enough to trade through the day, which markets can absorb shocks without halting, and how much private disorder the system can digest before the sovereign backstop must intervene. The visible crisis often begins with prices. The real crisis often begins earlier, inside queue discipline, collateral demands, and doubts about whether netting and finality will hold through the close. A sovereign that does not understand that sequence will arrive late to its own emergency.

The defense of clearing is true. Without netting and legally protected finality, modern market volume would be more expensive, less scalable, and more prone to opaque bilateral contagion. The critique is also true. Clearing concentrates authority, privileges insiders with direct access, compresses risk until it becomes politically invisible, and writes intricate loss hierarchies that only become publicly legible after failure. A serious payment state must govern both truths simultaneously. It must preserve the efficiencies that make modern markets possible while resisting the tendency for efficiency to metastasize into unexamined concentration.

The question is therefore governance. Who qualifies for direct access. What collateral is demanded and how procyclical those demands become. How transparent the loss waterfall is to those who will bear it. How cross-market dependencies are mapped before stress rather than discovered during it. Whether emergency liquidity can reach the core quickly enough without granting private rulebooks de facto sovereignty over public crisis timing. These are not secondary issues. They are statecraft. A system that cannot contain default inside the clearing core will force the sovereign to socialize panic outside it. A system that contains default through privileges too opaque to defend will preserve order at the cost of legitimacy. Governing means deciding where to accept that trade and where to redesign the architecture so the trade is less cruel.

This chapter belongs immediately after deposits because the deposit engine creates the claims the public uses as money, and clearing decides how those claims and their market relatives survive contact with one another at scale. Deposits teach the public to believe in sameness. Clearing teaches the system to manage difference. Deposits create private promises under public rule. Clearing compresses those promises into a daily order of movement, margin, and completion. If deposits are the first chamber in which private balance sheets manufacture money-like life, clearinghouses are the chamber in which the system decides how much of that life can actually be carried to finality without demanding more apex settlement than the architecture can comfortably provide.

The chapter closes where it began, with the illusion of completion. Modern finance depends on people believing that movement and settlement are nearly the same thing most of the time. That belief can be sustained only because institutions exist that sort, net, collateralize, queue, and contain obligations before the public experiences them as finished. Those institutions are not neutral. They are governors of time, access, and sacrifice. They make scale possible by deciding who may economize on liquidity, who must prefund, whose default is survivable, and when an argument ends. A society that ignores them is not ignoring plumbing. It is ignoring one of the constitutions under which its money actually lives.

CLOSING DOCTRINE

Clearinghouses and finality institutions are the hidden governors of scale. They make modern money and markets possible by compressing gross obligations into net positions, rationing the liquidity required to complete them, and pre-writing the order in which loss will be contained when a participant fails. Netting is not merely efficiency. It is controlled substitution of institutional trust for gross funding. Finality is not merely legal technique. It is the point at which the system chooses continuity over reopenability and makes that choice binding. Between message completion and legal finality lies the true territory of modern payment power: a governed interval in which sequence, collateral, queue position, and recognized authority determine whether an instruction becomes money in fact or remains an obligation in transit. A monetary order that depends on these institutions without governing them constitutionally will eventually discover that private rulebooks are allocating public time and public risk without adequate political mandate. A durable payment state therefore requires more than fast rails and functioning queues. It requires sovereign mastery of who owns the compression, who controls the sequence, and who is sacrificed to preserve the appearance that payment was simple all along.

CHAPTER 14

CROSS-BORDER GATEKEEPERS

MESSAGING, CORRESPONDENTS, AND ACCESS

The exporter believed the sale was complete when the goods left the warehouse. The invoice had been accepted, the shipping documents were in order, the buyer's bank had sent the instruction, and the domestic account manager said the funds were on the way. On paper, nothing was missing. In practice, almost everything that mattered still sat outside the exporter's reach. The message had to travel through institutions the exporter had never chosen, across compliance screens the exporter could not see, through time zones the exporter did not govern, and into correspondent relationships whose continuity depended on a hierarchy far larger than the transaction itself. For two days the firm treated the receivable as if it were nearly cash. By the third day, payroll was close, inventory replacement was delayed, and the credit line that had looked precautionary on Monday had become the only bridge between production and embarrassment. The payment had not failed. It had entered the part of the world system where money stops being local law and becomes licensed passage.

That is the subject of this chapter. Domestic money can appear sovereign because the state names the unit, taxes in it, protects its legal core, and stands behind final settlement within its own perimeter. Cross the border and the meaning of money changes. The claim is no longer judged only by domestic legality or domestic payment architecture. It must now survive translation into shared message standards, acceptance by foreign institutions, scrutiny through compliance filters, passage through correspondent chains, conversion through liquid currency corridors, and settlement in a hierarchy whose decisive nodes may sit entirely outside the legal world of buyer and seller. Cross-border payment is therefore not merely domestic payment at a longer distance. It is domestic payment submitted to external rank. The gatekeepers of that process do not always hold the funds themselves. Often they govern something more important: whether the request for movement is recognized, routed, trusted, repriced, delayed, narrowed, or allowed to remain inside the corridor long enough to become usable final value.

The first illusion in cross-border finance is that communication and payment are close cousins. They are not. A message saying funds should move is not the movement of funds. A standardized instruction is not discharge. A bank can truthfully say that a transfer has been sent while the underlying value remains contingent on later acceptance, screening, settlement-window availability, correspondent willingness, currency conversion, and the continued legal-operational compatibility of the institutions in the chain. This distinction matters domestically and becomes brutal internationally. At home, delays can often be explained, absorbed, or backstopped within a common legal perimeter. Across borders, the distance between message and money becomes a field of power. A claim can be valid, funded, documented, and still immobile because the infrastructure that interprets, relays, screens, and completes the instruction is governed elsewhere.

"The message is not the money." The line sounds obvious until one recognizes how much of global commerce depends on people forgetting it. Cross-border payments operate through layered functions that ordinary users compress into a single expectation. One layer standardizes the instruction so institutions can read one another. Another layer determines whether the sending institution is trusted enough to enter the corridor without enhanced friction. Another layer holds correspondent balances through which claims can ultimately be adjusted. Another layer screens names, destinations, counterparties, sectors, and jurisdictions against compliance obligations. Another layer handles currency conversion or bridges the claim through a more liquid intermediate unit. Another layer settles the residual value at the end of the route, often through claims anchored higher in the world monetary order than the currencies of buyer and seller alone. A user sees one payment. The architecture sees a sequence of permissions. That sequence is where sovereignty narrows.

The second illusion is that once an instruction is admissible it is effectively paid. Cross-border systems have at least three distinct thresholds that are constantly confused in commerce and occasionally confused in statecraft: access, passage, and finality. Access is being allowed to submit a message into the recognized language and routing perimeter at all. Passage is being allowed to move through the corridor without being stopped, repaired, repriced, delayed, or returned. Finality is the point at which value has arrived in a form that the destination layer treats as discharged and no longer subject to ordinary reversal or administrative hold. A firm can have access and still fail passage. A payment can have passage and still lack finality because a downstream institution has not released funds as available. A state can have the legal right to pay and still lack operational finality because external corridors control whether its payment becomes recognized discharge outside its borders.

The chapter must therefore make the chain physical. Imagine one commercial payment as a living object moving through rooms, each room staffed by someone who can say yes, no, later, repair, more information, different route, different currency, different timing, or unacceptable risk. The firm instructs its bank. The bank formats the message correctly. That gets the instruction into the first room: admissibility as language. The instruction then encounters a second room: admissibility as identity. If the originator data, beneficiary data, or documentation fields are incomplete or inconsistent, the instruction is returned for repair or held. If it passes, it enters a third room: admissibility as counterparty risk, where an intermediary may apply heightened scrutiny because the sending bank is outside a favored tier, the destination bank is outside a favored tier, or the corridor itself is treated as fragile. If it passes, it enters a fourth room: admissibility as corridor risk, where route selection matters because some paths are faster but narrower, others are slower but more tolerant, and some are closed without announcement. If it passes, it enters a fifth room: currency conversion, where value may need to be translated through an intermediate unit because liquidity in the direct pair is thin or because settlement infrastructure in the destination prefers a more central bridge. If it passes, it enters a sixth room: settlement timing, where the instruction may sit until windows align and the correspondent balances are available. If it passes, it enters a seventh room: release, where the destination institution decides whether funds are immediately usable, available after a delay, or held pending further checks. Only after that does the recipient experience finality.

Each room is a veto point. None of the commercial parties owns the rooms. They rent the right to pass through them by maintaining a banking relationship with an institution that itself rents access through correspondents and standards. This is why cross-border payment is not a simple extension of domestic payment. Domestic payment ends inside one legal perimeter with one ultimate settlement core. Cross-border payment crosses multiple perimeters and therefore accumulates multiple veto points. The system calls these veto points risk controls. The user experiences them as uncertainty, delay, and dependence. The state experiences them as a limit on sovereign usability outside its borders.

Messaging became central because the world needed a shared language of financial instruction long before it had anything resembling a shared sovereign authority over money. Standards solved this by making messages legible across institutions, time zones, legal systems, and operational cultures. But legibility is not neutrality. The institution or network that defines the message standard also defines what information must accompany the instruction, what fields matter, how errors are handled, what level of precision is mandatory, and what kinds of ambiguity are intolerable. Standards therefore do not merely facilitate movement. They determine who can speak in a financially recognizable voice. A bank outside the accepted standard cannot insist that its instruction be honored on the strength of local law or customer urgency. It must translate itself into the recognized language of the corridor. Translation costs money, invites delay, and increases the chance that an instruction will stall over a mismatch that would never have mattered inside a fully domestic system.

The chapter's first pressure scene belongs inside the admitted message. A manufacturer pays a supplier across a border. The paying bank formats the instruction correctly, the sending interface accepts it, and the treasury staff tells management the transfer is complete from their side. Yet one field triggers secondary review in an intermediary because a counterparty's name resembles another on a risk list, because a document reference is incomplete, because the goods description sits too close to a controlled category, or because the route now touches a jurisdiction treated as higher concern. The payment is suspended inside procedure. The buyer believes it has paid because it has complied with its domestic obligations and released the instruction. The seller believes it has not been paid because usable value has not arrived. Both are right from within their layer. Access existed. Passage failed. Finality did not occur. The error in ordinary commerce is that all three thresholds are compressed into one word: paid.

Correspondent banking gives this architecture its monetary depth. A bank cannot usually settle everywhere in the world directly in every currency that matters. Instead, it relies on correspondent institutions that hold accounts for one another, maintain balances in key currencies, and stand inside the operational and legal corridors through which international claims can be discharged. A correspondent relationship is therefore not just a service arrangement. It is delegated access to another bank's place in the hierarchy. The respondent bank rents reach, credibility, and settlement proximity through the correspondent. That arrangement can make global commerce possible for smaller institutions and weaker states. It can also make them dependent on institutions whose risk tolerance, compliance posture, and strategic preferences they do not control.

"Access is rented before it is owned." That proposition defines the correspondent layer more honestly than the softer language of network participation. A local bank may advertise international capability to its customers, yet what it often possesses is conditional passage through another bank's balance sheet and rulebook. That passage can be repriced, narrowed, delayed, or terminated. In calm periods the dependency feels manageable because the route is familiar and the correspondent has little reason to disturb profitable routine. In stressed periods the dependency becomes the whole story. A correspondent can de-risk a category, shorten tolerances, raise information demands, or exit a corridor entirely, leaving the respondent bank legally intact inside its own jurisdiction but operationally diminished in the monetary world beyond it.

The second pressure scene belongs to the bank one layer down. A midsized domestic bank serves exporters, importers, and remittance customers. It has no ambition to redesign world finance; it only needs stable passage through the major currency channels its customers rely on. One of its key correspondents decides that the jurisdictions, sectors, or client profiles associated with this bank now carry more risk than the relationship justifies. Nothing dramatic is announced publicly. Deadlines shorten. Investigatory requests expand. Some transactions take longer to clear. Others are returned for repair. Fees rise. Eventually the correspondent exits. The domestic bank has not failed, and no law inside its home country says it cannot keep serving its customers. Yet its customers now live in a different monetary reality. Trade payments take longer. Remittances cost more. Import financing tightens. What changed was not money in the abstract. What changed was access to the institutions willing to stand between local claims and global settlement.

The compliance layer hardens that condition into a structure that can be weaponized without spectacle. Cross-border payment is inseparable from identity verification, screening, anti-illicit-finance obligations, counterparty risk checks, and documentation demands embedded in the message itself. Defenders argue, with reason, that without this architecture the world would be more hospitable to evasion and dangerous opacity. Critics argue, also with reason, that these same obligations give gatekeepers extraordinary power to ration access, over-comply to avoid penalties, and force entire sectors, regions, or client groups into slower, more expensive, or less reliable corridors. Compliance is both prudence and hierarchy. It is also a channel through which geopolitical pressure can operate through ordinary payment sequence. When gatekeepers tighten interpretation, slow approvals, or withdraw correspondent capacity, the action can be defended as risk management rather than declared as coercion, even when the aggregate effect is coercive.

The ordinary firm feels this first as time and price. A small exporter does not describe its difficulty as a problem of transnational admissibility. It describes it as a longer cash-conversion cycle, more expensive trade finance, documentary fatigue, and the constant need to answer questions that larger firms with established routes seem able to answer once and then forget. The cross-border system imposes a tax not only in fees but in uncertainty. When payment-arrival time becomes less predictable, inventory planning changes. Firms hold larger precautionary balances. Suppliers demand earlier payment or stronger counterparties. Credit insurers recalculate. The gatekeeper's delay becomes the firm's margin compression.

The chapter's intimate scene should show the cost in the body of a business. A distributor expects payment from a major customer on Thursday. The customer's bank portal shows instruction complete. The distributor schedules supplier payments and payroll for Thursday afternoon. Then a corridor delay ripples backward through a chain the distributor never sees. The instruction was complete as message, but the underlying value had not yet crossed into finality. A downstream correspondent held release pending a documentation repair that had nothing to do with the distributor's performance. By late afternoon the distributor is drawing on an expensive emergency line to avoid missing payroll. Nothing has been stolen. No one has declared default. Yet the difference between access, passage, and finality has appeared as financing cost, managerial humiliation, and thinner margins. That is cross-border gatekeeping made physical.

A sovereign-level pressure scene makes the larger truth unavoidable. A country faces no declared embargo and no formal financial war. Its domestic banks remain licensed. Its laws remain unchanged. Yet external correspondents reduce exposure, dealers widen conversion spreads, screening delays lengthen, and the cost of moving value through dominant corridors rises across exactly the sectors most dependent on imported inputs. Fuel purchases take longer to settle. Medical imports require more working capital. Exporters begin invoicing differently to reassure counterparties. Domestic banks allocate scarce external payment capacity to the most urgent clients and quietly push others to the back of the line. The state discovers that domestic legality means little once external admissibility tightens. Its currency remains sovereign at home while the international life of its claims is being rationed abroad. This is pressure without spectacle. It does not require a blockade when permission can simply become slower, narrower, and more expensive.

The reserve-order implication must now be stated harder. Dominant corridors matter not only because they are widely used, but because they sit at the points where cross-border finality is easiest to achieve. A currency becomes structurally powerful when its institutions occupy the routing core: the correspondents that clear, the dealers that bridge, the compliance interpretations that become global defaults, and the settlement endpoints that others must approach to complete discharge. Under that structure, geopolitical pressure can operate through ordinary payment sequence without dramatic rupture. Raise screening standards. Narrow correspondent appetite. Increase documentation burdens. Shorten cutoffs. Slow approvals. Widen conversion spreads. Each step can be defended as prudence. Together, they can function as a lever on another state's working capital, import capacity, and domestic stability. The power is not only in the symbol of the currency. It is in the corridors that make international money movement ordinary for some and conditional for others.

The official defense of the architecture remains true. Shared message standards, correspondent networks, and compliance frameworks reduce friction and make global commerce possible at scale. They create enough common language and screening discipline that institutions can deal across distance with less fear than a fully improvised world would generate. But the critique is equally structural. The same architecture concentrates power in a relatively small number of institutions and dominant-currency corridors; it allows private actors to make public-geostrategic decisions through de-risking and access withdrawal; and it turns technical standards into instruments of admission and exclusion. Efficiency and hierarchy arrived together, and any state that pretends otherwise will misunderstand how cross-border pressure actually works.

The present-day implication is severe for serious statecraft. Building domestic payment speed is not enough. Building domestic banking scale is not enough. A country that wants real monetary resilience must ask harder questions. How many of its trade and remittance corridors depend on a narrow set of correspondents. How exposed its institutions are to external message standards they do not shape. How much of its foreign-exchange settlement passes through dominant-currency bridges. Whether its firms can withstand longer settlement intervals without widespread liquidity strain. Which sectors would choke first if admissibility tightened. Whether emergency import categories have alternative routes or merely comforting assumptions. A finance ministry that cannot answer these questions does not yet know the border conditions of its own monetary order.

The hardest truth is the simplest one. A state may fully govern the law of money inside its territory and still discover that the movement of its claims across borders depends on institutions that owe it nothing beyond contract and compliance. That is not a theoretical weakness. It is a ranked condition in the world system. When access is smooth, the condition hides behind ordinary commerce. When access tightens, it reveals that part of international monetary life is governed not by your own law, but by your position in other people's corridors. Cross-border payments do not merely test efficiency. They test whose permission still matters after domestic legality has finished speaking.

CLOSING DOCTRINE

Cross-border payment is not domestic payment at greater distance. It is domestic payment submitted to an external hierarchy of message standards, correspondent balance sheets, compliance screens, dealer liquidity, and dominant-currency corridors. Access is admission to speak in the recognized language. Passage is continued permission to move through the corridor without being stopped or repaired. Finality is the point at which value arrives as discharged obligation in a form the destination layer must honor. Between those thresholds lies the governed interval where gatekeepers allocate time and enforce hierarchy. Dominant corridors matter because they hold the routing core, and routing core power allows geopolitical pressure to operate through ordinary payment sequence without formal rupture. In the world economy, the border is not only where goods stop. It is where payment asks permission, and permission can be narrowed quietly until a sovereign discovers how much of its monetary life outside its territory was always rented.

CHAPTER 15
RETAIL RAILS
THE INTERFACE THAT HIDES THE STATE

The purchase approved in less than a second. A tap, a soft vibration, a green mark, and the customer walked away carrying coffee and the ordinary confidence that the monetary order had done its job. Behind the counter the merchant's screen echoed the same small certainty. Approved meant paid. It meant closure. It meant the argument was over. Yet nothing final had happened in the place where finality lives. What had happened was permission, not discharge. A network had authorized a promise to pay later, at netted scale, on a schedule whose timing, reversibility, and dispute rights were governed by rules the customer had never read and the merchant could not renegotiate. The retail interface had delivered its most valuable product: the feeling that the settlement machine is personal, instantaneous, and frictionless, even when the underlying architecture is layered, conditional, and dependent on a hierarchy of intermediaries whose work begins precisely where the user's certainty ends.

Retail rails are the part of the payment state most citizens experience as reality. They are also the part least likely to be recognized as state-craft. People do not speak of sovereignty when a card clears or a wallet shows funds as available. They speak of convenience. They speak of technology. They speak of apps and speed. That language is the interface doing its job. The interface hides two truths that matter for governance. First, retail payment is usually not final settlement. It is a managed sequence in which authorization, posting, clearing, settlement, and legal discharge occur at different times and under different dispute rules. Second, the state is present even when it appears absent. The state supplies the unit, the legal perimeter, the bank licensing regime, the dispute forum, the supervision that keeps institutions legible to one another, and the apex settlement asset that makes the system credible when fear rises. Retail rails do not replace those functions. They route them through a surface that makes public authority feel like private ease.

The last chapters established the deposit engine and the clearing core, then showed how cross-border gatekeepers convert international payment into licensed passage. Retail rails now show how the monetary order keeps legitimacy at home. Retail legitimacy is not built by speeches or balance sheets. It is built by ordinary completion. Wages arrive. Bills are paid. Small merchants are funded. Payroll teams release files at the last practical minute because the system has taught them that next-morning availability is not hope but routine. Families do not think about settlement windows because grocery purchases, school fees, transit swipes, and utility debits have trained them to treat digital movement as a natural extension of possession. The public judges the monetary order not by its theory but by its reliability at the kitchen table, at the register, and in the inbox that confirms salary availability before the first coffee is poured. That makes retail rails politically decisive. If wholesale markets freeze, officials can speak to institutions, deploy backstops, and restore order with visible force. If retail rails degrade, the breakdown becomes intimate. People experience it as humiliation, lost time, late wages, missed rent, failed deliveries, added fees, and the sudden realization that a life built on digital completion can be forced back into cash-like caution overnight.

The interface has become so intimate that millions of people now plan their lives not merely around money, but around expected speed. A household schedules rent for the morning because wages are "always there" by dawn. A payroll team submits later than prudence would once have allowed because same-day or next-morning movement has become a routine assumption embedded in labor management. A restaurant owner orders perishables against projected weekend card takings because Monday availability has been normalized into purchasing discipline. A home-health worker accepts multiple small jobs from different platforms because each platform promises rapid payout and the worker's grocery logic now depends on whether those promises are fulfilled by evening rather than by week's end. A contractor pays crews before being fully paid by the client because prior payment experiences have taught him to treat incoming transfers as quasi-immediate. Retail speed is therefore no longer just a convenience delivered by the payment system. It is a behavioral constitution distributed across households, firms, landlords, payroll departments, and local supply chains. The rails do not merely move money faster. They redefine what everyone downstream believes prudent timing looks like.

"Approved is not final." That sentence sounds like pedantry until it becomes the difference between a calm day and a political crisis. In retail payments, approval is a promise that the system intends to settle later, subject to rules, disputes, and reversals that protect consumers, protect networks, and allocate fraud risk. Finality, by contrast, is the point at which the system withdraws permission to treat the payment as unpaid. Retail rails deliberately blur that boundary because the economy requires speed at the surface. Yet the same system must preserve reversibility in certain cases because fraud containment and consumer protection are also legitimacy functions. Retail payment is therefore governed by a paradox. The public wants payment to feel irrevocable when buying groceries, boarding a train, or paying a caregiver. The public also wants payment to be reversible when deception drains a paycheck or a scam empties a savings balance. The retail interface resolves this paradox not by solving it, but by concealing it within sequence. Felt completion is delivered first. Legal finality arrives later, sometimes much later, and only after the system has reserved the right to reopen the event under certain conditions. That interval between felt completion and legal closure is where power sits, because power is the ability to decide which reversals are permitted, whose story is believed, how quickly funds are made available, and who bears the loss while the system investigates.

A retail payment system has more layers than ordinary users are allowed to see comfortably. The first layer is authorization: a near-real-time judgment about whether the payer's instrument is permitted to promise payment. The second layer is posting: the user-facing representation of that event in the payer's and sometimes the recipient's interface. The third layer is clearing: the aggregation and calculation of obligations among institutions, often netted to economize on liquidity. The fourth layer is settlement: the actual movement of value in a form the system treats as apex discharge between participating institutions. The fifth layer, often hidden inside legal documents rather than interfaces, is challenge, reversal, and recognized closure: the point at which the obligation can no longer ordinarily be reopened except under exceptional process. A household sees one event. A merchant sees one event. A payroll clerk sees one event. The system executes several, each with its own operational and legal posture. Retail rails are designed to make the first layer feel like the last layer most of the time. That is not a technical quirk. It is a political design choice because modern commerce cannot run if ordinary people must think in settlement stages every time they buy lunch or send money to a relative.

The system manufactures trust through concealment. Authorization tells the consumer yes. Posting tells the consumer the yes belongs to them. Clearing tells institutions what they actually owe after offset. Settlement decides when those residual obligations move in apex money. Legal discharge decides when the system will stop entertaining the claim that the payment was unpaid, fraudulent, or misallocated. The interface compresses these into one human impression because confidence at the surface depends on compression. But compression has a cost. The user builds life on the assumption that the early stage is functionally equivalent to the final stage. When that assumption breaks, the system does not merely create a technical exception. It destroys a rhythm people had mistaken for a right. The state's problem begins there, because once enough people feel the gap between promise and finality directly, the interface stops being convenience and becomes evidence that the monetary order had been asking them to believe in a fiction stronger than the underlying sequence could support.

The compression is never perfect, and its imperfections are where governance becomes visible. A restaurant owner sees approved receipts all weekend and assumes Monday will bring usable funds to cover payroll and inventory. Then a dispute wave hits the system because fraud patterns rise, a network tightens risk scoring, and the merchant's category is deemed more vulnerable. The owner is not accused of wrongdoing, yet settlement timing shifts. Funds are held longer. Reserves are not the owner's vocabulary; liquidity is. Payroll is. The owner learns that approval is a status, not a guarantee, and that the right to hold money-like completion belongs to the payment state, not to the merchant's expectations. The payment system is not a neutral conduit. It is a ranked claims architecture that can change the speed and certainty of money for entire categories of activity without negotiating with each merchant individually. That is governance by interface, and its force is sharper precisely because it often arrives without any visible official standing beside it.

The interface does more than hide sequence. It hides hierarchy. Some institutions and participants live closer to the settlement core and therefore enjoy faster posting, lower fees, more reliable availability, looser reserve holds, and cheaper access to working liquidity. Others live farther away and pay for it in time and cost. The consumer often experiences this as a difference between instant and two days, as if the difference were merely technical. In fact it is often the difference between being able to settle obligations using the system's own elasticity and having to wait for the system to deliver that elasticity after it has protected itself. The merchant who receives faster availability is being trusted. The merchant whose funds are held is being subordinated until further proof. The household that can move funds instantly is being served by an institution with robust routing and access. The household that waits is being served by an institution that must approach the core indirectly, or one whose risk profile forces more caution from intermediaries. Retail rails therefore allocate dignity. They decide whose life can proceed without pause and whose must live inside pending.

A pressure scene makes this allocation concrete. A gig worker completes a week of jobs and expects payout on Friday night. The platform marks the payout as sent. The worker's wallet shows a positive balance, yet availability is delayed because the receiving institution classifies the payment as higher risk for reasons that have nothing to do with the worker's character and everything to do with routing, category, and compliance posture. Rent is due Saturday morning. The landlord's automated debit does not care about pending. A fee posts. The worker spends Saturday making calls, proving identity, and enduring the soft contempt hidden inside "for your protection." The money arrives later and everyone insists the system worked as designed. That insistence is technically correct and politically destructive, because the system has just taught the worker that the monetary order is fast for those who can afford to wait and slow for those who cannot. Retail rails become legitimacy machinery when they are reliable. They become legitimacy accelerants when they are not.

A household builds more around those rails than public language admits. Grocery timing, rent timing, salary timing, subscription timing, childcare timing, transport timing, and emergency borrowing decisions are all increasingly synchronized to the expectation that interface speed is reality rather than surface representation. A parent who sees a balance at 7:00 a.m. uses that sight as if it were settled fact. A landlord, utility, or school fee system does the same from the other side. The interface has therefore become a distributed planner of household life. When it misfires, the household does not experience a technical inconsistency. It experiences a breach in the rhythm by which modern life stays governable. That is why retail payment failures are politically larger than their nominal values suggest. A missed institutional transfer of great size can remain invisible. A failed wage, bill, medicine purchase, or grocery payment becomes a public verdict on whether the monetary order respects ordinary existence.

Merchants and payroll teams internalize the same rhythm from another angle. A payroll manager at a midsized firm now times submission not with old-fashioned conservatism but with the confidence supplied by retail rails that almost never visibly fail. That confidence becomes part of treasury optimization. Funds remain invested or used elsewhere until late in the cycle. Liquidity buffers are thinned because next-day movement is treated as ordinary. A small merchant does the same in miniature, paying suppliers once weekend receipts show as posted and assuming Monday availability will bridge the gap. A beauty salon orders products on Tuesday based on Monday receipts that still carry quiet reversal and timing risk beneath the interface. A food truck operator buys fuel against an incoming processor settlement that appears close enough to possession to justify action. The interface is therefore not just a layer of convenience over money. It is the metronome by which small operators choreograph survival.

Retail rails also change behavior at scale by changing what people expect to be possible. Faster transfers shorten household cash buffers because people rely on the system's speed as their buffer. Businesses hold leaner liquidity because they expect settlement to arrive on schedule. Payroll teams push release windows later because instant or same-day movement has become an operational assumption rather than a marketing phrase. That creates efficiency in calm and fragility in stress. If the system slows, the public does not merely experience inconvenience; it experiences the collapse of its own liquidity planning. The payment state then discovers that retail speed is not simply a consumer feature. It is a macroeconomic assumption distributed into millions of private and corporate decisions. A fast retail rail therefore carries a hidden requirement: it must either be resilient enough to remain fast under pressure or it must have governance mechanisms capable of slowing selectively without triggering broad loss of confidence. Selective slowing is itself a political act, because it means deciding which transactions remain ordinary and which become exceptional.

"The interface is the perimeter." That proposition explains why retail rails cannot be treated as harmless customer experience. The interface determines where identity is verified, where compliance is enforced, where fraud is triaged, where access is denied, and where monetary life becomes legible to the system. This is why the retail layer attracts both innovation and contestation. Whoever controls the interface can shape user behavior, capture data, impose fees, assign risk labels, and, in extreme cases, deny access or reroute flows. The state cannot ignore this because the interface is where citizens decide whether the monetary order feels legitimate. In earlier eras, cash performed this function by making discharge immediate and anonymous. In digital retail rails, the function shifts to platforms and bank-ledgers that can decide whether a payment is allowed, delayed, reversed, or frozen. The state must govern these powers or risk discovering that private intermediaries have acquired practical sovereignty over everyday money usage.

The data layer deepens that sovereignty. The interface does not merely route payment; it captures identity, timing, location, counterparties, behavioral regularities, device signatures, spending patterns, payout habits, dispute frequency, and transaction contexts that can be turned into risk scores, commercial leverage, targeted pricing, exclusion decisions, and new forms of financial ranking. A person with the same nominal balance can live in a different monetary world depending on how legible, profitable, low-risk, or compliant the system judges that person to be. The merchant with modest chargebacks but thin margins may be treated as more dangerous than a larger merchant whose scale makes losses tolerable. The worker whose identity signals do not align neatly across databases may face holds that others never see. The family that lives in a geography or category the system associates with higher fraud may experience money as more conditional than a family elsewhere, even when both hold the same legal unit. If the payment state permits the interface layer to become an opaque scoring regime, then money begins to behave differently not only according to balance-sheet strength but according to data-status. The public will experience that as arbitrariness long before it acquires the vocabulary to describe it.

Exclusion begins quietly. It rarely starts with a declared ban. It starts with an account under review, a transfer unavailable for instant release, a merchant category assigned stricter reserve treatment, a payout corridor turned off, an identity mismatch that cannot be corrected in real time, a risk flag that no human being with decision-making authority is willing to explain. The interface tells the excluded user that the system is protecting itself, others, or the user. What it often means is simpler and harsher: the user is no longer legible enough, profitable enough, or low-risk enough to move with ordinary dignity. That is why the interface does not merely move money; it decides who is legible enough to move at all. In a society where wages, bills, transport, and food increasingly depend on those rails, practical illegibility is a form of partial monetary exile.

Fraud and dispute resolution are where the interface's hidden constitution becomes visible. Retail payment systems must manage deception at scale, and deception is relentless because the interface is where the money is easiest to touch. The design choice is unavoidable: either the system allows irreversible retail payments and then leaves victims to absorb losses, or it allows reversibility and then imposes uncertainty and cost on merchants and networks. Either choice creates a distributional map. Irreversibility protects merchants and networks at the expense of households. Reversibility protects households at the expense of merchants and, ultimately, the price level they face. The system resolves the conflict through rules: time windows for disputes, evidentiary requirements, liability allocations, merchant category controls, identity verification standards, and scoring systems that decide who is trusted. This is not merely consumer protection. It is monetary governance because it determines whether retail deposits behave like final money or conditional claims at the interface.

A second pressure scene shows how this becomes institutional. A small retailer suffers a fraud wave that triggers disputes. The retailer did not commit fraud, but the system does not distinguish innocence and vulnerability in the same way a moral mind does. It distinguishes loss patterns. The retailer's access to fast settlement is tightened. Reserve holds are imposed. Fees rise. The retailer is forced into higher liquidity buffers simply to operate, and those buffers become a cost that pushes prices upward or squeezes margins downward. The retailer's neighborhood experiences the result not as prudential design but as one more reason the digital economy seems cheaper for large chains than for small operators. The official defense calls it prudence. The lived experience calls it punishment without appeal. If the system cannot provide credible recourse, the payment state will produce resentment that can be misdirected politically in ways that destabilize broader monetary consent.

Retail rails also hide the state through the way they create the illusion of private settlement. A wallet balance looks like money outside the banking system even when it is merely a representation of bank-held deposits or claims on a regulated institution. A stored-value balance can feel cash-like even when its finality depends on the same bank and settlement core the user imagines they have bypassed. This matters because the interface can attract the public by implying it has escaped banks and official machinery, while in reality it has simply moved the user to a different point in the same hierarchy. The user gains convenience. The interface provider gains data and fee leverage. The banking system still provides settlement. The legal core and backstop remain essential. Retail rails are therefore a stage on which monetary myths are performed for profit and for legitimacy. If the state does not insist on clarity about what is deposit, what is claim, what is protected, and what is truly final, then the public will be taught a story about money that will not survive the next stress event.

The retail layer is also where the system's most dangerous ambiguity lives: availability. A balance can be posted without being settled. Funds can be shown without being fully usable. A merchant can be credited while still subject to reversal. A consumer can see a number that is real enough to spend in one context but not real enough to move in another. These are not bugs. They are governance choices designed to reconcile speed, fraud protection, and liquidity constraint. Yet every such choice creates the possibility of moral hazard and political outrage, because the system is effectively telling some users that money is a promise today and others that money is a fact today. When those differences track wealth, institutional status, geography, or platform privilege, the payment state becomes a legitimacy problem.

A third pressure scene belongs in a weekend outage, because outages reveal the extent to which the interface has become the economy's operating assumption. A software update fails at a core node of the retail payment ecosystem. For several hours, authorizations are unreliable. Merchants shift to cash-like alternatives, but many customers do not carry them. Grocery stores ration transactions. Fuel purchases become awkward. Hospitals demand different payment methods for nonemergency services. Families discover that their access to money is not a metaphysical right but a sequence dependent on network synchronization. The official role remains mostly invisible until it is needed. Then institutions coordinate, liquidity is positioned, fraud defenses are adjusted, emergency communication begins, and the system gradually returns to ordinary completion. The public experiences inconvenience. The payment state experiences a legitimacy hazard: if retail completion cannot be trusted, the public begins hoarding the most final form it can access, and hoarding is how a retail trust event can become a systemic liquidity event.

This is where retail smoothness must be connected to back-end fragility with sharper force. The interface can remain beautiful while the basement fills with stress. Households see instant movement. Merchants see approved sales. Payroll teams see completed releases. Beneath that surface, institutions are netting positions, extending intraday credit, managing fraud reserves, funding collateral needs, and relying on wholesale liquidity conditions that can deteriorate without warning. The smoother the surface becomes, the more intensely the back end must absorb the burden of making speed appear natural. If that back-end elasticity is built on thin buffers, concentrated intermediaries, or shadow liquidity promises, then retail grace is being financed by structures the public never sees and cannot price. That combination is politically explosive because when the surface slips, ordinary users do not conclude that hidden wholesale arrangements failed. They conclude that money itself has become unreliable. A system that trains the public to expect effortless completion and then reveals dependence on brittle support structures is not merely technically fragile. It is legitimacy-fragile.

The strongest counterargument insists that retail rails are not statecraft, merely private competition delivering better customer outcomes. There is truth in that. Competition can reduce costs, improve speed, and expand access. Better interfaces can pull informal activity into formal rails and broaden the compliance perimeter in ways states quietly prefer. Yet the counterargument fails when it treats the retail layer as separate from the settlement core. Retail rails can be private, but they cannot be sovereign on their own. They require the unit of account, the legal perimeter, the bank chartering regime, the dispute forum, and the settlement architecture that makes promised payments credible at scale. When retail rails grow systemically important, the state cannot treat them as just another market. Their outages become public events. Their fraud dynamics become political scandals. Their fee and availability policies become distributional disputes. Their data and identity rules become power. Retail rails are the interface that hides the state, which means they are also the interface through which the state is judged.

The chapter's present-day implication is unavoidable. If monetary legitimacy matters, the retail interface must be governed as a constitutional zone even when private firms build the product surface. That governance has to be more than consumer-protection slogans. It must be architecture. It must specify which claims are protected-like and which are merely contractual. It must impose clarity about reversibility, availability, hold practices, and dispute standards. It must manage the competition between speed and fraud containment without allowing the system to become fast only for those it already trusts. It must prevent the interface from becoming a private choke point that can deny access arbitrarily, extract rents, or rewrite money usage through opaque rule changes. It must also ensure that retail speed does not hollow out the system's ability to slow safely under stress, because the system will need to ration time during panic and the public will tolerate that rationing only if it believes the rationing is governed rather than predatory.

Retail rails also quietly prepare the ground for the next chapter's subject. The more the interface promises instant money, the more the system must manufacture liquidity elsewhere to make instant money feel true. That elsewhere is often shadow liquidity: off-balance-sheet credit, wholesale funding, private liquidity promises, and nonbank structures that behave like money until they seize. Retail rails therefore do not only hide the state. They increase pressure on the rest of the system to provide time on demand. When the interface is fast, the back end must be elastic. When the back end is elastic, shadow structures proliferate. The system then becomes more efficient and more fragile in the same breath. Retail rails are the smiling front door of a building whose basement fills with combustible material whenever the front door is made too easy to open.

The deepest truth is that the interface is not secondary to the monetary order. It is the public face through which ordinary life decides whether the order deserves trust. A society can survive complex wholesale structures it does not understand. It cannot easily survive daily evidence that money is conditional for ordinary people while being treated as immediate for institutions and favored channels. The interface therefore performs a constitutional function. It translates hierarchy into a livable story. The question for statecraft is whether the story remains close enough to the truth that the public will continue believing it when pressure arrives. If the gap grows too wide, the next slowdown, outage, fraud wave, or exclusion error will not be heard as technical explanation. It will be heard as confession.

CLOSING DOCTRINE

Retail rails are not merely payment products. They are the interface layer through which the payment state earns legitimacy and through which hierarchy becomes lived experience. Authorization creates permission, not discharge, and the system survives by compressing the feeling of completion at the surface while managing posting, clearing, settlement, reversibility, fraud triage, data-based ranking, and legal closure beneath it. The gap between approval and finality is governance territory: it allocates time, assigns liability, decides availability, determines who is legible enough to move without friction, and decides who bears loss while the system investigates. A fast interface is a macroeconomic promise distributed into millions of private liquidity plans, which means slowing the interface under stress is never just operations; it is political triage. Retail smoothness can coexist with wholesale and data-layer fragility for long periods, but when the surface slips the public judges the whole monetary order through the failure of that one intimate layer. A state that does not govern the retail interface as a constitutional perimeter will eventually discover that private intermediaries have acquired practical sovereignty over availability, identity, exclusion, and the public meaning of money itself. The interface hides the state until it fails, and then the public judges the state anyway.

CHAPTER 16
SHADOW LIQUIDITY
THE SYSTEM THAT RUNS UNTIL IT SEIZES

The first sign of trouble was not a collapse. It was a question asked twice. A funding desk called a counterparty and asked for the morning roll on the same terms as yesterday. The answer did not refuse. It asked for more collateral. The desk adjusted and sent the substitution. Ten minutes later the counterparty asked again, quieter this time, for a different kind of collateral, and for a slightly larger buffer. Nothing had defaulted. No headline had moved. Yet a line had been crossed inside the system's bloodstream. Liquidity had begun to demand proof. Proof had begun to demand hierarchy. The day's funding was still running, but it was running on thinner trust, and the thinness was the warning.

Shadow liquidity is the system that makes modern finance feel faster, richer, and more flexible than its settlement core should allow. It is the private machinery that manufactures time on demand by turning collateral into cash-like funding, by turning promises into near-money through rolling agreements, by netting and rehypothecating claims until they behave like a usable surplus of settlement capacity. It is called shadow not because it is secret, but because it sits adjacent to the formal monetary hierarchy while borrowing the credibility of that hierarchy. Shadow liquidity looks like liquidity most of the time. It is spendable in practice, fundable at scale, and accepted by institutions as if it were safely convertible into the apex claim whenever needed. Then a stress arrives that reclassifies it. The same instruments that were treated as money-like become treated as conditional, and the system discovers how much of its daily stability had been financed by a promise to refinance.

The previous chapters built the visible chambers of the payment state: deposits as privately manufactured money under public rule, clearing as the compression machine that makes scale possible, cross-border gatekeepers as licensed passage, retail rails as the legitimacy interface. Shadow liquidity is what lives behind all of them. Retail speed is felt as immediate because wholesalers can fund the machine that underwrites immediate behavior. Clearing can net and compress because participants can obtain collateralized funding to survive the intraday and overnight intervals that netting creates. Cross-border corridors can be priced and bridged because dealers and intermediaries are willing to warehouse currency risk and provide settlement liquidity across time zones. Deposits remain just money most days because institutions can convert assets into cash-like funding when flows go one-sided. Shadow liquidity is therefore not a separate financial curiosity. It is the private time-allocation layer that keeps the payment state moving faster than its apex money should strictly permit.

"It is only a roll." That is the most dangerous sentence in this chapter because it is true until it is fatal. The architecture of shadow liquidity is built on short maturity and repeated renewal. A loan that matures tomorrow is safe today if it will certainly be renewed tomorrow. A funding position that must be rolled each morning is stable if the market's habit of rolling is treated as a near-law. A security that can be pledged overnight for cash-like funding is money-like if the pledge will be accepted again tomorrow on roughly the same terms. This is how a system creates usable liquidity without the state issuing more apex settlement claims. It manufactures time by treating renewal as routine. The fragility is that renewal is never a right. It is a preference held by counterparties, and preferences change abruptly when fear arrives.

The public usually imagines money as a balance and liquidity as a synonym for possession. The system knows better. A visible balance is not the same as immediate funding capacity. A large asset position is not the same as cash. A solvent institution is not the same as a liquid one. Shadow liquidity lives inside those differences. It is the bridge between owning claims and being able to survive the timing of obligations. That bridge is private, priced, revocable, and deeply hierarchical. It works by allowing institutions to treat high-quality claims as temporary substitutes for final settlement, but only so long as lenders and counterparties agree to maintain that fiction. The moment enough lenders stop agreeing, the bridge does not gradually weaken. It can vanish at a speed that makes balance-sheet strength look irrelevant for long enough to become politically dangerous.

The difference between visible money and borrowed liquidity is the hinge on which the whole chapter turns. Visible money is what the user sees: a posted balance, a credited account, a nominal asset value, a line on a statement. Borrowed liquidity is what the institution must secure to honor the timing expectations that those visible balances invite. An institution can show abundant assets and still fail if it cannot borrow against them in time. A fund can look rich and still be forced to sell. A bank can appear well-capitalized and still experience acute pressure if cash-like funding disappears faster than formal solvency can matter. A business can have receivables and still miss payroll because receivables are not liquid enough soon enough. The public routinely confuses balances with access because most days the system works hard to make the distinction disappear. Shadow liquidity is the machinery that erases the distinction in calm and reveals it brutally in stress.

Shadow liquidity has a clean mechanism and an ugly politics. The clean mechanism is collateral transformation. An institution holds assets that cannot be spent directly as money. It pledges those assets for short-term funding. That funding is used to settle obligations, finance inventories, support market-making, and bridge time between receivable and payable. The pledged assets remain on the balance sheet, but their liquidity has been extracted through a contract. The contract is typically short, often overnight, sometimes a few days, rarely long enough to feel comfortable when the world shifts. The ugly politics is that only some assets are eligible for this treatment at scale, only some institutions can borrow against them cheaply, and only some counterparties can demand the lowest buffers. Shadow liquidity therefore reproduces the hierarchy of money in a private register. It sorts collateral. It sorts borrowers. It sorts counterparties. It allocates time to those who can pledge the right objects and speak from the right position in the network.

To understand how deep that sorting runs, the chain has to be made tactile. Picture one highly rated bond, plain enough to look boring on a portfolio screen. In calm times it is not just a security. It is a key. One dealer uses it to borrow overnight cash. That borrowed cash finances a market-making inventory. The inventory supports prices for investors who believe they can enter and exit without penalty. Another institution that receives the bond as collateral is comfortable because it believes the bond can itself be reused or sold quickly if needed. A clearing member relies on the dealer's continued functioning to meet variation flows without disturbing its wider book. A corporate issuer pricing debt that afternoon benefits from orderly markets made possible by that dealer's funded inventory. A bank treasury desk counting on normal settlement conditions can hold slightly less idle cash because the chain of funded confidence remains intact. A payment processor extending intraday tolerance benefits indirectly because the wholesale system remains calm enough that back-end liquidity is available on familiar terms. That one bond has now helped support a lattice of promises far larger than its face value. It has become not just an asset, but a bearer of time.

Multiply that example by thousands of objects and the tactile truth becomes unavoidable. Shadow liquidity is a civilization of re-usable confidence. A modest group of high-grade collateral objects can anchor layers of funding, market-making, margin support, settlement tolerance, and everyday payment normality far beyond what a simple ownership model would imply. The stability of the whole arrangement depends not just on the collateral existing, but on orderly reuse continuing without interruption. The moment one layer in the reuse chain refuses to continue on old terms, all the other promises supported by that object must either find replacement time or begin collapsing inward. This is why shadow liquidity feels abundant until it suddenly feels scarce. Its abundance is not the abundance of cash. It is the abundance of permission to keep using the same trustworthy objects to support successive layers of temporary funding.

"Haircuts widen." Another sentence the system learns to fear. A haircut is the system's way of admitting that collateral is not cash. It is the buffer demanded between the pledged asset's current value and the cash-like funding advanced against it. In calm periods, haircuts are treated as technical. In stress, they become constitutional. A widening haircut is not merely a change in funding cost. It is a demand for additional collateral at the precise moment collateral is hardest to spare. It forces asset sales to raise eligible collateral. It forces institutions to shrink balance sheets rapidly. It converts price movements into funding crises because declining collateral value and rising haircuts compound, demanding more assets to secure the same funding at the exact moment asset values are falling. This is how a liquidity problem becomes a fire-sale problem and then becomes a solvency problem.

The chapter's first pressure scene belongs inside that compound. A dealer finances a portfolio of liquid securities through short-term secured borrowing. The portfolio is diversified, the daily price movement seems manageable, and the borrowing is rolled each morning as a habit older than the current team. One morning the market's tone changes. A few assets drop. The dealer expects modest variation and sends it. Then haircuts widen. The dealer must deliver more collateral for the same cash. To deliver it, the dealer must either post higher-grade assets it was holding for other needs or sell assets to obtain the preferred collateral. The sale itself pushes prices lower, which widens haircuts further, which forces more sales. Nothing in this sequence requires a formal default to begin. The system can seize while everyone is still trying to behave. Shadow liquidity turns small shocks into large forced motion because it ties funding to collateral value in real time and demands immediate adjustment.

The decisive cruelty of the mechanism is that it punishes institutions before any slow legal process can rescue them. Insolvency is still a legal category, still something tribunals and restructuring specialists know how to process. Shadow illiquidity is faster and less forgiving. It tells an institution that yesterday's respectable balance sheet is irrelevant if today's collateral will not fund the obligations due before the close. It tells a treasury desk that asset quality in the long run is less important than acceptable collateral in the next two hours. It tells a market-making desk that it can be right about value and still die of sequence. This is why shadow liquidity belongs in a book about the monetary state. It is a system for rationing time privately, and time is the first asset that vanishes in panic.

Shadow liquidity is also built on chains, not single links. A pledged asset can be re-used. A cash-like advance can be reinvested. A collateral claim can be rehypothecated, meaning the same object becomes the basis for multiple layers of funding in sequence. This is not always malicious. It is a structural response to scarcity. The system wants more usable settlement capacity than the supply of apex money provides. It creates that capacity by reusing collateral and by trusting that the chain will remain intact long enough for each participant to roll their positions. Reuse is efficiency until it becomes opacity. The more a single asset supports multiple funding promises, the more the system's stability depends on everyone agreeing about who has priority if the chain breaks. That returns us to the book's root doctrine. Money is not just promise. It is ranked promise. Shadow liquidity multiplies promises faster than it can comfortably guarantee the ranking under stress.

The second pressure scene belongs in the moment the chain is questioned. A large institutional lender calls for substitution. It does not want a certain class of collateral this morning. It wants higher-grade collateral. The borrower complies by drawing on its own inventory, which removes those higher-grade assets from other uses. Another counterparty then requests the same upgrade. The borrower begins scrambling. It tries to borrow the high-grade collateral by lending out lower-grade collateral, but the market is tightening everywhere at once. When the borrower cannot upgrade enough collateral quickly, it begins selling assets to obtain what the market will accept. Those sales pressure prices, which tighten funding further. The chain has not broken yet, but it is being asked to prove itself. That is what stress really is in shadow liquidity: a demand to prove convertibility today rather than relying on a reputation built in calm periods.

This is also where visibility diverges from importance. The public may never hear the name of the instrument being rejected or the exact corridor in which substitution failed. What it feels later are the consequences: a dealer stepping back from making markets, a bank revising liquidity assumptions, a fund pulling back from certain assets, a corporate credit line repriced more harshly than any local manager expected. A system held together by rolling private time can absorb many ordinary days without public narrative. The day it cannot, the public sees only the outer symptoms while the actual seizure begins in collateral rooms and funding screens it never knew existed.

Shadow liquidity is often defended as self-discipline. That defense has force. Collateralized borrowing and short maturity impose market discipline. If an institution becomes weak, its funding should become more expensive or unavailable. If an asset becomes risky, haircuts should rise. In theory, this is a private risk-control system that reduces the need for public backstops. The critique is that discipline can become panic faster than it becomes prudence, and when it becomes panic it tends to punish not only the weak but anyone forced to move in a crowded corridor at the same time. The same architecture that disciplines risk-taking can also create systemic acceleration into collapse, because funding withdrawal is both rational for the individual and destructive for the system when everyone does it simultaneously. Shadow liquidity therefore contains a structural contradiction. It is designed to allocate time efficiently in calm and it allocates time brutally in stress.

"Do you have the collateral." That question becomes sovereign when asked at scale. In a shadow liquidity regime, the system's immediate survival depends on whether institutions can produce eligible collateral on demand. Not any collateral. Collateral that the market, the clearing core, and the most cautious lenders will accept. The practical result is that collateral eligibility becomes a form of currency in its own right. Those holding it can fund. Those lacking it must pay, wait, or sell. This is where the payment state and shadow liquidity fuse. The state may define legal tender, but the market defines which collateral buys time inside the funding machine. Under stress, the state often intervenes precisely by expanding what counts as acceptable collateral for official liquidity support or by providing a backstop that turns previously conditional assets into fundable objects. The state becomes the dealer of last resort not because it loves markets, but because the collapse of shadow liquidity collapses the payment state's ability to maintain ordinary completion.

The third pressure scene belongs in the world of an ordinary operating business, because that is where shadow tightening stops sounding like a market problem and starts sounding like a managerial sentence. A midsized manufacturer relies on a revolving facility to buy inputs three weeks before customer payments arrive. The facility's legal terms have not changed. The relationship manager has not grown hostile. Yet funding conditions at the bank have tightened because the bank's own short-term liquidity has become more expensive and less predictable. The manufacturer is told that the line remains open, but at a higher spread, with stricter reporting, with tighter collateral language, and with less tolerance for late receivables. The business does not care that a collateral corridor seized two layers above it. It now has to choose between carrying less inventory, delaying expansion, or paying materially more to bridge the same calendar gap it bridged last month at lower cost. This is shadow liquidity entering the real economy not as apocalypse, but as narrower time.

But narrower time is not only a matter of higher rates. It is operational compression. The manufacturer had been ordering inputs with a three-week cushion and paying suppliers on thirty-day terms because its revolving line and customer-payment rhythm allowed those calendars to overlap. Once the bank shortens tolerance and draws harder lines around receivables, the calendar itself changes. Orders must be smaller. Deliveries must be staged rather than batched. A shift that could have been added next month is postponed because the working-capital gap can no longer be carried comfortably. The purchasing manager spends more time sequencing invoices than negotiating price. Production planning turns from expansion to choreography. Nothing dramatic has happened in law. Nothing visible has happened in the consumer's wallet. But the business has lost time, and lost time is one of the most expensive forms of monetary tightening because it forces every decision to become shorter, meaner, and more defensive.

A smaller operator feels it even more intimately. A local distributor once paid vendors in ten days because incoming receivables, card settlements, and a modest line of credit created enough overlap to make the rhythm work. Then the line becomes more expensive and more conditional, card settlements are held longer by risk controls elsewhere in the chain, and a supplier sensing broader caution insists on shorter terms. The distributor is not ruined. It is squeezed. Deliveries are staggered. Inventory thins. Staff hours are cut one day a week. The owner starts calling customers sooner, not because they have become less trustworthy, but because the calendar can no longer tolerate the old slack. The customer sees emptier shelves and slower fulfillment. The political system sees no headline event. Yet the true event has already happened: private time has become scarce, and scarcity has moved from funding desks into ordinary commerce.

Another business feels the same squeeze through payroll. A regional service firm has enough revenue on paper, enough contracts, and enough receivables booked to appear healthy. What it lacks is elastic time. A bank that used to let expected receivables bridge payroll for two or three days now wants money actually in before extending the same comfort. The payroll team starts releasing files earlier, then delaying reimbursements, then asking managers to postpone contractor hours. None of those moves sound like shadow liquidity in ordinary speech. They sound like budget discipline, belt-tightening, operational caution. Yet underneath them sits the same event: borrowed liquidity has become harder to obtain, so visible balances and booked income no longer convert into spendable timing with the old ease. This is how a hidden funding regime rewrites the internal culture of firms long before it appears in speeches about credit conditions.

Shadow liquidity also operates through nonbank promises that behave like cash substitutes. Institutions hold instruments that can be redeemed daily, used as margin, or treated as near-cash for operational needs. These instruments are often perceived as safe because they are short-term, diversified, and professionally managed. Their safety, however, depends on the same condition as the rest of shadow liquidity: the ability to convert assets into cash without needing to sell into a falling market. If too many holders demand immediate liquidity at once, the manager must sell assets or impose gates, fees, or delays. The public learns, again, the book's core lesson: the appearance of money depends on the capacity to provide discharge at scale. Shadow liquidity offers that capacity in normal times by relying on the market's willingness to refinance. When refinancing becomes scarce, the promise reveals its conditional nature.

This conditionality is not a footnote. It is the practical reason modern crises spread through funding channels faster than through old-fashioned insolvency. A traditional bank run is visible. People line up. A modern funding run is invisible until it is everywhere. It occurs through haircuts, margin calls, collateral substitutions, shortened maturities, and the quiet refusal to roll positions. It is run by institutions, not households, and it moves at the speed of messaging rather than at the speed of bodies. The payment state can be forced into emergency posture before the public has even noticed, because the wholesale machine that finances retail normality has already started rationing time. That is why shadow liquidity is a constitutional subject. It determines how quickly a system can slide from calm routine into crisis triage.

The reserve-order implication is unavoidable even domestically. A system whose shadow liquidity is built on a narrow set of collateral types, a narrow set of central nodes, and a narrow set of balance-sheet intermediaries is efficient in calm and brittle in stress. Concentration is the enemy of resilience because it turns a single corridor's fear into the whole system's fear. Yet the same concentration is attractive because it produces scale and low cost. This is the recurring theme of the payment state. Every gain in efficiency creates a new dependency. Every dependency becomes a lever under stress. Shadow liquidity is the most delicate lever because it sits at the intersection of collateral value, short-term confidence, and the need to settle continuously.

The state's role in this chapter is not to moralize about private markets. It is to see them clearly. Shadow liquidity is not an optional add-on. It is part of the modern monetary constitution because it supplies time where apex money is scarce. The question is therefore governance. How much shadow liquidity the system should tolerate. Where it is concentrated. Which collateral chains are essential. Which institutions are systemically decisive. How quickly official backstops must be able to convert conditional collateral into fundable assets without turning private risk-taking into a permanent claim on public rescue. The payment state cannot prevent shadow liquidity from forming. It can decide whether shadow liquidity is mapped, constrained, diversified, and backstopped in a way that preserves sovereignty rather than forcing emergency improvisation every time the private corridor tightens.

Here the political contradiction should be stated more nakedly. The state needs shadow liquidity because without it modern finance would move more slowly, hold more idle balances, and fund less activity. The very speed and abundance that make advanced monetary systems productive depend on private actors manufacturing time beyond the stock of final settlement money. Yet the state must also stand ready to rescue the system from that same private abundance when the refinancing promise fails. This is not a side tension. It is the heart of the arrangement. Public authority permits a private liquidity machine to make the economy feel richer and more continuous than apex money alone would allow, and then public authority is summoned whenever that machine begins to unwind. The system is privatized in gain, socialized in sequence, and periodically re-publicized in panic. No state can govern modern money seriously without admitting that contradiction.

The contradiction is heavier than it first appears because the state is not merely rescuing private excess. It is rescuing the continuity of everyday life that private excess had been financing invisibly. When the state backstops shadow liquidity, it is preserving payroll calendars, merchant settlement routines, inventory chains, funding markets, payment guarantees, and the very expectation that a posted balance or approved transfer will continue to mean what ordinary people think it means. That does not make every rescue wise. It makes every rescue politically entangled. The authority that refuses to intervene may defend discipline while allowing the payment state's tempo to break in public. The authority that intervenes may preserve tempo while teaching the market that private leverage enjoys an eventual public floor. The contradiction cannot be solved by rhetoric because it is architectural. The state wants the system fast, broad, and inventive in calm, then stable, obedient, and shrinkable in stress. Shadow liquidity is the mechanism through which those desires coexist until they do not.

The strongest official defense insists that shadow liquidity is not a defect but a feature that allows modern economies to finance more activity with less idle cash, making capital allocation more efficient and lowering the cost of credit. That defense is true in part. The honest counter is that efficiency purchased through short-term refinancing is a form of leverage on confidence, and confidence is not a stable resource under stress. A system built on rolling promises must either accept periodic seizures or design backstops that prevent seizure. Backstops then create moral hazard and political risk. There is no pure solution. There is only architecture and trade. The duty of statecraft is to choose the architecture that makes the trade survivable.

This chapter also sets the stage for the next chamber in the Part. If shadow liquidity is private time manufactured through collateral chains, token rails attempt to manufacture finality and programmability through new ledger forms. Token rails promise faster settlement and clearer collateral movement. They also introduce new concentration risk and new forms of gatekeeping at the platform layer. The payment state is moving toward systems that look more direct, more real-time, and more automated. Shadow liquidity teaches why those promises must be examined with suspicion. The faster the system tries to move, the more it must decide where time comes from in stress. Shadow liquidity has been the traditional answer. It runs until it seizes. The next design will run until its own failure mode appears, and those failure modes will be different but not gentler.

The deepest truth is that shadow liquidity is not the exception to the monetary order. It is one of the hidden ways the order achieves ordinary abundance. The public sees stable balances and assumes money is there. Institutions see asset inventories and assume liquidity can be borrowed. Businesses see receivables and assume time can be bridged. All of those assumptions are correct until the private corridors that transform claims into time begin to close. Then the distinction between money and financed access comes roaring back. What had looked like abundance is revealed as choreography. What had looked like possession is revealed as sequence. What had looked like private market convenience is revealed as a public problem waiting for a sovereign answer.

CLOSING DOCTRINE

Shadow liquidity is private time. It is manufactured by turning collateral into cash-like funding through short maturity, rolling contracts, and chains of reuse that borrow credibility from the apex monetary hierarchy without being the apex itself. It makes the payment state feel faster and more abundant than the supply of final settlement money would otherwise permit. Its failure mode is not usually insolvency first. It is withdrawal of passage: the refusal to roll, the widening of haircuts, the sudden demand for higher-grade collateral, the acceleration of margin calls, and the forced sale that converts liquidity stress into price collapse and then into solvency loss. The visible money users think they possess and the borrowed liquidity institutions rely on to honor that visibility are not the same thing, and modern stability depends on keeping that difference hidden in calm without being destroyed by it in stress. Shadow liquidity is disciplined in calm and contagious in panic because individual prudence becomes collective seizure when everyone seeks the same collateral at once. The state relies on shadow liquidity to keep the system fast, broad, and abundant, yet must intervene whenever that same private abundance begins collapsing into forced deleveraging. That contradiction is not a flaw at the edge of the order. It is one of the terms on which the order operates. A state that does not map, constrain, and prepare backstops for shadow liquidity will be forced into emergency triage when private corridors tighten, and the triage will be more expensive, more politically corrosive, and more sovereign-threatening than preemptive governance would have been. Shadow liquidity runs until it seizes, and when it seizes the payment state discovers how much of its ordinary completion had been financed by a promise to refinance.

CHAPTER 17
TOKEN RAILS
PROGRAMMABLE CLAIMS AND NEW CONCENTRATION RISK

The trade looked cleaner on the new rail than it ever had on the old one. The buyer's treasury desk could see the asset, the payment instruction, the compliance checks, the conditional release logic, and the settlement state all on one screen, arranged with the kind of clarity that makes complexity feel solved rather than merely rearranged. The seller liked the promise even more. No more waiting through layered confirmations from institutions that never touched the goods. No more guessing which intermediary had slowed the chain. No more watching value and title move in separate worlds and trusting that the lawyers and operations teams would eventually stitch the two together. The token would move when the condition was met. The ledger would update. The claim would settle. That was the pitch, and in calm conditions it sounded less like persuasion than like relief.

The treasurer saw efficiency. The operations lead saw fewer breaks, fewer reconciliations, fewer delayed calls from counterparties asking which version of the ledger was the real one. The regulator saw a different object entirely. The regulator saw a claim whose speed depended on a platform, whose transfer depended on identity controls, whose legal meaning depended on wrapper documents and custody arrangements, and whose apparent finality might dissolve the moment public law, insolvency procedure, or emergency authority arrived to remind the rail that code did not outrank the state. All three were looking at the same system. They were not looking at the same reality.

Then a day arrived when the platform operator pushed a rules update, one validator cluster slowed, a custody dependency tightened, and a transfer that had been described as self-executing suddenly became a matter of who controlled the code, who controlled the keys, who controlled the node permissions, whose legal wrapper governed the asset, and whose version of finality the system would honor when the clean line of logic broke under stress. The rail had not removed power. It had hidden power inside software sequence and platform governance, where it could be exercised faster than law could argue with it and more opaquely than ordinary users had been taught to expect.

This chapter enters the next chamber of the payment state by following a temptation that is now too serious to dismiss and too dangerous to romanticize. If old rails are layered, delayed, message-heavy, and crowded with intermediaries, perhaps token rails can compress the chain. Perhaps a programmable claim can carry both asset and payment logic together. Perhaps settlement can be made faster, collateral can move more visibly, and operational frictions can be reduced by writing legal and financial conditions into the rail itself. That temptation is serious because parts of it are real. Token rails can reduce reconciliation burdens, tighten operational sequence, and change how institutions manage settlement windows, collateral mobility, and conditional execution. But they do not abolish hierarchy. They relocate it. The old system distributed power across correspondents, clearinghouses, custodians, compliance screens, banks, settlement institutions, registrars, and legal forums. The token system promises to simplify that arrangement while quietly creating new choke points: platform operators, validator governance, code standards, identity attestation layers, custody dependencies, oracle dependencies, cloud concentration, permissioning authorities, legal wrappers, emergency pause rights, and the institutions that decide whether a tokenized claim counts as money, collateral, title, or merely a contractual echo of something more final elsewhere.

"Code can move sequence. It cannot abolish ranking." That proposition belongs near the front because the language around tokenization is often built on a comforting illusion. The illusion says that if claims become digital objects on a synchronized ledger, then timing problems become software problems, and software problems can be solved by better design. The deeper reality is harsher. Money is not slow because paper is old. Money is slow where hierarchy, legal priority, compliance, dispute risk, convertibility uncertainty, custody fragility, and jurisdictional conflict require institutions to pause, verify, rank, and sometimes refuse. Token rails can compress parts of that process. They cannot remove the need to decide which claim is authoritative, which ledger counts, who may update it, what happens when a smart rule conflicts with public law, whose custody is trusted, whether off-chain assets really back on-chain representations, and who has the power to halt, reverse, freeze, or override execution when fraud, error, panic, or judicial intervention appears. Programmability changes the location of judgment. It does not eliminate judgment.

Token rails become attractive because they promise a different sequence. In the older chain, asset transfer, payment instruction, compliance review, title verification, and settlement often sit in distinct institutional layers, joined by message and legal convention rather than by one synchronized operational object. In the token imagination, the claim itself can carry execution conditions. A delivery can release payment. A pledge can revalue automatically. A transfer can refuse unauthorized addresses. A coupon can distribute itself. A collateral call can trigger the moment thresholds are reached. A trade can appear to settle as one act rather than as several linked acts stretched across time and institutions. That is not fantasy. It is a genuine operational shift. The problem is that each act of compression raises the stakes of the platform that now hosts the compressed sequence. If several institutional decisions once distributed across many actors are now embedded in one rail, the rail becomes more efficient in calm and more constitutionally important in stress. This is where concentration risk begins, not as an afterthought, but as the price of elegance.

"A programmable claim is still a claim." The sentence sounds obvious, but much of the excitement around token rails depends on forgetting it. A token can represent central-bank money, a commercial-bank deposit, a fund share, a bond, warehouse inventory, a stable liability, a custody entitlement, a repo claim, a secured receivable, a carbon unit, a shipping document, or a mere promise that some off-chain institution will honor the token holder's rights later. These are not the same thing. They are ranked claims wearing a similar software costume. The interface makes them look alike because they move through similar wallet and ledger environments. The constitutional question is what stands behind each token when pressure arrives. If a tokenized deposit is only as good as the issuing bank's balance sheet and legal regime, speed has not converted it into apex money. If a tokenized bond settles faster on-chain, it does not become liquid under stress without a buyer, a funding corridor, and legal priority outside the code. If tokenized collateral moves more visibly, that does not mean it can support unlimited leverage without the old problem of reuse, substitution, and ranking returning through new channels. If a tokenized invoice is financed more quickly, that does not mean the debtor's obligation has become sovereign-grade money. It means the platform has accelerated a private claim while inheriting responsibility for what happens when the acceleration outruns legal clarity or liquidity support.

The taxonomy matters because it decides whether the rail is a settlement perimeter or a representation layer. A token can be final money on the rail only if the rail itself is recognized as the final settlement book, not merely as a mirror, wrapper, or staging area. If redemption into apex settlement remains external, the rail can be fast while remaining conditional. That conditionality is not a minor caveat. It is the difference between a rail that changes monetary architecture and a rail that changes operational convenience while leaving sovereignty and finality largely unchanged. Many token systems are strongest precisely where their marketing is least honest: they are highly effective coordination tools sitting on top of older sovereign and banking structures they cannot replace but often prefer not to name too loudly.

The first pressure scene belongs at issuance, because tokenization begins with a claim about representation. A platform advertises tokenized high-grade instruments to institutions that want intraday mobility and programmable settlement logic. The instrument is marketed as if old frictions have been dissolved. Then the first serious question arrives: where is the legal claim perfected. On the platform's ledger. In the custodian's books. In the issuer's register. In the governing law of the trust, omnibus account, or special-purpose wrapper that stands behind the tokens. Suddenly the object is no longer a technological convenience. It is a ladder of dependency. If the token holder has a direct legal claim on the underlying asset, the platform is one kind of rail. If the holder has only a contractual claim on an intermediary who promises exposure to the asset, the platform is another. If the token can move instantly but redemption remains tied to old settlement windows, the rail has accelerated transfer without fully accelerating discharge. The treasurer likes the speed anyway because speed changes treasury practice. The operations lead likes the shared state because shared state cuts errors. The regulator, if serious, does not begin with speed. The regulator begins with rank: who has the direct claim, what happens on insolvency, who controls redemptions, who can freeze transfers, and what forum decides the meaning of ownership when the software record and the legal record diverge.

This is where token rails become operationally seductive. They reduce reconciliation between ledgers because shared state appears to eliminate endless message comparison across firms. They make delivery-versus-payment logic more tightly coupled. They allow collateral to be posted, valued, and monitored with more visible sequence. They reduce some temporal waste created by traditional operating hours and fragmented books. For treasury functions, margin management, securities operations, and cross-institution coordination, those gains are real. The operations lead feels them first. Break rates fall. Exceptions narrow. Call volume declines. There are fewer late-day disputes over whose record is current. A treasury desk can optimize buffers more tightly because conditional execution is more visible. A collateral team can move faster because assets look transferable rather than trapped in layered custody. These are not cosmetic improvements. They affect staffing, operating cost, and the practical geography of financial time.

The danger begins when operational elegance is mistaken for constitutional completion. A platform can show synchronized state while still depending on off-rail custody, off-rail law, off-rail emergency authority, and off-rail institutions to decide what happens when fraud, coding error, identity challenge, jurisdiction conflict, insolvency stay, sanctions order, or liquidity shock appears. Software can shorten the path between decision and execution. It cannot make the meaning of finality independent from public order. The operations lead may celebrate the disappearance of friction. The regulator must ask which friction has merely been hidden and where it will return under pressure.

The second pressure scene belongs at the exact point where automation collides with governance. A tokenized collateral arrangement has been designed to call margin automatically when prices breach a threshold. In calm conditions this is praised as discipline. No pleading, no delay, no human hesitation. Then volatility spikes in a way the designers considered improbable but not impossible. Margin calls propagate simultaneously across the platform. Assets must be posted into the accepted collateral set immediately or positions are liquidated automatically. The old system had frictions that slowed destruction as well as completion. The new rail has fewer frictions, which means the protective mechanism can become an accelerant. A participant that might once have negotiated a brief extension now faces self-executing seizure or forced sale.

The treasurer sees a screen filling with calls that are technically valid and financially impossible to satisfy all at once. The operations lead sees the platform behaving exactly as specified and begins to fear that specification itself has become the problem. The regulator sees the oldest pattern in a new costume: a system that removed human delay in the name of efficiency has also removed one of the last discretionary barriers against synchronized self-harm. The platform operator now faces the most revealing dilemma in modern finance. To preserve credibility, the rules should run. To preserve system stability, the rules may need to pause. A rail built to remove discretion discovers that discretion was not an accident at the edge of finance. It was one of the tools by which institutions prevented elegant rules from becoming elegant cascades. The rail can be made strict, fast, and fair in code terms. It can also be made fragile in systemic terms. When both cannot be true at once, someone must decide which principle survives the day.

"Automation does not remove politics. It front-loads politics into design." That line matters because token rails redistribute conflict from the moment of execution to the moment of architecture. The old rail asks, in real time, who approves, who clears, who may reverse, who must report, who bears liability, and when a dispute is paused for review. The new rail asks those questions earlier, in code design, governance documents, permissions, validator rules, emergency keys, oracle standards, attestation procedures, fallback paths, and legal wrappers. The user sees cleaner execution and assumes cleaner legitimacy. But legitimacy has not become simpler. It has been pushed upstream into technical and legal design choices most users will never see. The same decision that once would have been made by a clerk, custodian, or judge at the time of friction is now embedded in a platform rule, a governance vote, a paused module, an administrator key, or a code standard written months earlier. The politics has not gone away. It has become less visible until the day it becomes absolute.

The third pressure scene belongs at the seam where on-rail execution meets off-rail law. A court order arrives requiring an asset freeze against a party in a commercial dispute. On the old rail, the bank or custodian would execute the freeze through familiar legal procedures. On the token rail, the asset is already moved, pledged, or embedded in a smart contract that is mid-execution. The operations team watches the contract continue toward completion because, in code terms, the conditions remain satisfied. The legal team insists the transfer must stop. The platform's governance group is pulled in to decide whether to use an emergency override. A judge believes the matter is straightforward because public law is public law. The platform operator knows it is not. If the rail honors the court order, it reveals that "immutable" was always conditional on governance. If it refuses, it risks being cut off from the legal and banking infrastructure it depends on for serious use. The platform therefore complies, then explains the compliance as exceptional. The market learns a harder truth. The rail can be programmable, but it cannot be sovereign in the face of public law. The more economically important the rail becomes, the less plausible it becomes that it will outrank courts, insolvency administrators, supervisors, or emergency public authority when they arrive with orders that disrupt software sequence.

That seam scene should be understood not as an embarrassing anomaly but as the central constitutional exposure of token finance.

"Programmable finality" is only finality within the perimeter of conditions the platform is permitted to treat as decisive. The moment a higher legal authority asserts a conflicting claim, the platform must either yield, fragment, or detach itself from the world of regulated finance. Most serious platforms will yield. They will remain connected to banks, custodians, central institutions, courts, and regulated counterparties by accepting that code can define sequence but not ultimate legal legitimacy. The sovereign consequence is straightforward. Token rails cannot be understood simply as software systems. They are legal-operational hybrids whose practical meaning depends on who gets the last word when on-rail logic and off-rail authority collide.

Token rails intensify the question of custody. In the older architecture, custody may be slow, expensive, and full of layered institutions, but the user at least knows there is a custodian. In token systems, custody can become psychologically ambiguous. A user may feel like direct possession has replaced institutional dependence because the token sits in a wallet-like environment. Yet key control is not the same as legal claim. If the underlying asset remains in a custodian or reserve account governed by traditional law, then key possession gives operational control over transfer but not necessarily insulation from the institution holding the backing. If key loss, smart-contract vulnerability, platform pause, or jurisdictional freeze can impair access, the token user has traded one dependency map for another. In some cases the new map is better. In others it is more fragile precisely because the user mistakes cryptographic control for legal independence.

The fourth pressure scene belongs there, at the seam between software possession and institutional dependence. A corporate treasurer keeps tokenized cash claims on a permissioned rail described as more flexible than ordinary deposit movement. During a stress event, the treasurer can see the tokens, can verify ledger ownership state, and can initiate transfers inside the platform. Yet redemption into conventional bank balances slows because the issuing institution imposes extraordinary controls, the platform activates risk rules, or the external settlement corridor has not expanded to match the rail's internal speed. On-screen possession remains intact. Usable liquidity outside the platform is rationed. The treasurer's team discovers that the treasury dashboard had been showing not money in the most practical sense, but a claim whose convertibility depended on institutions the token rail had not replaced. The old lesson returns in a sharper form because the interface had trained them to expect more. A visible digital balance is not the same as unconstrained liquidity. The token exists. The claim remains conditional on the architecture that stands behind it.

The fifth pressure scene belongs in the nonfinancial economy, because token rails are often sold as if they will solve problems for trade, inventory, and mid-sized enterprise cash flow. A logistics firm adopts a tokenized receivables and settlement platform because it promises faster invoice-financing cycles and tighter linkage between delivery and payment. For a while, the improvement is real. Invoices are tokenized, pledged, and financed quickly. The operations lead feels relief because fewer documents go missing in transit between systems and fewer counterparties argue over status. Then a platform rule change tightens acceptable counterparties and modifies the data feed used to verify delivery events. Some receivables that previously qualified now settle into review. Funding against them slows. The firm has not become weaker in the real economy. Goods still moved. Customers still owe payment. But the platform has changed the legibility of those receivables to the financing rail, and that change narrows time. Drivers are paid later. Fuel purchases become more cautious. Inventory expansion pauses. Managers cut back on taking marginal-but-profitable jobs because working-capital timing can no longer tolerate uncertainty at the platform layer. The firm experiences token governance as working-capital austerity. The technology did not fail. It governed. That is the point.

This is why identity and data become more central, not less, on token rails. A programmable financial object cannot reliably enforce compliance, eligibility, collateral standards, or transfer rules unless the system knows enough about participant identity and status to sort them. The rhetoric of open rails collides with the operating demands of regulated money. To keep claims legally admissible, platforms need onboarding rules, whitelists, sanction filters, transfer permissions, entity resolution, and some method of determining whether a receiving wallet belongs to a qualified participant. The more serious the asset, the more serious the identity layer becomes. The result is not liberation from control but denser control through new architecture. The platform now decides not only whether a token exists, but whether a participant is legible enough to touch it, transfer it, pledge it, or redeem it under ordinary conditions. Tokenization turns questions of identity into questions of liquidity more directly than many legacy rails ever did.

"If identity is weak, programmability becomes theater. If identity is strong, programmability becomes power." This is a central tension. A weak identity layer invites fraud and legal uncertainty. A strong identity layer allows the platform to enforce rules with extraordinary granularity. It can separate retail from institutional users, domestic from foreign, permitted sectors from restricted sectors, compliant from pending, high-grade collateral from merely visible collateral. It can prevent certain transfers from happening at all. It can embed policy into the rail. That may be desirable in some contexts. It may also create new forms of strategic exclusion, new dependencies on identity providers and attestation services, and new political battles over who governs access to rails that increasingly host financial life. Once identity and money are fused in the same programmable perimeter, exclusion becomes real-time. A bank account closure once required procedural drag. A platform-level exclusion can render a participant operationally inert in moments.

The sixth pressure scene belongs there. A small commodities intermediary operating legally but in a sector the platform begins to classify as higher review risk discovers that its wallets remain visible yet functionally constrained. Transfers to certain counterparties no longer complete automatically. Pledges into preferred collateral pools move into review. Redemption windows lengthen. Nothing has been criminalized. No public decree announces a new policy. The platform has simply revised risk logic and identity thresholds. The intermediary experiences this as an unexplained narrowing of working-capital freedom. Its counterparties interpret delays as weakness. Financing becomes more expensive because timing uncertainty now attaches to the firm itself. This is not old-fashioned exclusion through formal legal prohibition. It is exclusion through degraded legibility. The rail has decided that the firm can still exist but not move with ordinary dignity.

Concentration risk in token rails is not only market share. It is architecture. A system can have many visible nodes and still be concentrated in the places that matter: code maintenance, emergency authority, legal wrapper, cloud hosting, data feeds, issuance permissions, conversion pathways, and recognized settlement into the rest of the monetary system. A platform can claim distribution and still rely on a narrow set of validators, a narrow set of smart-contract libraries, a narrow set of key-management systems, a narrow set of custody institutions, and a narrow set of governance actors who can patch, pause, or redirect the rail. A sovereign reader should care less about whether a rail calls itself distributed than about whether it has diversified failure points, transparent override procedures, legal clarity, and credible fallback paths outside a single vendor or governance circle.

The seventh pressure scene belongs in the cloud, because token rails often inherit digital concentration faster than their promoters admit. A permissioned settlement platform is marketed as resilient because it runs across multiple institutional participants. Then a cloud-region outage, a key-management failure, or a data-feed synchronization error stalls updates across a meaningful portion of the network. The ledger is not corrupted beyond repair. It is simply not available in the timing assumed by users. That is enough. A collateral transfer misses the margin window. A tokenized cash leg lags the asset leg. A payment that looked atomic becomes a timing mismatch. A treasury desk that had optimized buffers to the minute must suddenly find conventional liquidity. An operations team that had reduced exception staffing must improvise manual fallback procedures it has barely rehearsed. A supervisor watching the event realizes the rail was not merely a technical experiment. It had become a live settlement dependency. Participants discover that real-time had been dependent on infrastructure concentration they did not think of as monetary because it wore the clothing of technology rather than finance. Cloud dependency becomes monetary dependency by another name.

Token rails invite another illusion: that programmability can solve the old dispute between liquidity and finality by making money conditional in cleaner ways. Escrow logic, conditional release, and automated compliance can reduce certain ambiguities. But the old conflict returns as soon as the world becomes adversarial rather than routine. Who decides whether the data feed was wrong. Who decides whether a contract behaved as intended or merely as written. Who decides whether an emergency override was legitimate or abusive. Who decides whether token holders rank directly against the issuer or only through an intermediary wrapper. None of these are code-only questions. They are legal and constitutional questions whose answers determine whether a programmable rail becomes a public utility, a private chokepoint, or a hybrid that inherits the burdens of both. The faster and cleaner the rail appears, the more violent the revelation becomes when users discover that the old questions were never deleted, only hidden inside design documents and governance clauses.

The official defense deserves respect. Token rails can reduce waste. They can shorten settlement intervals. They can make collateral mobility more legible. They can reduce reconciliation burdens and open new ways of coordinating trade finance, securities operations, and complex cash management. Under the right design, they can lower operational risk in places where the old system relies on fragmented books and delayed message alignment. All of that is real. The critique is equally structural. The same rails can concentrate power inside code governance, identity control, cloud dependence, issuer dependence, and legal wrappers that users do not understand until pressure arrives. They can accelerate good sequence and bad sequence alike. They can convert platform rule changes into economy-wide timing shocks. They can make money look more direct while increasing dependence on a smaller number of institutions whose failure or discretion becomes systemically meaningful.

The state's role in this chapter is not to decide whether tokenization is fashionable. It is to determine where token rails belong in the hierarchy of claims and what happens when their logic collides with public order. Are tokenized deposits merely another form of deposit representation. Can they be supervised and backstopped within the banking perimeter. Are tokenized collateral movements legally perfected in ways that survive insolvency. Can emergency override powers be exercised without destroying trust in the platform. How are cloud, validator, and data dependencies mapped. Which participants are allowed direct access. Which identity systems govern legibility. Which legal jurisdictions control the rail when operations, issuers, validators, and users span borders. How are ordinary commercial users protected when platform-level rule changes alter financing rhythms they never consented to as macro-level governance. A token system cannot answer these questions through code alone. A sovereign that pretends otherwise is outsourcing constitutional design to platform engineering.

The political contradiction is sharp. The state wants what token rails promise. It wants faster settlement, clearer auditability, more precise compliance, more mobile collateral, and a payment architecture modern enough to preserve competitiveness and strategic relevance. Yet the state must also fear what token rails concentrate. If too much payment, collateral, and deposit representation migrate onto a narrow set of platforms, standards, or issuers, the state may discover that it has traded slow institutional fragmentation for fast institutional concentration. The old system dispersed friction across many layers. The new one can disperse less and fail harder.

The contradiction is even harsher when stated plainly. Token rails promise private speed. If they succeed, they become systemic. If they become systemic, they cannot be left fully private when continuity is threatened. The result is familiar in structure even if new in form: private actors innovate the speed layer, the public sector inherits the failure layer. A state that wants the benefits of programmable claims without public responsibility for their collapse is dreaming. A state that assumes it can absorb the collapse without shaping the architecture in advance is derelict. Token rails force the same uncomfortable recognition as shadow liquidity. Faster private abundance tends to become public obligation the moment continuity is threatened.

The contradiction should be pushed further because this rail is not merely another payment technology. It is an attempt to relocate discretion into design and then sell the relocation as neutrality. In calm periods, that strategy works. Treasurers see efficiency, operations teams see cleanliness, platforms see fee growth, and policymakers see innovation. In stress, the camouflage burns off. Someone must decide whether a paused rail counts as failure, whether a freeze is lawful, whether a rollback is permissible, whether a validator set can be changed, whether an issuer can suspend redemption, whether a governance vote can alter the rights of participants mid-crisis, and whether a public authority can compel changes to a rail advertised as self-executing. The more important the rail becomes, the more certain it is that these decisions will not remain private forever.

The chapter closes by returning to the architecture already built in this Part. Deposits taught that private money lives under public rule. Clearinghouses taught that finality belongs to governed sequence. Cross-border gatekeepers taught that access is licensed passage. Retail rails taught that the interface hides the state. Shadow liquidity taught that private time finances ordinary abundance until refinancing fails. Token rails gather these lessons and compress them into new objects. A tokenized claim can look direct while still depending on issuer balance sheets, custody law, identity controls, cloud infrastructure, validator governance, and state-defined convertibility. Its novelty is operational. Its hierarchy is ancient. The question is not whether token rails are new. They are. The question is whether sovereigns and system architects will mistake the new wrapper for an escape from the old truths. They should not. The old truths will still decide who gets paid, who can move collateral, whose claim counts, who is legible enough to participate, and who has the authority to stop the machine when it runs too cleanly toward the wrong conclusion.

CLOSING DOCTRINE

Token rails do not abolish hierarchy. They relocate it into code governance, identity architecture, custody design, cloud concentration, validator control, oracle dependence, and the legal wrappers that determine whether a programmable claim is money, collateral, title, or merely a contract wearing faster software. A programmable claim remains a ranked claim, and faster sequence does not remove the need to decide who may issue, who may transfer, who may halt, whose data feed counts, whose validator set rules, whose legal forum governs, and what stands behind convertibility when pressure arrives. Token rails can reduce reconciliation, tighten conditional execution, and make certain funding and settlement processes more legible, but they can also accelerate liquidation, deepen dependence on narrow platforms, and fuse identity with liquidity in ways that intensify strategic exclusion and platform-level austerity for ordinary commercial users. The state wants the efficiency, visibility, and speed these rails promise, yet it will be forced back into the picture whenever private platform abundance begins to threaten continuity, legal priority, or public trust. The private sector may write the first version of the rail, but if the rail matters, the state inherits the constitutional burden. Tokenization changes the location of power more than the existence of power, and any sovereign that mistakes programmability for neutrality will discover too late that the new concentration risk was the old hierarchy rewritten in software.

PART FOUR
CRISIS IS GOVERNANCE
HOW PANIC REVEALS THE TRUE HIERARCHY OF MONEY

PART IV – CRISIS IS GOVERNANCE

The first hour of panic is always quieter than the later story. Phones light up before streets do. Funding desks stop joking. Treasury teams stop optimizing and start counting. A risk officer who has spent years insisting the institution is liquid discovers that liquidity is not a feeling and not a ratio. It is a set of permissions granted by other institutions in real time, and permission is the first resource to vanish when everyone wants the same thing at once. A depositor does not arrive thinking about architecture. A depositor arrives thinking about rent, payroll, a mortgage payment, a child's tuition, a weekend that must not be interrupted by humiliation. A corporate treasurer does not arrive thinking about theory. A treasurer arrives thinking about whether vendors will ship tomorrow if the payment that is "in process" becomes "under review." The system does not announce that it is entering crisis. It simply starts asking for proof in places where it used to accept routine.

In the first hour, panic behaves like a minor administrative shift. It hides in small frictions that are easy to misread. A counterparty asks for a little more collateral. A settlement window that normally clears without attention now insists on earlier cutoff. A transfer that would have posted instantly sits in pending for thirty minutes with a sterile note about verification. A funding roll that never required a call now requires a call. A junior operations lead notices an unusual number of exceptions and tells herself the queue will clear by afternoon. These are not yet disasters. They are the first signals that the hierarchy has begun to reappear, because crisis is not initially the absence of money. Crisis is the sudden scarcity of trusted time.

"In a panic, time is the first asset that disappears."

That sentence sounds like metaphor until it is read as a physical description of how crises actually unfold. Crisis begins as a compression of deadlines. Collateral that could be posted tomorrow must be posted by noon. Funding that could be rolled weekly must be rolled overnight. Transfers that were accepted on trust now require documentation. Settlement that was treated as ordinary becomes queued behind special review. The speed of the system changes first, and speed is not cosmetic. Speed is solvency when obligations mature faster than assets can be sold without loss. When time compresses, hierarchy becomes visible because only some actors can buy time cheaply. Others must sell assets to obtain it, and forced selling is how funding stress becomes price collapse, and price collapse is how a rumor becomes a balance-sheet event.

Part IV is where the book stops letting the reader imagine that money is a stable object governed by policy instruments in a clean, continuous world. This Part treats crisis as the governing act of the monetary state, because crisis is the moment the system reveals what it truly is: a hierarchy of ranked claims defended by backstops, enforced by legal priority, and stabilized through triage. The quiet truth is that most monetary orders are not designed in peace. They are designed in response. They become constitutional when fear arrives and forces a decision about who will be saved by speed, who will be sacrificed to delay, and which promises will be treated as money when money is scarce.

It is tempting to imagine crisis as interruption, an external shock to an otherwise functioning machine. The more accurate frame is harsher. Crisis is not a break from governance. Crisis is governance revealed in its pure form, stripped of the politeness that routine allows. In routine, everyone can pretend equivalence holds. Deposits feel the same. Collateral feels fungible. Settlement feels automatic. Loss allocation can remain a paragraph in a contract nobody reads. In crisis, equivalence breaks. Some deposits become "good" deposits because they sit in institutions with stronger backstops or faster access to settlement. Some collateral becomes "real" collateral because it can be pledged into the corridors that still move. Some payments become final because they reach the apex ledger before the doors tighten. Others become pending, then disputed, then irrelevant.

Crisis therefore begins as a reclassification. Claims that had been treated as interchangeable are re-ranked in practice. Funding instruments that had been treated as routine are suddenly treated as conditional. Counterparties that had been treated as peers are suddenly treated as exposures. Legal language that had been background becomes foreground because law is where priority lives, and priority is what everyone fights about when value is insufficient to satisfy all promises. The system is forced to discover what it really believes, because crisis is the moment when belief must be translated into sequence. It is not enough to say claims are safe. The system must move them safely through congested corridors, and in congested corridors, someone is always moved first.

The first day has a recognizable choreography, and this Part begins by naming it because naming it is itself a form of sovereign clarity. There is a point when treasury stops trying to price funding and starts trying to obtain it at any price. There is a point when risk stops calibrating models and starts identifying which counterparties can destroy the institution in hours rather than in quarters. There is a point when the operations team stops treating exceptions as annoying and starts treating exceptions as signals that the pipe itself is narrowing. There is a point when legal counsel stops discussing hypothetical stays and starts drafting real ones. There is a point when communications teams stop polishing language and start negotiating how to speak without creating a run. Crisis governance is not only about money. It is about the sequence of recognition: who admits stress first, who denies it longest, and which denial becomes fatal because it delays action until action must be violent.

A sovereign reader should notice something uncomfortable here. The system often performs calm long after calm has ended because performance itself is a tool. If the public sees fear, fear multiplies. If counterparties sense weakness, they tighten. If markets smell forced selling, they front-run it. This is why crisis governance is partly theatrical. Yet the theater is not mere manipulation. It is a defensive instrument used to buy time, and time is what crisis steals first. The state must therefore perform stability while manufacturing stability, and manufacturing stability requires interventions that can never be fully revealed in real time without destroying the very confidence they are intended to preserve. That paradox is not a moral flaw. It is the operating condition of crisis governance.

This Part therefore begins with a sentence that changes how every future crisis looks. Crisis is not a failure of policy to achieve a target. Crisis is the moment when the hierarchy of claims becomes the operating interface of the economy. In calm, hierarchy is infrastructure. In panic, hierarchy is public life. The state does not merely manage interest rates and publish reassurance. The state decides which claims are upgraded into money and which claims are left to behave like lawsuits.

Runs and freezes are the first chamber of that decision. A run is not merely people withdrawing cash. A run is the collective decision to upgrade from a lower-grade claim to a higher-grade claim because the hierarchy has become visible. A freeze is the system's answer when it cannot honor all upgrades at once without collapsing. Both are acts of ranking. Both force institutions and states to decide whether they will preserve legitimacy by providing conversion, or preserve solvency by denying it, or attempt the most politically dangerous maneuver of all: providing conversion for the few while insisting nothing has changed for the many. A run tests whether the system's promises are genuinely convertible. A freeze tests whether the system can ration convertibility without destroying consent.

The difference between a contained event and a contagious event is rarely the magnitude of loss at the start. It is the speed with which the system can reassure itself, in practice, that obligations will still reach finality. A solvent institution can be killed by sequence if it cannot meet today's calls. A healthy market can seize if participants doubt whether netting will still hold through the close. A payment system can become politically explosive if households begin seeing that "pending" is not a technical note but a rationing device. Crisis spreads when people stop believing the system can end arguments on schedule.

Lender of last resort is the next chamber because it is the institutional device that turns an abstract sovereign promise into operational time. A lender of last resort is not a comforting phrase. It is constitutional power. It does not only supply liquidity. It decides what counts as eligible collateral, which institutions qualify as solvent enough to deserve rescue, what penalties will be imposed for accessing emergency support, and how visible the rescue will be to the public whose consent must be preserved. Liquidity support is never neutral, because liquidity is never neutral in a hierarchy. It reaches some balance sheets first, through some corridors, at some prices, with some stigma, under some conditions. The order of rescue becomes the order of survival. The state's capacity is measured not by how loudly it can declare stability, but by how quickly it can deliver final settlement to the places where delay would become contagion.

Crisis also reveals the most underappreciated political technology in modern finance: collateral. In routine, collateral looks like credit hygiene. In crisis, collateral is the language the system uses to decide who gets time. Haircuts widen. Eligible sets narrow. Substitution requests become relentless. Funding maturities shorten. The same asset that supported a week of funding now supports a day, then an hour, then nothing. Institutions that relied on the market's habit of refinancing discover that habit is not a right. They begin selling what they can, not what they should. That is how collateral breakdown becomes fire sales. Fire sales are not only price movements. They are forced transfers of wealth and control, because the actors with time can buy assets from the actors without time. The system says it is discovering prices. In reality, it is redistributing survival capacity through sequence.

The most important thing to understand about collateral in crisis is that it turns the abstract question of trust into a concrete question of eligibility. The system does not ask whether you are honest. It asks whether you can deliver acceptable objects right now. Those with the right objects remain inside the corridor. Those without must sell into the corridor to obtain them, and selling into the corridor is exactly how the corridor becomes crowded and violent. This is why crises accelerate. The scramble for eligible collateral creates a scramble for funding. The scramble for funding creates forced sales. Forced sales create price declines. Price declines expand haircuts. Expanded haircuts demand more collateral. The loop is not moral. It is mechanical. Crisis governance exists to break the loop before it consumes the settlement core.

Resolution authority sits in the middle of this Part for a reason. Resolution is the state admitting that rescue is not the only tool. It is also admitting that when failure is unavoidable, the system must still be governed. Someone must assign losses. Someone must decide whether a firm can be wound down without detonating payment, clearing, or deposit confidence. Someone must decide which creditors are subordinated, which contracts are stayed, which counterparties are protected, which executives are removed, and which liabilities are converted into equity-like pain. Resolution is crisis governance written in legal procedure. It is how the state tries to preserve the continuity of money and payments while allowing some balance sheets to die. Done well, it prevents panic from becoming permanent subsidy. Done poorly, it teaches the market that risk will always be socialized or that law cannot be trusted to rank claims predictably under stress. Either lesson changes future behavior, because crisis memory is one of the few forms of education markets never forget.

"When panic arrives, the state discovers which promises it cannot afford to treat as ordinary."

This sentence frames the unavoidable contradiction at the core of modern monetary legitimacy. The system relies on private promise-making to achieve scale. It relies on banks, dealers, money-like funds, payment platforms, and shadow liquidity channels to make everyday life fast and abundant. Yet when those private promises begin to collapse into forced deleveraging, the same state is summoned to rescue continuity. Refuse rescue and the payment state's interface fractures in public. Provide rescue and the state becomes the insurer of private risk-taking. Attempt a middle path and the state must perform triage with surgical precision: enough support to prevent contagious collapse, enough loss allocation to preserve discipline, enough clarity to preserve legitimacy, enough ambiguity to prevent immediate runs into the apex claim. Crisis makes that balancing act unavoidable because the market's own discipline tool is withdrawal, and withdrawal is contagious.

The Part's governing thesis can now be stated without softness. Crisis is the moment when the state decides whether the hierarchy remains governable. That decision is made through time allocation. Who is allowed to settle today. Who is delayed until tomorrow. Who is told to accept a substitute instrument. Who is granted emergency liquidity against collateral that would not be accepted in calm. Who is allowed to roll funding and who is forced to unwind. Who is permitted to borrow at the sovereign perimeter and who is left to the market's discipline. Every one of those choices allocates survival. Every one of those choices becomes political once households, employment, and supply chains begin depending on them.

This is why crisis cannot be treated as a technical episode for specialists. When payment and funding systems tighten, businesses shorten terms, households hoard liquidity, and consumption becomes defensive. The state then faces a second crisis layered on the first: not only a crisis of financial continuity, but a crisis of social consent. People will accept triage only if they believe it is governed rather than predatory, and they will judge governance not by doctrine but by whether wages clear, whether bills can be paid, whether small merchants can fund payroll, whether ordinary completion is preserved for most people most of the time. Crisis governance therefore lives in two places at once. It lives in wholesale pipes, and it lives in household dignity.

Part IV ends with global backstops rather than treating them as an international footnote because crisis rarely stays domestic. Even an event rooted in one jurisdiction travels through funding markets, correspondent corridors, foreign exchange hedges, trade finance, and the global appetite for the highest-grade settlement asset. Some states can issue the claim the world upgrades into. Most cannot. The gap between those categories becomes brutally visible in crisis, because a country can have legal authority at home and still face an external shortage of settlement claims it cannot manufacture. Global backstops exist because the world economy cannot function if every crisis forces states to defend their currencies alone against global liquidity preference. Those backstops are not gifts. They are conditional rescue. They are leverage. They are the international version of lender of last resort: a mechanism that preserves continuity while quietly determining which states must accept conditions to obtain time.

Part IV therefore takes a position that serious officials often hesitate to say aloud. Crisis management is not an emergency add-on to a monetary system. It is the proof of the system's constitution. The order that claims to be market-based reveals itself as governance-based the moment markets demand settlement in the highest-grade claim. The order that claims to be rules-based reveals which rules matter when discretion must decide who is saved by speed. The order that claims to be sovereign reveals how dependent sovereignty is on access to external liquidity corridors, trusted collateral, and global backstops when the public upgrades away from domestic promises.

The Part's deeper structure is hidden but relentless. Runs reveal the hierarchy. Lender of last resort reveals who can manufacture time. Collateral breakdown reveals the private machinery that creates fragility. Resolution reveals how losses are reassigned without destroying the payment state. Global backstops reveal that crisis is not only domestic governance but also international ranking. Each chapter is a different chamber of the same truth: the monetary state is most real when it is forced to choose.

The reader should be prepared for an unsettling recognition as this Part opens. In normal times, people argue about money as if it were a policy variable, a confidence trick, or a neutral measure. In crisis, money becomes a matter of doors: doors to settlement, doors to collateral eligibility, doors to emergency liquidity, doors to legal stays, doors to insured claims, doors to external lines. The system's architecture is the map of those doors. Crisis is the moment the doors become the economy.

This Part begins at the point where fear stops being psychology and becomes sequence, and sequence becomes law.

CHAPTER 18
RUNS AND FREEZES
THE OLD FEAR IN MODERN FORM

The line outside the branch is never the first line. The first line forms on screens. It forms when depositors move balances from one institution to another in the same unit, with no intention of leaving the currency at all. It forms when corporate treasurers instruct sweeps into the safest institution they can name, because payroll is due and the week cannot tolerate a delay disguised as a technicality. It forms when a small business owner prepays suppliers, not because prepayment is efficient, but because prepayment is closure. It forms when a platform changes payout timing by a few hours and thousands of users read that tiny shift not as operations but as omen. By the time bodies appear at doors, the run has already moved through faster pipes, and the institutions that will survive have already been separated from those that will not by the one thing that matters most in a panic: whether they can still turn promises into timely discharge.

A panic, in its oldest meaning, is a demand for cash. In modern form that demand is rarely for paper. It is for finality, for immediate usability, for the claim that cannot be questioned in the next hour. Cash now includes the apex settlement claim used inside the core. It includes immediate access to insured-like deposits that are believed to be paid even if the institution fails. It includes the ability to move balances out of danger before a freeze turns movement into permission. The fear has not changed. The object of fear has become more abstract because the system's surface has become more abstract. The public still wants the same thing it has always wanted in a run: a claim that ends arguments before tomorrow's obligations arrive.

Runs and freezes are the first chamber of crisis governance because they are the simplest form of hierarchy becoming visible. In calm periods, deposits look interchangeable. You are told your balance is money, and in ordinary life it behaves like money. You pay bills. You receive wages. Your card works. Your transfer arrives. Your employer's payroll file clears before breakfast. Your rent leaves on schedule. Your utility debit posts without conversation. That smoothness is not proof of equivalence. It is the product of a system that spends enormous effort making equivalence feel natural. In stress, that effort collapses into triage. People stop asking whether the unit is stable and begin asking whether their specific institution will be able to honor the timing of their obligations. The run is the public turning from the unit to the issuer, from money as a general concept to my money as a claim on a particular balance sheet and a particular corridor of settlement.

A freeze is the system's reply when it cannot honor everyone's upgrade demand simultaneously without destroying itself. The freeze is rarely announced with the language that would make its meaning honest. It arrives as delays, holds, extended processing, heightened verification, reduced limits, earlier cutoffs, temporary maintenance, additional review, operational exceptions, and the administrative phrase that says nothing while doing everything: temporary measures. The freeze is the moment the system admits, by action rather than by speech, that convertibility is scarce. In theory, money ends arguments. In a freeze, the argument is paused because the system cannot afford to end all arguments at once.

The run is not a moral event. It is not proof that the public is irrational. It is a rational response to a structure in which some claims are safer than others under stress. A depositor who can move early reduces exposure. A treasurer who upgrades early protects payroll. A fund that redeems early avoids being trapped behind gates. A merchant who routes settlement through the strongest platform is not making a philosophical statement. She is trying to preserve Monday. The collective effect is destabilizing, but the individual act is prudent inside the hierarchy the system built. Instability comes from a fact the system works hard to hide in calm: deposits are not equal. They are ranked by the perceived strength of the issuing institution, by the speed and certainty of access to the settlement core, by the legal protections attached to the liability, by the credibility of official rescue, and by the market's belief about whether rescue will arrive in time. A run is that ranking becoming behavior.

The most important correction to popular intuition is that runs are often about time more than about loss. People do not only run because they fear losing money. They run because they fear being trapped in pending while obligations mature. A guarantee that pays eventually can be perfectly sincere and still fail to stop a run, because eventually does not pay rent tomorrow and it does not meet payroll Friday afternoon. A firm can believe it will recover in a legal sense and still upgrade immediately because its survival is paced by settlement timing. The public speaks about safety. The system is governing a calendar. In crisis, the calendar becomes a weapon because every hour of uncertainty redistributes power toward whoever already holds the highest-grade claim.

The modern run begins with silence. A risk team watches outflows that are still within ordinary noise but trending in one direction. A treasury desk notices that overnight funding is a touch more expensive, not because the institution is insolvent, but because counterparties have moved from indifference to caution. A large client calls with an awkward question about intraday limits and transfer cutoffs. The relationship manager answers calmly and tries not to sound offended. The question itself is the signal. The client is no longer treating the bank as a neutral pipe. The client is testing the bank as a potential point of failure. That test is contagious because every large actor watching the system asks the same question at roughly the same time, and the act of asking tightens the corridor even before any money moves.

In older systems, a run was slowed by physical friction. Movement took time. Withdrawal took time. Transport took time. Those frictions were miserable in ordinary life and protective in crisis. Modern payment systems have removed much of that friction. That is a triumph in daily commerce and a danger in panic. The faster the upgrade can occur, the less time authorities have to respond before the run becomes irreversible. Speed reduces daily waste. Speed also reduces crisis time. This is why the modern state cannot design crisis tools as if the run is a weekend event. The run is an intraday event, and its most decisive moments occur before a press statement can be reviewed without legal edits.

Runs also migrate. When banks become hard to run physically, the run moves to the next closest layer. Wholesale runs occur when short-term lenders refuse to roll funding. Collateral runs occur when haircuts widen and certain assets become unacceptable as time-buys. Platform runs occur when users attempt to exit token claims into bank deposits or state-backed balances. Fund runs occur when investors redeem money-like shares into bank balances. Stable-value runs occur when holders attempt to leave a promise before the promise is tested. The same panic, different corridor. The shared structure is upgrade demand. The shared constraint is that not everyone can upgrade simultaneously, because the system's apex money is scarce relative to the volume of lower-grade claims built on top of it.

The anatomy of a run is easiest to see from inside a balance sheet. The institution begins the day with a liquidity buffer calibrated to normal outflows. It holds settlement assets, highly liquid instruments, and contingent lines designed for routine. When outflows rise, the institution sells liquid assets or borrows against collateral. That is still normal. When outflows accelerate and wholesale funding tightens simultaneously, the institution meets a harsher reality: selling assets in size moves prices against it, and borrowing against collateral requires counterparties willing to lend. Those counterparties are watching the same outflows. Their willingness tightens precisely as the need increases. A run is not only the public withdrawing. It is the entire funding ecosystem coordinating against the institution in real time, not out of malice, but out of self-preservation.

There is a point in every run when the institution stops being judged by what it owns and starts being judged by how quickly it can turn ownership into settlement. That is the moment sequence defeats valuation. The institution can be solvent in a long-horizon sense and still fail because the short-horizon corridor closes. This is why crisis kills by timing before it kills by arithmetic. It is also why the state's crisis tools are tools of time. The state does not rescue because it loves balance sheets. It rescues because it fears what happens to the payment state when timing collapses publicly.

A run has a second engine once forced selling begins. Asset sales reduce balance-sheet strength, which increases perceived risk, which accelerates outflows, which forces more sales. Even if the assets are fundamentally sound, selling into a stressed market imposes losses that can become self-confirming. The public rarely sees this loop directly. It sees its consequences: tightened credit, widening spreads, nervous institutional behavior, delayed settlements, funding repricing, and the eventual weekend communiqué that tries to compress complex triage into a simple story of restored confidence. The system calls that story stabilization. The public calls it either rescue or favoritism depending on which side of the triage it experienced.

A freeze is the mirror act. It is the system refusing to allow the run to complete. It is the rationing of convertibility. There are multiple kinds of freezes, and their variety is diagnostic. A bank freeze can appear as transfer limits, delayed withdrawals, delayed availability, or unspoken discouragement of large outbound wires. A platform freeze can appear as paused redemptions, suspended transfers, narrowed eligible counterparties, or mandatory review on movements that once cleared automatically. A fund freeze can appear as gates, fees, side pockets, or delayed settlement of redemption requests. A market freeze can appear as spreads so wide that selling becomes punitive or as the refusal to quote at all. A clearing-related freeze can appear as sharply higher margin requirements and narrower eligible collateral, which forces some participants out and protects others. A state freeze can appear as emergency legal stays, bank holidays, capital controls, or the quiet instruction that certain payments will not be prioritized until further notice. Names vary. The function persists. The system denies time to some claimants to preserve time for the core.

A freeze is rarely experienced as a neutral safety measure by those frozen. It is experienced as subordination. The claimant is being told that the claim is still valid but not payable now. In a society paced by timing, not payable now is already harm. It may be necessary harm. It is still harm. This is why freezes become political quickly. They are governance performed as delay. A sophisticated state understands that the technical defensibility of a freeze does not guarantee its legitimacy. Legitimacy depends on distribution, narrative, and lived consequence. If households and small firms experience delay as humiliation, they will remember humiliation longer than they remember technical explanations.

The distribution of freezes is where the hierarchy becomes socially dangerous. The system is built to protect settlement and clearing continuity because those are the corridors through which contagion spreads fastest. That design means the core is defended first. Edge claims are easier to delay without immediate systemic collapse. Edge claims belong to households and small firms, the very actors whose consent sustains the monetary order politically. Crisis governance therefore carries an unavoidable tension. Protect the core and you preserve the machine. Delay the edge and you damage legitimacy at the point where legitimacy is judged. A state that ignores this will preserve solvency and lose consent, and consent is the long-run asset no backstop can print.

A modern run often begins with behavior that looks like ordinary prudence. Large firms concentrate cash at the safest institution. Payment processors route flows through the most reliable corridors. Platforms tighten release rules. Banks shorten credit terms to conserve liquidity. Funds sell the most liquid holdings first because those are the only holdings that can be sold without immediate stigma. None of these acts are called a run by those performing them. Each is framed as standard risk management. Yet together they produce the run's distinctive pattern: a rapid, silent reallocation of safety toward the core and away from the periphery. The periphery then experiences stress not because it was reckless, but because it was downstream of other actors' defensive reclassification. This is how a run becomes social. It is not only depositors racing for safety. It is firms, platforms, funds, and intermediaries reallocating safety in ways that make weaker institutions weaker, which forces weaker institutions to treat weaker clients more harshly. Crisis is a cascade of rationing.

The household sees this cascade late and feels it early. A salary that usually appears before dawn arrives at noon. A transfer that usually settles in minutes remains pending through the afternoon. A landlord's debit posts while the payroll credit still sits in review. A grocery purchase is declined because an available balance turned out to be conditional. None of these events need to involve ultimate loss to become politically explosive. They are enough to teach the public that money is a timing arrangement with institutions, not merely a number. Once that lesson becomes common knowledge, runs become easier in the next episode because people no longer assume pending is temporary inconvenience. They assume pending is the beginning of rationing.

The state often comforts itself by pointing to guarantees and insurance-like protections as if legal promise cancels fear. In practice, guarantees work only if the public believes they will be honored quickly enough to preserve ordinary life. Timing is the substance. A guarantee with slow payout invites runs because it confirms that people may be trapped in pending during the most dangerous period. This is why crisis tools must be designed for speed and for public legibility. A backstop that is large but slow can fail to stop a modern run because the run is not asking, will I be paid eventually. It is asking, will I be paid in time to avoid ruin.

The state's crisis choreography therefore has a grim precision. It must supply liquidity without broadcasting desperation. It must support institutions without turning rescue into a permanent subsidy. It must impose conditions without creating stigma so strong that institutions refuse to use the facility and die. It must reassure depositors without promising what cannot be delivered quickly. It must coordinate among multiple authorities whose mandates were designed for calm. It must do all of this while the run is executing digitally and the freeze is becoming visible at the household interface through delays that look small but feel personal. This is why crisis is governance. Only governance can coordinate a system in which rational actors doing rational things will otherwise stampede into the same corridor and collapse it.

The strongest counterargument insists that markets can discipline institutions without public rescue and that repeated rescues create moral hazard. This counterargument is not wrong. It is incomplete. A system that permits full discipline through collapse must also accept that collapse will reach payment, employment, and public order quickly because finance is now the timing layer of the whole economy. The state can choose discipline through collapse. It should then be honest about what it is choosing: a willingness to let the payment state fracture in public, with all the social consequences that follow. Most states are unwilling to choose that. They prefer a hybrid: discipline where possible, rescue where necessary, and a narrative that insists the rescue was exceptional even when the structure makes rescue recurrent. Runs and freezes are the moments when that narrative is tested.

There is one more truth that must be said without softness. The run is the public and the market trying not to be late. The freeze is authority deciding who must be late. In a crisis, the penalty for being late is not embarrassment. It is subordination. The system can handle loss if loss is ranked and contained. The system cannot handle generalized doubt about whether payments will complete on time. Runs and freezes are therefore the first chamber of crisis governance because they force immediate choices about convertibility, timing, and ranking. Those choices will be made either by markets through stampede or by the state through triage. The only question is whether the triage is designed, lawful, and legible enough to preserve consent.

CLOSING DOCTRINE

A run is an upgrade demand: the collective attempt to convert lower-grade claims into higher-grade claims before the corridor narrows. A freeze is rationing: the system's denial of immediacy to some claimants to preserve the settlement core for the whole. Modern runs are faster because the pipes are faster, which means crisis tools must be designed for operational speed rather than for rhetorical reassurance. The public confuses balances with access in calm because the system works to make convertibility feel natural; crisis restores the distinction violently, and that restoration is where legitimacy is won or lost. Guarantees stabilize only when they are believed to deliver usable timing, not merely eventual legal recovery. Delay is a form of subordination, and subordination becomes political the moment households and small firms experience pending as a governing condition rather than as a technical note. A state that cannot manage upgrade demand without humiliating the public will face a crisis of consent alongside a crisis of liquidity, and once consent fractures the hierarchy becomes harder to govern in the next panic, not easier.

CHAPTER 19
LENDER OF LAST RESORT
RESCUE AS CONSTITUTIONAL POWER

The call never arrives as philosophy. It arrives as a request for time. A treasury desk that spent the previous week funding itself without ceremony now asks whether the window is open, what collateral will be accepted, how long funds can remain outstanding, whether usage will be visible, whether usage will be interpreted as weakness, and whether taking the money will save the institution long enough for private funding to return or merely announce to the market that private funding has already judged the institution and found it wanting. The caller speaks in operational language because operational language is the last language left when panic begins. Yet the fear underneath is older than the institution itself. Will the corridor stay open long enough to meet today's obligations. Will the firm reach tomorrow as an institution or only as a legal problem.

On the other side of the line, officials do not ask whether the institution deserves sympathy. They ask whether its failure would propagate through payments, settlement, funding chains, payroll chains, merchant acquiring, corporate liquidity, collateral valuation, and confidence before law and procedure could catch up. They ask whether the firm is illiquid or merely unloved, whether the collateral is usable or merely visible, whether the stress is idiosyncratic or systemic, whether rescue will stop contagion or invite it, and whether the public can be told that this is liquidity support rather than quiet triage. By the time the first facility opens, doctrine has already moved from theory into sequence. The state is no longer discussing money. It is deciding who receives time in a world where time has become the rarest claim.

A lender of last resort is often described as a safety valve, a technical instrument, or a central banking function that appears only when private markets malfunction. That language is too mild for the work being done. The lender of last resort is a constitutional power of the monetary order because it decides which institutions can exchange temporarily suspect claims for immediately usable settlement capacity when ordinary funding corridors have begun to close. It is not merely a faucet of emergency funds. It is a ranking device. It decides what counts as eligible collateral, which institutions qualify as sufficiently important or sufficiently solvent, what penalty will be charged, what stigma will attach, what secrecy or publicity will surround access, what maturity will be offered, how renewals will be handled, and how far the state is willing to extend its own balance sheet so that the private hierarchy of money does not collapse into liquidation. The facility does not rescue everyone. It reveals whom the state cannot afford to let run out of time.

"In panic, the state lends not only money, but sequence."

This is the chapter's threshold truth. Emergency lending is usually described as liquidity, yet liquidity in crisis is never merely volume. It is timing plus credibility. Funds that arrive tomorrow may not stop a run today. A collateral schedule that is legally sound but operationally slow can fail in the face of intraday outflows. A facility that exists in law but cannot be accessed without public humiliation may be unusable even when technically open. A window that accepts the wrong collateral may preserve appearances while missing the actual point of pressure. The lender of last resort governs the tempo at which the system can continue behaving as if ordinary completion remains ordinary. If rescue comes too late, the institution may already be subordinated by markets before the state speaks. If rescue comes too broadly, the market may learn that private risk carries an embedded public put. This is why the facility is constitutional power rather than administrative routine. It protects convertibility by deciding when private claims will be upgraded into public time.

The historical argument for such power began with a recognition that remains modern in every essential respect. Private institutions issue liabilities that behave like money in calm because the public believes those liabilities are convertible into a more final claim when needed. The problem appears when too many holders attempt conversion together. No private institution can meet universal upgrade demand on its own, because its liabilities exceed the immediately liquid assets it can deploy without destroying itself. This is not scandal. It is architecture. Banking, dealer finance, market-making, and money-like funds all work by maturity mismatch and by confidence that not everyone will demand the top claim simultaneously. The lender of last resort arose because the state discovered that private discipline alone could not coordinate this collective-action problem. If everyone runs to the exit at once, even a solvent institution can fail by sequence. An authority with the power to create or mobilize the apex settlement claim is therefore needed to prevent convertibility stress from turning into generalized collapse.

The classic formula survives because it compresses rescue and discipline into one sentence: lend freely, against good collateral, at a penalty rate. Its elegance is also its concealment. Every word hides a governance question. Freely for whom. Good according to which mark, under what law, and with what haircut. Penalty high enough to deter casual dependence or low enough to prevent stigma from becoming fatal. In a real panic, the state must decide under uncertainty whether collateral that looked unquestionably good yesterday remains good today, whether an institution that is solvent can survive market suspicion long enough to prove solvency, and whether a penalty designed to preserve discipline will instead advertise weakness and intensify the run. The facility's doctrinal simplicity conceals operational discretion. Crisis governance is the disciplined use of discretion without admitting it is discretion.

The real mechanism begins where ordinary funding ends. A bank, dealer, or systemically important intermediary loses access to private funding at tolerable terms. Outflows rise. Counterparties ask for more collateral, shorter maturities, stronger documentation, earlier settlement, larger buffers, and less optimism. Assets that could normally be financed become difficult to pledge without punitive haircuts. The institution can still own good assets in the long run and still be unable to bridge the next six hours. That is the emergency lender's domain. The state offers settlement-capable funds against collateral when the market will not. In doing so, it interrupts the loop in which rising outflows force asset sales, asset sales depress prices, depressed prices widen haircuts, and wider haircuts produce more outflows. The facility is not a gesture of confidence. It is an attempt to halt a specific sequence before sequence becomes insolvency.

This can be said another way because it must be. The lender of last resort is not primarily in the business of making weak institutions feel better. It is in the business of keeping timing failure from spreading through the payment state. A payroll bank that fails today can trigger real-economy fear tomorrow. A dealer that cannot fund inventory by noon can impair price formation by the close. A settlement intermediary that cannot obtain intraday liquidity can turn ordinary payment delay into public panic within hours. Emergency lending exists because the state cannot allow every timing failure to be tested through liquidation. It must decide when liquidation is discipline and when liquidation is a public event whose consequences exceed the firm.

Here the chapter must insist on a distinction that becomes decisive in panic. Liquidity is not solvency. Solvency is a balance-sheet claim about assets exceeding liabilities over time. Liquidity is the ability to meet obligations as they mature. Crisis kills by liquidity first because liquidity is a timing constraint that can destroy a solvent institution before valuation has a chance to speak. This is why lender of last resort is not a charity and not merely a macro tool. It is an anti-sequence-collapse tool. It keeps liquidity failure from becoming solvency failure by denying the market the ability to force immediate liquidation at the worst possible time.

The first pressure scene belongs at the window or its functional equivalent, because that is where doctrine collides with stigma. A bank can technically borrow, yet hesitate because the market may interpret borrowing as evidence that private funding has already dried up. The institution delays using the facility designed to keep it alive. Treasury officers tell themselves they can bridge one more day through asset sales, client calls, careful language, and borrowed calm. Supervisors quietly urge earlier usage because they can see the outflows and they know the next day's funding desk will be less friendly. Senior management fears that early usage will be inferred, priced, and amplified. This hesitation is not irrational. Emergency facilities are often designed to be penal and exceptional, which means they carry social meaning inside markets. The institution needs time, but the act of asking for time may cost it more time elsewhere. A rescue instrument that stigmatizes rescue too heavily can fail not because it lacks money, but because it cannot be used early enough to matter.

This tension reveals why lender-of-last-resort design is never merely financial. It is communicative. The state must decide whether emergency borrowing will be made unattractive enough to preserve discipline or ordinary enough to be used before collapse. Too much stigma and firms arrive late, making rescue larger, uglier, and more politically corrosive. Too little stigma and firms incorporate public liquidity into routine strategy, thinning private buffers and externalizing fragility. Between those poles lies the most delicate design requirement of all: the facility must be respectable enough to be used and unattractive enough not to become habit. The irony is that a facility can be perfectly designed on paper and still fail if the market's social interpretation makes its use synonymous with terminal weakness. Panic is not only economic. It is reputational and reflexive.

The decision-making room should be named because it is where the constitutional act occurs. A supervisor sits with outflow data, watching the tempo of withdrawals and the tempo of collateral mobilization. A payments operator watches settlement queues and sees whether the institution is beginning to miss daylight cutoffs. A markets team watches whether spreads are widening as counterparties price the rumor of stress. Legal staff watch what can be done without inviting immediate challenge. A communications group works on sentences intended to sound calm enough to reassure and vague enough not to trigger the next question. An official watches the calendar of public events and understands that a visible failure today will be interpreted as incompetence tomorrow. In that room, liquidity means a set of synchronized acts that must occur before the close. It means collateral must be valued, accepted, and advanced against. It means the institution must be able to settle its obligations in the core asset. It means the market must be prevented from concluding that this institution is the one that cannot be trusted to make it to tomorrow. The room is not debating theory. It is selecting which sequences will be permitted to continue.

"The window must be open before the market believes it is needed."

This captures the sequencing problem. Emergency facilities stabilize best when their existence is credible in advance, their access rules are understood, their collateral schedule is operationally workable, and activation does not itself announce institutional disgrace. If officials wait for public evidence of collapse before acting, they are already late. If they open too early or too broadly, they may be accused of insuring speculation or socializing private risk. The lender of last resort therefore works best when it is structurally prepared and politically deniable: visible enough to reassure, quiet enough not to become the headline that triggers the next wave of fear. That paradox is not a flaw. It is part of the instrument.

The second pressure scene belongs inside the collateral schedule. In calm periods, collateral frameworks look technical. In crisis, they become public law in operational form. An institution brings assets. The question is not whether the institution believes the assets are sound. The question is whether the state will lend against them, at what valuation, with what haircut, with what concentration limits, with what margining, and under what continuing conditions. A narrower schedule preserves the purity of the public balance sheet and draws a bright line around public support. A wider schedule can stop a broader collapse because crises are often driven not by worthless assets but by temporarily unfundable ones. The moment the public lender widens the schedule, however, it does more than inject liquidity. It changes the hierarchy of money. Claims that markets had begun to reject are lifted back into motion by sovereign permission. This is not merely rescue. It is temporary re-legislation of what counts as fundable value.

The state therefore confronts a problem that cannot be solved by formulas alone. If it lends only against assets the market already trusts, its intervention may be too narrow to matter. If it lends against assets the market increasingly distrusts, it may preserve continuity while absorbing future losses and teaching the market that borderline assets may eventually be elevated by public support. The crucial distinction is rarely good versus bad in the abstract. It is illiquid due to panic versus impaired due to reality. In real time, that distinction is hard. Officials are forced to decide under uncertainty, because waiting for certainty is itself a decision to permit sequence collapse.

The lender of last resort is therefore judgment under fire, wrapped in collateral language and executed at settlement speed.

The third pressure scene belongs beyond traditional banks, because modern panics travel through dealer balance sheets, money-like funds, key funding markets, and systemically important nonbanks. If a dealer cannot finance inventory, market-making collapses and core prices become unreliable. If a money-like fund cannot honor redemptions without asset fire sales, the run migrates into the corporate cash management layer. If payment intermediaries cannot fund intraday exposures, retail normality fractures. The lender of last resort then extends beyond one window. It becomes a family of facilities and operations aimed at holding together the timing layer of the economy. This widening is not optional. It is the state admitting that the monetary hierarchy is larger than the formal banking perimeter it might prefer to police.

Widening is also perilous. The more the state extends emergency support beyond traditional banks, the more it risks becoming the ultimate liquidity provider to private structures that were designed to behave like money without being governed like money. Yet the state cannot ignore those structures once they become the time engine of daily commerce. This is the recurring contradiction of modern monetary governance. Private innovation manufactures speed and abundance. The state inherits the failure mode when speed becomes fragility. A serious state cannot pretend it will never support nonbank corridors if those corridors have become essential to settlement, payments, or corporate liquidity. It can, however, demand architecture in exchange: tighter supervision, clearer capital and liquidity buffers, narrower permissible leverage, more transparent collateral chains, and resolution regimes that assign losses when support is withdrawn. The lender of last resort is therefore not just rescue. It is leverage. It is how the state forces the private system to accept discipline after panic without causing panic during the moment of rescue.

The fourth pressure scene belongs in the household and business layer, because emergency lending is often discussed as if it operates only in rarefied balance-sheet space. A regional employer is not reading collateral schedules, yet its ability to meet wages may depend on whether its bank can pledge assets into the public facility before the close. A small manufacturer may never hear the facility's name, yet its revolving line may remain open next week only because the bank's liquidity position stabilized under official funding. A grocery supplier may keep shipping through a chaotic week not because confidence spontaneously returned, but because a payment intermediary was quietly backstopped and ordinary completion was preserved. Public lending enters daily life as continuity. The public may never see the support. It feels the absence of support immediately when continuity breaks.

This is why the lender of last resort cannot be evaluated only by whether it saves a particular institution. It must be judged by whether it preserves the broader architecture of convertibility, settlement, and public trust at a cost the polity can bear. Rescue that preserves one balance sheet but teaches the market that all large risk will be socialized corrodes discipline. Rescue that preserves doctrinal purity while allowing payroll systems, merchant payments, and core funding markets to fracture corrodes legitimacy. The state is not choosing between morality and markets. It is choosing among losses: loss of discipline, loss of continuity, loss of public consent, loss of sovereign balance-sheet strength. The point of emergency lending is not to eliminate loss. It is to decide where loss will sit so that the hierarchy remains governable.

A popular misconception imagines the lender of last resort as a giant pool of money waiting to be dispensed. In practice it is a bundle of authorities, legal protections, operational channels, collateral frameworks, counterparty definitions, stigma dynamics, and communication choices. The institution must be able to lend lawfully, value collateral quickly, deliver settlement-capable funds immediately, monitor use, coordinate with supervisors, and reassure the public without implying that every future panic will be treated the same way. It must also operate within a political environment in which elected actors may fear being seen as rescuing financiers while the public may punish visible inaction more harshly than quiet support. The constitutional power therefore depends not only on monetary capacity, but on the surrounding legal and political willingness to let that capacity be used in time.

The strongest counterargument insists that repeated recourse to last-resort lending creates moral hazard and rewards institutions that chose fragile funding models. This is true often enough that it cannot be brushed aside. A facility that is too generous or too predictable can encourage thin liquidity buffers, complacent risk management, and overreliance on collateral that will be accepted publicly even if privately discounted. Yet the rival proposition, that the state should stand aside and allow the market to discipline aggressively in real time, must be tested under actual panic conditions rather than under classroom cleanliness. If standing aside means the payment state fractures, payrolls fail, merchants lose access to daily funding, and a broader run begins because the public sees that even systemically important institutions can be left without time, then discipline through nonintervention has ceased to be a market lesson and become a political choice to permit social damage in pursuit of purity. The honest debate is not rescue versus no rescue. It is architecture: how much fragility the system should permit in calm, how much stigma emergency support should carry, how wide the collateral net should be, how losses should be assigned afterward, and how private actors should be constrained so that public time is not consumed as routine fuel.

Comparison across eras clarifies what is structural. In earlier banking systems, emergency lending centered on note convertibility and reserves. In contemporary systems, the same logic extends into secured funding, dealer balance sheets, money-like funds, clearing member liquidity, and payment intermediaries. What has changed is the corridor. What has not changed is the reason intervention becomes unavoidable. The public and the market try to move upward in the hierarchy together. The state responds by deciding whether, how, and through whom upward movement will be subsidized. The older form made this visible in queues at branches. The newer form makes it visible in facilities, collateral schedules, and extraordinary operations. Different surface, same constitutional act.

Present-tense relevance is severe. A payment state built on fast digital movement, lean buffers, shadow liquidity, token rails, and concentrated clearing cannot wait to invent a lender-of-last-resort architecture during panic. It must already know which institutions matter, which collateral can be widened under stress, which facilities can reach nonbank transmission channels, how stigma will be managed, how public language will preserve trust without overstating certainty, and how emergency support will be paired later with supervisory, legal, or structural consequences. A sovereign that can issue public money but cannot direct it into the right corridor at the right hour does not possess full crisis capacity. It possesses the symbol of sovereignty without the sequence of sovereignty.

"The lender of last resort is where sovereignty becomes operational or is exposed as incomplete."

This is the late hard truth. A state that cannot lend against the collateral its system actually uses, to the institutions its economy actually depends on, at the speed panic requires, will discover that formal authority is weaker than it appears. It will then be forced into improvisation, and improvisation in panic is expensive, politically humiliating, and structurally educational in the worst way. Markets remember where the state hesitated. The public remembers where the state protected the core but let the edge absorb the shame. Future runs become easier when those memories harden.

The contradiction should be stated one final time without softening it. The state relies on private liquidity creation in calm because private balance sheets, market-making, repo, funds, dealers, and payment intermediaries make the economy faster, broader, and more productive than a narrow public-money core could on its own. Yet the same state must step in when those private circuits begin to fail, because if it does not, private issuers and intermediaries will either collapse or become de facto sovereigns by deciding which claims still move. Emergency lending is the instrument through which the state prevents private timing power from becoming outright constitutional power. The moment private funding markets close, the state must decide whether the right to determine sequence remains public or is surrendered to panic. That is the deepest reason lender of last resort belongs in this book's constitutional core.

The chapter ends where it began: with time. The lender of last resort is not best understood as a pool of funds or an emergency kindness. It is the power to manufacture time when private time disappears. It is constitutional because the hierarchy of money cannot survive panic if no authority can decide which claims will continue moving. It is political because any such decision socializes some risk and redistributes some survival. It is operational because timing, collateral, stigma, law, and communication determine whether the authority works before the run outruns it. Money is a hierarchy in calm. The lender of last resort proves who governs that hierarchy in panic.

CLOSING DOCTRINE

The lender of last resort is constitutional power exercised through time allocation. It upgrades selected private claims into settlement-capable liquidity when market funding and convertibility have begun to fail, and in doing so it reveals which institutions, collateral forms, and payment corridors the state cannot afford to let run out of time. Collateral schedules, haircuts, stigma, and access rules are not technical details at the edge of crisis response. They are the instruments through which rescue, subordination, and triage are decided. A facility that is too stigmatized fails because institutions arrive late; a facility that is too generous fails because private fragility becomes public habit. The state relies on private liquidity creation in calm to keep the economy fast and abundant, yet must prevent private intermediaries from becoming de facto sovereigns by demanding public time whenever their abundance collapses into forced deleveraging. That contradiction is not episodic. It is structural. A state that cannot manage it with speed, clarity, and credible post-crisis discipline will either lose legitimacy by allowing timing failure to reach households or lose discipline by turning emergency liquidity into routine entitlement.

CHAPTER 20
COLLATERAL BREAKDOWN
FUNDING STRESS, HAIRCUTS, AND FIRE SALES

The first break is not a default. It is a substitution request. A counterparty that has accepted a certain class of collateral every day for years asks, with polite urgency, for a different class today. It is framed as routine housekeeping. It is not. It is the market admitting that yesterday's objects no longer buy the same amount of time. The borrower complies once, because compliance is easier than argument. Ten minutes later, the same counterparty asks for a larger buffer. The borrower complies again, because the alternative is to lose funding. A third request arrives, and now it is not a request but a condition: deliver higher-grade collateral by a fixed hour or the trade will not roll. The borrower looks around the balance sheet and discovers the most frightening fact in modern finance. The assets are still there, but the doors they used to open are tightening, and the time those assets used to purchase has been rationed away.

"Haircuts widen before headlines."

Collateral breakdown is the moment that sentence becomes an operating law. In calm, collateral looks like prudence. In panic, collateral becomes the constitution that decides who gets to live inside the funding corridor and who is forced out into liquidation. The system's day-to-day stability depends on the conversion of assets into funding. That conversion depends on collateral eligibility, valuation, and the market's willingness to treat a pledge as sufficient proof. When willingness changes, the financial system does not merely become more expensive. It becomes less continuous, because continuity is financed by rolling funding and rolling funding is financed by acceptable collateral.

This chapter is about the most misunderstood crisis mechanism in modern monetary systems. People think crises are about losses. Losses matter, but the system often collapses before losses are realized, because it collapses by timing. Collateral breakdown is timing collapse expressed as a reclassification of what counts as fundable value. It is the market saying, in the language of haircuts and eligibility, that it no longer trusts the conversion path from your assets to tomorrow's payment obligations. You may still be solvent. You can still die.

The modern economy is built on collateralized time. Banks and dealers finance inventories through secured borrowing. Market participants pledge securities to obtain cash-like funding. Clearing systems demand margin and variation payments to contain default contagion. Payment and settlement intermediaries rely on intraday funding tolerance that is itself supported by collateral and credit. Corporate treasurers use collateralized facilities to bridge receivables and payables without holding large idle balances. In calm, these arrangements feel like plumbing: present collateral, obtain funding, roll tomorrow, repeat. In panic, the loop breaks because the system does not merely demand collateral. It demands better collateral, faster collateral, more collateral, and sometimes collateral that can only be obtained by selling the very assets whose price is already falling.

To make the mechanism physical, follow one collateral object. In calm, it functions like a key. It can be pledged in the morning for funding. It can be reused as needed. It can be moved across desks as a general-purpose time-bearer. It supports market-making inventory, margin postings, and settlement smoothing. Then stress arrives and the key stops working in half the doors. Not because the metal changed, but because the lock has been replaced. The collateral object is still good in the long run, yet its immediate usability is reduced. Haircuts widen. Eligibility narrows. The key becomes heavier because it buys less time. The institution must now carry more keys to open the same doors, and it discovers that it does not have enough keys. That shortage is collateral breakdown experienced as reality rather than as vocabulary.

This is the first recommendation folded into the chapter's body: treat collateral not as a category but as a traveling permission slip. In calm, permission slips are rubber-stamped. In crisis, every stamp becomes conditional. The same object can be usable at 9:00 a.m., questioned at noon, and rejected by 4:00 p.m. not because its nature changed but because the system's appetite for delay vanished. Collateral is therefore not only about value. It is about the willingness of other institutions to treat your pledge as sufficient to let you pass. A panic is a collapse of that willingness.

A haircut is the system's confession that collateral is not cash. It is the buffer between the pledged asset's market value and the cash-like funding advanced against it. In routine, haircuts are narrow enough to feel like technical detail. In stress, haircuts become the mechanism by which the system forces deleveraging. A widening haircut is not a modest repricing. It is an immediate demand for more eligible collateral to secure the same funding. If the borrower cannot produce additional eligible collateral, the borrower must shrink. Shrinkage usually means selling assets. Selling assets in a stressed market pushes prices lower. Lower prices trigger larger haircuts. Larger haircuts demand more collateral. The loop feeds itself.

This loop is the fire-sale engine. Fire sales are not merely selling in a bad market. Fire sales are forced liquidation driven by funding constraints rather than valuation judgment. A firm sells not because it believes the asset is overpriced, but because it needs eligible collateral now, and the only way to obtain it is to sell what it owns into whatever bid remains. Fire sales transfer wealth and control because the actors with time can buy assets from the actors without time. The system calls this price discovery. The honest description is that time scarcity is selecting winners.

Here the second recommendation is integrated: sharpen the difference between visible wealth and fundable wealth. In calm, marks and balances are treated as if they can be converted into time with minimal loss. In panic, the system discovers that what you own and what you can fund are different realities. An institution can have a large asset base and still be forced into liquidation because the assets are not acceptable in the corridors that remain open. A firm can show a healthy balance and still fail because the haircuts demanded against its assets have widened beyond what it can satisfy. Visible money is what you can show. Fundable money is what can pass through today's doors. Collateral breakdown is the moment the public and many institutions learn that the two are not the same.

The first pressure scene belongs inside the secured funding desk, because that is where collateral breakdown becomes visible earliest. A dealer finances a book of assets through overnight secured borrowing. Each morning, the dealer rolls funding, posts collateral, and receives cash. The dealer believes this is stable funding because the contract is secured and has rolled for years. Then the market posture changes. Lenders demand higher haircuts and insist on narrower eligibility. The dealer must post more collateral for the same cash. The dealer's collateral inventory is finite. It can respond by posting its highest-grade assets, but those assets were already allocated to other critical needs. It can respond by selling assets to obtain higher-grade collateral, but selling pushes prices down, which widens haircuts further. It can respond by shrinking the book, which reduces market-making capacity and widens spreads across markets, pushing prices down again. In a short window, the dealer discovers that the book's survival depends less on long-run value than on immediate fundability.

A second desk feels the same stress through substitution cascades. One lender refuses a class of collateral the dealer thought was safe. The dealer substitutes. Another lender tightens concentration limits. The dealer substitutes again. The dealer now begins moving collateral around the balance sheet like a frantic logistician, not like an investor. The dealer's job is no longer to price assets. It is to keep doors open. Every substitution consumes the best collateral and leaves the rest of the balance sheet more exposed. This is how collateral breakdown drains resilience invisibly before a public failure occurs. The institution appears intact until it suddenly cannot meet a call, because the best assets have already been used to buy time in other corridors.

This is the third recommendation folded into the narrative: show how collateral breakdown becomes forced liquidation within a single day. The sequence is not dramatic. It is administrative. A refusal to roll on existing terms forces substitution. Substitution consumes the best collateral. The next call arrives and there is no longer enough best collateral. The institution sells assets to obtain what the corridor will accept. Selling pushes prices down. Price moves trigger larger margin calls. Larger calls require more cash. More cash requires more selling. At no point does the institution need to be "wrong" on long-run value. It simply needs to be short on time. That is why collateral breakdown is so lethal. It converts small frictions into forced motion before deliberation can catch up.

The second pressure scene belongs inside the clearing perimeter, because clearing turns collateral breakdown into synchronized motion. A clearing member holds positions that require margin. In calm, variation payments are routine and margin levels feel stable. In stress, price volatility spikes and margin requirements rise rapidly. Variation calls arrive in larger size and at faster tempo. Members must deliver cash or eligible collateral on strict timelines. If one participant delays, the system tightens further because the clearing mechanism is designed to protect itself by becoming more demanding. This is not malicious. It is self-preservation encoded in rules. Yet it means stress becomes synchronized. Many participants are asked to produce the same kind of collateral at the same time. Those who can produce it survive. Those who cannot must sell assets to obtain it. Those sales push prices lower, which generates more variation calls, which generates more selling. Clearing transforms dispersed fear into a coherent demand for time, and that demand expresses itself as collateral.

"In crisis, margin is not a number. It is a command."

The command has two meanings. It commands you to deliver eligible assets now. It also commands you to liquidate if you cannot. The clearing rulebook does not need to hate you. It can destroy you without emotion by enforcing a timetable. That timetable is why collateral breakdown spreads so fast. It is not primarily a story of people changing their minds. It is a story of contracts enforcing sequence under stress.

The third pressure scene belongs in the nonfinancial economy because collateral breakdown does not remain inside finance. A mid-sized manufacturer relies on an asset-backed facility secured by receivables and inventory. In calm, the borrowing base is calculated with predictable haircuts and the firm runs a steady rhythm: inputs purchased, inventory built, goods shipped, receivables collected. Then stress hits and lenders tighten. Haircuts on receivables increase. Eligibility rules narrow. Advance rates drop. The manufacturer is told the line remains open but the available amount is lower, the reporting cadence is tighter, and the recalculation is more frequent. This is not just higher rates. It is operational narrowing of time. The firm must now pay suppliers sooner because its own financing window is shorter. It must hold more cash idle because it cannot trust conversion from receivables into funding at the old tempo. It must reduce inventory because inventory can no longer be financed at the same scale. It shrinks activity not because demand vanished but because time became expensive.

The fourth pressure scene is the same mechanism hitting payroll. A service firm with steady contracts discovers that its payroll account can no longer rely on the same intraday cushion. The bank insists on earlier funding of the payroll file because the bank itself is managing tighter settlement exposure and higher internal liquidity demands. The firm's payroll team does not describe this as collateral breakdown. It describes it as new procedures, new deadlines, and more conservative cash management. The effect is the same. The business loses slack. Slack is time, and time is what crisis steals first.

This is the transmission channel that makes collateral breakdown politically explosive. The public rarely notices haircuts. The public notices empty shelves, delayed wages, tightened credit, canceled projects, and the quiet increase in fees that appears as prudence from lenders and punishment from borrowers. Collateral breakdown is a crisis mechanism that can destroy ordinary life without a single dramatic default event. It works through tightening eligibility and shortening timing. That is why it is so effective and so corrosive.

Collateral breakdown also reveals the system's deepest contradiction. In calm, the financial system manufactures abundant private liquidity by pledging and reusing collateral. It builds claims on top of claims because the market is willing to treat certain assets as near-cash when pledged. This structure is productive. It also creates fragility because it depends on continuous rollovers and stable haircuts. When fear arrives, the same structure demands immediate conversion into the top claim. It discovers there is not enough top claim to satisfy everyone simultaneously. The system then attempts to manufacture top claim by selling assets, which depresses prices and worsens the shortage. This is why collateral breakdown is not only a market event. It is a governance event. The state is pulled in because only the state can decide whether to expand eligibility, provide backstop funding against collateral the market has begun to reject, or allow the fire-sale loop to continue until the system shrinks violently enough to restore private confidence.

The state's interventions at this stage are often described as liquidity operations, yet the true content is collateral politics. When public authority broadens what it will accept as eligible collateral, it is not merely providing funds. It is telling the system which assets will be treated as time-bearing even when the market doubts them. When it applies haircuts, it is deciding which losses will be borne privately and which will be deferred. When it lends at certain terms, it is deciding whether stigma will deter use or whether ease of access will prevent collapse. When it supports certain corridors first, it is deciding which pathways of settlement matter enough to keep open. Collateral policy is therefore not a footnote. It is a constitutional act. It decides whose assets remain money-like under stress.

The political contradiction must land without softness. The state often insists it does not pick winners, that it simply preserves system functioning, that it simply supplies liquidity against sound collateral. Yet collateral eligibility is the act of picking. It is the act of declaring which private objects will be treated as time-bearing when private markets have begun to reject them. In calm, this looks like technical administration. In crisis, it is revealed as hierarchy management. The state can either admit that it is governing the hierarchy or pretend it is not and allow the market's panic classification to become a liquidation regime. Either choice is governance. The only question is whether governance is acknowledged and disciplined or denied and improvised.

The cleanest description of the state's dilemma is also the most uncomfortable. If the state refuses to lend widely against collateral, it preserves discipline and protects its balance sheet, but it may allow a spiral that destroys payment continuity and forces losses through fire sales that were not required by long-run value. If the state lends widely, it can stop the spiral and preserve continuity, but it risks becoming the marginal buyer of time for private actors who built fragile structures in calm. Either choice has consequences. The state cannot avoid choosing. The only question is whether it chooses early enough to avoid the worst forced sales or late enough that its eventual intervention must be larger, more politicized, and more openly protective of the core.

The chapter must also name the asymmetry that becomes visible during collateral breakdown. Institutions closest to the apex settlement asset can often obtain funding more easily because their collateral is already in accepted form, their access to official time is clearer, and their counterparties trust them longer. Institutions farther from the core experience haircuts widening sooner and eligibility narrowing faster. Nonbanks often face the harshest version because they may not have direct access to public time. They rely on intermediaries who pull back precisely when needed most. This asymmetry means collateral breakdown redistributes market structure. It pushes activity toward the core and away from the edges. It rewards access and punishes dependence. This is crisis as structural consolidation.

Collateral breakdown is also a story about information under stress. In calm, market participants can pretend they know what assets are worth because trading is continuous and funding is routine. In stress, prices are shaped by forced selling and forced selling is shaped by haircuts, and haircuts are shaped by fear, and fear is shaped by incomplete information about who is exposed and who will be rescued. The system enters a feedback loop where prices stop being pure signals and become outcomes of governance and funding sequence. This is why crisis pricing cannot be read as a simple market verdict. It is a hybrid of valuation, funding constraint, and institutional power. A state that mistakes fire-sale prices for fundamental truth can amplify the spiral by treating forced prices as evidence that assets are worthless rather than temporarily unfundable. A state that ignores price signals entirely can socialize genuine impairment and destroy discipline. The correct posture is governed judgment: which price moves represent genuine impairment and which represent forced timing.

The last pressure scene belongs in the legitimacy layer. When households see prices falling and credit tightening, they suspect the system is rigged. When businesses see borrowing bases shrink and covenants tighten in the same week their orders remain strong, they suspect finance has become predatory. When citizens hear that collateral eligibility is being expanded for institutions while households are told to endure tighter conditions, they see favoritism. Some perceptions are inaccurate in technical terms. They can be politically true because crisis governance is judged by distribution. The state cannot govern collateral breakdown with technical excellence alone. It must govern with awareness that the public reads time allocation as moral allocation.

Collateral breakdown belongs to the constitutional core of this Part because it is where the system's claim-ranking becomes a daily fact. It is where liquidity becomes command, where haircuts become policy without being called policy, and where the state's rescue choices become visible not as speeches but as who is forced to sell first.

CLOSING DOCTRINE

Collateral breakdown is crisis in its most mechanical form: a reclassification of what assets can buy time, enforced through widening haircuts, narrowing eligibility, shortened maturities, and synchronized margin demands. It kills by sequence before it kills by valuation, because a solvent institution can fail if it cannot fund itself today. Fire sales are the system's forced conversion of assets into time, and they transfer wealth and control toward those who can still obtain funding when others cannot. Clearing and margin systems accelerate this process by turning dispersed fear into synchronized collateral commands on strict timetables. The public confuses visible wealth with fundable wealth in calm because the system makes conversion feel natural; collateral breakdown is the moment conversion becomes permission and permission becomes scarce. The state is pulled in because only public authority can interrupt the loop by lending against collateral the market has begun to reject, yet doing so turns collateral policy into a constitutional act that decides whose private objects remain money-like under stress. The state may deny that it picks winners, but eligibility is selection, and selection is governance. A monetary order that cannot govern collateral breakdown cannot govern crisis, because collateral is the language by which modern systems decide who stays inside the corridor when time becomes scarce.

CHAPTER 21
RESOLUTION AUTHORITY
HOW LOSSES ARE REASSIGNED

The institution does not fail in public the way it fails in spreadsheets. In spreadsheets, failure is a minus sign that grows until it becomes undeniable. In public, failure is a series of operational humiliations: counterparties shortening terms, haircuts widening, clients moving balances, internal funding desks burning through the best collateral to survive another day. Then a Friday arrives when the question is no longer whether the firm is solvent on paper, but whether it will open on Monday without tearing a hole in payments, clearing, payroll, and the quiet assumptions that make ordinary money feel ordinary. By that point, the real crisis is no longer the institution's weakness. The real crisis is the system's dependence on the institution continuing to behave as if it is still a trusted node.

Resolution authority exists because bailout and liquidation are both politically and operationally insufficient once a financial system becomes dense enough to be life-support. A bailout preserves continuity by socializing loss, but teaches the market that private risk carries an eventual public floor. A liquidation preserves discipline by letting failure occur, but can fracture the payment state by turning one firm's collapse into a cascading interruption of settlement, collateral, and credit. Resolution is the state's attempt to do the hardest thing: allow failure while preserving continuity, impose losses while keeping critical functions alive, punish risk without detonating the machinery that households and firms depend on for daily completion.

"No creditor should be worse off than in liquidation." (Financial Stability Board, Key Attributes of Effective Resolution Regimes, 2014)

This line looks procedural until one recognizes what it is actually doing. It is not a moral guarantee. It is a legitimacy constraint on violence. Resolution reassigns losses through state power, often rapidly and with partial information, and then claims the result is lawful because it is bounded by a counterfactual: what would have happened in ordinary insolvency. The phrase is the system admitting that crisis governance cannot be pure discretion. It must be disciplined by a rule that can be defended after the fact, because the public will accept triage only if triage can be framed as governance rather than looting.

Resolution begins with a blunt recognition that crisis always creates: some institutions cannot be allowed to fail as a pure market event because their failure would become a public event. The state's task is therefore not to prevent loss. The task is to decide where loss will sit and how quickly it will be recognized, while keeping settlement, payments, and basic credit channels from collapsing into a generalized freeze. If the lender of last resort manufactures time, resolution authority decides who pays for the time that was manufactured, and what form that payment takes.

The first mechanism is seizure, which in this context means the state taking control of the failing institution's operating body before the market can tear it apart. This is often misunderstood as a dramatic political act. In practice it is a race against the weekend. The institution is bleeding credibility. Outflows are rising. Collateral is tightening. Clearing corridors are becoming hostile. If the state waits for perfect information, the system may already be broken by Monday morning, not because the firm's assets were worse than believed, but because the firm lost the ability to settle on time. Resolution therefore begins where panic begins: with time as the scarce resource. The authority moves to freeze the destructive sequence, not by calming markets with speech, but by changing legal control of the balance sheet before the balance sheet's timing failure becomes a system-wide event.

Here the first recommendation is integrated as texture rather than commentary: make the weekend choreography feel like a control-room script. By late Friday, supervisors are not counting ratios. They are counting hours. They are watching which payments must settle before close, which margin calls will hit at open, which counterparties will refuse to roll at dawn, which clients will move balances before breakfast, and which contractual triggers will fire automatically if the institution is perceived as failing. A resolution team knows it has one non-negotiable goal: keep critical functions from losing access to the settlement core. A legal team knows it must be able to impose stays and transfers without inviting instant injunctions. An operations team knows that if payment files do not run on Monday, the crisis becomes public in a way no balance-sheet recapitalization can undo. A communications team knows that a sentence can trigger a run just as efficiently as a withdrawal button, because markets upgrade on language as well as on numbers. Resolution begins in this choreography because the choreography is the system's real anatomy under stress.

Continuity of critical functions is the second mechanism. A modern large institution is not merely a lender. It is a payment processor, a custody node, a clearing member, a source of intraday liquidity, a provider of credit lines that keep payroll and inventory moving, and a legal counterparty in thousands of contracts that assume it will still exist tomorrow. Liquidation treats the institution as an asset pool to be sold. Resolution treats the institution as an operating system that must keep running while ownership and losses are rewritten. That is the conceptual pivot. In liquidation, the firm is dismantled to satisfy claims. In resolution, the firm is stabilized long enough to avoid destroying the system that surrounds it.

"Maintain continuity of critical functions." (Financial Stability Board, Key Attributes of Effective Resolution Regimes, 2014)

This phrase is where the politics lives. Once the state admits certain functions must continue, it has admitted it is willing to protect the system from the market's full discipline, at least long enough to transfer, recapitalize, or unwind without detonating settlement. The market hears protection. The public hears favoritism if pain is not seen to fall on the right parties. Resolution tries to solve that perception problem by making loss allocation explicit: shareholders are wiped first, then creditors absorb losses according to rank. The system is kept alive, but ownership is punished. Continuity is preserved, but someone pays.

The split between good and bad is the third mechanism, and it is more physical than the language suggests. Resolution often requires moving critical operations into a bridge structure that can keep paying, settling, and processing while losses are concentrated elsewhere. This is the institutional equivalent of isolating infection without stopping the heart. Deposits and basic payment channels continue. Critical contracts are honored or transferred. Employees keep systems running. Meanwhile, impaired assets, legal exposures, and subordinated liabilities are separated so they can be written down, converted, or unwound without dragging the payment state into the grave with them. The public sees one firm. Resolution sees two bodies: the living machine that must keep running and the loss bucket that must be owned by someone other than the public if legitimacy is to survive.

The fourth mechanism is bail-in, which is the core innovation of modern crisis governance: recapitalization by forced conversion of private claims into loss absorption. Bail-in is the state declaring that the hierarchy of claims will be used not only to allocate losses after liquidation, but to prevent liquidation by converting some creditors into the new buffer that keeps the institution solvent enough to operate. This is the most honest alternative to bailout, because it says openly what bailout often tries to hide. The system will be stabilized by reallocating loss, and the loss will fall on those who knowingly held risk-bearing claims rather than on taxpayers in the first instance. The difficulty is that bail-in is politically clean and operationally brutal. It changes property rights rapidly, under stress, with markets watching for how the rules will be applied next time. If it looks arbitrary, future funding costs rise. If it looks captured, legitimacy collapses. If it looks timid, the state is accused of protecting creditors by stealth. Resolution authority therefore must do two things simultaneously: act fast enough to preserve continuity, and act predictably enough to preserve credibility after the event.

Here the second recommendation is integrated: sharpen ordinary insolvency versus resolution by showing how close-out rights can kill continuity even when assets exist. Ordinary insolvency proceeds through court-managed ranking and liquidation. It is slow enough that an operating institution with critical payment functions cannot survive it without becoming a public emergency. Counterparties with termination rights exit as soon as triggers are met. Secured creditors seize collateral. Setoff rights are exercised by those who can. Liquidity drains out of the firm faster than any administrator can organize an orderly sale. The legal system may still be functioning, but the payment system cannot wait for legal functioning. Resolution exists because contract law, applied at scale in panic, is a liquidation machine. It is not evil. It is simply too fast and too self-protective to preserve systemic continuity. Resolution authority therefore includes the power to pause close-outs, transfer contracts, and override certain private rights temporarily so the market cannot liquidate the firm by contract before the state can impose an orderly ranking.

Bail-in should be felt, not merely defined. The creditor does not experience bail-in as doctrine. The creditor experiences it as a regime change in the meaning of the instrument. A claim that was treated as safe enough to hold as a liquidity buffer becomes, overnight, a loss-absorbing layer. A funding desk that treated that claim as money-like collateral must now reclassify it as suspect. A treasury team that held the instrument because it always trades discovers that it no longer trades because nobody wants to be the last holder of a claim that can be converted into pain by sovereign decision. This is where resolution reshapes market memory. Once creditors believe bail-in is real, they price instruments differently in calm. They shorten maturities, demand higher spreads, shift toward safer claims, and avoid complexity they cannot model. That is the disciplining function of credible resolution. It imposes an ex ante cost on fragile funding models by making creditors fear conversion in the next panic.

Here the third recommendation is integrated: make bail-in and loss reassignment tactile by showing the creditor's day. A large holder wakes up to notice that its balance still exists on the screen but has been transformed in legal substance. The holder's internal risk committee meets and decides whether this class of claim can still be treated as liquid in any future stress. The answer becomes no, which means the firm reduces exposure system-wide, not only to the resolved institution. That reduction tightens funding conditions across the sector. The state has preserved continuity in one weekend and imposed discipline that will echo through pricing for years. That echo is intended. It is also dangerous if it is too violent, because it can starve the system of stable funding and make the next crisis faster. Resolution is therefore a weapon that must be used with calibration. It cannot be used as theater. It must be used as design enforcement.

This is also where the line between resolution and run becomes thin. If creditors suspect that a class of liabilities will be bailed in, they will attempt to exit before conversion. They will not call this a run. They will call it prudent risk management. It is a run. Resolution is therefore always threatened by the behavior it is designed to discipline. Announce bail-in too clearly and you trigger preemptive exits. Announce it too vaguely and you lose credibility. The only stable solution is preparation in calm: clear liability hierarchies, credible buffers, credible supervisory enforcement, and credible system-wide backstops so that disciplining one institution does not trigger a stampede across the whole system.

The legal architecture matters more than rhetoric because the modern crisis system is full of contractual tripwires that are rational in isolation and dangerous in aggregate. Early termination rights protect counterparties. Setoff rights protect creditors. Collateral triggers protect lenders. Cross-default provisions protect those who do not want to be last. In generalized stress, these protections become a liquidation engine. If every counterparty closes out simultaneously, the institution is liquidated by contract before the state can impose an orderly ranking. Resolution authority therefore includes the power to impose brief pauses, not as mercy, but as a way to prevent the contractual machine from executing liquidation faster than governance can assign losses.

The first pressure scene belongs inside that pause, because it is where orderly is made real. A clearing member is wobbling. Variation calls are rising. Counterparties are tightening. The institution is still making payments, but it is doing so by burning its last eligible collateral. On Friday afternoon, counterparties begin preparing to close out exposures at the first legally permissible moment. The institution's operations team sees the same thing from the inside: fewer incoming payments, more outgoing demands, and a settlement queue that is growing in ways that feel like suffocation. The resolution team must decide whether to impose a stay that prevents close-outs, whether the stay will be recognized across borders, and whether the stay itself will be read as confirmation that the institution is failing. If the stay is not credible, counterparties will still run through other channels. If the stay is too broad, the market will assume future stays are likely and begin shortening maturities across the system in anticipation. A stay is both lifesaving and reputationally radioactive. It buys hours by overriding private rights. It also teaches creditors what sovereignty can do to contracts in panic.

The second pressure scene belongs at the clearing membership seam, because that seam determines whether continuity is real or theatrical. A firm can be placed into resolution and still fail systemically if it loses clearing membership, loses access to payment rails, or loses access to intraday liquidity. The most dangerous question in the resolution room is therefore not whether the balance sheet can be recapitalized on paper. It is whether the firm will be allowed to settle. If infrastructures treat the firm as toxic, they deny it access even if legal ownership has changed. A bridge structure with a clean balance sheet still needs counterparties willing to transact, clearinghouses willing to accept, and payment systems willing to process. Resolution is therefore not only legal restructuring. It is a credibility transplant. It must move not only assets and liabilities but also the market's willingness to treat the entity as a functioning node. This is why resolution planning obsesses over operational continuity, collateral positioning, and access to key infrastructures. Without those, the resolution is just a statement that arrives too late.

The third pressure scene belongs at the boundary between the firm and the public. A business client calls to confirm that payroll will clear on Monday. The relationship manager wants to say yes because saying no would trigger an immediate move of balances that would worsen the institution's condition. The manager also knows that false assurance could become fraud if the firm is resolved over the weekend and payments are delayed. The client is not asking for solvency ratios. The client is asking whether the payment state will behave like the payment state or like a courtroom. This is why resolution cannot be evaluated only by legal elegance. It must be evaluated by whether it preserves ordinary completion for those who cannot survive the system becoming a legal seminar in real time.

The fourth pressure scene belongs inside political leadership because resolution is legitimacy management under fire. If a large institution is resolved, headlines follow. Opponents will claim either that the state rescued elites or that the state allowed crisis to unfold. Supporters will claim either that the state preserved stability or that the state imposed accountability. The reality is usually harsher: the state is trying to prevent a payment fracture while keeping the public from concluding that money is a private privilege protected by public force. The state must prove the hierarchy is governable and that governance is not captured. The only way to prove this is through visible loss allocation. Yet visible loss allocation can intensify market fear if holders of similar instruments at other firms begin rushing to exit before they are next. Accountability can trigger contagion if it is not paired with credible system-wide backstops. This is the distinctive cruelty of resolution. It must be strong enough to punish and gentle enough not to collapse the system while punishing.

Cross-border reality makes this harder and more violent. Large institutions live in multiple legal jurisdictions. Their assets, liabilities, and operations are scattered. A resolution imposed in one country may not be recognized cleanly in another. Creditors may race to seize assets in friendly courts. Local regulators may ring-fence assets to protect domestic creditors. These acts are rational from each jurisdiction's perspective. In aggregate, they fracture the continuity resolution is designed to preserve. Ring-fencing feels like defense to the nation doing it. It feels like sabotage to the home authority trying to maintain a single orderly ranking. This is why resolution authority is also geopolitical. In a global system, the ability to reassign losses predictably across borders is itself a form of monetary power, because it determines whether the system can be stabilized without resorting to blunt national measures that fragment markets and intensify crisis transmission.

Resolution also tests the state's honesty about the hierarchy it pretends is invisible. In calm, officials speak as if markets price risk and failures occur cleanly. In crisis, the state reveals that some failures are intolerable and some are permitted, some creditors are protected and others are sacrificed, some functions are treated as public necessities and others are treated as private business. Resolution is the moment the state stops pretending it does not govern the hierarchy and instead governs it explicitly. That explicitness can save legitimacy if loss allocation looks disciplined. It can destroy legitimacy if loss allocation looks improvised or biased.

The strongest official defense of resolution is that it is the responsible middle path: preserve critical functions, impose losses on shareholders and creditors, protect depositors and payment continuity, and avoid turning every crisis into a taxpayer bailout. This defense is serious. It is incomplete unless it includes the harder truth that resolution only works when embedded in preparation. Institutions must be structured with resolvability in mind. Loss-absorbing buffers must exist in forms that can be written down quickly. Operational continuity must be planned so critical functions can be transferred or maintained. Data and legal entity maps must be clean enough that authorities can act without guessing. Without this preparation, resolution becomes a word used to describe an improvised weekend rescue. Preparation turns resolution from a fantasy into a credible threat, and credible threat is what disciplines behavior in calm.

The public's counterargument is visceral. Why should anyone be protected at all. Why should the state preserve any institution whose failure is the consequence of private choices. Why should the payment state be built such that the collapse of one institution can threaten ordinary life. This counterargument is not foolish. It is a demand for a different architecture. Resolution is the state's admission that the current architecture already exists, already entangles daily life, and cannot be unwound instantly during panic. The state can promise redesign after crisis. During crisis, it must govern the system it has, not the one it wishes it had. Resolution is constrained sovereignty: decisive action constrained by dependencies tolerated in calm.

The chapter's deeper claim is severe. Resolution authority is where the monetary state shows whether it can convert panic into lawful order without turning law into paralysis. It is where the hierarchy is made explicit and then defended as legitimate. It is where losses are not merely discovered but assigned. Assignment is not optional. If the state refuses to assign losses, the market assigns them through fire sales and runs. If the state assigns losses carelessly, the market withdraws trust and future funding costs rise across the system. If the state assigns losses in a way that appears captured, the public withdraws consent, and consent is the long-run collateral of monetary order.

Resolution is governance in its purest form. The state takes control, preserves critical functions, imposes a ranking, and forces the system to accept that ranking as binding. The act is violent in the legal sense, because it overrides private expectations. The act is merciful in the systemic sense, because it prevents private liquidation from becoming public breakdown. The only question that matters is whether the violence is disciplined enough to be called law and whether the mercy is limited enough to be called accountability.

CLOSING DOCTRINE

Resolution authority exists because modern systems cannot choose between bailout and liquidation without either destroying legitimacy or destroying continuity. Resolution is the state's method for reassignment of loss under sovereign control while keeping critical functions running, which means it is crisis governance written into legal and operational sequence. The legitimacy hinge is predictability: losses must follow a credible hierarchy and respect the constraint that creditors should not be worse off than in liquidation, otherwise crisis governance becomes arbitrary power dressed as procedure. The operational hinge is timing: resolution must move faster than contract-driven liquidation, close-out cascades, collateral breakdown, and clearing access loss, otherwise the market will execute a disorderly ranking before the state can impose an orderly one. Bail-in is the decisive tool because it recapitalizes continuity by forcing private creditors to absorb losses, and it is credible only when creditors believe conversion is real and therefore price it in calm. Cross-border ring-fencing is the standing threat because jurisdictional conflict can fracture continuity and turn resolution into fragmentation. Resolution must be lawful enough to preserve future funding and violent enough to prove accountability, and the space between those demands is where crisis governance either becomes legitimate or becomes a permanent wound.

CHAPTER 22
GLOBAL BACKSTOPS
SWAPS, MULTILATERAL SUPPORT, AND CONDITIONAL RESCUE

The request arrives as a technical cable and a political confession at the same time. A central bank governor signs it, not because he enjoys the humiliation of asking, but because the domestic system has begun to experience an external truth that no statute can repeal. The country's banks can be solvent in local law and still fail in global practice if they cannot obtain the settlement claim demanded by trade, external debt service, fuel imports, margin calls, and correspondent banks that will not move without comfort. A finance minister reads the balance of payments numbers and sees that what looked like a manageable problem last month has become a calendar problem this week. The exchange rate is moving, and not in a way that can be defended cheaply. Local rates can be raised, but raising them fast enough to stop outflows will crush domestic credit. Capital controls can be tightened, but tightening them will fracture the business sector that needs external inputs. Reserves can be spent, but reserves are a finite stock, and a finite stock is a magnet for panic once the market believes the stock is being consumed with no replenishment.

This is where global backstops begin. They begin not as benevolence but as hierarchy, because the question under stress is never, is this country legal. The question is, is this country admissible. Admissibility is the right to pass through the world's settlement corridors without paying an extreme premium in time and spread. When admissibility tightens, domestic authority becomes less relevant than external clearance. A state can be sovereign and still be rationed by the world's willingness to roll its funding, accept its collateral, clear its payments, and treat its promises as recognizable enough to trade. Global backstops exist because the world cannot endure a system in which every crisis forces each country to solve a global liquidity shortage alone. They also exist because those who control the backstops obtain leverage that looks like assistance and functions like governance.

The reader should hold a simple, brutal distinction in mind as this Part reaches outward. Domestic crisis is fought with domestic time. Global crisis is fought with external time. Domestic time can be manufactured by a central bank that controls the apex claim inside its legal order. External time must be obtained through conversion corridors not fully under domestic control. This is why global backstops are not a niche topic. They are the international version of the lender of last resort, and they expose the reserve order as a crisis machine rather than merely a trade convenience.

"The Fund's role is to give confidence to countries through its financing and the policies that accompany it." (International Monetary Fund, operational doctrine)

The wording matters because it admits the twin structure of global rescue. Financing is the visible instrument. The policies are the hidden instrument. Confidence is the target, but confidence is not a feeling. Confidence is the market's belief that obligations will be discharged on schedule and that the creditor hierarchy will be defended. The global backstop is therefore not simply a loan. It is a package of claims about discipline. It is the world's way of deciding whether a country's promises will remain money-like enough to trade, or be subordinated into suspicion.

In domestic crises, the lender of last resort supplies time against collateral. In global crises, time is supplied against sovereignty itself. The collateral is the state's future fiscal capacity, its willingness to reprioritize spending, its ability to raise revenue, its political capacity to enforce adjustment, and its credibility in the eyes of external institutions whose own legitimacy depends on making rescue appear conditional rather than sentimental. The state asks for liquidity. The world asks for discipline. The bargaining occurs inside that contradiction.

The mechanism must be stated cleanly. A country facing external stress encounters a shortage of settlement claims it cannot manufacture. Even if it issues its own currency, it cannot issue the currency demanded for imports, external debt, and cross-border margining without converting through markets that may now be closed or punitive. The country's banks and firms are then forced to scramble for the needed settlement claim, often by selling local assets, drawing down reserves, or borrowing at escalating premiums. That scramble becomes an exchange-rate collapse, a domestic banking squeeze, and a sudden contraction of trade credit. The state can try to defend by raising rates, but high rates can destroy domestic credit faster than they restore external confidence. The state can impose controls, but controls can freeze legitimate commerce and produce a parallel market that signals deeper weakness. The state can spend reserves, but spending reserves can accelerate the run if the market believes the stock will be exhausted. The shortage is therefore not merely financial. It is strategic. It is a shortage of external time.

To make that shortage physical, follow one import transaction. A fuel buyer contracts for shipment. The invoice is denominated in an external settlement claim. The buyer's bank must obtain that claim, not in theory, but in a form acceptable to the seller's bank and to the correspondent corridor between them. The buyer's bank attempts to source it through the market. Spreads are wide. Liquidity is thin. The bank can obtain the claim, but only at a punitive price, or only in fragments that require repeated transactions that each leave traces of desperation. Each transaction triggers compliance checks, documentation, and risk committee review because counterparties are nervous. The bank then tries to send payment. The correspondent asks for additional information and holds the payment in review because the country's risk classification has tightened. The seller's bank asks for assurance that the payment is final and not subject to reversal, freeze, or local restriction. The shipper asks for confirmation before unloading. The buyer's government pleads that fuel is essential. The corridor does not care that fuel is essential. The corridor cares that it is paid in the right claim, at the right time, through the right institutions, with the right assurances.

This is the first recommendation folded into the chapter's machinery: show the invisible veto points. The crisis is not only a shortage of foreign settlement claims. It is a shortage of passage. Every step in the transaction passes through gates: market acquisition gate, compliance gate, correspondent gate, settlement gate, finality gate, and then, if the crisis deepens, repatriation and convertibility gates. A country can have money locally and still fail to buy fuel because its money is not admitted without heavy haircut into the corridor that turns local promise into external discharge. Global backstops exist to reopen the corridor by supplying external time and by certifying discipline to the gatekeepers who control passage.

A second transaction reveals the human reach even more sharply because it is smaller and therefore more exposed to delay. A small pharmaceutical importer tries to pay for a shipment of basic medicine. The bank advises using a larger correspondent chain to improve acceptance. The fees rise. The documentation burden expands. The supplier insists on prepayment rather than post-delivery settlement because the supplier does not trust the corridor. The importer must now fund the purchase earlier, which requires more working capital. Working capital is already scarce because domestic credit is tightening in response to the external crisis. The importer cannot obtain the needed external claim without paying a punitive spread, and cannot obtain the domestic credit without pledging collateral that the bank now haircuts more aggressively because the bank is defending its own external position. A crisis that began as "the external account" now appears as empty shelves. The state experiences it as macro constraint. Households experience it as scarcity. Both are true.

Global backstops were created to address this structural scarcity, but they do so through design choices that embed hierarchy. There are three principal channels, and each carries a different form of leverage. The first is swap lines between central banks, framed as technical liquidity tools but functioning as selective corridors of privilege. The second is multilateral crisis financing, providing balance-of-payments support with explicit conditionality as the price of access. The third is development and regional financing mechanisms repurposed in crisis, sometimes as emergency budget support, sometimes as trade-finance stabilization, sometimes as liquidity buffers for critical imports, always carrying governance constraints and alignment signals that determine who gets passage and under what terms.

The first pressure scene belongs in the swap line request because it is where rank becomes instantaneous. A swap line allows one central bank to obtain foreign settlement claims from another in exchange for its own currency, with an agreement to reverse later. The public story describes stability and cooperation. The operational story is sharper. A swap line is a corridor through which foreign settlement claims can be injected into a domestic banking system quickly enough to halt a run on external funding. It is the cleanest backstop because it is fast. It can be large. It can be executed through central bank operations rather than through legislative improvisation. It can restore market belief that external payments will continue. Yet it is also selective. It is not offered universally. It is a privilege extended to those judged systemically important, strategically aligned, or institutionally trusted enough that assistance will not be treated as waste or as political surrender.

"Swap lines are not global money. They are membership."

This is not a slogan. It is a functional description. A country with swap access can supply external settlement claims to its banks in the hour of need. Its banks can continue funding trade and rolling external exposures at tolerable spreads. Importers can continue paying for critical goods without turning every invoice into a crisis negotiation. A country without swap access must acquire external settlement claims in stressed markets, pay punitive spreads, and ration domestic credit to protect external obligations. This difference is not philosophical. It is the difference between a crisis that can be stabilized and a crisis that becomes an economic contraction through import compression and credit collapse. A swap line converts a geopolitical relationship into a funding advantage. The public may call this cooperation. The market reads it as rank.

This is the second recommendation embedded as contrast. Imagine two countries hit by the same external shock. One has access to an official corridor for the key settlement claim. The other does not. The first can meet external demand without draining reserves at panic speed. The second must drain reserves to buy time, which signals weakness, which accelerates outflows, which forces more draining. The first can keep domestic banks functioning with external liquidity support. The second sees domestic banks tighten credit, raise rates, and shorten terms to defend their own external position. The first sees the exchange rate stabilize earlier. The second sees the exchange rate become a public countdown. In both cases, the domestic legal system may be stable. The difference is access to external time. That is what swap lines buy.

Yet swap lines also carry a deeper governance implication that must be stated without romance. They create a tiered system of crisis privileges. Access is not merely about liquidity. It is about the world deciding which states are trusted enough to receive immediate time without a program, and which must submit to program discipline in exchange for time. This is why swap lines are coveted. They reduce the need for public humiliation. They reduce the need for immediate austerity. They reduce the need for capital controls. They preserve more domestic autonomy precisely because they deliver external time quickly. Those without access must pay for time with visible adjustment, visible conditionality, and often visible political cost.

The second pressure scene belongs inside the multilateral negotiation, because that is where conditional rescue becomes explicit. A finance ministry team arrives with numbers and urgency. The external account is deteriorating. Reserves are falling. Debt maturities are near. The country needs money quickly to prevent the exchange rate from turning into a domestic banking crisis. The multilateral institution asks for a program: fiscal measures, monetary measures, structural reforms, transparency commitments, and a schedule of actions designed to convince markets that the country will not waste the funds and that it will restore the ability to service obligations without continuous external rescue. The country experiences this as intrusion. The institution experiences it as the only way to justify lending into a political system it does not control. Both are correct.

The third recommendation is integrated here: conditionality is calendar governance. A program does not only adjust aggregates. It rewrites domestic time. Subsidies are reduced or retargeted, which changes household survival calendars. Public procurement is tightened, which changes contractor cash flow calendars. Tax measures are accelerated, which changes business planning calendars. Public employment and wage bills are reviewed, which changes political calendars. Credit conditions are tightened, which changes private investment calendars. Interest rates are raised not only to stabilize the exchange rate but to signal discipline to external holders who are deciding whether to roll. The program is experienced not as macro language but as reordered days: when the government pays, who it pays first, which arrears are tolerated, which imports are prioritized, and which sectors are asked to shrink so external obligations can be honored. That is why conditionality is never neutral. It is political scheduling imposed under duress to restore admissibility.

Conditionality exists because global backstops are reputational. The institution lending is itself a node in the hierarchy of confidence. If it lends without conditions and the borrower fails anyway, the institution's credibility is damaged and future rescue becomes harder. If it lends with conditions that are politically impossible, rescue fails through noncompliance and crisis deepens. If it lends with conditions that are too harsh, adjustment can crush domestic legitimacy and produce political instability that undermines economic stabilization. Conditionality is therefore not merely reform. It is the price of belonging to the world's discharge corridor, imposed in the name of credibility, negotiated in the language of sovereignty, and felt by the population as the loss of control over the calendar of domestic life.

A second scene inside conditionality makes the contradiction sharper because it shows how the state's internal authority is constrained by external gatekeeping even when the program exists. The government announces measures. It expects the announcement to calm the market. The market waits for disbursement and watches whether the disbursement is timely, whether it is large enough, and whether it is paired with steps that convince creditors that the state will not reverse course under domestic pressure. The state can announce discipline. It cannot announce admissibility. Admissibility is granted by the corridor once it believes the discipline. The gap between announcement and corridor behavior is where panic lives, and it is why program design must care about speed, not only about totals. A country can have a program in principle and still suffer a run in practice if the corridor believes the program is politically fragile.

The third pressure scene belongs in the domestic banking system as the program is discussed, because this is where global becomes intimate. Bank treasurers watch external lines tighten. Importers discover trade finance is more expensive and slower. Firms that rely on external inputs begin rationing production because settlement timing is no longer reliable. Households see the exchange rate move and change behavior, not because they understand the external account, but because they understand that prices will rise and jobs will be threatened. The government can announce a program, but announcement alone does not restore the corridor. What restores the corridor is the combination of immediate financing, credible fiscal and monetary steps, and the market's belief that external obligations will be honored without improvisation. Until that belief returns, the economy behaves as if the country has been downgraded in the hierarchy of money, because it has.

A sovereign reader should notice the structural irony. The state enters a global program to restore autonomy, yet the program requires constraints that reduce short-term autonomy. The promise is that discipline now buys freedom later. The risk is that discipline now becomes politically untenable, leading to program failure, deeper panic, and a permanent increase in the country's cost of external time. This is why global backstops are conditional rescue rather than pure insurance. They require the borrower to trade political discretion for continued access to the corridor.

The fourth pressure scene belongs in development and regional credit in crisis, because the line between development and stabilization is thinner than most publics realize. When external liquidity tightens, states often need foreign settlement claims not only to pay bondholders but to keep fuel, food, medicine, and critical industrial inputs moving. Development institutions can provide emergency support, guarantees, and trade-finance facilities that keep imports flowing when private finance retreats. They can provide risk-sharing structures that allow local banks to continue issuing trade instruments rather than hoarding external liquidity. They can fund critical supply-chain continuity directly through project disbursements structured to pay foreign suppliers, ensuring the money becomes external discharge rather than disappearing into domestic budget gaps.

This is the fourth recommendation made central: development credit in crisis is not only finance. It is a continuity mechanism for the physical economy. Consider how a trade-finance guarantee facility functions in panic. A local bank wants to issue a letter of credit for a vital import. The foreign supplier's bank distrusts the local bank because country risk has risen. The guarantee facility stands behind the transaction, converting a risky private promise into a promise the corridor will accept. The goods move. The factory stays open. The supermarket shelves are stocked. The public sees no guarantee. The public sees continuity. This is where development institutions become crisis institutions. They do not merely lend. They certify. They bridge admissibility. They keep the physical economy from collapsing into shortage while macro stabilization is negotiated.

A second development-credit scene makes the governance content clearer. A state needs spare parts for power generation. Without them, electricity rationing begins, and electricity rationing turns a financial crisis into a social crisis. A development lender structures a facility that pays foreign suppliers directly, tied to procurement oversight and monitoring. The parts arrive. The grid remains stable. The state avoids rolling blackouts that would have destroyed political legitimacy. Yet the price of this continuity is not just interest. It is governance constraints: procurement rules, auditing rights, reporting obligations, and sometimes restrictions on domestic discretion that outlast the crisis. Support preserves stability and embeds monitoring. The line between assistance and governance is not a conspiracy. It is the mechanism. The corridor must trust the funds are used for continuity rather than for escape. Trust is purchased through control.

The strongest defense of global backstops is that they prevent local crises from becoming global collapse. Without external liquidity support, many countries would be forced into abrupt adjustment, massive import compression, and disorderly defaults that would harm both the country and the global system. This defense is serious. The critique is also serious. Backstops can entrench hierarchy by making access conditional on alignment and compliance. They can convert crisis into leverage, allowing creditors and powerful states to extract concessions. They can impose adjustment that stabilizes external accounts while damaging domestic legitimacy. They can create dependence if governments begin to treat official rescue as periodic rather than exceptional. The reality is neither benevolence nor conspiracy. The reality is that in a hierarchy of money, the ability to supply external settlement claims is power, and power is exercised under the appearance of assistance.

The chapter must clarify the three distinctions that determine outcomes in global crisis, because these distinctions are where states and publics misread their own position. The first is access versus adequacy. A country can obtain some external liquidity and still fail if the amount is too small or arrives too slowly to change market behavior. A line that is credible but delayed can be worse than a line that is smaller but immediate, because panic is a race against timing. The second is passage versus finality. A country can appear to have financing while still being unable to discharge obligations on time if correspondent corridors remain hesitant, documentation burdens intensify, or domestic banking systems cannot transmit the external liquidity into the right channels. The third is rescue versus reset. A country can be rescued from immediate collapse and still be left with a debt structure, import dependency, or banking fragility that makes the next crisis inevitable. Backstops buy time. They do not substitute for solvency, institution-building, and credible domestic governance.

A further contradiction must be stated without romance. The global system needs a backstop network because private finance retreats in panic and because the world economy cannot survive if every retreat forces abrupt national collapse. Yet every backstop network creates a map of privilege. Some states have standing corridors. Others do not. Some can obtain foreign settlement claims quickly. Others must negotiate under duress and accept conditions that would be politically impossible in calm. This privilege is not incidental. It is one of the ways the reserve order reproduces itself. The system's top settlement claim is not only a medium of exchange. It is the basis of emergency time. Those who can obtain it under official arrangements hold a different class of sovereignty than those who cannot.

The most revealing moment in global crisis is not when the program is announced. It is when external counterparties resume ordinary behavior. When trade finance prices normalize. When banks roll funding without drama. When merchants stop hoarding external settlement claims. When households stop treating the exchange rate as a countdown. These changes occur only when the market believes the state has regained access to external time and will defend that access through policy choices that are politically sustainable. This is why global backstops are conditional rescue. They are bridges built out of money and discipline. If discipline is not credible, the bridge collapses. If discipline is credible but politically explosive, the bridge may hold long enough to restore external confidence while destroying internal consent. In either case, the crisis has not been solved. It has been moved.

The final implication is uncomfortable but necessary. Global backstops are part of the world's monetary constitution. They determine which countries can stabilize quickly, which must endure prolonged adjustment, which can protect domestic employment while restoring external confidence, and which must sacrifice domestic stability to satisfy external admissibility. They are tools of stability. They are also tools of leverage. A state that does not map its backstop options, its swap eligibility, its multilateral channels, its development-credit corridors, its reserve adequacy, and its dependence on specific settlement pathways does not fully understand its own crisis capacity. It is governing in calm with a blind spot that becomes fatal in panic.

CLOSING DOCTRINE

Global backstops exist because many states cannot manufacture the external settlement claims demanded in panic, and without an official corridor the scramble for those claims becomes exchange-rate collapse, trade credit rationing, and domestic banking stress that spreads into households through shortage and inflation. Cross-border crisis is not only a shortage of currency. It is a shortage of admissible passage through corridors filled with invisible veto points, where compliance, correspondent discretion, and finality concerns can delay or block settlement even when funds exist in principle. Swap lines are the fastest form of external time, but they operate as selective membership rather than universal insurance, turning geopolitical trust into a funding advantage that can stabilize one country while forcing another into punitive market acquisition. Multilateral support stabilizes by pairing financing with conditionality because credibility is the asset being purchased, and the price of credibility is calendar governance; the borrower trades discretion for admissibility. Development and regional mechanisms become crisis tools when private finance retreats because they can guarantee trade and finance essential imports, yet they can also embed long-run dependency through monitoring and corridor control. In global crisis, domestic legality is not enough. Admissibility is the real constraint, and whoever supplies the scarce settlement claim supplies discipline with it.

PART FIVE

THE PRIVATE CHALLENGE

STABLECOINS, CRYPTO, AND THE BATTLE FOR THE INTERFACE

The next system fight does not begin with ideology. It begins with a tap. A user opens a phone, sees a balance that feels global, sends value across a border as if borders were a bureaucratic rumor, and receives a confirmation in seconds. The user does not ask what claim backs the balance, what ledger decides finality, what court would enforce redemption, or whose discretion can freeze the account. The user asks only whether it worked. When it works often enough, the user begins to treat it as money, because habit is the first currency of legitimacy and convenience is the first proof most people require. The state can insist on definitions. The user will follow the interface until the interface fails.

The merchant's experience is even simpler. A customer pays. The merchant sees approval, sees funds appear, sees the dispute risk framed as manageable, sees fees framed as transparent, and experiences a kind of calm the merchant did not know could exist in payments. The merchant is not trying to rebel. The merchant is trying to survive. When a private rail offers cheaper acceptance, faster access to funds, fewer reversals, and fewer weekend gaps, the merchant adopts it the way merchants have always adopted anything that reduces uncertainty. This is not cultural. It is arithmetic. Yet arithmetic is how monetary sovereignty is challenged, because the interface that removes friction becomes the place where public trust is manufactured without public permission.

A treasury team watches the same phenomenon from a colder angle. They do not care about narrative. They care about timing. They see a private rail that operates continuously, settles outside bank hours, offers programmable conditional payments, and can be used to move value across subsidiaries without waiting for traditional cutoffs. The team starts using it not because it is romantic, but because it is operationally superior in certain tasks. Once the tool is used, it becomes part of working-capital rhythm. Once it becomes part of rhythm, it becomes part of the economy's calendar. And once it becomes part of the calendar, it becomes part of the state's crisis problem whether the state likes it or not.

This Part begins with that relocation of habit, because habit is how the private challenge wins before any law is changed. The private rail does not need Parliament. It needs daily usage. It needs merchants and payroll teams and cross-border senders building routines around its speed. It needs the public learning to treat "available" as a natural right rather than as a privilege produced by settlement plumbing. If the public learns that money means instant movement, constant availability, and application-level dispute resolution, then the state's slower layered settlement architecture begins to feel like an insult. People do not start by rejecting the state. They start by routing around friction. That routing becomes structural.

Private money always presents itself as choice. It presents itself as escape from friction, escape from delay, escape from the state's slow procedures and visible rules. The deeper truth is that private money, at scale, is never an escape from governance. It is a proposal to relocate governance into new hands: issuers, custodians, platforms, compliance gatekeepers, code maintainers, and the standards bodies that decide who is legible enough to move. This is the first recommendation embedded as doctrine: name governance relocation as the real object, not "innovation." The state's problem is not that private challengers exist. The state's problem is that the challengers are competing for the public's habit, and habit is the raw material of monetary legitimacy. If enough economic life organizes around a private rail, the state is eventually forced to either absorb it, subordinate it, or watch the interface become the de facto constitution of payment life.

"The interface is where trust is manufactured."

The sentence belongs early because it is the hinge between daily experience and constitutional machinery. Most people do not experience money as settlement finality, legal priority, and crisis facilities. They experience it as a card that works, a transfer that arrives, a balance that is available, and a dispute that does not ruin their week. If a private system delivers that experience more consistently, the public begins to treat it as money regardless of what the law says. The state can insist on legal categories. The public will live inside usability. That is why the private challenge is not a niche sector problem. It is a legitimacy problem.

The state's first instinct is often to treat this as novelty or threat. Novelty invites dismissal. Threat invites prohibition. Both instincts are inadequate. Dismissal fails because the interface can become systemic before the state admits it. Prohibition fails because it drives activity into darker corridors, increases backlash, and often increases the allure of the exit narrative by confirming that the state fears losing control. The serious posture is architectural clarity: define which private claims are permissible, define what disclosure must be enforced, define what redemption rights exist, define what backstops exist or do not exist, and define where the interface can innovate without quietly rewriting sovereignty. This is the second recommendation embedded as stance: do not argue morals, govern perimeters.

This Part is not a morality play about innovation versus regulation. It is a struggle over who defines the settlement perimeter and who owns the user's experience of money. The private sector's advantage is speed, design, and distribution. The state's advantage is finality, legal priority, and the ability to impose binding closure on unwilling parties. The private sector tries to copy the feel of state money while living outside the state's constraints. The state tries to preserve the monopoly on finality while not losing the interface. Each side is trying to control the public's intuition of what money is supposed to feel like, because intuition determines which claims are accepted in calm and which claims are run toward in panic.

The supervisory room is where this stops being abstract, and this is the third recommendation folded into the opening: give the reader the institutional vantage that makes the dilemma inevitable. In that room, officials do not begin with slogans. They begin with flow maps. They ask which private instruments are being used to pay wages, which merchant sectors are adopting which rails, which custodians and banks are holding the reserves that back stable-value promises, which redemption paths terminate in the public settlement core, and which concentrations would become a run corridor if confidence breaks. They do not need to believe private money is dangerous to know it is now a crisis object. Any private claim that behaves like money in calm will demand to be treated like money in panic. The state can deny responsibility in speeches. It cannot deny the public's expectation once daily life depends on the rail.

The room's real question is not whether private rails are popular. It is whether private rails have become a route for systemic runs. Officials look at how quickly a private issuer could be forced into fire-sale liquidation if holders demand redemption simultaneously. They look at whether the issuer's reserves sit inside the banking system and therefore inside the state's own crisis perimeter. They look at whether redemption pressure would become pressure on specific banks, specific money markets, and specific settlement nodes. They look at whether a stable-value claim that markets treat as cash-equivalent is in fact a short-term funding instrument whose stability depends on markets staying calm. They look at the quiet but unavoidable political reality: if a private rail becomes the way wages are paid, merchants are settled, and cross-border remittances are sent, then a failure will not be experienced as "a private product failed." It will be experienced as money failed. And once it is experienced as money failed, the public will demand that the state fix it.

This is the trap the private challenge sets for the state, and it is not necessarily malicious. It is structural. Private issuers and platforms want to operate as if they are outside sovereign discipline in calm, yet they become indistinguishable from the payment state in crisis because the public will not accept that the interface is private when the interface has become daily necessity. This is why stable-value claims are not merely products. They are proto-backstop claims. Their success writes a political obligation the state did not sign but will be expected to honor.

The Part begins with the exit fantasy because the exit fantasy is the story private money tells to make relocation of power feel like liberation. Money without the state. Settlement without permission. Finality without courts. Stability without sovereign backing. Identity without surveillance. The fantasy is attractive because it offers a clean moral narrative: the individual against the apparatus. The fantasy is also incomplete because money at scale is not a tool for solitary freedom. Money at scale is a system for binding strangers to obligations over time. Binding strangers requires enforceable closure and credible loss allocation. When the private system grows large enough, it either recreates those functions through private governance or it relies on the state's courts and enforcement while claiming independence. The state's task is to see through the narrative and classify the reality.

Here the fourth recommendation must land as a governing dilemma, not as rhetoric. The private sector wants the state's finality without the state's discipline. It wants the public's trust without the public's liabilities. It wants money-like status without being forced to behave like money under stress. The state wants private innovation without private sovereignty. It wants faster payments, cheaper cross-border transfer, and better user experience without letting a private issuer become a de facto central bank through control of the interface and the issuance of widely used money-like claims. These desires are incompatible without architecture. That is why this Part is not about whether private money is good or bad. It is about which perimeter rules prevent the private system from becoming the state's crisis problem while still allowing genuine improvements in the interface.

This Part therefore proceeds as a sequence of constitutional questions disguised as product questions. Who is allowed to issue a stable-value claim. What is the claim on reserves, and under what law. Who holds the reserves, and what happens on custodian insolvency. Are reserves segregated or commingled. Is redemption a right or a promise. Is redemption same-day or conditional. Can redemption be gated. Can transfers be frozen. Who can freeze them. What counts as final settlement on the rail. What happens when the rail's "confirmation" collides with court-ordered reversal, fraud, or sanctions. Who bears loss in a run. Who is paid first, and who waits. The public never asks these questions in calm. The state must ask them before calm ends.

The Part then moves to stablecoins because they are the most direct private attempt to manufacture money-like claims while borrowing credibility from the state. A stablecoin promises a unit stable enough to spend, settle, and hold across platforms. It can be used as collateral. It can be moved continuously. It can be embedded in programmable logic. Yet its stability is not self-generated. It is derived from reserves, custody, legal rights, and the ability to redeem into public money. This creates a contradiction that cannot be escaped. If stablecoins become systemic, they become public problems, because runs will be contagious and redemption pressure will target the banking and settlement core. The issuer will claim it is private. The public will demand rescue when redemption breaks. The state must decide in advance whether these claims are allowed to become money-like at scale, and if allowed, what perimeter of supervision, disclosure, reserve composition, custody constraints, audit discipline, and redemption enforceability is imposed to prevent a private issuer from becoming a de facto monetary sovereign.

The Part then moves to crypto rails more broadly because rails can outlive any one issuer. Even when a token fails, the habit of routing around friction can persist. The rail becomes an expectation: continuous operation, near-instant confirmation, application-level dispute resolution, and a user experience that treats finality as a screen message rather than as a legal event. This is why the private challenge is ultimately a challenge for the state's monopoly on the meaning of completion. A private rail can deliver confirmation quickly. The state's system delivers discharge. If the public cannot tell the difference, the rail wins the interface battle until a crisis teaches the difference violently. The state's strategic question is whether it will allow that teaching event to occur at scale, or whether it will discipline private rails before the public is trained to assume private confirmation equals sovereign finality.

The Part then moves to custody because custody is where private sovereignty quietly concentrates. A user can be told they hold a token directly and still be dependent on custody institutions, key managers, access policies, and platform rules that can be changed overnight. Custody is not merely safekeeping. It is gatekeeping. Whoever controls custody controls freeze capability, transfer permissioning, and sometimes the practical ability to redeem. Custody is therefore the private analogue of the settlement core. It is where the rail's promise becomes either credible or cosmetic. A state that focuses only on issuance while ignoring custody is governing the label and losing the substance.

The Part then turns to identity and data because scale requires legibility. The private challenge often frames itself as freedom from surveillance, yet scale requires compliance, and compliance requires identity, and identity requires data. The issue is therefore not whether private rails will govern identity, but who will control the identity layer and how exclusions will be executed. The state excludes through law and due process, at least in principle. Private platforms exclude through terms of service, risk models, and opaque compliance standards that can change overnight. A public system can be tyrannical. A private system can be arbitrary. The danger is not only surveillance. The danger is that the gatekeeping function migrates into private hands and becomes less contestable because it is framed as product policy rather than as public power.

The Part then moves to sovereign digital currency because this is the state's counter-move: reclaim the payment front end without surrendering finality, priority, and crisis capacity. The state is not only defending the unit. It is defending the interface and the data trail that determines who is legible, who is included, and who can be excluded. A sovereign digital currency is not only a payment instrument. It is a redesign of the state's ability to enforce identity, impose compliance, and deliver finality directly to users. It can increase inclusion. It can also increase control. This is why it becomes politically contested. Private systems frame it as surveillance and coercion. States frame it as modernization and sovereignty. The real question is whether the state can design a public interface that preserves trust without turning monetary life into a permissions regime the public rejects.

The Part then turns to policy in code because programmability is the next battlefield. Programmability promises a world in which conditions are enforced automatically: taxes withheld, subsidies targeted, funds restricted, compliance embedded, transfers constrained by identity, and money designed to behave differently depending on context. This is seduction and danger in the same sentence. Programmability can reduce fraud and increase policy precision. It can also create a system in which money is no longer a general claim but a segmented instrument, with different permissions for different people. That segmentation can become a quiet caste system if not governed with extreme discipline. The state will be tempted by programmability because it offers control. Private platforms will be tempted by programmability because it offers product differentiation and fee power. The public will be tempted by programmability because it offers convenience until the day it becomes denial. This Part treats programmability not as a feature but as a constitutional rewrite of what it means for money to be general.

The Part then faces the same contradiction that drove Part IV, now in private form. Private rails want to be treated as ordinary in calm and exceptional in crisis. They want to offer speed without bearing the full cost of stability. They want to claim neutrality while making governance choices through code updates, listing decisions, custody policies, and compliance models. They want the public to treat them as money and the state to treat them as private until the moment panic arrives. The state must decide whether it will allow that asymmetry to stand. If it does, it will eventually be forced to rescue under worse terms, because the interface will be systemic by the time it breaks. If it does not, it must impose perimeter rules that either force private rails to behave like regulated money or limit them to narrow use cases where failure will not become a public emergency.

Finally, the Part ends where it must end: rule. If the private challenge is a contest for interface, then rule is the state's answer: identity standards, compliance regimes, settlement finality boundaries, disclosure mandates, redemption rights, and the hard decision about which private claims can be upgraded into public time in a panic. The state cannot win the interface battle with prohibition alone. It must either offer a better public interface or impose perimeter rules that force private interfaces to operate as regulated representatives of public money rather than as independent monetary sovereigns in disguise. The outcome will shape not only payment convenience but also crisis stability, because the interface becomes the route through which runs travel.

Part V therefore makes one doctrinal claim that governs every chapter that follows. The private challenge is not primarily about technology. It is about sovereignty relocating into design, custody, data, and standards. Whoever governs those layers governs money's lived reality. The state can preserve the symbol of money while losing the interface, and if it loses the interface long enough, it will eventually be forced to rescue the interface's failures anyway, because the public will not accept a system in which the money it uses daily cannot be converted into the money that ends arguments when panic arrives. The private sector wants the public's habit and the state's backstop without the state's discipline. The state wants private innovation without surrendering finality. That contradiction is the engine of this Part, and it will be resolved not by speeches but by architecture.

CHAPTER 23
THE EXIT FANTASY
MONEY WITHOUT THE STATE

The first pitch is always personal. A founder sits across from an investor and describes money as a kind of imprisonment that most people do not notice because the bars are painted the color of normal life. Fees that arrive without explanation. Transfers that arrive late without apology. Weekend gaps treated as if time itself can be closed for maintenance. Accounts frozen by a message that reads like a verdict. Identity checks that feel like suspicion. A system that can exclude you with a form letter and still call itself neutral because it is following policy. The founder does not begin with macroeconomics. The founder begins with insult. Why should a payment wait. Why should a ledger be closed. Why should a citizen need permission to move what the citizen owns. The investor nods because the emotional frame is correct. People do experience monetary systems as inconvenience and humiliation, and the humiliation is not incidental. It is how a complex hierarchy of claims is made tolerable to those who live on the surface. The founder then makes the move that turns grievance into a monetary proposal. Replace the issuer. Replace the ledger. Replace the rules. Replace the gatekeepers. Make money a protocol and make settlement a function of code.

The pitch is persuasive because it does not sound like finance. It sounds like dignity. It offers a world in which a user is not a supplicant and a merchant is not a hostage to disputes arriving months later. It offers a world in which a balance is not a request and the weekend is not a cage. The exit fantasy does not need to convince the user that central banking is illegitimate. It needs to convince the user that the interface is unfair. Once the user believes the interface is unfair, a replacement interface can be adopted as moral repair. That is how technical systems acquire political constituencies without campaigning. They win not by persuading legislatures. They win by persuading calendars.

The seduction is not theory. It is a sequence of small wins that become a worldview. A young worker is paid on a Friday and sees value appear instantly in an application that also handles spending, transfers, and cross-border gifts. The worker learns, without reading any doctrine, that money is supposed to be immediate. A small merchant watches a weekend rush and sees funds become usable without waiting for bank hours. The merchant learns that money is supposed to be continuous. A contractor sends support to family across a border and sees the value arrive quickly, without the sender feeling interrogated, without the recipient waiting days, without fees changing midstream. The family learns that money is supposed to be borderless. None of these people believe they are making a constitutional choice. They believe they are reducing friction. Friction reduction becomes habit. Habit becomes expectation. Expectation becomes legitimacy.

The habit capture is faster than most states admit because it is built out of ordinary life. It is a payroll-to-rent week that runs smoothly enough times that the user begins to treat smoothness as a right. On Monday, rent is due. On Tuesday, a utility payment is scheduled. On Wednesday, a small loan payment is expected. On Thursday, groceries and commuting costs land like clockwork. On Friday, wages arrive again and the cycle repeats. When a privately governed rail makes this cycle feel immediate and continuous, the user stops thinking in terms of settlement and starts thinking in terms of availability. Availability becomes moral. If the system can move value instantly, then delay feels like theft. If the system can operate continuously, then weekends feel like a scam. If the system can confirm completion in seconds, then any dispute that reopens the past feels like a violation of reality.

This is why the state's first error is dismissal. The fantasy survives not on theory but on daily pain. Dismissal treats private rails as toys until they have already trained a generation of users to measure money by interface behavior rather than by legal discharge. The state's second error is to treat the fantasy as purely ideological. The fantasy is operational. It is a product strategy aimed at adoption. It offers speed, constant uptime, and the appearance of finality. It offers the feeling of ownership without the sensation of permission. It offers a ledger that cannot be altered easily, a rulebook that cannot be rewritten by committee, and a form of value that can be carried across borders without asking anyone's consent. Even when these claims are only partially true, the experience is attractive enough to capture habit, and habit creates constituency. Constituency becomes bargaining power, because once enough people live inside an interface, the state is no longer governing a system. The state is negotiating with a reality.

The exit fantasy should be named precisely, because precision is how the state escapes both romance and panic. It is not primarily a claim about price stability or macro policy. It is a claim about governance substitution. It says that the functions associated with sovereign money can be replicated by protocol: issuance rules, transfer rules, settlement rules, and a form of finality that does not rely on courts. It says trust can be manufactured by transparency and math rather than by institutions and law. It says monetary order can be sustained by voluntary participation rather than by coercive enforcement. It proposes a world in which law becomes commentary on a ledger it does not control.

The fantasy's central sleight of hand is to treat the removal of one class of intermediaries as the removal of power. Scale does not permit powerlessness. Scale requires identity discipline, fraud containment, dispute handling, custody, liquidity provision, and a stable interface ordinary people can use without fear. Those functions can be performed publicly under law, or privately under platform policy, but they must be performed somewhere. The fantasy calls these requirements edge cases until the system is large enough that the edge becomes the center.

The first chamber of the fantasy is issuance. Constrained issuance looks like moral purity because it speaks to a real fear: states can abuse their ability to create money and distribute that money in captured ways. The fantasy frames scarcity as honesty and treats a rule fixed in code as superior to discretion exercised by officials. There is truth in the fear. There is also a trade. A system that cannot expand its supply of safe settlement claims in crisis forces adjustment through collapse rather than through stabilization. It converts political abuse risk into panic fragility risk. It also converts policy discretion into a different kind of discretion, because rules in code do not maintain themselves. People maintain them. Someone decides what constitutes a legitimate upgrade, how emergencies are handled, who can change parameters, and how the community enforces those choices. The fantasy sells constrained issuance as the elimination of human choice. In practice, it relocates human choice into governance structures that are less visible to ordinary users and often less accountable to public law.

That relocation matters more than the scarcity narrative because it reveals where sovereignty is actually moving. The user is told that the protocol is neutral because it is automated. The user is not told that automation depends on maintenance, maintenance depends on governance, governance depends on legitimacy, and legitimacy in private systems is often enforced by control over interfaces, liquidity access, and listing standards. The state can argue with scarcity claims forever and still miss the point. The point is not whether scarcity is virtuous. The point is who gets to decide how the system behaves when reality does not match the rulebook, because reality always arrives eventually.

The second chamber is settlement. The fantasy promises settlement without permission, which is appealing because permission is where modern payment life feels humiliating. Yet settlement at scale is not merely updating a ledger. Settlement is discharge that binds third parties. It is what ends disputes when counterparties refuse to cooperate. A private ledger can record completion. It cannot by itself force a creditor, a court, an employer, a tax authority, or an insurer to treat that completion as discharge in all relevant domains. This is where the fantasy is strongest on screen and weakest in law. The ledger can be incontrovertible within its own community. The wider world can still contest whether that ledger entry has the legal meaning the user assumed it had.

The third chamber is finality, and this is where the fantasy wins adoption by a quiet substitution. Confirmation equals finality. A user sees a confirmation and feels safe. A merchant sees a confirmation and ships goods. A platform shows a receipt and calls the payment complete. A sovereign system treats finality as a legal state defended by rules, institutions, and enforcement powers that survive dispute and insolvency. A private system often offers finality that is conditional: conditional on network health, conditional on governance not being contested, conditional on custody not failing, conditional on an interface not reversing access through its own rules, and conditional on courts not later treating the transfer as stolen, coerced, fraudulent, or in violation of public policy. The fantasy attempts to replace legal finality with computational finality. The state must make the difference visible without sounding like it is defending friction for its own sake.

This is where a single week in ordinary life becomes the state's lesson plan, whether the state wants it or not. On Monday, a household expects rent to clear. On Tuesday, a utility payment is scheduled. On Wednesday, a small loan payment is due. On Thursday, groceries are purchased. On Friday, wages arrive again. When the private rail behaves smoothly, the household learns a promise: the money is always there, always movable, always immediate. When the promise breaks, the household does not interpret it as a technical incident. The household interprets it as a betrayal. Pending becomes a moral word. Review becomes an accusation. Additional verification becomes humiliation. The household's balance still exists, but the household cannot use it to discharge obligations due in the real world. The fantasy collapses in one sentence spoken out loud at a kitchen table: it says I have it, but I cannot use it. That sentence is where private confirmation stops being comfort and becomes rage.

The fourth chamber is identity. The fantasy begins by promising movement without permission. At scale, movement without permission collides with crime, sanctions, fraud, and tax enforcement. The system then faces a choice. Either it remains a narrow rail used by those willing to accept elevated risk and legal ambiguity, or it becomes a mainstream rail and adopts identity controls, screening, and exclusion mechanisms. This is where the fantasy breaks in slow motion. A rail that touches payroll, merchant settlement, and consumer savings becomes a political object. Political objects attract regulation. Regulation demands identity. Identity demands data. Data creates gatekeeping. Gatekeeping recreates permission. The fantasy can delay this outcome. It cannot abolish it without remaining marginal.

Private governance reappears here, not as an accident but as a law of scale. To preserve mainstream access, the rail must adopt compliance standards. Those standards must be enforced somewhere, which means gatekeepers: platforms that approve accounts, custodians that hold reserves, liquidity venues that decide which conversions are allowed quickly and which are delayed, and interface providers that can cut off access instantly with no courtroom in sight. These gatekeepers acquire powers that look increasingly sovereign in practice. They can freeze, exclude, reorder, and ration. They do so in the language of safety and compliance rather than law, which means actions can be less transparent and less contestable. The exit fantasy promised liberation from arbitrary power. The reality can become migration into a different kind of power executed through terms of service and risk models rather than courts.

The fifth chamber is custody, where the fantasy compromises itself without admitting it. The ideology of self-custody is simple: if you hold the keys, you hold the money. The operational reality is that most users do not want the responsibility of key management, loss recovery, inheritance planning, and security against theft. They want the experience of self-custody with the protections of institutional custody. That preference produces intermediaries. Intermediaries produce concentration. Concentration recreates power. Custodians become the points where freezes occur, recoveries occur, compliance occurs, and losses are allocated when failures occur. Once custody concentrates, the private system begins to resemble the banking system it sought to replace, except legal protections may be thinner and crisis backstops ambiguous.

Custody concentration also produces a new map of vulnerability. A rail may be decentralized in ideology and concentrated in practice. Users may believe they transact with a protocol. In reality, they transact through a handful of custodial institutions and interface providers whose risk decisions govern the system's lived reality. A private system can therefore be open at the narrative layer and controlled at the choke point layer. The policy mistake is to govern the narrative and ignore the choke points. The private challenge wins when the state argues about decentralization while power concentrates in custody and interfaces.

The sixth chamber is liquidity, where the fantasy learns it cannot live without market makers, conversion venues, and deep pools of immediately usable value. A permissionless rail can move an entry at any hour, but economic life demands conversion between forms, and conversion is governed by liquidity. Liquidity is never neutral. It is provided by institutions that demand spreads, impose conditions, manage inventory, and pull back when fear arrives. If liquidity concentrates, then the rail's practical openness becomes conditional on a few institutions continuing to make markets. When those institutions tighten, the rail's promise of constant availability becomes conditional. The user learns that immediacy on screen is not the same as immediacy in conversion, and conversion is where money becomes usable in the wider world.

The seventh chamber is collateral, where the fantasy mutates into something more dangerous than protest. When private claims can be pledged as collateral, used in margining, or treated as cash equivalents in internal treasury operations, they become part of funding architecture. That is success. It is also danger, because collateral usage creates procyclical fragility. When the asset is rising, it supports leverage. When the asset falls, margin calls arrive, haircuts widen, and forced selling begins. If a private asset becomes collateral widely enough, its volatility transmits stress into institutions otherwise regulated, because collateral chains bind balance sheets through the demand for time. The fantasy does not die here. It becomes an internal participant in the state's financial machine while still claiming it is outside the machine. That is how private claims become public problems.

The decisive seam that exposes the fantasy is the collision between off-rail law and on-rail execution. On the rail, a transfer can be irreversible in technical terms. Off the rail, the world remains full of legal claims: stolen funds, coerced transfers, fraud, insolvency preferences, property disputes, and state enforcement. When a court orders restitution, the private rail cannot reverse history. It can only pressure intermediaries to freeze accounts, compel custodians to block withdrawals, and force interfaces to deny access. The user who believed in pure finality discovers a different truth: irreversibility does not eliminate governance. It forces governance to reappear as freeze power rather than reversal power. The system becomes a place where funds can be trapped by gatekeepers and unlocked only by those with influence over the custody and compliance layer. Authority returns. It returns without the public ceremony that usually admits authority exists.

This is where the fantasy becomes strategically dangerous, because it trains the public to expect one moral world and delivers another. The promise is freedom from the state's arbitrary delays. The delivered reality can be exposure to private delays that are less appealable and less explainable. The promise is money that cannot be censored. The delivered reality can be money that is censored by platform policy. The promise is neutrality. The delivered reality is a new hierarchy of who is legible and who is not, enforced by risk models behind an interface that still calls itself permissionless.

The decisive event that will determine the future of the exit fantasy is not the bull market. It is the first mass run in which ordinary users attempt to convert private claims into sovereign claims simultaneously, not because they hate the rail but because they need certainty. In that moment, the private system discovers whether it has a backstop or only a narrative. The state can pretend this is not its problem. The public will not accept refusal if the private rail has become part of wage life, merchant settlement, and household savings. That is why this chapter sits at the beginning of Part V. It trains the reader to see the private challenge as a contest for the interface that inevitably becomes a contest for the backstop.

The strongest defense of the fantasy is that the state deserves competition. Monopoly breeds complacency. Payment systems can be slow, exclusionary, expensive, and humiliating. Surveillance can expand beyond what citizens consider legitimate. Cross-border corridors can be weaponized, leaving smaller states exposed. This defense is not wrong. It is incomplete. Competition can discipline the state's interface. It can also create a parallel system that concentrates power in fewer hands and fewer transparent institutions, because a winner-take-most platform can control access to payments, identity legibility, custody, and dispute handling without the public constraints that bind state institutions. Competition can produce a private sovereign. The state's answer cannot be to ban competition. The answer must be to ensure that any private competitor that behaves like money is governed like money, and any private competitor that cannot accept those obligations remains limited in its claims on public trust.

This is the chapter's central strategic question. Can a system deliver money-like finality without sovereign enforcement. The honest answer is that it can deliver a form of completion within a bounded community, but the moment it tries to become general money, it collides with enforceable discharge, legal priority in insolvency, consumer protections, identity governance, and crisis backstops. The fantasy can deny these needs. It cannot remove them. If it refuses them, it remains a niche system where participants accept elevated risk and legal ambiguity. If it accepts them, it becomes a regulated system that resembles the state's architecture more than its rhetoric admits. The fantasy then survives only as branding, not as constitutional reality.

A statecraft reader should also see the geopolitical implication without needing any public name. The fantasy is an attempt to route around dominant corridors. It promises cross-border settlement without reliance on correspondent networks. It promises an external unit that can be held without exposure to foreign financial statecraft. It promises smaller states can diversify away from reserve dependence by adopting a neutral protocol. Yet the moment the protocol becomes systemic, it acquires its own concentrations: custodians, stable-value issuers, liquidity venues, compliance chokepoints, software dependencies, and infrastructure providers running critical pieces of the network. Those concentrations become targets of pressure. A protocol does not abolish statecraft. It relocates it. A state that understands this will map the new chokepoints and treat them as strategic infrastructure rather than as novelty.

The state's correct posture toward the exit fantasy is neither worship nor dismissal. It is classification. What is this claim. Who governs its ledger. Where does its finality come from. Who bears its losses under stress. Which corridor does it use for upgrade into sovereign claims. Which custody and identity points can freeze or exclude. Which concentrations will become panic targets. Once those questions are answered, the fantasy becomes an object of statecraft rather than an object of belief.

CLOSING DOCTRINE

The exit fantasy is a governance substitution attempt that begins as convenience and matures into a claim about finality without the state. A private rail can produce completion within a bounded community, but general money requires enforceable discharge, legal priority under insolvency, identity governance, consumer protection, and a credible backstop when upgrade demand arrives. As systems scale, intermediaries reappear through custody, compliance, and liquidity concentration, recreating gatekeeping in forms that can be less transparent and less contestable than public law if left outside discipline. The decisive seam is the collision between off-rail law and on-rail irreversibility, which forces authority to reappear as freeze power and exclusion rather than reversal, revealing that governance was never abolished, only relocated. The decisive stress event is the mass upgrade attempt, when holders seek conversion into sovereign claims and the private promise is revealed as dependent on public settlement corridors, public law, and public crisis capacity. The state's task is to classify private claims, map their dependencies into the public core, and decide in advance whether they are permitted to behave like money under stress; if permitted, they must carry money obligations and accept money discipline, and if not, their marketing, distribution, and collateral usage must be constrained so the public is not trained to expect sovereign protection for a private promise.

CHAPTER 24
STABLECOINS
PRIVATE ISSUERS, PUBLIC DEPENDENCE

The first time a stable-value token becomes real to a household is not when the household reads a technical paper. It is when the household uses it like checking. A paycheck hits, the balance updates, and the household begins to treat the number on the screen as ordinary money because it behaves like ordinary money. Rent is scheduled. Groceries are covered. A transfer to family clears quickly. The household does not examine reserve composition. The household does not ask what court would enforce redemption. The household does not track custodial concentration or settlement windows. The interface does the quiet work of persuasion: if it behaves like money, it is money. That is the stablecoin's conquest. It makes a private claim feel like a public claim by borrowing the user's habit before the user asks what supports the claim.

The merchant's version is even more immediate. The merchant receives payment, sees confirmation, and treats the token as spendable inventory because it clears faster than alternatives and because dispute burden feels lighter. The merchant's supplier accepts it, or accepts it often enough that the merchant begins to rely on it. Payroll is timed against it. Weekend settlement becomes normal. The merchant does not experience a "private instrument." The merchant experiences a shorter cash conversion cycle, and a shorter cash conversion cycle feels like relief. Relief becomes dependence quickly because the merchant's life is a sequence of deadlines and thin margins.

Stablecoins are not the exit fantasy's pure form. They are the compromise that made the private challenge plausible at scale. The exit fantasy promised money without the state. Stablecoins promise money that feels like the state's unit while living in a privately governed channel. They do not ask the public to accept volatility. They ask the public to accept a familiar unit in an unfamiliar legal wrapper. That is why they are potent. They do not need to win an argument about sovereignty. They need only to win daily usability, because usability writes political expectation faster than statutes do.

A stable-value claim is not proven by how it trades when nobody is afraid. It is proven by how it redeems when everyone is afraid. That seems obvious when stated plainly, yet stablecoin marketing works by training the public to treat price stability in calm as if it were an enforceable right in stress. This is the first improvement to make the chapter heavier. The chapter must keep dragging the reader back to the only place where stability becomes real: redemption into the apex claim, on time, at par, without conditions that appear only when conditions are most damaging.

"A stable-value token is a digital claim designed to maintain a stable value relative to a reference unit." (international consultative definition, 2020)

Read the sentence carefully. It is not a guarantee. It is a statement of design intent. Designed to maintain stable value is not the same as guaranteed to maintain stable value, and this distance between intent and guarantee is the stablecoin's central political trick. It allows a private issuer to market stability while preserving a boundary between a public obligation and a private promise that is blurry enough to preserve optionality when stress arrives. The state's job is to remove that blur before the public learns the difference through a run.

The mechanism is simple in outline and ruthless in consequence. An issuer accepts money-like funds and issues a token claim. The issuer holds reserves. The issuer promises redemption at par into the reference unit, under stated conditions, within stated timelines, through stated channels. If the promise is credible, the token circulates and the market treats it as near-cash. If the promise is doubted, holders attempt redemption. Redemption pressure forces the issuer to convert reserves into money quickly. If reserves are liquid and uncontested, the issuer survives. If reserves are illiquid, encumbered, concentrated in one custodian, subject to legal dispute, or operationally gated, the issuer delays or fails. Delay is enough. Delay teaches the market that the claim is not cash. Once the market learns that, the run accelerates because nobody wants to be last holding a claim marketed as stable.

Stablecoins therefore live inside the oldest monetary logic in a new costume. They are short-term liabilities that promise par redemption. They function like deposits for users and like cash-equivalent buffers for treasurers, yet they often sit outside the full discipline that protects par redemption in the banking system. Their stability is not self-generated. It is borrowed from the public money they redeem into and from the public institutions that make redemption possible. This is the chapter's governing proposition. Stablecoins are private issuers with public dependence. They can only be stable at scale if they are anchored to the settlement core, the legal enforcement system, and the crisis capacity of the state, even when they insist otherwise.

The stablecoin's appeal is not abstract. It is operational. It offers continuous movement, near-instant transfer, and an interface that behaves as if settlement were a screen event rather than a legal event. It also offers portability across platforms that ordinary bank balances cannot always deliver without friction. For a household, it feels like digital cash with global reach. For a merchant, it feels like faster receivables. For a corporate treasury team, it can feel like a buffer that is deployable at any hour. The stablecoin's danger is that this smoothness is a surface effect produced by a private claim riding on public foundations. When foundations are tested, the surface can crack without warning.

The chapter must make that training effect intimate rather than theoretical. A household builds routines around the stablecoin balance. Autopay is scheduled. A landlord accepts the token. A gig platform pays out in it. The household begins treating the stablecoin wallet as the place where money lives, not because of ideology but because it is where money behaves politely. Then the first small disruption arrives. It is not a collapse. It is a banner that says congestion. It is a redemption queue that says pending. It is a customer support message that says additional verification required. The household's balance still exists on screen, yet the household cannot convert it into the form needed for obligations due Monday morning. The household does not experience this as "private credit risk." The household experiences it as money becoming conditional at exactly the worst moment. That is the instant the stablecoin crosses from private product into political object, because political life begins where ordinary people discover that what felt like a right is actually permission.

The second improvement is to make the stablecoin's fragility feel like a chain of chokepoints rather than one balance sheet. The label stable hides distinct architectures that behave differently in stress. Some designs are full-reserve in spirit, holding only the highest-grade liquid assets and offering tight redemption terms. Others chase yield by holding longer-duration instruments, taking credit risk, or concentrating exposures. Some depend on affiliated market makers for liquidity. Some depend on one custodian, one prime broker, one settlement corridor. Some reserve the right to gate redemptions. Some reserve the right to suspend redemptions. Each variation changes the run mechanics and changes how quickly public dependence becomes public liability. A state that regulates the word stable will fail. A state must regulate the claim structure.

Reserve composition and reserve control are the center of gravity. If the issuer holds reserves as immediately available central-bank money, the run mechanism is mostly operational: can redemption be processed fast enough, and can the issuer keep its rails functioning while processing the surge. If reserves are held in short-term government instruments, the run mechanism becomes market depth: can the issuer sell into stress without haircuts that break par. If reserves are held in bank deposits, the run mechanism becomes bank concentration: redemption becomes outflow pressure on a narrow set of banks, which then tightens domestic credit to defend their own liquidity. If reserves are held in privately issued short-term instruments, the run mechanism becomes credit. If reserves are mixed, the run mechanism becomes uncertainty, because holders cannot see which slice will be sold first and which slice will be stuck. Uncertainty is the run's accelerant because it turns rational caution into simultaneous exit.

"A claim is stable only to the extent it can be redeemed, at par, on demand, under stress." (doctrine distilled from crisis practice)

This is an engineering requirement. The stablecoin is not proven by its price in calm. It is proven by its redemption behavior in a week when everyone wants out. Any design that cannot meet that requirement is not a stable money substitute. It is a liquidity instrument wearing a stability costume. That costume can survive in calm. It dissolves in a run.

The first pressure scene belongs inside the issuer's treasury desk, because this is where stability is manufactured day by day. The desk is not thinking about ideology. It is thinking about inflows, outflows, and how to keep reserves positioned so redemptions can be met without selling at the wrong moment. In calm, the desk's problem is efficiency: keep reserves liquid enough to meet redemptions while earning enough yield to fund operations and distribution. In stress, efficiency becomes fragility. Yield becomes a liability because yield is purchased by giving up immediacy. The desk begins shortening assets, moving into the most liquid instruments, concentrating risk in what it believes will remain bid even under pressure. That repositioning is rational. It is also a signal. Counterparties see it. Custodians see it. Liquidity venues feel it. The issuer's internal behavior becomes external information, and external information becomes public fear.

The second pressure scene belongs inside custody, because custody is where stablecoins quietly resemble the banking system they claim to bypass. Reserves sit somewhere. They are held by custodians and banks operating under public law. They are subject to operational holds, compliance reviews, legal disputes, and risk decisions by institutions that must protect themselves first. An issuer can promise redemption. A custodian can slow the movement of reserves if it fears liability or if it is responding to a directive. The issuer can be solvent and still fail the run if it cannot access its own reserves quickly enough to deliver the reference unit. This is the stablecoin's hidden dependency: the issuer's promise is only as good as the custodial chain's willingness and capacity to move the underlying settlement claim on demand.

Make the chokepoints explicit, because this is where the illusion of simple money becomes real complexity. There is a reserve asset gate, where the issuer discovers what can actually be sold quickly in size without creating a haircut spiral. There is a custody gate, where reserves must move through institutions with their own risk appetites and legal obligations. There is a compliance gate, where redemption requests can be delayed or denied for reasons that the user experiences as arbitrary. There is a banking rail gate, where settlement windows and operational cutoffs create timing scarcity. There is a messaging gate, where public reassurance that tries to calm can accidentally confirm weakness and accelerate the run. A stablecoin run is rarely one failure. It is a chain of small denials that converts a stable claim into a subordinated claim, and once subordination is visible, the run becomes rational for everyone at once.

The third pressure scene belongs in merchant settlement, because merchants carry the economy's pulse. A merchant sees token payments arrive and treats them as cashflow. The merchant uses that cashflow to restock. The merchant uses that cashflow to pay staff. The merchant relies on the stablecoin's promise that redemption is routine. When redemption slows, the merchant's supplier starts adding conditions, demanding prepayment in a different form or charging a premium for accepting the token. The merchant's margin compresses overnight. Inventory shrinks. Staff hours are cut. The merchant does not describe this as a stablecoin run. The merchant describes it as the business suddenly having less time. Less time is what crisis feels like in the real economy.

The fourth pressure scene belongs in a nonfinancial firm's operations, because this is where the stablecoin's failure becomes a timing shock rather than a finance story. A logistics firm uses the stablecoin to settle cross-border invoices quickly, because the traditional corridor has more friction and the stablecoin corridor feels continuous. When redemption becomes uncertain, counterparties begin demanding earlier payment, or demand a different settlement form, or demand a premium for accepting the token. The logistics firm begins holding more idle cash to protect timing. Holding more idle cash reduces investment. Reduced investment reduces capacity. The firm looks to the banking system for a credit line to bridge the gap and discovers that banks have tightened because stablecoin redemption pressure is pulling liquidity toward the core. The firm experiences stablecoin stress as compressed working capital, not as a debate about private money.

The fifth pressure scene belongs inside the supervisor's view, because this is where "private issuer" becomes "public dependence." A supervisor sees that stablecoin reserves are concentrated in a small set of banks and short-term markets. A supervisor sees that redemption pressure would translate into fast outflows from those banks. A supervisor sees that those banks will respond by pulling back credit, hoarding liquidity, and tightening terms for ordinary business clients. The supervisor also sees that stablecoin issuers and platforms have trained merchants and households to treat the token as money-like. The political risk is obvious. If a run freezes merchant settlement and household access, the public will not accept the explanation that the token was private. The public will experience it as the payment state malfunctioning. This is how the stablecoin becomes a backstop claim even if no law says it should be.

The stablecoin's public dependence also appears in the redemption promise itself. Redemption is usually executed through the banking system. The issuer relies on bank accounts, payment rails, and settlement windows. If those rails become constrained in stress, redemption slows. If redemption slows, the token trades at a discount, and the discount becomes a public signal that the claim is subordinated. Once the claim is visibly subordinated, it stops behaving like money and starts behaving like a risky instrument. The run accelerates because no rational holder wants to be the last person holding a discounting claim that was marketed as stable.

The chapter must sharpen a distinction the public rarely sees until it is too late: price stability versus redemption stability. A stablecoin can trade slightly off par in routine conditions for microstructural reasons and still be stable. Redemption instability is different. When redemptions are delayed, limited, gated, or selectively honored, the stablecoin's stability claim is broken even if the token's market price is temporarily held near par by liquidity providers. Market price can be supported by trading behavior. Redemption cannot be faked when holders demand conversion into the reference unit. Redemption is the test. Everything else is performance.

A serious counterargument insists stablecoins can be safer than banks because they can be backed by high-quality reserves and because ledger transparency can reduce hidden leverage. This can be true when reserves are truly high quality, custody is resilient, redemption rights are legally enforceable, reserves are segregated, and the issuer cannot rehypothecate or obscure the balance sheet. Under those conditions, the stablecoin begins to resemble a narrow-bank claim: a money-like liability backed by liquid assets, redeemable at par, structured to avoid maturity mismatch. The state's response should not be denial. The state's response should be classification. If the claim is built as a narrow-bank substitute, it must be governed as a narrow-bank substitute. It cannot be allowed to use banking-like stability narratives while avoiding banking-like discipline.

Another counterargument insists stablecoins improve payment competition and reduce cross-border dependency on dominant corridors. That too can be true in daily use. Yet routing around friction does not abolish statecraft. It relocates it. The stablecoin becomes dependent on custodians that hold reserves, jurisdictions that govern those custodians, compliance standards that determine legibility, and banking rails that execute redemption. If the stablecoin becomes systemic, it becomes strategic infrastructure and therefore becomes a target of pressure, whether by markets or by states. The corridor may look different. The dependency remains.

The third improvement is to make the political contradiction land heavier and earlier, because this is the heart of the stablecoin problem. In calm, an issuer can grow by marketing stability while preserving legal optionality. In crisis, that optionality becomes a public injury. The issuer will insist delays are temporary, gates are prudent, and reserves are sufficient. Users will see only that money is no longer behaving like money. Merchants will see that settlement is no longer dependable. Firms will see timing shrink. Supervisors will see liquidity pulled toward the core. The state then faces the choice it always faces when a money-like claim becomes systemic: allow the run to proceed and accept broader spillovers, or intervene to preserve continuity, which confirms that the stablecoin was always a public dependence instrument. The state cannot escape the choice by pretending stablecoins sit outside monetary architecture. Once stablecoins become widely used, their failure mode becomes an internal failure mode of the payment state.

The worst posture is ambiguity. Ambiguity permits growth on a public-money feel while preserving private-money escape hatches in the terms. Ambiguity trains the public to expect par safety and then delivers subordination. That is how legitimacy breaks. A state can tolerate small private failures. A state cannot tolerate a mass public lesson that the unit people used as money was never money when it mattered, especially if the state allowed the claim to market itself as stable while avoiding enforceable discipline.

The chapter must also name the stablecoin's power map, because Part V is about the interface war and stablecoins are an interface weapon. The issuer controls issuance and redemption policy. The custodian controls the movement of reserves. The major liquidity venues control price and therefore public perception. The distribution platforms control habit and therefore dependence. The compliance gatekeepers control legibility and therefore inclusion. When the system is calm, these powers feel administrative. In stress, they become sovereign-like. They determine who can redeem first, who is delayed, whose accounts are frozen, and which transactions are permitted. Stablecoins do not remove governance. They compress governance into private hands and then ask the state to tolerate the arrangement because it feels modern.

This is why stablecoins are the central private challenge of this Part. They are the cleanest attempt to take the state's unit, reproduce it as a private claim, distribute it through private interfaces, and normalize it as daily money before the state decides whether the claim is permitted to become systemic. Once normalized, the stablecoin becomes a political hostage. The state is told that disciplining it will harm consumers and merchants who now depend on it. The issuer gains leverage by becoming indispensable. This is not a conspiracy. It is the predictable result of building a money-like product without first settling whether the state will treat it as money in crisis.

The chapter therefore ends with a hard but necessary point. A stablecoin can either be a narrow, clearly bounded instrument, with clear disclosure that it is not public money and can break under stress, or it can be permitted to become money-like at scale, which requires the state to impose money obligations: reserve discipline, custody resilience, enforceable redemption, and explicit rules about whether and when public backstops will be available. If the state refuses to make this choice, the market will make it during panic, and the market's method of choice is a run.

CLOSING DOCTRINE

Stablecoins are private issuers that borrow public credibility through the promise of par redemption into the state's unit, which makes them public dependence instruments even when they claim independence. Stability is not proven by calm trading or by on-screen confirmation. It is proven by stress redemption, because a claim is only money-like to the extent it can be converted into the apex claim on demand without delay, gates, or contested custody. Reserve composition is the mechanism of survival and the first source of fragility, because yield is purchased by giving up immediacy; custody control is the hidden choke point, because the issuer's promise is only as good as the custodial chain's ability and willingness to move the underlying settlement claim. As stablecoins scale, their runs transmit into banks, short-term markets, and settlement corridors through reserve liquidation and redemption flows, forcing the state into triage whether it wants that responsibility or not. The only durable posture is explicit architecture: either constrain stablecoins to remain bounded and clearly risky, or govern them as money by enforcing reserves, redemption rights, custody segregation, disclosure discipline, and crisis rules before the public learns the difference through panic.

CHAPTER 25
SOVEREIGN DIGITAL CURRENCY
RECLAIMING THE PAYMENT FRONT END

The state does not build a sovereign digital currency because it wants a new gadget. It builds one because it is losing the front end of money while still being held responsible for the back end. Private platforms have taught users to expect instant availability, continuous operation, and an interface that treats confirmation as completion. They have trained people to treat fees, delays, weekend gaps, and reversals as proof of incompetence or capture. In that environment, the state can preserve the unit and still lose the lived definition of the unit. The state can keep its currency as the legal reference and still watch daily payment life migrate into privately governed apps, privately managed custody stacks, and private settlement corridors. Once that happens, sovereignty becomes an afterthought: the state is still expected to rescue and stabilize, yet it no longer owns the channel through which citizens experience money.

This is not a philosophical injury. It is an operational humiliation with political consequences. When a private rail tightens, the citizen blames the state because the citizen experiences money as a public promise, not as a private product. When a platform freezes accounts under a risk policy, the citizen does not feel the subtlety of corporate terms. The citizen feels exclusion from economic life. When a merchant's receipts become delayed, discounted, or conditionally usable, the merchant does not care whether settlement is technically in process. The merchant cares that payroll is due and inventory must be ordered. The state can declare the rail private. The public will not accept the declaration once that rail has become daily habit. This is the interface problem in its harshest form: the state carries legitimacy liability for a surface it does not control.

A sovereign digital currency is the state's counter-move. It is a bid to reclaim the payment front end, not by nostalgia but by architecture. It is the attempt to deliver public finality through a user experience that can compete with private interfaces without surrendering legal priority, crisis capacity, and enforceable discharge. The point is not that citizens crave direct public money on a phone. The point is that the state cannot tolerate an interface vacuum where private systems define what money feels like and then demand public rescue when private promises fail. A state that does not defend the front end will be forced to defend it anyway, but under worse terms, with less legitimacy, and with fewer levers, because the levers will be embedded in private systems that do not answer to public obligation.

The serious frame is statecraft, not modernization. Money is a governed architecture of claims. The interface through which claims move is the public's experience of governance. When the interface is private, the governance that matters in daily life becomes private: account access, freeze decisions, dispute logic, data capture, and the quiet setting of norms about who is legible enough to move at full speed. A sovereign digital currency is therefore not only a payment rail. It is a fight over who owns legibility, who owns transaction data, and who owns the power to include and exclude. That fight is why sovereign digital currency becomes politically combustible. The promise is inclusion and resilience. The fear is surveillance and control. Both are plausible because both are produced by the same mechanism: direct reach.

"CBDC is a digital form of central bank money that is different from balances in traditional reserve or settlement accounts." (Bank for International Settlements, 2020)

The phrase matters because it clarifies what is changing. This is not a new messaging system glued onto old settlement. This is a new public claim type, or a new public access model, or both. It shifts where the apex claim can be held, how it can be used, and who can touch it. That shift alters the hierarchy of money whether policymakers admit it or not. It changes citizens' exit options in stress, banks' funding expectations in calm, and the state's ability to deliver continuity directly rather than through intermediaries that can become choke points.

The chapter's objective can be stated without softness. The objective is to prevent the interface from becoming a private constitution. If the interface becomes private, private actors define daily monetary reality through design choices: what speed is normal, what reversals are tolerated, what fees are acceptable, what identity burdens are required, what disputes are adjudicated, and what exclusions are executed quietly. In calm, these decisions feel like product policy. In stress, they become monetary governance because they determine who can move and who is stuck. A sovereign digital currency is the state's attempt to ensure that a public baseline exists, anchored in public finality, whose access cannot be withdrawn by private policy and whose operation cannot be silently reprioritized by a platform's incentives.

The first design question is the most politically sensitive because it determines whether the instrument is a currency modernization or a balance-sheet redesign. What exactly is being issued. If the instrument is a direct claim on the central bank, then the state is offering apex money to the public in a form that can compete with private claims. This can improve safety for households and reduce dependence on private issuers. It can also destabilize banks in stress if depositors shift rapidly from bank deposits into the apex claim. That shift is not hypothetical. It is rational behavior for anyone seeking certainty when fear arrives. A sovereign digital currency, if widely accessible, creates a new and faster exit route from bank liabilities into the apex asset. Even before a crisis, the existence of that exit route changes bargaining power. Depositors demand more. Banks pay more. Banks lend differently. The mere presence of an easy upgrade path into the apex claim tightens bank funding conditions over time, because it introduces competition for the safest form of money.

The state cannot avoid this trade by pretending the instrument is only a "payment layer." If it is a direct public claim, it is a structural change to the hierarchy of claims. That means the design must decide how to manage deposit migration dynamics without undermining the instrument's credibility. Limits, frictions, tiered remuneration, and conversion policies are not technical details. They are the political controls that determine whether the banking system remains a primary credit engine or becomes a narrower credit broker funded differently. A state that offers apex money to the public without designing the banking consequence is designing a run mechanism and calling it innovation.

Here the state faces a tri-lemma that should be stated plainly because it is where political disappointment is born. A sovereign digital currency cannot maximize inclusion, maximize bank stability, and maximize privacy all at once without accepting tradeoffs that will become visible under stress. If the state maximizes inclusion by making the apex claim widely available with minimal friction, it increases the risk of rapid migration out of deposits in panic unless it imposes limits or builds a new bank funding architecture. If it maximizes bank stability by restricting access, imposing strong frictions, or making the public claim unattractive in normal times, it may fail to provide the public baseline that prevents private platforms from becoming the default interface. If it maximizes privacy with strong compartmentalization, it will face pressure from enforcement authorities to expand visibility and it will face public skepticism if privacy exists only as a promise rather than as an enforceable boundary. The state must choose a posture and defend it, because the public will experience the tradeoffs whether they are named or not.

The second design question is distribution, and distribution is governance. The state can issue the instrument and rely on private intermediaries to distribute it, manage wallets, perform identity checks, and provide customer service. This avoids turning the central bank into a retail institution and it can scale faster because existing networks already touch citizens. It also preserves intermediaries as gatekeepers. If intermediaries remain the place where identity is verified, access is granted, and disputes are handled, the state has modernized settlement while leaving legibility and exclusion inside private systems. That may be acceptable if the state's goal is only efficiency. It is inadequate if the state's goal is to prevent private platforms from becoming the de facto constitution of payment life.

The alternative is public baseline access: a design where every citizen and lawful resident can hold a wallet claim that cannot be arbitrarily withdrawn by private policy. That baseline can be delivered through public channels or through tightly constrained private channels with enforceable obligations. It can be designed to ensure that a citizen can always pay rent, buy food, and receive wages even if a private platform locks accounts. This is inclusion as dignity rather than inclusion as marketing. Yet baseline access also concentrates power because the state becomes the direct provider of a rail that touches daily life. If the state builds baseline access, it must build visible restraint, because direct reach without restraint is the architecture of a permission regime, and a permission regime will be resisted.

The third design question is privacy and data. A sovereign digital currency produces data, and data is not a byproduct. Data is the interface's shadow. The state must decide what can be seen, by whom, and under what conditions, and these decisions must be designed to survive crisis politics rather than merely announced in calm. If transactions are visible in real time to authorities, the rail becomes a surveillance layer by default. If transactions are visible only under strict legal process, the state must build technical compartmentalization so that "only under process" is true in practice rather than true in theory. If transactions are stored in ways that allow intermediaries to monetize and profile, the state has created a public rail that feeds private extraction and exclusion. Privacy is therefore not an optional feature. Privacy is the boundary line between a public utility and a monitored permission system.

The fourth design question is resilience. A payment state that depends entirely on connectivity is a fragile state. If a sovereign digital currency becomes a primary rail, it must be treated like critical infrastructure: continuity under outage, resilience under cyberattack, and graceful degradation without turning the economy into a queue of failed payments. This requirement is not technical vanity. It is legitimacy. A private platform can fail and call it downtime. A public rail cannot fail without teaching citizens that their money is conditional on network health. If the rail cannot maintain continuity under stress, it will become a political liability and private alternatives will gain moral fuel again, because the public will interpret failure as governance failure.

The fifth design question is interoperability, because an isolated public rail is not a reclaimed interface. It is a niche. Citizens live inside mixed payment ecology: cards, bank transfers, merchant platforms, payroll providers, and cross-border corridors. A sovereign digital currency that cannot interact smoothly with those systems will feel like an inconvenience rather than a baseline. Yet interoperability is also where power hides. If interoperability is mediated by a handful of private gateways, then private gatekeeping reappears at the conversion seam. The state can issue apex money and still lose the interface if the only usable paths into and out of the rail are controlled by private gateways. A serious design must therefore treat conversion seams as political seams: where friction, fees, and exclusion can be imposed quietly.

The sixth design question is programmability, and it cannot be postponed because even if the state refuses programmability, private competitors will market it. Programmability promises that money can carry conditions: taxes withheld automatically, subsidies targeted precisely, funds restricted for defined uses, compliance embedded at the moment of transfer. This promises precision. It also threatens generality. General money is money that can be used for any lawful purpose. Conditional money can become segmented money, and segmented money can become stratification if certain groups receive money that is more restricted than others. Programmability can be a tool for reducing fraud and improving delivery. It can also become the mechanism through which money is turned into a policy leash. If the state chooses programmability, it must defend generality as a constitutional principle rather than as a policy preference, because segmented money is a political fracture waiting to happen.

The necessity of a sovereign front end becomes obvious when it is felt as ordinary life rather than as design debate. A household uses a private wallet because it is easy. Wages arrive there. Bills are paid there. The household stops thinking of money as an institution and starts thinking of money as a screen. Then a compliance review triggers. The wallet is locked. The household cannot pay rent. The landlord does not care that the lock was executed by a private policy model. The landlord cares that rent did not arrive. The household calls customer service and receives a scripted delay. The household goes to a bank and discovers the bank cannot restore access because the bank does not control the wallet. The household goes to the state and discovers the state can warn and scold but cannot reopen the rail in time because the rail is private. The household experiences this not as inconvenience but as abandonment. That abandonment is the interface vacuum made visible. A sovereign digital currency is the state refusing to allow daily economic participation to be contingent on private discretion alone.

The merchant scene is sharper because merchants are where legitimacy becomes public. A merchant accepts private money-like claims because customers want to pay that way. Settlement is fast. Fees are lower. Disputes are fewer. Then a stress event arrives. Redemptions slow. Liquidity providers widen spreads. The merchant's receipts are still visible but less usable. Suppliers begin demanding different forms or charging premiums. The merchant holds bigger buffers, cuts inventory, and delays hiring. The merchant's pain becomes the neighborhood's pain. The state can stabilize banks and still fail the merchant if the merchant's payment life is mediated by private rails that the state cannot compel to behave as a public utility. This is the seam that makes the sovereign front end politically inevitable. The state is not building a new rail to win a product contest. The state is building a baseline so commerce does not become hostage to private gating when panic arrives.

The bank funding conflict is where the state must show discipline rather than optimism. A sovereign digital currency changes the exit option for depositors. In calm, depositors may not move. In fear, they will. Banks see this and respond. They compete harder for deposits, they hold more liquid assets, and they tighten lending standards. Credit becomes more expensive at the margin. Some lending becomes shorter-term. The economy feels this as a slow squeeze that arrives even without a headline crisis, because banks are pricing the new public exit option into their balance sheet discipline. The state must decide whether it wants that discipline to force banks into safer funding structures, or whether it wants to preserve the current model and accept design limits that reduce the sovereign digital currency's attractiveness as a full substitute. The state cannot pretend that it is issuing a neutral instrument. It is issuing an exit path, and exit paths change systems.

The political fear crystallizes around surveillance because the state's temptation is real. If the state builds a rail that provides fine-grained visibility and fine-grained control, the temptation to use it will expand, especially under crisis politics. Authorities will argue for broader access to combat fraud, crime, sanctions evasion, and tax avoidance. Those arguments will often be sincere. The public will fear mission creep, and mission creep is not a conspiracy. It is institutional gravity. The only credible answer is restraint embedded in architecture and enforceable law: compartmentalization that makes mass monitoring difficult by design, legal thresholds that cannot be bypassed by convenience, and governance that treats privacy as a boundary on power rather than as a slogan. If the state cannot demonstrate restraint, citizens will treat sovereign digital currency as a control project and will flee toward private alternatives even if those alternatives are riskier, because people will accept financial risk to avoid political fear.

This is why a sovereign digital currency is a renegotiation of the relationship between citizen and monetary state. It can restore trust by making public money feel modern and dependable, anchoring daily payment life in public finality rather than in private confirmation. It can also destroy trust by making money feel like a monitored permission slip. The state cannot ask for trust. It must earn trust through restraint that is visible in design, not merely promised in speeches. It must also earn trust through competence that is visible in continuity, because the public will judge the rail not by its ideals but by whether it works when the week is tight and fear is rising.

"Cash is a public interface. Its digital successor must be a public interface too, or the interface will belong to private sovereigns by default." (doctrinal principle distilled from payment-state reality)

The sentence is not nostalgia. It is warning. Cash is not merely anonymous. Cash is a baseline: a way to transact without permission from a platform and without dependence on a risk model. If the digital economy has no baseline with public obligations, then private rails become the baseline, and private rails will govern inclusion, exclusion, data capture, and dispute logic in daily life. The state will still be blamed when those choices hurt citizens. Sovereign digital currency is the state acknowledging that the baseline must exist in the digital realm, and that the baseline must be governed as a public utility rather than as a product.

CLOSING DOCTRINE

Sovereign digital currency is the state's counter-move in the interface war: an attempt to reclaim the payment front end so that public finality is delivered through a public-standard user experience rather than through privately governed rails that can tighten, gate, and exclude at the worst moment. If the instrument is a direct public claim, it changes the hierarchy of money by bringing the apex asset closer to households and merchants, strengthening resilience but also creating a faster exit from bank deposits in panic unless limits, frictions, or bank funding redesign absorb the shift. Distribution is governance because whoever distributes controls legibility and exclusion; a public rail either modernizes settlement while leaving gatekeeping to intermediaries or provides baseline access that cannot be withdrawn by private policy, accepting the political burden of direct reach. Data and privacy are constitutional because the rail's legitimacy depends on restraint that is real in architecture and enforceable in law, not merely promised, since fine-grained visibility and fine-grained control become irresistible under crisis politics. Resilience and interoperability are legitimacy conditions because a baseline that fails in outage or becomes hostage to private gateways is not a baseline at all.

Programmability is the next battlefield because conditional money can become segmented money, and segmented money can become political stratification unless generality is defended as a boundary. A sovereign digital currency succeeds only if it closes the gap between retail smoothness and sovereign finality without turning money into a permission regime; otherwise it either fails adoption or wins adoption and loses legitimacy, which is simply failure delayed.

CHAPTER 26
POLICY IN CODE
PROGRAMMABILITY, CONTROL, AND CONTESTATION

The most dangerous sentence in modern monetary design is also the most seductive: we can make money do the right thing automatically. The promise is efficiency. The promise is precision. The promise is fewer loopholes, fewer frauds, fewer delays, and fewer human bottlenecks. The promise is that the state can deliver benefits without leakage, taxes without evasion, and compliance without the slow violence of paperwork. The promise is also control, because automatic means the rule executes whether the citizen agrees or not, and it executes at transaction speed, without the friction that used to create time for debate, discretion, and appeal. Programmability is therefore not a feature. It is an argument about relocating sovereign choice into code, and code is law that runs on rails rather than in courtrooms.

Programmability enters the public conversation through convenience, not ideology. A merchant wants payments that reconcile themselves. A payroll team wants wages that arrive with withholding already handled. A treasury team wants conditional release tied to delivery and verification. A welfare agency wants restrictions that prevent diversion by predatory actors. A regulator wants compliance embedded so prohibited flows are blocked before they become scandals. Each desire is rational. Each also pulls money away from being a general claim and toward being an instrument with conditions. That pull is the beginning of contestation, because general money is the one thing a society shares even when it disagrees about everything else. When money becomes conditional, society begins to split not only by income and class, but by the rule sets attached to people's balances, by which payments clear smoothly and which payments are forced into review, by who carries script-free money and who carries money that arrives already wearing restrictions.

"Code is law." (digital governance maxim, late 1990s)

The phrase is old because the reality is older than the phrase. Any payment system already has rules. Programmability is not the invention of rules. Programmability is the relocation of enforcement into automatic execution, with fewer human intermediaries and less discretionary delay. That relocation changes what citizens can contest. Under traditional regimes, people fight the state through courts, politics, and administrative appeals. Under code regimes, people fight the system by trying to avoid the rule, by seeking alternative rails, or by protesting legitimacy after the rule has already acted. Politics does not disappear. Politics is compressed into design decisions and then hidden behind execution, and execution is harder to reverse once it becomes routine.

The state's temptation is obvious. Money already expresses governance. Taxes create demand. Benefits distribute capacity. Enforcement defines admissibility. The state already shapes the economy through the rules around money, and the state already leans on private institutions to carry much of the reputational and operational burden of that rule. Programmability offers a way to do this with less friction, fewer intermediaries, and more measurable outcomes. It promises that public spending can be tagged, traced, and restricted. It promises that fraud can be prevented rather than prosecuted after the fact. It promises that sanctions can be enforced at the moment of transfer rather than through slow litigation. It promises that the state can govern without constantly pushing the burden onto banks and platforms and then blaming them when enforcement is uneven. From the state's perspective, programmability looks like sovereignty regained.

From the citizen's perspective, programmability can look like the end of neutrality. The citizen is not wrong to fear that a programmable rail can become a moralizing rail. When money is general, a citizen can spend lawful funds as the citizen chooses. When money becomes conditional, a citizen's choices can be shaped, constrained, or punished automatically. Restrictions can begin as targeted protections and then expand as the default posture of the rail. The line between protection and paternalism is not a technical line. It is a political line, and once the line is encoded, it becomes the daily reality for anyone living inside that payment interface.

The chapter therefore begins with the simplest constitutional claim: money's generality is not an accident. It is a social truce. General money is money that can be used for any lawful purpose, and that generality protects citizens from being sorted into rule classes at the point of spending. It is the guarantee that the state's distribution of capacity does not carry an invisible script deciding how a person is allowed to live. Programmability threatens that truce because it makes scripts easy to attach and cheap to enforce. Once scripts exist, the question becomes who receives script-free money and who receives scripted money. That distribution becomes a new political hierarchy, and hierarchies at the payment layer do not stay quiet for long because they touch dignity every day.

The first pressure scene belongs inside a benefits office, because this is where programmability's promise is most sympathetic and its danger is most visible. An agency is trying to deliver support quickly while preventing diversion by predatory actors who exploit vulnerable recipients. A programmable payment seems like a humane solution. Funds can be restricted to essential categories. Funds can be made non-transferable to known exploitative channels. Funds can be timed to reduce immediate seizure by creditors. The agency sees protection, and recipients may even welcome it when it blocks the worst forms of exploitation. Then the system meets ordinary life and the categories reveal their blunt edges. A recipient tries to buy medicine and the payment is blocked because the merchant category is misclassified. A recipient tries to pay rent and the landlord's payment channel is flagged as noncompliant because the landlord's account structure does not fit the system's model. A recipient tries to buy groceries and discovers that the cheapest store in the neighborhood is not approved while the more expensive approved store clears instantly. The recipient is not debating theory. The recipient is trying to live without being treated like a suspect.

Under older regimes, a denial can be appealed, delayed, negotiated, or explained. Under code regimes, a denial is instantaneous and often opaque. The citizen receives a refusal without a human decision-maker present. That absence of a human face can reduce certain forms of bias. It can also remove accountability because the citizen cannot confront the rule's author. The citizen is told, in effect, that the system says no, and the system becomes the state's voice. If the system is wrong, trust is not damaged at the margin. It is damaged at the root, because the citizen learns that the rail is not merely moving money; the rail is deciding what money is allowed to mean.

The second pressure scene belongs inside a small business payroll run, because this is where programmability becomes time pressure rather than policy rhetoric. A small firm uses an automated payroll process that calculates withholding, clears wages, and files compliance obligations. In a programmable environment, a payment can be held because a rule flags an identity mismatch, a location anomaly, or an employer classification conflict. The payroll team is not trying to evade. It is trying to pay people on time. The staff do not experience "risk management." They experience instability. The owner experiences humiliation because the owner must explain why wages did not land. A system built to prevent abuse has now imposed reputational damage on legitimate commerce because it executed without discretion. This is where programmability becomes political: the public does not revolt against a rail that blocks criminals; the public revolts against a rail that punishes ordinary life by mistake and then offers no rapid remedy.

The third pressure scene belongs inside a merchant dispute, because this is where programmability turns into leverage. A merchant sells goods and expects payment. Under conditional logic, payment can be tied to delivery confirmation, quality verification, sensor data, or customer acceptance. In theory, this reduces disputes. In practice, it shifts bargaining power toward whoever controls verification. A large buyer can set conditions that are easy for itself to satisfy and hard for a small supplier to satisfy perfectly, and the script executes regardless of context. The supplier that would normally negotiate a late payment now confronts a system that cannot be persuaded. Working capital becomes conditional on a classification decision, a timestamp, a scanning event, and sometimes on data that can be wrong. The supplier experiences programmability as less time. Less time is leverage. Programmability therefore becomes contestation not only between citizen and state but between large actors and small actors, because code can become a weapon of contract enforcement that favors the powerful by default.

The mechanism beneath these scenes is not mystery. It is classification. Programmability requires the system to decide what a payment is, not only that a payment occurred. It must classify the payer, the recipient, the purpose, the category, the jurisdiction, the compliance status, the risk score, the eligibility state, and the conditions that must be satisfied before execution. Once classification exists, error becomes inevitable because classification is a model of reality and models misread the world. Under traditional systems, misreads can be negotiated by human judgment and corrected through after-the-fact remedies. Under programmable systems, misreads can prevent action at the point where action matters most, because the payment is the action. A coded rail therefore turns classification accuracy into civil peace. The system does not merely need to be fair. It must be seen to be corrigible, because citizens will tolerate inconvenience they can appeal and will not tolerate denial they cannot contest.

This is why the chapter must make a clean distinction that becomes decisive once money is coded: policy in money versus policy through administration. Policy in money means the condition is embedded in the claim itself or in the rail's execution logic so that the restriction travels with funds and follows the recipient into every transaction. Policy through administration means the state uses code to administer eligibility, delivery, and fraud reduction while preserving money's generality by keeping restrictions narrow, time-bound, and contestable. The difference is constitutional. When policy is in the money, restriction becomes a permanent marker of status, and money becomes a tagging system for citizenship. When policy is through administration, the state can deliver efficiently without issuing second-class money. The state will be tempted to embed policy in the claim because it is powerful and visible. The state should resist that temptation except under narrow, emergency-like conditions, because second-class money becomes a durable source of political fracture.

"Money must remain a general claim for lawful use, or it becomes a sorting tool." (doctrinal principle of generality)

This line is not sentimental. It is defensive architecture. A society can tolerate targeted restrictions in emergencies. It cannot tolerate permanent segmentation without consequences because segmentation makes the payment state a ranking machine in the most intimate places: groceries, rent, commuting, childcare, and medical care. Once people believe the rail is sorting them into categories of legitimacy, they will seek exit even at financial cost because people accept economic risk to escape humiliation. Exit is not always ideology. Exit is often dignity. This is how careless programmability strengthens the private challenge: it gives private rails a moral narrative as escape from state-coded indignity, even if those private rails are riskier.

The state's most common error is to treat programmability as if it were merely a compliance upgrade. It is not. It is a change in the location of discretion. Under older systems, discretion was applied by humans in banks, in agencies, in supervisors, and in courts. Under programmable systems, discretion is applied by design choices, by parameters, by thresholds, by categories, by exception lists, and by the governance process that decides who can change those parameters. The state can claim it is removing discretion by automating enforcement. It is actually relocating discretion into a smaller group of designers, model owners, and rule maintainers. If that group is not governed with auditable process and real oversight, programmability becomes a quiet transfer of power from visible institutions into technical committees that can change daily life with an update.

This is where crisis politics becomes decisive. The infrastructure is built in calm and expanded in fear. A scandal erupts. A prohibited flow is discovered. A political coalition demands immediate action. Programmability offers immediate action: expand the block list, widen screening, restrict categories, enforce purpose constraints more aggressively, tighten identity thresholds, lower the risk tolerance for ambiguous behavior. Each move is justified as temporary. Temporary measures persist because they are easier to keep than to unwind. Once the infrastructure exists, expansion is cheap. Cheapness is the danger. When enforcement becomes cheap, the rail's default posture drifts from permission to restriction without any formal constitutional moment. The constitutional change occurs through parameter updates, not through public debate.

A serious state must therefore treat programmability as constitutional power requiring explicit restraint. Restraint is not a press release. It must be embedded in the rail's governance and the rail's remedies. It requires narrow scopes, clear authority boundaries, auditable change control, and appeal mechanisms that operate fast enough to matter in daily life. It requires a doctrine of generality that functions as a presumption: the default state of money is general, and any deviation must be limited, publicly justified, and reversible. It requires a doctrine of remedy: the system must be able to correct itself quickly when it denies lawful life. If a programmable rail cannot reverse its own mistakes or provide rapid restitution, it will be experienced as cold power, and cold power breeds exit narratives faster than it reduces fraud.

The private sector's role complicates the picture because private platforms already run rule systems that behave like law. They classify transactions. They set velocity limits. They freeze accounts under risk policies. They decide what identity proofs are acceptable. They define what counts as suspicious by model. Programmability does not invent private control. It expands its range and accelerates execution. If the state refuses to build a disciplined public programmable layer, private programmable layers will govern by default, and they will do so without public obligations. If the state builds a programmable public layer without restraint, the public will resist and private exit narratives will gain moral fuel. This is why programmability is contestation. It is a fight over who defines normal economic behavior and who bears accountability when those definitions harm people.

The myth that programmability automatically improves fairness must be broken without hesitation. Automatic enforcement can reduce certain kinds of discretionary discrimination by removing human discretion in specific moments. It can also encode bias more efficiently if the inputs and classifications are biased. A system that flags certain neighborhoods, occupations, or transaction patterns as higher risk will impose more friction on those populations. That friction will be justified as model output rather than as prejudice. The harmed individuals will experience exclusion that cannot be argued with, and they will experience it repeatedly, transaction by transaction, until life becomes a sequence of denials. This is how a technical system becomes a legitimacy crisis. Programmability therefore requires not only legal oversight but classification oversight, because a coded rail is a decision-making system whether or not it is described as one.

A further danger is the emergence of invisible money classes without formal announcement. Once a rail can attach conditions, it becomes easy for different programs, different agencies, and different political coalitions to demand their own conditions. One stream of funds arrives with spending restrictions. Another arrives with geography restrictions. Another arrives with time restrictions. Another arrives with automatic garnishment logic. Another arrives with tax collection embedded. Individually, each restriction can be defended. Collectively, the result is that different citizens live under different money. This is not simply inconvenient. It is a redesign of citizenship. People with script-free money experience freedom. People with scripted money experience management. The public will name this stratification even if policymakers refuse to.

The strategic center of the chapter is the contradiction between enforceability and legitimacy. The state wants enforceability because enforceability is how the system stays clean, stable, and credible. The citizen wants legitimacy because legitimacy is how the system remains a common utility rather than a tool of discipline. Programmability strengthens enforceability. It can weaken legitimacy if it turns money into permission. The state's success depends on whether it can use programmability to reduce fraud and improve delivery without creating second-class money that marks recipients and narrows their lives. The private sector's success depends on whether it can offer programmability as convenience while avoiding accountability for the denials and exclusions programmability inevitably produces.

The operational insight that determines survival is simple and brutal: programmability will be judged where it hurts, not where it helps. When the system works, nobody notices. When the system denies a payment, the denial becomes personal, and it becomes personal at the worst time because denials matter most when someone needs to transact. A programmable rail must therefore be built with fast remedy as a first-class design requirement. Even if certain transfers are irreversible, the system must provide rapid paths to restitution, error correction, and humane escalation. Otherwise, the rail will be experienced as cold power. Cold power is what fuels exit narratives, and exit narratives strengthen private challengers even when those challengers are less safe.

Programmability also changes the meaning of compliance. Under older systems, compliance is often an admission process and an enforcement process. Under programmable systems, compliance becomes continuous. Every transfer becomes a compliance event. This can reduce crime. It can also turn ordinary life into a sequence of micro-judgments. A society can tolerate occasional scrutiny. It cannot tolerate constant suspicion without backlash. This is why programmability, if used broadly, becomes a contest over the presumption of innocence at the payment layer.

The chapter closes with necessary clarity. Programmability will expand because private systems will continue embedding it, and states will be pressured to match the precision private systems market. The real question is whether programmability will be governed as a narrow administrative tool or allowed to become a general control substrate. If it becomes a control substrate, the payment state becomes a political battleground and exit narratives strengthen. If it is governed narrowly, with generality protected and remedies built in, programmability can improve delivery without rewriting the citizen's relationship to money. The choice is not whether code will execute rules. The choice is whether the rules will execute as governance with restraint or as discipline by default.

CLOSING DOCTRINE

Programmability is policy power relocated into execution: rules that used to be debated, administered, and appealed become conditions that run automatically at transaction speed. Its promise is precision, fraud reduction, and lower enforcement friction; its danger is that conditional money can become segmented money, and segmented money can become a hierarchy of citizenship at the payment layer. The constitutional hinge is generality: money must remain a general claim for lawful use, with restrictions narrowly justified, time-bound, and rapidly appealable, otherwise the rail becomes a sorting machine that trains people to seek exit as dignity. The institutional hinge is accountability: a coded rail must include auditable change control, visible authority boundaries, and fast remedies for error, because denial without recourse becomes legitimacy damage that spreads faster than any technical benefit. The political hinge is crisis cheapness: once the infrastructure exists, expansion is easy, and easy enforcement becomes permanent enforcement unless restraint is embedded as architecture rather than promised as intent. The strategic hinge is contestation: if the state does not build disciplined programmability, private platforms will govern by default; if the state builds expansive programmability without restraint, the public will resist and the private challenge will gain moral fuel. A programmable payment state succeeds only if it can embed enforcement without turning money into permission.

CHAPTER 27
REASSERTING RULE
IDENTITY, COMPLIANCE, AND SETTLEMENT FINALITY

When private money grows, it does not merely compete with the state's instruments. It competes with the state's ability to define what counts as payment. That is the quiet threat beneath every innovation narrative. A state can tolerate competing interfaces. It cannot tolerate competing definitions of discharge, because discharge is how obligations end and how public order avoids becoming a series of private disputes. The private challenge therefore forces the state back to first principles: who is allowed to move value, under what identity, through which rails, toward what endpoints, and with what consequences when rules are violated. Reasserting rule is not a crackdown. It is the state deciding whether money remains a governed public architecture or becomes a patchwork of private corridors whose failures are socialized only after they rupture.

The first mistake states make is to treat rule as an add-on. Rule is not added after adoption. Rule determines whether adoption becomes stability or becomes systemic fragility. When private rails scale, they create a second perimeter of trust built on convenience and marketing rather than enforceable finality. In calm, that works because smoothness is mistaken for safety. In stress, the second perimeter becomes a run corridor because everyone tries to upgrade into the apex claim at once. The state then discovers it has allowed a private front end to train the public to expect public safety while preserving legal structures that allow private gating and private loss shifting. Reasserting rule means closing that ambiguity. It means forcing private claims that behave like money to carry money obligations, and forcing private rails that market completion to meet finality standards that survive stress.

The chapter's argument is simple, and it is the simplest arguments that usually govern systems. The monetary state governs through three levers that look administrative until crisis makes them visible: identity, compliance, and finality. Identity is who the system recognizes as a legitimate participant. Compliance is what behaviors the system permits at transaction speed. Finality is the moment the system declares that the argument is over. Private challengers can innovate around many things, but they cannot escape these levers if they want to scale. They can only relocate them into private hands. The state must decide whether it will allow that relocation or impose a perimeter that keeps these levers within public governance.

Identity is the first gate, and it is not a single check. It is a lived credential chain. A person is recognized by documents, biometrics, device reputations, address histories, employer verifications, behavioral patterns, and the quiet reputational scores created by institutions that decide what looks normal. In calm, identity feels like onboarding. In stress, identity becomes a throttle. A system can decide that certain people must prove themselves repeatedly, that certain neighborhoods require more proofs, that certain jobs trigger more reviews, that certain transaction patterns are suspicious even when lawful. Procedure becomes distributive power because procedure determines who moves at full speed and who is forced into delay.

This is where private identity governance becomes a hidden constitution. A platform can change what it accepts as proof without a public vote. It can tighten thresholds overnight because its liability model shifts. It can treat certain patterns as high risk because a regulator has applied pressure or because a fraud wave has spiked. The platform will call this prudence. The citizen experiences it as exclusion. The citizen's problem is not that identity exists. The citizen's problem is that identity becomes revocable by private policy in ways that are hard to contest. A state can be challenged through courts and politics. A platform can deny you with a template and still claim neutrality.

At scale, identity cannot be optional. Fraud, coercion, theft, sanctions, and tax enforcement are not edge cases in mass payment life. They are daily pressures that determine whether a rail can exist in a lawful society. The real question is therefore not whether identity will exist. The real question is whether identity will be portable, contestable, and governed by public standards, or whether identity will be a proprietary credential controlled by a few platforms who can exile people from economic life without meaningful remedy. If identity becomes proprietary, the state will have allowed private actors to define membership in the economy. That is sovereignty relocation in its most intimate form.

Compliance is the second gate, and compliance is not merely screening. Compliance is admissibility at transaction speed. It is the system's method of deciding which transfers are allowed to pass and which are blocked, delayed, or frozen. In older regimes, compliance is executed through intermediaries who screen and report, and the friction of that process creates time for explanation and appeal. In newer regimes, compliance becomes embedded at the rail level through continuous monitoring, programmable constraints, and automatic denial. This can reduce crime. It can also create a society of constant suspicion if it is expanded without restraint. The state's task is not merely to require screening. The task is to define proportionality, to define remedies, and to prevent compliance from becoming an invisible class system where some people move frictionlessly and others live inside review. The most corrosive form of exclusion is not a formal ban. It is practical immobility delivered as endless friction.

The chapter must make compliance feel tactile as a timing weapon, because timing is where governance becomes solvency. A merchant receives receipts and expects to pay suppliers, staff, and rent on schedule. A compliance hold delays settlement. The merchant's supplier responds by demanding prepayment or adding a premium. The merchant's payroll runs tighter. Inventory shrinks. Customers see empty shelves and assume failure. The merchant experiences compliance as less time, not as law. Review becomes solvency the moment working capital is thin. This is how a technically "reasonable" compliance tightening becomes a political event. Integrity does not pay invoices, and nobody forgives a system that protects itself by starving ordinary commerce of time.

Finality is the third gate, and it is where the state must be hardest because finality is what separates money from promise. Private rails can deliver confirmation quickly. Confirmation is not discharge. Discharge is a legal state defended by the order. Finality is the moment the order declares the transfer irrevocable and unconditional, that the obligation is discharged, and that third parties must honor that discharge. Private systems can approximate finality within their own community. They often cannot provide finality that binds the wider world unless they are anchored to public law and public settlement assets. The state must enforce a clean distinction: marketing that implies finality must be matched by architectures that can deliver finality, and architectures that cannot deliver finality must be barred from presenting themselves as money-equivalent.

"Final settlement is the irrevocable and unconditional discharge of an obligation." (international settlement standard, 2012)

This definition is not academic. It is the boundary line between a payment system and a messaging system. If a rail cannot specify where finality occurs, who defends it, and what happens under insolvency and fraud, then the rail has not produced money. It has produced conditional completion that becomes fragile when fear arrives. The state's first duty is to prevent conditional promises from being treated as public money without public discipline, because that is how runs are manufactured.

The public experiences the finality problem as betrayal because the interface trains people to equate confirmation with completion. A user sends money and sees a receipt. The user assumes the obligation is ended. A merchant ships goods because the interface indicates completion. Later, the transfer is disputed, flagged, frozen, reversed, or rendered unusable through off-rail intervention, or because the recipient is under review, or because the system's redemption corridor tightens. The public does not experience this as risk management. The public experiences it as money failing to be money. This is why finality cannot be treated as a branding term. Finality is a property that must be defended through architecture and law. If a system cannot defend it, it must not sell it.

The first pressure scene belongs inside a compliance desk during a crisis week. Abnormal flows appear. Thresholds tighten. Holds widen. More accounts are frozen. Each action can be justified individually. Collectively, ordinary commerce begins to slow. Merchants see receipts trapped. Workers see wages delayed. Families see transfers pending. The rail claims it is protecting integrity. The public experiences money becoming conditional. The state is asked to intervene, yet the state does not control the platform's model. Reasserting rule means preventing the payment state from being outsourced to opaque models whose crisis behavior becomes a political event without public accountability.

The second pressure scene belongs in a bank supervisor's view. Private stable-value claims hold reserves inside banks. Redemption stress becomes bank outflow stress. Banks tighten credit. The economy slows. The public blames the state for tightening even though the trigger was private. The supervisor recognizes the loop: private issuers create money-like claims, the public treats them as safe, redemption runs transmit into banks, and the state is forced to stabilize banks, which stabilizes private claims indirectly. This is public dependence expressed as supervisory reality. Reasserting rule means deciding whether private issuers will be permitted to create money-like claims at scale without being subject to money-like discipline. If permitted, they must be brought into a perimeter where reserves, redemption, and custody are governed with enforceable standards. If not permitted, distribution and marketing must be constrained so the public is not trained to expect par safety for a private promise.

The third pressure scene belongs in an ordinary household's week because this is where legitimacy is lost quietly and then all at once. A household receives wages through a private interface. The interface flags the account under a model. The household cannot pay rent. The household cannot transfer to family. The household is told to wait. The household learns that inclusion is not a status; it is a continuously revocable privilege. The household does not care whether the model is statistically prudent. The household cares that money has become permission. Reasserting rule means ensuring baseline access to the monetary system is governed by public standards and remedies rather than private policy alone, because a society cannot remain stable if large populations experience money as contingent on opaque scoring.

Reasserting rule is also border governance, because cross-border payment is where private and public corridors collide and where dependency becomes visible. Private rails market borderlessness. In reality, cross-border settlement depends on admissibility: identity standards, compliance screening, corridor acceptance, and the ability to discharge obligations in jurisdictions that do not treat private ledgers as final. The border becomes the place where statecraft operates quietly. A country can have domestic legality and still be rationed in cross-border passage if external admissibility tightens. Payments can be delayed. Additional proofs can be demanded. Conversion can be priced at punitive spreads. Liquidity can be throttled. All of this can occur without dramatic rupture. It occurs as ordinary sequence: more questions, more holds, higher haircuts, slower settlement. Reasserting rule therefore includes treating connections as strategic infrastructure, because connection points are where runs travel and where pressure can be applied through ordinary payment sequence.

The state's practical toolkit for reasserting rule is perimeter clarity enforced by law and supervision. Define permitted claim types and forbid ambiguous marketing that implies public money status without public obligations. Define reserve and custody standards for any private claim that promises par redemption into the state's unit. Define redemption rights and prohibit discretionary gates that appear only under stress. Define identity standards and require portability so exclusion cannot be executed as permanent platform exile without due process. Define data rules that limit extraction and profiling that turn the interface into a surveillance business. Define settlement standards that separate confirmation from discharge and require clear finality points for any system that wants to call itself money-like.

The deeper work is refusing to socialize private promises by accident. The state must refuse to allow private firms to build money-like products at scale on the marketing implication of public safety while preserving the legal ability to gate, delay, and shift losses under stress. It must force clarity. Either a claim is public-like and therefore must accept public discipline, or it is private and therefore must be marketed and structured as private risk. Ambiguity is the toxic middle. Ambiguity manufactures runs because it trains the public to expect safety and then reveals subordination abruptly.

The contradiction remains political. The state needs private innovation to keep the interface modern, yet must prevent private issuers from becoming de facto monetary sovereigns. The state needs intermediaries for distribution, yet must prevent intermediaries from becoming unaccountable gatekeepers. The state needs compliance to preserve integrity, yet must prevent compliance from becoming permanent suspicion. The state needs finality to preserve order, yet must prevent finality claims from being sold without finality capacity. Reasserting rule is therefore not a one-time crackdown. It is continuous perimeter maintenance: defining what the system will honor and refusing to honor what would force rescue without control.

CLOSING DOCTRINE

Reasserting rule is the monetary state's refusal to outsource legitimacy while still socializing failure. Identity, compliance, and settlement finality are the gates through which monetary reality is produced: identity decides membership and legibility, compliance decides admissibility at transaction speed, and finality decides when the argument ends with binding discharge. Private systems that scale cannot escape these gates, they can only relocate them into private hands, where exclusion can become less contestable and delay can become a timing weapon that turns review into solvency pressure for ordinary commerce. Finality is the nonnegotiable boundary between messaging and payment, and any rail that markets money-equivalence must be anchored to enforceable discharge that survives stress, not merely to rapid confirmation. Cross-border connections are strategic infrastructure because corridor gatekeeping can constrain domestic autonomy through ordinary payment sequence without dramatic rupture. The perimeter task is claim classification and disciplined access: impose reserve, custody, and redemption standards on par promises, separate confirmation from legal discharge, enforce identity portability and proportional compliance remedies, and prevent ambiguous private instruments from training the public to expect public safety without public obligations. If the state fails this perimeter work, private interfaces become the lived constitution of money, and the state will still be forced to rescue when those interfaces break, which is sovereignty surrendered twice: once in calm, and again in crisis.

PART SIX

THE RESERVE ORDER

CURRENCY AS GEOPOLITICAL INFRASTRUCTURE AND LEVERAGE

A reserve order is not a medal. It is an operating environment. It is the set of habits, contracts, collateral conventions, settlement corridors, and crisis reflexes through which the world decides what it will accept when it needs an obligation to end. In calm, this environment is mistaken for neutrality because it works smoothly and because its benefits are distributed invisibly through lower spreads, easier refinancing, and quieter payment life. In stress, neutrality dissolves because the reserve order reveals its true nature: it is a hierarchy of upgrade rights, and hierarchy is power whenever time is scarce. The reserve order is therefore best understood not as a ranking of currencies but as the world's geopolitical infrastructure for settlement, liquidity, admissibility, and loss allocation under fear.

The system's central fact is that a top currency is not top because it is loved. It is top because it is demanded. Demand is a discipline machine. When global institutions are forced to hold, borrow, invoice, and settle in one unit to remain competitive, the issuer of that unit acquires capacity that looks like magic to outsiders and looks like routine to insiders. Outsiders see the issuer fund itself more cheaply, absorb shocks more smoothly, and run larger balance sheets without immediate penalty. Insiders see a different reality: dominance drags global fear into domestic politics, and the issuer becomes responsible for stabilizing a system it does not fully control. Privilege grants room. Privilege also grants entanglement. Entanglement becomes constraint when domestic politics resists the backstop role and when the distributional consequences of being the world's refuge become visible at home.

Reserve order is built first through the unit of account, because quoting is the beginning of dependency. The world prices certain goods and contracts in one unit because the unit is convenient, deep, and widely accepted. Invoicing creates habit. Habit creates liquidity because more trades in the unit produce more participants, more hedging instruments, and more secondary markets. Liquidity then creates collateral preference, because the liquid instrument is the instrument others are willing to accept without argument. Once the unit's liabilities become preferred collateral, the currency's status stops being a trade story and becomes a funding story. Funding is where discipline is written. A state can boast about trade share and still be punished by funding markets. A state can be politically popular and still be forced into tightening when refinancing becomes expensive. Funding markets do not obey speeches. Funding markets obey eligibility, haircuts, and the fear of being trapped.

The reserve order is governed day to day by the collateral ladder. In calm, the ladder looks broad. Many assets are accepted, and the system behaves as if equivalence holds. In stress, equivalence breaks. Eligibility narrows, haircuts widen, and margin calls demand a specific kind of claim: the claim that ends arguments fastest. This is where the top currency's privilege becomes concrete. Its short-term public liabilities and the instruments tightly linked to them are treated as the nearest thing to cash in the global machine. The privilege is not that these instruments yield more. The privilege is that they clear more easily. When time becomes scarce, clearing ease is the most valuable economic attribute because it prevents forced liquidation and preserves solvency long enough for institutions to survive.

A collateral ladder is also a legal ladder. Collateral is not merely an asset. It is a property right that must be enforceable quickly when counterparties fail. This is where the reserve order becomes institutional. The world prefers collateral not only because it is liquid, but because it is governed by legal and operational standards that make enforcement predictable and fast. Predictability is what allows institutions to accept collateral at scale, and fast enforcement is what makes a pledge useful when panic compresses time. The top currency's infrastructure tends to dominate here because it bundles deep markets, standardized documentation, reliable custody chains, and dispute systems that preserve confidence that pledges can be turned into usable settlement without becoming litigation. That bundle is not an accident. It is infrastructure built over decades.

Reserve order also governs through settlement corridors, and corridors are the world's invisible border crossings. A cross-border payment is not a single act. It is a sequence of checkpoints: identity verification, compliance screening, documentation validation, correspondent acceptance, liquidity provision, and settlement into a final claim that third parties treat as discharge. Each checkpoint contains a veto point. A document can be rejected. A beneficiary can be flagged. A bank can be de-risked. A corridor can be narrowed. A payment can be delayed until additional proofs arrive. In calm, these veto points are background noise. In stress, they become power because they allocate time and determine who remains admissible. A state may have domestic legality, functioning courts, and formal sovereignty, and still discover that external admissibility tightens. The result is that domestic autonomy is priced not by domestic law but by corridor access. Reserve order is the system that makes corridor access the condition of participation in global trade and finance.

The mechanism is felt most clearly by those who must transact. An importer pays the daily pricing tax. The supplier demands the apex unit because the supplier can fund inventories more cheaply when invoices clear in the unit the world prefers. The importer's bank demands more documentation, more lead time, and more liquidity buffer because it must keep the corridor open and because corridor failure can turn a routine payment into reputational risk for the bank. The importer's cost is not only spread. The importer's cost is precaution: higher cash buffers, tighter supplier terms, more frequent hedging rolls, and more fragile planning. The importer experiences this as commercial annoyance. It is reserve order discipline: the world's preferred unit is quietly shaping domestic working capital norms.

A commodity trader experiences the same discipline through collateral and margin. In calm, domestic assets may be accepted as margin or as repo collateral. In stress, haircuts rise and the "acceptable" set narrows toward apex collateral. The trader is forced to sell domestic assets to obtain apex claims, not because domestic assets are worthless, but because domestic assets are not accepted quickly enough when the market is afraid. The trader's forced sales transmit stress back into domestic prices, domestic banks, and domestic politics. A private portfolio decision becomes a sovereign liquidity event because the reserve order converts margin calls into cross-border demand for the apex unit.

A local bank treasury desk experiences the discipline as a calendar and as a reputational cliff. In calm, short-term funding in the apex unit is rolled as routine. In stress, counterparties demand shorter tenors, larger buffers, and cleaner collateral. The bank can obtain domestic liquidity from its own central bank. It cannot obtain apex liquidity from its own central bank. The bank becomes dependent on external markets, which means dependent on external confidence. Confidence is not just about solvency. It is about admissibility. A bank that becomes suspected, even briefly, can be forced into defensive behavior that hurts domestic credit provision. This is how reserve order turns global fear into domestic tightening without any decree.

Reserve status is therefore not primarily a question of national pride. It is a question of whose liabilities function as the world's upgrade endpoint. A non-issuer that borrows in the top currency is buying cheaper funding in calm and selling itself vulnerability in stress. The vulnerability is arithmetic. A liability that must be paid in a unit you cannot create becomes a sovereign exposure even when the borrower is private because, in stress, the private borrower's failure becomes employment failure, supply-chain failure, and tax failure, and the state is forced to manage consequences without controlling the unit of settlement. The reserve order amplifies this exposure because demand for the apex unit rises precisely when it is hardest for non-issuers to obtain. That timing is what makes reserve order a discipline machine.

The sequence from foreign-currency funding to domestic austerity is best understood as time scarcity, not ideology. A finance ministry faces a widening funding gap because external investors pull back. Short-term liabilities denominated in the apex unit must be refinanced. The ministry can tighten fiscal policy, raise rates, impose controls, seek external support, or compel domestic institutions to absorb issuance. Each choice carries internal political cost. What triggers the crisis is not simply fear about domestic fundamentals. What triggers it is that refinancing now requires collateral and spreads the state cannot provide easily, and that the apex unit required for settlement has become expensive to obtain. Domestic reforms do not instantly create apex liquidity. A government can announce austerity and still see spreads widen if the market believes austerity will collapse growth and reduce repayment capacity. The reserve order constrains domestic autonomy without a treaty, through the price of time and through the corridor's power to demand proof, collateral, and compliance at machine speed.

This is how the top currency sets terms. The terms are not speeches. The terms are documentation burdens for corridor passage, collateral requirements for funding, legal certainty for enforcement, and operational standards for admissibility. A non-issuer internalizes these terms quietly. It reforms supervision to match external expectations. It adjusts disclosure standards. It builds compliance capacity. It changes market infrastructure. It holds reserves as insurance. It does these things not because it worships the top currency, but because it cannot afford exclusion from the corridors that clear trade and funding. Reserve order is governance by interface at global scale: standards, eligibility, documentation, and settlement procedures that shape domestic institutions without requiring overt conquest.

The issuer's privilege creates a constraint shift rather than constraint absence. The issuer can run a larger balance sheet without being punished as quickly because the world treats the issuer's liabilities as the place to hide when fear spreads. This does not mean the issuer faces no constraint. It means the constraint arrives differently. Instead of a sudden external funding stop, the issuer faces internal political fights over inflation, distribution, and the legitimacy of using national balance-sheet capacity to stabilize a global system. Liquidity privilege shifts the constraint from external solvency to internal governance, which is a different constraint and often a more survivable one. Yet survivable is not costless. Domestic legitimacy becomes part of global stability because if the issuer's politics reject the backstop role, the entire system learns that the apex claim is no longer unconditional. That lesson would reorder the world, and the fear of that lesson is itself a stabilizing force that pressures the issuer to keep performing the role.

Reserve order is also the mechanism by which blocs rise and stumble. A shared currency area can create deep markets and a large internal payment space. It can reduce external dependency and build the scaffolding of an alternative corridor. Yet the world watches crisis performance, not ambition. A bloc that cannot preserve internal fungibility under stress, that must improvise backstops through slow bargaining, or that allows internal fragmentation of deposit confidence will be treated as conditionally usable. Conditionality is enough for the reserve order to punish because fear does not buy conditional assets when an unconditional refuge is available. Reserve order therefore rewards not only size but coherence: fast finality, credible backstops, consistent supervision, and the ability to allocate losses without dissolving into moral war.

Leverage in a reserve order is not only formal prohibition. Leverage is the ability to change admissibility, slow passage, raise documentation burdens, and narrow corridors in ways that shift the cost of time onto targeted actors without dramatic rupture. A state can be squeezed without a blockade. A firm can be constrained without a public ban. A corridor can be weaponized by making it expensive, slow, and uncertain. These moves operate through ordinary payment sequence, which is why they are effective. They resemble compliance. They feel like prudence. They function as pressure. The reserve order is the infrastructure that makes such pressure possible because it concentrates settlement and collateral preferences into a narrow set of corridors that must be used by those who want to participate at scale.

For serious decision-makers, the reserve order should be treated as a design environment, not as fate. Non-issuers can reduce vulnerability by building domestic currency credit markets, limiting foreign-unit borrowing, diversifying reserves prudently, strengthening institutional credibility that supports admissibility, and cultivating alternative corridors without assuming network inertia will dissolve quickly. These actions are costly. They are the cost of autonomy. Issuers must manage the legitimacy of the backstop role, maintain deep and open markets, preserve predictable rule enforcement, and avoid allowing domestic political conflict to undermine the belief that the apex claim remains usable in stress. These actions are costly too. They are the cost of privilege.

The reserve order, then, is not a story about who is greatest. It is a story about who sets the terms of time. Time is the scarce asset in crisis. The unit that can be obtained quickly, pledged widely, and settled finally becomes the unit that determines who survives without forced liquidation. The corridors that clear that unit become the corridors through which the world's commerce, credit, and politics must pass. Currency becomes infrastructure, and infrastructure becomes leverage because it shapes what is possible before anyone argues about what is desirable.

CHAPTER 28
LIQUIDITY PRIVILEGE
THE TOP CURRENCY SETS THE TERMS

The reserve order begins as a convenience story and ends as a discipline story. In calm, the top currency feels like a neutral tool. It is the unit invoices clear in, the unit reserves are held in, the unit global prices are quoted against, the unit short-term funding prefers, the unit markets treat as closest to cash when distance, language, and legal difference would otherwise make trust expensive. In stress, neutrality disappears because the world discovers what it has built: a single apex corridor through which the demand for safety concentrates, and a single issuer whose liabilities become the settlement refuge for everyone else's fear. The privilege is not admiration. The privilege is demand, and demand at the moment of fear is the most valuable form of power a monetary system can generate because it converts preference into compulsion, and compulsion into terms.

Liquidity privilege is therefore not a compliment. It is an operating fact. It means the top currency's instruments clear at the narrowest spreads, are accepted as collateral with the smallest haircuts, and are treated as the easiest claim to pledge when time becomes scarce. It also means that when balance sheets tighten globally, the first instinct of institutions is not to hold their own domestic assets. The first instinct is to reach for the apex claim because the apex claim is what other actors accept without negotiation. This is why reserve status is not primarily about prestige. It is about the settlement perimeter: which liabilities are treated as the final answer when everybody wants the argument over, and which liabilities are treated as conditional promises that must be discounted, delayed, or defended.

Liquidity privilege is reproduced long before crisis makes it visible. It appears as a daily pricing tax paid by those who are not issuers, collected quietly through spreads, documentation, and eligibility. An importer in a mid-sized economy orders machinery priced in the apex unit because that is what the supplier demands. The importer's bank quotes a spread. The spread is not only compensation for credit risk. It is compensation for corridor risk: the risk that liquidity in the apex unit tightens, that settlement slows, that documentation burdens rise, that conversion becomes more expensive at the wrong moment, and that an external compliance choke point can turn a routine payment into a queue. The importer treats this as business friction. It is the reserve order operating in miniature: a daily transfer of margin to the issuer's corridor because the corridor is where global trust concentrates and where global disputes are ended most cleanly.

A commodity trader experiences the same structure differently. In calm, the trader funds positions cheaply in the apex unit, posts acceptable collateral, rolls exposure, and treats liquidity as routine. In stress, the trader discovers that the list of acceptable collateral is not a list. It is a hierarchy that hardens suddenly. Haircuts widen. Margin calls arrive sooner. Funding tenors shorten. The trader's own domestic assets, which were acceptable yesterday, are treated today as conditional and tomorrow as suspect. The trader does not describe this as geopolitics. The trader describes it as the market becoming tight. Yet tightness is the language the reserve order uses to enforce discipline without speeches, because the reserve order governs by rationing time.

A local bank treasury desk experiences liquidity privilege as a calendar. In calm, it can obtain apex-unit funding through markets, run a matched book, and treat rollover as ordinary. In stress, the desk finds that counterparties ask for more collateral, better collateral, faster settlement, and cleaner documentation. The desk can obtain domestic liquidity from its own central bank. It cannot obtain apex liquidity from its own central bank. The desk discovers that its survival now depends on access to a corridor controlled elsewhere. The reserve order is that corridor becoming the condition of survival, and survival is what converts a market preference into a political constraint.

The top currency's privilege is not merely that it is used. It is that it is used as the unit in which uncertainty is priced and in which safety is settled. A unit becomes apex when it performs three jobs at once. It is the preferred unit of account for key contracts, so commercial life is organized around it. It is the preferred unit of settlement for key markets, so financial life must clear through it. It is the preferred unit of collateral when fear rises, so crisis life accelerates toward it. These three functions lock together. Quoting creates habit. Habit creates liquidity. Liquidity creates collateral preference. Collateral preference creates crisis reflex. Crisis reflex creates further liquidity. The reserve order is self-reinforcing because fear is self-reinforcing, and the top currency is the channel through which fear is most cheaply soothed.

"In times of stress, demand for the safest and most liquid assets rises sharply." (macro-financial assessment doctrine)

The line is not descriptive ornament. It is the engine of hierarchy. Stress does not merely raise risk premia. Stress reorganizes the system around a narrow set of claims treated as cash-like beyond dispute. The question is not why markets behave this way. The question is which institutions and legal structures produce the belief that a given claim will remain usable when everything else becomes conditional. Liquidity privilege is the accumulation of that belief over decades, locked in by collateral conventions, payment corridors, clearing arrangements, custody chains, documentation standards, and the habit of pricing global goods and global funding in a particular unit.

To see the mechanism clearly, begin with collateral because collateral is where hierarchy becomes arithmetic. A collateral system is a ranking system. In calm, many assets are acceptable, and participants behave as if a wide set of collateral is close enough to equivalent. In stress, the list narrows. Eligible becomes scarce. Haircuts widen. A pledge that yesterday was treated as sufficient becomes marginal today and unusable tomorrow. The system's language is technical. The effect is political. When collateral eligibility tightens, it is not only a market event. It is a time allocation event. Those who can pledge apex collateral meet margin calls and continue operating. Those who cannot are forced to sell, forced to shrink, and forced into more expensive funding. Liquidity privilege is the privilege of having the collateral the world reaches for when time is scarce, which is the same as having the collateral that prevents forced liquidation when panic arrives.

The collateral ladder is also how the top currency sets terms without announcing them. Eligibility lists, haircuts, margin schedules, settlement cutoffs, and custody acceptability become a global rulebook because they determine which assets can be converted into usable settlement quickly. A non-issuer can insist its domestic assets are safe. The market can still haircut them harshly because safety is not the only requirement in crisis. Usability is the requirement. Usability is the ability to be pledged, accepted, and settled without argument, because argument is the cost nobody can afford when funding is rolling day by day. The apex unit's liabilities are usable because the world believes they will clear, settle, and remain convertible under stress. That belief is not mystical. It is enforced through deep markets, institutional continuity, and the expectation that the issuer can provide liquidity to its own system without waiting for permission from others.

This is where the reserve order becomes discipline rather than convenience. The world's funding system does not punish weakness in speeches. It punishes weakness in haircuts. A state can have domestic legality, a functioning court system, and credible internal institutions, and still discover that its assets are treated as conditional outside its borders because they cannot be converted quickly into the apex claim during fear. Conditionality becomes a spread, and spreads become policy because spreads decide how much room the state has to maneuver. The reserve order does not need to issue commands. It prices time. A state with cheap time can stabilize. A state with expensive time must tighten, improvise, or beg.

The most common misunderstanding of the reserve order is to treat it as a ranking of national greatness. That interpretation flatters politics and obscures mechanics. The reserve order is better understood as a stack of permissions embedded in global finance. Who can fund in their own liabilities at scale without paying a penalty. Who can borrow long and lend short without being punished instantly. Who can absorb global demand for safe assets without losing market access. Who can provide the world's preferred collateral without surrendering control of crisis tools. These are not symbolic privileges. They are balance-sheet privileges. Balance-sheet privileges become state capacity when stress arrives, because state capacity is time, and time is purchased with liquidity.

The issuer's privilege creates a constraint shift rather than constraint absence. The issuer can run a larger balance sheet without being punished as quickly as others because the world treats the issuer's liabilities as the place to hide when fear spreads. This does not mean the issuer faces no constraint. It means the constraint arrives differently. Instead of a sudden external funding stop, the issuer is more likely to face an internal political fight over inflation, distribution, and the legitimacy of using national balance-sheet capacity to stabilize a global system. Liquidity privilege shifts the constraint from external solvency to internal governance, which is a different constraint and often a more survivable one, because internal governance can be renegotiated through politics while external solvency is renegotiated through panic.

The non-issuer's side is harsher because the constraint arrives as arithmetic, not debate. A central bank in a smaller economy watches banks and firms accumulate obligations in the apex unit because it is cheaper, deeper, and easier to roll. This looks rational in normal times. It is also the construction of dependency. The central bank can provide domestic liquidity in domestic money. It cannot create the apex unit. If markets refuse to roll short-term funding in the apex unit, domestic banks must obtain it somewhere else or liquidate assets to repay. The moment becomes brutal because it is not about preference. It is about mismatch. A liability that must be paid in a currency you cannot create is a sovereign exposure, even if the borrower is technically private, because the borrower's failure becomes employment, supply, and tax collapse, and the state is then forced to manage consequences without controlling the unit of settlement.

"Foreign-currency liquidity shortages can arise suddenly and propagate quickly through financial systems." (central bank liquidity doctrine)

This is the hinge. Currency mismatch becomes crisis channel. The reserve order makes the apex unit the preferred funding unit for cross-border activity, and that preference encourages borrowing in the unit. Borrowing creates rollover risk. Rollover risk creates panic dynamics. Panic dynamics force actors to seek the apex unit at the same time, tightening apex-unit funding markets and raising the apex unit's price in terms of other currencies. This is how the reserve order amplifies itself in stress: demand rises precisely when non-issuers cannot manufacture supply, which means the penalty for not being the issuer is paid exactly when the system is most unforgiving.

Liquidity privilege therefore turns the world into a system of uneven upgrade rights. The issuer can always provide its own liabilities to its domestic system. Non-issuers must earn access through reserves, market confidence, corridor acceptance, institutions willing to lend, and political alignment that determines whether emergency access is extended. The reserve order is not merely a market equilibrium. It becomes a geopolitical equilibrium because emergency liquidity is never purely technical. It is extended through relationships, conditions, and discretionary choices reflecting power. Even when no explicit conditions are written, dependency is itself a condition because it shapes future choices and narrows the space of what is politically possible.

The sovereign constraint sequence is best understood as time scarcity, not ideology. A finance ministry faces a widening funding gap because external investors are pulling back. Short-term liabilities denominated in the apex unit must be refinanced. The ministry can tighten fiscal policy, raise rates, impose controls, seek external support, or compel domestic institutions to absorb issuance. Each choice carries internal political cost. What triggers the crisis is not simply fear about domestic fundamentals. What triggers it is that refinancing now requires collateral and spreads the state cannot provide easily, and that the apex unit required for settlement has become expensive to obtain. Domestic reforms do not instantly create apex liquidity. A government can announce austerity and still see its spreads widen if the market believes austerity will collapse growth and therefore reduce repayment capacity. The government can announce reform and still see its currency fall if the market believes reform will arrive too late to meet refinancing calendars. The reserve order constrains domestic autonomy without a treaty, through the price of time and through the corridor's power to demand proof, collateral, and compliance at machine speed.

This is how the top currency sets terms. The terms are not speeches. The terms are the documentation burdens that must be satisfied for corridor passage, the collateral that must be pledged for funding, the legal certainty that must be provided for settlement, and the operational standards that must be met for accounts and institutions to remain admissible. A non-issuer internalizes these terms quietly. It reforms bank supervision to match external expectations. It adjusts disclosure standards. It builds compliance capacity. It changes market infrastructure. It holds reserves as insurance. It does these things not because it worships the top currency, but because it cannot afford exclusion from the corridors that clear global trade and funding. The reserve order is governance by interface at global scale: standards, eligibility, documentation, and settlement rules that shape domestic institutions without requiring overt political conquest.

A cross-border transaction makes the mechanism physical. A payment begins as a domestic instruction and becomes a sequence of checkpoints: identity verification, sanctions screening, documentation verification, correspondent acceptance, liquidity provision, and settlement into the apex claim. At each checkpoint, there is a veto point. A document can be rejected. A beneficiary can be flagged. A bank can be de-risked. A corridor can be narrowed. A payment can be delayed until additional proofs arrive. Each veto point can be justified as compliance or prudence. Collectively, they form a geopolitical infrastructure because they determine which states and firms can move value at full speed. When a state discovers that domestic legality means little once external admissibility tightens, it learns the reserve order's true structure: the top currency sets terms through the corridors that define usable completion.

The non-issuer responds by trying to reduce dependency, but each response is a form of paid autonomy. Reserve accumulation is one response, but reserves are expensive because they are foregone domestic investment and because they tie national policy to maintaining external confidence. Domestic invoicing mandates are another response, but mandates can raise costs if counterparties demand risk premia and if hedging markets are shallow. Capital controls can preserve liquidity but can damage long-term trust if applied bluntly. Alternative corridors can reduce vulnerability but face network inertia and acceptance constraints. Each response is a way of buying time. None is free. Liquidity privilege creates a strategic burden for non-issuers: decide how much autonomy to buy through buffers and how much dependency to accept for cheaper funding, knowing that cheap funding often arrives with invisible covenant: remain admissible, remain predictable, remain aligned enough that the corridor remains open in fear.

The issuer's side of the story is not romantic either. Liquidity privilege pulls global stress into domestic politics. When the world demands apex assets, domestic conditions can tighten or loosen in ways not chosen solely for domestic reasons. The issuer's central bank may be forced to stabilize domestic markets and, in doing so, stabilize global markets because global markets are anchored to the apex unit's funding system. Fiscal authorities may find deficits easier to finance in stress, but domestic voters may interpret that ease as moral hazard or exploitation by outsiders. The issuer must manage legitimacy: being the world's refuge without appearing to sacrifice domestic stability for global rescue. Liquidity privilege is power, but it is also entanglement, and entanglement can become domestic political constraint because the issuer's internal distribution fights are now linked to the world's demand for safety.

"The provision of liquidity can preserve stability while creating dependency." (central bank cooperation doctrine)

The sentence captures the reserve order's quiet control channel. Emergency liquidity is not merely money. It is conditional access to time. Time is what prevents forced liquidation. Time is what prevents a bank run from becoming insolvency. Time is what prevents a sovereign from being forced into sudden policy reversal.

When a state or institution obtains time through access to the apex unit, it often accepts conditions, explicit or implicit, about alignment, transparency, and behavior. Even when conditions are not written, dependency shapes the future because it alters which choices feel feasible and which choices feel suicidal. That is power without declarations.

Liquidity privilege therefore sets the terms of trade in a deeper sense than tariffs or agreements. It sets terms by deciding which claims are treated as cash-like and which are treated as conditional. It sets terms by deciding which assets are eligible collateral and which are discounted. It sets terms by deciding which payment corridors clear smoothly and which experience friction. It sets terms by deciding who can refinance cheaply in crisis and who must pay a panic premium or seek rescue. This is why reserve order is geopolitical infrastructure. It is settlement reality shaping national options through ordinary funding mechanics, and it is why reserve order endures even when politics changes because the corridor is built into routine.

The strongest counterargument is that reserve status can shift naturally as economies grow and markets evolve, and that no issuer holds privilege forever. The reserve order can change. Yet it changes slowly because network systems reward defaults and punish experiments during fear. Challengers must not merely be large. They must be trusted in stress. They must offer deep markets, reliable finality, predictable rule enforcement, credible collateral, and a corridor that remains open when pressure rises. Until a challenger proves these traits across crises, the system returns to the apex currency by reflex, because reflex is the cheapest decision when fear is expensive, and because institutions that manage other people's money are paid to avoid reputational catastrophe, not to pioneer.

The residue for decision-makers is simple. Liquidity privilege is structural advantage anchored in settlement hierarchy, collateral conventions, and crisis access. Non-issuers who ignore it build balance sheets stable only in calm and then discover in stress that external acceptance governs domestic autonomy. Issuers who misunderstand it overestimate their freedom, ignore the domestic political costs of being the world's refuge, and mismanage the legitimacy of the backstop role they inevitably play. The reserve order is where monetary architecture becomes geopolitical leverage through ordinary funding, ordinary collateral, and ordinary payment sequence.

CLOSING DOCTRINE

Liquidity privilege is the reserve order's operating advantage: the top currency's claims are treated as the quickest upgrade into acceptance when fear makes time scarce, tightening spreads, lowering haircuts, and turning the issuer's liabilities into the system's settlement refuge. The privilege is reproduced in crisis, not declared, because stress concentrates demand for a narrow set of claims and forces non-issuers to seek the apex unit precisely when they cannot create it, converting currency mismatch into a run channel. The top currency sets terms through collateral ladders, eligibility lists, documentation burdens, and corridor admissibility, which means domestic legality does not guarantee external passage and external passage prices time. Non-issuers therefore live inside uneven upgrade rights and must buy autonomy through buffers, infrastructure, and constraint, while the issuer lives inside entanglement and must manage the domestic legitimacy of being the world's refuge. Reserve order is geopolitical infrastructure precisely because it governs through ordinary settlement sequence: spreads, haircuts, holds, and rollovers that quietly determine who can move and who must adjust.

CHAPTER 29
BLOC MONEY
SHARED CURRENCY, FRACTURED SOVEREIGNTY

The crisis meeting starts with a spreadsheet and ends with a question nobody wants to ask out loud. A finance minister in a member state of a currency bloc is staring at a refinancing calendar that has stopped looking like ordinary debt management and started looking like a countdown. Auctions must clear. Banks must roll funding. Firms must meet payroll. The unit in which all of it is denominated is the same unit used by richer neighbors, yet the interest rate the minister is being quoted feels like a foreign price imposed on a domestic polity. The minister's central bank cannot devalue and cannot print a separate national currency to buy time. The minister's parliament can tighten budgets, but tightening budgets can collapse growth and worsen the debt path, which makes the market demand even more compensation for risk. Inside a bloc, the state has surrendered one escape valve and discovered that the remaining valves are political, slow, and humiliating, and humiliation is not a mood in these systems, it is a constraint that shapes what leaders dare to do next.

The humiliation is not only fiscal. It is social and intimate. A shared unit creates a shared expectation of sameness, and sameness becomes a promise the bloc must defend every day. In calm, the promise is invisible because most people do not test it. In stress, the promise becomes a daily referendum because households, merchants, banks, and governments begin deciding whether a unit held there is as safe as a unit held here, whether a deposit in one jurisdiction clears with the same speed and certainty as a deposit in another, whether an invoice paid from a peripheral bank carries the same reputational cleanliness as an invoice paid from a core bank. The moment that question becomes ordinary, the bloc's monetary project stops being economics and becomes legitimacy transmission under fear.

"The conversion rates shall be irrevocably fixed." (founding treaty clause of a currency union)

The line is often presented as a triumph of integration. In practice, it is a redesign of sovereignty. Irrevocably fixed means you do not have a national currency to adjust. It means you cannot use exchange-rate movement to absorb shocks. It means adjustment must occur elsewhere: wages, prices, taxes, spending, migration, and credit. It also means markets do not treat all members as equally safe simply because they share a unit. Markets treat members as different credit risks inside a single unit, and that difference becomes a political event because the unit removes the distance that used to separate domestic policy from external pricing. In a national currency, a widening spread can be narrated as "the currency weakening," and the narrative gives politics a face to argue with. Inside a bloc, the spread is the face. The spread is a verdict delivered in the same unit citizens use to buy bread, which is why bloc crises feel personal so quickly.

Bloc money begins as shared stability and often becomes shared constraint. The promise is that a common unit eliminates currency risk inside the bloc, deepens trade, lowers transaction costs, and creates a larger and more liquid financial area. Those promises can be real. Yet the promise that matters most in crisis is implicit: if we share the unit, we will share the safety. The implicit promise is never fully written because writing it would require writing the fiscal constitution of the bloc, and blocs are built by compromise. Compromise can build a unit. Compromise struggles to build a backstop. This is the chapter's core mechanism. A currency union is easy to announce and hard to govern because the true difficulty is not issuing a unit. The difficulty is deciding who bears losses when imbalances accumulate and fear arrives, and deciding it fast enough that the decision looks like rule rather than like panic bargaining.

A shared currency creates two different unions at once. It creates a monetary union, where payment and settlement occur in the same unit and the internal exchange rate disappears. It also creates an implicit credit union, because banks, insurers, pension funds, and households begin to treat cross-border claims inside the bloc as near-domestic. A deposit in one member feels as spendable as a deposit in another, at least in calm. A bond issued by one member can be held by institutions in another as if the unit itself were the guarantee. This is the bloc's great efficiency. It is also the bloc's great danger, because it encourages the accumulation of cross-border exposures that become politically explosive when the market reintroduces credit differentiation inside the shared unit. The unit removes the visible boundary. The credit risk returns as a hidden boundary that appears suddenly in stress, and hidden boundaries are always experienced as betrayal.

The first structural tension is between a single monetary authority and multiple fiscal authorities. A shared unit implies one interest-rate policy, one settlement core, and one apex liquidity provider for the bloc's banking system. Yet budgets, taxes, welfare obligations, and political legitimacy remain national. In calm, this is manageable because markets price risk modestly and because growth covers imperfections. In stress, the bloc discovers it has centralized the power to create the apex settlement claim while leaving the responsibility for debt and social order dispersed. The result is recurring bargaining crisis: the monetary authority can stabilize banks with liquidity, but it cannot legitimize transfers, and national parliaments can legitimize budgets, but they cannot create the unit they owe. The bloc becomes a machine that can produce money and cannot easily produce solidarity, and in a bloc, solidarity is not a virtue, it is an operational requirement because the unit is a shared promise.

The second structural tension is bank-sovereign entanglement inside a unit that forbids devaluation. Banks hold large amounts of member-state debt because it is liquid, because convention and regulation treat it as usable collateral, and because it is convenient for balance-sheet management. Governments depend on banks because banks are primary buyers of domestic issuance and because banks distribute credit to the domestic economy. In calm, this looks like national financial development. In stress, it becomes a loop. If the sovereign is questioned, bank balance sheets are questioned because sovereign holdings lose market value and because funding markets demand more collateral. If banks are questioned, the sovereign is questioned because the sovereign is expected to rescue domestic banks and because recession deepens. In a national currency, the state can sometimes break this loop by using monetary tools and by letting the exchange rate absorb some adjustment. Inside a bloc, the state cannot devalue and cannot create a national settlement asset. The loop becomes harder, and politics becomes the primary stabilization channel. Politics is slower than panic. That timing mismatch is the bloc's core vulnerability, and it is where "shared unit" becomes "fractured sovereignty."

The third tension is internal imbalances without an internal exchange rate. In a shared unit, current-account differences do not produce currency depreciation inside the bloc. They produce accumulation: surpluses in some members and deficits in others, financed through cross-border credit. In a fully unified fiscal and banking union, such imbalances can be absorbed through automatic stabilizers and risk sharing. In a partial union, imbalances accumulate as claims between banking systems and as private exposures later discovered to be public problems. The deficit member experiences cheap financing until the moment it does not. The surplus member experiences export advantage until the moment it becomes the creditor facing potential loss. The bloc's politics then turns into an argument over morality: who was prudent, who was reckless, who should pay. Moral arguments are attractive because they make complex mechanics feel simple. They are also destructive because they turn what is fundamentally a design problem into a blame war, and blame wars are the substitute systems build when they cannot allocate losses cleanly and must still preserve consent.

"There shall be no assumption of the commitments of another member." (treaty-style clause commonly used in currency-union design)

This is the second sentence that defines bloc money's fracture line. No-assumption clauses are meant to prevent moral hazard and protect domestic taxpayers. They also create ambiguity about the backstop. Ambiguity is survivable only when the market believes a backstop exists anyway. When the market doubts, spreads widen, banks tighten, and the bloc discovers that it cannot both deny shared risk and preserve shared stability. The clause becomes a bargaining chip rather than a credible rule, and the bargaining happens in crisis time, which means it is always late.

The mechanics of lateness appear first as spreads and then as money-speed differences inside the same unit. A household in a stressed member hears a rumor that a local bank is under pressure. The household does not need to hate the bloc. The household only needs to protect itself. It moves savings toward an institution in a safer jurisdiction or toward a perceived safer bank inside the bloc. The household experiences the act as prudence. The bloc experiences it as an internal run. A small business owner begins to hear a new phrase from suppliers: pay from a core bank, not a local bank, because a payment that arrives from the wrong corridor might be delayed, questioned, or simply treated as a sign of fragility. The owner learns that one unit is shared and payment reputation is not. A municipal payroll office is told by its treasury bank that liquidity is tighter and that settlement timing may slip. The payroll office discovers that the bloc's unit is common and its cashflow certainty is not. The result is a political injury that arrives through invoices and wages, not through manifestos.

This is what internal fungibility means in practice. Fungibility is not a slogan. It is the lived equality of the unit across jurisdictions and institutions. If a unit held in one member is treated as less safe than a unit held in another, then the bloc does not have one currency in the only sense that matters. It has a shared symbol and fractured confidence. The bloc can preserve legal sameness. It cannot preserve economic sameness without a credible backstop and a credible loss-allocation mechanism, because the market will create its own hierarchy inside the bloc if the bloc refuses to name one.

Internal fungibility is maintained by settlement architecture and by the willingness to treat central-bank money as common rather than national. Payments inside a bloc clear through a shared core. Liquidity support can be extended to banks across the bloc if the monetary authority treats collateral and supervision as common. Yet the political legitimacy of losses remains national unless fiscal union exists. This creates the bloc's recurring compromise: liquidity can be common, solvency responsibility is contested. Liquidity prevents immediate collapse. Solvency determines who pays. The longer liquidity substitutes for solvency decisions, the more the bloc converts time into resentment. Time is purchased, but the bill arrives as elections, coalitions, and constitutional fights, because citizens can tolerate emergency support and rarely tolerate indefinite emergency support that feels like hidden transfer or hidden punishment.

The chapter must treat the settlement layer as an active actor, not a backdrop. In a bloc, settlement is where sameness is performed. A shared settlement core makes a payment instruction appear uniform across borders. Yet the moment liquidity provision, collateral acceptability, and supervisory trust become differentiated by jurisdiction, settlement stops being a neutral highway and becomes a political border disguised as a technical process. Banks in stressed members find that collateral is accepted with harsher conditions, that haircuts rise, that counterparties shorten tenors, that cross-border lines are reduced quietly. None of this requires the bloc to announce a split. The split emerges as sequence: a payment that posts but does not feel final, a transfer that clears but arrives slower, a credit line that renews but at punitive price. This is how a shared unit fractures without changing its name.

Bloc money is therefore not merely a monetary choice. It is a choice about where discipline lives. In a national currency, discipline can arrive through inflation, devaluation, and domestic policy tightening. In a bloc, discipline arrives through credit spreads, conditional assistance, and internal wage and price adjustment because the exchange rate cannot move. This shifts the burden of adjustment onto domestic labor markets and domestic politics. It also shifts the burden of legitimacy onto institutions that may be perceived as external, even if they are jointly governed. The bloc's institutional challenge is legitimacy transmission: can the bloc impose discipline without being experienced as foreign rule. If it cannot, the bloc becomes unstable even if its economics are sound, because monetary unions fail politically before they fail arithmetically.

The morality war is not a side show. It is the bloc's replacement for a missing constitution of loss. Surplus members narrate deficits as irresponsibility, because that story protects domestic consent by converting a structural design problem into a behavioral indictment. Deficit members narrate conditionality as punishment, because that story protects domestic consent by converting a structural design problem into external domination. Both stories can contain partial truths. Neither story resolves the mechanics. The mechanics require a decision about who bears losses and on what terms. When a bloc cannot make that decision cleanly, it makes it through time: delays, partial facilities, conditional packages, incremental commitments, and constant renegotiation. That is why bloc crises feel repetitive. Repetition is what happens when a system tries to govern a fiscal constitution through improvisation.

A sovereign-level pressure scene makes the design problem unavoidable. A member state faces recession and rising debt ratios. It cannot devalue. It cannot print a national settlement asset. It can tighten budgets, but tightening deepens recession and can worsen debt dynamics by shrinking the denominator that makes the ratio survivable. It can seek assistance, but assistance comes with conditions that look domestically like external governance, and even when those conditions are rational, rationality does not guarantee legitimacy. Domestic politics polarizes. The state begins to lose not only market access but political coherence. The union's partners face their own politics. They can extend support, but support looks like transfer. They can refuse, but refusal risks fracture of the shared unit and therefore risks larger losses. The bloc discovers that monetary architecture has turned into a bargaining problem over solidarity and punishment. This is not a failure of economics. It is the consequence of building a shared unit without fully socializing the backstop that makes a unit credible in panic.

The chapter must also show how the same shared unit produces different lived money for different actors the moment stress hits. Households experience it as deposit safety anxiety and the sudden need to choose where to keep savings. Small businesses experience it as supplier distrust and pricing premiums attached to the origin of payment. Municipalities experience it as the cost and timing of payroll funding and the political shame of being forced to cut services because credit lines tighten. Banks experience it as collateral and corridor scarcity. The shared unit remains, and yet the speed and certainty attached to the unit diverge. A bloc can survive many economic disputes. It struggles to survive when its citizens discover that the same unit carries different privileges depending on where it is held.

Bloc money also changes the reserve-order picture in a subtle and often misunderstood way. A bloc currency is often created partly to reduce external dependency on the top currency. It can succeed in creating a larger internal market and a deep pool of safe assets. Yet the bloc's internal fractures can prevent it from becoming a full alternative apex. The world watches crisis performance. External holders do not need to dislike the bloc to treat its assets as conditionally usable under stress. Conditionality is enough. If a bloc must improvise rescue packages, invent new facilities mid-crisis, and negotiate conditionality with visible political pain, it teaches outsiders that the unit is a shared instrument with contested backstop. Outsiders then price that contestation as risk precisely when they are looking for unconditional refuge.

A corridor scene makes this external pricing mechanism concrete. A global investor holds bloc assets because returns are attractive and markets are deep. In calm, the investor treats bloc assets as near-apex. In stress, the investor asks a single question: will I be trapped. Will settlement remain smooth. Will collateral remain eligible. Will legal commitments hold without political fracture. The investor does not need to predict collapse. The investor only needs to fear that the bloc will respond with restrictions, delays, or political conflict that makes liquidity uncertain. The investor then shifts toward the top currency's claims, not because of ideology, but because the top currency is where the system has learned to hide when politics becomes loud. This is how internal bloc fracture risk becomes external reserve-order constraint. A bloc can be large and still be priced as conditional if its backstop is politically contested, and conditional is precisely what the reserve order penalizes when fear is expensive.

The strongest defense of bloc money is that it forces discipline and prevents irresponsible monetary policy at the national level. That defense holds in one sense. Removing the national printing press can prevent inflationary abuse and can stabilize expectations. Yet the defense fractures under stress because discipline is not merely preventing abuse. Discipline is also ensuring continuity. A system that imposes discipline by forcing immediate internal adjustment can create political breakdown, which then creates financial breakdown. The bloc can prevent one kind of abuse and still produce another kind of fragility: fragility from mismatch between centralized monetary power and decentralized fiscal legitimacy. The discipline story is incomplete unless it includes the backstop story, because discipline without backstop becomes austerity under panic, and austerity under panic is how democratic consent collapses.

The chapter must also tell the truth about what makes bloc money work when it works. It works when internal financial supervision is unified enough that banks are not treated as national fiefdoms. It works when collateral standards are consistent enough that liquidity provision does not become disguised transfer. It works when settlement infrastructure preserves fungibility and when emergency facilities can be deployed quickly enough to prevent runs from becoming political movements. It works when fiscal rules are credible enough to prevent persistent imbalances from becoming moral wars, and when some form of risk sharing exists so shocks do not force one member into depression while another accumulates surpluses without responsibility. In other words, it works when the bloc treats money as a shared governance project rather than a shared symbol, because symbols do not backstop deposits and do not clear funding markets when fear arrives.

That is why bloc money is fractured sovereignty by design. Sovereignty is not abolished. It is redistributed. Monetary sovereignty is centralized. Fiscal sovereignty remains national. Legal sovereignty is mixed. Political legitimacy remains local. The system can be stable only if these sovereignties are stitched together by institutions that can act quickly in panic and by political arrangements that can assign losses without dissolving into resentment. If the stitching is weak, the bloc becomes a machine that produces periodic existential crises, because panic will always test where the true backstop lives and whether the bloc's promise of sameness is rule or theater.

CLOSING DOCTRINE

Bloc money is a shared unit that removes the exchange-rate escape valve while leaving fiscal legitimacy dispersed, converting many macro adjustments into political bargaining under crisis time. Irrevocably fixed conversion is a sovereignty redesign that shifts discipline onto wages, credit spreads, and conditional assistance because devaluation is no longer available, which means adjustment is experienced domestically as social strain rather than as currency movement. The union's core vulnerability is fungibility under stress: if deposits, collateral, and payment speed are not treated as equally safe everywhere, the currency fractures in lived reality even if the symbol remains. No-assumption clauses can limit moral hazard in calm and create fatal ambiguity in panic unless a credible backstop and a credible loss-allocation regime are built alongside them, because liquidity can be common while solvency responsibility is contested. Internal imbalances and bank-sovereign entanglement become more dangerous inside a shared unit, turning time bought by emergency facilities into resentment when moral narratives substitute for missing constitutional machinery. Externally, bloc assets are priced by crisis performance: outsiders treat a shared unit as conditional if its backstop is politically contested, which limits the bloc's ability to become an unconditional reserve refuge even when markets are deep. Bloc money succeeds only when the bloc governs its unit as a shared public architecture, capable of preserving fungibility quickly in panic and allocating losses legitimately, rather than as a shared symbol whose backstop is negotiated only after fear has already begun to fracture the union.

CHAPTER 30
CHALLENGER STRATEGY
RAILS, RESERVES, AND INCREMENTAL CAPTURE

The meeting is not held in public, and it is not framed as rebellion. It is framed as risk management. A governor sits with a finance minister, a reserve manager, and the heads of payments, markets, and supervision. On the table are three files that look unrelated to anyone outside the room: a map of correspondent relationships and their failure points, a reserve report that admits what buffers really are and what they are not, and a technical plan for new cross-border rails that promises redundancy and efficiency. The governor does not ask how to dethrone the top currency. The governor asks a colder question: if the corridor tightens tomorrow, what still clears, what still settles, what still counts as usable money at the boundary, and what humiliations will be demanded as the price of time. Challenger strategy begins there, because no serious state attempts to replace an order before it can survive the order's pressure.

"Reserve status is earned in crisis, not announced in policy." (threshold doctrine used inside reserve management)

That sentence is not pessimism. It is an operating constraint. A challenger can grow in trade share, build a deep domestic market, and still fail at the moment that matters because the reserve order is a system of panic reflexes. In panic, institutions do not choose the currency with the boldest narrative. They choose the currency whose instruments remain usable under stress, whose corridors remain open, whose collateral remains eligible, whose legal protections remain predictable, and whose liquidity can be obtained without pleading. Challenger strategy is therefore a staged campaign of credibility, not a declaration of sovereignty. It is incremental capture: capture of payment sequence, capture of settlement routine, capture of collateral acceptability, capture of reserve habit, and capture of the belief that holding the challenger is not a trap.

The first principle is that dominance is not one lever. It is a stack. The top currency dominates because it sits at the top of multiple stacks simultaneously: unit of account, settlement corridor, collateral ladder, and crisis backstop. Challengers usually fail because they attack the visible layer, the symbol, and ignore the operating layers that govern acceptance. The symbol is not where power sits. Power sits in upgrade rights: the right to convert a claim into usable settlement when fear arrives. If a challenger cannot supply upgrade rights reliably, it cannot displace the incumbent. It can carve a zone. It can build a regional perimeter. It cannot become the refuge.

The second principle is that reserve displacement is plumbing before it is politics. Challengers win first by changing where payments route and what institutions must hold to keep routing smooth. This is why rails matter. A rail is not only a message path. A rail is a permissions path. It determines whose compliance rules apply, whose identity standards are required, which data fields must be furnished, which legal jurisdiction governs disputes, and which settlement asset is required at the end. A challenger that builds alternative rails is not merely building redundancy. It is building a corridor where gatekeeping is different, where admissibility terms are different, and where emergency access can be granted by a different authority. This is the first quiet capture: once enough payments route through a new corridor, the corridor's standards become the new normal for participants who must transact to survive.

Yet rails alone do not create money. Rails create motion. Money requires a credible end state. A cross-border system can route around incumbent messaging and still fail if settlement remains dependent on incumbent collateral or incumbent-unit conversion at the last mile. This is the first trap of "new rail" thinking: bypassing one choke point while leaving the final hinge anchored to the old corridor. If the last mile still clears in the incumbent's unit, the challenger has built a detour that ends at the same gate. Detours still matter because detours create bargaining leverage and crisis options, but detours are not replacement. Replacement requires a complete stack: routing, clearing, settlement, and a credible legal definition of discharge that third parties will honor even when politics is loud and credit is scarce.

The third principle is that reserves are not passive savings. Reserves are corridor insurance and corridor signaling. They buy time at the boundary, and time is the scarce asset in crisis. A challenger that wants to reduce dependency must treat reserves as a strategic portfolio designed for panic, not a yield strategy designed for calm. The reserve manager's job is not to optimize returns. The reserve manager's job is to keep imports flowing, keep external obligations current, keep domestic banks from seizing when rollover tightens, and keep the state from being forced into policy surrender at the worst moment. A challenger strategy therefore begins by admitting that, for a long time, the incumbent's unit remains the emergency tool even for those trying to escape it. This is the central contradiction of transition: you cannot exit dependency by denying it. You exit by building alternative capacity while preserving enough incumbent access to avoid collapse during the build.

This contradiction produces the fourth principle: incremental capture must happen along the margin, not through dramatic rupture. The reserve order punishes rupture because rupture creates trap fear, and trap fear reverses diversification instantly. A challenger that wants adoption must look boring in the ways that matter: predictable convertibility, predictable settlement, predictable legal recourse, predictable corridor behavior under stress. Boring is not branding. Boring is trust. The challenger must also resist domestic temptation to prove strength through sudden controls or sudden rule changes that trap foreign holders. The moment foreign holders believe exit can be blocked, reserve ambition dies, because reserve status is a bet on being able to leave. The fastest way to kill a challenger is to teach the world that the challenger's unit becomes a cage in crisis.

The fifth principle is that the unit of account is not conquered directly. It drifts. Quoting moves when routines move, and routines move when treasurers are rewarded for reducing friction and punished for taking blame. This is why incremental capture begins inside corporate policy rather than inside speeches. A multinational treasury desk rewrites its invoice templates so that a portion of supplier contracts can be paid in the challenger's unit. Not because the desk believes in a new world, but because the desk discovers that settlement in the challenger's corridor is cheaper, faster, and less prone to discretionary holds. A procurement team accepts the change because it reduces fees and reduces operational headaches. Hedging desks build the necessary instruments because there is now flow. Accounting systems update because there is now routine. The currency enters the firm's life not as ideology but as default. This is how unit-of-account share changes: through bureaucratic adoption that becomes habit and then becomes necessity.

Commodity settlement is the next arena where quoting drifts. A buyer offers to pay in the challenger's unit for a discount. A seller accepts only if the seller can convert the unit into usable collateral quickly, can hedge exposures cheaply, and can repatriate proceeds without fear of discretionary trap. The decision is made by risk managers who care less about grand strategy than about operational certainty. When enough of these transactions clear smoothly, banks build product around them. Once banks build product, more trade flows shift. The reserve order is not conquered by rhetoric. It is chipped away by the accumulation of boring operational wins that reduce blame risk for the people who decide what unit is used.

The sixth principle is that collateral is the real battlefield. The reserve order is ultimately a hierarchy of acceptable pledges. The incumbent dominates because its short-term public liabilities are treated as the highest-grade pledge for margin calls and emergency funding. Challengers must build a comparable collateral object: a short-term claim in their own unit that markets treat as liquid, legally safe, easily custodied, and reliably convertible in stress. This is not merely an issuance question. It is a legal and institutional question. Who can hold the collateral. How easily it can be pledged across borders. Whether title and priority are enforceable quickly. Whether insolvency rules are predictable. Whether enforcement is fast enough to matter when panic compresses time. Whether custody chains are trusted. Whether market depth exists that can absorb forced sales without collapse. Foreign holders do not price only yield. They price enforceability and speed. They price the probability that, if something breaks, they will be paid without having to litigate inside a political storm. That probability is what outsiders call safety, and what insiders must build as rule.

The seventh principle is the external lender-of-last-resort problem, and it is the wall most challengers avoid naming. A currency can be domestic and still become regional. A currency can be regional and still fail to become reserve because reserve status implies that, in global stress, foreigners need the unit and can obtain it. The incumbent's unit is demanded globally in panic, which means global institutions build balance sheets that require access to it. A challenger that wants reserve status must eventually supply liquidity beyond its borders or build an architecture through which liquidity can be obtained without humiliating negotiation. This does not mean open-ended rescue. It means credible perimeter liquidity: facilities, collateralized lending structures, and crisis procedures that foreign counterparties believe will function when fear is high. Without perimeter liquidity, a challenger remains conditional. Conditional is tolerated in calm and abandoned in panic.

The perimeter liquidity question is also a domestic politics question because it requires the challenger to accept that foreign institutions will hold its liabilities and will demand liquidity at moments that may be politically inconvenient. A challenger that wants the world to hold its unit must accept that, in a crisis, supplying liquidity to the external perimeter can look domestically like helping outsiders. If domestic politics treats that act as betrayal, the challenger will hesitate, and hesitation will be priced immediately as conditionality. Reserve status is not only a financial achievement. It is a political discipline: the ability to keep corridors open and to maintain predictable behavior even when the domestic mood wants punishment.

The eighth principle is legal finality as the antidote to trap fear. Trap fear is not irrational. It is how institutions protect themselves from political intervention. If foreign holders suspect that, in stress, courts will be slow, enforcement will be discretionary, custody will be politicized, or priority will be rewritten, they will not hold the challenger at scale. They may trade it. They may use it opportunistically. They will not treat it as reserve. A challenger strategy must therefore treat finality and enforcement as reserve infrastructure. It must build a legal environment where collateral can be enforced, titles are respected, insolvency priorities are predictable, and changes to rules are bounded by procedure. These are not "legal niceties." They are the difference between a unit that can be held by strangers and a unit that can only be held by friends.

The ninth principle is convertibility discipline, which is the knife edge between credibility and collapse. The reserve order is built on the belief that the apex claim can be converted into what is needed quickly. Challengers must offer a credible convertibility promise without offering an open-ended guarantee that would exhaust buffers. If convertibility is too tight, adoption stalls because foreign holders fear trap risk. If convertibility is too loose, the challenger becomes vulnerable to attack and depletion because it promises exit it cannot finance. The middle path is staged credibility: widen access only as market depth, collateral acceptability, perimeter liquidity tools, and legal predictability become real. This is why transition is slow. Slow is not failure. Slow is the price of building a currency that can survive a crisis without improvisation. Improvisation is what the reserve order punishes most, because improvisation teaches the world that rules are not rules when fear arrives.

The tenth principle is that the reserve order is rarely replaced by one challenger in a single leap. It is constrained by partial successes that change bargaining power. A state that can route trade payments through a non-incumbent corridor has options during dispute. A state that can settle key imports in a different unit reduces immediate vulnerability to corridor tightening. A region that builds a liquidity pool reduces the need for emergency access at the worst moment. These moves do not dethrone the incumbent. They change the terms of dependence. They reduce the incumbent's ability to impose discipline unilaterally. Incremental capture is therefore often less about replacement and more about creating credible alternatives that force the incumbent corridor to remain open, cheaper, and less discretionary because a credible alternative exists. Competition becomes restraint.

The strongest defense of the status quo is that a single apex corridor reduces coordination costs and stabilizes global trade. A world of multiple reserve candidates can become a world of higher transaction costs, fragmented liquidity, and increased crisis volatility because safe-asset demand is spread across thinner markets. This defense has force. It is the reason institutions prefer a default. Yet it is incomplete because it ignores how the same default concentrates coercive power and concentrates systemic fragility into a narrow set of choke points. A single apex corridor stabilizes until it is used as leverage, and it creates global vulnerability by making global liquidity dependent on one issuer's domestic politics. The reserve order is therefore a trade between efficiency and autonomy. Challenger strategy exists because states are deciding that the autonomy cost of a single apex corridor is no longer acceptable, even if the efficiency cost of diversification is real.

Challenger strategy ends, for serious officials, as a checklist disguised as geopolitics. Build rails that can route and clear. Build collateral instruments that can be pledged. Build legal finality that can be trusted. Build reserves that buy time. Build hedging markets that reduce trap fear. Build supervisory credibility that lowers haircuts. Build crisis governance that can supply perimeter liquidity without improvisation. Then, and only then, ask markets to hold the unit at scale. Everything else is performance.

CLOSING DOCTRINE

Challenger strategy is incremental capture, not declaration: reserve status is earned in crisis performance through usable convertibility, collateral acceptability, corridor reliability, and trusted finality. Rails matter because they relocate gatekeeping and define admissibility, but rails alone do not create money unless settlement can finish without permission from the old corridor. Reserves are time insurance at the boundary, not portfolios, and time prevents forced liquidation and policy humiliation. The core battlefield is collateral and law: a challenger must build short-term public liabilities that are pledgeable with predictable enforcement, narrow haircuts, trusted custody, and stable insolvency priority, otherwise foreign holders price trap risk and exit at the first shock. The hard wall is perimeter liquidity: without credible ability to supply the unit beyond its borders in stress, a challenger remains conditional and is abandoned in panic. The hidden cost is domestic restraint: reserve ambition requires predictable rules and convertibility discipline even when politics wants punishment. The reserve order is rarely replaced at once; it is constrained when credible alternatives exist, because alternatives force the incumbent corridor to behave.

CHAPTER 31
MULTILATERAL INSTRUMENTS
EMERGENCY LIQUIDITY AND QUIET CONTROL

The first signal is never a declaration. It is a delay that arrives as a polite question. A bank's compliance team requests additional documentation for a transfer that cleared without friction for years. A corporate treasury desk is told a counterparty bank is reassessing exposure and will shorten settlement windows. A shipping insurer receives notice that a familiar corridor now requires a different chain of attestations before coverage can attach. None of these moves is framed as a sanction. Each is framed as prudence. Yet together they change the price of time. The corridor war is fought precisely here, in the ordinary sequence of payment life, where admissibility can be narrowed quietly until a state discovers it is negotiating for access to its own trade.

Payment access is statecraft because modern sovereignty depends on cross-border passage. A state may govern its domestic unit and still be unable to settle for imports, refinance external obligations, or receive export earnings without corridors operated, supervised, and reputationally defended outside its borders. The corridor is therefore not merely plumbing. It is the infrastructure through which a state converts domestic legality into external usability. When corridors are open, the state experiences autonomy. When corridors tighten, the state experiences constraint that feels like market pressure until it recognizes that the pressure is concentrated at specific veto points controlled by institutions that can say yes, delay, or quietly say no, while still claiming they are only following policy.

Corridor wars thrive on misrecognition because payment is assumed to be binary. Allowed or banned. In reality, payment access is graded, and grading is where leverage lives. A transfer can be authorized and still be slowed. It can be posted and still be held. It can be cleared and still be reversible in practice because the receiving institution can freeze. It can reach a messaging milestone and still fail to become usable value because the last-mile bank refuses crediting until additional proofs arrive. These distinctions sound technical. They are political. A state that cannot distinguish access, passage, and finality is a state that will be surprised when its payment life becomes conditional in crisis, because the corridor war rarely begins with "no." It begins with "not yet," and "not yet" is how scarcity is made without confession.

The clean way to feel the difference is to watch one payment move through its lifecycle. A corporate treasury desk initiates an urgent transfer for a critical import shipment. The payment is authorized internally. The bank accepts the instruction. The platform shows confirmation and a reference number, which is enough for an inexperienced user to believe the obligation is ended. In the back end, the transfer enters screening. A data field is incomplete or a beneficiary name triggers a similarity match. The payment is flagged and held. The bank requests clarification. The treasury desk responds with documents that satisfy internal counsel but do not satisfy the corridor's preferred format. A second hold is applied. The shipment is delayed. Demurrage begins. The importer's factory reduces production. Workers are sent home early. The payment is still "in process," and yet the economy is already adjusting. This is the corridor war in its most ordinary form: the power to turn an instruction into a queue and to make a state pay for time through scarcity that looks like business disruption rather than political pressure.

This is why the corridor war's primary weapon is the compliance choke point. Compliance is not only a legal requirement. It is a gating technology. It decides which identities are legible, which counterparties are admissible, which industries are tolerated, and which transactions become suspicious by default. In calm, compliance appears as routine screening and reporting. In pressure, compliance becomes a rationing system that can be tightened selectively with plausible deniability. The corridor does not need to announce exclusion of a state or a sector. It can require more proof, shorten deadlines, widen holds, narrow acceptable documentation, and increase the cost of error until counterparties retreat voluntarily. Retreat is the corridor's ideal outcome because it produces compliance without coercive theater.

"Access is granted by institutions that can deny without calling it denial." (corridor doctrine line used by payment strategists)

The phrase captures the essence. Corridor wars are not usually fought by overt prohibition. They are fought by raising the operational cost of passage until targeted actors cannot move at scale. This is why corridor leverage is so effective. It looks like risk management. It feels like compliance. It functions like pressure. And because it operates through private institutions, it can be deployed without the drama that would trigger immediate retaliation or political mobilization.

The private intermediary is not a bystander. It is the corridor's executive arm. Risk committees decide whether a counterparty is worth the scrutiny load. Compliance teams decide how narrow tolerance should be. Correspondent banks decide which relationships are worth maintaining. Insurers decide whether coverage attaches at the old price or at a punitive premium, which changes trade viability. Custodians decide whether certain collateral remains acceptable, which changes liquidity access. Clearing members decide whether to extend intraday credit, which determines whether a payment sequence flows or seizes. None of these decisions must be described as geopolitics, and that is precisely why they become geopolitics. Corridor wars are governance by private policy executed at scale under public legal cover.

A state experiences corridor tightening first through its firms, because firms are where payment friction becomes scarcity. An importer discovers that paying for critical inputs now requires longer lead times and higher fees because banks are unwilling to take compliance risk. A commodity buyer discovers that suppliers demand payment through specific banks, in specific jurisdictions, with specific attestations, or shipment will not be released. An exporter discovers that receiving proceeds triggers more holds and more questions, delaying payroll and inventory procurement. A logistics operator learns that insurance now attaches only when payments route through a narrower set of corridors. The state sees macro consequences later: inflation in imported goods, liquidity stress in banks, reduced investment because planning becomes fragile. Corridor wars convert payment friction into domestic scarcity, and scarcity becomes politics quickly because scarcity does not arrive as policy debate. Scarcity arrives as empty shelves, layoffs, and rising prices that feel like betrayal of normality.

Corridor wars are fought through data because legibility is membership. Modern rails demand data fields that are then used to classify transactions, counterparties, and patterns. The actor that sets the data standard sets classification reality. Classification reality determines who is suspicious, who is routine, and who is excluded. If a state's firms cannot supply demanded data, they become high-friction by default. If a state's institutions cannot assure demanded identity integrity, they become suspect by default. Data therefore becomes a sovereignty issue because a state can have citizens and firms and still find that those citizens and firms are not legible enough to move at full speed in dominant corridors. The corridor does not need to punish overtly. It can simply treat the non-legible as slow, and slowness is punishment in a system where supply chains run on timing.

The next layer is collateral and liquidity, because corridors prefer counterparties who can post the right pledge and settle without drama. Corridors clear faster and cheaper for actors who can pledge eligible collateral and obtain liquidity in the right unit. In pressure, collateral requirements tighten and liquidity tenors shorten. A state's banks may still have assets, but if those assets are not acceptable to corridor counterparties, the banks cannot fund. The banks then pull back from domestic credit. The domestic economy slows. The state is forced into emergency measures to preserve stability, and those emergency measures can reduce external confidence further, tightening corridors again. Corridor wars therefore create feedback loops that look like market cycles but are driven by concentrated veto points in cross-border payment infrastructure.

A sovereign-level pressure scene shows how quickly corridor tightening becomes national humiliation. A finance ministry must pay for food and fuel imports. The funds exist in domestic currency and even in reserve holdings, but payment is delayed because intermediaries demand additional proofs and because the preferred settlement path has become reluctant. The ministry can accept higher spreads, reroute through longer corridors with less certainty, or negotiate directly with gatekeepers for exceptions. The negotiation itself is humiliation because it reveals that sovereignty at the boundary is conditional on the corridor's willingness to grant passage. The ministry learns, in a way no textbook can teach, that legal tender at home does not buy discharge abroad.

The next humiliation is subtler and more instructive: the attempt to reroute. The ministry directs payments through an alternative corridor. The alternative corridor works at small scale, but at crisis scale it demands the same thing the dominant corridor demands, because the alternative still touches banks that must protect themselves from secondary risk. Additional documentation is required. A different chain of identity attestations is demanded. Settlement cutoffs are earlier. Buffer requirements are higher. The ministry discovers that rerouting is not choosing a new wire path. Rerouting is entering a new admissibility regime. Admissibility is the corridor's real power. A state can build an alternative corridor and still be subject to corridor discipline if the alternative's gatekeepers fear contagion from the dominant corridor's standards. This is how corridor wars propagate: pressure spreads through reputational risk and through the universal desire not to be the weak link that attracts enforcement.

The corridor war is also fought through insurance and shipping, because trade depends on more than payment. A corridor can tighten by making payments expensive, but it can also tighten by making trade risky. If insurance coverage becomes conditional on routing through approved banks or on producing specific attestations, then the corridor has gained leverage without touching the payment itself. Firms comply because they must. The corridor's standards become embedded in commercial contracts, and embedded standards are the most durable form of power because they reproduce themselves through private agreement rather than through state decree.

Corridor wars alter alliance behavior and accelerate fragmentation. States that fear tightening corridors diversify payment paths, build regional clearing arrangements, pre-position liquidity buffers, and sign bilateral settlement agreements. These moves are described as de-risking. They are escape routes. The reserve order does not collapse when escape routes are built. It is constrained, because credible alternatives reduce the ability of a dominant corridor to impose discipline without cost. Yet alternatives are hard because networks reward defaults, and defaults are embedded not only in payment rails but in custody chains, legal predictability, insurance attachment, and collateral acceptability.

The deepest truth of corridor wars is blowback. Once corridors are used as leverage, actors build counter-corridors, and counter-corridors change the world's liquidity geometry. More buffers are held. More inventories are kept. More settlement occurs in smaller pools. More hedging is duplicated. More collateral is trapped in ring-fenced structures. The world becomes less efficient and more volatile because the premium for redundancy rises. The corridor power that once reduced transaction costs becomes the reason transaction costs rise. This is why corridor wars are dangerous even for the corridor's owner. Weaponized corridors eventually create a world in which everyone hoards time and hoards liquidity, and hoarding is the enemy of growth. Corridor leverage can win a short-term concession and still lose the long-term stability that made the corridor valuable in the first place.

Corridor wars are won by credibility more than by threat. Corridors tighten because counterparties can be risky, unstable, or simply too expensive to monitor. Tightening can be prudence. It can also be pressure. The line is rarely clean, which is why corridor wars can spiral. When actors interpret every compliance tightening as geopolitical intent, trust collapses and fragmentation accelerates. When fragmentation accelerates, the world pays a collective tax: higher transaction costs, thicker buffers, and more frequent liquidity shocks. Corridor leverage therefore becomes self-defeating if deployed as routine statecraft, because the corridor's dominance is a product of trust and trust cannot be taxed indefinitely without dissolving.

The state's strategic task is not only to complain about corridor power. It is to build corridor resilience, and corridor resilience is built with the same seriousness as military logistics because payment is the logistics of trade. Corridor resilience has four pillars. First, institutional legibility: identity integrity, documentation capacity, clean governance, and supervisory credibility that reduce de-risking incentives. Second, liquidity resilience: sufficient buffers in the units needed for settlement and domestic tools to prevent corridor stress from becoming domestic bank failure. Third, routing redundancy: alternative rails and relationships that can carry trade payments when one path tightens, with pre-negotiated standards rather than improvised pleading. Fourth, finality clarity: settlement endpoints that produce discharge the state can rely on without hidden reversibility. A state that lacks any of these pillars will experience corridor wars as repeated humiliation because each tightening forces improvisation, and improvisation is what corridors punish by raising the cost of time further.

Corridor wars end where they began: with time. When a corridor can slow you, it can discipline you, because slowing forces bigger buffers, worse terms, and policy concessions to regain passage. When you can route around a corridor, you can negotiate because you have options. Options are sovereignty at the boundary. The reserve order concentrates options in a few corridors. Challenger strategies attempt to multiply options. The corridor war is the struggle between concentration and redundancy, and the outcome determines whether payment access remains a neutral utility or becomes the world's quiet battlefield, fought through sequence rather than through speeches.

CLOSING DOCTRINE

Corridor wars are payment statecraft executed through graded access: admissibility, passage, and finality can be tightened selectively through documentation burdens, identity standards, data requirements, collateral eligibility, insurance attachment, custody acceptability, and liquidity terms without formal rupture. The corridor's power is the power to price time by turning instructions into queues, raising error costs, and inducing voluntary retreat by counterparties who fear compliance exposure, which converts payment friction into domestic scarcity. Because cross-border usability depends on corridors, domestic sovereignty can be undermined by external admissibility even when domestic legality is intact, and rerouting is itself governed by the legibility standards of the new path. Data standards and classification become membership systems, collateral ladders determine who can clear quickly when fear narrows eligibility, and private risk committees become geopolitical instruments by deciding what is tolerable under the cover of prudence. Corridor resilience therefore requires institutional legibility, perimeter liquidity buffers, routing redundancy, and trusted finality so that tightening in one path does not become national humiliation. If states fail to build this resilience, payment access becomes leverage by default, fragmentation accelerates, and the global system pays a tax in thicker buffers, higher costs, and more frequent liquidity shocks, producing a world where money moves slower precisely when it is most needed.

CHAPTER 32
FINANCIAL STATECRAFT
EXCLUSION, FREEZES, SEIZURES, SIGNALING

The decision is made in a room that feels more administrative than strategic, which is the point. There are binders, draft notices, legal memos that read like dry weather, and a short list of institutions whose names recur across trade finance, correspondent banking, commodities settlement, insurance attachment, and custody chains. The officials are not debating the target's moral status. They are debating the architecture of pressure. Which permissions are removed first. Which corridors are narrowed. Which assets can be immobilized quickly. Which claims can be subordinated without triggering a wider run. Which allies must be notified to avoid gaps that convert a targeted measure into a global scramble. The power here is not primarily persuasion. It is the power to re-rank claims and reprice time at the boundary. Financial statecraft is the practice of turning monetary infrastructure into leverage without having to declare war.

The first thing to understand is that these instruments are graded, not binary. Exclusion, freeze, seizure, and signaling are often described as separate tools, but in operation they are a ladder. The ladder begins with stigma. Stigma raises compliance cost. Higher compliance cost reduces willingness to intermediate. Reduced willingness narrows corridors. Narrowed corridors slow settlement. Slower settlement forces counterparties to demand safer routes, safer banks, safer formats, and earlier payment. That demand induces voluntary retreat. Voluntary retreat is the applying state's most efficient pressure channel because it is scalable, deniable, and self-reinforcing. If voluntary retreat is insufficient, the ladder climbs. The system begins to hold, then to block, then to immobilize, then to appropriate. The target experiences this as sudden punishment. The applying state experiences it as controlled escalation of admissibility. Both perspectives are true because financial statecraft is a technique for making private actors do the work while the state sets the liability environment in which those private actors must survive.

Exclusion is the cleanest instrument and the most misunderstood. People describe exclusion as being cut off, as if a plug is pulled and the target goes dark. In reality, exclusion is almost always staged. It begins by redefining visibility and suspicion. Once a counterparty becomes categorically suspicious, every transaction becomes more expensive to process because documentation burdens rise, exception handling becomes routine, and the reputational penalty for error expands. Banks react by narrowing risk appetite, shortening maturities, and demanding stronger proofs. Insurers react by raising premiums or attaching conditions. Clearing members react by tightening collateral requirements and shrinking intraday credit. Custodians react by adding enhanced review to instructions. None of this is yet a freeze. It is the pre-freeze economy, where the target remains technically connected but functionally slowed. The pressure is in choosing where to apply the first friction, because friction is triage. It decides whose trade survives, whose funding rolls, and whose transactions drift into queue.

The first scene is rarely the dramatic block. It is the conference call between a large bank's risk committee and its general counsel. A notice has arrived that creates a new expectation: certain flows are now intolerable, or tolerable only with burdens that make them uneconomic. The bank does not ask whether it agrees. The bank asks what it can prove. Which data fields must be captured. Which counterparties are higher risk by default. How quickly systems can be updated to prevent prohibited transactions without blocking lawful ones. Every answer produces an operational change, and operational change produces economic consequence. Onboarding tightens. Threshold rules narrow. Manual review expands. Correspondent exposure shrinks. The bank's private policy becomes the state's instrument because the state has pushed the bank into a new liability posture. This is how financial statecraft scales: private enforcement executed at transaction speed under the shadow of public penalty.

"If you control the settlement perimeter, you control the speed of commerce." (operational doctrine line)

Speed is the scarce asset in modern trade and modern finance. A system can absorb higher prices. It cannot absorb persistent uncertainty about whether payment will clear, whether funds will be credited, and whether the corridor will remain open when a shipment is mid-ocean and financing is mid-roll. Exclusion works first by making speed unreliable. Once speed is unreliable, counterparties retreat voluntarily. Voluntary retreat is efficient pressure because it denies the target without requiring the state to issue a universal ban that would expose the state to direct retaliation and would force the applying state's firms to reveal their own dependencies.

Exclusion has a second face that matters even more: exclusion through legibility. A state can be excluded not only because it is forbidden, but because it is unintelligible to the dominant corridor's risk systems. If beneficial ownership is opaque, if registries are unreliable, if identity documents are not trusted, if court enforcement is unpredictable, the network behaves as if the jurisdiction is toxic even absent formal action. Banks de-risk. Correspondents withdraw. Trade finance dries. Payment corridors become thin and expensive. In this sense, exclusion is not merely a policy. It is a structural property of the network. Financial statecraft exploits this by raising the perceived cost of legibility until the target cannot meet requirements quickly, and then the system excludes by default. Default exclusion is the most durable exclusion because it is reproduced through private caution rather than through state decree.

The freeze is the next rung, and the freeze is not merely immobilization. It is reclassification plus instruction. A freeze tells every intermediary that touching the asset is risky in a new way. That risk is not only about legality. It is about liability, reputational exposure, and the operational cost of exception handling. A freeze can be applied to an individual account, a group of entities, a category of transactions, a security position, or an entire corridor class. It can be executed through banks, through custodians, through payment intermediaries, through insurers, through clearing members, and through the legal architecture that gives those actors the right and obligation to stop honoring certain claims. A freeze turns usable claims into contested claims, and contested claims are discounted claims. The discount spreads beyond the named target because intermediaries do not want to be the weak link. The halo of avoidance is the amplification mechanism.

The freeze's power is temporal. It introduces frozen time. Frozen time is not merely delay. It is the inability to plan because even if the asset exists, it cannot be relied on as working capital or as pledgeable collateral. Firms inside the target economy learn to hoard usable money, to prepay, to demand harsher terms, to shorten supply chains, to thicken inventories, and to redesign contracts so that settlement occurs earlier and in safer forms. These are not ideological choices. They are adaptations to degraded usability. The state does not need to block every transaction. It only needs to make enough transactions unpredictable that the private sector self-insures, and self-insurance is contraction.

Seizure is narrower and more psychologically decisive. Freezes immobilize. Seizures transfer. A seizure is the state asserting that the asset is not merely blocked but appropriable under law, and that law will be defended through courts, police power, and custody chains. Seizure is a signal to every holder watching that property rights at the boundary are conditional on political status. That conditionality can be morally justified in the case at hand. The mechanism remains dangerous because it teaches a general lesson: assets held in jurisdictions that can seize are assets whose priority can be rewritten by sovereign decision. The reserve order relies on the belief that apex assets are safe because rule is predictable. Seizure is a stress test of that belief. It can strengthen deterrence and still impose long-run cost in trust if used carelessly, because every seizure is also a reminder that custody is sovereignty made operational.

Signaling ties the ladder together, and it is often the most important instrument. Financial statecraft is not only what the state does. It is what the state makes other actors expect. A signal can be delivered through designation, warning, enforcement action, quiet guidance to regulated institutions, or the mere choice of which cases are prosecuted and which are settled. The signal changes private behavior before the state acts again. Firms and banks are paid to anticipate the next restriction, not to wait for it. Once the signal is credible, the system tightens itself. That self-tightening is what makes pressure effective at scale, because the corridor's private guardians do the work in advance and often do more than the state formally required.

The signal travels fastest through liability fear. A bank can survive losing a customer. A bank cannot survive being accused of enabling forbidden flows. So the bank avoids risk, and avoidance becomes over-compliance. Over-compliance is not a mistake from the statecraft perspective. It is the amplifier. The state sets the penalty posture. Private intermediaries choose the safest path, which is broad retreat. Broad retreat is precisely how a targeted measure becomes systemic pressure without the state having to expand the target list openly. This is why financial statecraft is often described as "outsourced." Outsourcing is the structure. Private actors enforce at scale because they cannot afford not to.

Trade finance is where the ladder becomes visible to ordinary life. A bank that used to confirm letters of credit for a route begins refusing or pricing them punitively. Not because the goods are illegal, but because the corridor is now politically toxic. Insurers raise premiums or require additional attestations. Shipping firms demand payment upfront rather than on delivery. Suppliers demand settlement through safer banks in safer jurisdictions with safer documentation formats. Each step is a private adaptation to a public expectation. The state does not need to freeze every shipment. It only needs to make the route expensive enough that commerce shrinks. Shrinking commerce shrinks state capacity because fewer imports arrive, fewer exports clear, and fewer tax receipts flow. Financial statecraft becomes national pressure through ordinary commercial sequence.

The first lived consequence inside the target is not ideological. It is operational humiliation. The finance ministry can point to reserves on paper. The central bank can point to domestic liquidity tools. Yet imports must be paid through corridors that require admissibility, documentation, and counterparties willing to touch the transaction. When counterparties retreat, the state learns the distinction between having money and having usable money. Usable money is money that discharges obligations in the corridors that matter. Financial statecraft exploits hierarchy by turning certain claims into second-class claims at the boundary. Second-class claims do not vanish. They clear slower, cost more, and are more likely to be trapped. Time scarcity appears. Time scarcity becomes rationing. Rationing becomes politics at home because it forces visible tradeoffs in wages, subsidies, and public order.

A second consequence is internal private self-protection, which is the mechanism that turns external pressure into domestic crisis. Firms begin hoarding the foreign unit needed for imports. Banks raise spreads, tighten credit, and shorten tenors. Households demand cash, goods, or safer stores of value because they do not trust that external settlement will remain stable. The domestic currency weakens. Prices rise. The government imposes controls to stop outflows. Controls reduce confidence further because they confirm fear. The state's own defensive moves become part of the statecraft effect because they teach the market that the target is trapped. Financial statecraft works best when it induces the target to misstep, not because missteps are inevitable, but because missteps are common under time scarcity.

The delivery system that makes these tools real is custody and clearing, which is where law becomes immediate economic consequence. Modern wealth sits in custodial chains. Modern liquidity sits in clearing chains. Custodians execute freezes by refusing to settle delivery instructions, blocking transfers, and holding positions in place. Clearing members execute pressure by tightening margin, shrinking intraday credit, narrowing eligible collateral, shortening default tolerances, and increasing the cost of participation. Insurers execute pressure by refusing coverage or attaching conditions that effectively prohibit trade. Correspondents execute pressure by declining relationships and rerouting flows through narrower networks. These actors are not merely service providers. They are the gates. A freeze that cannot be implemented through custody is a speech. A seizure that cannot be implemented through custody is a threat. A corridor restriction that cannot be implemented through clearing and insurance is a slogan. This is why the reserve order's power is not only legal. It is operational. It sits in the private institutions that can execute a reclassification instantly.

The applying state must manage spillover because networks amplify. A targeted exclusion can become a general tightening if intermediaries decide broad avoidance is the safest posture. Broad avoidance can lock out legitimate commerce, trigger unexpected shortages, and provoke retaliation that fragments corridors further. The disciplined practice of financial statecraft is not maximal pain. It is targeted pain with controlled blast radius. This requires network competence: knowing the topology, key correspondents, custody dependencies, collateral loops, insurance bottlenecks, and where a hold will cascade into a liquidity run. The applying state that neglects topology will impose pressure and then discover it has also tightened its own supply chains and its allies' balance sheets.

Blowback is not hypothetical. It begins at home through prices and through business lobbying. If targeted measures raise global commodity prices, domestic inflation rises. If corridor fragmentation raises transaction costs, domestic firms pay more. If counter-corridors emerge, domestic financial institutions lose corridor rents and informational advantages. If global buffers rise, global growth slows, feeding back into domestic demand. Domestic manufacturers that depend on imported inputs face higher costs and longer lead times. Domestic exporters face retaliatory documentation burdens. Domestic voters experience higher prices and lower growth and ask why policy is making life more expensive. Financial statecraft is not free power. It is a trade between immediate leverage and long-run system stability. In an interdependent world, instability returns as cost.

The target adapts, and adaptation is where the long-run architecture changes. A targeted state begins rerouting trade through regional intermediaries. It begins settling through smaller corridors with higher costs and longer times. It begins building inventory because payment reliability is reduced. It begins using state-owned conduits because private firms cannot access corridors reliably. It begins creating special purpose import and export entities to minimize touch points. It begins using prepayment and offset structures that resemble barter in modern dress. Each adaptation reduces the effectiveness of the original pressure and increases enforcement complexity. Complexity is where evasion grows. The more fragmented the system becomes, the harder it becomes to police, because monitoring cost rises and adversaries exploit seams. Financial statecraft therefore carries a long-run trade: pressure now can produce a less governable system later.

The most disciplined statecraft accounts for this trade by offering a credible ladder back. Pressure is stronger when it isolates the target from high-quality corridors while leaving a path for compliance and reintegration. If there is no reintegration path, the target will build a parallel system permanently. If there is a path, internal factions face a choice: accept conditions and regain corridor access, or accept isolation and pay permanent costs. This is why signaling matters. Signals can offer both threat and ladder. The ladder must be credible in practice, otherwise pressure becomes permanent fracture and the target's best strategy becomes permanent evasion. Permanent evasion is the worst outcome for the applying state, because it produces a world where enforcement tools are blunter and less effective.

The applying state's most delicate problem is legitimacy. These instruments rely on private intermediaries enforcing public expectations, and private intermediaries enforce most willingly when they believe the rule is bounded, lawful, and stable. If intermediaries suspect that policy is arbitrary, expansive, or opportunistic, they respond in two ways that weaken statecraft over time. They overcomply in ways that create spillover and political backlash, and they reduce exposure to the corridor altogether by pushing clients toward alternative systems. Allies respond similarly. Legitimacy is therefore not moral theater. It is the practical condition for coordinated enforcement and controlled blast radius.

The hardest truth is that financial statecraft is now one of the primary ways international order is enforced. It is enforced through exclusion from correspondent networks and payment rails, through freezes that immobilize claims inside custody chains, through seizures that rerank property rights, and through signals that change private risk behavior before new measures are issued. These instruments operate by exploiting the hierarchy of money: the difference between having a claim and having a claim that settles quickly and finally in the corridors that matter. They also operate by exploiting concentration: most high-value cross-border flows pass through a limited set of institutions whose compliance posture sets the global default.

The strongest defense is that these tools are necessary to preserve integrity and to stop the system from becoming criminal infrastructure. That defense has force. A payments network that cannot exclude criminals becomes criminal. A financial system that cannot freeze proceeds of corruption invites corruption. A custody chain that cannot immobilize stolen assets loses trust. The discipline is to hold this truth without turning it into an excuse for careless power. Dual-use tools require dual-use restraint. Without restraint, the world responds not by becoming law-abiding but by becoming evasive. Evasion is not only about bad actors. It becomes a general design goal for states that fear being next. That is how enforcement, if overused, produces a less enforceable world.

The practical implication is that exclusion, freezes, seizures, and signaling must be treated as instruments that reshape architecture, not as isolated actions. Each use teaches the world something about the system's priorities and its willingness to subordinate claims. Each use shifts incentives for corridor building, custody diversification, and reserve posture. Each use changes the probability that a targeted actor seeks reintegration versus permanent parallelism. A state that uses financial statecraft without an architectural view can win a moment and lose a decade by hardening fragmentation and encouraging counter-corridors that make future enforcement harder. A state that uses it with an architectural view can preserve corridor legitimacy while still applying pressure where it is effective, because it understands that the ultimate objective is not the spectacle of pain, but the management of incentives at the boundary.

CLOSING DOCTRINE

Financial statecraft is leverage built from ranked permissions: exclusion raises stigma and compliance cost to slow commerce, freezes immobilize by reclassifying assets as toxic to touch, seizures transfer control through custody chains, and signaling reshapes private behavior so the system tightens itself before new measures are issued. The power is not merely punishment; it is the ability to turn usable money into conditional money at the boundary, forcing voluntary retreat and converting payment friction into domestic scarcity and domestic political strain. Custodians, correspondents, insurers, and clearing members are the delivery system that turns law into immediate economic consequence, and their over-compliance often amplifies targeted measures beyond formal scope. The strategic risk is spillover and blowback: repeated weaponization hardens fragmentation, thickens buffers, raises transaction costs, and accelerates counter-corridors that reduce future enforceability. Disciplined use therefore requires controlled blast radius, credible ladders of reintegration, and procedural legitimacy, because the reserve order endures only if its corridors remain trusted as law-governed architecture rather than feared as discretionary power.

PART SEVEN
THE SPLINTERING SYSTEM
PARALLEL RAILS, COMPETING STANDARDS, WEAPONIZED INTEROPERABILITY

The splintering does not announce itself with a flag or a treaty. It starts as a procurement decision, a compliance revision, a routing preference, and a contingency plan that is never filed under geopolitics. A bank's payments team adds a second path for cross-border settlement because its first path has become unreliable under pressure. A finance ministry orders reserve managers to pre-position liquidity in a different jurisdiction because availability has begun to mean permission. A regional clearing group tightens membership rules and calls it prudence, while everyone in the room understands it is also perimeter construction. A shipping insurer rewrites its conditions so that coverage attaches only when payment arrives through a corridor it trusts, and suddenly the corridor is not only a financial route but a commercial border. The system does not fracture because someone wants it to fracture. It fractures because too many actors learn, from experience, that the world's money can be slowed, flagged, frozen, and repriced by gatekeepers who do not need to announce that they are governing.

The first new seams are cut by private institutions trying to survive liability. A global bank's risk committee reduces exposure to certain correspondent relationships not because the flows are illegal, but because the compliance ambiguity has become unpriceable. The committee does not say it is aligning with anyone. It says it is protecting the franchise. It tightens onboarding, demands more beneficial ownership proof, shortens settlement windows, and quietly routes payment instructions away from corridors that have become politically loud. Meanwhile, a corporate treasury desk revises its policy manual. It creates a dual-routing playbook: a primary corridor for calm, a secondary corridor for stress, and a third corridor as an emergency manual path that is more expensive but less likely to be throttled. None of this is described internally as a geopolitical decision. It is described as resilience. Yet once enough banks and treasurers behave this way, resilience becomes architecture: the world stops being one network and becomes a map of preferred routes that reveal who is trusted and who is merely tolerated.

A second seam is cut by insurers and commodity intermediaries because commerce cannot tolerate ambiguous finality. An insurer learns that claims are harder to collect when payments touch certain corridors. It responds by rewriting coverage triggers so that a shipment is insurable only if the payment clears through a narrower set of institutions and arrives with a specified documentary chain. A commodity intermediary responds similarly. It does not refuse to trade. It adds conditions: prepayment in specified forms, documentation in specified formats, settlement through specified banks, collateral posted with specified custodians. These conditions look like commercial caution. They are border construction. Once written into contracts, they become self-enforcing standards that replicate across markets. The splintering system becomes real not when states declare new rules, but when private contracts begin assuming different money in different perimeters, and when ordinary firms discover that "same unit" no longer means "same passage."

The reserve order taught states that currency dominance is not unit-of-account habit alone. It is settlement privilege, collateral preference, and corridor control. The private challenge taught states that alternative instruments can scale only if they anchor to rule, identity, and finality that survive stress. The corridor wars taught everyone that access can be throttled without formal rupture. This Part begins where those lessons become irreversible: when enough institutions decide that dependence is not theoretical risk but live operational exposure, and they begin building a world that can route around power. That decision is defensive. It is also strategic. Once defensive duplication becomes normal, the system stops being one machine with one set of defaults and becomes an archipelago of perimeters, each with its own standards, its own admissibility tests, and its own definition of what counts as safe completion.

"Interoperability is never neutral; it is the right to pass." (payments architect's maxim)

A single global network feels efficient because it collapses choice into default. Default is cheap. Default is also a hidden constitution because it decides whose data standards apply, whose identity tests are required, whose compliance posture governs, and whose legal system is treated as the final forum when disputes metastasize. When interoperability is easy, the world treats it as a property of technology. When interoperability becomes contested, the world discovers it was always a property of permission. The same message format that once looked like convenience becomes a border device. The same hygiene practice becomes a gate. The same settlement endpoint becomes a strategic dependency that can be tightened, priced, or denied.

Weaponized interoperability is the practice of turning standards into selective passage. A bloc can claim it is merely protecting integrity while it designs identity rules that certain outsiders cannot satisfy cheaply. It can claim it is merely modernizing data while it demands fields and attestations outsiders cannot provide without rebuilding registries and compliance systems. It can claim it is merely managing risk while it requires documentation chains that route commerce through preferred intermediaries. The standard's stated purpose is safety. The standard's operational effect is sorting: it determines who is legible enough to move at full speed and who is forced into exception handling. Exception handling is where costs rise and time becomes scarce. Scarcity is where power lives.

The splintering system is therefore not merely a multiplication of rails. It is a multiplication of sovereignties inside money. Each bloc, each corridor, each clearing group, each identity regime, each compliance stack begins to behave like a state within the state's money because it assigns membership, determines admissibility, and allocates time. The older monetary order had a visible hierarchy: central bank money at the top, deposits below, shadow claims below that, and cross-border corridors as the external skeleton. The splintering order introduces a sideways hierarchy across the old one. The question becomes less what is the unit and more which network will honor it, less what is legal tender and more which corridor will treat it as discharge, less what is collateral and more which custodian will accept it under stress. The state still issues law. The network now decides whether law can travel.

This Part is not a forecast of inevitable disintegration. It is an anatomy of incentives that now reward redundancy even when redundancy is expensive. Every time a corridor is used as leverage, every time a freeze becomes normal, every time an insurer or custodian adds a new exclusion rule, the rational response for those who can afford it is to build alternative paths. Alternative paths require alternative standards. Alternative standards require alternative identity. Alternative identity requires alternative data governance. Alternative governance produces alternative centers of liquidity. Alternative centers of liquidity create new dependencies, because the moment a regional pool becomes important, it gains the same capacity the old center had: to decide who clears quickly and who waits. Fragmentation can be escape and trap at the same time.

The first mechanism to hold is that fragmentation is often chosen by private institutions before it is chosen by states. A large bank does not need a policy shift to reduce exposure to a corridor it believes will become politically toxic. It only needs a change in liability posture. A clearing member does not need a law to tighten membership. It only needs a new definition of what risk it will tolerate. A payment platform does not need a treaty to demand new data fields. It only needs a compliance expectation that makes old fields insufficient. These shifts appear as governance choices inside private committees. They become geopolitical facts when enough balance sheets respond the same way. The splintering system is built by repetition of small decisions across thousands of institutions that all fear being last to adapt, because the penalty for being last is not theoretical, it is the run and the freeze.

The second mechanism is that standards, once competing, become borders. One bloc's identity proofs are not recognized by another. One bloc's privacy assumptions are incompatible with another's surveillance assumptions. One bloc's compliance model demands data another bloc's law forbids sharing. The resulting friction is not an accident. It becomes a strategic moat. If your firms cannot satisfy the other bloc's onboarding requirements, your firms become slow by default. If your banks cannot produce the other bloc's beneficial ownership trace, your banks become suspect by default. If your payment messages cannot carry the data fields the corridor demands, your payments become exceptions by default. Exception handling is where fees grow, delays multiply, and commerce shrinks. The standard is no longer a common language. It is a filter that decides who is legible enough to speak.

This is where fragmentation becomes domestic politics. Maintaining multiple standards is expensive. Large firms can afford to maintain multiple compliance stacks, multiple identity stacks, multiple data retention practices, and multiple treasury playbooks. Smaller firms cannot. Fragmentation therefore redistributes advantage toward scale and toward those with institutional fluency. That redistribution becomes a domestic legitimacy risk because it concentrates mobility inside the firms and banks that can pay the fixed cost of being multi-perimeter. The state may build fragmentation to reduce external dependency and discover it has intensified internal inequality in access to cross-border commerce. The external solution becomes an internal fracture.

The third mechanism is that perimeters create domestic gatekeepers. A rail that matters becomes governable. A regional liquidity pool that matters becomes political. A consortium that sets standards becomes a quasi-regulator. The state may discover it has escaped one dependency only to create another because any rail that becomes important becomes a gate, and any gate becomes a site of extraction, discrimination, and control. The question is not whether gatekeeping will exist. It will. The question is whether gatekeeping will be accountable and whether the state can prevent its own rules from being outsourced to a small set of operators whose incentives are private survival rather than public continuity.

The fourth mechanism is crisis relocation. In an integrated system, crises spread through obvious bridges: funding markets, correspondent chains, and shared collateral ladders. In a splintering system, some bridges are severed, so some shocks are contained. Yet the remaining bridges become more important and therefore more fragile. When fewer corridors connect blocs, each corridor carries more strategic weight. It becomes a high-value target for cyber pressure, regulatory retaliation, and market runs. The system can therefore become both more insulated and more brittle. Insulation reduces contagion speed. Brittleness increases catastrophe risk when bridges fail. Fragmentation does not eliminate systemic risk. It relocates systemic risk into interfaces and into the concentrated bridges that remain.

The paradox that follows is economic thickening. A splintering world increases buffer demand because uncertainty rises. Firms hold more inventories. Banks hold more liquid assets. Governments hold more reserves. Clearing systems demand more collateral. Everyone hoards time. Hoarding time is rational under contested interoperability. Hoarding time is also contractionary. It reduces investment, reduces growth, and increases the political appetite for further protection, which can accelerate fragmentation again. The system becomes self-thickening: more perimeters create more uncertainty, more uncertainty creates more buffers, more buffers create slower growth, slower growth creates more political volatility, and volatility makes corridors more cautious, which tightens perimeters further.

The strategic implication for serious officials is uncomfortable. If the world splinters, you do not solve vulnerability by building your own rail alone. You solve vulnerability by controlling the full stack that makes a rail sovereign: identity, compliance, liquidity, collateral, custody, and finality. If you cannot supply those, you will depend on someone who can, and that dependency will become the new lever used against you. The splintering system rewards states that can build complete internal architectures and penalizes states that build only the visible front end while leaving decisive layers external. It also punishes states that confuse redundancy with resilience. Redundancy is two routes. Resilience is two routes that can finish, in crisis, without begging for admissibility. The difference is the difference between a contingency plan and a sovereign capacity.

This Part is the threshold where the reader must stop thinking in terms of the payment system and start thinking in terms of competing payment constitutions. Each constitution defines membership, admissibility, and finality differently. Each constitution claims legitimacy. Each constitution produces its own hierarchy of claims. The splintering system is the world learning to live inside multiple constitutions at once and discovering that the price is not only higher fees and thicker buffers, but a new kind of strategic uncertainty: which constitution will rule your transaction when the transaction crosses a border, and what happens when constitutions disagree.

The decisive chamber ahead is therefore not a technology chamber. It is a sovereignty chamber disguised as interoperability.

CLOSING DOCTRINE

The splintering system begins as private adaptation and becomes public architecture: liability fear pushes banks, insurers, custodians, and clearing members to duplicate routes, tighten standards, and embed corridor preferences into contracts, turning resilience plans into permanent perimeters. Weaponized interoperability converts standards into border devices by making identity, data, and compliance selectively satisfiable, grading access through delay and exception handling rather than overt bans. Fragmentation reduces dependence on a single center while multiplying interface conflict and concentrating risk into the bridges that remain, producing a system that can be simultaneously more insulated and more brittle. The domestic cost is redistribution: multi-perimeter compliance and routing privilege scale actors and creates new gatekeepers inside each bloc, making external autonomy a potential internal legitimacy crisis. The strategic test of this Part is whether states can build full-stack sovereignty over identity, liquidity, collateral, custody, and finality, because a rail without those layers is a detour that ends at someone else's gate.

CHAPTER 33
PARALLEL NETWORKS
BUILDING A WORLD THAT CAN ROUTE AROUND POWER

The first meeting is held by operations, not by diplomats, because splintering begins where embarrassment begins: on the day a payment that was supposed to be boring becomes a problem nobody can solve quickly. A treasury desk at a mid-sized exporter has a shipment on the water and a supplier demanding confirmation of funds. The bank portal shows the transfer as sent. The supplier's bank shows nothing. Hours become a day. A day becomes penalties. The exporter's finance team discovers that sent is not completion; it is hope, and hope is not a settlement state. In a stable order, hope is cheap because settlement is routine and delays are exceptions that can be explained. In a pressured order, hope becomes a cost center because the corridor can slow without calling it a denial, and every hour of uncertainty changes inventory timing, production scheduling, and reputational standing with counterparties whose own financing depends on reliable receipt. The chief financial officer does not talk about geopolitics. The chief financial officer talks about burn rate, contractual breach, and which bank will still move money if the corridor tightens again next week.

The second meeting happens inside a bank's risk committee with a different tone: controlled, legalistic, almost bored. The committee is reviewing its correspondent map. Certain routes now carry a higher penalty for error, and error is no longer an internal mistake; it is a regulatory event that can trigger fines, supervisory intervention, reputational damage, and the loss of privileged access to other corridors. The committee does not say it is leaving a corridor. It says it is reducing exposure. That reduction is implemented through smaller credit lines, narrower transaction categories, longer holds, stricter documentary requirements, and refusal to serve customers whose flows attract scrutiny. It is implemented by routing instructions away from high-liability gateways and toward corridors that are less politically loud. The bank calls this prudence. The target calls it punishment. The world experiences it as slowness. Slowness is how fragmentation becomes real without requiring anyone to announce it.

The third meeting is held by a central bank's payments division, and it sounds like engineering until the conversation becomes unmistakably sovereign. The staff has been told to build redundancy. Redundancy does not mean a backup server. It means a second cross-border path that can clear and settle even if the dominant network narrows access, demands proofs the state cannot provide at speed, or imposes holds that convert routine settlement into political humiliation. The staff drafts a plan for a parallel arrangement with allied counterparties: messaging standards, participant eligibility, settlement assets, operating hours, liquidity provision, dispute handling, and an emergency protocol for when a member fails. The plan is titled like a technical project, but it is a constitution in miniature. It defines membership, admissibility, and the practical meaning of discharge inside the new perimeter.

A fourth meeting is held by an insurer's underwriting desk, and it completes the picture. The underwriters are not thinking about monetary theory. They are thinking about claims collectability and legal enforceability under stress. The desk has learned that a payment route can be "approved" and still be held long enough to strand a shipment, trigger demurrage, and cascade into a dispute that becomes expensive to litigate. So the insurer rewrites its conditions. Coverage attaches only if payment arrives through a corridor the insurer trusts, with documentary evidence the insurer can audit quickly, and with a settlement sequence the insurer believes will survive a dispute. The insurer calls this risk management. It is also perimeter construction. Once these clauses appear in trade contracts, the splintering system stops being a story about rails and becomes a story about commerce: if you cannot pay through the right corridor, you cannot ship, and if you cannot ship, you cannot trade at scale.

"A payment system is a promise about what still works when nobody trusts anyone." (industry maxim)

Parallel networks are built when that promise fails in one corridor and the cost of failure becomes politically unbearable. The common myth is that payment networks splinter because leaders want symbolic independence. The truth is more prosaic and more dangerous. They splinter because repeated episodes of throttling, freezes, documentation shocks, and sudden risk reclassification teach private institutions to protect themselves, and those private protections become architecture. Once enough banks, treasurers, insurers, and clearing members assume that a dominant corridor can be used as a lever, the rational response is to build a corridor that cannot be pulled by that lever. That response is defensive. It is also strategic. A second corridor does not merely move money; it changes bargaining power by making denial expensive for the gatekeeper, because the threatened actor can reroute rather than beg.

Parallel networks begin with messaging and end with settlement, and confusing the two is how naive plans fail. Messaging is the language used to send instructions. Settlement is the act that changes balance sheets and ends disputes. A state can build an alternative messaging layer and still remain dependent on the old order if settlement must still be completed through the old corridor's banks, custody chains, and collateral conventions. That is why serious parallel-network building is not an app. It is a stacked project. It must replicate the minimum set of functions that make a corridor sovereign in practice: identity, compliance, routing, liquidity, collateral, custody, settlement finality, and crisis default handling. If any of these layers remains external, the parallel network is a detour that still ends at someone else's gate.

The opening move is usually described as resilience because that word sells internally. The actual move is perimeter construction. A bank signs additional correspondent relationships that look redundant until the day one route tightens. A corporate treasury desk rewrites its policy so that major supplier classes can be paid through two banks in two jurisdictions, with pre-approved document packets that satisfy multiple compliance stacks. A platform rewrites its data fields so that outbound messages carry additional identity attestations, because those attestations reduce the chance of being slowed by receiving banks. An insurer changes contract terms so that coverage attaches only if payment passes through defined corridors. A commodity intermediary rewrites settlement conventions so deliveries are released only after specified confirmations. The private sector's daily operating rules begin encoding a map of which perimeters are considered safe. That map becomes the new reality of commerce. It is not ideological. It is actuarial.

The state enters later, and when it enters it often misreads what has already happened. The state sees fragmentation as a lever it can pull. The private sector sees fragmentation as a survival measure it has already begun. A state that tries to create parallel networks without acknowledging private liability fears will build a network nobody uses. Adoption requires that the network reduce blame risk. Blame risk is the hidden governor of corporate money. The treasurer who chooses a new corridor and gets trapped is punished. The treasurer who stays with the default corridor and gets trapped can blame the world. Parallel networks must therefore be designed to feel less like a bet and more like a routine: predictable rules, predictable enforcement, predictable convertibility, and predictable crisis behavior.

Three drivers produce most parallel-network buildouts, and each driver produces a different network temperament. The first driver is strategic exclusion. When a state or bloc learns it can be throttled, it begins building a corridor that cannot be throttled by the same gatekeepers. This corridor prioritizes internal autonomy over external convenience. It will accept higher cost as the price of sovereignty. It will often adopt narrower membership and stricter internal surveillance because it must prevent infiltration and prove integrity to its own members. It will also tend to route through state-linked institutions because private institutions fear the liability of being the backbone of a politically contested network. The second driver is data conflict. When jurisdictions cannot agree on privacy, identity, or data-sharing requirements, interoperability becomes political. Parallel networks arise because a single corridor cannot satisfy contradictory legal demands. One perimeter demands deeper data disclosure, broader screening, and longer retention. Another perimeter forbids certain disclosures, requires localization, or refuses foreign oversight. The split is a legal split disguised as technical architecture. The third driver is crisis insurance. Even allies build parallel paths when they discover that a single dominant corridor concentrates fragility. A major outage, a cyber event, or a liquidity freeze teaches institutions that redundancy is not a luxury. Parallel networks, in this case, are built not to escape power but to survive accidents, yet the effect is similar: redundancy reduces centrality, and reduced centrality reduces any one corridor's ability to impose terms.

The anatomy of a parallel network begins with membership because membership is how trust is manufactured and how exclusion is enforced. A network must decide who may connect, under what conditions, and with what obligations. The decision is never purely commercial. Membership determines who gets fast passage and who must clear through intermediaries. In a unified corridor, membership tends to expand for scale. In a splintering system, membership becomes security perimeter. Networks tighten access because they fear infiltration, evasion, and secondary penalties. Tight membership creates coherence and reduces risk. Tight membership also creates hierarchy because nonmembers must clear through members, paying fees and accepting delays. Parallel networks therefore reproduce gatekeeping. They do not abolish it. They transfer it.

The settlement asset is the next chamber, and it is where many parallel networks quietly confess their dependence. A network can message instructions all day and still fail if it cannot settle final claims. Settlement requires a base claim treated as final within the perimeter. Some perimeters rely on central bank liabilities. Others rely on designated settlement institutions backed by public guarantee. Some rely on pooled account structures, where members pre-fund a shared settlement pool and transfer claims inside that pool. Pre-funding reduces credit risk. It increases buffer cost. Buffer cost is tolerated when corridor risk is feared. This is how fragmentation raises global liquidity demand: each perimeter demands its own buffers, and each buffer is a slice of liquidity removed from lending, investment, and ordinary commerce.

Liquidity is the chamber where most parallel networks either become real or become symbolic. Settlement systems fail not because messages cannot be sent but because liquidity is not available at the right time in the right unit. In a unified system, liquidity can often be sourced through deep markets and widely accepted collateral. In a splintered system, liquidity is more local, more political, and more conditional. A parallel network must decide whether it will provide intraday credit, under what collateral rules, and who will backstop a member's shortfall. Without intraday credit, payment queues lengthen and commerce slows. With intraday credit, risk concentrates in the network's operators and in whichever institution provides the backstop. This is where network design becomes statecraft. A network that cannot backstop its own queues becomes unreliable under stress, and unreliability kills adoption because unreliability produces blame.

Collateral is the engine that allows liquidity to be extended without turning the network into a charity. If members can pledge high-quality collateral, the network can extend intraday credit and keep settlement smooth. If collateral is limited, the network becomes a pre-funded system, and pre-funded systems demand larger buffers. Larger buffers reduce velocity and growth. Collateral rules are therefore a political choice disguised as risk policy. Which assets count. What haircuts apply. What custody arrangements are acceptable. What happens when collateral values move. Who bears loss if collateral enforcement is contested. These are not back-office questions. They are the constitution of the new corridor, because they determine who can move quickly and who must wait, and waiting is solvency when margins are thin.

Custody is the chamber where property rights become operational. In an integrated order, custody chains are trusted by habit. In a splintered order, custody becomes a contested infrastructure. A parallel network must decide which custodians are accepted, under what audit standards, and what legal regime governs title transfer. If custody is ambiguous, collateral is discounted. If collateral is discounted, intraday credit shrinks. If intraday credit shrinks, payment queues grow. If queues grow, commerce slows. The chain is mechanical and unforgiving. Parallel networks therefore cannot be built as "payment pipes" alone. They require custody governance that convinces counterparties that assets are real, title is clear, and enforcement is swift enough to matter when panic compresses time.

Default handling is the chamber that separates a corridor from a rumor. A network must define what happens when a participant fails: how positions are netted, how collateral is seized, how losses are allocated, and how settlement continuity is preserved for non-defaulting members. Without clear default handling, the first failure becomes a run because every member fears being the next trapped in an unresolved dispute. Default handling is also where the new corridor reveals its politics, because loss allocation always produces winners and losers. If the corridor allocates losses in a way perceived as biased, it will not attract broad adoption. If it allocates losses in a way perceived as too generous, it may become a magnet for risk-taking. The corridor must therefore engineer discipline without cruelty, because cruelty collapses legitimacy and generosity collapses solvency.

"Redundancy is expensive until the day it is cheaper than humiliation." (reserve manager's line)

A state can tolerate inefficiency. It cannot tolerate repeated episodes where it must beg for corridor access to pay for essentials. A firm can tolerate higher fees. It cannot tolerate a corridor that holds funds unpredictably and turns routine settlement into reputational crisis with suppliers. Parallel networks are an attempt to price autonomy into routine before panic prices it into catastrophe. That is why buildout occurs even when economists complain about fragmentation. The complaint is correct in the narrow sense: fragmentation raises transaction costs and reduces netting efficiency. The complaint is incomplete in the strategic sense: fragmentation lowers single-point dependency and reduces the ability of any one gatekeeper to allocate time unilaterally. States are paying for option value, and option value becomes visible only when the corridor tightens.

Standards are the chamber where parallel networks either remain interoperable pluralism or harden into blocs. A messaging standard determines data fields, identity formats, and compliance signals required for a transaction to be processed automatically rather than manually. Manual processing is where delays and discretion live. Automated processing is where speed lives. Therefore, the entity that sets the standard sets the price of speed. A standard can be designed to be broadly compatible across regimes, preserving passage with friction. A standard can be designed to embed one bloc's legal assumptions, turning the standard into a border device. This is the moment interoperability becomes weaponized: the corridor is not closed; outsiders are made slow by default.

Weaponized interoperability works through legibility. If a standard requires deeper beneficial ownership trace, more granular transaction purpose codes, tighter identity attestations, and stricter provenance for funds, the corridor can claim it is improving integrity. It is also shifting the burden of proof onto outsiders. Outsiders must rebuild registries, upgrade identity systems, and accept surveillance demands to remain legible. The corridor does not need to exclude. It can insist on legibility. Those who cannot comply become exceptions. Exceptions become holds. Holds become trade contraction. Pressure is executed through sequence rather than decree, and sequence is harder to contest because it is administered by private institutions in the name of safety.

Parallel networks impose a new global tax through buffer hoarding. In a unified corridor, netting economizes on settlement assets because obligations can be offset across a wide pool. In a splintered world, netting pools shrink and become perimeter-specific. Shrinking pools increases gross settlement demand. Higher gross settlement demand increases the amount of liquid assets banks must hold. Banks then lend less, or lend at higher cost, because liquidity buffers are costly. Firms respond by holding more working capital. Governments respond by holding more reserves. Clearing systems respond by demanding more collateral. Everyone hoards time. Hoarding time is rational under contested passage. Hoarding time is contractionary. It slows investment, slows trade, and raises political volatility, which feeds back into corridor caution. This is how fragmentation becomes self-thickening rather than self-stabilizing: the system thickens its own friction because fear makes redundancy mandatory.

The bridge is the most fragile element in parallel networks because no large economy can fully insulate itself from cross-border trade, capital flows, and commodity settlement. Even hardened perimeters need interfaces. Interfaces are where translation occurs between standards, identities, and compliance expectations. Translation is expensive. Translation is also where evasion hides. A bridge institution that translates between regimes becomes a valuable node for illicit flows and a valuable node for intelligence gathering. The bridge becomes a security concern. The natural response is stricter screening. Stricter screening slows passage. Slower passage drives more parties to look for alternative bridges. The system begins to behave like water under pressure: it flows through whatever channels remain open, and it erodes the institutions that try to contain it. Parallel networks do not end corridor wars. They relocate corridor wars into bridge management.

A bridge-bank scene shows how quickly the bridge becomes political. A large bank in a neutral jurisdiction becomes the preferred conduit between perimeters because it can satisfy multiple standards and has a reputation for reliable execution. Volume concentrates there because treasurers follow reliability and because insurers and commodity intermediaries begin writing contract language that implicitly privileges the bank's corridor. Once volume concentrates, the bank becomes a choke point. Regulators notice. Counterparties notice. The bank's risk committee tightens controls to avoid becoming an enforcement headline. Those tightened controls slow the bridge. Firms complain that the alternative corridor is no longer fast. The state demands speed. The bank demands safety. Safety creates friction. Friction creates more fragmentation. The bridge becomes the place where the new order's contradictions show up first: the desire for autonomy collides with the reality that someone must carry liability, and liability concentrates where translation occurs.

The cyber layer turns brittleness into a strategic hazard. In a unified system, redundancy exists inside the dominant corridor. In a splintered system, redundancy exists across corridors, but each corridor's internal security may be uneven, and bridges become high-value targets because a bridge compromise can leak data across regimes or can allow manipulation of routing and documentation. The more perimeters exist, the more interfaces exist. The more interfaces exist, the more attack surface exists. Attack surface is not only technical. It is procedural: identity proofing, document verification, custody instructions, and exception handling. Attackers target the seams because seams are where humans must override automation. Parallel networks therefore require not only new rails but new governance of overrides, because overrides are where fraud becomes systemic and where corridor trust collapses.

Parallel networks also create domestic distribution problems, because being multi-perimeter is a fixed-cost business. Large firms can afford multiple compliance stacks, multiple identity stacks, multiple data retention practices, and multiple treasury playbooks. Smaller firms cannot. The result is consolidation of cross-border capability inside a few banks and a few large firms. Those firms become domestic gatekeepers. They can price access. They can decide whose payments go first when liquidity is tight. They can shape standards by lobbying because they become essential. A state that builds parallel networks under the banner of sovereignty can discover it has created a domestic oligopoly of passage. That creates legitimacy risk, because ordinary firms and households experience sovereignty as higher fees, more paperwork, and less ability to transact across borders. The promise is autonomy. The lived experience is bureaucracy. Bureaucracy becomes politically explosive when it is perceived as serving elites who can afford compliance while trapping smaller actors in exceptions and delays.

Crisis behavior changes in a splintered system. Some bridges are severed, so some shocks are contained. Yet remaining bridges become more important and therefore more fragile. Fewer bridges carry more load. More load makes each bridge a higher-value target for cyber pressure, regulatory retaliation, and market runs. The system becomes both more insulated and more brittle. Insulation reduces contagion speed. Brittleness increases catastrophe risk when bridges fail. Many policymakers celebrate insulation and ignore brittleness. Brittleness is where the next crisis hides, because bridge failure is not slow tightening; it is a cliff. A cliff inside a payments system is a political emergency because it produces immediate scarcity even when fundamentals are sound.

The strongest defense of integrated networks is efficiency and the belief that global commerce requires a common language. That defense is real. A single dominant corridor reduces friction, reduces buffer demand, and improves netting efficiency. Yet it ignores the political cost of dependence on a corridor that can be weaponized. Integrated networks are stable only as long as gatekeepers are perceived as lawful, predictable, and restrained. Once that perception shifts, private actors diversify regardless of cost because the cost of being trapped is greater than the cost of redundancy. Parallel networks are what actors build when trust becomes a liability rather than an asset.

The practical implication for serious officials is not that fragmentation is good or bad. It is that fragmentation is a design environment that must be governed or it will govern you. A state that wants resilience must build full-stack capacity inside its perimeter: identity integrity, compliance discipline, liquidity provision, collateral standards, custody capability, and credible finality. A state that builds only a rail without those layers builds a detour that still ends at someone else's gate. A state that builds those layers but cannot discipline domestic gatekeepers will discover it has created private sovereignty inside the new perimeter, and private sovereignty allocates time and access according to private survival rather than public continuity. The splintering system does not abolish hierarchy. It multiplies hierarchies.

The minimum stack checklist is therefore not a slogan but a failure map, and each missing layer produces a predictable crisis that the market will punish immediately. Without identity integrity, the corridor becomes a laundering magnet and is shut out by others. Without compliance discipline, the corridor becomes a liability magnet and is abandoned by members who fear secondary penalties. Without liquidity backstops, the corridor becomes a queue machine in stress and loses adoption because "works in calm" is not a value proposition. Without credible collateral rules, intraday credit shrinks and netting efficiency collapses, forcing pre-funding and raising buffer cost until commerce slows. Without custody capability and clear title transfer, collateral is discounted, haircuts rise, and the corridor becomes expensive because enforcement is uncertain. Without finality, nothing is money; everything is reversible promise, and reversibility becomes panic because nobody can treat receipt as discharge. Without default handling, one member's failure becomes everyone's run because no one trusts the corridor to allocate loss without improvisation. Each missing layer teaches the world that the corridor is conditional. Conditional corridors are tolerated in calm and abandoned in panic. Abandonment is how the market votes against your architecture.

Parallel networks are therefore not the end of power. They are the relocation of power into new perimeters, new standards, and new gatekeepers. They can reduce the ability of any single dominant corridor to impose discipline unilaterally, but they also increase the number of places where discipline can be imposed, because each perimeter acquires its own levers: membership, data demands, collateral rules, liquidity access, custody recognition, and the definition of finality. The world that results is not flat. It is layered. It is not free. It is expensive. It is not immune to crisis. It is vulnerable in new ways, because interfaces are where crises are born and bridges are where crises jump.

CLOSING DOCTRINE

Parallel networks arise when corridor dependence becomes an operational exposure: repeated throttling, holds, and reclassification teach banks and firms that sent is not settlement and that speed is permission granted by gatekeepers. A messaging alternative is not a monetary alternative unless the full stack is rebuilt through membership rules, settlement assets, liquidity provision, collateral eligibility, custody capability, default handling, and a credible definition of finality that survives stress. Weaponized interoperability turns standards into border devices by pricing passage through legibility requirements and exception handling rather than overt bans, shifting burdens onto outsiders until outsiders become slow by default. Fragmentation reduces single-point leverage while trapping liquidity in perimeter-specific buffers, raising the global price of time and shifting advantage toward scale actors that can afford multiple compliance stacks, which creates new domestic gatekeepers and new legitimacy risks. Bridges become the new choke points, and choke points attract the same pressures the splintering system was built to escape, which is why resilience requires full-stack capacity and accountable gatekeeping inside each new perimeter rather than a symbolic rail that still ends at someone else's gate.

CHAPTER 34

DATA AND IDENTITY BORDERS

INTEROPERABILITY BECOMES POLITICAL

The first border is a spreadsheet, and it sits on a compliance officer's second monitor like a quiet threat. The list of required fields has grown since last quarter. There are new identity attestations, expanded beneficial ownership traces, richer transaction purpose codes, extended provenance questions, and a set of flags that do not accuse anyone of wrongdoing yet still force a transaction into manual review. None of it is framed as ideology. It is framed as integrity. Yet each new field is a toll. Every field that must be supplied is a cost paid by the sender and a discretion granted to the receiver. When the list grows long enough, passage stops being a function of money and becomes a function of legibility. The firm that can produce the proofs moves quickly. The firm that cannot becomes an exception. Exceptions are where delays, fees, and silent denials live. The border is not the message. The border is the standard that decides whose message is treated as routine.

The second border is a call from a correspondent bank, and it arrives with a tone that is polite precisely because it is not negotiable. A corporate treasurer is told a long-standing relationship is being reviewed because the bank's compliance posture has changed. The treasurer is asked to deliver more documentation, faster, in a format that can be audited, and the treasurer hears the same phrase twice: demonstrate controls. The bank is not asking for proof of innocence. The bank is asking for proof of insurability. If the treasurer cannot supply that proof, the bank will quietly reduce service, narrow limits, and reroute payments through slower channels. The treasurer cannot argue with the bank because the bank's risk committee is not debating fairness. The bank's risk committee is debating liability. Liability is the new tariff.

A third border appears in the least dramatic place: a payroll run. A mid-sized import-dependent manufacturer has staff to pay on Friday. The firm's working capital normally turns smoothly because invoices clear, receivables arrive, and credit lines roll with minimal friction. This week, a major customer's payment is held for additional documentation, and the customer insists the payment has been made because the customer's portal shows sent. The manufacturer's treasurer cannot pay employees with sent. The treasurer needs credited funds. The firm draws on its bank line, and the bank charges a higher spread because it has learned to price the new uncertainty: settlement risk disguised as compliance review. The firm's human resources director hears the word delay and treats it as existential because delay is how trust inside a workforce fractures. The new tariff is not a visible tax. It is the interest margin paid for the privilege of surviving corridor uncertainty, and it compounds quietly until the firm's competitiveness is rewritten without anyone changing a tariff schedule.

Standards are borders when compliance decides speed. (payments supervisor's maxim)

In the integrated order, standards felt like coordination. They enabled automation, reduced errors, and lowered cost. In the splintering order, standards become selective passage. They determine whose identity is legible, whose data is admissible, whose privacy is acceptable, and whose oversight is trusted. A technical change can therefore function like a geopolitical measure without being announced as one. The state does not need to ban a corridor. It can raise the standard until outsiders cannot satisfy it cheaply. The resulting friction looks like prudence and functions like a tariff paid in time. Time is the most expensive tariff in a world where supply chains run on timing and credit runs on settlement certainty, because delay at the wrong moment breaks working capital, breaks production schedules, and breaks the informal trust that makes counterparties extend terms in the first place.

The older tariff regime was visible. Goods were taxed at borders. The newer tariff regime is procedural. Data requirements act as toll gates, and toll gates can be adjusted without parliamentary debate. An exporter can price a customs duty into a contract. An exporter cannot price a hold into a contract with the same confidence because a hold is not an announced number. It is a probability that shifts with enforcement mood, supervisory pressure, and the corridor's evolving liability posture. That uncertainty becomes a premium built into every deal, a buffer built into every treasury plan, and a skepticism built into every counterparty relationship. The tariff is paid in thicker liquidity cushions, earlier payments, smaller trade volumes, and wider spreads, and those costs compound because every actor up the chain copies the caution of the actor who touches the corridor most directly.

Standards become borders through three layers that behave like a single machine: identity, data, and oversight. Identity is the question of who a participant is and whether that participant can be held accountable. Data is the question of what is known about the transaction and whether that knowledge is sufficient for screening, audit, and enforcement. Oversight is the question of who watches the watchers, whose regulators are trusted, and whether the corridor believes that a participant's controls are real. A corridor can tolerate weak identity if it trusts oversight and can audit quickly. It can tolerate imperfect data if it trusts identity and oversight and can remediate. It cannot tolerate all three being contested. The moment trust collapses in any layer, the standard tightens, and tightening makes outsiders slower by default. Slower by default is the definition of a border in a payments system.

Identity is the first battlefield because identity is membership. A system that cannot attribute activity to accountable actors becomes a magnet for fraud and illicit flows, and once it becomes a magnet it becomes a liability for every intermediary touching it. In an integrated order, identity regimes tended to converge on minimums because friction was costly and dominant corridors preferred expansion. In a splintered order, identity regimes diverge because blocs embed different assumptions about privacy, surveillance, and sovereignty. One perimeter demands deep disclosure and continuous monitoring as the price of passage. Another perimeter treats deep disclosure as political submission and forbids exporting certain identity data. The result is not merely disagreement. The result is incompatibility, and incompatibility is a border because it forces routing through trusted translators who can satisfy both regimes or through slower manual processes that create queue. Queue is the functional equivalent of a customs line, except it moves unpredictably and can stretch without warning.

The identity border does not only sort foreigners. It sorts domestic actors as well. A country can have a unified legal system and still contain multiple degrees of legibility inside it. A large bank can maintain identity assurance at a level that foreign corridors recognize. A smaller bank cannot. A multinational can build compliance teams to assemble proof packets quickly. A family-run exporter cannot. When identity standards become borders, the domestic economy develops a fast lane and an exception lane. The fast lane is not only about size. It is about institutional fluency: the ability to speak the corridor's language without friction. Fluency becomes a competitive advantage.

Competitive advantage becomes a political advantage. This is how standards turn into domestic distribution.

Data becomes the second battlefield because data is power. The actor that sets the data fields sets the classification reality. Classification determines what is suspicious, what is routine, what is blocked, and what is escalated. In practice, classification governs commerce because anything classified as ambiguous becomes slow, expensive, and fragile. Data standards also determine who can be excluded quietly. If a corridor requires a certain beneficial ownership trace and a sender cannot provide it, the corridor does not need to accuse the sender of wrongdoing. It can treat the sender as noncompliant and therefore slow. Slowness is exclusion by other means, and it is a more politically survivable form of exclusion because the corridor can claim it is merely enforcing standards.

The data border has a second purpose beyond screening: it is a regime of memory. The more fields required, the more a corridor knows, and the longer it can know it. Data retention practices are not only administrative. They decide what can be reconstructed after the fact. In a world of financial statecraft, reconstruction is power, because reconstruction allows enforcement to be applied retroactively, and retroactivity is how risk committees become fearful. Fearful risk committees are how standards become self-enforcing borders. When firms and banks believe that today's transaction might be judged later under tomorrow's expectations, they tighten today. That tightening is the hidden tax of ambiguous standards: it forces private actors to overpay for safety now to avoid liability later.

Oversight becomes the third battlefield because oversight is how trust is outsourced. A corridor cannot personally verify every participant's integrity. It relies on the participant's regulators, auditors, and internal control systems. When oversight trust is high, corridors allow automation and low friction. When oversight trust is low, corridors demand more data, impose more holds, and prefer narrower membership. Oversight therefore functions like sovereign credit. A trusted supervisor creates corridor speed for its institutions. A distrusted supervisor creates corridor friction for its institutions. This is why standards are statecraft: they translate institutional credibility into transaction velocity. The new tariff is often paid by jurisdictions with weaker oversight reputations even when their firms are individually well-run, because a corridor cannot cheaply distinguish the clean from the risky once it distrusts the system that certifies cleanliness.

Oversight is also where politics hides most easily, because oversight can be withheld without calling it denial. A corridor can say, truthfully, that it lacks confidence in another jurisdiction's enforcement. It can say, truthfully, that it cannot rely on another jurisdiction's registries. It can say, truthfully, that it is protecting its own system. The effect is still pressure. Oversight mistrust is the most efficient justification for tightening standards because it is hard to refute quickly. Oversight reform takes years. Corridor tightening can take a week. That timing mismatch is itself a lever.

The practical consequence is a new politics of documentation. Firms discover that a payment is no longer only a transfer of value. It is a packet of proofs, assembled under time pressure, that must satisfy multiple regimes simultaneously: the sender's compliance obligations, the intermediary's risk tolerances, the receiver's admissibility requirements, and the corridor's evolving standards. Large firms can build teams and systems to generate packets at scale. Smaller firms cannot. The border therefore redistributes advantage toward scale, because scale can afford legibility. Legibility becomes a form of capital, and like any form of capital, it concentrates. A firm with legibility can negotiate terms. A firm without legibility is offered take-it-or-leave-it conditions: prepayment, higher prices, narrower routes, and longer lead times. The border is not written on a map. It is written into the operating cost of being believed.

A small manufacturer illustrates the lived cost. The firm is profitable and compliant in its own jurisdiction. It sells to a customer across a border now governed by a tighter corridor. Payments begin to be held because documentation is incomplete in the new format. The firm hires compliance support. The firm upgrades software. The firm still gets held because a beneficial ownership chain in its jurisdiction is not recognized as sufficiently transparent by the receiving corridor. The firm is not accused of wrongdoing. It is treated as slow. Slow payment forces the firm to hold more cash. More cash forces the firm to invest less. Less investment forces the firm to fall behind. Falling behind forces the firm to raise prices. Raising prices makes the firm less competitive. A border has been erected without a tariff line being written, and the border's effect is to turn working capital into a privilege.

Standards also create a new class of intermediaries: translators. Translators are banks, platforms, and service firms that specialize in converting one regime's documentation and identity into another regime's admissibility. Translators charge fees because translation is costly and because translation carries liability. Translators also become chokepoints, because everyone who cannot speak the dominant standard directly must pass through them. The splintering system therefore creates a new tariff revenue stream not for states but for those private actors who control translation and exception handling. Exception handling is the dark matter of the new order: it is where discretion lives, where delays hide, where blame risk accumulates, and where the most profitable fees can be charged under the language of safety.

The translator's business model is also a governance model. To translate, a firm must decide which proofs count, which attestations are trustworthy, and which risks are tolerable. Those decisions resemble regulation, but they are executed by private actors with private incentives. The state may discover that sovereignty has been defended at the border only by outsourcing power to translators inside the border. That creates a new internal politics: who licenses the translators, who audits them, who holds them accountable when they overreach, and what happens when they become essential enough to dictate terms to everyone else. Standards as borders thus become standards as domestic power. The border does not stop at the frontier. It spreads inward through the firms that control legibility.

The state experiences standards as both shield and constraint. As shield, higher standards reduce illicit flows and protect the integrity of the domestic system. As constraint, higher standards can lock domestic firms out of corridors if other blocs refuse to recognize domestic identity and oversight regimes. The state therefore faces a strategic choice: harmonize standards to preserve passage, or assert sovereignty and accept higher friction. Harmonization can look like submission, because it requires adopting another perimeter's data demands and oversight expectations. Assertion can look like isolation, because it forces domestic firms into slower routes and higher compliance costs. In a splintering system, there is rarely a free choice. There is only a choice about which cost to pay and which domestic coalition will bear it.

Standards become borders most sharply when they collide with domestic law. A jurisdiction may forbid sharing certain data, require localization of records, or impose limits on how identity information can be exported. A corridor may require exactly that data for passage, and require it quickly enough that manual workarounds cannot scale. Firms then face an impossible situation: comply with domestic law and become slow or excluded abroad, or comply abroad and violate domestic law. The state responds by building parallel corridors that match domestic law. Parallel corridors reduce dependence on incompatible standards. They also deepen fragmentation, because they harden the perimeter where different assumptions are enforced. This is the feedback loop: standards conflict produces parallel networks, and parallel networks harden standards conflict by making each bloc more comfortable living inside its own rules and less willing to compromise at the border.

The border effect is not only in trade. It is in finance. A bank that cannot satisfy a corridor's identity and data requirements is treated as a higher-risk counterparty. Higher-risk means higher haircuts on collateral, shorter funding tenors, higher margin requirements, and more intrusive monitoring. Those conditions tighten domestic credit even if the domestic economy is stable, because banks pass their increased funding cost to firms and households. Standards thus become monetary conditions without being called monetary policy. A corridor can tighten standards in the name of integrity and still cause a measurable tightening of credit in the jurisdictions that become slow by default. That tightening can be politically explosive because it is experienced as recession pressure with no visible policy author and no obvious lever to reverse.

A supervisor sees the same story from another angle. The supervisor can keep domestic banks solvent in domestic currency. The supervisor cannot make foreign corridors recognize domestic standards. The supervisor can publish regulations. The supervisor cannot force a foreign corridor's risk committee to treat domestic compliance as sufficient. The supervisor therefore begins to treat recognition as a national asset that must be managed. That management includes improving registries, strengthening audit capacity, raising enforcement credibility, and sometimes aligning domestic rules with external expectations even when alignment is politically unpopular. The state is pulled into a new form of diplomacy: standard diplomacy, where recognition is negotiated through technical agreements, joint examinations, data-sharing protocols, and mutual trust arrangements that are fragile precisely because they are political while pretending to be technical.

A standard is a treaty that does not admit it is a treaty. (regulatory realist's line)

When standards are borders, the most important agreements are not about tariffs or quotas but about which identity proofs are recognized, which data is shareable, which audits are accepted, which supervisors are trusted, and which enforcement actions are credible. Recognition becomes the currency of passage. Recognition can be granted, suspended, or conditioned. Conditioning is the modern tariff schedule. Suspension is the modern embargo, except it can be partial, quiet, and plausibly deniable. This is why standards become the new tariffs: they are adjustable pressure instruments embedded in everyday sequence, and sequence is where firms live.

The splintering system introduces a new asymmetry: the dominant standard can claim universality. The challenger standard must either translate or accept regionality. Translation requires bridges. Bridges become chokepoints. Chokepoints attract leverage. This is how standard power reproduces itself even when rails multiply. A bloc can build a parallel network and still find that global commerce demands translation into the dominant standard at some point in the chain because critical suppliers, insurers, and lenders live inside that standard's perimeter. The new tariff is therefore not always paid at the customs gate. It is paid at the translation gate, where a transaction is converted from one regime's legibility into another's.

The domestic distribution consequence is severe and delayed. Large firms build legibility factories: compliance teams, data systems, identity verification processes, and contractual templates that satisfy multiple regimes. They become multi-perimeter by design. Smaller firms cannot afford that overhead. They become dependent on translators and large banks. Dependence means higher fees, worse terms, and slower execution. Over time, this consolidates cross-border commerce inside larger players. Consolidation then feeds political resentment because the rhetoric of sovereignty is experienced as the reality of concentrated privilege. If standards are borders, then the most politically sensitive question becomes who gets the fast lane and who is left in the exception lane. The exception lane is not merely slow. It is humiliating, because it forces smaller actors to prove innocence repeatedly while larger actors pass as trusted by default.

Standards reshape the crime-and-enforcement landscape, and the change is paradoxical. Higher standards reduce some kinds of illicit flows by making anonymity expensive. Higher standards also increase the value of document fraud and identity fraud because passage depends on proof packets. The border moves from the dock to the document, and the criminal response moves from smuggling goods to smuggling legitimacy. That forces corridors to tighten further, increasing friction for everyone. The system can become more secure and more bureaucratic at the same time, and bureaucracy is itself a cost that reduces dynamism.

The cyber layer intensifies the border effect because standards are implemented by software and software fails at scale. A corridor that demands more data fields and more attestations increases its attack surface. Each additional field is a potential injection point for falsification, each additional attestation is a potential target for compromise, each additional translator is a potential point of failure. In a splintered system, multiple standards create multiple systems, and multiple systems create more interfaces where humans must override automation. Overrides are where fraud becomes systemic and where accidents become crises because override decisions are often made under time pressure with incomplete information. Standards therefore do not simply filter transactions. They shape where the system is brittle.

A pressure scene shows how standards become diplomatic force without being named. A state's firms are not formally prohibited.

They are simply asked, more and more often, for enhanced documentation, faster, and in a new format that the state's registries cannot produce at scale. The state's banks begin losing correspondent relationships. Trade finance becomes more expensive. Firms complain. The state calls the corridor and asks for clarity. The corridor replies with technical language: improve your controls, raise your transparency, align your ownership practices, strengthen your enforcement. The state hears a demand for governance change delivered through a payment standard. The state is being asked to redesign domestic institutions to maintain passage. That is the new tariff regime: governance paid as the price of speed.

The targeted state responds in three ways that reshape the system. It can comply, redesigning registries and oversight to regain legibility, which may improve integrity but can create domestic backlash if compliance is perceived as external submission. It can resist, accepting slower passage and building parallel perimeters, which may preserve sovereignty narratives but raises costs and concentrates commerce inside large actors who can afford translation. Or it can split, creating a two-track system: one set of firms and banks aligned to the dominant standard for global passage, another set aligned to domestic rules for internal legitimacy. The two-track system is politically unstable because it creates a visible hierarchy of citizens and firms inside the same national economy: those with the privilege of passage and those without.

The most important consequence of standards as borders is that they relocate economic power from price to permission. In older stories, trade competitiveness was about cost and quality. In the splintering system, trade competitiveness is also about legibility and admissibility. A firm can be efficient and still be slow. A firm can be innovative and still be treated as high-friction. A bank can be solvent and still be treated as suspect. Those classifications are not purely economic. They are institutional and political. They depend on standards that encode values: how much privacy is tolerated, how much data must be shared, how much surveillance is normal, and whose oversight counts as trustworthy. The new tariff is therefore cultural as well as financial, because passage now requires aligning with a regime's definition of acceptable visibility.

The border can also be turned inward as an instrument of domestic control. A state that adopts high standards gains a powerful internal sorting device: it can decide who is legible enough to receive finance, who is legible enough to transact across borders, who is legible enough to participate in modern commerce. This can reduce crime and raise integrity. It can also become an exclusion engine if the costs of legibility fall unevenly. If the poor pay more to be documented than the rich, if the small business pays more to be compliant than the multinational, then the standard becomes a domestic tariff on participation. This is one of the hard truths of the splintering system: standards do not only defend sovereignty; they reshape citizenship in practice by deciding who can move at speed.

Standards are also a method of enforcing hierarchy without calling it hierarchy. A corridor can maintain openness formally while making it operationally expensive for outsiders to participate at full speed. This is the soft border: no ban, only friction. The soft border is more durable than the hard border because it preserves plausible deniability and because it can be tightened or loosened without drama. The soft border also creates a psychological discipline. Firms begin internalizing that certain counterparties are risky not because they are bad but because they are slow. Slowness becomes stigma. Stigma becomes avoidance. Avoidance becomes exclusion. The corridor does not need to act again. It has turned private risk preference into a border.

A second scene makes the mechanism intimate: a small merchant importing components for local assembly. The merchant has two options. Use the dominant corridor and accept the documentary burden, the occasional holds, and the rising fees. Or use a translator who promises speed but charges more and demands prepayment. The merchant chooses the translator because the merchant's business cannot survive unpredictability. The merchant's choice becomes the translator's market power. The translator's market power becomes the translator's ability to set terms. The merchant is now paying a private tariff for legibility. The state may celebrate sovereignty. The merchant experiences extraction. Over time, enough merchants make the same choice and the translator becomes a domestic gatekeeper. Domestic gatekeepers become political actors because they control passage. This is how standards as borders create new domestic hierarchies even as they claim to defend national autonomy.

The chapter's deeper warning is that border standards are contagious. Once one bloc tightens standards to protect itself, others respond by tightening their own standards, either to protect integrity or to protect sovereignty. Tightening produces friction. Friction produces parallel rails. Parallel rails produce new standards. New standards produce more friction at interfaces. The system can enter a phase where every perimeter is rationally responding to the last perimeter's tightening, and the world ends up with thicker bureaucracy, higher costs, and lower resilience because interfaces become the places where crises concentrate. The splintering system is not only fragmentation of rails. It is fragmentation of shared reality about what counts as a valid identity and a valid transaction. When reality fragments, commerce slows not because people refuse to trade, but because they cannot agree on the proof needed to trade without fear.

The strategic challenge for states is that standards policy is now economic policy. Standards decide who can transact quickly, who can finance cheaply, and who can operate at scale across borders. Standards also decide who can be excluded quietly without overt bans. A state that ignores standards governance will discover that its firms are slow by default and that slowness becomes competitiveness crisis. A state that weaponizes standards without restraint will accelerate fragmentation and create counter-standards that make enforcement harder and commerce more expensive. Standards are therefore not merely tools. They are constitutions of passage, and constitutions cannot be rewritten daily without producing instability.

The practical response for serious officials is uncomfortable, because it is not glamorous. It is institutional grind. Build registries that produce trusted ownership traces. Build identity systems that are auditable without becoming predatory. Build supervisory credibility foreign corridors can recognize without treating recognition as a favor. Build data governance that protects domestic legitimacy while enabling enough sharing to preserve passage. Build translator capacity without allowing translators to become unaccountable gatekeepers. Build domestic protections so that the cost of legibility does not become a domestic inequality engine. These are not slogans. They are the difference between being fast by default and being slow by default, and in a splintering system, slow by default is a national constraint that feels like poverty even when the state is rich in resources.

CLOSING DOCTRINE

In a splintering system, standards become borders: identity proofs, data fields, and oversight recognition determine who moves at speed and who becomes an exception, and exception handling is the new tariff paid in time, liquidity buffers, and blame risk. Because corridors can tighten standards without formal bans, selective legibility becomes a lever that grades access through holds, documentation demands, and liability-driven retreat rather than overt prohibition, translating institutional credibility directly into transaction velocity. Standards politics redistributes advantage toward scale actors who can manufacture proof packets and toward private translators who monetize incompatibility, creating new domestic gatekeepers and legitimacy risk even when the public narrative is sovereignty. States face a strategic trade between harmonizing to preserve passage and asserting sovereignty at the cost of friction, and collisions between corridor requirements and domestic law harden fragmentation by forcing parallel perimeters. The decisive struggle is not only over rails but over which standards become unavoidable, because the standard that defines normal defines the border, and the border that defines speed governs the economy without announcing itself.

CHAPTER 35
REGIONAL LIQUIDITY POOLS
THE RETURN OF BLOC MONEY

The first sign is a calendar invite with a title that sounds technical and harmless: settlement resiliency working group. The people who accept it do not think of themselves as building a new monetary order. They think of themselves as preventing embarrassment. A payments director wants to avoid the day a cross-border queue becomes a domestic political scandal. A reserve manager wants to avoid the day imported essentials must be paid for by pleading for corridor access. A bank treasurer wants to avoid the day intraday credit evaporates because collateral is suddenly judged in someone else's court. Their language is operational. Their motive is sovereign. They have learned that a rail without liquidity is a highway without fuel, and that the only reliable fuel in a crisis is the fuel you can supply inside your own perimeter.

The second sign appears not in a ministry but in a warehouse. A fuel importer has contracts to deliver to power plants and distribution depots on a schedule that assumes money moves with the same routine as ships. The importer's payments team is told that a familiar corridor now requires enhanced proof packets for every large transfer, and that exceptions will be reviewed manually. Manual review means time. Time means demurrage, contract penalties, and emergency purchases at worse prices. The importer does not write op-eds about sovereignty. The importer rewrites its treasury policy: more pre-funded balances in the bloc's settlement institutions, more buffers held in the bloc's preferred collateral, and a new rule that shipments only leave port when payment is credited, not when payment is "sent." This is the return of bloc money as lived reality: the border has moved from a customs gate to a liquidity gate, and the importer's survival depends on which gate can be opened on demand.

A regional liquidity pool begins as an insurance device, which is why it is politically sellable. It is designed to keep trade flowing if a dominant corridor tightens or if a global funding market freezes. Its promise is simple: members will not be forced to scramble for external settlement assets at the worst moment because the bloc will provide a usable settlement claim inside the bloc, and will backstop the queues that turn fear into collapse. The deeper meaning is sharper. A pool is not merely shared liquidity. It is shared discipline. Whoever can allocate liquidity can allocate time, and whoever can allocate time can allocate solvency when obligations are due. A liquidity pool is therefore a decision about who is inside the perimeter, what counts as acceptable collateral, and which institutions will be treated as protected when stress arrives.

Liquidity is political because it decides whose deadlines matter. (treasury maxim)

The older global order hid this truth by giving the world one dominant upgrade endpoint. The apex corridor could supply the settlement asset the world reached for when fear rose, and the rest of the system organized around that reality. The splintering system reveals the cost of dependence. If the world's fuel can be throttled by external gatekeepers, then fuel becomes sovereignty. Regional pools are an attempt to manufacture sovereignty by building an internal fuel supply that can be mobilized quickly and defended legally. They are also an attempt to reduce humiliation, because humiliation is what happens when a state's domestic legality cannot buy external discharge and the country must negotiate for passage to pay for essentials.

The pool is built through a stack, and the stack must be complete or the pool becomes a speech. The stack is not complicated in concept. It is complicated in politics. The stack has four chambers that decide whether the pool is real. The first chamber is the settlement asset. The second chamber is the collateral constitution. The third chamber is the distribution mechanism, meaning who receives liquidity and on what terms. The fourth chamber is loss allocation, meaning what happens when a member fails or when collateral is insufficient. If any chamber is weak, the pool will fail in crisis in a predictable way, and predictable failure is how markets teach a bloc that solidarity was conditional.

The settlement asset is where the pool decides what "money" means inside the region. There are only a few plausible choices, and each choice carries a political fingerprint. The most straightforward approach is to settle through central-bank liabilities inside the bloc, using a shared settlement platform that allows member institutions to transfer claims that are, inside the perimeter, final. This approach is clean because it anchors finality to public balance sheets, but it requires the bloc to harmonize operational standards and to accept that central banks are now jointly responsible for a shared settlement space. A second approach is a pooled claim backed by member sovereigns, a regional settlement claim that functions as a common internal fuel even if member currencies remain distinct. This approach can reduce reliance on any single central bank's liabilities but raises immediate governance questions: who issues, who backs, what happens if one member's politics turns against backing. A third approach is a hybrid: a settlement token that functions as an internal settlement unit with strict conversion rules into member central-bank money at defined points and under defined collateral terms. Hybrid designs promise flexibility. They also risk ambiguity, and ambiguity is poison in a crisis because it invites disputes about whether settlement is final or merely provisional.

The collateral constitution is the treaty the pool writes without calling it a treaty. Collateral is not merely what supports liquidity. Collateral is what defines which balance sheets are considered trustworthy inside the bloc. Eligibility lists and haircut schedules are political hierarchies rendered as arithmetic. If a member's sovereign paper is eligible with narrow haircuts, that member has a privileged capacity to generate liquidity in crisis. If another member's paper is accepted only reluctantly, with wide haircuts and tight limits, that member is treated as second class inside the union it joined to avoid being second class outside. The collateral constitution therefore must balance stability against equality. Stability demands that the pool accept only assets that can be liquidated or enforced without legal chaos. Equality demands that membership not be humiliation by another name. The pool survives only if members believe the collateral constitution is strict enough to protect the perimeter and fair enough to justify solidarity.

The distribution mechanism is where politics becomes time. A pool that can act in crisis must have pre-authorized channels: intraday credit lines, emergency settlement windows, collateral substitution rules, and a priority scheme for scarce liquidity. If distribution is too automatic, it creates moral hazard and can funnel support to the loudest balance sheets regardless of merit. If distribution is too discretionary, it creates uncertainty and therefore runs. The distribution mechanism must also decide whether liquidity is provided broadly to keep payment life smooth or targeted narrowly to protect systemic nodes. Broad distribution is politically popular. Narrow distribution is often financially necessary. Every pool eventually faces the moment when it must choose between letting a non-systemic actor fail to preserve discipline and supporting that actor because failure would become a political crisis. That choice reveals whether the pool is a technocratic device or a political union in embryo.

Loss allocation is the chamber everyone wants to ignore until it is too late. A pool must decide what happens when collateral values move, when a member's bank fails, when a member's sovereign is under stress, or when a payment disruption triggers default cascades. Without a loss allocation rule, the first failure becomes a run because members fear improvisation. With a loss allocation rule that is perceived as unfair, the pool becomes politically intolerable because support becomes a transfer union by stealth. The pool therefore needs a loss allocation regime that is explicit enough to prevent panic and bounded enough to preserve legitimacy. Bounded does not mean painless. It means predictable. Predictability is what turns fear into calculation, and calculation is what prevents stampedes.

These chambers are the constitution. The pool's public story is solidarity. The pool's private story is governance. The pool will be judged not by the speeches that announce it but by the first week it is tested under stress. Stress tests are not conducted by committees. Stress tests are conducted by treasurers, clearing desks, and households watching whether the shelves stay stocked and whether the payroll clears. That is why regional pools are the return of bloc money. Money in practice is the ability to settle without begging, and a pool is an attempt to make settlement a regional right rather than an external permission.

The first trade is speed versus discipline, and it is unavoidable. A pool that can act quickly must have pre-agreed rules, pre-positioned collateral, and pre-authorized decision rights. If every disbursement requires political debate, the pool becomes a speech rather than a backstop. Yet pre-authorizing decision rights concentrates power in operators: the governing board, the settlement agent, the collateral committee, the supervisors who can declare an emergency. Operators decide who gets liquidity first. First access becomes survival advantage. Survival advantage becomes political controversy. The pool therefore imports the core contradiction of every backstop: it must be powerful enough to end panic and restrained enough to remain legitimate. Restraint cannot be purely moral. It must be procedural, because procedure is what keeps winners from being seen as favorites and losers from being seen as enemies.

The second trade is solidarity versus moral hazard. A pool promises that members will support each other when fear rises. That promise stabilizes the bloc by reducing the incentive for each member to hoard individually. Yet the same promise can encourage risk-taking if members believe the pool will absorb their mistakes. This is not a theoretical risk. It is the central risk of shared liquidity. A pool must therefore be built with surveillance and conditionality, but surveillance and conditionality are precisely what members resent because they feel like loss of sovereignty. The tension is structural: the region wants autonomy from external discipline, but autonomy requires internal discipline, and internal discipline feels like external control when it is imposed by a regional institution rather than by a national one.

The third trade is inclusion versus defensibility. Wide membership increases scale, deepens markets, and makes the pool more credible. Wide membership also increases attack surface. A weak member can become a conduit for illicit flows, a target for external pressure, or a source of unstable collateral. Narrow membership increases defensibility but reduces usefulness. The pool therefore has a perimeter problem: it must choose who is legible, who is trusted, and who is excluded. Exclusion is politically costly because it can fracture alliances. Inclusion is financially costly because it increases the backstop's exposure. The pool is therefore not only a financial instrument. It is a map of regional trust.

A bank treasury scene shows how bloc liquidity becomes lived reality, because the pool's true function is not heroic rescue but everyday avoidance of forced liquidation. A mid-tier commercial bank runs payments for importers, manufacturers, and consumer merchants. In calm, it funds cross-border activity by borrowing in external markets and using standard collateral. In a tightened world, external markets become expensive and conditional. Collateral haircuts widen. Tenors shorten. Counterparties demand intraday margin earlier. The bank holds assets and has profitable customers, but it cannot obtain external funding at acceptable terms because corridor standards have tightened and collateral has been downgraded by foreign risk committees. The bank turns to the pool. The pool provides intraday credit against eligible collateral. The bank meets settlement cutoffs without dumping assets into a falling market. The bank's customers experience this as normality: payroll clears, shipments arrive, shelves are stocked. The bank experiences it as survival by permission. The state experiences it as sovereignty by architecture.

The pool's collateral list is the real treaty. It decides which assets count as safe inside the bloc. It decides which securities are acceptable, which loans can be pledged, which claims are treated as liquid, and which are treated as suspect. Collateral eligibility is where bloc money becomes governance because it determines which national balance sheets can be turned into immediate liquidity. A pool that accepts only the strongest members' assets will preserve strict stability and destroy political cohesion. A pool that accepts everyone's assets at equal terms will preserve political cohesion and risk collapse when the weakest collateral is tested. The solution, if it exists, is not equality. It is a politically survivable hierarchy: transparent haircuts, clear limits, and predictable pathways by which a member can improve its collateral standing through reforms that are not humiliating. If the pathway feels like punishment, the pool will be resisted. If the pathway feels like discipline shared for collective stability, the pool can endure.

The pool also changes reserve behavior, and reserve behavior is where bloc money becomes real at the sovereign level. In the old order, members hoarded external reserves because they feared external corridors tightening. In a pool, members can substitute some external reserves with claims on the pool, but only if they believe the pool will perform in crisis. That belief is not created by speeches. It is created by legal enforceability, funding capacity, and the credibility of the largest members. This is the hidden heart of bloc money: the pool is only as strong as the political willingness of the largest members to be backstops when domestic politics turns against solidarity. The pool must therefore solve a credibility problem that is not technical. It is political endurance. If domestic politics can veto solidarity at the moment of crisis, the pool becomes conditional, and conditional liquidity is not liquidity when fear rises.

The most underestimated feature of bloc pools is that they are also standards engines. A pool requires shared messaging, shared identity standards, shared compliance assumptions, shared collateral documentation, and shared legal definitions of finality. Those requirements produce a regional standard. Once a regional standard exists, firms and banks build systems around it. That is how bloc money becomes real: not only through liquidity, but through routine. Routine is the mechanism by which a regional perimeter becomes default. Defaults create lock-in. Lock-in creates power. The pool therefore is not just a crisis facility. It is a daily machine that gradually relocates the region's commercial habits away from external corridors.

Pools interact with parallel networks the way fuel interacts with roads. A parallel network can route messages and instructions. A liquidity pool can supply settlement fuel. When both are built together, a region can reduce dependence on external corridors. When only one exists, dependence remains. This is why serious regional strategies treat pools and rails as a pair. Rails without pools are detours that end at an external fuel station. Pools without rails are fuel without highways. The return of bloc money is the return of the regional stack: internal routing, internal liquidity, internal collateral standards, internal custody recognition, and internal finality rules.

The hardest problem for a pool is crisis allocation. Crisis allocation is where legitimacy is tested because it is where scarcity is distributed. A pool must decide whether to prioritize trade settlement for essentials, bank funding for systemic institutions, or liquidity for markets that are politically sensitive. It must decide whether to support a member whose policies are viewed as reckless. It must decide whether to impose conditionality in crisis, when conditionality can deepen panic. It must decide whether to let a member suffer to preserve discipline, risking fracture, or to support the member and absorb political backlash. Every choice is political. That is why bloc money is not monetary cooperation. It is shared governance under stress.

The chapter's governing contradiction is simple: the pool is built to avoid external discipline and external humiliation, and it can only succeed by importing discipline inward. External corridors impose discipline through time scarcity: tightening access, widening spreads, forcing austerity choices. A pool replaces some of that external discipline with internal discipline: shared surveillance, shared collateral rules, shared crisis procedures. That can preserve regional autonomy at the boundary, but it shifts conflict inward. The conflict becomes a fight over who controls the pool and whose priorities are embedded in its rules. In a splintering system, that fight is unavoidable because the region cannot have sovereignty without accepting that someone must decide how sovereignty is exercised in crisis.

The return of bloc money therefore has a double edge. It reduces vulnerability to external corridor leverage. It also creates a regional hierarchy that can be used as leverage within the bloc. A smaller member may discover that it has escaped one dependence only to enter another: dependence on the bloc's largest institutions and on the bloc's standards. Bloc money is not pure liberation. It is reallocation of power. The question is whether that reallocation is more tolerable than the old dependence, and that question will be answered not in calm but under stress, because stress is when gatekeeping becomes visible.

The pool's first chamber in full detail is the settlement asset, because everything else rests on what the bloc treats as final inside its perimeter. The design choice is not a matter of elegance. It is a matter of whether outsiders believe the pool's settlement is real and whether insiders trust it enough to treat it as money. If settlement is anchored to central-bank liabilities, then finality is clear inside the perimeter, but the pool becomes a coordination mechanism among sovereign issuers, which means politics is never far. If settlement is anchored to a pooled claim, then the pool creates a new regional instrument that can behave like bloc money, but it must answer questions that cannot be postponed: who guarantees redemption, under what conditions, and what happens if one member refuses to honor its share in crisis. If settlement is anchored to a token-like internal unit, the pool risks creating ambiguity about finality and about who bears loss when conversion is stressed. Ambiguity is the enemy of crisis operations because ambiguity forces negotiation, and negotiation is the one thing a payment system cannot afford when queues are growing.

The settlement asset also determines how the pool behaves in diplomacy. A pool that settles in member central-bank liabilities is implicitly a coalition of sovereign issuers, which means it can be viewed as a regional public infrastructure. A pool that settles in a pooled claim begins to resemble a regional issuer, which attracts external scrutiny and internal political fights about who controls issuance. A pool that settles in a hybrid internal unit can be dismissed as symbolic until stress reveals whether conversion is real. Symbolic pools do not deter corridor leverage because gatekeepers measure not announcements but performance. The pool's asset must therefore be designed to perform under the same pressure that motivated its creation. It must be usable when fear rises, and it must be legally defensible when disputes arise.

The second chamber is collateral, and collateral is where solidarity becomes measurable. A pool's collateral constitution must decide two things simultaneously: which assets are pledgeable and how much liquidity those assets can generate. That is eligibility plus haircut. Eligibility without haircuts is charity. Haircuts without eligibility is exclusion by another name. The pool must also decide what it will not accept, because refusing certain collateral is how it draws the perimeter line between members who can be supported automatically and members who must be supported politically. The refusal line becomes the bloc's internal border.

Collateral also carries a time dimension that outsiders often miss. The pool's collateral is not just a pledge. It is a pledge that must be enforceable quickly. If collateral cannot be seized and liquidated without legal conflict, it is not collateral in crisis; it is a lawsuit. A bloc that cannot harmonize, at least operationally, the enforceability of collateral across its members will discover that the pool's liquidity is conditional on the jurisdictions where enforcement is strong. That creates an internal hierarchy that can become politically intolerable because it means some members are effectively under guardianship during stress. The pool must therefore build legal pathways for collateral enforcement that are fast enough to matter and legitimate enough to be accepted. If it cannot, the pool becomes a confidence game rather than an infrastructure.

The third chamber is distribution, which is where the pool becomes an allocator of time. Distribution is not simply "lend and repay." It is the rulebook for intraday credit, queue management, collateral substitution, and emergency settlement extensions. In normal times, the pool can pretend it is a technical facility. In crisis, it becomes a traffic controller. It decides which payments clear first, which institutions receive liquidity, and which transactions are delayed. That is solvency allocation because delayed settlement can trigger defaults. Distribution therefore must be designed to prevent the pool from becoming a political tool for favoritism while still allowing it to act quickly. This is why pools build pre-agreed triggers: objective thresholds that allow automatic liquidity provision and automatic tightening when risk rises. Yet triggers are themselves political, because the triggers embed judgments about what counts as systemic and what counts as tolerable pain.

Distribution is also where the pool's purpose can shift without anyone admitting it. A pool built to support trade settlement can become, under pressure, a mechanism to support government funding indirectly by accepting sovereign collateral more generously. A pool built to support banks can become a mechanism to support certain sectors by prioritizing payment categories. These shifts are understandable. They are also dangerous if they become opaque because opacity invites suspicion and suspicion invites withdrawal. A pool survives when members believe the rules will be applied as promised, not when members believe the operators have good intentions.

The fourth chamber is loss allocation, and it is the pool's darkest room because it contains the answer to the question nobody asks aloud: who pays when the pool is wrong. Loss allocation appears in three situations. The first is participant default. A member bank fails to repay intraday credit or fails to meet margin. The pool must seize collateral and cover obligations. The second is collateral impairment. Collateral values fall or become legally contested. The pool must decide whether to demand more collateral, impose losses on the borrower, or absorb losses as a collective. The third is sovereign stress. A member sovereign's assets are questioned, and the pool must decide whether to continue treating that sovereign's collateral as eligible. Each choice affects the pool's credibility and the bloc's political cohesion.

If the pool socializes losses too easily, it creates moral hazard and domestic backlash in stronger members. If it refuses to socialize losses, it risks panic in weaker members and fractures the bloc at the moment it is supposed to demonstrate solidarity. The pool's survival depends on a loss allocation scheme that is strict enough to deter reckless behavior and flexible enough to prevent collapse. That sounds like a contradiction because it is one. The only way through is transparency about the scheme before crisis, because surprise is what makes politics explosive. Surprise is what turns technical decisions into accusations of betrayal.

A port scene makes the stack tangible, because bloc money becomes real when it keeps essentials moving without begging. A country in the bloc imports fuel, fertilizer, and spare parts. Under corridor tightening, external settlement becomes slow and expensive, and suppliers demand prepayment in the safest unit. The bloc's pool provides a different routine. The importer pays in the bloc's settlement claim. The seller's bank accepts because it can convert that claim into eligible collateral inside the pool or into member central-bank liabilities through pre-agreed conversion channels. The insurer accepts because proof packets and finality are standardized. The port releases the shipment because payment is credited, not merely sent. The public sees fuel arriving and assumes the system works. The system works because the bloc has built internal liquidity and internal finality. That is bloc money: not a new symbol, but a new ability to discharge obligations inside a protected perimeter without external permission.

Yet the same scene contains the seed of conflict. The pool's collateral constitution may favor some members' assets. The pool's conversion channels may be easiest in the largest member's markets. The pool's governance may be dominated by the largest member's institutions. Smaller members can experience the pool as a corridor of their own, with its own gatekeepers and its own prices. The pool must therefore manage a legitimacy problem inside the bloc: it must not reproduce the humiliation it was built to avoid. If smaller members feel they have traded external dependence for internal dependence, they will comply in calm and defect in stress. Defection in stress is the one outcome that can destroy the pool's credibility permanently.

The return of bloc money therefore requires that the pool not only exist but be credible as a collective commitment. Credibility is not the size of reserves. Credibility is the belief that rules will be honored under stress. That belief must be produced. It is produced by prepositioned collateral, by legal enforceability, by a clear chain of decision authority, by the demonstrated willingness of the largest members to act, and by the demonstrated willingness of smaller members to accept discipline. Discipline is not punishment. Discipline is the acceptance that solidarity requires constraints on behavior. Without constraints, solidarity becomes a transfer with no end, and transfers with no end become politically fatal.

There is also a second, quieter reason pools return: they allow the bloc to internalize netting. In the integrated order, netting often relied on global corridors and global market plumbing. In a splintered order, netting across perimeters becomes harder because standards diverge and legal finality is contested. Regional pools re-create a netting space where obligations can be offset and settled with less reliance on external fuel. That netting space reduces gross settlement demand inside the bloc, which reduces the amount of buffers members must hold, which reduces the cost of being inside the bloc. This is how bloc money becomes attractive not only politically but economically. Yet netting spaces require trust, and trust requires governance. The pool's ability to net safely depends on its default handling and its collateral discipline. A pool that nets without discipline becomes a mechanism for importing risk from one member into all members. A pool that disciplines without flexibility becomes a mechanism for excluding weaker members and hardening internal hierarchy.

A second bank scene shows the everyday mechanics that make the pool either stabilizing or resented. A bank treasurer begins the day with obligations due at multiple cutoffs. Some are internal to the bloc. Some are cross-perimeter. Under stress, external cutoffs are tighter and external holds are longer. The treasurer's fear is not bankruptcy in the abstract. The treasurer's fear is missing a cutoff because missing a cutoff triggers a cascade: counterparties tighten, collateral demands rise, and depositors become anxious. The pool offers intraday liquidity against eligible collateral. The treasurer can meet bloc cutoffs reliably. The treasurer still struggles with cross-perimeter cutoffs. The treasurer begins shifting business toward bloc settlement because it is more reliable. That shift reduces the bank's external dependency and increases the bloc's internal volume. Internal volume deepens the pool's importance. The pool becomes more central. The pool's governance becomes more consequential. This is how bloc money grows: not through edict, but through operational preference for what clears.

The pool's governance regime is where the return of bloc money becomes the return of bloc politics. Governance must answer three questions that cannot be finessed. Who decides. On what basis. With what accountability. If governance is too technocratic, it will be attacked as illegitimate when it makes distributive choices. If governance is too political, it will be too slow and too compromised to act when panic requires speed. The pool therefore creates a new class of political operators: officials and institutional heads who must act like crisis governors in a domain that is formally financial but practically sovereign. Their success will be judged not by speeches but by whether queues were cleared, whether shortages were prevented, and whether the bloc avoided humiliating dependence on external fuel.

The pool also becomes a mechanism for setting regional standards, and standards are borders. A pool that works requires shared data fields, shared identity rules, shared compliance posture, and shared legal definitions of finality. These requirements embed a regional "normal." Once a regional normal exists, firms adjust systems. Banks adjust processes. Insurers adjust contracts. The region becomes an ecosystem. Ecosystems are sticky. Sticky ecosystems attract more internal trade and more internal settlement. That internalization reduces external leverage, because leverage works best when everyone must pass through the same chokepoint. A bloc with a functioning pool can route more of its life through its own infrastructure, which means external pressure must be applied at narrower interfaces. Narrower interfaces can still be powerful. They are also easier to hedge because the bloc can plan for them. Planning is the difference between vulnerability and constraint.

None of this eliminates the pool's internal tension. The pool, by design, allocates time. Time allocation in crisis is solvency allocation. Solvency allocation becomes political allocation when failures spill into employment and public order. A pool that is honest about its purpose will therefore build a political narrative that can survive crisis: a narrative of mutual defense, shared discipline, and bounded solidarity. A pool that hides behind technical language will be seen as deceitful when it makes hard choices. Deceitful governance is fragile governance. Fragile governance is the one thing a pool cannot afford because fear attacks the weakest point first, and the weakest point is legitimacy.

The pool's external implication is also strategic. A bloc that can supply its own settlement fuel reduces the dominance of external corridors. That does not necessarily dethrone the apex unit. It reduces the apex unit's monopoly on being the only usable answer in panic for that region. That reduction matters because it changes bargaining power in corridor wars. If a bloc can keep essentials moving internally, external tightening becomes less immediately catastrophic and therefore less coercive. Coercion works by creating immediate scarcity. Scarcity works by creating panic. Panic works by forcing capitulation. A pool interrupts that chain by providing time. Time is what allows a state to negotiate rather than surrender.

The pool's weakness is that it must be believed before it is tested, and belief is difficult to manufacture in a world already scarred by broken promises. Members will ask whether the pool will truly perform in a severe crisis, whether the largest members will truly provide support, whether collateral rules will truly hold, whether governance will truly act quickly. The pool cannot answer these questions with persuasion. It must answer them with design. Pre-positioned collateral. Automatic triggers. Transparent limits. Clear conversion channels. Enforceable legal frameworks. Demonstrated routines in smaller stresses that build confidence. Routine is how confidence is made. Confidence is how a pool becomes money-like.

The chapter's deepest claim is that bloc money returns because the splintering system forces regions to choose between external dependence and internal governance. External dependence is cheaper in calm and humiliating in stress. Internal governance is expensive in calm and stabilizing in stress. Regions build pools because they have experienced the price of humiliation and decided that paying for internal governance is cheaper than being disciplined by external gatekeepers when time is scarce. Yet internal governance is not free. It creates internal hierarchies, internal gatekeepers, and internal political fights over who deserves liquidity and under what conditions. The return of bloc money is therefore not the end of monetary politics. It is the relocation of monetary politics to the regional level, where it will be fought as a struggle over standards, collateral, and crisis discretion.

CLOSING DOCTRINE

Regional liquidity pools are the return of bloc money because liquidity is the fuel of settlement and fuel is sovereignty when external corridors can be tightened, delayed, or denied. A pool is not only shared liquidity; it is shared discipline, because the settlement asset, collateral constitution, distribution mechanism, and loss-allocation regime determine who receives time when fear makes time scarce. The pool's credibility depends on pre-authorized governance powerful enough to act in crisis and legitimate enough to survive domestic backlash, and on solidarity strong enough to hold when politics turns against it. Pools therefore reduce external vulnerability by importing discipline inward: they harden regional standards, create internal hierarchies through collateral eligibility and membership, and shift crisis allocation into regional politics. In a splintering system, blocs build pools to avoid humiliation at the boundary, but the price is that monetary sovereignty becomes shared governance, and shared governance is tested only when the region must decide which failures to absorb and which failures to allow.

CHAPTER 36
EVASION, ARBITRAGE, AND THE NEW SMUGGLING
SEAMS AS MARKETS

The seam is where the profit is. Not because people suddenly became more dishonest, but because the splintering system multiplied borders that do not look like borders. One corridor demands one identity proof. Another corridor recognizes a different identity proof. One perimeter treats a data field as mandatory. Another treats it as optional. One bloc's compliance posture is strict and audited. Another bloc's posture is thin and discretionary. The result is not merely fragmentation. The result is an economic opportunity: move through the place where rules disagree, and you can turn disagreement into margin. The seam is the new port, and the smugglers of the new age do not always move contraband. They move legitimacy, passage, and timing.

A compliance director at a large bank calls it leakage. A trader calls it basis. A logistics operator calls it rerouting. A small business calls it survival. A state calls it evasion. These are different moral frames for the same mechanical truth: when systems have borders, the borders create rents. Rents are collected by those who can navigate, translate, and exploit the gaps. The splintering system increases the number of gaps. It therefore increases the number of rents. What used to be a single global routine becomes a set of competing routines, and the space between routines becomes a market because the space between routines is where discretion lives, and discretion can be priced.

Where standards diverge, arbitrage is born. (market maxim)

In an integrated order, arbitrage existed, but it was constrained by a shared core of standards and by a shared sense of what completion meant. In a splintered order, the core itself fractures. Identity, compliance, settlement finality, collateral eligibility, custody recognition, and documentation burdens vary by perimeter. Each variation creates a spread between fast money and slow money, between legible money and suspect money, between collateral that counts and collateral that is discounted, between completion that is final and completion that is provisional. Those spreads invite actors to move assets, claims, and transactions into the perimeter where they are treated most favorably, then back into the perimeter where they can be spent, pledged, or converted at higher status. This is how seams become markets. The market is not always visible as a single exchange. It is visible as a pattern: the rise of translators, the rise of expedited handling, the rise of routing services, the rise of contract clauses that quietly embed corridor preferences, the rise of fee schedules that charge for speed and for ambiguity resolution, and the rise of private guarantees that promise "it will clear," a promise that is not about creditworthiness but about admissibility.

The chapter's first claim is that evasion is not only criminal. It is structural. When the cost of compliance rises and the cost of delay becomes unbearable, legitimate actors begin seeking alternative routes. They use translators, intermediaries, and contractual forms that reduce exposure to the strictest corridors. They change invoicing patterns. They prepay. They net obligations privately. They settle through regional pools. They redesign supply chains so that settlement occurs through jurisdictions with lower friction. None of this is necessarily illegal. It is the private sector responding to a world where passage is uncertain and time is expensive. The state may label it evasion because it reduces visibility. The firm may label it resilience because it preserves operations. The system experiences it as reduced governability because fewer flows pass through the corridors where oversight is strongest, and the corridors that remain visible become saturated with the highest-liability traffic, which causes them to tighten further, which increases seam value again.

A small importer makes the structure intimate. The importer brings in components for local assembly and sells to domestic retailers. The business lives and dies on timing and on the ability to pay suppliers without drama. A supplier abroad changes terms because the supplier's bank has begun treating the importer's corridor as high-friction; payments that used to clear routinely now fall into manual review often enough to be dangerous. The supplier demands prepayment. The importer cannot prepay without borrowing. The importer's bank offers a line but raises the spread because it is now pricing corridor uncertainty as a credit factor. The importer begins routing payments through a translation service that claims it can produce proof packets in the right format and can select the right path for passage. The importer pays a fee for speed and predictability. The importer is not trying to hide. The importer is trying to survive. Yet the importer has moved from a transparent corridor into a less visible one, because less visible is often the price of fast. This is the seam economy at its most ordinary: compliance friction becomes working-capital stress, working-capital stress becomes routing changes, routing changes reduce visibility, reduced visibility triggers tightening, tightening increases friction again.

The second claim is that the same seams that allow legitimate rerouting also allow illicit laundering. Proof packets become valuable. Identity attestations become tradeable. Translators become chokepoints, and chokepoints attract corruption because a chokepoint can sell passage. When standards become borders, the object being smuggled is not always a good. It is a compliant-looking story that allows a transaction to be treated as routine. This is the return of the old logic of trade fraud in new dress: re-label, re-route, re-document, and move through the weakest verification regime, not necessarily to break a law openly, but to exploit the fact that the strict corridor cannot cheaply verify reality at distance when the documents look correct on the surface.

The modern smuggler's core asset is not a ship or a warehouse. It is an ability to manufacture legibility. Legibility is the property a corridor demands before it grants speed. If a corridor's standards require certain fields, certain attestations, and certain traceability, then the actor who can manufacture those artifacts reliably can sell speed to everyone else. The actor who can manufacture them dishonestly can sell speed and invisibility to those who need both. This is why seams create moral ambiguity. The same service that helps a legitimate small firm survive can also help an illicit actor hide. The service is neutral in advertising. The use is not neutral in consequence. The system's difficulty is that it cannot easily distinguish the two once documentation becomes a product.

A scene inside a translation firm shows how the new smuggling is assembled without romanticizing it. The firm advertises itself as a compliance service. It collects documents, verifies identities to the extent it can, and prepares proof packets in the format required by strict corridors. It has relationships with banks that can clear through multiple perimeters. Its fees are justified as expertise. Over time, demand grows. The firm becomes essential to small exporters who cannot afford internal compliance teams and cannot absorb unpredictable holds. A second business line quietly emerges: expedited handling. Expedited handling is sold as premium service, but it is also a discretion point where staff decide which packets are complete enough to pass without escalation. In a splintered system, complete enough is not a neutral standard. It is a value judgment, and value judgments can be bought, not always through explicit bribery, but through structural incentives: preferred-client lists, priority review fees, performance metrics that reward throughput, and relationships with upstream institutions that expect volume and do not want exceptions. Corruption arrives when discretion is monetized and oversight is thin, because selling passage is the easiest business model a chokepoint can adopt.

The third claim is that arbitrage increasingly targets time, not price. In older markets, arbitrage meant buying cheap in one place and selling dear in another. In a splintered payment system, arbitrage means settling fast in one perimeter and settling slow in another, then capturing the financing spread created by delay. If a firm can move money through a corridor that credits quickly, it can finance inventory cheaply, meet supplier deadlines without prepayment, and keep production smooth. If its competitor is stuck in exception handling, the competitor must hold larger buffers or borrow at higher cost, which is a hidden tax that accumulates until it becomes a competitive disadvantage. The arbitrageur sells fast passage as a service, which means the arbitrageur becomes a private corridor. Private corridors are where statecraft and markets collide, because a private corridor is neither fully accountable like a public system nor fully constrained like a regulated bank, and yet it can become systemically important as firms cluster around what works.

A bank treasurer sees this as balance-sheet pressure. Funds held in review are funds that cannot be deployed. Deployment is profit. The treasurer therefore seeks counterparties who can guarantee fast settlement. Those counterparties demand fees, collateral, or side arrangements. Over time, a shadow market forms: a market in passage. The participants are not only criminals. They are firms and banks trying to reduce the uncertainty tax imposed by contested standards. The result is a new layer of shadow liquidity built not on credit risk alone but on corridor risk. This is the subtle transformation that changes the system's temperature: leverage begins to grow on the basis of "will clear" rather than "is solvent," and "will clear" depends on standards and discretion that can tighten overnight. Corridor risk becomes the new hidden rate. Those who can hedge it become rent collectors. Those who cannot hedge it become slow, and slow becomes fragile.

The seam economy is not a single phenomenon. It is a taxonomy of arbitrages created by border multiplication. Each class is different in mechanics and in enforcement failure mode, and the chapter becomes heavier when the reader sees the classes distinctly. The first class is time arbitrage, which sells speed through routing, pre-approval, and translator capacity. The second class is legibility arbitrage, which sells admissibility by manufacturing proof packets and by structuring entities and transactions to look routine. The third class is collateral arbitrage, which upgrades assets from discounted status in one perimeter to eligible status in another by moving them through custody and documentation regimes. The fourth class is custody arbitrage, which exploits differences in title recognition and enforcement tempo across jurisdictions. The fifth class is jurisdictional arbitrage, which relocates the legal "birth" of a transaction to the weakest regime and then imports it into a stricter regime with a compliant narrative. When a system fractures, these arbitrages do not appear one by one. They appear together, because they reinforce one another. Time arbitrage requires legibility arbitrage to prevent holds. Collateral arbitrage requires custody arbitrage to make pledges enforceable. Jurisdictional arbitrage requires legibility arbitrage to make the story credible. The seam market is therefore a connected economy, not a set of isolated tricks.

Time arbitrage becomes an industry because time is the scarce asset in a modern credit economy. A firm that can promise settlement within a predictable window can offer better commercial terms and can operate with lower buffers. That advantage is worth paying for. Once firms pay for it, intermediaries build products around it: priority routing, pre-approved proof packet templates, multi-corridor accounts, and contractual settlement guarantees that are, in practice, guarantees of passage rather than guarantees of value. Passage guarantees are dangerous because they transfer corridor risk from the buyer to the seller, and corridor risk is not fully hedgeable when standards tighten suddenly. Sellers then demand collateral or fees, which makes passage guarantees into a premium service. Premium services tend to be purchased by those with scale. Scale becomes speed. Speed becomes profit. Profit becomes lobbying power. The seam market becomes a political actor because it sits between commerce and the state.

Legibility arbitrage is older than the term, because every system that requires proof produces a market in proof. What changes in a splintered system is that proofs multiply and become inconsistent across perimeters. In a unified regime, a firm learns the forms, the fields, and the routines. In a splintered regime, the firm must satisfy competing routines simultaneously, and the easiest path becomes to outsource. Outsourcing creates translators. Translators create chokepoints. Chokepoints create discretion. Discretion creates rents. This is why legibility arbitrage quickly becomes an inequality engine. The firms that can afford internal compliance factories remain in the strict corridors and receive routine treatment. The firms that cannot afford internal factories pay tolls to translators and accept slower passage. Their commerce becomes more expensive, and expensive commerce becomes fewer transactions, less growth, less resilience. The seam market is not only about evasion. It is about who can afford to be legible.

Collateral arbitrage is the seam market's most institutionally dangerous form because it turns perimeter disagreement into leverage. In a splintered system, an asset can be eligible collateral inside one pool and discounted inside another. That difference creates a spread. Actors seek to "upgrade" collateral by moving it into the perimeter where it is treated as high-grade, borrowing against it there, then using the proceeds or the claim in another perimeter where the borrowed liquidity can purchase goods or finance activity. The system can tolerate small amounts of this. It cannot tolerate large amounts because collateral arbitrage creates hidden interconnectedness across perimeters that claim to be insulated. It is insulation theater. When stress hits, the links become visible as margin calls and forced sales. The seam economy therefore recreates contagion pathways even in a fractured network, because leverage seeks the cheapest funding and the easiest eligibility, then carries that leverage across borders.

Custody arbitrage exploits differences in title and enforcement speed. If one jurisdiction recognizes a custody transfer as final quickly and another recognizes it slowly or contestably, then assets can be repositioned to avoid freezes, to avoid seizures, or to gain eligibility in a particular collateral regime. The actors who can do this at speed have an advantage in crisis. They can move out before a gate closes. They can post collateral where it counts before haircuts widen. This is why custody regimes become strategic terrain. The border is not only in payment messages. It is in asset location. In a splintered system, asset location becomes a political choice because asset location determines which sovereign can freeze, seize, or rerank. Custody arbitrage is therefore a seam market in sovereignty itself: the ability to move claims into the jurisdiction whose rules you prefer before the other jurisdiction's rules trap you.

Jurisdictional arbitrage is the most visible and the most politically inflammatory because it looks like cheating even when it is legal. A transaction is structured so that it is legally and documentarily "born" in a regime where requirements are light, then "matures" into a regime where it can be spent at higher status. The mechanism is paper, not trucks. An invoice is rewritten. A counterparty is swapped. A ship-to address is changed to a hub that can re-export with new documentation. A financial claim is booked through an affiliate. A beneficial owner is hidden behind layered entities in a jurisdiction that does not provide fast transparency. The strict corridor sees a packet that passes basic checks. The strict corridor cannot cheaply prove that the packet is a story designed for the seam, because the strict corridor is not physically present where origin claims were created and because data sharing across perimeters is contested. The seam is exploited. The corridor tightens. Tightening raises friction. Raised friction increases seam value. That is the self-thickening loop of fragmentation.

A logistics scene makes jurisdictional smuggling feel like an operating rhythm rather than a morality play. A shipment moves through a hub because hubs are where documentation and routing can be standardized. The hub is efficient. The hub is also a seam. In a splintered world, hubs become more valuable because they can produce documentation that satisfies multiple perimeters, and they can do it at scale. That value attracts legitimate traffic and traffic that wants to borrow legitimacy. The hub becomes a sorting machine: some goods are routine, some are exceptional, and the line is drawn by paperwork rather than by physical inspection. Paperwork becomes the traded commodity. The state that believes it is governing goods discovers it is now governing narratives, and narratives are harder to verify at scale because verification requires cooperation across perimeters that no longer share a single trust regime.

The seam market's fourth claim, deepened, is that the seam economy increasingly manufactures "completion" as a product. Completion used to be an institutional fact: settlement finality recognized by the system. In a splintered order, completion becomes perimeter-specific, and the ability to achieve completion across boundaries depends on translation capacity, admissibility, and sometimes relationships. That dependence invites intermediaries to sell completion. They sell it as a guarantee, as a premium routing service, as a "managed payment" that includes proof packet assembly and pre-clearance checks. The buyer pays to remove uncertainty. The seller extracts margin by controlling the route. Completion becomes a rent. When completion becomes a rent, the payments system has ceased to be a neutral public infrastructure and has become a market in permission. Markets in permission are politically volatile because permission is supposed to be rule-bound, not auctioned.

A corporate procurement office makes the rent visible without melodrama. The procurement director is told that a supplier will raise prices unless the buyer can guarantee faster settlement. The buyer asks its bank for solutions. The bank offers a premium routing option that relies on translator capacity and pre-approved proof packets. The buyer pays. The supplier is paid. The deal closes. The economy continues. Yet the buyer has now paid a private tariff for speed. Multiply that private tariff across thousands of transactions and it becomes a macro drag, a transfer from productive activity to passage management. Passage management is now an industry. Industries lobby. Lobbying shapes standards. Standards create seams. Seams create industries. The seam economy becomes self-reinforcing because it feeds on the very fragmentation it helps manage.

The fifth claim is that enforcement becomes less effective as fragmentation grows. Not because enforcement agencies lose will, but because enforcement must police multiple perimeters with incompatible standards. If one bloc demands deep data and another forbids sharing it, enforcement cooperation becomes contested. If one corridor's identity proof is not recognized by another, tracing becomes slow. If settlements occur through regional pools and bilateral offsets, visibility declines. If private translators and bridge institutions carry more volume, enforcement becomes dependent on the integrity of private chokepoints. Chokepoints are where pressure is applied and where corruption concentrates. A splintered system therefore becomes harder to govern because it has more interfaces, more translators, more private routines, and more places where discretionary overrides can hide.

A bank compliance scene shows how enforcement can succeed locally and fail systemically. A bank's compliance team is told that risk tolerance must shrink. Shrinking tolerance means more transactions flagged, more holds, more escalations. The team responds by over-complying because over-compliance is safer than under-compliance. The bank's legitimate clients begin suffering delays. Those clients change behavior: they route through less visible corridors and avoid the bank's gate. The bank becomes cleaner on paper and less central in commerce. The state sees the bank's improved posture and assumes control is increasing. In reality, control is relocating. The system's visible corridors become stricter while the invisible corridors become busier. This is the core tragedy of seam enforcement: tightening at the center can increase activity at the edges if the incentives for rerouting are stronger than the incentives for compliance, and in a splintered system, rerouting incentives are strong because the cost of being delayed is existential for many ordinary firms.

The sovereign pressure scene is the hinge where this becomes monetary governance rather than a policing problem. A finance ministry discovers that stricter standards have reduced some illicit flows but have also pushed legitimate commerce into less visible routes. Tax receipts weaken. Capital flight increases. Trade becomes harder to monitor. The ministry responds by tightening controls, tightening oversight, tightening documentation demands, because tightening feels like control. Tightening pushes more commerce into alternative corridors that are harder to see, because commerce is trying to avoid the cost of being held. Visibility declines further. The ministry becomes trapped in a cycle where each tightening intended to restore control produces more evasion because the seams have multiplied. This is how the new smuggling becomes a state problem. It is not only about crime. It is about governability. The state's ability to see its own economy depends on which corridors commerce uses. When commerce moves to escape friction, the state becomes blind, and blindness is fiscal weakness. Fiscal weakness forces the state to borrow more or tax harder. Borrowing more and taxing harder intensify domestic stress. Domestic stress increases political anger. Political anger increases demands for tighter controls. The loop tightens again.

The moral ambiguity at the center of the seam economy is not a side note. It is the reason the era is unstable. A small importer routing through a lower-friction corridor to keep shelves stocked is not the same as a criminal laundering proceeds. Yet both use the same seams. The enforcement apparatus struggles to separate survival routing from illicit routing, especially when proof packets can be purchased and when documentation can be made to look routine by professional translators. The result is over-enforcement, which punishes legitimate actors and pushes them outward, and under-enforcement, which emboldens criminals and erodes trust in the system. Both outcomes increase political anger. Political anger increases the demand for tighter controls. Tighter controls increase friction. Friction increases seam value. The loop tightens, and each turn of the loop makes the state less certain about who it is targeting, which is exactly how legitimacy collapses: not when the state is weak, but when the state is seen as both harsh and ineffective.

The seam economy also produces a new domestic hierarchy because legibility becomes a paid resource. Firms that can afford compliance factories can remain inside strict corridors and enjoy routine treatment. Firms that cannot afford compliance factories become dependent on translators and on smaller intermediaries that specialize in routing. That dependency is expensive and precarious. The public story will be integrity. The lived story, for smaller actors, is that modern commerce requires paying for legibility. When legibility becomes a paid service, the seam market becomes a distribution engine: it shifts margin from ordinary producers to the intermediaries who control passage. Distribution engines become political targets when economic stress rises, because people can tolerate inequality that feels abstract and cannot tolerate inequality that feels like a toll booth they must pass every day to do ordinary business.

The seam market reshapes credit in ways that are easy to miss until they are too large to ignore. Banks price corridor uncertainty as a credit factor. Firms that rely on slow corridors must hold more liquidity. Holding more liquidity reduces investment. Reduced investment slows growth. Slower growth increases fiscal stress. Fiscal stress increases enforcement hunger because the state wants revenue and wants control. Enforcement hunger increases tightening. Tightening increases seam value. The macro loop is the micro loop scaled. This is why the chapter belongs in monetary statecraft rather than in a separate "crime" discussion. Evasion and arbitrage become macro mechanisms when they reorganize the path by which commerce clears and when they reallocate who gets to operate at speed.

A household-level scene makes the political transmission clearer without melodrama. A household is paid when an employer's receivables clear. The employer's receivables are held more often because proof packets are incomplete under a tightening standard. The employer draws on credit more often to bridge holds. Credit becomes more expensive because banks are pricing corridor risk. The employer delays hiring and delays wage increases. The household sees prices rising because suppliers are charging for prepayment and for uncertainty. The household cuts spending. The employer's demand softens. Layoffs begin. The household's story is simple: money is not arriving as reliably, and everything costs more. The household does not care whether this is called enforcement, standards, or geopolitics. The household experiences it as economic insecurity. Economic insecurity becomes political anger. Political anger becomes pressure for visible action. Visible action often means tighter controls and harsher enforcement. Harsher enforcement increases seam value. The seam economy becomes a political driver, not an underground curiosity.

The system's defenders will argue that stricter standards are necessary, and they are right in the narrow sense. Standards that are too weak invite crime and corruption. The problem is that in a splintered system, raising standards inside one perimeter does not eliminate demand. It displaces demand. Displaced demand finds seams. Seams are where standards are weaker, where oversight is thinner, where translation is opaque, and where discretionary overrides can be purchased. The system becomes a contest between tightening and displacement. If tightening is unpredictable, it makes displacement more valuable because compliance becomes a gamble. If tightening is stable and transparent, compliance can become routine and displacement becomes less valuable because the seam premium shrinks. Predictability becomes the forgotten anti-smuggling tool, because predictability reduces the profitability of selling "certainty" through private toll booths.

This is where the chapter must be explicit about the statecraft mistake that repeats. States often treat the seam economy as a moral failure and respond with moral intensity: more bans, more lists, more punitive actions, more rhetoric. Moral intensity does not reduce seam value. Seam value is set by friction and by disagreement. If perimeters disagree and if friction is high, seam value remains high. High seam value will attract sophisticated actors who can pay for documentation craftsmanship and who can build translator networks. A state that responds with moral intensity without addressing the structural drivers will increase friction for ordinary actors and leave seam value attractive for sophisticated actors, which produces the worst outcome: the state becomes harsher to the compliant and less effective against the capable. That outcome erodes legitimacy, and legitimacy is an enforcement resource. Once legitimacy erodes, gray routing becomes socially acceptable, and when gray routing becomes socially acceptable, governability declines sharply because the line between survival and evasion dissolves in public perception.

The practical conclusion is that seams will not be eliminated. They will be managed. Management is not a slogan. It is a design problem and a governance problem. Management requires integrity at translators and bridges, because those institutions are where proof packets are assembled and where passage is sold. If translators are not governable, the state has subcontracted border control to private actors whose incentives are fee extraction and throughput. Management requires coordinated oversight across perimeters, because otherwise criminals will always route through the weakest regime and legitimate actors will follow because speed clusters where standards are loosest. Management requires domestic legitimacy, because a system that makes legitimate commerce too costly will force ordinary actors into gray routes. Gray routes are where the line between evasion and survival dissolves, and once that line dissolves, every enforcement action becomes politically contested, which makes enforcement slower, which increases seam value again.

Managing seams therefore becomes a form of monetary governance because seams are not merely routes. They are pricing mechanisms for permission. When seam markets grow, the economy's effective cost of capital rises for those in the exception lane, trade volumes shrink, and liquidity hoarding increases. Those outcomes are monetary conditions by another name. They affect inflation through supply, employment through contraction, and financial stability through corridor risk. A state that treats seam management as a technical law-enforcement matter will miss that it is managing the economy's passage layer, and the passage layer is where money becomes usable. Usability is the currency of state capacity in a splintered system.

The splintering system creates a paradox for statecraft. Standards are raised to protect integrity and regain control. The raising of standards increases the value of seam navigation, which creates new private gatekeepers and new corruption incentives. The state can respond by tightening again, but tightening again increases the incentive to build parallel systems and monetize translation. The only stable path is to build standards that are strict enough to deter crime and predictable enough to allow legitimate actors to comply without being crushed by friction, while simultaneously making translator chokepoints governable rather than sovereign. Governable does not mean destroying them. It means auditing them, licensing them, and designing the system so no single translator becomes the sole gateway for an economy's commerce. Monopoly chokepoints are where smuggling and corruption become systemic because monopoly chokepoints can sell passage without fear of competition or scrutiny.

The chapter's final truth is that seam markets are not an aside. They are an inevitable byproduct of border multiplication. Every border is a place where value can be re-ranked. Every re-ranking is an opportunity to profit. In a splintering order, the system is thick with re-rankings: recognition in one perimeter, suspicion in another; eligibility in one pool, discount in another; routine in one corridor, exception in another; custody enforceable here, contestable there. Seams are where those differences are turned into cash. A state that ignores seams will find that its standards produce blindness. A state that attacks seams blindly will find that its enforcement produces paralysis and pushes commerce into deeper shadows. The statecraft problem is therefore to make the seam premium small enough that ordinary commerce does not need the seam, while making the illicit seam costly enough that sophisticated criminals cannot live there comfortably. That is not a moral aspiration. It is a governability requirement in a world where money is no longer only an instrument but a set of permissions distributed across competing perimeters.

CLOSING DOCTRINE

In a splintering system, seams become markets because divergent standards create spreads between fast money and slow money, legible money and suspect money, eligible collateral and discounted collateral, and actors convert those spreads into profit by selling passage, selling timing, and selling compliant-looking narratives through translators, routing services, custody positioning, and jurisdictional relabeling. Evasion is therefore not only criminal; it is structural: legitimate firms reroute to survive time scarcity while illicit actors exploit the same gaps to launder identity, documentation, and provenance, turning proof packets and discretion points into tradable goods. Translators and bridges become chokepoints that monetize incompatibility and concentrate corruption risk, while enforcement becomes harder because incompatible perimeters reduce cooperation, slow tracing, and push volume into less visible routes, producing a cycle where tightening raises friction, friction raises seam value, and seam value increases both gray survival routing and deliberate illicit tradecraft. The stable objective is not seam elimination but seam premium suppression: standards must be strict and predictable enough to make routine compliance viable for ordinary commerce, while translator chokepoints must be governable enough that passage cannot be privately auctioned at scale, because once passage is auctioned, monetary governance has been subcontracted to the market that profits from the border itself.

CHAPTER 37

FRAGMENTED CONTAGION

WHEN BRIDGES FAIL AND PANIC FINDS THE SEAMS

The first hour feels like a technical incident because the system has trained its users to treat friction as a service outage, not as a sovereign event. A settlement platform posts a status update that an interface is degraded. A clearing window is extended by thirty minutes. A queue forms. A bank's operations floor treats it as nuisance work: extra calls, extra reconciliations, extra apologies to corporate clients who want certainty and will accept theater if it comes with a timestamp. In a unified order, this becomes a footnote because the system has redundant depth inside a shared regime of recognition, and recognition is the quiet agreement that turns sent into done. In a splintering order, the same event becomes a stress fracture because the world has fewer bridges that matter more, and every bridge carries not only volume but political meaning. The system does not panic because one message fails. The system panics because nobody can agree, in real time, on what complete means across perimeters, and in a payments world, not complete yet is a weapon even when nobody intends it to be.

The second hour exposes the difference between redundancy and resilience. A payment can be rerouted, technically. The alternate corridor accepts the instruction, then asks for a proof packet that is not immediately available because the sender's identity regime is not native to the alternate corridor's standard. Manual review begins. Manual review means time. Time means inventory not released, payroll uncertainty, margin calls unanswered. The treasurer learns a brutal lesson: a second path is not an option if it cannot finish at speed under the rules of the path. In this world, the bridge is not a wire. The bridge is an agreement about admissibility, custody, collateral, and finality that holds under stress, and agreements are exactly what panic tests first because panic is the moment when every party asks, silently, whether the other party will still honor the routine when honoring the routine becomes costly.

In crisis, the question is not where money is. The question is where money is usable. (trader's line)

Fragmented contagion is what happens when usability becomes contested across perimeters and when the remaining bridges become both overloaded and politically sensitive. In the old integrated story, contagion was a fire that spread through obvious channels: funding markets, common collateral ladders, and shared settlement infrastructure. In the splintering story, contagion becomes stranger. Some fires burn out at perimeter walls because internal settlement is protected by internal pools and internal finality. Other fires jump unexpectedly through the few remaining bridges, and when they jump, they jump with greater force because the bridge carries concentrated volume and concentrated distrust. The result is a system that can look safer on paper because it is less interconnected, and then behave more violently in practice because the connections that remain are choke points whose failure is a cliff.

The first mistake officials make in this environment is to read the early signal as a localized outage rather than as a recognition event. The degraded interface is not merely a software matter. It is an ambiguity injector. Ambiguity forces discretion. Discretion forces delay.

Delay forces self-protection. Self-protection is what turns a queue into a run. The splintering system is built out of multiple recognition regimes, each with its own definition of what counts as routine, what counts as exceptional, and what counts as suspicious. When an interface degrades, transactions that would have flowed automatically become candidates for exception handling. Exception handling is where the system's human beings appear, and human beings are where liability is priced and fear is expressed. The system becomes fragile not because it lacks technology, but because it has multiplied the number of points at which a human must decide whether to let money pass, and multiplied the number of reasons a human can cite to justify caution.

Fragmented contagion has a rhythm that repeats across episodes, and the rhythm matters because it is where early signals are misread as noise. First, a localized disruption begins, often technical, often mundane, often plausibly harmless. Second, uncertainty spreads about whether the disruption is technical, regulatory, or political, because in a splintered system these categories overlap and participants have learned that holds can be policy without being named as policy. Third, institutions respond by hoarding liquidity inside their own perimeters because the safest action is always to defend one's own cutoffs. Fourth, hoarding reduces the availability of bridge funding and bridge settlement. Fifth, reduced bridge settlement turns localized disruption into cross-perimeter scarcity. Sixth, scarcity triggers self-protection by firms and households, which turns payment uncertainty into an economic slowdown. Finally, the state is forced to choose between defending internal stability and preserving external passage, and that choice reveals the system's real hierarchy because each choice creates a different set of losers who will become loud quickly.

The splintering system changes the anatomy of panic because panic is no longer only about solvency. It is about recognition, and recognition is a layered gate. In a unified order, the apex claim ends arguments broadly. In a splintered order, you can hold a claim and still be unable to use it where you need to use it because recognition is perimeter-specific. Recognition has conditions: identity proofs, data fields, compliance posture, custody acceptability, and the corridor's appetite to avoid being blamed later. When panic rises, conditions tighten. Tightening is rational for each gatekeeper. Tightening is also contagion for the system because tightening moves the border inward. The boundary of what counts as routine shrinks, and what was money-like becomes conditional. Conditionality is the gas of panic because it makes everyone reach for the few claims that are still unconditional, and reaching concentrates pressure at the bridges that can still convert one perimeter's claims into another's without becoming an exception factory.

A bridge failure does not need to be a collapse. It can be a hold. A hold is a pause that becomes a rumor. A rumor becomes a queue. A queue becomes a liquidity event because liquidity is timed. Timed liquidity is what keeps banks from missing cutoffs. Missed cutoffs become defaults in systems that run on sequence. This is why payment systems are always crisis systems in disguise. They are machines that convert time into continuity, and when time is withheld, continuity breaks quickly. When continuity breaks quickly, politics arrives because politics is how societies allocate pain they did not budget for.

The timeline of failure in a fragmented system is best understood as a cutoff cascade. A bank has incoming flows expected by a certain hour. Those incoming flows fund outgoing obligations due by a later cutoff. The incoming flows are delayed. The outgoing obligations remain due. The bank can bridge the gap with intraday credit if eligible collateral is available in the right custody and recognized in the right perimeter. If collateral is eligible only inside one perimeter but the outgoing obligation sits in another perimeter, collateral translation is required. Translation is slow because translation is not only moving an asset; it is making an asset legible under a different set of rules. Slow is dangerous. The bank then protects itself by delaying outgoing payments, which spreads the hold outward. The hold outward becomes a rumor in the corporate sector. The rumor triggers defensive actions: suppliers demand prepayment, lenders shorten terms, clients withdraw balances, and treasurers shift activity toward perimeters that are still clearing reliably. Each defensive act makes the bridge weaker. A technical event becomes a systemic event not because the event was large, but because it hit the seam where time is converted into trust.

The contagion is fragmented because the system's perimeters absorb shocks differently. One bloc has a strong internal liquidity pool, a tight internal identity regime, and a clear internal definition of finality. Inside that bloc, payments continue with tolerable friction. Another bloc is more dependent on bridges for ordinary commerce. That bloc experiences the same interface degradation as scarcity because it cannot substitute internal settlement for external passage. A third bloc has internal finality but weak translation capacity at the border, so it can keep domestic life moving and still fail at the boundary, which means trade becomes the first casualty. The mosaic is what makes this era hard to read. The shock does not appear everywhere at once as a single price move. It appears as uneven delays, uneven holds, uneven shortages, uneven bank behavior, and uneven political panic. Unevenness is what produces accusations of unfairness and exploitation, and accusations are what harden perimeters further.

The splintering system produces a new kind of contagion: interface contagion. Interface contagion occurs when a disruption in one perimeter causes tightening of admissibility in another perimeter, not because the other perimeter has direct exposure, but because the other perimeter fears being the weak link through which risk is imported. The fear is reputational and legal. A bridge institution that processes questionable flows can be punished. So bridge institutions tighten first, and tightening is how the system defends itself. Yet tightening is also how the system transmits stress. Every defensive act by a bridge is a friction increase for the actors who relied on the bridge. Friction increases working-capital needs. Increased working-capital needs widen spreads. Wider spreads reduce trade. Reduced trade reduces volume. Reduced volume reduces liquidity. Reduced liquidity increases fragility. The system does not need a solvency shock to spiral. It needs a recognition shock that becomes a liquidity shock through time.

A short, brutal operational fact sits under the macro story: cash is a timing instrument. Firms do not hold cash because they enjoy it. They hold cash because they cannot tolerate uncertain settlement. When settlement becomes uncertain, cash buffers rise. Rising buffers are contractionary because they are idle. When cash buffers rise across thousands of firms simultaneously, the economy slows even if nothing "fundamental" has changed. The splintering system can therefore create recession pressure without a classic financial crash, because the mechanism is not insolvency first, it is timing uncertainty first. The macro signal appears later. The micro signal is immediate: suppliers changing terms, banks shortening credit, firms delaying hires, households cutting spending because pay arrives late or because prices rise due to supply contraction.

The role of custody is where "insulated" systems share fatal seams even when they claim autonomy. Payments can be perimetric. Assets are not. Assets sit in custody chains that span perimeters because global finance built custody as an efficiency machine long before it understood custody as geopolitical terrain. In a splintered system, custody becomes a bridge in disguise. A custody bridge can fail through law, through cyber, through political pressure, or through risk committee retreat. When custody bridges fail, collateral becomes trapped. When collateral becomes trapped, liquidity becomes scarce. When liquidity becomes scarce, payment queues become credit events. This is how custody turns into a jump point of contagion: a custody dispute is not a legal footnote in crisis; it is a liquidity event with political consequences.

Collateral translation is the other jump point. In a unified system, eligible collateral is broadly eligible and can be converted through deep markets. In a splintered system, eligible collateral is perimeter-specific. A security can be treated as high-grade inside one bloc and discounted inside another. A pledge can be enforceable inside one regime and contestable inside another. A haircut can be stable inside one pool and volatile at the border. When an interface incident occurs, institutions do not only hoard cash. They hoard universal collateral, meaning the assets they believe will be pledgeable in more than one perimeter. Hoarding universal collateral drains liquidity from everywhere else. That drain forces sales of less-accepted assets. Forced sales depress prices. Depressed prices widen haircuts. Wider haircuts force more sales. The loop is familiar, but in a splintered system it is not synchronized globally. It is synchronized at seams: the selling pressure concentrates in the assets whose acceptability is contested across perimeters. Those are exactly the assets most held by actors who sit at the border: importers, exporters, bridge banks, translators, and mid-tier institutions that rely on cross-perimeter funding. The seam becomes the liquidation engine.

A clearing desk's view of this world is simple and merciless: obligations that miss cutoffs become defaults, and defaults are processed through rule, not sympathy. When collateral values are uncertain and settlement is delayed, clearing mechanisms demand more margin. Margin calls arrive earlier and larger because uncertainty is treated as risk. Margin calls are the system's way of turning doubt into cash. In a splintered system, margin calls become border weapons unintentionally, because margin can only be posted in eligible forms, and eligible forms differ by perimeter. A participant that can post eligible collateral meets the call and survives. A participant that cannot post eligible collateral sells assets, borrows at punitive rates, or fails. Failure then triggers further tightening. Tightening then increases exceptions. Exceptions then delay settlement. Delay then increases margin calls again. The system becomes a machine for amplifying recognition stress into solvency stress.

The corporate experience is not margin calls. It is my bank changed terms. A major retailer imports goods across multiple perimeters. Its treasury has routines built around predictable settlement and predictable release of inventory. A bridge disruption causes payments to be held. Suppliers demand prepayment for future shipments because they cannot finance uncertainty. The retailer's treasury draws more heavily on short-term funding. Short-term funding becomes expensive because bridge uncertainty widens spreads and because banks conserve liquidity for their own cutoffs. The retailer reduces orders and shrinks inventory. Shrinking inventory becomes price increases and shortages. Households experience inflation and scarcity. The treasury's original problem was a payment hold. The economy's problem becomes reduced supply. Payment fragility becomes political fragility because the shortage does not feel like an abstract macro story; it feels like daily life becoming thinner.

A mid-tier bank's experience is more precise and more brutal. The bank's treasury desk manages cutoffs. It relies on intraday credit and predictable settlement. A bridge disruption delays incoming funds. Outgoing obligations remain due. The bank uses internal liquidity first. Internal liquidity is finite. It turns to its regional pool. The pool provides relief, but only against eligible collateral. The bank's collateral includes assets treated as first-class inside the bloc and assets treated as second-class. Second-class collateral receives worse haircuts and tighter limits. The bank learns the bloc's hierarchy in arithmetic. It meets cutoffs, but the experience changes behavior. It shifts business away from cross-perimeter exposures and toward internal settlement. That shift reduces bridge volume and reduces bridge liquidity. Reduced bridge liquidity increases bridge fragility. The system thickens its own border because surviving institutions retreat into the perimeters that protect them.

This is the first core mechanism of fragmented contagion: perimeter flight. In a unified order, flight is toward the apex claim. In a splintered order, flight is toward the safest perimeter. A safe perimeter is the one with the strongest internal finality, the strongest internal liquidity support, and the least contested recognition regime. When a shock hits, actors do not only seek safe assets. They seek safe jurisdictions of finality. They seek safe corridors of recognition. They seek safe data regimes where a transaction will not be held because a field is missing or a proof is nonstandard. Perimeter flight reduces cross-perimeter activity, and reduced cross-perimeter activity makes bridges weaker, because bridges are sustained by volume and by trust. Trust decays quickly when exceptions multiply.

Bridges weaken mechanically because bridge business is complex and expensive. It requires staff, systems, compliance capacity, and capital. If volume falls and liability risk rises, bridge institutions shrink their activity. Shrinking activity raises costs and increases manual review. Manual review increases delays. Delays increase perimeter flight. The loop tightens. The system becomes a self-fulfilling prophecy: fear of bridge fragility causes actions that make bridges fragile. The integrated order had depth that could absorb fear. The splintering order has interfaces that amplify fear because each interface is a discretionary point where a human can decide to be cautious, and caution is contagious when liability is asymmetric.

The second core mechanism is collateral fragmentation. In a unified system, collateral hierarchies exist, but apex collateral is widely accepted and convertible. In a splintered system, collateral acceptability becomes perimeter-specific. An asset can be eligible inside one bloc and discounted or unrecognized inside another. This creates a new kind of panic: collateral panic, where institutions hoard the assets that remain universally pledgeable and dump assets whose pledgeability is contested. The hoarding reduces liquidity. Reduced liquidity forces more selling. Selling depresses prices. Depressed prices widen haircuts. Wider haircuts force more selling. The loop is familiar. The new feature is mosaic tightening, with some perimeters experiencing extreme stress and others experiencing relative calm. That mosaic is politically dangerous because it creates narratives of unfairness that drive policy reactions, and policy reactions tighten standards again, increasing friction and multiplying seams.

Collateral fragmentation also creates a hidden vulnerability in regional pools. Pools stabilize perimeters by allowing eligible collateral to be transformed into intraday credit. Pools embed hierarchy by declaring which collateral is eligible and at what haircut. When a crisis tests a member's collateral, the pool must choose: tighten haircuts to protect the pool or maintain support to protect the member. Tightening haircuts protects the pool but can destabilize the member, triggering domestic crisis and backlash. Maintaining support protects the member but can destabilize the pool if losses threaten collective credibility. This is the internal contagion channel of bloc money: the pool is a stabilizer until it becomes the mechanism by which one member's weakness becomes a regional political fight, and political fights are a poor substitute for settlement finality when cutoffs are hours away.

The third core mechanism is standards shock. Standards are borders. In a splintered system, standards can tighten quickly in response to perceived risk. Tightening is justified as integrity protection. Tightening also functions as a sudden tariff: new documentation burdens, new identity attestations, new data fields required for automatic processing. Firms that cannot comply immediately become exceptions. Exceptions become holds. Holds become liquidity stress. Liquidity stress triggers risk committee tightening. Tightening produces more exceptions. Standards shock is therefore a contagion channel, and it is more dangerous than overt prohibition because it can be enacted quietly and amplified by private over-compliance.

Standards shock produces a rumor economy with macro consequences. A firm hears a payment was held because a purpose code was insufficient. Another firm hears a shipment was delayed because an attestation was missing. Firms add buffers and change contract terms. Suppliers demand prepayment. Buyers demand discounts. The system becomes less trusting even if the shock was localized. Localized enforcement becomes generalized caution because the line between routine and exception becomes unpredictable. Predictability is the lubricant of payments. When predictability fades, everyone hoards time, and time hoarding is the start of recession.

The fourth core mechanism is translation capture. As standards diverge, translators become essential. Translators are bridge banks, service firms, and platforms that convert one regime's legibility into another's. Translators reduce friction and therefore become valuable. Their value gives them power. In crisis, their power becomes systemic risk because they become chokepoints. If a translator fails operationally, fails legally, is targeted by enforcement, or is compromised by cyber attack, the flows that depend on it do not reroute easily because translation capacity is not infinite. Fragmentation creates concentration in a new place. The integrated order concentrated power in a few global corridors. The splintering order concentrates power in a few translators between corridors. Translators become the new bridges. Bridges are where contagion lives.

Translation capture produces a distribution effect that becomes political quickly. When translation is scarce, translation is expensive. The largest firms buy speed. The smallest firms wait in exceptions. The difference becomes politically explosive because it creates an obvious story: those with institutional privilege can keep trading; those without it are trapped by paperwork and delay. Exceptions are disproportionately borne by those who cannot generate proof packets quickly, cannot pledge eligible collateral, and cannot pay for translator capacity. In a splintered system, inequality in legibility becomes inequality in survival, and survival inequality is the kind that turns technical disputes into street anger.

The fifth core mechanism is legal clash. A transaction final in one perimeter may be contestable in another. A custody instruction enforceable in one regime may be stayed in another. An insolvency priority clear in one jurisdiction may be challenged in another. In calm times, these clashes are managed through legal process. In crisis, legal time is too slow for financial time. Actors respond by refusing exposure. Refusal is withdrawal. Withdrawal is contagion. Legal clash becomes a panic channel because it turns the question of payment completion into a question of forum: whose court, whose definition, whose priority. When forum becomes contested, the safe choice is to hold claims that do not require forum recognition to be usable. Those claims are scarce. Scarcity creates runs.

A custody clash becomes a cliff when conflicting instructions arrive. A custodian receives a demand to ringfence assets for local creditors and, simultaneously, a demand from another perimeter to transfer those same assets immediately to protect a different set of claims. The custodian delays because acting on either instruction creates legal exposure. The delay becomes visible to counterparties as nonperformance. Counterparties withdraw. Withdrawals force more delay because the custodian must triage. Triage creates accusations of favoritism. Accusations invite political pressure. Political pressure widens the conflict. The custody bridge that was an efficiency machine becomes a battlefield, and the battle produces liquidity stress because trapped assets cannot be pledged where they are needed.

The sixth core mechanism is information fragmentation. In a unified system, pricing and settlement information is coherent enough that counterparties can judge risk quickly. In a splintered system, information becomes perimeter-specific. Different corridors have different visibility. Different pools have different transparency. Different standards produce different classifications. A counterparty can be solvent and still be slow because it is not legible in the corridor you must use today. Uncertainty about legibility is more corrosive than uncertainty about credit because credit can be priced. Legibility becomes binary at the moment of processing: routine or exception. Exception is slow. Slow is dangerous. Actors avoid exposure to uncertain legibility. Avoidance reduces liquidity. Reduced liquidity increases fragmentation.

Fragmented contagion evolves from technical incident to credibility crisis because credibility is what makes private actors intermediate. If bridge institutions believe standards, enforcement, or legal frameworks can shift unpredictably, they reduce exposure. Reduced exposure slows commerce. Slowed commerce increases political anger. Political anger produces policy responses. Policy responses tighten standards, impose controls, or pressure institutions to prioritize domestic stability. These responses stabilize interiors and worsen bridges, because external counterparties interpret domestic controls as increased trap risk. Increased trap risk causes more withdrawal. Withdrawal causes more tightening. The system becomes a sequence of defensive moves that generate the panic they are meant to prevent.

The political feedback loop is sharper in a splintered order because the measures that stabilize interiors can poison external recognition. A state can keep domestic banks alive by providing liquidity, but if it does so by restricting outflows, prioritizing domestic settlement, or pressuring institutions to conserve external claims, external counterparties interpret it as convertibility risk. Convertibility risk is fear that claims will be trapped, re-ranked, or delayed. Convertibility risk is a reason for bridge institutions to tighten. Tightening reduces external passage. Reduced passage increases domestic scarcity. Domestic scarcity increases pressure for stronger measures. Stronger measures increase convertibility risk again. The loop is why fragmented panic can escalate rapidly even without a classic solvency problem. The system is not collapsing because it has no assets. It is collapsing because it cannot agree on what it will honor across borders at the moment honoring across borders is expensive.

The state's dilemma is therefore not merely to backstop. It is to choose which perimeter to defend and at what cost. Stabilizing domestically can require restricting outflows, tightening controls, or prioritizing internal payment continuity over external settlement. Those choices preserve domestic order and accelerate external fragmentation because external counterparties interpret them as evidence that convertibility is conditional. Preserving external trust can require honoring external obligations even when doing so drains internal liquidity and forces austerity through time scarcity. The splintering system forces states to confront an older truth: you cannot be fully sovereign at home and fully reliable at the boundary without paying a cost in buffers, discipline, and institutional credibility.

The end-state of a fragmented panic is simultaneity without coordination. On the same day, a household experiences wages arriving late and prices rising. A small firm experiences suppliers demanding prepayment and banks tightening lines. A mid-tier bank experiences cutoffs becoming cliffs and haircuts widening. A large importer experiences shipments delayed because credited funds are not recognized fast enough to release goods. A custodian experiences conflicting instructions and delays transfers to avoid choosing a side. A ministry experiences reserves draining while external passage remains uncertain. Each actor experiences a rational fear. The fears align. The aligned fears become a self-reinforcing panic, and fragmentation prevents a single authoritative calming mechanism from reaching all actors at once.

Managing fragmented contagion requires a new crisis doctrine because old doctrines assumed a shared endpoint. The new doctrine begins with mapping bridges, not markets. Which translators matter. Which custodians matter. Which corridors are essential for essentials. Which perimeters tighten standards first. Which data fields create mass exceptions. Which legal clashes freeze custody transfers. Which pools have credible loss allocation. Mapping is not academic.

It is the only way to see cliff edges, and in a splintered system cliff edges sit at the least replaceable translation nodes.

Emergency recognition must be pre-negotiated because crisis is precisely when recognition fails. Minimum shared proofs for essentials, temporary acceptance of defined attestations, and pre-agreed exception handling for critical flows are not luxuries. They are what prevents every shock from becoming a border event. Without them, each perimeter tightens to protect itself, and tightening breaks bridges that could have shared liquidity.

Buffer design must reflect interface risk. Assets pledgeable in multiple perimeters, collateral pre-positioned in multiple custody regimes, operational capacity to generate proof packets quickly, redundant translation capacity that can be activated without improvisation, and contractual structures that reduce the probability that essential flows are trapped behind standards shock are the new insurance. It is expensive in calm. It is cheaper than humiliation in stress.

Legitimacy management must be built into crisis doctrine because crisis tools redistribute advantage. If banks are supported, favoritism is alleged. If households are supported, discipline is alleged to be broken. If essentials are prioritized, winners are said to be chosen. These accusations cannot be eliminated. They can be managed by rules announced before crisis. Improvisation looks like favoritism. Pre-announced prioritization looks like governance even when it is painful. Pain without governance produces rupture.

The final conclusion is sober: fragmentation does not remove contagion. It changes contagion's geometry. It reduces some global spread while increasing the violence of interface failure. It relocates systemic risk from the center to the seams. In a splintered system, systemic risk is the failure of translation, recognition, and finality at interfaces where commerce must still cross even when politics wants separation. That failure announces itself first as queues, holds, exceptions, missed cutoffs, and shortages, and by the time macro indicators reflect it, political indicators have already moved.

CLOSING DOCTRINE

Fragmented contagion is contagion through recognition: shocks transmit less through a single global center and more through interface failures where standards diverge, translators concentrate, custody chains clash, collateral becomes perimeter-specific, and finality is contested across regimes. Insulation contains some fires, but brittleness increases because fewer bridges carry more load, and a bridge disruption becomes a cliff when rerouting cannot finish under foreign admissibility rules and proof-packet exceptions multiply. Panic takes the form of perimeter flight and liquidity hoarding, which weakens bridges further and turns technical holds into economic scarcity that falls unevenly on actors forced into exception lanes. Regional pools stabilize interiors but import discipline inward through collateral hierarchies and loss allocation, creating internal contagion when solidarity is tested. Managing this geometry requires mapping critical translators and custody nodes, pre-negotiating emergency recognition for essentials, designing buffers for interface risk, and anchoring crisis legitimacy in pre-announced prioritization, because in a splintering system the seams are where both markets and politics break first.

PART EIGHT

FAILURE MODES AND FINAL DOCTRINE

HOW THE SYSTEM BREAKS NEXT, AND HOW TO REDESIGN IT

The warning arrives as a quiet message from an operations lead who has learned, through repetition, that the fastest way to be ignored is to sound alarmed. The incident is described in the language of routine: elevated latency, intermittent authentication failures, partial degradation in a service tier that most executives do not know exists. The front end still works for most users. Retail transfers appear to post. The dashboards show green because green is a summary of yesterday's assumptions, not today's pressure. Inside the machine, the truth is sharper: the same few infrastructure layers are carrying more and more of the order's settlement life, and the layers are converging in ways that turn local disturbance into broad paralysis. The system has spent decades diversifying instruments and multiplying rails. It has spent the same decades concentrating execution into fewer technical and legal choke points.

"Amateurs talk strategy. Professionals talk logistics." (attributed military maxim)

In money, logistics is not trucks and warehouses. Logistics is identity, connectivity, compute, authorization, posting, queuing, netting, custody, collateral, and the legal moment of discharge. It is the hidden choreography that makes claims usable. A modern monetary order can survive many failures of opinion. It cannot survive repeated failures of execution. Execution is the part the public never sees until it breaks, and when it breaks, legitimacy breaks with it because legitimacy in money is the public's belief that the system can close arguments on schedule. The point of the next sequence is not to decorate the system with new tools. The point is to understand the failure modes that are now structural, because when failure becomes structural, crisis policy becomes improvisation, and improvisation is the shortest path from financial stress to political rupture.

The first lived evidence of structural failure is rarely a dramatic crash. It is a Wednesday. Payroll files are submitted. Benefit debits are scheduled. Merchant batches are queued. Households see a "processing" icon and assume it will resolve because it always resolves. A ministry's cash managers see expected inflows that fund expected outflows, and assume sequence will hold because sequence is what the state depends on to avoid borrowing for routine life. Then a utility layer—neither the central bank nor a commercial bank—misbehaves. An authentication service rejects valid credentials intermittently. A message format validation routine begins flagging a common field as malformed. A queue management module begins throttling traffic as if it were defending against attack. Nothing is "down." Yet completion becomes selective. Some payments post. Others stall. The system does not fail in one stroke. It shifts into triage without admitting it.

A triage state is the most dangerous state because it creates the appearance of continuity while generating unfairness. Retail users see some transfers succeed and others fail. Merchants see some settlements credited and others delayed. Firms discover that the term "sent" now includes a hidden question: will it finish today. Banks discover that settlement cutoffs are cliffs because the queue has become discretionary. A ministry discovers that routine cash forecasting is now a political problem because benefits that arrive late are not "late," they are betrayal, and betrayal is not measured in basis points. The order survives the day. It loses legitimacy that day, because legitimacy is made of reliable closure, and triage is closure rationing without consent.

The splintering system was supposed to reduce dependence by multiplying perimeters. It does reduce some kinds of exposure. It also creates a deeper problem: fragmentation raises translation load, and translation load concentrates in the institutions and technical stacks that can still bridge perimeters. When perimeters disagree, bridges become more valuable. When bridges become more valuable, they attract volume. When they attract volume, they become single points of failure. That is the first failure mode of the era: fragmentation can concentrate risk rather than disperse it. The system becomes a patchwork on paper and a narrow throat in practice. The throat is where the system chokes, and the choke rarely looks like a single outage. It looks like a rising share of transactions marked for manual review, rising queue times, rising holds, rising exceptions, and rising collateral demands designed to protect those who remain willing to intermediate.

The second failure mode is standards-driven rationing masquerading as integrity. Standards tightening is presented as risk control, and risk control is necessary. Yet in a system that runs on sequence, standards tightening is time rationing. Time rationing becomes liquidity rationing because delayed settlement forces actors to hoard cash and hold higher buffers. Liquidity rationing becomes solvency triage because obligations do not wait for standards to relax. The new system breaks less through spectacular collapses and more through quiet queueing: exceptions, holds, deferred settlement, collateral haircuts, custody disputes, delayed discharge that turns "payment" into a ladder of conditional states. Conditional states produce doubt. Doubt produces hoarding. Hoarding produces contraction. Contraction produces political blame, and blame hardens perimeters further. This spiral looks, to the public, like incompetence or sabotage, and looks, to practitioners, like prudent defense. Both descriptions can be true at once, which is why this era is politically combustible: the system can be rational and still be intolerable.

A finance minister does not experience these failure modes as theory. A finance minister experiences them as a calendar that stops cooperating. External obligations still exist. Internal politics still exist. Import needs still exist. The banking system still must clear payroll. Yet the passage between these requirements becomes less reliable because execution has become more brittle. The minister can raise rates, cut spending, impose controls, negotiate support, threaten retaliation, or seek alternate corridors. None of these actions restores execution if execution has failed for technical or infrastructural reasons. None of these actions restores trust if the public begins to believe the machine's promises are conditional. The failure mode is no longer "the market lost confidence." The failure mode is "the machine cannot finish." A machine that cannot finish is not a monetary order. It is a set of aspirations with invoices attached.

The third failure mode is concentration hidden behind vendor neutrality. The system's daily life increasingly depends on a small number of infrastructure domains that were never designed to be monetary sovereigns: compute platforms, identity providers, messaging layers, cybersecurity contractors, operational utilities whose decisions can slow, exclude, or freeze flows. The public still imagines money as issued by central banks and intermediated by banks. The reality is that money's usability is increasingly mediated by technical operators whose incentives are different from the state's incentives and whose legal obligations are shaped by contracts more than constitutions. That gap between imagined sovereignty and operational sovereignty becomes lethal under pressure because authority is misassigned. When the order breaks, officials reach for policy instruments. The break is in execution. Execution cannot be commanded by speeches when the choke point is a contract, a configuration, or a private operator's liability posture.

A central bank governor confronted with an incident that threatens settlement continuity does not need a lecture on technology. The governor needs a clear power map: which technical layer can halt the queue, which legal layer can compel continuation, which institutions can provide intraday liquidity if posting is delayed, which custodians can transfer collateral if a bridge freezes, which alternate pathways exist that are not merely available but usable under current admissibility rules. Most systems do not have this map in a single coherent form. They have fragments: risk reports, cyber playbooks, vendor contracts, supervisory assessments, contingency memos written after the last stress. Fragmentation of knowledge is itself a failure mode because the machine runs on sequence and sequence does not pause while committees compare documents.

The fourth failure mode is algorithmic reflex. Markets and operations desks increasingly rely on automated controls: risk limits that tighten when volatility rises, margin timetables that accelerate when spreads widen, fraud filters that become more aggressive when anomalies appear, routing engines that divert traffic when latency increases, queue managers that throttle to preserve stability. Each control is rational inside its own objective. In aggregate, the controls can synchronize withdrawal. The system's human beings then discover they are governing emergent behavior, not a set of decisions. Emergent withdrawal meets a brittle execution layer and produces a cliff: flows that were routine become exceptional at scale, and exceptional at scale is simply another name for paralysis. This is why legitimacy can evaporate quickly when the machine's behavior becomes inexplicable to its users. In money, inexplicable is indistinguishable from unfair, and perceived unfairness is where politics arrives.

The fifth failure mode is cryptographic fragility. The system increasingly relies on cryptography not only in private finance but in identity, authentication, messaging integrity, tokenized settlement designs, and the auditability of records. Cryptography is treated as permanent foundation because it is mathematical. Yet mathematics is only permanent relative to compute and technique. When compute changes sharply or technique changes abruptly, what looked like a foundation can become a trapdoor. A cryptography shock is not only about digital assets. It is about the integrity of the system's proofs: identity, authorization, signatures, custody control, auditability. If proofs can be forged at scale, the system cannot know who is speaking to it, and if it cannot know who is speaking to it, it cannot enforce ranking, finality, or discharge reliably. That is not a technology issue. That is the collapse of admissibility itself, and admissibility is the first gate of monetary order.

The sixth failure mode is climate as collateral stress rather than climate as morality. When physical shocks become more frequent and transition mandates re-rank assets, collateral values change in ways that can be abrupt and politically contested. The system can tolerate slow repricing. It cannot tolerate sudden repricing of what counts as eligible collateral for credit creation and settlement liquidity. When collateral is re-ranked, funding becomes more expensive for some sectors and regions. Those sectors and regions do not experience this as environmental policy. They experience it as exclusion. Exclusion becomes political conflict. Political conflict becomes pressure on central banks and supervisors. Pressure can produce exceptions. Exceptions can produce fragility. The climate channel therefore becomes another way the system's ranking of claims becomes politically explosive, because collateral is the place where policy meets balance sheets without polite language.

The seventh failure mode is legal discontinuity. Under stress, perimeters discover that what looked like a shared settlement world was actually a patchwork of forums with different definitions of finality, different clawback powers, different insolvency priorities, different emergency authorities. A payment can be posted and still be contested. A custody transfer can be instructed and still be stayed. A collateral pledge can be documented and still be reranked. In calm, these differences are managed by time and process. In crisis, legal time is too slow for payment time. Actors respond by withdrawing exposure. Withdrawal is the contagious act. Legal discontinuity turns bridges into cliffs because bridges rely on predictable recognition across boundaries. When recognition becomes a forum fight, the safest choice is to hold only what does not require argument. That choice concentrates demand and produces runs.

These failure modes share a single theme: the system breaks at the conversion points where private intention becomes public fact. Authorization becomes posting. Posting becomes clearing. Clearing becomes settlement. Settlement becomes discharge. Collateral becomes liquidity. Identity becomes admissibility. Custody becomes enforceability. Each conversion is a gate, and each gate can be tightened under pressure. A state that governs only the instruments and not the gates governs symbolism, not power. The gates are where sovereignty lives because the gates decide who can finish.

The redesign doctrine begins with naming the breakpoints that matter most. The first breakpoint is identity and authentication, because without reliable attribution the system cannot enforce penalties, cannot prevent fraud at scale, and cannot maintain trust in admissibility. The second breakpoint is queue control, because queue control is time allocation, and time allocation becomes solvency allocation when cutoffs approach. The third breakpoint is custody mobility, because trapped collateral becomes trapped liquidity, and trapped liquidity becomes payment failure. The fourth breakpoint is collateral eligibility, because eligibility is the upgrade path from private assets to public settlement capacity. The fifth breakpoint is translator capacity, because in a fragmented world, translators are the true bridges, and bridges are where crises become systemic. The sixth breakpoint is legal finality, because without a defendable endpoint, every transaction remains contestable and contestability is the enemy of scale.

Each breakpoint carries a specific betrayal story when it fails, and betrayal stories are what make technical incidents politically fatal. When identity breaks, innocent users are excluded and criminals pass, and the public concludes the system is unjust and incompetent. When queues break, some payments clear and others do not, and the public concludes the system favors insiders. When custody breaks, assets are trapped and the public concludes property rights are conditional. When collateral eligibility breaks, credit becomes scarce for some regions and sectors and the public concludes policy is punishment. When translators break, commerce becomes slow and expensive and the public concludes the state has lost control. When finality breaks, the past becomes unsafe and the public concludes money itself is unreliable. This is why failure modes are governance: they determine which betrayal stories will dominate politics when pressure arrives.

A redesigned system therefore must be built not only for efficiency but for graceful failure. Graceful failure does not mean no pain. It means pain allocated under rules the public can recognize as coherent and bounded. Graceful failure means queue policies that prioritize essentials transparently. It means collateral policies that can tighten without becoming arbitrary. It means custody mobility that can function under legal stress. It means translator redundancy so no single bridge becomes a choke point. It means emergency recognition rules that keep essentials moving without turning every transaction into an exception. It means a legal doctrine of finality that is defendable and not casually reversible. These are not technical preferences. They are legitimacy protections.

The chapters that follow are not a tour of fashionable risks. They are a descent into the system's brittle chambers. The first chamber is infrastructure concentration: the quiet single point of failure hidden inside diversification theater. The second chamber is cyber conflict: the recognition that payments are battlefield terrain because disabling settlement is coercion without formal war. The third chamber is machine markets: algorithmic feedback loops that can manufacture sudden scarcity and sudden legitimacy collapse. The fourth chamber is proof shock: the day authentication and signature trust becomes doubtful and the system must rebuild admissibility under pressure. The fifth chamber is climate and collateral: the re-ranking of assets under stress and the way mandates collide with backstop politics. The sixth chamber is final doctrine: design principles that treat money as governed architecture of ranked claims, not as a set of instruments, and that treat sovereignty as operational control over discharge, finality, collateral eligibility, and exclusion, not as rhetoric.

The reader does not need to be persuaded that these risks exist. The reader needs to be persuaded that the system's architecture makes them governable or not governable. Some risks can be buffered. Some require redesign. Some require choosing dependencies to accept and dependencies that are politically intolerable. The deeper truth is that resilience is not a property you can purchase after the fact. Resilience is a design choice embedded in where the system concentrates, how it authenticates, how it settles, how it ranks collateral, and how it assigns loss. The system breaks where those choices were made for efficiency and assumed to be reversible. Under pressure, efficiency becomes fragility, and reversibility becomes illusion.

The final doctrine to be earned in this sequence is not a slogan about stability. It is a doctrine about sovereign capacity under failure. Sovereign capacity is the ability to keep settlement life functioning when markets are afraid, when bridges are contested, when standards tighten, when proof becomes doubtful, and when collateral is re-ranked. A system that cannot keep payment life functioning will face political rupture regardless of its macro intentions, because the public cannot be asked to trust a machine that cannot finish. The system's most dangerous vulnerability is not that it is complex. The vulnerability is that it is complex in ways that hide who is responsible when it fails. Hidden responsibility turns technical outages into legitimacy crises, because the public will not accept nobody as an explanation for missing wages, missing inventory, and missing discharge.

CLOSING DOCTRINE

Failure modes are governance because they reveal which institutions, technical layers, and legal regimes control usability when pressure arrives. Fragmentation can reduce exposure while concentrating dependence in fewer translators and infrastructure stacks, turning bridges into cliffs. Standards tightening is not only integrity; it is time rationing, and time rationing becomes liquidity rationing, and liquidity rationing becomes solvency triage. Infrastructure concentration relocates operational sovereignty into contracts and technical operators; cyber conflict weaponizes settlement continuity; machine feedback can synchronize retreat faster than committees can coordinate; proof shock threatens admissibility by undermining identity and authorization; climate and collateral re-rank eligibility under political pressure; legal discontinuity turns settlement into forum fights that produce withdrawal. The redesign imperative is therefore not to add instruments but to harden execution: map breakpoints, diversify true single points, pre-negotiate emergency recognition for essentials, preserve defendable finality, keep custody and collateral chains enforceable, and design queue and collateral policies that fail gracefully under stress, because a monetary order that cannot finish cannot govern.

CHAPTER 38

CLOUD CONCENTRATION

THE NEW SINGLE POINT OF FAILURE

The call comes from a room that is never photographed. The room has no flags, no polished lecterns, no ceremonial language. It has screens, incident channels, and a tired rhythm of people who speak in short clauses because every extra word is a second that should have been used to keep the queue moving. The payments day is already in motion. Payroll files are in flight. Merchant batches are staged. Treasury outflows are scheduled against expected inflows. The public sees confirmation screens and assumes completion is a promise. Then the confirmations stop arriving on time. Not everywhere. Not cleanly. Just enough that the operators feel the shift in their bodies before any minister hears the phrase "degraded service."

The first message from the infrastructure team tries to be calm because calm buys minutes and minutes buy options. A core dependency is experiencing elevated latency. Authentication requests are intermittently failing. An upstream routing layer is throttling traffic to protect itself. None of this is described as an outage because outage implies a single switch flipped from on to off. What is happening is worse: the machine is entering triage while still appearing to function. Some institutions are finishing their day. Others are stacking exceptions faster than they can clear them. The state's payments spine is now a set of queues whose behavior depends on a private operator's incident posture, not on any public promise the state has made to its own citizens.

"We built for scale. We did not build for blame." (reliability engineer, internal incident review)

Cloud concentration is the modern single point of failure disguised as modernization. The surface story is rational: consolidate infrastructure, reduce legacy fragility, gain elastic capacity, standardize security practices, improve resilience through redundancy. The deeper story is political: the system has relocated operational sovereignty into a narrow set of technical layers whose governance is contractual, whose failure modes are opaque to most officials, and whose incident decisions can ration completion at the worst possible moment. In a monetary order, rationed completion is a form of power because completion is where private intention becomes public fact. The question is not whether cloud infrastructure is useful. The question is whether the monetary state understands what it has concentrated, where it has concentrated it, and what it can compel when the concentration misbehaves.

The first illusion cloud concentration produces is vendor neutrality. A ministry sees multiple banks and multiple payment providers and assumes diversity. A central bank sees multiple participants and assumes redundancy. A supervisor sees multiple compliance programs and assumes independence. Underneath, those institutions can share the same few infrastructure dependencies: the same compute regions, the same identity providers, the same key management services, the same routing edges, the same logging and monitoring stacks, the same incident coordination pathways. Diversity on the surface can hide monoculture underneath. Monoculture is not an insult. It is a design property, and design properties become fate under stress.

The second illusion is that availability means usability. A cloud system can remain technically reachable while becoming unusable for critical flows because latency, throttling, and intermittent authentication failures convert routine into exception. Exception is where time is rationed. Time rationing becomes liquidity rationing. Liquidity rationing becomes solvency triage as cutoffs approach. This is the sequence that makes cloud concentration a monetary problem, not a technology problem. It is not the server that matters. It is the timing of settlement and the legal expectations built around that timing. A payments system that cannot finish on schedule does not merely inconvenience commerce. It breaks the state's promise that obligations can be discharged reliably inside its own domain.

The third illusion is that multi-region equals independent. Many institutions believe they have solved concentration by distributing workloads across multiple locations. They are often distributing compute while keeping control planes, identity roots, and key management centralized. That design can survive hardware failures and still fail catastrophically when a control plane degrades, when identity services throttle, when a key store becomes unreachable, or when an automated security response triggers protective shutdown across locations simultaneously. The system can be spread out geographically and still share a single nervous system. When the nervous system misfires, the limbs do not matter.

The first lived evidence of this failure mode is rarely a dramatic crash. It is a Wednesday. Payroll files are submitted. Benefit debits are scheduled. Merchant batches are queued. Households see a processing icon and assume it will resolve because it always resolves. Inside the banking system, teams do what they have trained themselves to do: they trust sequence. Then a utility layer—neither the central bank nor a commercial bank—misbehaves. An authentication service rejects valid credentials intermittently. A message validation routine begins flagging a common field as malformed. A queue management module begins throttling traffic as if it were defending against attack. Nothing is "down." Yet completion becomes selective. Some payments post. Others stall. The system does not fail in one stroke. It shifts into triage without admitting it.

A triage state is the most dangerous state because it creates the appearance of continuity while generating unfairness. Retail users see some transfers succeed and others fail. Merchants see some settlements credited and others delayed. Firms discover that the word "sent" now includes a hidden question: will it finish today. Banks discover that settlement cutoffs are cliffs because the queue has become discretionary. A ministry discovers that routine cash forecasting is now a political problem because benefits that arrive late are not "late," they are betrayal, and betrayal is not measured in basis points. The order survives the day. It loses legitimacy that day, because legitimacy is made of reliable closure, and triage is closure rationing without consent.

Cloud concentration becomes systemic not because everyone uses the same provider for everything, but because the same critical functions converge into a small set of shared dependencies. Identity and authentication converge because institutions cannot manage dozens of internal identity schemes and still satisfy modern security demands. Key management converges because audit and control requirements punish ad hoc cryptography and reward managed systems. Routing converges because performance incentives push traffic toward the same optimized edges. Monitoring converges because incident response needs unified telemetry. Even when providers differ, the architectural pattern can converge: the system depends on a small number of identity roots, a small number of key vaults, a small number of routing choke points, and a small number of incident coordination channels. The result is correlated behavior under stress, and correlated behavior is hidden systemic risk because it looks like coincidence until it becomes simultaneity.

The splintering system intensifies this because fragmentation raises translation load. When perimeters disagree, bridges become more valuable. When bridges become more valuable, they attract volume. When they attract volume, they become single points of failure. Cloud concentration feeds this by giving bridge institutions strong incentives to consolidate translation and screening stacks into the same infrastructure domains. Translation is compute-heavy, data-heavy, and liability-heavy. Liability-heavy functions seek standardized environments with the strongest security posture and the strongest audit trails. Those environments are often the same few technical domains. The system becomes a patchwork on paper and a narrow throat in practice. The throat is where it chokes.

The choke does not look like silence. It looks like a rising share of transactions marked for manual review. It looks like rising queue times. It looks like rising holds justified as integrity measures. It looks like "in progress" statuses that do not finish before cutoffs. It looks like dashboards that show partial success and therefore encourage denial. It looks like phone calls from corporate treasury teams asking why they can see "accepted" but cannot see "credited." It looks like small businesses refreshing banking apps and seeing nothing wrong until the supplier calls demanding prepayment for the next shipment. The system's failure mode is fog, and fog is contagious because it forces each actor to defend itself, and self-defense is how liquidity disappears without any official decision to tighten.

Standards tightening turns that choke into a contraction engine. Standards tightening is presented as integrity, and integrity is necessary. Yet in a system that runs on sequence, standards tightening is time rationing. Time rationing becomes liquidity rationing because delayed settlement forces actors to hoard cash and raise buffers.

Liquidity rationing becomes solvency triage because obligations do not wait for standards to relax. The modern system breaks less through spectacular collapses and more through quiet queueing: exceptions, holds, deferred settlement, collateral haircuts, custody disputes, delayed discharge that turns payment into a ladder of conditional states. Conditional states produce doubt. Doubt produces hoarding. Hoarding produces contraction. Contraction produces political blame, and blame hardens perimeters further. This spiral looks, to the public, like incompetence or sabotage, and looks, to practitioners, like prudent defense. Both descriptions can be true at once, which is why this era is politically combustible: the system can be rational and still be intolerable.

The monetary state's predicament begins with an uncomfortable distinction: policy control is not execution control. A finance minister can change tax timing. A central bank can supply liquidity. A supervisor can demand capital. None of those actions makes an identity service respond. None of those actions makes a validation layer stop rejecting messages. None of those actions forces a throttled queue to advance. Liquidity can prevent insolvency. Liquidity cannot create completion if completion is throttled. The state's traditional crisis logic assumed pipes worked and balance sheets were stressed. Cloud concentration creates the opposite risk: pipes fail, then balance sheets become stressed as a consequence. The state can be powerful on paper and helpless at the choke point if it never secured governance rights over the choke point.

A central bank governor confronted with an incident that threatens settlement continuity does not need a lecture on technology. The governor needs a clear power map: which technical layer can halt the queue, which legal layer can compel continuation, which institutions can provide intraday liquidity if posting is delayed, which custodians can transfer collateral if a bridge freezes, which alternate pathways exist that are not merely available but usable under current admissibility rules. Most systems do not have this map in one coherent form.

They have fragments: risk reports, cyber playbooks, vendor contracts, supervisory assessments, contingency memos written after the last stress. Fragmentation of knowledge is itself a failure mode because the machine runs on sequence and sequence does not pause while committees compare documents.

The power map begins with the simplest and least glamorous fact: whoever controls identity controls access, and access is the first gate of money. If authentication fails intermittently, systems choose safety over availability. Safety over availability means rejecting flows rather than risking fraudulent acceptance. Rejecting flows creates exceptions. Exceptions create delay. Delay becomes liquidity stress. In a crisis, the choice to favor safety can be correct for integrity and catastrophic for continuity. The state must decide, in advance, where it wants the system to sit on that tradeoff, because allowing private operators to decide it under pressure is allowing private operators to decide who gets to finish.

The second lever is routing and throttling. Modern systems throttle to protect themselves from overload and attack. Throttling is defensive. Throttling is also rationing. Rationing is political when it determines whose payment completes and whose does not. Throttling policies often treat all traffic as equivalent. In a monetary system, traffic is not equivalent. A retail purchase delayed is inconvenience. A payroll batch delayed is household shock. A settlement obligation delayed into cutoff is default risk. A sovereign outflow delayed can widen spreads and trigger external suspicion. If the system cannot differentiate criticality under stress, it rations blindly, and blind rationing produces the worst legitimacy outcome: random winners, random losers, no explanation.

The third lever is key management. A system can remain "up" while losing the ability to authorize because keys cannot be accessed, rotated, or validated at the required pace. A partial key management failure forces systems into freeze posture. Freeze posture is often correct because moving money without reliable authorization is a fraud invitation. Freeze posture is economically violent because it halts discharge. This is the moment cloud concentration becomes constitutional: a private technical failure can force the settlement perimeter into freeze without any formal declaration of emergency. The public will ask why the state cannot simply order resumption. The state will discover it can order domestic institutions to try, and domestic institutions can still be unable to act because the choke point is not the domestic institution.

The fourth lever is telemetry and observability. Observability is power because in a failure you cannot govern what you cannot see. Cloud systems generate logs and metrics, but access to those logs is gated by contracts, security constraints, and liability fear. A bank may not be able to share logs quickly with supervisors without internal approvals. A provider may not be able to share root cause details quickly without legal review. Delayed telemetry turns incident response into guesswork. Guesswork turns decision-making into caution. Caution becomes delay. Delay becomes contraction. The paradox is sharp: the system becomes more measurable in theory and less governable in practice when the needed visibility is trapped behind organizational boundaries that do not dissolve under emergency.

The fifth lever is incident coordination itself. When a dependency degrades, the first question becomes: technical fault, cyber interference, or policy disguised as technical behavior. In a splintered world, actors cannot assume benign explanation. Suspicion makes response slower. Slower response makes queues longer. Longer queues make the system appear weaker. Apparent weakness invites opportunistic attacks and panic behavior. Panic amplifies load. Amplified load worsens degradation. The incident becomes self-thickening. Cloud concentration makes this worse because it increases blast radius: a single degraded service creates correlated trouble across many institutions at once, making it harder to separate signal from noise, and harder to separate signal from noise is how everyone chooses the conservative posture at once.

A mid-tier bank's treasury desk experiences cloud concentration as a mismatch between cutoff time and queue time. Outgoing obligations still exist. Incoming expectations still exist. The desk relies on intraday credit and predictable posting to avoid holding excess cash. The moment posting becomes uncertain, behavior changes. It hoards. It shortens terms. It delays outflows where it can, even if delaying outflows damages relationships, because missing a cutoff damages survival. Multiply that behavior across banks and the system tightens without any policy rate move. The public will describe it as "banks got strict." The reality is that cloud triage translated into monetary contraction through timing uncertainty.

A corporate payroll team experiences the same concentration as humiliation. The file is submitted. Confirmation is received. Then employees call because wages have not arrived. The payroll team is not in the incident channel. It is at the end of the blame chain. It has no authority to force completion, yet it is held responsible by people whose lives are organized around predictable receipt. This is how legitimacy is lost in practice: not through ideological arguments about money, but through repeated moments when ordinary completion becomes conditional and no one can name who is accountable. The most corrosive phrase a society can learn is "it is still processing" when "still processing" means "we do not know."

Cloud concentration is also a hierarchy problem because not all users experience a degraded dependency equally. Large institutions buy redundancy, pre-position failovers, maintain parallel stacks, negotiate priority support, and keep specialized personnel to intervene quickly. Smaller institutions cannot. When a shared dependency degrades, the large institution has better visibility and faster escalation paths. The small institution waits behind the same queue it serves. The result is a distributional event: some actors regain completion faster than others. Defenders call this rational because scale buys performance. The public experiences it as favoritism because the state promised equal treatment in discharge. Equal treatment in discharge is one of the few moral claims money can credibly make. Once that claim is visibly false, politics arrives quickly, and politics will not accept "the contract terms were different" as a justification.

The mechanism of concentration is not mysterious, but it is layered, which is why it hides. A modern payment life cycle runs through identity and authentication, message validation, routing, fraud controls, posting, reconciliation, settlement, logging, monitoring, and incident coordination. Each layer can be provided by different services, but operationally those services often live inside the same small set of providers and the same small set of regions because cost and performance incentives reward consolidation. Institutions move workloads for agility, adopt managed services for convenience, standardize identity because it reduces overhead, centralize key management because security teams demand it, centralize monitoring because incident response needs unified telemetry. Each step is rational. The combined outcome is concentration of the system's ability to operate into a narrow set of levers. When those levers misbehave, the system degrades not in clean outage but in partial completion, and partial completion is where the system becomes politically dangerous because it is unfair without admitting it is being unfair.

The strongest defense of cloud migration is real: large providers invest in security and redundancy at a scale individual institutions cannot match. They patch faster. They hire deeper teams. They run multiple locations. They absorb surges. They standardize. These arguments are not wrong. The failure is to treat them as sufficient. Redundancy inside a provider is not redundancy across providers. Multiple locations are not independent if they share control plane dependencies. Elasticity does not help if authentication fails. Deep security does not help if incident response prioritizes the wrong workloads. Standardization does not help if it becomes correlated behavior and correlated behavior creates correlated failure.

The test that matters is not calm performance. The test is political pressure. Under political pressure, private operators protect themselves first. Protecting themselves often means conservative throttling, conservative disclosure, and conservative restoration priorities. Those choices are rational for liability. They can be disastrous for sovereign continuity. Sovereign continuity means the ability to keep discharge usable for the society on schedule, especially for wages, benefits, and essential commerce. If restoration priorities are set by private incident playbooks and private liability calculations, the state's promise becomes contingent on a contract the public never saw and never consented to.

The central strategic question becomes blunt: who controls the queue when the queue becomes the economy. The queue is where payment becomes real. In calm, the queue is invisible and treated as plumbing. In stress, the queue becomes a rationing device, and rationing devices are political. If the state does not control or pre-govern queue behavior, the state will be blamed for outcomes it did not choose. Blame forces improvisation. Improvisation is crude: blanket freezes, emergency mandates that harm commerce, punitive measures that satisfy anger and worsen fragility. The path from cloud degradation to policy overreach is short because the public does not tolerate "a vendor issue" when wages do not arrive.

A benefits-day incident shows how cloud concentration forces a fiscal decision within hours. Disbursements are scheduled on a day that is part of the social contract, not a discretionary favor. A degraded dependency delays posting unevenly: some recipients are paid, others are delayed. The minister faces a legitimacy crisis: citizens compare outcomes and conclude the state chose winners. The state did not choose winners. The queue did. Yet the state must answer. The minister is offered two options. Wait for completion and accept anger now, or initiate emergency alternative disbursements and accept reconciliation chaos later. Emergency disbursements can create duplicates. Duplicates can be recovered later, but recovery itself becomes political because recovering "overpayments" looks like punishment for a failure the citizen did not cause. The minister chooses between anger now and scandal later, and neither choice restores the simple condition the public actually wants: predictable completion. The failure mode has become a political trap.

A sovereign external payment shows how the same incident becomes a credibility event beyond the border. A sovereign has an external obligation due. The instruction is scheduled early to avoid cutoff risk. The instruction is accepted, then stalls because the authorization layer is degraded and the validation routine has shifted into conservative mode. The payment is not rejected. It is pending. In a market, pending is uncertainty, and uncertainty has a price. Counterparties widen terms immediately because they cannot wait for narrative clarity. The sovereign now faces a choice: attempt to reroute through alternate channels, which may be slower and more expensive, or accept the delay and absorb reputational damage. Fundamentals did not change. Execution did. Yet markets reprice on execution because execution is what makes promises real. Cloud concentration becomes a channel by which technical incident becomes sovereign spread.

A third scene shows how the incident becomes an industrial shock without ever being called "a crisis." A port operator will not release high-value cargo until payment is credited under the operator's rules. The buyer's bank shows "sent" and cannot show "credited." The seller's bank will not ship the next tranche until it sees funds. Insurers tighten because documentation is now incomplete. The transaction falls into exception handling across multiple institutions simultaneously. Cargo sits. Demurrage accumulates. Supply schedules slip. A factory manager sees missing components as downtime, not as "latency." Workers are sent home. Retail prices rise weeks later, and the public experiences it as inflation and incompetence, not as cloud triage. The failure mode is transmission: an execution interruption becomes a production interruption and then becomes a political narrative that blames the state even if the state never touched the technical layer that failed.

Officials often respond to this reality by declaring "sovereign cloud" or "national infrastructure" as the answer. The instinct is understandable: bring choke points under domestic control. The risk is that "sovereign" becomes a label without capacity. Building truly sovereign infrastructure requires deep technical competence, disciplined procurement, governance structures that prevent contractor capture, and insulation from politicized interference with security posture. Many states will not have these conditions. They will produce a domestic version of concentration risk with weaker operational excellence. Sovereign capacity is not a flag on a server rack. It is the ability to keep the queue moving under stress. A weak sovereign cloud is not sovereignty. It is a new dependency with fewer exits.

The redesign doctrine therefore starts with architecture, not slogans. If cloud concentration is a single point of failure, then the system must build true multi-homing for critical functions. True multi-homing is not "we can migrate in theory." It is active-active or at least warm standby with tested cutover for identity, key management, routing, and core settlement posting. Tested means practiced under realistic load, not demonstrated in a slide. The monetary state must be able to force the cutover decision when necessary, because cutover is itself a rationing decision: some transactions will be lost, duplicated, or delayed in the transition. If the state does not control cutover doctrine, the state does not control the moment when the economy's completion state changes.

Multi-homing also requires a sober acceptance that certain managed conveniences are political liabilities. Convenience is not free. Convenience is dependency. Dependency is tolerable when it is explicit, priced, and governed. Dependency becomes dangerous when it is hidden, assumed, and treated as technical. Identity-as-a-service is convenient until identity becomes the gate at which commerce is held. Key management-as-a-service is convenient until key management becomes the point at which authorization is frozen. Centralized observability is convenient until observability becomes the bottleneck that delays diagnosis and forces rumor. The redesign doctrine does not require rejecting managed services. It requires refusing to allow managed services to become ungovernable sovereign levers.

Queue governance is the second redesign principle because the queue is the economy when stress arrives. Queue policies should prioritize essentials by design: payroll, benefits, critical supply chains, and settlement obligations that prevent cascading defaults. Prioritization must be rule-bound and pre-announced because improvisation looks like favoritism. If prioritization is not pre-announced, officials will avoid it for fear of scandal, and the system will ration randomly. Random rationing is the fastest path to political rupture because it creates the sense the state has become arbitrary. The technical layer will insist it cannot prioritize because it does not know the semantic meaning of transactions. That is precisely why governance must be designed: transaction criticality must be representable in a form the system can enforce without inviting fraud, and representable criticality is a governance decision, not an engineering detail.

Measured disclosure is the third redesign principle because in concentrated infrastructure events, disclosure is stabilization. Lack of disclosure creates rumor. Rumor triggers hoarding. Hoarding deepens the incident's economic footprint. Private operators fear disclosure because disclosure increases liability and invites attack. The state must design disclosure regimes that protect useful transparency without creating careless exposure. This is not solved by demanding "more transparency" as a moral good. It is solved by defining what incident information must be shared, with whom, on what timeline, under what secure channels, and with what legal protections. If incident disclosure is not governable, incident response will be slow, and slow is the same as expensive in settlement terms.

Degraded-mode capability is the fourth redesign principle because the public does not accept "we had an outage" as a reason for missing wages. Degraded-mode capability includes emergency settlement windows, emergency posting procedures that preserve later reconciliation, emergency liquidity policies that account for posting delays, and rules that prevent recipients from being criminalized for duplicates created by emergency disbursement. Degraded mode is not a technical fallback alone. It is a legitimacy fallback. The public does not forgive the initial failure. It can forgive a response that is coherent and bounded. It does not forgive a response that adds humiliation to delay.

Supervisory realism is the fifth redesign principle. Supervisors must stop treating operational resilience as a checklist and start treating it as a dependency map. Which critical payment and settlement functions share which providers. Which identity layers are shared across banks. Which key management services are single points. Which routing edges are common. Which monitoring and incident coordination stacks are common. Which contractual terms create veto points. Without this map, stress tests are incomplete because they simulate capital and liquidity without simulating completion. The system can be well-capitalized and still fail socially if it cannot settle. The failure mode is not insolvency. The failure mode is suspended discharge.

Procurement as monetary governance is the sixth redesign principle. Vendor contracts are not administrative details. They define who can see what, who can compel what, who can audit what, who owns logs, who controls keys, who decides escalation, who carries liability, who can terminate service, under what conditions, and with what notice. Those are power clauses. If procurement is handled as cost optimization, the state optimizes itself into dependency and discovers the price during crisis. If procurement is handled as sovereignty architecture, the state reduces the risk that private operators become accidental sovereigns.

A single clause can decide whether failure is governable. If logs cannot be accessed quickly by designated public authorities under secure emergency procedures, diagnosis slows and rumor dominates. If incident escalation is "best efforts" rather than a defined obligation, restoration priorities become private. If termination rights exist without continuity requirements for essential functions, the state has accepted sudden execution loss by contract. If key custody is controlled by a third party without emergency override arrangements, a key management fault becomes a sovereign freeze. None of these clauses are "technology." They are constitutional levers disguised as procurement language, and they decide who controls the queue under stress.

The chapter's counterargument deserves respect because many officials hold it and because parts of it are true. Concentration, they say, is not the problem; legacy is the problem. A few high-quality providers are safer than thousands of mediocre server rooms. Standardization and managed services reduce fragility. Centralization enables deep security. The private sector innovates faster. The state should not attempt to run infrastructure. The response is not to deny the operational gains. The response is to insist on the real test: what happens when liability fear tightens and when the incident is ambiguous enough that nobody wants to be the one who let a fraudulent payment through. In that moment, safety-first postures create system-wide throttling. Throttling is rationing. Rationing is governance. If rationing is conducted by private operators without public doctrine, the system fails politically even if it survives technically.

The final revelation is that cloud concentration changes the meaning of backstop. A central bank can backstop liquidity. A treasury can backstop credit. Neither can backstop execution if execution is throttled by infrastructure dependency. The new backstop must include operational backstop: the capacity to keep the queue moving, to keep discharge functioning, to keep settlement finality defendable even when a critical dependency degrades. That is a constitutional chamber of the monetary state because it is where sovereignty becomes operational in the most literal way: can the state make its own payments system finish.

This chamber also shows why the sequence that follows is not a collection of separate risks but a single architecture of vulnerability. Cloud concentration narrows choke points. Cyber conflict targets choke points. Machine markets can synchronize retreat at the same time choke points throttle. Proof shock attacks identity and authorization, which are already concentrated. Climate and collateral re-rank eligibility, which becomes more dangerous when custody and posting are brittle. Legal discontinuity turns technical disruption into forum fights over finality. The order's next failures will not be polite. They will be fast. They will be uneven. They will be blamed on officials who did not know the contracts they inherited were power documents.

CLOSING DOCTRINE

Cloud concentration is a monetary failure mode because it relocates operational sovereignty into a narrow set of technical and contractual choke points that can ration completion without declaring emergency. Availability is not usability: latency, throttling, and intermittent authentication convert routine flows into exceptions, exceptions convert time into scarcity, and scarcity converts delay into liquidity stress and solvency triage as cutoffs approach. The decisive levers are identity, queue control, key management, telemetry access, and incident coordination, because those layers decide who can speak to the system, who can finish, and how quickly the state can govern response. Concentration produces unequal completion because the largest actors buy redundancy and priority while smaller actors wait in exception lanes, turning technical incidents into legitimacy incidents. The redesign imperative is operational backstop: true multi-homing for critical functions, rule-bound queue prioritization for essentials, governable incident disclosure, maintained degraded-mode procedures, supervisory dependency mapping, and procurement treated as sovereignty architecture, because a state that cannot make its settlement perimeter finish on schedule does not fully control its monetary position.

CHAPTER 39
CYBER CONFLICT
PAYMENTS AS A BATTLEFIELD

The first sign is not a siren. It is a small, irritating asymmetry that begins to show up in the places where professionals hide annoyance because annoyance is how you admit you are not yet afraid. A bank's fraud model spikes for a narrow band of transactions that look ordinary: familiar merchants, familiar ticket sizes, familiar timing. A payments operator sees a rising percentage of soft fails, the kind that resolve after retry, and assumes network weather. A treasury desk sees a delay in an expected credit and assumes a counterparty's internal cutoffs slipped. A merchant processor notices an unusual pattern of reversals and assumes a temporary integration fault. Nothing here reads as an attack because modern systems produce noise constantly, and the most reliable way to miss a real event is to insist that real events announce themselves. The machine continues to function. That is the point. A payments battlefield does not need to destroy the system. It needs to introduce doubt into completion and to force the system into a defensive posture that rationing can exploit.

"The easiest way to break trust is to make truth expensive." (incident commander's remark, internal postmortem)

Cyber conflict becomes monetary conflict when it targets the conversion points where intention becomes discharge. An adversary does not need to steal balances to inflict national harm. It can slow posting, disrupt reconciliation, poison identity confidence, corrupt logs, trigger protective throttles, manufacture enough ambiguity that every gatekeeper chooses caution at once, and then let the defenders do the rest. Caution does not look like attack. It looks like compliance. It looks like integrity. It looks like risk management. Yet in a payments system, synchronized caution is contraction, and contraction is political. The system's most dangerous cyber vulnerability is not that it is digital. The vulnerability is that it must be fast to be economically useful and must be conservative to be legally defensible, and an adversary can force it to choose between those goals under pressure, then harvest the second-order consequences that arrive when completion is no longer routine.

The old mental model treated cyber as theft, sabotage, and espionage. That model is incomplete because it describes outcomes that can be counted and insured. The new model treats cyber as coercion through usability. If wages do not arrive on time, if firms cannot rely on suppliers being paid, if banks cannot rely on settlement finishing before cutoffs, the state faces political instability regardless of whether any money was "lost." People do not measure monetary order by balance-sheet integrity. They measure it by completion, which is the social fact money exists to manufacture. Cyber conflict that degrades completion attacks the state's legitimacy at the exact point where legitimacy is experienced as daily life, and it does so with an ambiguity that turns every explanation into a fight, because the public has learned that "technical problem" can also be a mask for favoritism, incompetence, or deliberate pressure.

The payments battlefield is attractive because it is deniable, scalable, and distributive. A visible strike is escalatory. A payment degradation can be framed as outage, weather, technical error, criminal fraud, or vendor mishap, and the system itself helps the attacker by offering plausible narratives that feel familiar enough to delay decisive response. It is scalable because a small exploitation at a shared dependency can create correlated effects across many institutions without revealing a single dramatic breach. It is distributive because the pain falls unevenly: smaller firms, weaker banks, and households living close to the margin suffer first from delay and uncertainty, while large institutions can buy resilience, reroute, and absorb buffers. Uneven pain is political fuel. An adversary does not need to break the system equally. It needs to create enough unevenness that ordinary people conclude either that the state has lost control or that insiders are being protected. The accusation can be false and still be politically lethal if the machine's behavior becomes inexplicable and lopsided.

The core proposition is strict: in a modern monetary order, the line between operational resilience and national security has dissolved, because payments are no longer a back-office function. Payments are the state's daily proof that it can close obligations and allocate time. When that proof is interrupted, the state must choose between admitting weakness and improvising control. Improvised control often arrives as restrictions that harm commerce, and harmed commerce becomes public anger, and public anger becomes pressure for retaliation, and retaliation invites further attack. Cyber conflict is therefore not an "IT risk." It is a governance trap with escalation dynamics, and those dynamics accelerate when defenders fear scandal more than they fear delay, because scandal fear produces the conservative posture that turns partial disruption into economic tightening.

To understand why this battlefield is new, hold one fact in view: modern payments are sequences of conditional states that only look like finality from the outside. Authorization is not posting. Posting is not clearing. Clearing is not settlement. Settlement is not discharge. Each stage has its own controls and its own veto points. An adversary does not need to break the final stage if it can break confidence in the intermediate stages, because intermediate uncertainty forces conservative behavior at the edges, and the edges are where commerce lives. When commerce begins to treat "sent" as "maybe," the economy tightens itself. The state's problem is that the public does not recognize the stages; the public recognizes only the promise. That mismatch between the hidden ladder and the visible promise is exactly what cyber coercion exploits.

The first category of payment-state cyber conflict is denial of settlement, which is rarely total and therefore rarely called what it is. The attacker's objective is to push the system into triage by degrading one or more choke points: identity, routing, validation, queuing, reconciliation, or logging. The system responds by throttling, imposing holds, tightening fraud filters, increasing manual review, and instructing staff to treat anomalies as suspicious. Each response is rational inside its own mandate. In aggregate, the responses create delay. Delay forces liquidity hoarding. Liquidity hoarding tightens credit. Tightened credit slows the economy. The attacker achieves macro effect without needing to steal. The state, if it responds publicly, risks panic. If it responds quietly, it risks looking incompetent when the public experiences repeated pending states that used to be rare.

A treasury floor scene makes denial-of-settlement coercion concrete without theatrics. A mid-tier bank is not "hacked" in the cinematic sense. It is being exhausted. Authentication retries rise, which means logins take longer and automated authorizations time out. Payments queue lengthens, which means posting lags behind submission. The bank's operations team increases staffing and adds overtime. Staffing cannot shorten a queue that is throttled upstream. Outgoing cutoffs approach. The treasury desk begins hoarding intraday liquidity and delaying noncritical outflows to protect survival. It delays vendor payments that do not trigger immediate contractual penalties and prioritizes obligations that would create immediate default. It also shortens intraday credit offered to smaller counterparties because it cannot tolerate uncertainty about incoming timing. A small firm that has never thought about intraday credit experiences this as "the bank is suddenly difficult." The small firm then starts paying earlier, holding more cash, reducing purchases, postponing hires. Multiply that behavior across thousands of firms and denial-of-settlement becomes a recession lever without an official rate change.

The second category is integrity attack: not slowing the machine, but making the machine doubt itself. The attacker aims at the system's ability to prove what happened, because proof is what makes a ledger governable. It can corrupt audit trails, poison logs, tamper with time synchronization so events cannot be ordered reliably, or degrade identity attribution so the system cannot say who authorized what. If the system cannot trust its own records, it cannot reconcile, cannot assign liability, cannot enforce penalties, and cannot prove completion. The system then chooses safety-first behavior: freeze, rollback, halt certain classes of flow, or demand additional proofs for everything. A payments system can tolerate fraud losses. It cannot tolerate uncertainty about whether its record is reliable, because record reliability is the basis for adjudication. A well-timed integrity scare can force conservative posture that halts discharge and thereby creates macro disruption, while defenders argue about whether they are under attack or merely "experiencing inconsistencies."

Integrity coercion is not always about tampering with balances. It is often about destroying confidence in reconciliation. Reconciliation is the quiet act that turns "we think it happened" into "we agree it happened." If reconciliation teams cannot certify, counterparties treat posting as provisional. Provisional posting changes behavior: merchants hold inventory, custodians hold transfers, banks refuse to redeploy credits, clearing participants demand more margin, and treasurers hoard more cash. The attacker's goal is not to make the ledger false in every entry. The goal is to make the ledger arguable, because arguable is what forces conservative behavior at scale. Arguable is also what forces committees, and committees are slow, and slowness is the same as contraction when the economy is organized around next-day completion.

The third category is coercion through compliance. Modern corridors include screening, AML controls, purpose coding, identity attestations, beneficial ownership routines, and strict anomaly detection. An attacker can exploit these by generating patterns that trigger over-compliance. It can create false positives at scale, causing legitimate flows to be held. It can manipulate data fields so transactions look suspicious. It can generate volumes that overwhelm manual review teams. The compliance apparatus tightens thresholds to protect itself. Tight thresholds create more holds. Holds create more panic. Panic creates more suspicious behavior because firms reroute and restructure, which looks like evasion. The system becomes trapped in a feedback loop where the compliance perimeter becomes the attack surface, and the defender's own integrity posture becomes the vector of economic disruption.

A manufacturer's finance team sees this first as a vague message: additional review required. The team cannot accelerate review because review is upstream. The supplier begins demanding prepayment. Prepayment is not merely a term change; it is a working-capital shock. The manufacturer draws on credit more often. The bank tightens the line because anomalies and delays now appear in cash flow patterns, and cash flow patterns are what credit models consume. The manufacturer cuts production to avoid inventory commitments it cannot finance. Workers are idled. Prices rise later. A politician calls it greed. A household calls it unfair. The attacker calls it success, because it has forced the defender to impose economic pain through its own compliance machine. Nothing in that chain required stealing money. The weapon was the defender's fear of being blamed for letting bad flows through.

The fourth category is targeted disruption at translators and bridges. In a splintering system, translators are the institutions and service layers that convert one regime's legibility into another's. They are the new choke points and therefore the cheapest targets. Attackers target them because degrading the translator has higher leverage than degrading a single bank. If a translator is degraded, thousands of legitimate flows become exceptions. Exceptions become delays. Delays become working-capital stress. Working-capital stress becomes macro stress. Translators also face concentrated liability, which makes them quick to throttle and quick to tighten, which turns a partial incident into broad rationing. The state cannot assume translators will behave as public utilities in crisis. They behave as liability managers. A cyber actor counts on that, because liability management looks like prudence and functions like choke.

A logistics and trade scene shows why translator targeting feels like "inflation" months later and like "no one knows why" in the middle. A buyer has goods moving through a hub, insured and financed under contracts that assume settlement in predictable windows. The translator corridor that normally handles proof packets is degraded. Payments that would have been routine become exceptions. Goods are not released because release rules require credited funds. Storage costs accrue. Insurance premiums adjust. The supplier changes terms because the supplier's own financing depends on timely receipt. The buyer reduces orders. That reduction is not ideology. It is time scarcity. Later, shortages appear. Prices rise. Politicians argue about causes. The attacker has forced a supply chain contraction through payment uncertainty, and the contraction looks like a market phenomenon rather than a hostile act.

The fifth category is data poisoning: not breaking the pipeline, but corrupting the signals that govern it. Payment operations and fraud prevention rely on models and rule engines. These systems are only as reliable as the data they ingest. Attackers can manipulate data to widen false positives, lock out legitimate users, approve fraudulent flows that then generate backlash, or trigger systemic tightening by creating patterns that look like coordinated criminal activity. Even without model exploitation, the attacker can create transaction patterns that cause risk committees to tighten globally. If risk committees tighten globally, liquidity disappears even in unaffected institutions because everyone moves to defensive posture at once. Cyber conflict targeting data thus becomes market conflict: it can synchronize caution and therefore synchronize contraction, and it does so by forcing defenders to distrust their own instruments of trust.

A sixth category, increasingly central, is identity capture and identity doubt. Payment systems assume identity as stable substrate: a customer is who the system says they are, a bank is who the network says it is, an instruction is authentic because credentials validate. If identity is compromised, defenders respond by tightening verification and reducing automated approvals. Tightening verification increases friction for legitimate users and pushes more activity into exception handling. Exception handling increases delay. Delay imposes economic cost. The attacker does not need to steal every identity. It needs to compromise enough identity signals that the system becomes uncertain about attribution. Attribution uncertainty forces conservative posture. Conservative posture is the attacker's macro lever because it turns the economy's speed into the economy's fragility.

A seventh category is time manipulation and sequence corrosion. Payment systems are sequence machines. They rely on ordering to reconcile, net, settle, and defend finality. If an attacker can corrupt or destabilize time synchronization, even partially, it can produce inconsistencies that force defenders to halt processes because they cannot prove ordering. A defender that cannot prove ordering cannot prove who owes what at which moment. The defender then chooses the only posture that avoids future scandal: stop and verify. Verification is slow. Slow is contraction. Time manipulation is therefore an integrity attack that does not need to alter balances; it only needs to make sequence uncertain. Sequence uncertainty becomes finality uncertainty. Finality uncertainty is where credit shrinks into caution.

The battlefield is shaped by political reality: attribution is slow and deniability is high. States hesitate to accuse. Institutions hesitate to disclose. Operators hesitate to admit breach. In that hesitation, rumor flourishes. Rumor is not neutral. Rumor makes actors hoard and reroute. Rerouting creates anomalies. Anomalies trigger compliance holds. Holds create delays. Delays create more rumor. The system becomes self-thickening, and the attacker's work is reduced because the system amplifies uncertainty for free. The most damaging cyber campaigns are often those that make defenders argue about whether an attack is happening while the economy begins to tighten, because tightening becomes visible to households before any official statement exists, and households fill silence with betrayal narratives that are emotionally rational even if technically wrong.

A critical distinction is the difference between a cyber incident and a cyber campaign. An incident is discrete. A campaign is a pattern designed to condition the system's behavior over time. Campaigns are more dangerous because they teach institutions to live in defensive posture. Defensive posture reduces efficiency and increases friction. Friction is a tax. A campaign can impose a tax without ever winning a battle. This is how payment-state coercion can be sustained: intermittent disruptions, intermittent anomalies, intermittent integrity scares, each one too small to trigger political escalation, together large enough to change how banks lend, how firms plan, and how households trust. The system survives each episode and becomes weaker as a result. That weakening is strategic effect.

A supervisor's view of campaigns is bleak because conventional macro tools miss the mechanism. Supervisors are trained to think in capital, liquidity, and conduct. A campaign changes those variables indirectly by changing behavior. If banks expect disruptions, they hold more liquidity and lend less. If firms expect delayed payments, they demand prepayment and carry larger buffers. If households expect wages might arrive late, they reduce discretionary spending. The macro environment tightens. Supervisors may respond by easing prudential constraints to encourage lending. Easing does not restore trust in execution. The problem is not risk appetite. The problem is completion confidence. A policy rate can be lowered. It cannot lower uncertainty about whether payments will clear if the attacker can live inside the system's daily noise and keep forcing defenders into cautious posture.

Cyber conflict interacts with infrastructure concentration in a reinforcing way. Concentration increases blast radius and creates correlated failure. Campaigns exploit correlated failure because correlated failure creates confusion and confusion slows response. Response slows. Queues lengthen. Institutions throttle. Throttling produces cutoff triage. Cutoff triage produces uneven completion. Uneven completion produces political anger. Political anger produces policy overreach. Policy overreach produces fragility. The architecture becomes a ladder of escalation: the attacker climbs by forcing defenders into blunt measures that harm themselves. The attacker's best weapon is not code; it is the defender's inability to accept bounded imperfection without reaching for dramatic restrictions that fracture commerce.

A central bank operations scene shows the dilemma at the apex without romanticism. Settlement delays appear across multiple participants. The central bank must decide whether to extend windows, provide additional intraday liquidity, relax certain operational requirements temporarily, or keep strict rules to protect integrity. Extending windows reduces default risk but increases uncertainty about finality, which can widen risk spreads and reduce willingness to intermediate. Providing liquidity prevents insolvency but does not help if the queue is blocked by authentication and validation. Relaxing operational requirements can keep flows moving but risks fraud and later scandal. Keeping strict rules protects integrity but creates mass delay that becomes political rupture. The central bank is forced to choose among bad options with incomplete information because attribution is uncertain and the incident's scope is unclear. The essence of the cyber battlefield is that it forces allocation decisions under ambiguity, and ambiguity is the defender's weakness because the defender must be accountable while the attacker can be deniable.

The public's experience of that dilemma is simple and ruthless. People do not care whether windows were extended. They care whether wages arrived and whether their card transactions worked. When the public sees inconsistency—some people paid, some not; some merchants credited, some not—the public concludes unfairness. Unfairness is an accelerant. A cyber actor understands this and aims not necessarily to turn everything off, but to create unevenness: enough failures to feel personal, enough successes to feel selective, enough silence to feel suspicious. Unevenness produces narrative. Narrative produces anger. Anger produces pressure for visible action. Visible action under cyber ambiguity is often miscalibrated, and miscalibration is how escalation becomes likely.

The state's immediate temptation is to treat cyber conflict as a secret war: classify, conceal, contain. Concealment can prevent panic. Concealment can also prevent the public from understanding why completion changed. When completion changes and the public receives no explanation, the public invents one. Invented explanations include corruption, favoritism, and incompetence. Those explanations damage legitimacy. Legitimacy damage makes future crisis management harder because the public's default assumption becomes betrayal. A state that conceals too much and a state that discloses too much both face danger. The governing problem is to design a disclosure posture that preserves trust without handing adversaries a map, and to do it before crisis, because disclosure designed under pressure becomes theater and theater rarely stabilizes a queue.

A second temptation is to militarize payments oversight in a way that harms commerce: blanket freezes, aggressive de-risking, broad controls that treat all anomalies as hostile. These moves can reduce some attack surfaces. They can also push legitimate commerce into seam markets and alternative corridors, reducing visibility and increasing gray routing. Gray routing increases unpredictability. Unpredictability increases false positives. False positives increase holds. Holds increase delay. Delay increases political anger. The state ends up fighting itself, and an attacker counts on that because a state that overreacts creates its own disruption and fractures its own legitimacy. The battlefield becomes a mirror: the defender's fear is weaponized as the defender's most damaging action.

A third temptation is to outsource response to private operators and treat it as technical. Private operators often have the best technical skill. They also have different incentives: liability minimization, contractual compliance, reputational containment. Those incentives produce conservative throttling, slow disclosure, and restoration priorities that favor large clients. The state cannot accept this as a private matter because the payments queue is a public allocation device under stress. If the state allows private incentives to govern queue allocation, the state will be blamed for outcomes it did not choose and could not control, and blame will force a political response later that may be worse than early coordination. The doctrine of payment defense therefore begins with an assertion of public authority over the sequence of completion, even if private actors operate the tools.

Cyber conflict demands a doctrine of operational sovereignty in defense. Operational sovereignty here means the ability to keep essential payment life functioning even when attack and uncertainty are present. That ability rests on five elements. The first is segmentation of critical payment functions so compromise of a peripheral channel does not contaminate the settlement spine. The second is hardened identity and key management with clear emergency override procedures that are auditable and limited. The third is queue governance that can prioritize essentials under stress without becoming an easy fraud target. The fourth is telemetry rights and rapid information sharing under secure protocols, because without shared visibility response becomes rumor-driven. The fifth is pre-negotiated coordination among central bank operations, major participants, and critical service providers so crisis decisions can be made quickly with known authorities and known responsibilities.

The hardest element is queue governance because it is where defense meets legitimacy. A queue policy that treats everything equally invites random rationing under load. Random rationing produces legitimacy collapse because it looks like arbitrariness. A queue policy that prioritizes essentials invites fraud attempts to masquerade as essentials. The system must make essentialness representable without being easily forged. That requires careful design: authenticated priority channels, strict eligibility rules, priority tagging tied to regulated originators, and post-event audit that punishes abuse without harming legitimate recipients. It also requires political doctrine about what counts as essential when the system is stressed, because essential is not only a technical label. It is a public promise about what society will protect first.

Degraded-mode doctrine is the second hard element because a campaign may never be fully "clean." The system may operate under persistent threat. The state must define what acceptable degraded mode looks like: which flows must remain finishable at all costs, which can be slowed, which can be temporarily constrained, and how to compensate those harmed by constraints. Without doctrine, every incident becomes improvisation, and improvisation becomes accusations of favoritism. A state that cannot explain degraded-mode priorities before crisis will be forced to explain them during crisis, which is the worst time to explain anything because everyone is angry, suspicious, and watching the machine misbehave in real time.

Legal and liability alignment is the third hard element because liability fear is the attacker's free amplifier. Private operators fear exposure for letting fraud through. Public officials fear scandal for allowing any abuse. In cyber conflict, zero fraud tolerance is not achievable without freezing the system, and freezing the system is itself a harm. The state must align legal frameworks and liability expectations to allow continuity-first behavior for essentials under defined rules, with defined audit and recovery processes. Without alignment, private actors choose conservative throttling and conservative throttling becomes macro disruption. Alignment is not leniency. Alignment is preventing liability posture from becoming the attacker's most reliable weapon.

The international dimension is the fourth hard element because border friction is the cheapest way to import scarcity. In a splintered order, cross-border payments run through translators and corridors that are easy targets. An attacker can disrupt trade settlement and force domestic scarcity without touching domestic retail rails. The state may keep domestic payments functioning while trade financing seizes. The public then experiences shortages and inflation and blames domestic policy. The attacker achieves macro effect through border disruption. This is why payment defense must include cross-border continuity for essentials and why emergency recognition matters: if perimeters cannot accept minimal proofs under stress, then a cyber campaign can exploit the border as a lever to force scarcity and political anger inside the state.

A sovereign-level scene makes border coercion feel real. A country relies on imported inputs for critical production. A cyber campaign degrades a translator corridor and triggers widespread compliance holds. Trade settlement is delayed. Suppliers demand prepayment in corridors perceived as safer. Domestic firms cannot prepay because working capital is tied up in receivables that are now clearing slower. Production slows. Domestic payments still "work" for retail users, which makes officials complacent until shortages appear. The economy contracts anyway because inputs do not arrive. The central bank can provide domestic liquidity. Domestic liquidity cannot buy external passage. The public experiences price rises and layoffs. The government faces protests. The attacker achieves political destabilization without touching domestic bank ledgers directly. Payments are supply lines, and supply lines are what war targets first even when there is no declared war.

Deterrence changes meaning in this environment. Attribution is slow and deniability is high. Threat alone cannot deter what cannot be named quickly. Deterrence must therefore include resilience, not only retaliation. If the state can keep essentials moving under attack, the attacker's strategic payoff declines. If the attacker cannot produce visible unevenness and humiliation, it cannot harvest political anger. Resilience is thus a deterrent tool: it reduces payoff. It is not softness. It is the denial of strategic effect. Yet resilience requires investment in boring capacities: dependency maps, redundant critical services, priority channels, auditable override procedures, incident disclosure frameworks, joint exercises that test coordination under ambiguity, and compensation rules that prevent emergency measures from becoming secondary scandals. This is what makes the doctrine difficult: it demands discipline in calm for a benefit that becomes visible only under stress.

The last truth is simple and harsh. A payment system is a public trust machine. Cyber conflict aims to make that machine either unfair or unreliable. Unfairness generates political rupture. Unreliability generates economic contraction. The attacker does not need to pick one. It can use small, repeated degradations to produce both. The state's response cannot be purely technical and cannot be purely political. It must be doctrinal: a defined way of choosing which obligations must remain finishable, a defined way of allocating time when time is scarce, and a defined way of preserving legitimacy when perfection is impossible, because perfection is not the goal under attack and pretending it is becomes the excuse for freezes that do more damage than the attacker ever could.

CLOSING DOCTRINE

Cyber conflict becomes monetary conflict when it targets the gates where intention becomes discharge: identity and authorization, routing and queue control, validation and compliance filtering, logging and auditability, custody and collateral mobility, and the sequence discipline that makes finality defendable. The objective is rarely total shutdown; the objective is triage and unevenness, because partial completion forces synchronized caution, converts delay into liquidity hoarding, and turns operational uncertainty into macro contraction and political anger without a single dramatic headline. Attackers coerce through usability by degrading choke points, poisoning proof, weaponizing false positives, exhausting translators, and relying on defenders' liability fear to produce conservative throttling that functions as cutoff triage. The state cannot backstop execution with liquidity alone; it must govern queue behavior for essentials, define degraded-mode priorities in advance, secure telemetry and coordination rights across critical operators, align liability so continuity-first decisions are possible under auditable rules, and build resilience as deterrence by denying strategic payoff. Payments are supply lines; if they cannot finish predictably under pressure, the monetary order loses legitimacy regardless of balance-sheet integrity.

CHAPTER 40
MACHINE MARKETS
FEEDBACK LOOPS AND FLASH LEGITIMACY

The first sell program does not arrive as a shout. It arrives as a change in the feel of the book, the kind of change only the people closest to execution notice before it becomes a headline. Quotes are still printing. Spreads are still there. Depth still exists in the way depth exists right before it disappears. A market-maker's screen shows a widening that should not be happening given the news flow, then a second widening, then a gap that looks like an error until you realize the gap is the new price. The desk does what it has been trained to do. It steps back. It reduces size. It protects itself. The venue does what it has been trained to do. It slows. It throttles. It widens bands. It triggers guardrails. Guardrails are the official face of stability. Guardrails are also the machine's way of confessing it cannot absorb the flow it is receiving.

The public story later is simple: a flash event. The professional story is uglier: the system briefly stopped believing its own prices, and when it stops believing its own prices it stops allocating risk, and when it stops allocating risk it stops financing itself. A modern monetary order can survive a day of bad news. It cannot survive a day when its market infrastructure produces prices that are not trusted as legitimate, because legitimacy in markets is the belief that prices emerge from a contest that is fair enough to be binding. When that belief cracks, funding becomes cautious, collateral becomes scarce, and sovereign backstops are invited into places they were never meant to govern.

Liquidity is not a quantity. It is a behavior. (senior market operator)

Machine markets are not a future problem. They are the present architecture of price, risk, and funding. The old narrative treated markets as human judgment aggregated by competition, the crowd as a stabilizer because no one mind could dominate. The current reality is that a growing share of market behavior is automated: algorithms that execute, algorithms that quote, algorithms that hedge, algorithms that detect anomalies, algorithms that enforce risk limits, algorithms that decide when to stop, and algorithms that decide what "stop" even means. Under calm conditions, this looks like efficiency. Under stress, it looks like synchronized retreat, because machines are not paid to be brave. They are paid to survive inside constraints, and constraints are designed to protect the institution, not the polity. The polity inherits the consequences because the polity depends on those institutions to intermediate its own debt, its own credit channels, and the ranking engine that governs collateral eligibility across the entire system.

The chapter's central question is not whether machines are good or bad. The question is where legitimacy lives when the market is an automated sequence, and what happens to sovereign capacity when legitimacy collapses faster than officials can name what collapsed. The traditional picture of crisis assumed you could watch prices move, infer fear, and respond with liquidity and signaling. Machine markets change the tempo and the target. They can move from ordinary to broken in minutes, and they can break without a single balance sheet failing, because what breaks first is the belief that the number is real enough to settle against. When that belief breaks, everything built on that belief becomes conditional: the value of collateral, the size of haircuts, the scale of margin, the willingness to make markets, the willingness to finance positions overnight, and the willingness of boards to permit risk at the exact moment the system needs risk-bearing to prevent collapse.

A market's price is not only information. It is a settlement instruction disguised as a number. When a price prints, collateral is revalued. Haircuts are recalculated. Margin is called. Risk limits are updated. Credit lines are adjusted. Credit committees are notified. Everything that matters in modern finance—the ability to borrow, to roll, to clear, to net, to settle—moves off that number. That means a price is a command issued indirectly, a command that forces people to move cash, sell assets, or retreat from lending. A market that produces prices no one trusts is not a market having a bad day. It is the system's ranking engine malfunctioning, because the ranking engine is what decides which claims can be upgraded into cash-like usability under stress and which claims become discounted and trapped.

Machine markets amplify fragility because they couple valuation and action more tightly than human markets ever could. In a human market, fear spreads through conversation, then through orders, and the friction of human coordination slows synchronization. In a machine market, fear spreads through code paths: a volatility spike triggers model updates, model updates trigger risk tightening, risk tightening triggers order withdrawal, order withdrawal triggers illiquidity, illiquidity triggers larger price moves, larger price moves trigger more volatility signals, and the loop closes faster than a committee can convene. This is not accidental. It is the logical outcome of building a system that treats speed as advantage and treats stop trading as safety. Safety tools are also discontinuity tools. Discontinuity is what creates legitimacy scars because discontinuity forces the system to admit that its own procedures cannot produce an authoritative price under pressure.

A desk manager's view captures the new reality without romance. The manager is not reading the news. The manager is reading constraints. The constraints say that when spreads widen past a threshold, quoting size must fall. When volatility rises past a threshold, the strategy must reduce exposure. When correlations break, the hedge must be recalculated, and when the hedge cannot be recalculated with confidence, the strategy must step away. Each rule is rational in isolation. Together, the rules mean that when stress rises, the market's suppliers of liquidity are obligated to stop supplying liquidity. The market then becomes a theater in which everyone observes liquidity evaporating as if it were weather, when it is actually pre-written policy embedded in risk engines and enforced without argument. The public will later ask why "the market" vanished. The answer is that it did not vanish. It complied.

This is why machine markets produce flash legitimacy events. Legitimacy fails before solvency because legitimacy depends on continuity, and continuity is what automated guardrails interrupt. When a venue halts, it is confessing it cannot process discovery in the moment discovery is needed most. When a venue reopens, it often does so with a discontinuous price, and discontinuity invites suspicion that someone moved first, that someone was protected, that someone exited through a door that was closed to others. Suspicion is corrosive because the market's claim to authority rests on the belief that everyone is bound by the same rules. Once participants believe rules are selectively applied, the market's prices become contestable. Contestable prices are toxic to collateralized finance because collateralized finance needs a number it can treat as binding without reopening the argument at every margin call.

The power map inside machine markets begins with a blunt observation: speed is not neutral. Speed decides who sees, who reacts, who is filled, and whose orders are treated as adverse selection. A system that measures and prices microseconds allocates advantage by infrastructure. That advantage is not merely profit. Under stress, it is survival. The fastest participants can pull quotes first, adjust risk first, avoid being the last liquidity provider standing, and avoid being harvested by those who know the book is about to thin. The slowest participants are left trading against a disappearing book, effectively paying a tax for being late. The system calls this efficiency. It functions as hierarchy. Hierarchy becomes political when the market's outputs determine retirement values, mortgage rates, corporate borrowing costs, and the state's own auction outcomes.

The second element of the power map is that liquidity provider is not a public title. It is a private strategy with private constraints. In calm, strategies compete and the market looks deep. In stress, strategies share a common reflex: reduce exposure. That shared reflex becomes synchronized retreat because they are trained on similar data, evaluated on similar metrics, constrained by similar risk committees, and threatened by the same margin regime. The market appears to run out of liquidity. What actually happened is that the market's liquidity suppliers followed their rules. The state can flood liquidity. It cannot force private strategies to quote if their constraints classify quoting as unacceptable risk. That is the mechanical face of a legitimacy crisis: the system cannot compel the behaviors it assumed would exist when it needed them.

The third element is that risk limits are now automatic. Automatic limits were built to prevent human hesitation from turning loss into catastrophe. They also prevent human discretion from stabilizing markets when discretion is needed most. In older regimes, a strong desk could choose to quote through turbulence, accept temporary pain, and profit later. In modern infrastructures, the desk may be prevented from doing so because a risk engine enforces shrinkage. The state can provide liquidity. It cannot easily force private risk engines to permit risk-taking. This is why policy can lose traction in flash events: the system is not asking for money first. It is refusing to intermediate, because intermediation has been redefined as unacceptable by a control path designed for self-preservation, not for public function.

The mechanism of flash legitimacy is a sequence of conversions that occur too quickly for narrative control. First, a price movement becomes a collateral movement. Second, a collateral movement becomes a haircut movement. Third, a haircut movement becomes a margin movement. Fourth, a margin movement becomes a liquidity movement, because margin calls demand cash or the nearest cash-like claim. When those conversions happen quickly, actors do not plan. They defend. Defense accelerates the conversion. The system turns price discovery into forced selling in minutes. The public sees a chart. Institutions experience a margin cascade that forces them to make decisions they will later describe as automatic because automatic is how you confess you had no choice.

A margin cascade begins with the apparently harmless fact that collateral is valued off market prices. That sounds obvious until you remember that in a machine market, prices can gap. When prices gap, collateral values collapse. When collateral values collapse, haircuts widen. When haircuts widen, borrowers must post more collateral or reduce positions. Reducing positions means selling. Selling into an illiquid book causes further price gapping. Further gapping causes further collateral collapse. The loop is familiar from older crises. The difference now is speed and automation. The loop can complete before a human can decide whether the initial price move was real, and once it completes, the question of real becomes irrelevant because the forced actions have already occurred.

The margin call is the crisis. (risk officer)

This is why machine markets are a failure mode of the monetary state, not merely of finance. When margin cascades occur, they force liquidation and therefore force loss allocation. Loss allocation is political when it spills into credit availability, employment, and sovereign borrowing conditions. The state is dragged in not because it wants to rescue speculators, but because a market infrastructure that cannot price without destabilizing collateral becomes a threat to the system's ability to fund itself and to fund the state itself. The backstop becomes constitutional power again, but now it is power applied to a machine whose failure happens at a tempo faster than public legitimacy can be maintained.

The first visibility at the apex rarely comes from the price print itself. It comes from the demands that follow the print. Requests for intraday liquidity rise sharply. Certain collateral becomes suddenly hard to finance, meaning it can only be financed at punitive haircuts or not at all. Dealers stop making two-way prices in instruments that were deep the day before. The system begins to behave as if it is in crisis even if no macro data has changed. That behavioral shift is the crisis. It is the market telling you that its internal rule-set has moved from discovery mode to defense mode, and defense mode is contagious because every institution's risk committee sees the same signals and reaches the same conclusion: do not be the last one standing.

Clearing becomes the hinge. Clearing is supposed to contain default. It does so by demanding margin and enforcing discipline. In calm, discipline looks prudent. In stress, it can look like gasoline. When volatility rises, margin models increase requirements. Increased requirements force participants to raise cash. They raise cash by selling assets. Selling assets raises volatility. Volatility triggers more margin. The clearing system is doing its job: protecting itself. The system as a whole experiences it as amplification. Clearing is a ranked-claims institution: it protects its own continuity first, then it protects members, then it protects the market. Under stress, that ranking becomes visible, and visibility of ranking is what produces legitimacy conflict, because those outside the protected perimeter conclude the game is designed to save insiders first.

The question becomes whether the monetary state wants system-wide stability to depend on private margin models updating at machine speed. If it does, it must accept that the system will tighten itself rapidly under uncertainty and that the state will be asked to choose between allowing liquidation and providing relief that looks like favoritism. If it does not, it must redesign how margin and liquidity interact, which is not a small reform. It is constitutional engineering because it changes who bears loss and when. There is no neutral option. There are only choices about where to place friction and how to distribute time when the machine is stressed.

Machine markets also change the meaning of fairness. Fairness is not a moral abstraction floating above microstructure. It is the belief that the rules of access, the rules of sequencing, and the rules of halting are stable enough that participants can plan and accept outcomes as binding. In a machine market, fairness becomes administrative reality: who receives data first, who can cancel orders faster, whose orders are protected by throttles, whose orders are rejected as too fast, whose trades are busted after the fact, whose losses are locked in. Each is a technical rule. Each is also a distribution rule. When a flash event occurs, those rules become politicized because the public and the legislature do not care about microstructure; they care about whether the machine favored the powerful.

A political staffer reading an incident report will see one sentence that matters: trades were canceled under predefined rules. Predefined rules are supposed to protect integrity. They also create the appearance that some participants were granted reversals while others were not. If reversals exist, the question becomes who qualified for reversal and why. That question is solvable in law and toxic in politics. The system can be correct and still lose legitimacy. Machine markets increase this risk because they produce more events where discontinuity and reversal are necessary to prevent collapse. Each necessary reversal creates another legitimacy scar. Scars accumulate into narrative. Narrative becomes political pressure. Political pressure demands reforms. Reforms that do not understand coupling can reduce liquidity further. The next flash event becomes more likely.

This is the meaning of flash legitimacy: legitimacy can fail instantly even when the system recovers operationally. The market may reopen. Prices may stabilize. Yet participants carry memory that the venue halted, that prints were discontinuous, that fills were uneven, that certain actors exited faster, that certain participants were forced to sell into a vacuum. That memory changes behavior. Behavior changes liquidity. Liquidity changes fragility. Fragility increases the probability of future halts. The system becomes conditioned. Conditioning is what turns a one-off flash event into a structural vulnerability, because conditioned participants step back earlier next time, and stepping back earlier makes the next event more likely to become a cliff.

The hinge is not a single date. It is the transition from human-centered discovery to machine-mediated discovery. Markets always had rules. The difference is that rules are now embedded in software and enforced at speed. The old hierarchy was social: relationship, reputation, and access. The new hierarchy is infrastructural: latency, co-location, privileged feeds, the ability to pay for visibility and the ability to pay for cancellation speed. The old crises unfolded over hours and days. The new crises can unfold in minutes. That tempo change matters because the state's legitimacy operates on human time. A minister cannot explain in minutes. A legislature cannot authorize in minutes. A court cannot adjudicate in minutes. The machine can break in minutes. The gap between machine time and political time is now a systemic risk, and it is not solved by better speeches, because the speech arrives after the margin call.

Machine markets also relocate discipline. In older regimes, discipline was imposed by capital and reputation: a firm that behaved recklessly would be punished by losses and counterparties. In machine regimes, discipline is imposed by models. Models embed assumptions about volatility, correlation, liquidity, and stress behavior. Models are calibrated on a past that may not resemble the future. When the world changes, models can impose discipline that is too tight, too fast, too synchronized. This is why relocation matters: discipline is no longer primarily the social consequence of bad judgment. It is the mechanical consequence of model design. Model design is governed by private incentives. Under stress, private incentives favor self-protection, and self-protection becomes systemically destabilizing when everyone does it at once.

A bank's risk committee becomes a sovereign-adjacent institution without admitting it. The committee does not issue law. It sets limits. Limits decide whether the bank supplies liquidity, finances clients, extends credit against collateral, clears trades, makes markets in government debt, warehouses inventory during volatility, or steps away to protect capital. In calm, limit-setting is prudence. In stress, limit-setting is allocation of time and money. If the committee tightens, the market tightens. If the market tightens, collateral becomes scarce. If collateral becomes scarce, the state's funding becomes more expensive. The committee's private decision becomes public consequence. That is a power map, and it is the kind of power map officials fail to see when they speak about "market sentiment" as if sentiment were the driver rather than the output.

Market infrastructure creates another power map. Venues set halting rules. Clearing venues set margin rules. Custodians and collateral agents set eligibility and mobility rules. Data vendors and feed standards set who sees what and when. None of these institutions are policy makers in a ceremonial sense. Yet they govern the system's ability to price, finance, and settle. Machine markets concentrate their authority because their rules are the code paths through which the entire system moves. When those rules trigger simultaneously, they can impose system-wide tightening that feels like a policy shock and is not. The state then faces a paradox: the system tightens without official tightening, and the public expects an explanation from officials who did not pull the lever that tightened.

Officials who treat market instability as mood will fail to govern. Mood is downstream. The upstream reality is microstructure coupled to margin. If you want to understand the next crisis, watch coupling points: how quickly prices move into haircuts, how quickly haircuts move into margin, how quickly margin moves into liquidation, how quickly liquidation moves into funding stress for institutions that provide basic market-making in the state's own debt, corporate credit, and essential commodity supply chains. This chain is the system's nervous system. Machine markets have made it faster and more sensitive. Sensitive nervous systems overreact. Overreaction is what a shock amplifies and what adversaries can exploit by pushing the system's reflexes rather than attacking its assets.

A sovereign funding scene makes the connection unavoidable. Government debt is often treated as anchor, the place where liquidity is deepest. Under machine stress, even deep markets can gap because providers who normally warehouse inventory step away when risk limits tighten. Bid-ask spreads widen. Auction outcomes become uncertain. Uncertain auction outcomes raise borrowing costs. Higher borrowing costs feed political pressure. Political pressure invites public blame of machines and speculators. Blame invites rule changes. Rule changes can reduce liquidity further if miscalibrated, because liquidity is behavior conditioned by rule expectations. The state discovers its funding is exposed to private machine behavior, and that exposure is sovereignty issue, because sovereignty depends on the ability to refinance without being held hostage by discontinuity in the ranking engine.

The social reach of machine markets is often misunderstood because the public imagines only speculators and traders. The more consequential channel is forced participation by institutions that are supposed to be boring. Pension funds, insurance portfolios, endowments, and liability-matching strategies do not trade because they want to win a day. They trade because governance requires it. Benchmark policies, rebalancing bands, duration targets, risk budgets, and mandate constraints force action in response to price changes. In a machine market, those governance rules collide with thinning books and automated retreat. The result is not a colorful trading story. It is the forced sale of public savings into discontinuity, followed by hearings and scandal and a political decision to regulate something that is not well understood.

A pension rebalancing desk experiences a flash event as a governance violation, not as a trading challenge. A board-approved policy mandates rebalancing bands. The policy exists to impose discipline and prevent drift. On an ordinary day, it stabilizes. On a flash day, it amplifies because the policy commands the desk to sell what is falling and buy what is rising to restore weights. The desk tries to execute. The book is thin. The book gapped. The venue halts. The halt freezes execution while liabilities do not freeze: benefits still must be paid; valuations still must be reported; risk committees still demand adherence to policy. When the venue reopens, the price is discontinuous. The desk completes the rebalance at worse levels. Losses become visible. The board asks why the desk sold at the bottom. The desk answers that it followed governance. The answer is correct and politically unacceptable, because governance that forces selling into a vacuum looks like incompetence even when it is rule compliance. This is flash legitimacy in the real economy: rules meant to protect beneficiaries become the channel through which beneficiaries are harmed, and the harm looks unfair because it is timed to the worst moment.

The interaction between passive structures and machine microstructure deepens fragility. Passive funds, systematic funds, and benchmark-driven mandates create predictable flows. Predictable flows are easy for fast actors to anticipate. Anticipation changes quoting behavior. When volatility rises, liquidity providers withdraw. Withdrawal makes flows more price-impacting. More price impact raises measured volatility. Measured volatility triggers more systematic selling. The loop closes. The public sees the market fell. The system experienced an automated demand to sell colliding with an automated refusal to provide liquidity. That collision is a design problem, not a mood.

A second institutional scene, inside a large asset manager, shows why the loop is not merely about panic but about risk budgets. The manager's mandate includes volatility control and drawdown limits. When volatility rises, the mandate forces reduction of exposure. The reduction is executed automatically across portfolios. The selling is not a judgment call; it is rule compliance. Rule compliance is the point: a machine market takes governance policies and turns them into synchronized orders. The result is that "prudence" becomes "pressure," and pressure becomes "gapping," and gapping becomes "margin," and margin becomes "forced selling" in instruments that were never meant to be traded like that. The manager can explain the logic to a committee. The committee will still face a public that saw retirement values fall in minutes and will demand a villain. The villain will be the machine, and once the machine is blamed, rule changes come fast, usually in the wrong places.

Corporate treasury feels the same loop from the opposite side, not as valuation but as funding conditions. A company that relies on short-term markets indirectly through banks experiences a flash event as sudden collateral tightening and sudden haircuts. Banks widen haircuts on collateral because prices are unstable and models demand caution. Haircuts widen. That makes liquidity more expensive. The treasurer hoards cash. Hoarding cash delays discretionary spending. Delayed spending shows up as postponed capital expenditure and postponed hiring. The corporate board blames uncertainty. The uncertainty is not philosophical. It is uncertainty about whether the system's prices will be stable enough tomorrow to support the same collateral terms. Machine markets transmit into the real economy not only through wealth effects, but through working-capital costs and the availability of short-dated credit, which are governed by haircuts that move with machine speed.

The clearing and settlement layer turns this into systemic danger because it turns price moves into obligations. Clearing protects itself by demanding margin. Margin is a claim on liquidity now. If margin demands rise quickly, participants must find cash now. Now is where panic lives, because now forces liquidation. Clearing venues are correct to protect themselves. Yet the system must decide whether it wants private self-protection to translate into public macro contraction at machine speed. If it does, it is choosing a system that will tighten brutally in the first minutes of stress. If it does not, it must build stabilizers that slow the feedback without destroying discipline. That stabilizer cannot be purely discretionary, because discretionary actions in flash events are accused of favoritism. The stabilizer must be rule-bound enough to be legitimate and flexible enough to be effective. That is the constitutional challenge, and it is constitutional precisely because it allocates pain and time under stress.

The most important paradox is that market safety tools can become funding weapons. Circuit breakers are designed to prevent disorderly trading. They can also concentrate loss on those who must trade during the halt window, including funds meeting redemptions, firms meeting margin calls, and dealers meeting settlement obligations. If trading is halted while liabilities continue to accrue, halts allocate time. Those with time can wait. Those without time are forced to act at reopen. Time is power. Halts allocate power. A state that authorizes halts is authorizing a distribution mechanism. If the distribution mechanism is not paired with liability-management tools, the system punishes those who cannot wait, and those who cannot wait are often ordinary institutions serving ordinary beneficiaries. That is where legitimacy breaks: not because halts exist, but because halts reveal that the system protects those who can delay and harms those who must finish.

Trade reversals are politically toxic for the same reason. Reversals exist to correct erroneous prints and preserve integrity. They also create the appearance that some participants were granted escape while others were not. The rules may be neutral. Outcomes will still be uneven because not all actors have equal ability to contest, equal ability to document, or equal ability to withstand loss while waiting for adjudication. Machine markets create more situations where reversals are invoked because discontinuities happen quickly and because automated strategies can create prints that look absurd in retrospect and therefore invite bust decisions. Each bust decision creates a scar. Scars accumulate into narrative. Narrative becomes political pressure. Political pressure can produce reforms that reduce liquidity. Reduced liquidity increases the probability that the next event will require another halt and another reversal. The system develops a self-harming cycle: it protects itself in the moment and loses legitimacy over time.

The doctrinal heart is the coupling chain: price to collateral, collateral to haircuts, haircuts to margin, margin to liquidation, liquidation to funding stress, funding stress to reduced market-making in the state's own debt and core credit channels. This chain is physical structure. A state that cannot see it cannot govern it. A state that sees it and refuses to engage it will be governed by it anyway, because the chain will impose its own policy in the form of forced tightening. A state that engages it must do so with humility about what can be controlled quickly and ruthlessness about what must be controlled structurally.

Structural control is not a vow to stop volatility. Volatility is not the enemy. The enemy is mechanical amplification that converts volatility into forced liquidation at a tempo that overwhelms liquidity supply. The objective should be to slow amplification so that liquidity suppliers can remain in the market without being punished instantly by adverse selection and without violating their own controls. That objective implies design choices: margin regimes that smooth increases rather than spike them, emergency liquidity that is automatic against high-grade collateral when volatility crosses defined thresholds, and microstructure rules that reduce the advantage of speed in ways that protect legitimacy. The objective is not moral anger at fast actors. The objective is to reduce the probability that liquidity suppliers vanish simultaneously because their constraint engines are built from similar assumptions and triggered by similar signals.

The second structural control point is collateral eligibility clarity under stress. If eligible collateral lists become ambiguous during flash events, liquidity freezes because actors cannot be sure what will be accepted tomorrow. Ambiguity forces hoarding of the highest-grade claims. Hoarding drains liquidity from everything else. The system becomes a hierarchy shock, and hierarchy shocks are destabilizing because they force sudden re-ranking of balance sheets. Eligibility is governance: it determines whether actors can upgrade holdings into usable settlement capacity during volatility. A state that wants stable markets must ensure that eligible collateral and haircut frameworks are defendable and predictable even when prices gap, because unpredictability of eligibility is the fastest way to transform a price move into a funding run.

The third control point is the design of halts in relation to funding obligations. If halts exist, the state must ensure halts do not trap participants in obligations they cannot manage. That means pairing halts with temporary funding relief mechanisms, with margin timing adjustments that prevent immediate forced selling at reopen, and with clear rules about how obligations accrue during halted periods. If halts freeze trading but not obligations, halts amplify stress. If halts are paired with liability management, halts can be stabilizing. The difference is governance: whether the system designed for the fact that time allocation becomes solvency allocation under stress.

The fourth control point is data and sequencing fairness. Fairness is the stability of access to information and the stability of sequencing rules. If the fastest participants can see and react materially earlier than others, those others will treat the market as predatory and will withdraw under stress, removing real-money liquidity that stabilizes. If withdrawal occurs, only the fastest remain, and the market becomes more reflexive and more brittle. Brittleness increases flash event probability. Flash events increase legitimacy scars. Scars increase political pressure. Political pressure produces poorly designed reforms. Reforms reduce liquidity. Reduced liquidity increases brittleness. The system becomes trapped in a spiral of mistrust. This is why data regimes are constitutional: they decide whether participants believe they can trade without being structurally harvested.

The fifth control point is supervisory realism about automated risk engines. Supervisors cannot treat liquidity as natural resource. It is engineered behavior. Behavior depends on constraints. Constraints are coded. If supervisors do not examine conditions under which major liquidity suppliers withdraw, they will be surprised repeatedly by synchronized retreat. They will respond with emergency liquidity and moral pressure. Moral pressure does not change code paths. To govern machine markets, supervisors must demand evidence: how quickly do limits tighten, what triggers quoting withdrawal, what triggers order cancellation, what triggers hedge suspension, what triggers internal halts, and how correlated are these triggers across major participants. The purpose is not to demand heroism. The purpose is to prevent the entire system from being built on the assumption that someone else will be brave when everyone's rules say step back.

Machine markets also embed a geopolitical vulnerability: perception warfare. A flash event does not need to be caused by an adversary to be exploited by an adversary. If the system produces discontinuity and reversal, a hostile narrative can frame it as rigging. If the public already suspects insiders, the narrative lands. The narrative increases political pressure. Political pressure can force destabilizing reforms. That is strategic effect: legitimacy scars become an attack surface. A resilient system therefore must aim not only to prevent flash events, but to prevent flash legitimacy collapses that are easily framed as corruption. That means designing transparency and rule-boundness into halts and reversals so that self-protection does not look like favoritism.

A final public scene makes the governance stakes explicit. A retirement account statement shifts sharply because prices gapped and then stabilized. The public hears that markets recovered. The public also hears that trades were canceled and that some participants were protected. Whether that is technically true does not matter at first. What matters is the conclusion that the system has hidden levers and that those levers are not for ordinary people. A system that looks like it has hidden levers invites populist pressure. Populist pressure invites blunt reforms. Blunt reforms can reduce liquidity and increase volatility. The next flash event becomes more likely. That is how legitimacy becomes a feedback loop: legitimacy is a stability input, and instability in legitimacy produces instability in the machine.

The defense of machine markets is real. Automation reduces certain human errors. It lowers transaction costs. It increases participation. It can provide liquidity in normal times. It can detect fraud. It can enforce discipline. These are genuine improvements. The counterargument is not nostalgia for human floors. The counterargument is to recognize that machine stability is conditional and conditional stability is dangerous when the system depends on it as if it were permanent. Under stress, automation synchronizes retreat. The state must design for the stress behavior, not the calm behavior. Calm behavior flatters efficiency. Stress behavior governs legitimacy.

The most important governing task is to map coupling, not merely observe volatility. Where does price feed directly into collateral valuation. Where do collateral valuations feed into haircut schedules. Where do haircut schedules feed into margin timetables. Where do margin timetables feed into forced liquidation. Where does forced liquidation feed into funding costs for institutions that intermediate government debt, corporate credit, and essential commodity supply chains. If you cannot draw the chain, you cannot govern it under pressure.

The second task is to slow amplification without freezing discovery. That implies smoothing margin increases, designing liquidity tools that provide temporary relief against high-grade collateral when volatility spikes, and designing microstructure rules that reduce the advantage of speed in ways that protect fairness. Relief must be rule-bound, not discretionary, because discretionary relief becomes scandal in flash events. Rule-bound relief shapes behavior ex ante. If liquidity suppliers believe the system will not punish them instantly with margin spikes, they can remain in the market longer, which reduces gapping and therefore reduces the very volatility signals that trigger retreat.

The third task is to treat margin models, halts, and microstructure as public-interest design. Private institutions will protect themselves first. They must. Yet when their protective behavior becomes systemically destabilizing, the state cannot pretend it is private. The state must have doctrine for how to break mechanical loops without rescuing individual bets, and doctrine for how to impose discipline ex ante through leverage constraints and ex post through predictable loss allocation. Moral hazard arguments are real. Legitimacy arguments are also real. A state that refuses to intervene on moral hazard grounds and then watches a margin cascade destroy the economy has protected doctrine and lost sovereignty. A state that intervenes without discipline invites reckless leverage. The doctrine must be structural and predictable enough that it does not look like favoritism when activated.

The chapter ends where it began: with the sensation of the book thinning. That sensation is not merely trader anxiety. It is a political signal. When the market cannot hold its own discovery process, the state will be asked to hold it. When the state holds it, it will be accused of distortion. When it refuses to hold it, it will be accused of abandonment. Machine markets are therefore constitutional machinery. They decide how quickly the ranking engine can malfunction, how quickly collateral can be re-ranked, how quickly private constraints can withdraw liquidity, and how quickly legitimacy can collapse. The state can either redesign the coupling chain before the next event or be forced to improvise in the moment, and improvisation is where legitimacy is lost fastest because improvisation looks like favoritism even when it is survival.

CLOSING DOCTRINE

Machine markets relocate monetary fragility from balance sheets into feedback loops: price prints become collateral revaluations, revaluations become haircut shifts, haircut shifts become margin calls, margin calls become forced liquidation, and forced liquidation becomes funding stress faster than political governance can respond. Liquidity is behavior governed by private constraints, so when volatility triggers automated limits, liquidity suppliers retreat together, turning risk control into synchronized contraction. Clearing and margin models protect their own continuity first, making them ranked-claims institutions whose protective actions can amplify stress at system speed. Flash legitimacy is the new systemic risk: halts, reversals, uneven fills, and microstructure advantage can make prices feel contestable, and contestable prices poison collateralized finance, trigger hierarchy shocks in eligibility, and invite political overreaction that can worsen liquidity. A serious state must map the coupling chain, slow mechanical amplification without freezing discovery, treat margin, halts, and microstructure as public-interest design, and build rule-bound fairness into access, sequencing, and emergency tools, because sovereignty is weakened when the ranking engine becomes too fast to remain legitimate and too brittle to remain trusted.

CHAPTER 41
CRYPTOGRAPHY SHOCK
WHEN TRUST MATH FAILS

The first meeting is called for an hour that signals urgency without admitting panic. People arrive with two devices, one for notes and one for a secure channel they pretend is optional. The agenda is written in language that protects careers: review threat posture, assess exposure, confirm contingency. The real agenda is simpler and harsher: decide whether the system's trust substrate can be relied on for another year. A deputy head of payments operations begins with what sounds like a technical update and lands it like a budget cut. A class of certificates will require emergency replacement. A subset of secure sessions can no longer be assumed secure against a particular kind of capture. A long tail of devices in the field cannot be patched quickly. The compliance lead asks whether this is material. The security lead answers that material is the wrong word, because the question is not whether losses can be counted. The question is whether the system's proofs remain proofs, because once proofs become arguable, every obligation becomes negotiable in practice even when the law insists it is not.

The room is not filled with cryptographers. It is filled with people who run closure. They manage cutoffs, exception queues, settlement windows, and the public's expectation that payment is not a request but a completion. For them, cryptography is not abstract. It is the invisible scaffolding that makes speed safe. When it holds, the system is smooth enough that the public believes smoothness is natural. When it cracks, smoothness becomes an expensive privilege purchased through added verification, added delay, and added exclusion. A payments operator can tolerate fraud incidents and still keep completion credible. A payments operator cannot tolerate widespread doubt about authorization, because authorization is what allows completion to be defended without reopening every transfer as a story. The moment authorization is questioned at scale, the system's only safe response is to slow, and slowing is how the state discovers that time is its most fragile asset.

Cryptography is the lock on the vault, and also the signature on the withdrawal slip. (security architect, internal briefing)

Cryptography shock is not a cinematic scenario where a secret code breaks and money disappears. It is a constitutional failure mode where the system loses the ability to bind claims reliably because the mechanisms that authenticate, authorize, and prove sequence become contestable. Contestable proof is corrosive in a way balance-sheet losses are not. A bank can survive a fraud loss. A system can survive a theft. A system cannot survive widespread doubt that authorizations mean what they say, because that doubt forces every gatekeeper to choose conservative posture, and conservative posture is how commerce freezes. The deeper point is that money is not primarily data moving. Money is dispute-ending. Dispute-ending requires proof that a discharge event occurred and is not open to plausible reversal. When proof becomes questionable, discharge becomes conditional. When discharge becomes conditional, credit shrinks into caution even if nobody touched an instrument or changed a target.

Modern monetary order rests on a quiet assumption most policymakers never have to articulate: trust can be mathematized and then operationalized at scale. Certificates, signatures, key exchanges, audited modules, and tamper-resistant devices allow strangers to transact without standing in the same room. These mechanisms allow money to be software without dissolving into mere messaging. When they work, the system feels natural. When they wobble, the system feels haunted: everything still runs, yet nothing can be treated as final until someone proves it. Proving it is slow. Slow becomes queueing. Queueing becomes rationing. Rationing under fear becomes politics, because people do not accept being placed in an exception lane without suspecting intent. That suspicion is the beginning of legitimacy collapse, and legitimacy collapse is the true systemic risk because it changes behavior faster than balance sheets change.

Cryptography shock arrives in two broad forms. The first is sudden: a practical break or near-break that forces emergency migration. The second is delayed: capture now, decrypt later; record now, forge later; hold evidence in escrow and wait for capability. The first form produces visible crisis because institutions must rotate, revoke, and reissue at pace while commerce does not pause. The second form produces invisible compromise that becomes visible at the worst time, when disputes arrive years later and rewrite the past through litigation. Both forms attack the same foundation: the system's ability to treat a record as authoritative without reopening every transaction as a question of testimony. A payments state can survive confidentiality loss with embarrassment. It cannot survive integrity doubt without becoming slower, more gated, and more unequal.

The system's vulnerability is often mis-described as "encryption risk." Encryption is one layer. The deeper danger is integrity and non-repudiation: whether the system can prove who authorized a payment, whether it can prove a message was not altered, whether it can prove an instruction was issued by the claimed party, whether it can prove that sequence cannot be rewritten without detection. These are the properties that make the ledger governable. If integrity is compromised, the record becomes arguable. If the record becomes arguable, finality becomes conditional. If finality becomes conditional, collateral becomes suspect and funding becomes timid. Timidity does not look like crisis. It looks like prudence, and prudence at scale is contraction.

The chapter's pressure point is authority. Money's authority in modern systems is mediated by cryptographic proof. Cryptographic proof is not decorative. It is how discharge is defended at machine speed. If that defense becomes questionable, the system responds by slowing and layering more checks. Those checks are not free. They increase the cost of payment, increase the cost of compliance, and increase the cost of cross-boundary passage. They also increase exclusion, because the actors who cannot generate the required proofs cheaply will be pushed into exception lanes. A cryptography shock therefore is always also a distribution shock, because it turns technical capacity into economic membership.

A payments operator experiences this as an immediate operational contradiction. The system has been designed to process at volume with low friction. Friction is minimized by trust in the cryptographic layer. If trust in the layer declines, the operator must either slow the system to add verification or accept higher fraud risk. Slowing creates queues. Queues create missed cutoffs. Missed cutoffs create defaults. Defaults create demands for backstop and political anger. Accepting fraud risk creates scandal. Scandal creates political pressure for harsher controls. Both paths force visible choices. The public experiences only one thing: completion used to be normal and now it is conditional. Conditional completion feels like the state is slipping, even if the state did not cause the vulnerability and even if the vulnerability is global.

Cryptography is an interlocking stack: identity issuance, trust chains, key management, signing protocols, authentication flows, secure communications, storage encryption, audit logging, and time discipline. A weakness in one layer can be survivable. A weakness that forces doubt across multiple layers becomes systemic. The systemic event is not the break itself. The systemic event is behavioral response: mass conservatism by gatekeepers and mass rerouting by users. Gatekeepers slow because they fear being blamed for fraud. Users reroute because they cannot afford delay. Conservatism and rerouting create exceptions. Exceptions create more conservatism. The system thickens its own borders.

The hidden power structure inside cryptography shock is key governance. Keys are sovereign instruments in software form. Whoever can issue, revoke, rotate, and validate keys controls who is legible, who is authorized, and which transactions can be treated as binding. Key governance sits in a narrow set of institutions: identity providers, certificate issuers, hardware module operators, platform administrators, and committees that determine which cryptographic suites remain acceptable. These institutions are not finance ministries. Yet they hold levers that can interrupt settlement, widen friction, and deny passage. When that authority is private, external, or concentrated, cryptography shock becomes sovereignty shock because the state's ability to keep its own payment perimeter functioning depends on actors outside the usual constitutional chain.

A simple scene reveals this without abstraction. A bank receives notice that a class of certificates must be replaced within a short window. The bank's core systems are patched and rotated with priority. The bank's downstream integrators are not. Smaller merchants and smaller institutions using older modules fail the new handshake. Their transactions begin to fail intermittently. Intermittent failure is worse than clean failure because it spreads blame and sustains uncertainty. The bank's operations team must decide: enforce strict verification and exclude laggards, or permit legacy fallback paths that are less secure. If it permits fallback, it may be blamed later when fraud occurs and the auditor asks why the bank kept a known-weak path alive. If it enforces strictness, it will be blamed now when commerce breaks and wages and purchases stall. The state is not in the room, yet the state will be blamed because the public does not separate bank security posture from monetary reliability when the payment surface becomes brittle.

That scene captures the first mechanism: migration is governance. Cryptography shock forces migration, and migration is not only a deployment. Migration determines who can transact. Every migration creates a seam between those who updated and those who did not, between those with modern hardware and those with older devices, between those who can rotate keys quickly and those who must wait on vendors. Seams become markets because someone will sell bridging services. Seams also become smuggling routes because someone will sell forged compliance and counterfeit attestations. Migration therefore does not merely harden security. It rearranges legibility, and legibility is membership in a payment state.

The second mechanism is evidentiary downgrade. In any dispute forum, evidence has hierarchy. Digital signatures and secure logs are treated as strong evidence because they are hard to forge and easy to verify. If a class of signatures becomes suspect or if a class of logs becomes tamperable, those records are treated differently. That treatment matters because it determines whether a payment can be treated as final without reopening underlying facts. If evidence becomes weaker, more disputes become litigable. More disputes increase the cost of transacting and the cost of financing, because financing depends on enforceability and enforceability depends on evidence. The system's legal core begins to buckle not because statutes changed, but because the proof those statutes rely on becomes questionable. The system shifts from closure by record toward closure by contest, and contest is what large economies cannot afford at scale.

The third mechanism is time weaponization. If cryptographic proof becomes questionable, time becomes the first rationed resource. Institutions lengthen holds, extend review windows, delay settlement until additional checks complete, and require step-up verification in ways that turn routine payments into exceptions. Delay is presented as prudence. Delay is also an economic weapon because it forces counterparties to hold liquidity and forces firms to finance working capital longer. In a system where speed is competitive advantage, generalized slowing functions like a tax imposed on commerce. The tax is not voted on. It is imposed by insecurity, and insecurity is never distributed evenly because the ability to produce proofs quickly is not evenly distributed.

When verification slows, liquidity becomes a hostage to time. (payments operations lead, escalation note)

The most damaging property of cryptography shock is that it attacks the system's ability to make tomorrow behave like yesterday. Monetary order is not stability in the sense of no change. It is stability in the sense of predictable closure. People build their lives around predictable closure: payroll on a day, rent on a day, supplier invoices on a day, benefits on a day, settlement cutoffs on a day. A cryptography shock does not need to break everything to break the social contract. It only needs to introduce uncertainty at scale about whether a transaction will finish on schedule and be defended as finished later. Once uncertainty enters, rational actors change behavior immediately. They hoard. They prepay. They demand buffers. Buffers reduce spending. Reduced spending becomes slowdown.

Cryptography shock is often discussed as if it were confined to specialized digital assets. That framing misses the larger reality: cryptographic primitives underpin nearly every modern financial operation. Interbank messaging relies on secure channels and signing. Retail payment authentication relies on device security and credential validation. Settlement messaging relies on integrity and sequence. Custody instructions rely on signatures and key control. Audit trails rely on logging that can be verified. A break in trust math is therefore a break in the system's ability to coordinate at volume. Coordination is what makes a high-volume economy possible. When coordination becomes expensive, the economy shrinks, and it shrinks in an uneven way that amplifies political tension: large institutions with modern infrastructure can adapt and keep flows in the fast lane; smaller institutions and peripheral regions are forced into degraded modes that feel like exclusion.

Cryptography shock therefore intensifies hierarchy. There are two hierarchies to see. The first is internal: within a domestic payment system, those who can authenticate and sign in the preferred way enjoy fast completion; those who cannot are routed into slower rails and manual review. The second is external: across borders, those who can satisfy dominant corridor standards achieve passage; those who cannot are treated as suspect, delayed, or excluded. Cryptography shock narrows acceptable proofs and raises the cost of compliance, turning both hierarchies from background noise into daily friction.

A corridor scene makes the external hierarchy tangible. A firm in a mid-sized economy attempts to pay a supplier through a corridor that tightened requirements. The payment instruction is valid domestically. The corridor refuses to treat it as routine because the identity attestation is not in the preferred format and the signing chain is not on the accepted list. The transaction becomes an exception. The exception triggers manual review. Manual review takes time. The supplier demands prepayment next time because it cannot finance uncertainty. The firm must hold more foreign liquidity. Holding more foreign liquidity is expensive. The firm raises prices or reduces output. The firm does not describe this as cryptography. It describes it as the world becoming harder, more suspicious, more bureaucratic. That hardness is how monetary hierarchy is felt: as a rising tax of proof and a rising scarcity of trusted completion.

The same mechanism becomes leverage even without intent. If dominant corridors adopt new standards faster than other perimeters can, compliance becomes a gate. Gates are where power sits. Even if standard tightening is justified as security, it functions as strategic exclusion if applied in ways certain states and institutions cannot meet quickly. This is not conspiracy. It is uneven capacity. The effect is the same: some actors keep their place in the fast lane; others fall into exception lanes, and exception lanes are where commerce becomes more expensive and where politics becomes angrier.

The strongest counterargument is that migration is routine. Algorithms age. Keys rotate. Systems upgrade. The world has always moved from weaker primitives to stronger ones. That is true. The pressure comes from tempo and scale. The modern system has more endpoints, more dependencies, more embedded devices, more third-party integrations, more cross-boundary interfaces than any prior monetary system. Migration that once affected a narrow set of institutions now affects millions of devices and thousands of firms. That scale makes coordination harder. Hard coordination means longer windows where mixed standards coexist. Mixed standards mean seams. Seams are attack surfaces. Seams are arbitrage surfaces. Migration becomes a period of elevated fragility even if the destination is stronger, because the process forces the system to tolerate incompatibility.

A retail payments scene shows how mixed standards become political quickly. A merchant's point-of-sale module is older. A firmware update is scheduled but delayed. A new requirement is rolled out across an acquiring network. The merchant begins seeing intermittent declines. Customers blame the merchant. The merchant blames the bank. The bank blames the vendor. The vendor blames a standards update. Meanwhile, the merchant's revenue becomes less predictable. Payroll becomes harder. Inventory orders are delayed. Local workers feel it as hours cut. Local politics sees it as incompetence. Mixed cryptography becomes mixed legitimacy: the state promised a reliable payment surface and cannot explain why the surface is brittle, because the cause is distributed across vendors and layers. The public experiences only the outcome: it used to work.

The true shock arrives when cryptography failure is not only compatibility but trust. Compatibility can be fixed with upgrades. Trust issues become litigation and institutional caution. If a new capability makes it plausible that a class of signatures can be forged or that captured traffic can be decrypted later, old transactions become suspect. The system then faces a terrible choice: treat past records as final and accept hidden fraud risk, or reopen past records and accept destabilization of confidence. Both options carry cost. A state that insists the past is final may be accused of protecting insiders and refusing justice. A state that reopens the past risks destroying the principle of finality that makes credit possible. This is where cryptography shock becomes constitutional: it threatens finality as a social promise, not only as a technical property.

A legal scene makes the conflict visceral. A dispute forum is presented with a set of signed instructions and logs. Under older assumptions, the signature is strong proof. Under a new threat model, the defense argues the signature cannot be treated as conclusive. The forum faces a choice: accept the record as binding and preserve finality, or accept contest and preserve a notion of fairness in the face of new vulnerability. Either choice has systemic implication. If the forum accepts contests broadly, lenders, custodians, and clearing participants see a new litigability risk, and litigability risk is priced as higher haircuts, higher margins, and more restrictive terms. If the forum refuses contests broadly, the public sees a state protecting the machine's convenience over individual justice. The state cannot avoid this. Cryptography shock forces the law to choose between closure and contest in a way that will be interpreted politically.

This is why cryptography shock is not merely a risk in the machine. It is a risk in the dispute system that defends the machine. A payment state is a set of procedures for turning disputes into closure. When proofs weaken, disputes expand. Expanded disputes burden the tribunals, slow adjudication, and increase uncertainty. Uncertainty is priced as friction. Friction becomes slower credit creation. Slower credit creation becomes slower growth. A state can publish optimism. It cannot publish away a rise in litigability.

The chapter's first hard truth is that cryptographic assurance is a public good inside a private supply chain. Most cryptographic modules, libraries, and infrastructures are built and maintained by private actors. Implementation is distributed across vendors, contractors, and internal teams. The payment state depends on this private supply chain for operational sovereignty. If the supply chain fails, the state must accept degraded-mode money or attempt emergency consolidation. Emergency consolidation is difficult because competence is specialized and the supply chain is global. The dependency therefore is strategic. It is one of the places where sovereignty is constrained by technical capacity, and where calm comfort becomes stress vulnerability.

The second hard truth is that cryptography shock is a hierarchy accelerator. Security improvements raise fixed costs: modern hardware, skilled teams, audited modules, compliance programs, key governance procedures. Fixed costs are easier for large institutions. Smaller institutions are pushed toward managed services and shared providers. Shared providers increase concentration. Concentration increases correlated failure. Correlated failure increases systemic risk. Therefore hardening, if not designed with distributed resilience in mind, can become fragility. The system becomes "more secure" in the sense of stronger primitives and "less sovereign" in the sense of more dependence on a narrow set of operators.

The third hard truth is that trust math is not only algorithms. It is also randomness, time discipline, and implementation. A scheme can be sound and still fail due to weak randomness, time drift, side-channel leakage, key reuse, poor certificate validation, or misconfigured fallback paths. Implementation failures can be exploited at scale precisely because systems are standardized. Standardization is necessary for interoperability. Standardization also creates common-mode vulnerabilities. The payment state cannot treat cryptography as a box it buys. It must treat it as a living governance regime that requires continuous verification, independent testing, and adversarial exercises. Without this, the system discovers weaknesses only when someone else finds them first.

A custody scene shows how proof doubt becomes liquidity stress in hours. A custodian receives an instruction to move collateral from one account to another so a bank can meet margin. The instruction is signed properly under the old scheme. Under the new threat model, the signature may be forgeable or replayable. The custodian cannot treat the instruction as routine. The custodian delays, demands additional proofs, routes through manual verification, and requires a second, independent attestation. Manual verification takes time. The bank that needed the collateral transfer to meet a margin call cannot meet the call. The bank sells assets instead. The sale depresses prices. Depressed prices widen haircuts. Haircuts generate more margin. A cryptography doubt has propagated into a market stress event. To the public, it looks like a market crash. Inside the system, it began as a signature doubt at a custody node where time cannot be extended without forcing liquidation.

The fourth hard truth is that cryptography shock is a fraud multiplier even when the system survives. During migration periods, fallback paths proliferate. Fallback exists to preserve continuity for older devices and older integrations. Attackers love fallback because fallback is where posture is weaker and monitoring is less mature. Institutions keep fallback quiet to avoid panic. Quiet fallback becomes invisible vulnerability. When fraud rises later, defenders tighten thresholds. Tight thresholds slow payments. Slowing payments creates contraction. The system can be forced into a cycle where the attempt to preserve continuity during migration creates conditions for later fraud, which then forces tightened controls that harm continuity anyway. Migration becomes a corridor of vulnerability.

The fifth hard truth is that cryptography shock complicates attribution in a politically poisonous way. If signatures become contestable, disputes about who authorized what become harder to resolve. Harder resolution means longer disputes. Longer disputes mean higher legal cost and more political demand for state intervention. Intervention risks politicizing the dispute forum. Politicized dispute forums destroy confidence. Confidence in money is the willingness to accept claims without litigating them. Cryptography shock increases litigability. Litigability increases friction. Friction shrinks credit. The system can remain solvent and still lose capacity, which is how a society becomes poorer without a single dramatic collapse.

The system's defense therefore must be designed around four imperatives that conflict under stress: preserve integrity, preserve finality, preserve continuity, preserve legitimacy. If integrity is pursued with maximum strictness in crisis, continuity can collapse. If continuity is pursued with maximum openness, integrity can collapse. Finality cannot be sacrificed lightly because finality is what makes credit scalable. Yet finality cannot be defended if proofs are contestable. Legitimacy cannot be preserved if outcomes look arbitrary or biased. The state must therefore design for bounded, auditable degradation rather than perfection. Bounded degradation means predetermined fallback regimes, predetermined priority flows, predetermined dispute and compensation procedures, and predetermined liability rules that prevent defenders' fear from turning into blanket freezes.

The first pillar is cryptographic agility as governance, not as marketing. Agility means the system can shift algorithms and key sizes without rewriting every dependency. In practice, this requires modular architectures, consistent certificate management, rehearsed rotation procedures, and staff capacity to execute migration quickly.

It also requires routine exercise, because the first time you attempt a complex rotation must not be during crisis. Agility is expensive. Agility is sovereignty: a state that cannot migrate its cryptographic substrate quickly is a state that will be forced into degraded-mode money by events outside its control.

Agility is also political discipline because it requires the system to accept regular disruption in calm to avoid catastrophic disruption in stress. Institutions dislike regular disruption because disruption is visible cost with invisible benefit. The state must make the benefit visible in doctrine: agility reduces seams, reduces mixed-standard windows, reduces reliance on fallback, and reduces the time adversaries have to exploit incompatibility. Agility is not a guarantee. It is a reduction in the duration of vulnerability, and duration is the currency of attack.

The second pillar is key governance as constitutional function. Key issuance and revocation must be distributed enough to avoid single points of failure and controlled enough to prevent weak links. Too centralized and the system becomes hostage to a small set of providers. Too distributed and the system becomes inconsistent and vulnerable. The answer is layered trust. Critical settlement functions depend on hardened, audited key governance. Retail interfaces can tolerate managed services only if managed services are bound by continuity obligations, audit obligations, and emergency disclosure obligations that function under stress. The state must know which layers can be outsourced and which layers must be directly governed, because outsourcing the wrong layer means outsourcing the ability to declare completion.

Key governance also requires disciplined revocation. Revocation is the ability to expel compromised identity quickly. Expulsion is necessary for integrity. Expulsion is also exclusion, and exclusion is political. A state that revokes aggressively can preserve integrity and create social unrest if legitimate actors are caught in the blast radius. A state that revokes timidly can preserve continuity and invite systemic fraud. The doctrine must define thresholds and processes that are rule-bound, not improvisational, because improvisational revocation looks like political persecution even when it is technical necessity.

The third pillar is evidence resilience. The system must preserve auditability across migrations. It must preserve time ordering. It must preserve non-repudiation under the new threat model. That requires dual-proof periods where both old and new proofs are recorded, strict timestamp discipline, secure logging that remains verifiable even if one primitive weakens, and procedures that allow later verification without turning every dispute into open-ended contest. Evidence resilience also requires dispute-forum readiness: courts and administrative forums must know what proofs mean under new regimes and must be prepared to handle dispute surges without turning into paralysis engines. A payment state that cannot adjudicate quickly cannot maintain credit, because credit depends on the expectation that disputes are bounded in time.

Evidence resilience also means defending sequence as a public asset. Time drift, inconsistent timestamping, and log gaps are not "technical details." They are the openings through which contest enters. Contest slows closure. Slow closure reduces trust in accepting claims from strangers. Accepting claims from strangers is how modern economies scale beyond kinship and proximity. Therefore time discipline is monetary discipline. A system that treats time as a monitoring problem rather than a constitutional requirement will discover its error when an adversary, or merely a complex migration, creates enough inconsistency that courts cannot resolve disputes cleanly.

The fourth pillar is continuity prioritization. If cryptography shock forces slowdown, the system must have predetermined priorities: wages, benefits, essential supply chains, critical settlement obligations that prevent cascading defaults. Prioritization must be rule-bound, not discretionary, because discretionary prioritization becomes scandal. Prioritization must also be protected from fraud, which means essentialness must be representable and authenticated without inviting attackers to masquerade as essential flows. That is a design challenge and a legitimacy challenge. The state must solve both or accept that every cryptography incident becomes social rupture.

The fifth pillar is concentration discipline. Cryptography upgrades often push smaller actors toward shared services. Shared services create choke points. Choke points become targets. The state must therefore require redundancy and multi-provider capability for critical functions. Without this, cryptography shock layered on infrastructure concentration becomes paralysis even if nobody intended it, because key governance and identity roots can be simultaneously stressed. The state must treat these dependencies as a single architecture rather than separate compliance checklists.

A counterargument insists private actors will solve this faster than the state can. Vendors and major institutions will upgrade because business depends on it. The state should not interfere. The critique is not private incompetence. The critique is incentive mismatch. Private actors optimize for liability, cost, and reputation. Under stress, that optimization can produce conservative throttling, selective restoration, and quiet exclusion of weaker counterparties. Those choices can be rational and still politically destabilizing. Cryptography shock is not only a security issue. It is a distributive and legitimacy issue. Only the state can impose doctrine balancing integrity with continuity for the public as a whole, because only the state carries the legitimacy burden when money fails in daily life.

Another defense insists cryptography shock is always discussed and never arrives. That defense is comforting because it allows budgets to be deferred. The reality is that cryptography risk does not need to arrive as a single dramatic day. It can arrive as chronic tightening: stronger requirements, heavier verification, longer holds, more exception handling, more costly compliance, more concentrated service provision. Chronic tightening is still shock, stretched. It still shrinks credit and increases exclusion. It still turns the payment state into a slower, more gated machine. It still creates political anger because it makes daily commerce less reliable. A shock that arrives as chronic friction is easier to ignore and therefore easier to allow to metastasize.

The last consequence is monetary diplomacy by proof. If blocs adopt different standards at different tempos, interoperability becomes political. Shared proofs become harder. Cross-border finality becomes more conditional. Corridors become more discretionary. These shifts can be defended as security. They also function as strategic exclusion if used intentionally or if they unintentionally exclude weaker states. A serious official must see that standard setting is not administrative. It is statecraft. Whoever sets proofs sets gates. Whoever sets gates sets terms of passage.

The chapter closes where it began, in a meeting that pretends not to be panic. The people in the room do not want to say the math failed, because math is the last neutral thing they believed in. They want the world to remain a place where you can prove what you did by pointing to a signature and a log. That desire is not philosophical. It is what keeps money from becoming argument. Cryptography shock is the moment when the system remembers that proof is not nature. Proof is architecture. Architecture must be governed. If it is not governed, it becomes fragility disguised as convenience, and fragility is what turns a modern payment state into a slower, angrier, more segmented society even without a single dramatic collapse.

CLOSING DOCTRINE

Cryptography shock is a failure of authority, not merely a security episode: when proofs become contestable, authorization becomes exception handling, exception handling becomes delay, delay becomes liquidity hoarding, and hoarding becomes contraction long before any balance sheet collapses. The systemic danger is integrity and non-repudiation, because a payment state cannot defend finality if signatures, logs, and sequence discipline are arguable, and once finality is conditional, credit shrinks into caution and disputes expand into governance crisis. Key governance is sovereign power in software form: whoever can issue, revoke, rotate, and validate keys controls legibility, access, and the practical boundary of discharge, while migration periods create seams that become both attack surfaces and profit centers. Security upgrades can accelerate hierarchy by raising fixed costs and pushing smaller actors into concentrated shared services, turning hardening into correlated fragility unless multi-provider resilience is enforced. A serious state therefore designs for bounded, auditable degradation: practiced cryptographic agility, layered key governance, evidence resilience through dual-proof and time discipline, rule-bound continuity prioritization for essential flows, and concentration discipline at identity and key choke points, because the monetary order fails fastest when trust math stops being invisible and becomes a daily argument.

CHAPTER 42
ENERGY SHOCK
THE PRICE OF SETTLEMENT

The first warning is not the headline. It is the invoice. A mid-sized manufacturer receives a revised power contract with a clause that reads like a threat disguised as arithmetic: pass-through pricing during volatility events, settlement within shorter windows, penalties for peak draw that used to be negotiated quietly. The manufacturer does not argue about the clause. The manufacturer calls the plant manager and asks whether shifts can be moved. Shifts cannot be moved without losing output. The manufacturer calls procurement and asks whether suppliers can be pushed to different schedules. Suppliers cannot be pushed without paying more. The manufacturer calls the treasurer and asks whether inventory can be reduced. Inventory cannot be reduced without risking missed orders. The manufacturer calls the bank and asks whether the working-capital line can be expanded. The bank answers that the line can be expanded on different terms, because the borrower's operating volatility has changed and because the system is now pricing energy as a liquidity risk rather than as a cost.

In the same week, an accounts payable manager at a distribution company sees the shock in the language nobody writes op-eds about:

revised payment terms from upstream suppliers and a new insistence on earlier settlement windows. Earlier settlement is not preference. It is upstream survival. When energy costs swing, suppliers shorten the time they are willing to carry receivables because receivables are promises and promises become fragile when expenses are unpredictable. The manager begins paying earlier, which means holding more liquidity, which means drawing credit more often, which means the bank's monitoring flags stress and tightens. A price shock becomes a timing shock. A timing shock becomes a credit shock. A credit shock becomes contraction, and contraction arrives without a formal declaration because the system's private terms have changed.

A utility operator sees the same event from the opposite side. It is not only that fuel prices moved. It is that predictability collapsed. Predictability is the true asset a grid sells, because predictability is what allows everything else to plan. When predictability collapses, everyone demands buffers. Buffers consume capital. Capital is credit. Credit is time. The operator hears the political narrative about gouging and greed and knows it is both understandable and incomplete. The deeper constraint is that the system must pay for reliability while reliability itself is becoming more expensive to produce. Reliability has a price. If the price is not paid through bills, it is paid through outages. Outages are worse than bills because outages ration by chaos rather than by rule, and chaos is a liability event for every institution whose legitimacy depends on predictable sequence.

Energy shock becomes monetary shock when the system discovers that the price of settlement includes the price of power. Modern payment systems do not settle in coin. They settle in data centers, networks, cloud services, fraud models, compliance filters, and the quiet labor of keeping the machine running continuously. Every element of that machine consumes energy. In calm, energy is treated as utility input, rarely mentioned in monetary doctrine. Under stress, energy becomes the physical constraint on financial continuity, and physical constraints are where monetary abstractions collapse into politics. The system can pretend it is digital. The grid will eventually remind it that digital is physical and physical is scarce.

Settlement is a physical act hidden behind digital language. (operations head, internal briefing)

The thesis is that energy is not merely an input to the economy. It is an input to monetary order. If energy becomes scarce, expensive, or unreliable, the system's ability to clear, net, and settle is degraded. Degraded settlement is not a nuisance. It is contraction mechanism because settlement ends disputes, releases collateral, and turns promises into closed facts. When settlement slows, collateral is trapped. When collateral is trapped, secured funding tightens. When secured funding tightens, credit shrinks. When credit shrinks, commerce shrinks. Energy shock therefore can function like a tightening of monetary conditions even if policy instruments did not move, because it tightens the economy's time budget and forces actors to purchase certainty with buffers.

The easiest way to misunderstand this is to treat energy shock as inflation alone. Inflation is visible symptom. The more dangerous mechanism is sequence disruption. If power costs rise sharply and reliability declines, critical operators—payment processors, clearing venues, identity providers, telecom backbones, data centers—face higher operating costs and higher interruption risk. Higher costs lead to fee increases and to prioritization decisions. Prioritization creates queues. Queues create delays. Delays create liquidity hoarding. The economic story that looks like higher costs becomes a monetary story that looks like completion reliability weakened. Reliability is what keeps credit cheap. When reliability weakens, the system becomes more conservative. Conservatism is tightening.

The speed at which this tightening propagates depends on the system's reliance on continuousness. Continuousness is the background promise that makes modern commerce feel effortless: always-on authorization, always-on posting, always-on customer support, always-on reconciliation, always-on fraud scoring, always-on compliance filtering. If energy volatility forces operators to degrade, continuousness becomes conditional. Conditional continuousness is not a partial inconvenience. It is a new distribution rule: those who transact through the most resilient rails remain "normal," those who transact through weaker rails become exceptions, and exceptions are where costs accumulate.

A payments operator experiences energy shock first as capacity discipline. Backups that used to be tested monthly are now tested weekly because outages are more likely. Generators consume fuel that is more expensive and harder to obtain. Cooling costs rise. The operator begins looking at which functions can be throttled during peak load to preserve core continuity. Throttling is presented as resilience. Throttling is also rationing. The operator must choose whether to preserve throughput or preserve scrutiny. If fraud scoring is throttled, losses rise and scandal follows. If scrutiny is maintained, more transactions fall into manual review. Manual review increases delay. Delay increases exception volume. Exception volume increases staffing cost. Staffing cost increases fees. Fees push smaller institutions into shared services. Shared services increase concentration. Concentration increases fragility. The shock therefore has an architectural consequence: it accelerates centralization of payment capacity, because only large operators can afford energy redundancy at scale.

A data-center operations lead experiences the shock as a triage manual no one wants to admit exists. Under grid stress, the lead must decide what remains live and what degrades. Degradation is rarely described as shut down. It is described as reduced functionality. Reduced functionality can mean lower-resolution monitoring, slower reconciliation, delayed batch posting, less frequent risk model refresh, slower settlement confirmations, and narrower customer support capacity. Each reduction increases disputability because a slower system produces more ambiguous states: authorized but not posted, posted but not cleared, cleared but not settled, settled but not confirmed. Those states are where users panic because they cannot tell whether money has moved or merely promised to move. Panic is behavioral. Behavioral changes become liquidity events.

A retail bank's operations director describes the same problem differently: an outage is not only downtime, it is a dispute generator. When systems go dark, transactions queue. When transactions queue, balances are not updated in real time. When balances are not updated, overdrafts rise and merchants see reversals. Reversals look like fraud. Fraud controls tighten. Tight controls produce more declines. Declines produce more customer calls. Customer calls overload support. Overloaded support reduces complaint resolution. Reduced resolution becomes reputational damage. Reputational damage triggers defensive behavior by customers: they move deposits to institutions perceived as safer. Deposit flight tightens weaker banks. Tightening reduces credit. Credit contraction is the macro symptom of a micro outage.

A household sees energy shock as double squeeze and trust test. Bills rise. Prices rise. Wages lag. Credit becomes more expensive because lenders price higher volatility and higher default risk. The household cuts spending. The spending cut is not sentiment. It is physics expressed through money. The household's belief in money's reliability is tested when payments fail during outages. If point-of-sale systems go down, if transfers are delayed, if receipts are uncertain, the household hoards cash or hoards balances in the institutions it trusts most. Hoarding is rational. Hoarding drains liquidity from weaker institutions. Weaker institutions tighten credit. Tight credit hits households again. The loop is how energy becomes financial stability: physical constraint becomes behavior shift that amplifies fragility.

A small business feels it through time scarcity. Energy volatility forces suppliers to shorten payment terms because suppliers cannot carry receivable risk when their own costs are unpredictable. Shorter terms force the business to finance working capital more aggressively. Financing becomes expensive because banks price volatility and because collateral is weaker when margins are squeezed. The business reduces inventory. Reduced inventory creates shortages. Shortages increase price volatility. Volatility increases margin requirements in hedges and increases bank caution. The physical shock becomes a financial tightening that feeds itself: higher volatility forces more conservatism, conservatism forces thinner inventory, thinner inventory forces more volatility.

The core mechanism is that energy volatility changes the value of time in the system. In a high-reliability world, settlement speed is assumed. In a volatile-reliability world, speed becomes conditional. Conditional speed changes risk pricing because the system is built on the assumption that obligations can be closed within known windows. When those windows become uncertain, credit lines are held back and buffers are demanded. Buffers consume capital and managerial attention. They also create hierarchy because large institutions can buy resilience and liquidity buffers more easily, while smaller actors are forced into slow lanes that function as an unlegislated tax. Taxes that are not legislated are politically corrosive because they feel like theft by procedure.

The monetary system contains energy-intensive chokepoints rarely discussed in public. Clearing systems and their risk engines, high-availability data centers, redundancy networks, cyber defense apparatus, and continuous surveillance in fraud and compliance scale energy consumption in the name of resilience. In an energy shock, resilience itself becomes expensive. Expensive resilience encourages consolidation. Large operators can afford multiple sites, multiple feeds, multiple backup systems, and dedicated fuel contracts. Smaller operators cannot. Smaller operators outsource to shared infrastructure. Shared infrastructure becomes systemic. Systemic infrastructure becomes a target. A shock that begins as fuel volatility becomes a structural shift toward concentrated settlement sovereignty in private hands, because the ability to afford resilience becomes the ability to remain a settlement node.

A bank treasury desk describes this shift as cost of funds and intraday risk. Settlement delays during grid stress create uncertainty about incoming flows. Uncertainty about incoming flows forces the desk to hold more liquidity and to shorten intraday credit offered to clients and counterparties. Shortening is defensive. It is also contraction. If many banks shorten simultaneously, firms lose working capital and must liquidate inventory or reduce payroll. The state can provide liquidity. Liquidity cannot restore power reliability. Liquidity bridges time. If the system repeatedly loses time to energy disruptions, bridging becomes chronic. Chronic bridging becomes fiscal and political stress because the backstop becomes a permanent subsidy to physical unreliability, and permanent subsidies are where legitimacy erodes when citizens perceive the system as expensive and still fragile.

Energy shock reshapes collateral hierarchies. Energy-intensive assets —data centers, industrial facilities, logistics hubs—become riskier if their operations depend on reliable power that is no longer cheap or stable. Financing terms tighten. At the same time, assets that secure energy supply or reduce dependence become more financeable because they reduce volatility. The collateral map shifts. Credit follows the shift. Regions and sectors that can stabilize energy access become credit-favored. Regions and sectors that cannot become credit-disfavored. This is not ideology. It is the system's re-ranking under scarcity, and re-ranking is distributive because it decides who can borrow to adapt and who is forced to shrink.

A sovereign-level pressure scene shows how energy becomes constraint on monetary sovereignty. A state faces higher import costs for energy. Its currency weakens. Domestic inflation rises. The central bank tightens to defend credibility. Tightening slows growth.

Slower growth reduces fiscal receipts. Fiscal strain reduces the ability to cushion bills. Reduced cushion increases volatility in household budgets. Volatility increases anger. Anger increases pressure to cap prices. Caps can preserve immediate stability and distort investment incentives, creating supply problems later. The state is forced into choices where every option has cost. The deeper point is that energy volatility forces monetary policy to fight on two fronts: price stability and payment stability. If payment stability is threatened by grid reliability, a technically correct stance becomes politically unsustainable because citizens judge the state by whether daily life functions, not by whether a target is met.

The most dangerous pathway is the failure of continuous settlement. Modern economies rely on continuous settlement at multiple layers: retail authorization, batch posting, clearing, netting, final settlement, reconciliation, reporting, dispute handling. If energy stress forces interruptions, backlogs accumulate. Backlogs require exception processing. Exception processing is human labor and manual oversight. Manual oversight introduces discretion. Discretion invites accusation. The state becomes trapped: if it prioritizes continuity by allowing discretionary overrides, it risks scandal; if it prioritizes integrity by refusing overrides, it risks paralysis. Energy shock turns into governance crisis because it forces the system to choose which values to sacrifice under physical constraint, and those sacrifices are experienced as unfairness.

A payroll office scene makes human transmission immediate. A city payroll administrator watches the batch file fail during an outage window. The file will be rerun, but rerun means delay. Delay means hundreds of employees are paid late. The phone rings. People do not ask about the grid. They ask why their money is missing. The administrator explains system issues, and system issues is heard as contempt because it offers no timeline and no remedy. Employees overdraft. Fees rise. Anger rises. Politicians demand accountability. A physically caused delay becomes socially interpreted as negligence or favoritism because money delays always feel intentional to those living close to the edge.

Energy shock also increases cyber vulnerability because degraded modes expand attack surface. When systems run under stress, they rely on fallback paths. Fallback paths are weaker. Attackers time campaigns to coincide with outages, when monitoring is overloaded and operators are restoring basic function. The state experiences clustering. Mechanically, it is predictable: physical disruption creates overload and exposure. Incidents rise. Conservative posture rises. Conservative posture tightens payments. Tight payments tighten credit. The loop deepens.

The interaction with scarcity makes energy shock more dangerous than a simple price move. Price moves can be hedged. Reliability failures cannot be hedged easily because they interrupt sequences. Sequence interruption is where the system loses its ability to manufacture closure. Closure releases collateral and permits credit expansion. If closure becomes intermittent, credit becomes episodic. Episodic credit is a condition of weak economies, because planning becomes harder and buffers become larger. Buffers are expensive and unequal.

A redesign doctrine for energy and settlement requires three parallel projects. The first is to treat payment infrastructure as critical energy infrastructure. This means demanding redundant power, verified backup capacity, geographic redundancy, fuel contracts for prolonged stress, and the ability to operate through sustained degradation without collapsing into discretion. It also means viewing certain private operators as essential nodes with public obligations, because their outages create public harm. The second project is to treat energy infrastructure as monetary infrastructure. If grids fail, money fails. The state must finance grid resilience not as utility upgrade but as stability project, because stable settlement is core public good. The third project is to design degraded-mode settlement that preserves legitimacy: clear priorities for essential flows, rule-bound queue governance, auditable override mechanisms, predetermined compensation frameworks that prevent "late wages" from becoming political rupture.

The political economy of these reforms is difficult because costs are visible and avoided crises are invisible. Yet energy shock will not wait for comfort. It arrives through invoices, through outages, through the quiet decision of a processor to throttle, through the quiet decision of a clearing venue to extend windows, through the quiet decision of a bank to shorten lines, through the quiet decision of suppliers to demand faster payment. The public experiences the aggregate as a society that feels less reliable and more expensive. The state's legitimacy is tested in that feeling, not in technical accuracy.

The price of settlement is therefore not only fees and spreads. It is power. If power becomes unstable, settlement becomes conditional. If settlement becomes conditional, collateral becomes sticky. If collateral becomes sticky, credit becomes cautious. If credit becomes cautious, commerce shrinks. The monetary state cannot afford to treat energy as external. Energy is the physical substrate of the ledger, and the ledger is the system's authority.

CLOSING DOCTRINE

Energy shock becomes monetary shock when power cost and reliability degrade the system's ability to clear, net, and settle, trapping collateral in queues, lengthening holds, and forcing credit to tighten as if by policy even when no instrument moved. Settlement is physical work hidden behind digital language, so grid stress converts into throttling, manual review, exception processing, and backlog accumulation, turning time into rationed asset and discretion into legitimacy hazard. Rising resilience costs push payment, clearing, and identity functions toward consolidation because only the largest operators can afford redundant sites and hardened power, converting energy volatility into concentrated private settlement sovereignty and correlated fragility. The macro effect is not only inflation; it is a revaluation of time that shortens terms, widens haircuts, increases buffers, and shifts collateral toward actors and regions that can stabilize energy access, while those who cannot are forced into slow lanes that function as an unlegislated tax. A serious redesign treats payment infrastructure as critical energy infrastructure, treats grid resilience as monetary stability finance, and builds rule-bound degraded-mode settlement with prioritized essentials, auditable overrides, and compensation logic, because a society whose settlement becomes conditional will experience contraction, inequality, and political anger long before it names the cause.

CHAPTER 43
FINAL DOCTRINE
DESIGN PRINCIPLES FOR SOVEREIGNTY, STABILITY, AND ADVANTAGE

The last room is never announced as the last room. It is called a coordination meeting, an interagency update, a stability call, a routine briefing that happens to be scheduled at the hour when sleep becomes an indulgence and certainty becomes scarce. Doors close softly. Phones are placed face down. A legal adviser brings a thin folder with the clauses that matter when promises become contested. A market-operations lead brings a dashboard that converts fear into numbers: queues, fails, spreads, cutoffs, intraday credit usage, margin calls arriving early, and margin calls arriving as if they are the same thing as justice. A head of supervision arrives with a list of institutions that are "fine" until the afternoon, and a list of dependencies that are "outsourced" until they become sovereign. A finance minister listens and realizes what ministers learn only when the machine is already moving against them: there are moments when the state does not decide so much as it chooses which constraint will become visible first. If it chooses to defend liquidity, inflation may rise. If it chooses to defend prices, unemployment may rise. If it chooses to defend convertibility, reserves may drain. If it chooses to defend domestic order, external passage may narrow. Each choice is a re-ranking of ranked claims, a reallocation of time, and a public declaration of legal priority even when officials insist no such declaration was made.

The modern system is built to make those choices appear technical until the day they cannot be hidden. On that day, the public asks a simple question with no patience for nuance: who is protected and who is sacrificed. Officials answer in the language of stability. The machine answers in the language of settlement: whose payment completes, whose collateral remains eligible, whose credit line remains open, whose margin call is bridged, whose account is restricted, whose claim is subordinated, whose loss is assigned to the future through a public balance sheet, and whose loss is assigned to the present through liquidation. This is the moment the audience for this book understands instinctively: policy is not the speeches, it is the gates. The gates are what the system enforces when the lights flicker.

In the end, money is a matter of belief. (central banker, private remark)

The remark is true and dangerously incomplete. Belief does not float. Belief is manufactured by procedures that produce closure, by enforcement that makes closure binding, and by institutions that defend finality under stress. Belief is the surface sheen of a harder architecture. Under it sits the machine: the unit of account that makes obligations comparable, the ledger regime that makes them admissible, the settlement pathways that convert promises into discharge, the collateral rules that determine which assets can be upgraded into liquidity, the legal priority schedules that allocate loss, and the backstops that decide when the state will convert private fragility into public obligation. When belief fails, it fails first at a gate: a payment is held; a security is no longer eligible; a corridor tightens identity requirements; a clearing venue raises margin and shortens timing; a custodian delays transfer; a bank's risk committee shortens terms; a market-maker withdraws quotes; an enforcement letter triggers over-restriction; a cloud incident disrupts visibility; a cyber event forces degraded mode; an insurer rewrites terms and collateral values change. The belief crisis is practical long before it is philosophical.

The purpose of this final doctrine is not to summarize the book and admire the symmetry. The purpose is to deliver a design grammar for those whose job is to govern the machine without pretending it is a morality play. A monetary order is not sustained by good intentions. It is sustained by the ability to make obligations end on schedule, to make record authoritative without being corruptible, to make liquidity available without turning rescue into theft, and to impose loss without turning failure into civil disorder. The doctrine is therefore the set of principles that separate a system that survives stress from a system that becomes hostage to its own seams. It is written for the only audience that matters when the machine is tested: finance ministers, central-bank governors, heads of supervision, sovereign advisers, bank chairmen, regulators, multilateral officials, and system architects. It is written in the language of consequences: what a design choice buys, what it costs, and how it fails when fear arrives.

The first truth a serious reader must accept is that neutrality is a story the system tells itself. Every design choice embeds distribution because every design choice embeds a hierarchy of access and a hierarchy of completion. The question is not whether distribution exists. The question is whether it is governed by rule and defended by legitimacy, or governed by discretion and defended by power. A system governed by discretion does not become flexible; it becomes purchasable, because discretion is the currency of favor. A system governed by rigid rule does not become fair; it becomes brittle, because rigid rule becomes cruelty when reality shifts. The doctrine here is design discipline: rule-bound enough to be legitimate, flexible enough to be resilient, explicit enough that the hierarchy the machine enforces under stress is visible before panic makes it visible in the ugliest way.

The Ordinary Breach That Ends Regimes

The foundational scene for the doctrine is ordinary and therefore easy to miss. A payroll file is transmitted. A receipt is generated. Employees assume wages will appear because wages are not experienced as credit; they are experienced as property. A back-end queue slows because a processor throttles under load, or a compliance filter runs heavier checks, or a data center drops into degraded mode, or an outage forces batch posting to slip. A subset of workers is paid late. The delay is small in system time and enormous in household time. Overdraft fees trigger. Rent payments bounce. Childcare payments fail. The worker does not parse authorization versus settlement. The worker knows only that the system promised completion and did not deliver it. Rumor spreads that some were paid and some were not, and whether the rumor is true becomes irrelevant because it feels true in a system that no longer produces reliable closure. That is how legitimacy collapses: not in speeches, but in missed obligations that people experience as betrayal.

The same breach repeats at corporate scale, with different language and larger numbers. A supplier's invoice is not paid on the day expected because the receiving firm's incoming receivables are held. The supplier tightens terms. The supplier demands prepayment. The receiving firm draws its line. The bank tightens because the bank sees volatility in flows. The firm reduces inventory. Inventory reduction becomes shortage. Shortage becomes price volatility. Price volatility triggers margin calls on hedges and tighter collateral demands on funding. What began as a payment hold becomes a working-capital crisis because the system turned time into scarcity.

The final version of the same breach repeats at sovereign scale. External admissibility tightens. Corridors slow. Documentation burdens rise. Reserve usage becomes visible. Visibility becomes narrative. Narrative becomes loss of confidence. Loss of confidence becomes funding stop. Funding stop becomes domestic austerity not as ideology but as time scarcity: obligations arriving without the ability to upgrade domestic claims into external settlement. The state then discovers a humiliating fact: domestic legality does not guarantee external passage. The doctrine below is designed to prevent these ordinary breaches from becoming regime endings by governing the gates before fear turns them into weapons.

I. Discharge Is the First Claim and the First Promise

Money begins where argument ends. A payment system that cannot produce discharge that third parties must honor is not a payment system. It is a messaging layer with legal theater attached. Discharge is the moment an obligation ends by rule. Without discharge, every transfer remains contestable; if contestable, every claim remains fragile; if fragile, credit shrinks; if credit shrinks, the economy becomes smaller and more violent in its bargaining because private enforcement returns as substitute for public closure. Discharge must be defined with precision and defended with enforcement that cannot be purchased. This is not a philosophical preference; it is the condition under which strangers will accept claims without carrying their own threat to enforce them.

The modern temptation is to treat discharge as user experience. "Instant" becomes marketing. "Real-time" becomes a public promise. Yet discharge is not speed; discharge is legal finality. Speed is operational. Finality is constitutional. A system can deliver fast posting and still lack finality if reversals remain available through broad discretion, if holds are routine, if settlement is conditional on later screening, or if legal claims can reopen the payment as if completion were a suggestion. A system that produces many "pending" states has surrendered its core job: ending the argument. Pending is not a neutral state. Pending is the return of bargaining under another name. It is the creditor's anxiety, the debtor's uncertainty, the banker's buffer demand, and the public's suspicion that some people have a faster lane.

Discharge also has a second function designers underweight because it does not sound like power: mercy. If discharge ends the creditor's right to pursue once payment is made, it prevents perpetual collection and perpetual dispute. Mercy is not sentiment; mercy is stabilization, because planning requires the belief that obligations can close. A society that cannot close obligations hoards and refuses risk. A society that closes obligations without discipline becomes cynical and extracts advantage through opportunistic default. The doctrine is to define discharge so that it binds both sides: it binds the creditor from endless pursuit, it binds the debtor from endless renegotiation, and it binds outsiders who finance the next transaction to treat closure as closure.

Discharge must be layered because different domains close differently. Retail systems require discharge that protects ordinary life from back-end complexity, because ordinary life cannot carry the burden of institutional conditionality without becoming politically combustible. Wholesale systems require discharge that survives stress in collateral markets and does not evaporate into discretion precisely when large obligations must close. Cross-boundary systems require discharge that remains coherent when legal regimes differ, because incoherent discharge is how corridors become gates and how commerce becomes an act of permission.

The failure modes of discharge are predictable and therefore unforgivable. False finality occurs when the interface tells users something is done while the back-end retains broad conditions and reversals. False finality produces political explosion because it converts technical process into perceived theft. Reversible finality occurs when the system preserves discretion to reverse under vague criteria; it looks like integrity until it becomes selective protection and destroys legitimacy. Fragmented discharge occurs when multiple perimeters have incompatible closure definitions, turning cross-boundary commerce into negotiated privilege.

A serious discharge doctrine therefore imposes a harsh discipline: decide where finality lives; decide what reversibility exists and under what narrowly defined process; decide which institution has authority to declare completion; and make that authority legally and operationally defensible against both error and capture. Discharge cannot be allowed to drift into "whatever the platform decides," because platform discretion is not sovereign legitimacy. It is private governance wearing the mask of security.

II. The Ledger Is a Constitution and Must Be Governed Like One

Every monetary order is a ledger regime. The ledger is not neutral bookkeeping. It is the institution that decides which obligations become enforceable facts and therefore transferable claims. It decides who may write, what counts as proof, when an entry becomes official, and how correction occurs without inviting opportunistic rewriting. It is where trust becomes procedure, and procedure is how strangers transact without private force. The state that treats its ledgers as databases is the state that will be surprised by crisis, because crisis is when database questions become constitutional questions: who is recognized, whose record is admissible, whose correction is permitted, whose error becomes permanent, whose claim can travel, and whose claim becomes trapped inside an account nobody trusts.

The doctrinal demand is to govern the ledger the way states govern constitutions: clarity, narrow amendment channels, defined authority, and protection against capture. Capture is the modern ledger risk because modern ledger authority is spread across committees, vendors, platforms, and internal control planes where "policy" is expressed as settings. A ledger that can be rewritten cheaply by insiders is not a ledger; it is a corruption machine. A ledger that cannot be corrected is not a ledger; it is a cruelty machine. The stable ledger is the one that can be corrected through admissible proof and due procedure while remaining resistant to opportunism.

Modern systems have multiplied ledgers: bank balance-sheet ledgers, payment platform ledgers, clearing ledgers, custodian ledgers, token ledgers, and the shadow ledgers inside risk engines that determine haircuts, margin, and access. Fragility emerges when these ledgers disagree about what is true, or when they can be made to disagree by an operator with an incentive to delay, exclude, or extract rent. A serious doctrine therefore requires ledger coherence: a disciplined map of how claims travel across ledgers, where they are upgraded into higher-grade settlement, where they can be reversed, and which ledger's entry is authoritative at the point of dispute. If coherence is not designed, coherence will be invented during crisis by whoever controls the bottleneck, and that invention will look like coercion because it will be coercion.

The ledger doctrine also includes identity. Identity is not a cultural debate in this frame; it is the mechanism that makes penalty meaningful and makes ledger entries attributable. A ledger without identity integrity becomes a theater of forgery. A ledger with identity integrity becomes a platform for credit. Yet identity can be weaponized because identity standards are gates. If identity standards shift unpredictably, are enforced unevenly, or are outsourced to operators whose incentives are not aligned with public legitimacy, exclusion becomes monetary policy by another name. The doctrine is layered membership: strict enough for enforcement and fraud resistance, predictable enough to avoid arbitrary exclusion, resilient enough to operate in degraded mode without collapsing into discretionary favoritism.

The system must also govern correction as legitimacy hinge. Too little correction produces brittle injustice: errors harden into permanent damage and the ledger becomes feared. Too much correction produces corrosive uncertainty: the past can be rewritten cheaply, so the future cannot be financed. The rule is not "be fair." The rule is "be correctable through disciplined channels." Disciplined channels are what allow outsiders to treat the record as reliable without personal trust. Personal trust does not scale. Disciplined correction does.

III. Finality First, Speed Second, Sequence Discipline Always

Speed without finality is illusion. Finality without speed can produce stagnation and shadow workarounds that move risk outside governable perimeters. The correct order is finality first, speed second, and sequence discipline always. A payment sequence has distinct states: authorization, posting, clearing, settlement, reconciliation, dispute handling, legal discharge. Users confuse these states because the interface compresses them into one impression: paid. The state must not confuse them. A state that confuses messaging completion with legal finality will be surprised by panic because it will believe obligations have closed when they remain conditional. Conditionality becomes weapon under stress because it allows gatekeepers to slow, hold, and reclassify while claiming integrity.

Sequence discipline sounds technical until the system produces ambiguous states that people experience as betrayal. Authorized but not posted. Posted but not cleared. Cleared but not settled. Settled but not confirmed. Confirmed and later reversed. Each ambiguity invites dispute. Dispute invites delay. Delay forces buffers. Buffers tighten credit. Tight credit spreads fear. Fear produces more disputes. The doctrine is to minimize ambiguous states, to define their legal meaning clearly when they exist, and to ensure that transitions between states are governed by rule rather than by discretionary staff actions that can be purchased or politicized.

Finality design must include queue discipline because queues are not nuisances; they are triage. Triage allocates time. Time allocation becomes solvency allocation when obligations are timed. Solvency allocation becomes political allocation when failure spills into employment, supply, and public order. A system that allows queue management to be discretionary will be accused—often correctly—of selective protection. The doctrine is rule-bound queue governance, auditable overrides, and explicit prioritization of essential flows in degraded mode. If essential prioritization is not defined in calm, it will be improvised in crisis, and improvisation will look like favoritism even when it is survival.

Finality design must include the coupling between settlement and collateral. When settlement is delayed, collateral is trapped. When collateral is trapped, funding tightens. Tight funding forces liquidation. Liquidation causes price gapping. Price gapping triggers margin and haircut changes. The system enters a self-amplifying loop. This is the moment macro language fails, because the collapse is driven by sequence and coupling rather than by a single policy instrument. The doctrine here is not "avoid volatility." It is "avoid mechanical amplification." Mechanical amplification is what converts a price move into forced liquidation through the coupling of valuation, haircuts, and margin. Finality that releases collateral on predictable timetables is one of the few stabilizers that can be designed without continuous discretionary rescue.

IV. Collateral Is Faith, Haircuts Are Discipline, Perfection Is Teeth

Collateral is where the system places its faith because collateral is what allows lending against uncertainty. Collateral eligibility lists, haircut schedules, margin timing, perfection rules, and custody mobility are the hidden constitution of credit. They decide which assets can be upgraded into liquidity, on what terms, with what documentation, under what custody regime, and with what speed. In calm, collateral doctrine is invisible. In stress, collateral doctrine becomes the command language of the system.

The principle is to treat collateral governance as statecraft. Eligibility must be explicit enough to be defended. Haircut logic must be coherent enough across institutions that it does not produce cliff effects when a single committee reclassifies a category and the market follows. Margin timing must be calibrated to avoid self-generated cascades. Perfection and custody chains must be clear enough that seizure and liquidation can occur without litigating basic title, because litigation freezes collateral mobility and frozen collateral is how solvent institutions become illiquid institutions in days. The system is often less afraid of loss than it is of ambiguity, because ambiguity destroys planning. The doctrine is to remove ambiguity where ambiguity becomes a panic channel.

Collateral doctrine must confront correlation. A system fails not only when collateral loses value, but when many assets lose value together and haircuts widen in synchronized fashion. Synchronized widening forces synchronized selling. Synchronized selling is systemic crisis. The doctrine is diversification with hierarchy: broad enough eligible sets to avoid brittle dependence, clear enough ranking so the system knows what is truly high-grade, and backstop facilities that stabilize temporarily without turning every asset into state-backed quasi-money permanently. Permanent expansion of eligibility is seductive because it calms panic. It also erodes meaning and invites leverage to rebuild on the assumption of rescue.

Collateral doctrine is distributive. Tightening eligibility re-ranks which sectors and regions can finance themselves. Loosening eligibility subsidizes risk and relocates loss into the public balance sheet. Both can be justified. Both must be governed. The doctrine is predictability and transition. Eligibility changes should not arrive as surprises during stress because surprises create cliff effects and cliff effects create panic and legitimacy loss. Transition is governance.

Perfection is the part most often treated as legal plumbing and then rediscovered as existential. If title is contestable, collateral is not collateral; it is an invitation to litigation. If litigation is likely, counterparties refuse exposure in crisis because legal time is slower than financial time. The doctrine therefore treats perfection, custody mobility, and enforceability as crisis tools, not as paperwork. A state that cannot move collateral quickly under law is a state whose backstop will be less effective because it will not be able to accept collateral without importing legal uncertainty into the public balance sheet.

V. Legal Priority Is the Hidden Constitution; Resolution Enforces It; Delay Is the First Weapon

Every monetary order eventually meets scarcity. Scarcity is where the system proves who it protects. Legal priority decides which claims are senior, which are subordinated, and which are sacrificed when value is insufficient. Priority is not an appendix. It is the constitution expressed as a schedule. Resolution enforces that schedule under pressure. Delay is the oldest crisis instrument because time is the first rationed asset when finality becomes scarce.

In calm, priority is ignored. In stress, priority becomes moral language because it determines who loses first. If priority is unclear, insolvency becomes a race. Races become privatized enforcement. Privatized enforcement becomes fragmentation. Priority prevents continuous brawling by forcing a ranking and forcing that ranking to be honored by third parties. That is how the system preserves continuity after failure: it assigns loss so activity can resume. The doctrine is to make priority legible enough that expectations match reality, because expectation mismatch is where panic becomes rage.

Resolution must be credible, rapid, and rule-bound. If resolution is slow, uncertainty spreads and funding freezes. If resolution is discretionary, legitimacy collapses because outcomes look like favoritism. If resolution is punitive without continuity protections, the system becomes fragile because fear of failure becomes fear of disorder, and fear of disorder drives runs earlier. The doctrine is to protect essential continuity and impose loss where risk was borne, in a way that can be defended as justice rather than revenge.

Deposit protection, emergency guarantees, and lender-of-last-resort facilities are all priority assignments in advance. They make certain claims senior by policy. This is not a moral embarrassment. It is design. The embarrassment is failing to govern the perimeter: protecting claims while allowing protected institutions to behave as de facto sovereign issuers without sovereign obligations. The doctrine is explicit perimeter, credible funding, discipline imposed on beneficiaries, and resolution tools that make failure survivable without turning rescue into permanent entitlement.

Delay, finally, must be governed as a crisis tool rather than allowed to appear as accident. Delay allocates time. Time allocation allocates solvency. Solvency allocation allocates political pain. A system that lets delay fall randomly will be accused of corruption. A system that designs delay, with explicit priorities and auditable queues, can defend it as triage rather than theft.

VI. Convertibility Is Discipline; Upgrade Rights Are Sovereignty; Runs Are Mass Upgrade Attempts

Convertibility is the promise that one claim can be upgraded into a higher-grade claim on known terms within known time. Convertibility is how hierarchies are managed. It is also how runs occur, because runs are mass upgrade attempts. If the system promises convertibility without capacity, it invites panic. If it denies convertibility without legitimacy, it invites revolt. Convertibility exists in layers: retail deposits to settlement claims, bank liabilities to central settlement assets, token claims to bank money, domestic money to foreign money through corridors, collateral to cash through secured funding and backstop facilities. Each layer has gates: documentation, eligibility, cutoffs, identity proofs, operational capacity, discretionary holds.

The doctrine is to map convertibility pathways explicitly and test them under stress conditions that include operational failure, not only price moves. Stress includes outages, queue overload, cyber incidents, legal holds, and cross-border tightening. If convertibility is not tested under operational stress, it will fail precisely when demand for upgrade spikes. The system then discovers that its promise was conditional in a way nobody admitted, and conditional promises are the fuel of runs because they create the fear that you will be the last one allowed to upgrade.

Convertibility is geopolitical discipline. Cross-boundary upgrade rights depend on correspondent networks, messaging standards, compliance regimes, and strategic exclusion decisions. A state that relies on external convertibility for essentials is dependent. Dependency is not an insult. It is a condition. The doctrine is to measure dependency, build buffers where dependency cannot be avoided, negotiate corridor access as continuous statecraft, and develop alternative passage where feasible without fantasy that symbols can substitute for corridors.

The reserve order is infrastructure rather than admiration. The top currency sets terms because it sets the easiest upgrade into usability under stress. That advantage is maintained through collateral conventions, settlement corridors, predictable legality, and credible backstops. Challengers who focus on issuance without corridors build claims that circulate in calm and seize in stress. Claims that seize in stress are not sovereignty. They are ornaments.

VII. Backstop Is Constitutional Power; Use It Like Law, Not Like Panic

Backstops prevent liquidity problems from becoming solvency problems and solvency problems from becoming social collapse. Yet backstops are also where the state can lose legitimacy because backstops can look like selective protection, and selective protection is the moral trigger of rupture. The doctrine is to design backstops as rule-bound, priced, and conditional facilities that can be activated quickly without improvisation. Improvisation is the enemy because improvisation looks like favoritism even when it is survival.

Rule-bound does not mean rigid. It means predictable triggers, clear eligible collateral, transparent haircut logic, clear penalty pricing or equivalent discipline, and a credible resolution framework that ensures the backstop does not become permanent subsidy to reckless leverage. It means the state can act at machine speed without appearing to invent rules mid-crisis. That is how legitimacy is preserved: not by pretending rescue is popular, but by making rescue defensible.

Backstop doctrine must include time discipline. Backstops buy time. Time preserves stability and creates dependency. External time creates geopolitical leverage. Domestic time creates distributional conflict. The state must be willing to say what time is being purchased and for whom: to prevent payment disruption, prevent fire sales, protect depositors, preserve critical market-making, sustain essential imports, prevent sovereign refinancing collapse. If purpose is unclear, the backstop becomes political target. If purpose is clear and discipline visible, the backstop can be defended as constitutional function rather than favoritism.

Backstop doctrine must include exit discipline. Permanent intervention is the path of least resistance. It is also the path to quiet nationalization without accountability: private profits preserved, public losses absorbed, incentives degraded, resentment sharpened. Exit must be condition-based: when finality and private intermediation return, the backstop shrinks; when they do not, the backstop demands restructuring rather than silently becoming permanent.

VIII. Concentration Is the New Fragility; Redundancy Is Sovereign Capacity

Modern fragility is concentration. Concentration appears as efficiency until it becomes a single point of failure. Cloud concentration, platform concentration, identity-provider concentration, custodian concentration, clearing concentration, data-feed concentration, compliance chokepoint concentration create a condition where an outage, a legal hold, or a cyber event interrupts settlement across the system. The system then discovers it does not have "risk." It has dependency. Dependency cannot be diversified away; it must be designed away through redundancy, substitutability, and governance.

Redundancy is expensive. Redundancy is sovereign capacity. A state that cannot route around a private platform failure is not fully sovereign in its payment perimeter. A bank that cannot route around a cloud incident is not safe; it is a bank with hidden fragility. A market that cannot function when a single data feed fails is not a market; it is a machine that produces numbers until it cannot. The doctrine is mandatory substitutability where failure would be systemic: multi-provider architectures, tested failover, independent time sources, independent identity verification channels, clear degraded-mode procedures that preserve legitimacy and avoid discretionary triage.

Concentration also creates power. The operator of a dominant node can impose documentation burdens, standards, fees, and exclusion decisions. That power can be used for integrity. It can also be used for rent extraction and strategic exclusion. The doctrine is to treat dominant nodes as public-interest institutions even when privately owned, subject to governance obligations commensurate with their role in settlement. This is architecture: if a private node can stop commerce, it is exercising sovereign-adjacent power, and sovereign-adjacent power must be governed or it will govern you.

IX. Interoperability Is Not Peace; It Is a Control Surface; Translators Become Gatekeepers

Interoperability is often sold as progress. It can be. It can also be weapon. Interoperability means systems can speak to each other, translate identity, translate claims, and transfer value across perimeters. That is beneficial for commerce. It is also beneficial for power because the translator becomes the gatekeeper. In splintering regimes, standards become borders. Identity diverges. Data requirements diverge. Compliance postures diverge. Finality definitions diverge. The seam between regimes becomes a market because divergence creates spreads between fast and slow money, legible and suspect money, eligible and discounted collateral. Arbitrage flourishes. Smuggling evolves from goods to proof packets and timing.

The system responds by tightening standards. Tightening thickens seams. Thick seams create more rents. Rents attract corruption. Corruption triggers more tightening. The loop becomes arms race in compliance and passage. The doctrine is deliberate interoperability: a clear theory of permitted flows, monitored flows, prohibited flows; minimum proofs for essentials; governance of translators as critical nodes; legal alignment sufficient to prevent "fast value" from landing in contested finality that detonates later as litigation and political scandal.

Interoperability must be bounded to preserve sovereign capacity. A state that allows external systems to define its identity standards and compliance rules surrenders autonomy through interface. A state that refuses interoperability entirely will be isolated and pay higher costs and lower growth. The doctrine is controlled permeability: open enough to trade, disciplined enough to preserve enforceable closure, designed to avoid single translation chokepoints that can be captured or coerced.

X. Strategic Exclusion Is Modern Statecraft; Uncontrolled Exclusion Creates Uncontrolled Fragmentation

Strategic exclusion is access denial, freezes, de-risking, corridor narrowing, and compliance pressure used to impose geopolitical cost through settlement systems. It works because it operates through ordinary payment sequence without dramatic formal rupture. It is effective precisely because it feels administrative. The doctrine is not to pretend it does not exist. The doctrine is to govern it.

If strategic exclusion is applied without clear authority, it becomes arbitrary power and invites retaliation. If applied through private over-compliance without accountability, it becomes shadow foreign policy run by risk committees and platform operators. If applied too broadly, it accelerates challenger corridors and parallel networks, reducing future leverage while increasing global fragility through splintering. The doctrine is constitutional discipline: triggers, boundaries, accountability, second-order consequence analysis. The point is control. Uncontrolled exclusion produces uncontrolled fragmentation, and uncontrolled fragmentation makes future crises harder to manage and easier to weaponize.

XI. Design Against Flash Legitimacy Collapse; Legitimacy Is a Stability Input

Modern crises can be fast. Fast crises are not only balance-sheet crises. They are legitimacy crises where markets stop believing their own prices, payment systems stop producing predictable completion, reversals and halts create suspicion, and the public concludes the machine is rigged. Once that conclusion lands, every rescue becomes morally suspect and every discipline measure becomes politically explosive.

The doctrine is procedural legitimacy built into the machine: rule-bound halts, rule-bound reversals, rule-bound queue priorities, auditable override channels, clear liability and compensation frameworks when system failure imposes cost on ordinary actors. The objective is not to avoid every incident. The objective is to avoid the impression that outcomes depend on insider access. Insider access is the political trigger.

This doctrine requires humility about automation. Automated risk engines and machine markets synchronize retreat. Synchronized retreat turns microstructure into macro tightening. Supervisors must examine withdrawal conditions and reduce common-mode triggers where possible: smoothing margin requirements, preventing procyclical haircuts from spiking at the worst moment, ensuring critical market-making in essential instruments does not depend on narrow set of private strategies whose constraints are correlated. Legitimacy is not solved by speeches. It is solved by rules that behave predictably under stress and by mechanisms that distribute pain in ways that can be defended. Pain is inevitable. Indefensible pain is rupture.

XII. Multilateral Instruments Are Architecture; They Allocate Time Through Conditionality

Multilateral support is often treated as rescue or charity. Inside the actual machine, it is liquidity and conditionality that shapes domestic policy by shaping access to time. It is part of the global ledger of admissibility: who is treated as creditworthy, under what documentation regime, under what policy constraints, and how quickly corridor gatekeepers will restore passage after an episode of fear.

For sovereigns, the doctrine is to treat multilateral liquidity as a layer of hierarchy, not as an external moral event. Support can stabilize. It can also impose dependency. It can also enforce convergence to standards favored by dominant corridors. Sometimes this is how coherence is preserved. Sometimes it becomes politically toxic if imposed without legitimacy.

For multilateral designers and sovereign negotiators, the doctrine is intelligible conditionality, minimized hidden discretion, preservation of domestic social stability while enforcing fiscal and monetary discipline, and coordination with corridor gatekeepers so support translates into actual passage and actual settlement, not merely domestic accounting relief. A rescue that does not restore admissibility buys little time. A rescue that restores admissibility at the price of political collapse accelerates long-run fragility. The purpose is not to be loved. The purpose is to keep the machine capable of closure, because closure is what allows reform to be paid for rather than screamed for.

XIII. Make the Payment State a State Function Again, Even When Operated in Partnership

The payment state is the set of institutions and rules that move money and declare completion. In recent decades, the payment state became a partnership between public authority and private infrastructure. Partnerships can work. They also conceal power. The doctrine is to make partnership explicit: which private nodes are critical, what obligations they have, what redundancy they must meet, what audit standards govern them, what public powers exist to compel continuity in emergency.

Without explicit governance, private operators become de facto sovereigns in their domains. They impose documentation burdens, widen fees, deny access, throttle flows, reshape settlement sequence. Often they do so in the name of integrity. The problem is incentive mismatch. They protect themselves first. The state is blamed anyway. Therefore the state must govern the payment state as infrastructure: resilience mandates, substitutability mandates, tested failover, emergency protocols that are rule-bound, accountability that matches systemic importance.

XIV. Advantage Is Design Discipline; Reserve Status Is Usability Under Stress

States compete over monetary advantage. Some advantage is inherited: scale, history, networks. Enduring advantage is design discipline: enforceable closure, liquidity without legitimacy collapse, legal priority without chaos, finality under stress, governed concentration, controlled interoperability, strategic exclusion without self-defeating fragmentation, backstop without surrendering sovereign capacity to private issuers.

Advantage accumulates as reputation that claims remain usable when fear rises. Usability is the test. Usability depends on settlement finality, collateral eligibility, convertibility pathways, credible backstops. This is why reserve order is infrastructure rather than admiration. The system that ends arguments reliably becomes the system others depend on.

The challenger doctrine is not to mint a new symbol. It is to build a corridor of trust: architecture that clears at scale, defends finality legally, provides liquidity to its nodes in crisis, imposes loss allocation credibly, governs identity without arbitrary exclusion, maintains interoperability without surrendering control to external gatekeepers. Challengers who cannot do this build claims that circulate in calm and seize in stress. Claims that seize in stress are not sovereignty. They are ornaments.

The Hard Counterargument, Tested Without Comfort

The official defense of existing architectures is familiar: imperfect but adaptive; private innovation improves efficiency; crises rare relative to daily success; complexity manageable through supervision and capital; heavy redesign risks unintended harm. The defense has weight. A system that tries to eliminate every failure mode can become brittle because over-control pushes risk into shadows and reduces adaptation capacity. A system that politicizes credit allocation can misprice risk and create fiscal burdens that become unsustainable. A system that mandates redundancy everywhere can impose costs that reduce growth.

The answer is to identify which layers are constitutional and which can remain competitive. Discharge, finality, legal priority, backstop governance are constitutional. They must be rule-bound and publicly defensible. Retail interfaces, credit products, and certain market services can remain competitive if failures are contained and if their claims cannot masquerade as public money without public obligations. Cloud services, identity providers, clearing venues, custodians cannot be treated as ordinary vendors if their failure interrupts settlement. They are infrastructure. Infrastructure demands governance not because the state loves control, but because the public cannot tolerate money failing as if it were an app.

The deeper counterargument is cynical: the system will always protect the powerful; doctrine is theater; crisis is where hierarchy is enacted; redesign is fantasy. The cynicism contains truth. Yet it is abdication. Hierarchy cannot be eliminated. It can be governed. Legal priority is hierarchy by design; without it, hierarchy appears as violence. Backstops are hierarchy by design; without them, hierarchy appears as runs and mass liquidation. The choice is explicit disciplined hierarchy or implicit discretionary hierarchy. The doctrine insists on the first because the second is how states lose legitimacy and then lose capacity.

The lender of last resort is there to lend, but not to be loved. (supervisory line)

The line is cold and correct. Rescue is constitutional power, not a popularity project. Yet rescue without doctrine becomes favoritism and favoritism becomes revolt. Discipline must be visible: conditionality, penalty logic, resolution of failed institutions, legal priority enforced. Love is not required. Legitimacy is required, and legitimacy is earned by procedures that withstand scrutiny.

The Practical Doctrine, Stated as Action

A doctrine that cannot be operationalized becomes prose. The audience here does not need prose. It needs action principles that can be applied to actual architectures, legal frameworks, institutional mandates, and cross-border dependencies. The following practical doctrine is sufficient to distinguish ceremonial reform from redesign.

The settlement endpoint must be identified, legally defended, and operationally resilient. If the system cannot say which ledger entry constitutes the final discharge fact for its highest-grade claims, it does not know what it is defending in crisis. If reversal conditions remain broad, finality is marketing, not law.

Convertibility pathways must be mapped as upgrade rights and tested as stress behavior, including operational failure. For each major claim type, the state must be able to answer: how does this claim upgrade into settlement, under what collateral and identity gates, on what time schedule, with what discretion, with what failure modes. Unknown gates become panic gates; panic gates become political gates.

Concentration nodes must be treated as infrastructure. If a node can interrupt settlement, it must meet redundancy and substitutability obligations. Substitutability must be tested, not promised. Degraded-mode behavior must be designed, not improvised. Improvisation allocates time and money by discretion, and discretion is the birthplace of scandal because it cannot be defended once the anger arrives.

Queue and triage must be governed openly enough to be defendable. Essentials cannot be preserved by prayer. They require explicit prioritization and rule-bound processing, with auditable overrides and compensation logic. A system that cannot explain why some payments were delayed and others were not will be accused of corruption even if it acted in good faith.

Collateral governance must be treated as constitutional project. Eligibility, haircut schedules, margin timing, perfection standards, custody mobility must be coherent enough that crisis does not become litigation over title and admissibility. The system must reduce mechanical amplification by smoothing pro-cyclical triggers where possible, because pro-cyclical triggers are how small shocks become cascades.

Identity must be hardened without turning identity gates into arbitrary exclusion. Identity standards must be predictable, layered, and resilient in degraded mode. Degraded mode must preserve integrity while keeping essentials moving, because degraded mode that collapses into discretionary favors poisons legitimacy faster than any fraud loss.

Resolution must match declared hierarchy. Protected claims must be explicit. Loss allocation must be credible. Speed must be real. A system that promises protection and fails to deliver it loses legitimacy.

A system that delivers protection while allowing private actors to harvest upside without discipline loses legitimacy too.

Cross-boundary dependency must be integrated into national doctrine. Corridor access, compliance expectations, strategic exclusion risk, external admissibility are boundary conditions of sovereign autonomy. Essentials require buffers. Buffers require financing. Financing requires political discipline. This is statecraft, not technicality.

Legitimacy must be designed as stability input. Procedural fairness under stress is not moral luxury; it is functional requirement because legitimacy governs behavior, and behavior governs liquidity. A system that repeatedly produces outcomes that look rigged will be forced into destructive reforms driven by anger. Anger is not a policy tool. Anger is what happens when the machine produces pain that cannot be defended.

The Closing Turn: Why This Doctrine Is Not Optional

A serious reader may still be tempted to treat these principles as useful but not urgent, accurate but not decisive, true but not actionable amid political noise. That temptation is the system's oldest self-deception. The machine will not ask permission before it fails. It will fail at a seam and rewrite politics. It will fail through a queue and rewrite legitimacy. It will fail through collateral re-rating and rewrite credit. It will fail through corridor narrowing and rewrite sovereignty. Its failures are not waiting for consensus because they are not ideological. They are mechanical.

The doctrine to carry forward is not that money is mysterious. It is that money is designed, and design choices are statecraft. The state that treats money as tool and not architecture will be surprised repeatedly by crises that appear to come from nowhere. Those crises did not come from nowhere. They came from gates that were built, outsourced, optimized, and then forgotten.

The final truth is quiet and severe: the system cannot be made safe by rhetoric because the system's danger is not rhetorical. It is mechanical. It is coupling of ranked claims to settlement finality, collateral to liquidity, convertibility to runs, concentration to fragility, interoperability to strategic exclusion, backstop to political legitimacy. The system will remain hierarchy. The only question is whether it will be hierarchy governed by law and doctrine or hierarchy governed by panic and improvisation.

In a crisis, you find out what your rules really were. (resolution practitioner)

That is the final frame. The rules are not what statutes proclaim in calm. The rules are what the machine enforces under stress: who clears, who settles, who gets paid first. This doctrine is the attempt to make those rules visible enough to be governed before the system teaches them again through rupture.

CLOSING DOCTRINE

Money is governed architecture, not symbol: discharge defines the end of obligation as a public fact, and a system that cannot defend finality under stress collapses into conditional messaging, expanded disputability, and credit contraction. The ledger is a constitution: it decides admissibility, transferability, enforcement, and correction, and sovereignty is compromised when the authoritative ledger of settlement and finality sits outside accountable governance or becomes capturable through settings and chokepoints. Collateral is the system's faith and haircuts are its discipline: eligibility, margin timing, perfection, and custody mobility determine which assets can be upgraded into liquidity, while mechanical amplification through pro-cyclical haircuts and synchronized retreat is the pathway by which ordinary price moves become cascades. Legal priority is the hidden constitution and resolution is its enforcement; backstop is constitutional power that must be rule-bound, conditional, and paired with credible loss assignment to remain legitimate. Convertibility is engineered discipline across layers and borders; interoperability is a control surface that creates gates, rents, and strategic exclusion; concentration turns private operators into sovereign-adjacent nodes whose redundancy is sovereign capacity. The enduring advantage belongs to the state that designs these chambers deliberately—finality before speed, redundancy before efficiency theater, explicit triage before discretionary rescue—because crisis does not create hierarchy; it reveals the hierarchy already embedded in the machine.

PART NINE
APPENDIX
RESEARCH, REFERENCE REGISTER, SOURCE CONCORDANCE, GLOSSARY +

This appendix is built to be used, not admired. It has four layers. The first layer is the research corpus: the institutional and legal body of work that defines what the monetary machine is allowed to do when fear arrives. The second layer is the reference register: the same corpus reorganized by the function it governs, so an operator can move from a question to the authoritative text quickly. The third layer is a chapter-to-sources concordance: a navigation instrument that ties each part of the book to the load-bearing authorities that define its boundary conditions. The fourth layer is an audit matrix: doctrine statements expressed as test questions, each mapped to the class of sources that define the answer. The matrix is not decorative. It is meant to be used in review sessions, supervisory examinations, and redesign workstreams.

This appendix is extensive by intent. A monetary state that cannot identify its sources will be governed by other people's sources. The goal is to make the machine legible enough to govern.

RESEARCH, REFERENCE & DATA SOUCE

This appendix is built to be used, not admired. It has four layers. The first layer is the research corpus: the institutional and legal body of work that defines what the monetary machine is allowed to do when fear arrives. The second layer is the reference register: the same corpus reorganized by the function it governs, so an operator can move from a question to the authoritative text quickly. The third layer is a chapter-to-sources concordance: a navigation instrument that ties each part of the book to the load-bearing authorities that define its boundary conditions. The fourth layer is an audit matrix: doctrine statements expressed as test questions, each mapped to the class of sources that define the answer. The matrix is not decorative. It is meant to be used in review sessions, supervisory examinations, and redesign workstreams.

This appendix is extensive by intent. A monetary state that cannot identify its sources will be governed by other people's sources. The goal is to make the machine legible enough to govern.

A. Research posture, boundaries, and selection rules

The research base was built from four rings. The first ring is primary rule and doctrine text: international standards, central bank operational descriptions, supervisory frameworks, and legal architectures that define record, discharge, settlement finality, eligible collateral, convertibility pathways, insolvency priority, close-out netting enforceability, and backstop authority. The second ring is market plumbing: clearing and settlement infrastructure mechanics, margin and haircut dynamics, repo and collateral chains, custody and beneficial ownership, and cross-border corridor sequencing. The third ring is crisis history treated as architecture: the documented interventions, rule changes, and facility creations that show what the state actually does when the machine cannot close everything at once. The fourth ring is theory treated as a lens: it is included only where it helps identify which gate is primary and why, and it is rejected wherever it substitutes ideology for enforceability.

Sources were prioritized when they define binding endpoints or binding gates. Opinion was not treated as authority. Data was used only where the measurement regime itself is official or institutionally anchored.

B. Corpus inventory by authority type

The corpus is presented by authority type first because authority type predicts enforceability.

B1. International standards and institutional doctrine

Bank for International Settlements, Committee on Payments and Market Infrastructures. Used to anchor definitions and risk taxonomies for payment systems, settlement finality, intraday liquidity, queue governance, cross-border payment sequencing, and the operational meaning of "final settlement" under stress.

CPMI-IOSCO, Principles for Financial Market Infrastructures. Used as the global reference spine for FMI governance, finality expectations, default management, liquidity risk, operational resilience, and the public obligations of market utilities.

Basel Committee on Banking Supervision. Used to anchor how supervisory liquidity and capital regimes hard-code balance-sheet behavior under fear, including the definition of high-quality liquidity buffers and stress assumptions that translate into credit contraction.

Financial Stability Board. Used to anchor nonbank financial intermediation mapping, shadow liquidity, market-based finance vulnerabilities, and post-crisis governance coordination.

International Monetary Fund. Used to anchor balance-of-payments constraint, reserve adequacy, capital flow management, sovereign refinancing fragility, multilateral conditionality as time allocation, and the external admissibility problem.

World Bank Group and regional multilateral development banks. Used to anchor development-credit mechanisms as architecture: guarantees, policy lending, project finance, and the institutional channels that localize development credit while interacting with external corridor admissibility.

Financial Action Task Force. Used to anchor identity, compliance, and admissibility as corridor borders, and to explain how standards divergence creates seam markets, de-risking, and private over-compliance as quasi-statecraft.

IOSCO. Used to anchor market governance, integrity expectations, and the systemic role of infrastructure utilities.

B2. National legal foundations and enforceability regimes

Commercial law and funds transfer law. Used to anchor record, transferability, negotiability versus contract claims, and the enforceable meaning of payment instructions and completion.

Secured transactions and perfection doctrine. Used to anchor when collateral is legally usable in stress and when legal uncertainty becomes a panic channel.

Insolvency and resolution frameworks. Used to anchor priority schedules, the treatment of secured claims, the enforceability of close-out netting, and the operational difference between collection and order under scarcity.

Settlement finality statutes and netting enforceability regimes. Used to anchor why clearing and settlement can scale without being reopened by later litigation, and how finality is protected as an institutional property.

Cross-border insolvency recognition frameworks. Used to anchor legal clash at the boundary as a systemic risk channel, especially where custody and collateral mobility becomes contested.

B3. Market infrastructure rule texts and operational descriptions

RTGS and high-value payment system operational descriptions. Used to anchor queue management, intraday liquidity, cutoffs, and the conversion of time into solvency.

Clearinghouse and CCP rule texts and public risk descriptions. Used to anchor margin timing, default management, loss allocation, and the institutionalization of netting as governance.

Repo market structure descriptions. Used to anchor collateral upgrade rights, haircut dynamics, and the difference between visible money and borrowed liquidity.

Custody and settlement system descriptions. Used to anchor beneficial ownership mechanics, custody chain mobility, and the points where legal time can freeze financial time.

Cross-border corridor and correspondent banking descriptions. Used to anchor access, passage, and finality as separate states governed by documentation burdens, screening, and private risk committees.

Operational resilience frameworks for critical nodes and third-party dependencies. Used to anchor concentration as sovereignty risk and degraded-mode governance as legitimacy preservation.

B4. Crisis history and intervention architecture

Classic lender-of-last-resort doctrine. Used to anchor time purchase with discipline, penalty logic, and collateral.

Dealer-of-last-resort and market backstop evolution. Used to anchor how states increasingly backstop market functioning and collateral liquidity, not only deposit funding.

Post-crisis reforms to clearing, margin, resolution, and operational resilience. Used to anchor the reality that the constitution of money is updated through crisis governance, not only through legislative theory.

B5. Theory lenses used only as mechanism clarifiers

Credit and state theories of money used to anchor the primacy of the unit of account, enforceable record, and taxation acceptance logic as demand engine, while insisting that this is operationalized through ledgers and settlement.

Monetary hierarchy literature used to anchor the claim that crisis is mass upgrade attempt and that the system's power sits in upgrade rights and collateral eligibility.

Market-instruments lenses used to anchor how instruments become money-like through eligibility, netting, settlement finality, and backstop expectations rather than through intrinsic character.

Currency competition lenses treated as counterargument to sharpen the claim that law, identity, custody, and finality are not optional layers that software can bypass at scale.

C. Reference register by governance function

This is the fast navigation layer. It organizes sources by the machine function they govern.

C1. Discharge, settlement finality, and payment sequencing

CPMI payment system doctrine and settlement risk taxonomy.

PFMI settlement finality, governance, and operational risk expectations.

National central bank operational descriptions of settlement and intraday liquidity.

Funds transfer legal frameworks defining completion, error correction, and liability boundaries.

C2. Ledger authority, admissibility, record, correction

Commercial law definitions of record and signature logic.

Evidence and business records logic as institutional practice for admissibility.

Audit and governance expectations for critical infrastructure.

Identity integrity standards and attribution mechanisms used for enforceability.

C3. Collateral eligibility, haircuts, margin, secured funding

Basel liquidity frameworks and HQLA logic.

BIS and FSB research on repo, haircuts, and collateral reuse.

CCP and clearing governance and margin timing expectations under PFMI.

Secured transactions and perfection law as mobility foundation.

C4. Insolvency, priority, resolution, close-out netting

Insolvency priority frameworks and secured versus unsecured treatment.

Resolution regime design and continuity tools.

Settlement finality and close-out netting enforceability regimes.

FMI default management and loss allocation governance expectations.

C5. Cross-border passage, corridors, admissibility, strategic exclusion

CPMI cross-border payment sequencing and improvement roadmap.

IMF external sector frameworks and reserve adequacy logic.

FATF standards, de-risking dynamics, and corridor screening logic.

Institutional analyses of correspondent banking and compliance divergence.

C6. Multilateral architecture and localized development credit

IMF program architecture and conditionality logic as time allocation.

World Bank and MDB lending instruments, guarantees, and project structures.

Blended finance and guarantee mechanism literature as domestic bankability engine.

Cross-border admissibility and corridor dependence sources linking external passage to domestic autonomy.

C7. Private rail, tokens, stable-value claims, and interface governance

BIS and IMF CBDC/tokenization analyses as sovereignty relocation study.

Supervisory materials on stable-value instruments and settlement risk.

PFMI concepts applied to new rails: governance, finality, operational resilience, default handling.

Identity and compliance standards as the programmable gate layer.

C8. Operational resilience, cloud concentration, cyber, degraded mode

PFMI operational risk expectations and resilience governance.

National supervisory operational resilience frameworks.

Critical third-party dependency doctrine.

Cyber resilience planning and degraded-mode governance practices.

D. Chapter-to-sources concordance

This section maps book sections to load-bearing sources. It is deliberately written so a reader can audit each chapter's mechanism spine quickly without hunting.

D1. Chapters on the first claim: discharge and finality

Load-bearing: CPMI definitions and settlement risk taxonomy; PFMI finality principles; central bank operational descriptions of settlement; funds transfer legal regimes.

Why: these sources define where "paid" becomes enforceable fact, and what reversibility is legally permitted.

D2. Chapters on ledger rule and admissibility

Load-bearing: commercial law record and transfer concepts; secured transactions enforceability; audit and governance standards for infrastructure; identity standards.

Why: these sources define which obligations become transferable claims rather than relational promises, and how correction preserves legitimacy without corruptibility.

D3. Chapters on credit creation, deposits, and hierarchy

Load-bearing: Basel liquidity and capital frameworks; central bank operational descriptions of reserves and settlement; monetary hierarchy scholarship; classic credit literature as lens.

Why: these sources explain why deposits feel same to households while ranking is enforced through convertibility, collateral, and settlement access at the institutional layer.

D4. Chapters on collateral, repo, shadow liquidity

Load-bearing: BIS and FSB repo and collateral reuse research; PFMI margin and default management expectations; secured transactions perfection doctrine; crisis backstop history.

Why: these sources explain how borrowed liquidity creates speed in calm and seizure in stress through haircut dynamics and margin timing.

D5. Chapters on crisis governance and backstops

Load-bearing: lender-of-last-resort doctrine; modern market backstop evolution; resolution frameworks; PFMI crisis expectations.

Why: these sources anchor that crisis is governance and that backstops are constitutional power with legitimacy risk.

D6. Chapters on cross-border dependence and reserve order

Load-bearing: BIS global liquidity; IMF external sector frameworks; CPMI cross-border sequencing; FATF admissibility standards and de-risking dynamics.

Why: these sources anchor the difference between access, passage, and finality and the ways dominant corridors set terms through admissibility.

D7. Chapters on multilateral development and localized credit

Load-bearing: IMF conditionality architecture; MDB lending and guarantee instruments; bankability and guarantee mechanism literature; external passage dependence sources.

Why: these sources anchor development finance as credit design interacting with external admissibility, not as spending narrative.

D8. Chapters on private rails, stable-value, programmable policy

Load-bearing: BIS/IMF CBDC and tokenization analyses; supervisory materials on stable-value; PFMI applied to new rails; identity and compliance standards.

Why: these sources anchor that private rails relocate sovereignty into code, identity, custody, and platform governance while remaining dependent on public finality under stress.

D9. Chapters on splintering and fragmented contagion

Load-bearing: CPMI cross-border payments; PFMI operational risk and governance; FATF standards divergence; operational resilience and third-party dependency doctrine.

Why: these sources anchor how seams become markets, translators become chokepoints, and bridge failure becomes cliff.

E. Doctrine audit matrix

The matrix below converts the book's final doctrine into test questions. Each question includes the source class that defines the authoritative answer. This allows a sovereign, supervisor, or system architect to audit an existing regime without relying on rhetoric.

E1. Discharge and finality

Test: Where is discharge legally declared for the system's highest-grade claims, and which ledger entry constitutes the enforceable end-state.

Authority class: CPMI final settlement definitions; PFMI finality expectations; national settlement system statutes and operational descriptions; funds transfer law.

Test: Under what narrow conditions can finality be reversed, who has authority to trigger reversal, and what compensation regime exists for erroneous reversals.

Authority class: funds transfer law; central bank and payment system rule texts; consumer and dispute liability frameworks.

E2. Ledger governance

Test: Who may write to the authoritative ledger, what proof is admissible, and how correction can occur without opportunistic rewriting.

Authority class: commercial law record definitions; infrastructure governance and audit standards; supervisory doctrine; internal ledger governance rules.

Test: Which private operators can alter ledger state by throttling, holding, or excluding, and what public accountability applies.

Authority class: operational resilience frameworks; critical third-party dependency doctrine; infrastructure governance standards.

E3. Convertibility and upgrade rights

Test: For each claim type, what is the engineered upgrade path into settlement, and what gates can tighten under stress.

Authority class: central bank operational doctrine; Basel liquidity and collateral frameworks; corridor and compliance standards; facility rule texts.

Test: What volume of upgrade demand can be met without discretionary rationing, and how rationing is governed if demand exceeds capacity.

Authority class: central bank liquidity facility design; payment system queue governance; crisis protocols.

E4. Collateral and haircuts

Test: What assets are eligible collateral for key facilities, what haircut logic applies, and how pro-cyclicality is mitigated.

Authority class: Basel liquidity frameworks; central bank collateral frameworks; PFMI margin governance; repo market mechanics research.

Test: Can collateral be perfected and mobilized at financial speed, and what legal clashes could freeze it.

Authority class: secured transactions law; custody and settlement system rules; cross-border recognition regimes.

E5. Priority and resolution

Test: What is the true priority schedule in insolvency, including any safe harbors, and can it be executed quickly without discretionary favoritism.

Authority class: insolvency and resolution law; netting enforceability regimes; resolution authority rule texts; PFMI default management expectations.

Test: What continuity obligations exist, who is protected, and how losses are allocated to preserve legitimacy.

Authority class: deposit protection frameworks; resolution regime design; crisis governance doctrine.

E6. Cross-border passage and strategic exclusion

Test: Which corridors are necessary for essentials, what admissibility standards govern passage, and what documentation gates can tighten without formal rupture.

Authority class: CPMI cross-border sequencing; FATF standards; correspondent banking and de-risking doctrine; IMF external sector frameworks.

Test: What is the state's plan for corridor tightening, and what buffers and alternate routes exist.

Authority class: reserve adequacy frameworks; trade finance and payment infrastructure planning; multilateral support options.

E7. Multilateral architecture and development-credit mechanisms

Test: How does multilateral support translate into actual corridor admissibility and restored passage, not just domestic accounting relief.

Authority class: IMF program design; corridor governance sources; MDB instruments and guarantees.

Test: How are local development credits structured to become bankable and enforceable while remaining compatible with external settlement requirements.

Authority class: MDB project finance instruments; guarantee mechanics; domestic enforceability law; external admissibility frameworks.

E8. Operational resilience and concentration

Test: Which nodes are single points of settlement failure, what substitution is tested, and what degraded-mode rules preserve legitimacy.

Authority class: operational resilience frameworks; PFMI operational risk principles; critical third-party dependency doctrine.

Test: How is cyber timing risk handled during degraded mode, and what queue priorities preserve essentials.

Authority class: cyber resilience doctrine; crisis protocols; payment system contingency plans.

F. Extended annotated bibliography for rapid executive use

This bibliography is organized by what the reader is likely to be trying to solve, not by academic discipline. Titles are given without links to preserve constraints, and each entry is described by what it governs.

F1. Finality and settlement

CPMI-IOSCO, Principles for Financial Market Infrastructures. Governs what FMIs must do to remain legitimate under stress: finality, liquidity risk controls, default management, and operational resilience.

CPMI cross-border payments roadmap corpus. Governs how cross-border payment sequences can be made faster and more transparent, and shows where frictions are governance frictions.

National RTGS operational descriptions. Govern how intraday liquidity and queue rules allocate time and prevent settlement from becoming disorder.

F2. Banking constraint and liquidity

Basel liquidity and capital frameworks. Govern bank behavior under fear and the definition of what counts as liquid enough to survive.

BIS global liquidity work. Governs the cross-border dimension of funding dependence and panic transmission.

F3. Collateral and shadow liquidity

BIS and FSB nonbank finance and repo work. Governs the speed layer of modern money and its seizure dynamics through haircuts and margin timing.

CCP governance literature under PFMI. Governs netting and margin as governance rather than as neutral arithmetic.

F4. Cross-border admissibility

FATF recommendations and guidance. Govern the identity and compliance borders that determine routine passage versus exception handling.

IMF external sector and reserve adequacy frameworks. Govern the sovereign's ability to withstand corridor tightening without losing domestic autonomy.

F5. Multilateral architecture and development-credit

IMF program architecture and conditionality literature. Governs time allocation and admissibility restoration as the core of rescue.

MDB instruments and guarantees. Govern how development-credit is localized through enforceable cash flows and risk allocation rather than through moral rhetoric.

F6. Interface battle and private rails

BIS and IMF digital money and tokenization analyses. Govern the sovereignty relocation question: identity, custody, finality, and platform governance.

Supervisory materials on stable-value instruments. Govern public dependence of private issuers under stress.

F7. Classic doctrine

Walter Bagehot, Lombard Street. Governs backstop discipline: lend to preserve the system without subsidizing panic as entitlement.

Classic credit and money scholarship used as interpretive lens, not as substitution for enforceability.

GLOSSARY OF TERMS AND GATE

This glossary is written as operational language, not academic language. Each term is defined so it can be pointed to inside a system diagram, a rulebook, a legal authority, or a crisis decision. Where a term is commonly used loosely in public, the definition here is narrowed so the machine remains legible.

Discharge is the enforceable end of an obligation under rule, binding on third parties, that terminates the creditor's right to pursue once proper tender has been made. Discharge is not a receipt, not a customer-facing confirmation, not a posting in an account display, and not a promise that reconciliation will occur later. Discharge is the legal event the order will defend.

Finality is the protected point after which reversal is not permitted except through narrowly defined, rule-bound channels. Finality is the system's red line because it is what makes payment do its primary job: end the argument.

Completion state is the explicit classification the system assigns to a payment or claim at each step of the sequence. If completion states are ambiguous, the system manufactures panic by producing "almost done" outcomes that users experience as betrayal.

Authorization is the permission state: the system has validated the initiator's right to attempt transfer under current controls. Authorization is a gate, not an end-state.

Posting is entry into an account ledger representation. Posting may occur before settlement and may be reversible. Treat posting as informational unless the legal regime treats it as discharge.

Clearing is the governed validation and obligation-building process that prepares claims for settlement, including netting where applicable, and includes membership rules, default handling, and loss allocation. Clearing is governance expressed through process.

Netting is the reduction of gross obligations to residual obligations under a binding, enforceable calculation. Netting becomes monetary only when refusal is punishable and the net result is enforceable.

Settlement is the transfer that changes the highest-grade ledger state the order recognizes as capable of producing discharge. Settlement is the act that turns intention into public fact.

Reconciliation is the alignment of records across ledgers after clearing and settlement actions. Reconciliation is necessary hygiene. It is not a substitute for finality.

Hold is an intentional delay inside the sequence due to screening, exception handling, operational degradation, dispute, or discretionary review. Holds allocate time; time allocation becomes solvency allocation in a timed system.

Exception is any state that falls outside routine processing and requires manual review or enhanced controls. Exceptions are the medium of contagion because they multiply uncertainty and widen discretion.

Queue governance is the rule set that governs order of processing under capacity constraint, including priority classes, maximum delay windows, and auditable override authority. Queue governance is crisis policy embedded in operations.

Triage is the explicit prioritization of flows when capacity is constrained. Triage is unavoidable in crisis. The only question is whether it is governed or improvised.

Degraded mode is the defined reduced-function state during outage, attack, energy stress, or overload. Degraded mode must be designed; otherwise it becomes discretion under stress.

Eligibility is the rule that a claim, asset, institution, or participant may be used for a defined purpose, such as collateral, facility access, or clearing membership. Eligibility is policy disguised as criteria.

Haircut is the discount applied to collateral value for funding, margin, or facility access. Haircuts are the system's fear price and discipline instrument.

Margin is collateral demanded to secure exposure. Margin timing is a crisis engine because time mismatch can force liquidation.

Collateral mobility is the operational and legal ability to move, pledge, substitute, and seize collateral at financial speed. If mobility fails, the backstop cannot work cleanly.

Perfection is the legal condition under which a security interest is enforceable against third parties. Unperfected collateral is litigation, not liquidity.

Convertibility is the engineered right to upgrade one claim into a higher-grade settlement claim on defined terms within defined time. Convertibility is how hierarchy is managed and how runs are triggered.

Upgrade right is the practical ability to obtain the apex claim when fear rises. A system's true hierarchy is the distribution of upgrade rights under stress.

Corridor is the sequence of institutions, standards, and gates that permits cross-boundary passage of claims into usable settlement. Corridors are geopolitical infrastructure because they allocate speed and admissibility.

Admissibility is the condition under which a claim, identity, or transaction is accepted as routine for passage and settlement. Admissibility is where compliance becomes border.

Translator is an institution or service that converts one regime's identity, compliance posture, or claim form into another's. Translators are chokepoints; chokepoints become power.

De-risking is corridor withdrawal by nodes due to perceived compliance or reputational risk. De-risking is exclusion executed through private balance sheets.

Backstop is the rule-bound power to provide time and liquidity to prevent mechanical collapse of settlement and collateral. Backstops are constitutional power because they allocate loss.

Resolution is the authority's process for imposing loss, maintaining continuity, and enforcing priority when institutions fail. Resolution is how the hidden constitution becomes public.

Priority is the ranked schedule of claims under scarcity. Priority is the constitution of loss allocation.

Mechanical amplification is the self-reinforcing loop where valuation shifts tighten haircuts and margin calls, forcing selling, driving prices further, tightening again.

Concentration node is any operator whose failure can materially interrupt settlement: cloud region, identity provider, processor, custodian, clearing venue, data feed, major translator. Concentration is dependency; dependency is fragility.

ACRONYMS AND INSTITUTIONAL ABBREVIATIONS

This list is compact on purpose. It covers only the abbreviations that recur as governing bodies, infrastructure categories, or constraint frameworks.

BIS: Bank for International Settlements

CPMI: Committee on Payments and Market Infrastructures

IOSCO: International Organization of Securities Commissions

PFMI: Principles for Financial Market Infrastructures

BCBS: Basel Committee on Banking Supervision

FSB: Financial Stability Board

IMF: International Monetary Fund

MDB: Multilateral Development Bank

FATF: Financial Action Task Force

AML/CFT: Anti–Money Laundering / Countering the Financing of Terrorism

RTGS: Real-Time Gross Settlement

FMI: Financial Market Infrastructure

CCP: Central Counterparty

CSD: Central Securities Depository

DvP: Delivery versus Payment

PvP: Payment versus Payment

HQLA: High-Quality Liquid Assets

LCR: Liquidity Coverage Ratio

NSFR: Net Stable Funding Ratio

KYC: Know Your Customer

STR: Suspicious Transaction Report

NBFI: Nonbank Financial Intermediation

DOCTRINE-TO-ACTION CHECKLISTS

Each checklist is written to fit on a single page and to force specificity. The goal is to make unknown gates visible before fear turns them into panic gates.

1) Settlement Finality Checklist

Identify the settlement endpoint and legal basis: which ledger entry constitutes the enforceable discharge fact for the highest-grade claim.

Identify reversals: which reversals are permitted after finality, by which authority, under what narrow rule, with what audit and compensation logic.

Map completion states: authorization, posting, clearing, settlement, reconciliation, dispute handling, discharge, and specify which states are user-visible.

Define queue governance: priority classes, maximum hold windows, auditable override authority, and the boundary of discretion.

Test degraded mode: outage and overload simulations that confirm essentials complete under rule and that ambiguity states are minimized.

2) Collateral Governance Checklist

Formalize eligibility and haircut principles: what counts, why, and how transition is managed to avoid cliffs.

Margin timing discipline: define triggers and smoothing logic to reduce mechanical amplification in stress.

Mobility and perfection: confirm collateral can be pledged, substituted, and seized at financial speed with clear title and clear enforcement.

Custody bottlenecks: identify custody dependencies and cross-boundary title risks that can freeze collateral under legal clash.

Backstop compatibility: ensure facility collateral rules do not import litigation risk into the public balance sheet.

3) Convertibility Mapping Checklist

Map upgrade paths for each claim type into settlement, including identity, collateral, time windows, and discretionary holds.

Measure capacity: quantify upgrade demand the system can meet without rationing and define rationing protocol when demand exceeds capacity.

Identify corridor dependence: map which upgrades require external passage and what buffers protect essentials.

Run mass-upgrade simulation: identify which claims convert, which are delayed, and how delays are governed and explained.

4) Crisis Queue Rules Checklist

Define essential flows: wages, benefits, utilities, critical imports, and critical market infrastructure obligations.

Define triage ordering: rule-bound prioritization and maximum delay windows per class.

Define override authority: who can override, evidence required, audit record, penalties for misuse.

Define compensation logic: remedy for system-caused delay costs that would otherwise become political rupture.

5) Concentration and Resilience Checklist

Identify concentration nodes: processors, cloud regions, identity providers, custodians, data feeds, clearing venues, translators.

Require substitutability: tested failover, independent time sources, independent identity channels, documented degraded mode.

Verify degraded-mode legitimacy: which functions throttle, which remain live, how triage is enforced without discretionary favoritism.

Cyber and energy coupling tests: confirm stress does not force manual discretion without audit.

6) Cross-Border Dependency Checklist

Map corridors for essentials and identify the gatekeepers.

Map admissibility gates: identity standards, documentation burdens, screening holds, de-risking triggers.

Buffer strategy: reserves, alternate passage plans, bilateral and multilateral options, domestic substitution where feasible.

Feedback risk: identify how domestic emergency measures can worsen external recognition and accelerate perimeter flight.

7) Multilateral Time Allocation Checklist

Define how multilateral support restores passage: what changes corridor gatekeeper behavior.

Conditionality clarity: required actions, sequencing, and domestic legitimacy plan.

Development-credit design: use MDB instruments to localize bankable credit compatible with external settlement.

8) Private Issuer Containment Checklist

Define money-like permissions: what private claims may be used for discharge and under what upgrade discipline.

Reserve and redemption discipline: prevent private promises of finality that cannot hold under stress.

Interface governance: ensure identity and compliance gates cannot become private monetary sovereignty.

Failure protocol: define resolution path without surprise political rescue.

RED FLAGS DIAGNOSTIC SECTION

These red flags are phrased as observable signals, not as moods. Each is a prompt to ask what gate tightened and why.

Exception rate rising in retail or wholesale processing, especially when concentrated in a corridor or institution.

Holds lengthening or becoming more discretionary, indicating that time allocation is shifting inside the machine.

Payment reversals or dispute volume rising, signaling false finality and growing mistrust.

Intraday liquidity spikes and repeated cutoff extensions, signaling time scarcity in settlement.

Haircuts widening pro-cyclically or margin timing tightening abruptly, signaling mechanical amplification risk.

Collateral eligibility narrowing quietly, indicating re-ranking of financeability.

Reliance increasing on a single translator, custodian chain, cloud region, or identity provider for critical flows.

Failover untested or degraded-mode procedures dependent on manual overrides without audit discipline.

Silent de-risking by corridor nodes, including correspondent withdrawal and rising compliance rejection rates.

Persistent gap between messaging completion and legal finality, visible as longer-lived ambiguous states.

Emergency discretion increasing without recorded, defensible triage logic, signaling legitimacy risk.

Insuredness cost spikes and collateral reclassification clusters, signaling slow-burning collateral failure modes.

CHAPTER CONCORDANCE AND SOURCE INDEX

This is a navigation instrument, not a bibliography. It tells internal teams where to go for load-bearing authority.

Discharge and finality: CPMI payment doctrine; PFMI finality and governance; central bank settlement operations; funds transfer legal regimes and liability boundaries.

Ledger authority: commercial law record and transferability; audit and admissibility practice; identity integrity standards; correction discipline and dispute procedure.

Collateral and shadow liquidity: BIS and FSB repo and nonbank mapping; PFMI margin and default management; Basel liquidity assumptions; perfection and custody mobility regimes.

Priority and resolution: insolvency priority frameworks; resolution authority tools; netting enforceability; PFMI default management and loss allocation; crisis facility precedents.

Cross-border dependence: BIS global liquidity; IMF external sector and reserve adequacy; CPMI cross-border sequencing; FATF admissibility; correspondent and de-risking dynamics.

Multilateral development-credit: IMF conditionality architecture; MDB instruments and guarantees; bankability and guarantee mechanics; corridor admissibility linkage.

Private challenge: BIS/IMF digital money and tokenization; supervisory stable-value regimes; PFMI applied to new rails; identity and compliance as programmable gates.

Crisis governance: lender-of-last-resort doctrine; modern market backstop evolution; operational resilience and critical third-party dependency; degraded-mode governance.

CLOSING FIELD DIRECTIVE

This book is a map of the machine that governs obligations when persuasion ends. The immediate task for any serious monetary authority is not to argue about symbols or narratives. The immediate task is to map the gates, name the settlement endpoint, defend finality, and make convertibility an engineered pathway rather than a promise. Harden collateral mobility so public liquidity can work without importing legal ambiguity. Govern haircuts and margin timing to reduce mechanical amplification. Identify concentration nodes and require tested substitutability, because redundancy is sovereign capacity. Pre-design triage and degraded-mode legitimacy rules so crisis does not force improvisation and improvisation does not become scandal. Treat cross-border corridors as statecraft, not convenience, and treat multilateral time allocation as architecture, not charity. A monetary order survives because it can end arguments on schedule and allocate time under stress without losing legitimacy. Everything else is commentary.

ABOUT THE AUTHOR

JAG DESAINT

Jag DeSaint is one of the rare voices in modern monetary statecraft who writes with the authority of mechanism rather than the comfort of abstraction. Where most discussions of money drift into ideology, personality, or headline politics, Jag DeSaint stays inside the machine: discharge, finality, admissibility, collateral discipline, margin timing, legal priority, corridor passage, and the quiet choreography of infrastructure that decides what "paid" means when fear arrives. His work does not treat these as technical details. It treats them as the constitution of the order, the place where sovereignty is actually exercised, and the place where states either retain control or discover—too late—that control has migrated into gates they no longer command.

Jag DeSaint's leadership in this space comes from a distinctive discipline: he refuses to separate law from operations, or policy from settlement, or public doctrine from private rule-setting. He writes as if the reader is responsible for outcomes, not narratives, and as if the reader understands that crises are not surprises but audits. In his framework, the question is never *"what do we believe about money."* The question is "where does finality live, who can delay it, who can reverse it, who can upgrade into it, and how does the system allocate time when time becomes scarce." That insistence—relentless, precise, and operational—turns his analysis into a practical advantage for decision-makers, because it gives them a language to interrogate systems that are usually protected by complexity and euphemism.

The signature Jag DeSaint contribution is clarity without simplification. He makes the hierarchy visible without turning it into a slogan, and he makes power legible without turning it into moral theater. His writing carries the reader from pressure to mechanism to consequence in the same cadence the system itself follows under stress: a hold becomes a queue, a queue becomes a liquidity event, a liquidity event becomes a collateral event, a collateral event becomes a solvency allocation, and a solvency allocation becomes politics. That sequence is the real story of modern monetary order, and Jag DeSaint writes it with a controlled intensity that keeps the subject unavoidably concrete.

The Monetary State is the culmination of that approach: a doctrine-level map of how monetary power is exercised through settlement architecture and legal enforceability, and how advantage is preserved through the governance of upgrade rights, collateral eligibility, corridor admissibility, and crisis tools that allocate loss. Jag DeSaint writes for the serious audience precisely because he assumes seriousness: finance ministers, central-bank governors, presidents, sovereign advisers, bank chairmen, regulators, multilateral officials, and system architects who cannot afford ornamental economics. The result is not a book that asks to be admired. It is a book that positions its author—and its reader—where the real levers are, and insists that the era ahead will be decided there: in finality, in admissibility, in infrastructure concentration, and in the disciplined governance of the gates that make money real.

OTHER WORK BY JAG DeSAINT

Jag DeSaint's work forms a single arc: how modern states preserve capacity when sovereignty is no longer tested only in parliaments and markets, but in settlement corridors, collateral regimes, identity gates, and platform governance. He writes for operators because he builds frameworks that survive stress. Each project follows the same discipline as his monetary doctrine: pressure first, mechanism second, power map third, failure point fourth, doctrine earned at the end.

The Payment State

A work on the front end of sovereignty: how retail speed, private interfaces, and identity standards quietly determine who is legible enough to move at all. Jag DeSaint tracks the layered sequence between authorization, posting, clearing, settlement, and legal discharge, then shows how the interface manufactures trust through concealment until an outage, a compliance surge, or a policy shift forces ordinary life to live on crisis time. The central theme is blunt: whoever governs the interface governs the public's lived experience of money, and lived experience becomes political constraint.

Corridors of Power

A study of cross-boundary dependence written as infrastructure, not diplomacy. Jag DeSaint maps how one transaction can pass through multiple invisible veto points before value becomes usable, and how corridor admissibility tightens without formal rupture. The work treats reserve order as geopolitical plumbing: documentation burdens, correspondent structure, custody acceptability, and the speed at which claims can be upgraded into the apex settlement asset. It is a book about leverage that does not announce itself as leverage.

The Collateral Constitution

Jag DeSaint's deep dive into how collateral is the system's theology and haircuts are its discipline. He explains why public debate fixates on rates while the machine is governed by eligibility lists, margin timing, and perfection rules that decide who can finance themselves when time becomes scarce. The work is also a warning: the modern system is stabilized by shadow liquidity and then rescued by public balance sheets when shadow liquidity collapses into forced deleveraging. The contradiction is not a scandal. It is the design problem of modern capitalism.

Crisis Is Governance

A doctrine manual built from case sequences rather than commentary. DeSaint isolates the repeatable pattern: ambiguous completion becomes a hold, the hold becomes a queue, the queue becomes a liquidity event, the liquidity event becomes a collateral event, and the collateral event becomes a political allocation of loss. He then argues that crisis management is not improvisation; it is constitutional execution, and legitimacy is preserved only when triage is rule-bound, auditable, and defensible.

Development Credit Architecture

A work aimed at sovereign and multilateral designers: how to localize development through credit design rather than through slogans. DeSaint treats development as a bankability problem: enforceable cash flows, guarantee structures, collateral maps, and corridor strategy that prevents external admissibility from becoming the bottleneck. It is a blueprint for building domestic credit capacity that survives external tightening.

The Private Challenge

Jag DeSaint's analysis of stable-value private issuers, token rails, and "policy in code" as a relocation of sovereignty into identity, custody, and platform governance. He shows why private money projects oscillate between exit fantasy and public dependence, and why programmable rails do not eliminate politics but compress it into compliance settings, upgrade rights, and discretionary exception handling. The work ends with a hard doctrine: private rails can innovate at the edge, but finality and discharge remain public facts, or the system becomes a patchwork of conditional promises.

ALSO BY JAG DESAINT

AUTHORED BOOKS

The Statesman — The Art of Dominion

A doctrine of state power for leaders who must command outcomes under legal, fiscal, and geopolitical constraint, showing how authority is built through institutions, incentives, and enforceable order rather than charisma. DeSaint maps dominion as architecture—control of rules, capacity, and timing—so power survives crisis, succession, and opposition.

Technomics — The Silent War

A field manual on how technology becomes sovereignty: standards, data regimes, supply chains, compute, and platforms weaponized into quiet coercion without a formal battlefield. DeSaint tracks how nations win by controlling critical nodes and choke points, and how "innovation" becomes the operating system of modern conflict.

Empire Born — Mother of God

A cinematic origin study of empire as a machine: myth welded to administration, devotion fused to discipline, and sacred narrative converted into enforceable rule. DeSaint shows how legitimacy is manufactured, how fear is organized, and how an empire is engineered to outlive betrayal from within and assault from without.

The Market — The Machinery of Capital

A deep dive beneath price into the infrastructure that makes capital real: rule, record, proof, custody, collateral, clearing, and settlement finality. DeSaint reveals markets as sequences of permissions, where advantage belongs to those who control visibility, timing, and the official mark that turns intention into fact.

www.ingramcontent.com/pod-product-compliance
Lightning Source LLC
LaVergne TN
LVHW052013200926
848481LV00005B/1475